W9-AWU-664

The Inclusive Classroom
Strategies for Effective Instruction
Second Edition

Margo A. Mastropieri
George Mason University

Thomas E. Scruggs
George Mason University

PEARSON

Merrill
Prentice Hall

Upper Saddle River, New Jersey
Columbus, Ohio

Library of Congress Cataloging-in-Publication Data

Mastropieri, Margo A.
    The inclusive classroom : strategies for effective instruction / by Margo A. Mastropieri
and Thomas E. Scruggs.—2nd ed.
        p. cm.
    Includes bibliographical references and index.
    ISBN 0-13-139799-0
        1. Inclusive education—United States. 2. Mainstreaming in education—United States. 3.
Classroom management—United States. I. Scruggs, Thomas E. II. Title.

LC1201.M37 2004
371.9'046—dc21   2003042024

Vice President and Executive Publisher: Jeffery W. Johnston
Acquisitions Editor: Allyson P. Sharp
Editorial Assistant: Kathleen S. Burke
Development Editor: Heather Doyle Fraser
Production Editor: Sheryl Glicker Langner
Production Coordination: Amy Gehl, Carlisle Publishers Services
Design Coordinator: Diane C. Lorenzo
Photo Coordinator: Cynthia Cassidy
Cover Designer: Linda Sorrels-Smith
Cover Art: ©Nicky Williams, a participating artist of VSA arts, *http://www.vsarts.org*
Chapter Opening Art: ©Very Special Arts, *http://www.vsarts.org*
Production Manager: Laura Messerly
Director of Marketing: Ann Castel Davis
Marketing Manager: Amy June
Marketing Coordinator: Tyra Poole
Photo Credits: Located on page iii.

This book was set in Weidemann Book by Carlisle Communications, Ltd. It was printed and bound by R. R. Donnelley
& Sons Company. The cover was printed by Phoenix Color Corp.

Copyright © 2004, 2000, by Pearson Education, Inc., Upper Saddle River, New Jersey 07458.
Pearson Prentice Hall. All rights reserved. Printed in the United States of America. This publication is
protected by Copyright and permission should be obtained from the publisher prior to any prohibited
reproduction, storage in a retrieval system, or transmission in any form or by any means, electronic,
mechanical, photocopying, recording, or likewise. For information regarding permission(s), write to:
Rights and Permissions Department.

Pearson Prentice Hall™ is a trademark of Pearson Education, Inc.
Pearson® is a registered trademark of Pearson plc.
Pearson Hall® is a registered trademark of Pearson Education, Inc.
Merrill® is a registered trademark of Pearson Education, Inc.

Pearson Education Ltd.
Pearson Education Singapore Pte. Ltd.
Pearson Education Canada, Ltd.
Pearson Education—Japan

Pearson Education Australia Pty. Limited
Pearson Education North Asia Ltd.
Pearson Educatión de Mexico, S.A. de C.V.
Pearson Education Malaysia Pte. Ltd.

10 9 8 7 6 5 4 3 2
ISBN: 0-13-139799-0

Photo Credits

Scott Cunningham/Merrill, pp. 5, 9, 35, 55, 66, 68, 82, 114, 161, 207, 226, 249, 262, 376, 390, 404, 410, 423, 466, 468, 486; Anthony Magnacca/Merrill, pp. 5, 17, 18, 23, 52, 120, 129, 174, 195, 199, 242, 254, 264, 280, 287, 319, 360, 413; Frank Siteman/PhotoEdit, p. 20; Elizabeth Crews/Elizabeth Crews Photography, pp. 32, 48, 202, 233, 235, 328; Cindy Charles/PhotoEdit, p. 49; Tony Freeman/PhotoEdit, pp. 63, 150, 210; Paul Conklin/PhotoEdit, pp. 72, 79; Doug Martin/Merrill, p. 76; Larry Hamill/Merrill, p. 95; Robin L. Sachs/PhotoEdit, pp. 98, 308; Phonic Ear Inc., p. 99; Myrleen Ferguson/PhotoEdit, p. 104; Streissguth, A. P., Landesman-Dwyer, S., Martin, J. C. & Smith, D. W., p. 106; Prentke Romich, p. 110; Bill Bachmann/Photo Researchers, Inc., p. 133; Jeff Greenberg/Visuals Unlimited, p. 140; Harcourt Brace and Company, p. 157; Cynthia Cassidy/Merrill, p. 159; Will Hart/PhotoEdit, pp. 161, 171; Todd Yarrington/Merrill, pp. 163, 401; Steve Skjold/Skjold Photographs, pp. 166, 170; T. Hubbard/Merrill, p. 177; James L. Shaffer, pp. 189, 355, 494, 506; Laura Dwight/Laura Dwight Photography, p. 222; Michael Newman/PhotoEdit, pp. 251, 373; David Young-Wolff/PhotoEdit, pp. 260, 287, 340, 431, 443; Bill Bachmann/PhotoEdit, p. 277; Richard Hutchings/PhotoEdit, p. 289; JRA Division of Macmillan/McGraw-Hill School Publishing Co., p. 375; Tom Watson/Merrill, p. 472; Daily Hampshire Gazette, p. 488.

Preface

One of the major features that will characterize classrooms of the new century is student diversity. Not only have classrooms become more diverse with respect to race, religion, and ethnicity, but also more students with disabilities than ever are being included in regular education classrooms. Data recently reported by the U.S. Department of Education indicate that nearly three-fourths of students with disabilities are now being served primarily within the general education classroom setting.

Unfortunately, today's teachers consistently report that they do not feel prepared to teach students with disabilities in their general education classrooms. Only about one-fourth believe that they possess skills necessary for effective inclusive teaching. We have written this book to give teachers a wide variety of proven and effective strategies for students with disabilities and other special learning needs.

Text Philosophy

There are in existence today a number of high-quality textbooks on inclusive education. This in itself is a notable advance from just a few years ago, and indicates an increasing awareness of the important role of inclusive education in today's schools. We wrote *The Inclusive Classroom: Strategies for Effective Instruction* to add our own perspective on inclusive education. According to this perspective, we believe that teachers certainly should be provided with necessary information regarding legal issues and the characteristics of students with disabilities and other special needs. In addition, however, we describe a variety of practical teaching and learning strategies that are directly relevant to the tasks and academic demands required of teachers in inclusive classrooms in today's schools.

However, we do not believe that "inclusion strategies" can be effectively implemented in the absence of overall effective teaching skills. That is, we believe that effective overall teaching and classroom management skills are necessary prerequisites for working with students with disabilities who attend inclusive classrooms. Therefore, we have described inclusion strategies within the overall framework of effective instruction and management of general education classrooms. The organization of this book reflects our perspective.

Text Organization

Part 1: The Fundamentals. The first section of this book presents the fundamentals of inclusive teaching, including information on the history of special education, the legal and political background of legislation for individuals with disabilities, and relevant, practical information on the Individualized Education Program (IEP). Chapter 2 provides specific information on strategies for consultation and collaboration with students, parents, and other school personnel, including special education teachers, paraprofessionals, and other specialized school personnel. Chapters 3 and 4 provide information on the various characteristics of specific disability areas identified in IDEA, the federal special education law, and general adaptations that can be made for each of these disability areas. Chapter 3 discusses higher-incidence disabilities, such as learning disabilities and speech or language impairments, that teachers are very likely to encounter in their classrooms. Chapter 4 covers lower-incidence disabilities, such as severe disabilities and visual impairments. Chapter 5 describes other special need areas not specifically covered under IDEA, including attention deficit hyperactivity disorder, at-risk students, and students with special "gifts" and talents.

Part 2: Developing Effective Teaching Skills. The second section of this book describes a range of strategies that can be applied across curriculum areas and grade levels to address special needs and particular problems. Chapter 6 describes the general teacher effectiveness strategies that have been demonstrated to be very helpful in promoting learning in inclusive settings. This chapter covers the variables most closely associated with student achievement, including engaged time-on-task, teacher questioning and feedback, and the most effective uses of praise, with specific reference to students with special needs. Chapter 7 describes behavior management strategies shown to be most effective for entire classrooms as well as for individual students. Chapter 8 provides strategies for the effective uses of peers to help accommodate diversity in classroom learning and behavior, including peer assistance, peer tutoring, and cooperative learning. These strategies can be used to transform classrooms into effective collaborative learning environments.

Chapter 9 describes strategies for promoting motivation and affect—two very critical components of successful classrooms, and a very common cause of concern for classroom teachers. Chapter 10 describes strategies for enhancing attention and memory, for entire classrooms as well as for individual students with special needs. In chapter 11 are strategies for teaching study skills, including organizational strategies, highlighting and outlining skills, listening and note-taking skills, and research and reference skills. Finally, chapter 12 describes assessment, and how adaptations can be made to accommodate the special needs of individual students as well as the classroom in general.

Part 3: Teaching in the Content Areas. The third part of this book describes specific academic areas and strategies that can promote learning in these areas for a wide variety of students. Chapter 13 describes learning in basic literacy areas, including reading, writing, and spelling, and how special problems in learning in these areas can best be addressed. Chapter 14 presents mathematics learning and effective strategies for promoting learning in a variety of different aspects of mathematics. Chapter 15 covers science and social studies learning and provides specific strategies to enhance learning for a variety of special needs areas. Finally, chapter 16 describes special strategies to improve learning and address special problems in such areas as art, music, physical education, and vocational education. In addition, strategies for facilitating transition to post-secondary, vocational, or community environments are described.

For the second edition we made numerous changes throughout the text, as a result of helpful suggestions from editors and reviewers, that we believe have greatly improved the text. These changes include more information on secondary-level and at-risk students; more reference to applications of technology and addition of a *Technology Highlight* feature; inclusion of *Questions for Reflection* for the *Research Highlights* (see text features); and chapter objectives. In addition, we have provided additional coverage and updated references to each chapter, to reflect findings from the latest research.

Text Features

Included also in this book are a number of special features that we hope will make it more useful and comprehensible.

- *In the Classroom* features have been designed to address very specific need areas, and may be used directly in classroom situations. One type of *In the Classroom* feature, "A Feature for Teachers," includes materials intended for use as resources that can be practically applied in inclusive classrooms. The second type of *In the Classroom* feature, "For

Sharing with Students," includes materials such as self-monitoring sheets, contracts, or study guides that can be directly utilized to provide assistance for students. In the second edition, this feature is now provided in the Companion Website.

- *Technology Highlight* features are found in individual chapters and provide information on technological applications relevant to the content of the chapter. These features provide up-to-date information on new technologies and how they can be employed to improve the academic or social functioning of students with special needs.
- *Research Highlights* explain the research behind certain teaching strategies developed for use with students with special needs. The descriptive nature within each Research Highlights allows the reader to verify and analyze the appropriateness of each strategy as it is used in the classroom. In the second edition, each Research Highlight contains resources for further information and Questions for Reflection, which can be answered online in the Companion Website.
- *Inclusion Checklists* summarize the strategies described in the chapter and should be particularly useful for teachers having difficulties with any area of teaching students with disabilities. The Inclusion Checklists are also helpful for finding immediate reference for specific strategies, pinpointing difficulties teachers might be having, or planning preferral interventions. Teachers may wish to consider the suggestions contained in the appropriate checklists prior to referring students for special education services. For example, if a teacher is considering referring a student for special education based on observed problems with attention or memory, she could first consult the Inclusion Checklist for chapter 10 for a list of possible interventions in these areas.
- *Classroom Scenarios* are cases that model how to identify students who should be referred for special services or who would benefit from specific teaching strategies.
- *Very Special Arts* (*http://www.vsarts.org*) is an international organization that promotes learning through the arts for individuals with disabilities. Each chapter opening illustration and the cover for this text are from the Very Special Arts collection and are original illustrations, completed by individuals with special talents who also have a disability.

In addition to the features discussed above, the text also contains the following:

- Margin notes connect the text with further elaboration of content, and refer the reader to other relevant sources.
- Relevant websites, listed by chapter in the Companion Website, are also referenced in the margin notes.
- CEC Professional Standards are listed at the end of each chapter where relevant. A complete listing of standards can be found on the Companion Website.
- An index is also included to make the text more accessible.

Supplements and Resources for the Instructor

Instructor's Manual and Test Bank
The Instructor's Manual is a comprehensive resource that includes chapter summaries, chapter outlines, overheads, a test bank, and suggested classroom activities for each chapter. A computerized version of the test bank is available on CD-ROM in Windows and Macintosh format, along with assessment software allowing professors to create and customize exams and track student progress.

Overhead Transparencies/PowerPoint Slides
A package of acetate transparencies is available for use with the text. The transparencies highlight key concepts, summarize content, and illustrate figures and charts from the text. These transparencies are also available on the Companion Website as PowerPoint slides.

Companion Website
Located at *http://www.prenhall.com/mastropieri*, the user-friendly website that accompanies this text provides online resources for professors as well as students.

The passcode-protected Professor Resources section for instructors includes an online version of the Instructor's Manual; downloadable PowerPoint lectures; and additional resources for effective instruction. The Syllabus Builder tool allows instructors to create and customize online syllabi online. To obtain a passcode to enter the Professor Resources section, contact your local Prentice Hall sales representative.

Additional Supplements for the Student

Companion Website

The Companion Website helps students gauge their understanding of the chapter content through the use of online chapter reviews and interactive multiple-choice chapter quizzes. It also provides links to websites mentioned in the text and a variety of other on-line resources.

Inclusive Classrooms: Video Cases on CD-ROM

Following examples of good teaching is one means of becoming an effective teacher. Simply reading and researching is not generally enough. But, witnessing meaningful teaching first hand, observing master teachers, and reflecting on the actions, decisions and artistry behind good teaching can bring you farther along on your journey toward becoming a better teacher yourself. The CD-ROM packaged in the guide that accompanies this text allows you to observe, reflect on, and learn from master teachers in their classrooms.

Purpose of the CD

The CD packaged in a guide that accompanies the text provides immediate access to living classroom examples of teaching and learning strategies for inclusion.

These examples are video clips, grouped by theme and classroom, which give the pre-service teacher a good picture of what inclusion looks like in a preschool, an elementary school, a middle school, and a secondary school. In each classroom, you will see a lesson that clearly shows the impact of inclusion on supporting students with challenging behaviors (preschool), classroom climate (elementary), assessment and planning (middle), and partial participation and cooperative learning (secondary).

Each classroom case contains 9 video clips. In each case, you will see how children with learning disabilities, attention deficit disorders, and mild/moderate disabilities are successfully engaged in the classroom community and in learning. Because of the natural supports and inclusive stance of the teachers and schools, it may be difficult to identify which children are indeed identified as having disabilities or in need of other accommodations.

To help connect the content featured in this CD-ROM to the chapter content and strategies in the text, we have packaged a guide with this text that enhances the CD cases with activities, applications, and connections to chapter content.

Acknowledgments

There are many individuals who contributed to the production of this book and to whom we are indebted. For the first edition, we thanked our editor, Ann Davis, for her initial encouragement of this undertaking and her continuous support for the project. Pat Grogg, editorial assistant, lent valued assistance on many occasions. Linda Montgomery, development editor, was particularly helpful in providing feedback, suggestions, and ideas for the first edition of this book as it was being written. Sheryl Langner, production editor, provided an invaluable service in editing the final version of the first edition. For the second edition, we would like to thank Allyson Williams Sharp, editor, Heather Fraser, development editor, and Amy Gehl, production coordinator. We feel the second edition of this text has been greatly improved by their imaginative and helpful ideas, suggestions, and support.

The reviewers also delivered much useful feedback and provided commentary on earlier versions of this book that were thoughtful, thorough, and professionally delivered. These reviewers included, for the first edition, Tammy Abernathy, Weber State University (UT); Marjorie A. Bock,

University of Missouri—Kansas City; Teri I. Burcroff, East Stroudsburg University of PA; Lynette K. Chandler, Northern Illinois University; Christine C. Givner, California State University, Los Angeles; Christy Hooser, Eastern Illinois University; Lloyd Kinnison, Texas Woman's University; Linda McCrea, Grand Valley State University; Robert G. Monahan, Lander University (SC); Marilyn Shank, University of South Alabama; and Qaisar Sultana, Eastern Kentucky University. For the second edition, we would also like to thank Rhonda S. Black, University of Hawaii at Manoa; Michael L. Daniel, Francis Marion University; Linda Schwartz Green, Centenary College; and Laura A. Reissner, Northern Michigan University.

Most of all, we thank the numerous individuals with whom we have had contact throughout our lives who have taught us about individuals with disabilities and teaching. Also included in our thanks are numerous special education professionals, whose research and publications form the core of substance for this book, and without whose contributions this book would not be possible. Finally, we would like to thank our parents, Janet Hunt Scruggs and Francis and Dorothy Mastropieri, who have always provided us with a continual source of support.

—M.A.M.

—T.E.S.

Educator Learning Center:
An Invaluable Online Resource

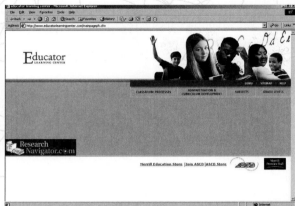

Merrill Education and the Association for Supervision and Curriculum Development (ASCD) invite you to take advantage of a new online resource, one that provides access to the top research and proven strategies associated with ASCD and Merrill—the Educator Learning Center. At **www.EducatorLearningCenter.com** you will find resources that will enhance your students' understanding of course topics and of current educational issues, in addition to being invaluable for further research.

How the Educator Learning Center
Will Help Your Students Become Better Teachers

With the combined resources of Merrill Education and ASCD, you and your students will find a wealth of tools and materials to better prepare them for the classroom.

Research
- More than 600 articles from the ASCD journal *Educational Leadership* discuss everyday issues faced by practicing teachers.
- A direct link on the site to Research Navigator™ gives students access to many of the leading education journals, as well as extensive content detailing the research process.
- Excerpts from Merrill Education texts give your students insights on important topics of instructional methods, diverse populations, assessment, classroom management, technology, and refining classroom practice.

Classroom Practice
- Hundreds of lesson plans and teaching strategies are categorized by content area and age range.
- Case studies and classroom video footage provide virtual field experience for student reflection.
- Computer simulations and other electronic tools keep your students abreast of today's classrooms and current technologies.

Look Into the Value of Educator Learning Center Yourself

Preview the value of this educational environment by visiting **www.EducatorLearningCenter.com** and clicking on "Demo." For a free 4-month subscription to the Educator Learning Center in conjunction with this text, simply contact your Merrill/Prentice Hall sales representative.

Brief Contents

PART 1   *The Fundamentals*

Chapter 1   *Introduction to Inclusive Teaching* 2
Chapter 2   *Collaboration: Partnerships and Procedures* 28
Chapter 3   *Teaching Students with Higher–Incidence Disabilities* . . 60
Chapter 4   *Teaching Students with Lower–Incidence Disabilities* . . 90
Chapter 5   *Teaching Students with Other Special Learning Needs* . . 124

PART 2   *Developing Effective Teaching Skills*

Chapter 6   *Effective Instruction for All Students* 154
Chapter 7   *Improving Classroom Behavior and Social Skills* 186
Chapter 8   *Promoting Inclusion with Classroom Peers* 220
Chapter 9   *Enhancing Motivation and Affect* 246
Chapter 10   *Improving Attention and Memory* 274
Chapter 11   *Teaching Study Skills* 304
Chapter 12   *Assessment* 334

PART 3   *Teaching in the Content Areas*

Chapter 13   *Literacy* 368
Chapter 14   *Mathematics* 408
Chapter 15   *Science and Social Studies* 446
Chapter 16   *Art, Music, Physical Education, Foreign Languages,
Vocational Education, and Transitions* 484

References 517
Name Index 561
Subject Index 571

Contents

PART 1   *The Fundamentals*

CHAPTER 1
Introduction to Inclusive Teaching 2

What Are the Educational Rights for Individuals with Disabilities? 5
The Least-Restrictive Environment 7
    Where Are Students with Disabilities Served? 7
    Mainstreaming and Inclusion 7
    Who Is Served Under IDEA? 8
    Other Instances of Classroom Diversity 10
Legal Foundations 10
    Legal Proceedings and Legislation 10
    Section 504 12
    Americans with Disabilities Act 12
    Individuals with Disabilities Education Act (IDEA) 12
    No Child Left Behind Act of 2001 14
Models of Service Delivery 16
    The Continuum of Services 16
    Where Are Most Students with Disabilities Served? 16
    What Are General Education Classroom and Consultation Services? 17
    What Are Resource and Self-Contained Services? 17
    Special Schools and Special Facilities 18
    What Other Related Services Are Available? 18
    Inclusion Movements 19
    What Does This Debate Mean for Teachers? 22
    Teacher Attitudes 23

CHAPTER 2
Collaboration: Partnerships and Procedures 28

Collaboration to Establish Need 31
    Shared Goals 31
Effective Communication 31
Collaboration and Communication for Intervention 34
    The Intervention Process 36
Collaboration for Referrals and Placements 40
Collaboration as Partnerships 50
    Partnerships Between Special and Regular Educators 50
    Designing Adaptations 50
    Co-Teaching 51
    Collaboration with Paraprofessionals 54
    Parents and Families as Partners 54

CHAPTER 3

Teaching Students with Higher–Incidence Disabilities

Teaching Students with Higher–Incidence Disabilities 60

Speech or Language Impairments 62
   Prevalence, Definitions, and Characteristics 62
   Causes of Speech or Language Impairments 63
   Issues in Identification and Assessment of Speech and Language Impairments 64
   Classroom Adaptations for Students with Speech or Language Impairments 64
Learning Disabilities 66
   Prevalence and Definitions of Learning Disabilities 66
   Causes of Learning Disabilities 68
   Issues in Identification and Assessment of Learning Disabilities 69
   Characteristics of Learning Disabilities 70
   Classroom Adaptations for Students with Learning Disabilities 72
Mental Retardation 75
   Prevalence and Definitions of Mental Retardation 75
   Causes of Mental Retardation 75
   Issues in Identification and Assessment of Mental Retardation 76
   Characteristics of Mental Retardation 77
   Classroom Adaptations for Students with Mental Retardation 79
Emotional Disturbance 80
   Prevalence and Definitions 80
   Causes of Emotional Disturbance 81
   Issues in Identification and Assessment of Emotional Disturbance 81
   Characteristics of Emotional Disturbance 81
   Classroom Adaptations for Students with Emotional Disturbance 84

CHAPTER 4

Teaching Students with Lower–Incidence Disabilities

Teaching Students with Lower–Incidence Disabilities 90

Visual Impairments 92
   Prevalence, Definitions, and Characteristics 92
   Classroom Adaptations for Students with Visual Impairments 93
Hearing Impairments 95
   Prevalence, Definitions, and Characteristics 95
   Educational Programming 96
   Classroom Adaptations for Students with Hearing Impairments 97
Physical Disabilities and Other Health Impairments 99
   Prevalence, Definitions, and Characteristics 99
   Physical and Health-Related Impairments 101
   Classroom Adaptations for Students with Physical Disabilities and Other Health Impairments 106
Severe and Multiple Disabilities 111
   Prevalence, Definitions, and Characteristics 111
   Classroom Adaptations for Students with Severe Disabilities 113
Autism 115
   Prevalence, Definitions, and Characteristics 115
   Classroom Adaptations for Students with Autism 117

CHAPTER 5

Teaching Students with Other Special Learning Needs 124

Students Served Under Section 504 126
    Definitions, Prevalence, and Characteristics of Attention Deficit
        Hyperactivity Disorder 126
    Causes of ADHD 127
    Issues in Identification and Assessment of ADHD 128
    General Classroom Adaptations for Students with ADHD 129
Gifted, Creative, and Talented 131
    Definitions, Prevalence, and Characteristics of Gifted, Creative,
        and Talented 131
    Issues in Identification and Assessment of Gifted, Creative,
        and Talented 135
    General Classroom Accommodations for Students Who Are Gifted,
        Creative, and Talented 136
Students Who Are Culturally and Linguistically Diverse 138
    Prevalence, Definitions, and Characteristics of Cultural and Linguistic
        Diversity 138
    Issues in Identification and Assessment 142
    General Classroom Adaptations for Students from Culturally and
        Linguistically Diverse Backgrounds 143
Students at Risk 145
    Definitions, Prevalence, and Characteristics of Students at Risk 145
    Issues in Identification and Assessment of Students at Risk 150
    General Classroom Adaptations for Students at Risk 151

PART 2   *Developing Effective Teaching Skills*

CHAPTER 6

Effective Instruction for All Students 154

Overview of Effective Instruction 155
Planning for Content Coverage 156
    Objectives 156
    Scope and Sequence 157
    Curriculum 157
    Pacing 158
    Planning for Learning 158
    Addressing Learning Problems 162
Using Effective Teaching Strategies 164
    Maximizing Academic Engagement (Time-on-Task) 164
    Making Effective Teacher Presentations 170
    Monitoring Practice Activities 176
    Review 178
    Formative Evaluation 179
    Components of a Model Lesson 179
Promoting Effective Inclusive Instruction: The PASS Variables 180
    Prioritize Objectives 180
    Adapt Instruction, Materials, or the Environment 181
    Systematic Teaching, or the SCREAM Variables 181
    Systematic Evaluation 181

CHAPTER 7
Improving Classroom Behavior and Social Skills 186

Managing Classroom Behavior 188
   Understanding Behavior Problems *188*
   Observe and Record Classroom Behavior *189*
   Use Effective Classroom Management Strategies *192*
   Handling Confrontations *206*
   Life Space Interviewing/Life Space Crisis Intervention *208*
   Schoolwide Discipline Systems *209*
Teaching Social Skills 210
   Social Skills Assessment *212*
   Train Students to Improve Social Skills *213*
   Choose Curriculum Materials Thoughtfully *214*
   Conduct On-the-Spot Training *214*
   Train for Generalization *216*
   Validate Treatments *217*

CHAPTER 8
Promoting Inclusion with Classroom Peers 220

Promoting Social Acceptance 222
   Circle of Friends *222*
   Special Friends *223*
Peer Assistance 224
   What Is Peer Assistance? *224*
   Peer Training *224*
Peer Tutoring 227
   Why Use Peer Tutoring? *227*
   Tutoring to Improve Academic Skills and Attitudes *230*
   Implementing a Tutoring Program *231*
   Classwide Peer Tutoring *231*
Cooperative Learning 235
   Important Teacher Functions in Implementing Cooperative
     Learning *236*
   Integrating Students with Special Needs into Cooperative Groups *240*
   Types of Cooperative Group Arrangements *241*
   Conflict Resolution *242*
   Advantages and Limitations of Cooperative Learning *243*

CHAPTER 9
Enhancing Motivation and Affect 246

Preconditions for Improving Motivation and Affect 248
   Create a Supportive, Organized Classroom Environment *249*
   Ensure Materials Are of an Appropriate Difficulty Level *250*
   Ensure That Tasks Are Meaningful *251*
   Create Task-Oriented, Not Ego-Oriented Classrooms *251*
Techniques for Improving Motivation and Affect .252
   Raising Students' Self-Esteem *253*
   Provide Opportunities to Increase Self-Efficacy *253*
   Teach Students to Set Goals *255*
   Train Students to Use Positive Attributions *256*
   Arrange Counseling Interventions When Needed *258*

Increase Students' Personal Investment in the Classroom *258*
Make Learning More Fun and Enjoyable *261*
Praise Students and Reward Their Efforts *265*

CHAPTER 10
Improving Attention and Memory 274

Attention 276
Attention and Students with Special Needs .276
Strategies for Improving Attention 276
Basic Skills and Problems 281
Extreme Cases of Attention Deficits 281
Memory 283
Aspects of Memory 283
Memory and Students with Special Needs 285
Preconditions for Improving Memory 285
Strategies for Improving Memory 285
Improve Memory with Mnemonic Techniques 292

CHAPTER 11
Teaching Study Skills 304

Tools to Develop Independent Learners 306
Help Students Develop Personal Organizational Skills 306
Promote Listening Skills 315
Note Taking 319
Research and Reference Skills 324
Teach Library Skills 324
Help Students Prepare Reports and Projects .326

CHAPTER 12
Assessment 334

Types of Tests 336
Adapting Tests for Students with Special Needs .338
Norm-Referenced Tests 338
Adapt Competency-Based and Statewide Assessment 340
Adapt Teacher-Made and Criterion-Referenced Tests 343
Using Curriculum-Based Measurement 347
Using Performance Assessment 350
Using Portfolio Assessment 355
Applications for Students with Special Needs 357
Teaching Test-Taking Skills 357
General Preparation Strategies 357
Strategies for Standardized Tests 358
Teach Specific Strategies for Standardized Tests 358
Teacher-Made Tests 361
Other Test-Taking Strategies 362
Grading and Scoring 363
Report Card Grades 363

PART 3   *Teaching in the Content Areas*

CHAPTER 13

Literacy 368

Reading 370
    Using Basal Textbooks 370
    The Whole Language Approach 371
    Reading Recovery 372
    Direct Instruction and Code Emphasis 373
    Adaptations for Promoting Word Identification 375
    Adaptations for Promoting Reading Fluency 382
    Technological Adaptations to Promote Reading 383
Reading Comprehension 383
    Strategies for Teaching Reading Comprehension in Inclusive Settings 384
    Instructional Adaptations that Foster Reading Comprehension 391
    Secondary Adaptations 391
Written Expression 392
    Handwriting 392
    Spelling 395
    Written Communication 398

CHAPTER 14

Mathematics 408

Mathematics Education 410
Mathematics and Students with Disabilities 411
Strategies for Teaching Math in Inclusive Settings 412
    Early Number Concepts 412
    Teaching Students to Count 413
    One-to-One Correspondence .414
    Helping Students Master Numeration 414
    Introducing Geometry in Early Years 414
    Addition and Subtraction Concepts 415
    Counting with Number Lines .415
    Writing Numbers 416
    Understanding Symbols 416
    Addition and Subtraction Computation 416
    Remembering Addition and Subtraction Facts 417
    Place Value and Regrouping .420
    Teaching Early Problem Solving with Addition and Subtraction 422
    Multiplication and Division Concepts 424
    Multiplication and Division Facts 424
    Calculators 426
    Arithmetic Vocabulary 427
    Multiplication and Division Algorithms 427
    Error Analysis for Diagnosis .429
    Problem Solving 430
    Metacognition and Mathematics 431
    Money 431
    Time 434
    Fractions 435
    Decimals 435
    Area and Volume Concepts 436

Algebra *436*
Mathematical Reasoning Problems *440*
Teach Functional Math *441*

CHAPTER 15

Science and Social Studies 446

Adapting Textbook/Content-Oriented Approaches 448
Adapting Science and Social Studies Instruction *448*
Effective Teacher Presentations *448*
Promoting Independent Learning from Textbooks *453*
Adapting Textbook Materials to Accommodate Diverse Learners *463*
Adapting Activities-Oriented Approaches in Science and Social Studies 467
Adapting Science Activities *468*
Social Studies Adaptations *475*
Inquiry Learning in Science and Social Studies 477
Use a Problem-Solving Model for Social Studies Instruction *478*
Promote Active Thinking with Guided Questioning *478*
Developmental Considerations *480*
Develop Students' Abilities to Use Deductive Reasoning *481*

CHAPTER 16

Art, Music, Physical Education, Foreign Languages, Vocational Education, and Transitions 484

Art, Music, and Physical Education 486
Teaching Strategies *488*
Foreign Languages *491*
Vocational and Career Education 492
Overview of Vocational and Career Education *492*
The Carl D. Perkins Vocational Education Act of 1984 . . . .*492*
Modifications for Students with Special Needs *493*
Instructional Strategies *501*
Transitions 503
What Does Transition Mean? *503*
Self-Advocacy and Self-Determination Preparation *506*
Assessment *508*
Curriculum *510*
Planning for Graduation *510*
Planning for Future Education *511*
Planning for Future Job Opportunities *513*
Planning for Independent Living Situations *514*

References 517

Name Index 561

Subject Index 571

Note: Every effort has been made to provide accurate and current Internet information in this book. However, the Internet and information posted on it are constantly changing, so it is inevitable that some of the Internet addresses listed in this textbook will change.

The Inclusive Classroom
Strategies for
Effective Instruction

Chapter 1

Ernestine Glidden, 12
Portland, Maine
"Untitled"

Introduction to Inclusive Teaching

Objectives

After studying this chapter, you should be able to:

- Understand federal laws protecting the educational services for students with disabilities.
- Compare and contrast the issues surrounding inclusive instruction for students with disabilities.
- Analyze several important court cases relating to students with disabilities, presenting a progression of increasing rights for students with disabilities.
- Describe the continuum of services available to students with special needs and the "least-restrictive environment" concept.
- Identify the disability categories served under IDEA.
- Summarize and describe the legal foundations, litigation, and legislation of students with disabilities such as IDEA (Individuals with Disabilities Education Act), Section 504 (Vocational Rehabilitation Act), and ADA (Americans with Disabilities Act).

In 1975, a law was passed by Congress that would change the face of public education in the United States. This law, the Education for All Handicapped Children Act (now known as the **Individuals with Disabilities Education Act,** or IDEA) specified that all children—including those with disabilities formerly excluded from school—were entitled to a free, appropriate public education. This law went far beyond any previous legislation in specifying that, to the greatest extent possible, this "special" education was to be provided in the **least-restrictive environment.** In other words, students with disabilities were to be educated to the greatest extent possible in the general education classroom. This book is dedicated to describing the means by which this "least-restrictive environment" can become a reality.

The passage of IDEA, and its subsequent amendments, has largely achieved its purpose. More than ever, students with disabilities now receive free, appropriate public education. Furthermore, this education is being provided more often in the general education classroom.

Before the passage of IDEA, students with disabilities were often denied access to public education (Johnson, 1986). In some cases, they were placed in institutions. In other cases, the parents were forced to pay for private schools, often in inappropriate settings. Today, all students with disabilities are legally eligible to a free, appropriate education suited to their needs. The following scenarios compare a case from many years ago with a similar case from today. As a result of IDEA and similar legislation, society has an increased understanding of individuals with disabilities, and is much better able to accommodate individual differences in the school, in the workplace, and in social settings.

HISTORICAL SCENARIOS

Mr. and Mrs. Patterson

In 1960, Mr. and Mrs. Patterson had a brand-new baby girl, Hope. The initial excitement about the successful pregnancy and delivery was soon shrouded by a dark cloud. They were informed by the doctors that their precious infant was retarded. Mrs. Patterson tells their story:

"We felt horrible when the physician informed us that our beautiful baby girl was retarded. I can still hear his words: 'You probably don't want to keep her. The state institution is the best place for infants like her. She really won't be able to learn anything. The staff at the institution will be able to take care of her better than you.' I immediately hated the doctor. How could he be saying this to me about my brand-new baby girl? I felt as if I was having a nightmare and that at any moment I would awake and find that everything was okay.

At first we were so angry and couldn't help thinking thoughts like: Why did this happen to us? We didn't do anything wrong; this is unfair! We looked for someone to blame. We blamed the doctors and the staff at the hospital. It must be their fault, it couldn't be ours! Then, gradually, we both felt so guilty. We racked our brains for things that we might have done incorrectly during pregnancy. Did I fall? Was I exposed to any harmful substances? We lived in an old apartment building, we had thought everything there was safe, but now we had second thoughts about everything. We didn't trust our own judgment anymore on anything. We didn't know who to turn to for help. We felt overwhelmed and lost. The only individuals we knew we could speak with were the doctors and staff at the hospital, who had already expressed their opinions to us.

We loved our baby and decided to keep her. She was very slow at developing. At first I was embarrassed to take her out of the house. We were always searching for effective ways to help her. Everything was so hard. Each little thing we did seemed like an enormous journey. When Hope reached kindergarten age she had passed some important developmental milestones. We knew she wasn't developmentally the same as other children her age, but we hoped that she might begin to catch up once she was in school.

Unfortunately, however, within the first week of kindergarten we were contacted by the school and asked to remove Hope from the school. We were told that she wasn't ready for school and that she took too much time away from the other children in the class. If we wanted Hope exposed to any educational program, the only solution available to us was to place Hope in the state institution's school.

We were again devastated with this horrible decision. We felt as if we had no educational option. We went through the identical grieving process as we did when Hope was born. We were angry and felt guilty for sending her away, but we sincerely believed we had no other options available to us. Although we made the best decision for us at the time, we still feel guilty."

Mr. and Mrs. Baxter

Imagine a family in similar circumstances as the Pattersons over 40 years later. Mr. and Mrs. Baxter have a brand-new baby girl, Holly. The excitement turns to dismay when they are informed by the doctors that their precious infant is severely developmentally delayed. This time, however, the Baxters have additional legal guarantees in place that will provide a free and appropriate education for their child in the least-restrictive environment, beginning with **early intervention services** *and continuing through supported employment options into adulthood. Some early intervention programs are available in their own community. Some of the program options are center-based, in which the intervention occurs at the school, some are home-based, in which the intervention takes place in the home, and others are a combination of center- and home-based programs. This means that Holly can participate daily in relevant educational programs in a variety of setting options.*

Additionally, established networks of organizations provide support to parents and families of children with disabilities. Although the Baxters will still have some of the same painful experiences that the Pattersons had, at least the federal government has mandated services for families with children with severe special needs. Mrs. Baxter tells her story:

Parents of children with disabilities face awesome responsibilities and challenges, including the need to advocate for the rights of their children.

"We felt horrible when the physician informed us that our beautiful baby girl would always be severely developmentally delayed. Her words still ring in my ears. 'Your baby is not normal!' We barely heard the rest of her statement: 'We have a staff of early childhood specialists and nurses who will be in contact with you later today.' We couldn't believe our ears. The doctor must have us mixed up with someone else. There must be a horrible mistake. How could anything be wrong with our brand-new baby girl? I felt as if I was having a nightmare and that at any moment I would wake up and find that everything was okay."

The Baxters, like the Pattersons, went through the same questions of "Why us?" and "What happened?" and the associated feelings of denial, anger, guilt, and aloneness. Later on the same day, however, the Baxters felt the support from an early childhood specialist and a nurse. As Mrs. Baxter reported:

"They explained the types of intervention services that were available for our baby and for us. At first everything seemed like a blur, but then as reality sank in we realized that we had hope for Holly again. Specialized services were available, she would receive assistance, and we would receive educational support. Although we still felt the anger and wanted to blame someone, we began to realize there were individuals and support services that would help us begin to adapt and provide appropriate services for our baby with special needs."

What Are the Educational Rights for Individuals with Disabilities?

Before the passage of federal legislation mandating services for students with disabilities, these individuals were routinely and legally excluded from school. Johnson (1986, pp. 1–2) documented several instances across the United States, including the following examples:

- In Massachusetts in 1893, a child with disabilities was excluded by a school committee because "he was so weak in mind as to not derive any marked benefit from instruction and further, that he is troublesome to other children. . . ." (*Watson v. City of Cambridge,* 1893).
- In Wisconsin in 1919, a 13-year-old with normal intelligence but physical disabilities was excluded for the following reasons:

  His physical condition and ailment produces a depressing and nauseating effect upon the teachers and school children; . . . he takes up an undue proportion of the teacher's time

The original special education laws and their amendments were referred to as the Education for All Handicapped Children Act. For clarity and consistency, in this text, we will refer to this law by its current acronym, IDEA.

and attention, distracts attention of other pupils, and interferes generally with discipline and progress of the school. (Beattie v. Board of Education of City of Antigo, 1919).

- In 1963, Nevada excluded students whose "physical or mental conditions or attitude is such as to prevent or render inadvisable his attendance at school or his application to study" (Nevada Revised Statutes, 1963).
- In 1971, Alaska excluded from school students with "bodily or mental conditions rendering attendance inadvisable" (Alaska Statutes, 1971).
- Virginia law in 1973 allowed school exclusion for "children physically or mentally incapacitated for school work" (Code of Virginia, 1973).

Today, these laws are no longer applicable. According to federal law, all students, regardless of disability, are entitled to a free and appropriate public education, including access to the general education curriculum. Since 1975, public education has truly become "education for all."

Along with increased rights of individuals with disabilities from legislation such as IDEA come increased responsibilities for teachers. General education teachers today have more students with disabilities in their classrooms than ever. In fact, nearly three-fourths of all students with disabilities currently receive all or most of their education in a general education classroom (see Table 1.1). Today, therefore, teachers must be especially aware of their responsibilities in providing appropriate instruction for students with disabilities.

Although more responsibilities are placed on the general education teacher, you should not consider them a burden. On the contrary, classroom diversity—whether in the form of gender, race, ethnicity, or ability—is something to be valued in its own right. Diversity provides a more exciting, dynamic classroom and the opportunity for students to learn that all people are not the same. Diversity provides opportunities for students to understand, respect, and value others for their differences. Finally, diversity provides the opportunity for you to use all of your imagination, skills, and resources, to be the best teacher you can be. In the end, effective inclusive teaching is about being the most effective teacher possible, and supporting all students to learn in the least-restrictive environment.

Table 1.1

Disability Categories, and Proportion of Students Ages 6–21 Currently Served 40% or More of the School Day in General Education Classrooms

Disability Category	Proportion of Students Served 40% or More in Regular Classrooms
All disabilities	75.9%
Specific learning disabilities	83.5%
Speech or language impairments	95.1%
Mental retardation	43.0%
Emotional disturbance	48.5%
Multiple disabilities	27.0%
Hearing impairments	58.3%
Orthopedic impairments	66.1%
Other health impairments	77.5%
Visual impairments	68.9%
Autism	33.5%
Deaf-blindness	23.4%
Traumatic brain injury	57.5%

Note: The data are from *Twenty-Third Annual Report to Congress on the Implementation of the Individuals with Disabilities Education Act* (Appendix A), 2001. Washington, DC: U.S. Department of Education.

The Least-Restrictive Environment

Where Are Students with Disabilities Served?

Critical to IDEA legislation is the concept of "least-restrictive environment." This phrase means that students with disabilities must be educated in the setting least removed from the general education classroom. To the greatest extent possible, students with disabilities are not to be restricted to education in special schools or special classrooms, but rather should have access to the same settings to which students without disabilities have access. When students with disabilities are educated, to any extent, in a different setting, there must be a compelling reason that this setting is in the student's best interest.

Mainstreaming and Inclusion

Mainstreaming was the first movement devoted to placement of students with disabilities within the general education classroom. Educators used the term **mainstreaming** to refer to the placement of students with disabilities—often part-time—into general class settings. Although this term is still used today, it often suggests an attitude that students with disabilities really belong to special education and that they only visit the general classroom. That is, the student is in reality the responsibility of the special education teacher, but for certain periods of the day is part of the mainstream environment. Advocates of mainstreaming two decades ago did not want to see students with disabilities placed in special classes for the entire school day, and argued that more exposure to the general classroom would be in everyone's best interest. Often, mainstreaming was thought to be something individual special education students could "earn," by demonstrating their skills were adequate to function independently in general education settings. More recently, the term **inclusion** has been used to describe the education of students with disabilities in general education settings. Although many definitions have been used to describe *inclusion,* the term is generally taken to mean that students with disabilities are served primarily in the general education classroom, under the responsibility of the general classroom teacher. When necessary and justifiable, students with disabilities may also receive some of their instruction in another setting, such as a resource room. Additional support can also be provided within the general education classroom, by paraprofessionals or special education teachers. Although this is a similar concept to mainstreaming, a critical difference of inclusion is the view of the general classroom as the primary placement for the student with disabilities, with other special services regarded as ancillary.

Effective inclusive teaching is about being the most effective teacher possible.

Many definitions for *mainstreaming* and *inclusion* are commonly heard in schools, but all definitions may not indicate exactly the same concept. In this text we will use the terms *inclusion* or *inclusive* to mean the practice of including students with disabilities and other special needs in the general classroom.

In addition to mainstreaming and inclusion, the term **full inclusion** is also used, referring to the practice of serving students with disabilities and other special needs entirely within the general classroom. In full-inclusion settings, all students with disabilities are served the entire day in the general classroom, although special education teachers and other personnel may also be present in the general classroom at times (Stainback & Stainback, 1990a).

Who Is Served Under IDEA?

IDEA is intended to provide necessary support services to students with disabilities. To accomplish this goal, students with disabilities are categorized in particular disability groups. It is important to remember, however, that all students served by IDEA are first human beings and individuals, capable of achievement, accomplishment, friendship, affection, and all other attributes of any other individuals. Disability status may not be a permanent characteristic of all individuals; in fact, most people can expect to be considered "disabled" at one time or another in their lives. This in no way detracts from their fundamental worth as human beings. In fact, it is this principle of individual worth that has inspired much of today's special education legislation.

In short, although students served under IDEA have been given a disability "label," it is important to consider the individual first, and then consider the label as a secondary factor, along with other characteristics that help identify the unique aspects of the individual. For this reason, it is recommended that "person first" language be adopted, whereby the individual is identified first, and disability characterizations, when necessary, are provided later (Blaska, 1993). For example, we speak of "students with hearing impairments," rather than "hearing-impaired students." It is also important to remember that we use these descriptions only when it is directly relevant to a situation. When it is not relevant to list hearing impairment as a characteristic, for example, we speak simply of "Amy," or "Richard," or "Ana." For example, Margo, as a high school student, was best friends with Carol, a student one year older. They played on the basketball team together, and spent much of their after-school time together. After several years of close friendship, Margo expressed surprise that Carol had not gotten her driver's license, even a year after her 16th birthday. Further, Carol went to a separate setting to take the SAT. When she asked Carol about these things, Carol revealed that she was legally blind. Margo was astonished to hear this—and this situation demonstrated clearly to her that many characteristics of individuals, such as warmth, caring, sincerity, and understanding, can be much more important than disability status. It also demonstrated that important relationships can be developed and maintained that have little or nothing to do with disability status.

General Characteristics

Students served by IDEA are distributed among 13 disability categories. Following is a brief description of each category (see U.S. Department of Education, 1999). Individual states may use different terminology. For example, Indiana refers to mental retardation as "mental handicap." These areas are described in more detail in chapters 3 and 4.

- **Autism:** Autism is a severe, lifelong disability manifested within the first 3 years of life. Major characteristics include impairments in communication, learning, and reciprocal social interaction.
- **Deafness:** Individuals with deafness have hearing impairments so severe that processing linguistic information through hearing is severely limited, with or without amplification, and educational performance is negatively impacted.
- **Deaf-blindness:** Individuals in this category have moderate to severe impairments in both vision and hearing. This is included as a separate category because of the unique learning needs presented, and specialized services required.
- **Emotional disturbance** (SED): This category includes individuals with a condition in one or more of the following areas during an extended period of time: (a) inability to learn, not due to intellectual, sensory, or health problems; (b) inability to build and maintain social relationships with peers and teachers; (c) inappropriate behavior and affect; (d) gen-

For information on many disability categories that can be found at the Website of the Council for Exceptional Children, go to the Web Links module in chapter 1 of the Companion Website.

eral pervasive depression or unhappiness; (e) tendency to develop fears or physical symptoms associated with school and personal problems; and (f) schizophrenia. According to the federal definition, SED is not intended to apply to socially maladjusted children unless they also are characterized as having serious emotional disturbance.

- **Hearing impairment:** Hearing impairments can range from mild to moderate to severe. The hearing loss, with or without amplification, affects educational performance and developmental progress. The impairment may be permanent or fluctuating, mild to profound, unilateral or bilateral. Individuals with hearing impairments are also referred to as "hard of hearing" or "deaf."

- **Mental retardation:** Mental retardation describes significantly below average intellectual functioning, as well as concurrent deficits in "adaptive behavior" (age-appropriate personal independence and social responsibility). Individuals with mental retardation may exhibit generalized problems in learning, memory, attention, problem solving, academic, and social functioning. It is manifested between birth and age 18, and negatively affects educational performance.

- **Multiple disabilities:** This category includes any individuals with two or more disabling conditions. However, this category often includes mental retardation as one of the categories, and is usually used when disorders are serious and interrelated to such an extent that it is difficult to identify the primary area of disability. It does not include deaf-blindness.

- **Orthopedic impairment:** Orthopedic impairments are associated with physical conditions that seriously impair mobility or motor activity. This category includes individuals with cerebral palsy or diseases of the skeleton or muscles, and accident victims.

All individuals with disabilities are, first and foremost, individuals.

- **Other health impairment:** This category includes chronic or acute health-related difficulties that adversely affect educational performance, and is manifested by limited strength, vitality, or alertness. It can include such health problems as heart conditions; sickle cell anemia; lead poisoning; diabetes; HIV, the virus that causes acquired immune deficiency syndrome (AIDS); or AIDS itself.

- **Specific learning disability:** This refers to a disorder in one or more of the basic psychological processes involved in understanding or using spoken or written language, which can result in difficulties in reading, writing, listening, speaking, thinking, spelling, or mathematics. The term *learning disabilities* does not apply to children with learning problems that are primarily the result of visual, hearing, or physical disabilities; mental retardation; emotional disturbance; or environmental, cultural, or economic disadvantage.

- **Speech or language impairment:** A disorder of articulation, fluency, voice, or language that adversely affects educational performance; or a severe communication deficit that may require the use of an augmentative or alternative communication system such as sign language, communication boards, or electronic devices.

- **Traumatic brain injury:** Traumatic brain injury is an acquired injury to the brain due to external force resulting in a total or partial disability or psychosocial impairment, or both, which negatively affects educational performance.

- **Visual impairment including blindness:** A visual impairment is a loss of vision that, even when corrected, affects educational performance. It may be mild to moderate to severe in nature. Students who are blind are unable to read print and usually learn to read and write using Braille. Students with low vision can usually read when the print is enlarged sufficiently.

In addition, children aged 3 to 9 can be classified as experiencing **developmental delay,** if they are experiencing developmental delays in one or more of the following areas: physical, cognitive, communication, social or emotional, or adaptive development, and who need special education and related services.

Definitions of major categories of specific disabilities, including incidence and prevalence, are topics on the Praxis *Special Education: Core Knowledge* Tests. For more information, including study guide and practice items, see Educational Testing Service (2002). For the ETS Web site, go to the Web Links module in chapter 1 of the Companion Website.

Detailed discussions of these disability categories are provided in chapters 3 and 4.

Other Instances of Classroom Diversity

IDEA provides service to most of the recognized disability areas. However, there are other sources of classroom diversity, not associated with disabilities, that you need to consider when planning and implementing classroom instruction. These areas include the following:

- **Culturally and linguistically diverse groups:** These students are culturally or linguistically different from the majority U.S. culture, or different from the teacher. Teachers should plan and implement instruction that is considerate of and sensitive to students' linguistic or cultural differences (Grossman, 1995).
- **At-risk:** Students characterized as "at-risk" exhibit characteristics, live in an environment, or have experiences that make them more likely to fail in school, drop out, or experience lack of success in future life (Frymier, 1992). These factors are many and varied, but they include "slow learners" not served by IDEA categories and individuals who have sociocultural disadvantages, are at-risk for suicide, or come from dysfunctional home environments (e.g., marred by drug or alcohol abuse, domestic violence, or child abuse). Such learners may require any of a variety of adaptations to help them succeed in school and later life (Stephens & Price, 1992).
- **Gifted and talented:** These students exhibit skills or abilities substantially above those of their age in areas such as academic achievement in one or more subject areas, visual or performing arts, or athletics. If the abilities of such students greatly exceed classroom standards or curriculum, special adaptations or accommodations may be appropriate. Although many states have passed laws providing for the identification and education of gifted and talented students, in many cases funding for gifted programs is not provided (Genshaft, Bireley, & Hollinger, 1995).

Legal Foundations

Legal and societal issues are topics on the Praxis *Special Education: Core Knowledge* Tests.

In the years following World War II, political change, litigation, and resulting legislation began to emerge that increased the inclusion of all groups of people in U.S. society. Most significant was the civil rights movement, which primarily addressed the rights of African Americans in U.S. society. This movement influenced the ideas on which much litigation and legislation involving individuals with disabilities are based. In the *Brown v. Board of Education* (1954) decision, the Supreme Court ruled that it was unlawful to discriminate against any group of people. With respect to school children, the Court ruled that the concept of "separate-but-equal" educational facilities for children of different races was inherently unequal. The justification for this ruling was found in the 14th Amendment to the U.S. Constitution, which states that individuals cannot be deprived of life, liberty, or property without due process of law.

Legal Proceedings and Legislation

People with disabilities also began to be identified as a group whose rights had been denied. In the years following *Brown v. Board of Education,* court cases were decided that underlined the rights of individuals with disabilities to a free, appropriate education. Other cases supported nondiscriminatory special education placement of individuals from minority groups in the United States. Some of the important court cases relating to individuals with disabilities present a progression of increasing rights for individuals with disabilities (see also Osborne, 1996; Rothstein, 1999; Yell, 1997):

- **1954:** *Brown v. Board of Education* (Kansas). The Supreme Court determined that "separate-but-equal" education is illegal.
- **1970:** *Diana v. State Board of Education* (California). The court ruled that children cannot be placed in special education based on culturally biased tests.
- **1972:** *Pennsylvania Association for Retarded Children (PARC) v. Commonwealth of Pennsylvania* and *Mills v. Board of Education* (District of Columbia) established the right to education for students with disabilities, and found that denial of education violates the 14th Amendment.
- **1977:** *Larry P. v. Riles.* A California court ruled that the use of standardized IQ tests for placement into special education classes for students with educable mental retardation was discriminatory.

- **1988:** *Honig v. Doe* (California). This decision was concerned with extensive suspensions of students with emotional disturbances from school, for aggressive behavior which the court determined was disability-related. The court ruled that a suspension of longer than 10 days was effectively a change in placement, requiring all the necessary procedures governing a change in placement.
- **1992:** *Oberti v. Board of Education of the Borough of Clementon School District* (New Jersey). A federal district court ruled that a self-contained special education class was not the least restrictive for a student with Down syndrome. The court ruled that school districts were obligated to first consider regular class placement, with supplementary aids and services, before considering alternative placements.

Along with this litigation, laws began to be passed that provided further support for the rights of students with disabilities. Some of these laws are summarized in Figure 1.1. In the following section, some of the most significant legislation involving individuals with disabilities is described (see also Osborne, 1996; Rothstein, 1999; Yell, 1997). This legislation includes **Section 504** of the **Vocational Rehabilitation Act,** the **Americans with Disabilities Act,** and the most significant law for special education, the Individuals with Disabilities Education Act (PL 94-142).

Federal legislation is numbered to reflect the number of the Congress as well as the number of the bill. Therefore, PL 94-142 was the 142nd Public Law passed by the 94th Congress.

1973	Section 504—Rehabilitation Act of 1973, U.S.C. Section 794: Recipients of federal funds cannot discriminate on the basis of disability.
1975	Education for All Handicapped Children Act (PL 94-142), 20 U.S.C. Sections 1400–1461: This law requires, and provides support to, states to implement a plan to provide free education and appropriate related services (on an individualized basis) to students with disabilities, including due process provisions. It requires Individualized Education Programs (IEPs) for each student served under this law. This law was amended in 1983, 1986, 1990, and 1997. The 1990 amendments also renamed this law the Individuals with Disabilities Education Act (IDEA).
1977	Final regulations of Education for All Handicapped Children Act are passed.
1978	Gifted and Talented Children's Education Act. This act provides financial incentives for state and local educational agencies to develop programs for gifted and talented students.
1983	Amendments to the Education of the Handicapped Act (PL 98-199): These amendments mandate states to collect data on students with disabilities exiting systems and to address transition needs of secondary students with disabilities. In addition, they provide incentives to states to provide services to infants and preschoolers with disabilities.
1984	Developmental Disabilities Assistance and Bill of Rights Acts (PL 98-527): These acts provide for the development of employment-related training activities for adults with disabilities.
1984	Perkins Act, 20 U.S.C. 2301, 2332–34: This act mandates that 10% of all vocational education funding must be for students with disabilities. Vocational education should be provided in the least-restrictive environment; secondary support is provided for students with disabilities.
1986	Education for All Handicapped Children Act Amendments (PL 99-457): These amendments encourage states to develop comprehensive services for infants and toddlers (birth through age 2) with disabilities and to expand services for preschool children (ages 3–5). After the 1990–91 school year, all states must provide free and appropriate education to all 3- to 5-year-olds with disabilities or forfeit federal assistance for preschool funding.
1986	Rehabilitation Acts Amendments (PL 99-506): These amendments provide for the development of supported employment programs for adults with disabilities.

Figure 1.1
History of Relevant Legislation

Section 504

Section 504 of the Vocational Rehabilitation Act of 1973 is a civil rights law that prevents discrimination against individuals with disabilities from any institution that receives federal funds, and provides for a free, appropriate public education (FAPE). Some private schools that do not receive federal funding may be exempt from Section 504. This law applies both to schools and to the workforce. Section 504 provides for equal opportunities in all aspects of education. Students may not be classified as disabled according to the IDEA guidelines, but they must demonstrate a significant learning problem that affects their ability to function in school. Under Section 504, disability is considered to be an impairment, physical or mental, that substantially limits a major life activity (Smith, 2001). Some students who may not be served under IDEA, because they do not meet the definitional requirements of one of the IDEA disability categories, can still obtain services under Section 504. For example, some students with attention deficit hyperactivity disorder (ADHD), as well as some students who require modifications for their severe allergies or asthma, may be covered under this law. Other types of disabilities likely covered under Section 504, but not IDEA, might include the following (Martin, 1992; see also Smith, 2001, p. 338):

- Students who had been placed in special education programs but have transitioned out;
- Students thought to be socially maladjusted, or who have a history of alcohol or drug abuse;
- Students who carry infectious diseases such as AIDS.

Students can be referred for Section 504 services by anyone, but are usually referred by teachers or parents. When a student has been referred, the school must consider the referral. If a group of knowledgeable school personnel believe the child is eligible, the school must then conduct an evaluation to determine eligibility and the nature of services needed to ensure a free, appropriate public education. The determination is made by individuals knowledgeable regarding the child, assessment procedures, and treatment options. The decision is based on professional judgment rather than by test scores and numerical indicators (Smith, 2001). Smith and Patton (1999) have provided a form that can be useful in determining eligibility. The form lists major life activities (such as caring for oneself, hearing, speaking, and learning), and provides spaces for school personnel to provide a description of the impairment, information sources, an assessment of severity and duration, and a determination of whether the limitation is substantial. If a student is considered eligible, the law does not provide funding; however, it does require that school personnel create a written plan that will help accommodate these special needs and provide an accessible environment. Accommodation plans can include a statement of student strengths and weaknesses, along with a list of accommodations to be implemented, and the person responsible for implementation. Accommodations are usually inexpensive, commonsense modifications intended to provide nondiscrimination and free, appropriate public education (Smith, 2001).

Americans with Disabilities Act

The Americans with Disabilities Act (ADA) was signed into law in 1990, and provided that individuals with disabilities should be provided with "reasonable accommodations" in the workplace, and that such individuals could not be discriminated against. ADA also included protections for individuals enrolled in colleges and universities. Adults with disabilities attending universities are also entitled to appropriate modifications in classes. These modifications, in many ways, parallel those made in public schools in compliance with IDEA. Major components of the ADA are given in Figure 1.2.

The Americans with Disabilities Act is of particular significance because of its aim to maximize the employment potential of millions of Americans with disabilities. It can be considered an important extension of IDEA, in that it provides for reasonable accommodations and nondiscriminatory treatment of individuals with disabilities beyond the high school years.

Individuals with Disabilities Education Act (IDEA)

This act is the major special education law. Originally signed in 1975 as the Education for All Handicapped Children Act, IDEA has been amended several times since then, most recently in 1997. The most important provision in IDEA is that all children, from 3 through 21 years of age, regardless of type or severity of disability, are entitled to a free, appropriate public education. Discretionary assistance is also provided to develop interagency programs for all young children with disabilities,

- Employers may not discriminate on the basis of disability.
- Employers may not ask if applicant has a disability.
- "Reasonable accommodations" must be provided in the workplace.
- New buses must be made accessible.
- Most communities must provide transportation.
- Rail service must accommodate individuals with disabilities within 20 years.
- Public locations—hotels, stores, and restaurants—are accessible.
- State and local governments may not discriminate.
- Telephone companies must provide adapted communication options for the deaf.

Figure 1.2
Major Components of ADA
Note: From *Americans with Disabilities Act Requirements: Fact Sheet,* 1990, Washington, DC: U.S. Department of Justice.

from birth to 3 years of age. This provision overrides previous legislation and decisions that limit the attendance of students with disabilities in public schools. Overall, six major principles have remained in the law throughout its amendments. These principles are as follows:

1. *Zero reject.* This principle requires that no child with a disability can be excluded from public education.
2. *Nondiscriminatory testing.* Schools are required to use a variety of nondiscriminatory methods to determine whether a student has a disability, and, if so, whether special education is required. Testing must not discriminate on the basis of race, culture, or ethnicity, and must be administered in the student's native language. A variety of measures is required so that placement decisions are not made on the basis of a single test score.
3. *Free and appropriate education.* Students who have been referred to special education must have an **individualized education program** (IEP) that details their special learning needs and mandates appropriate services. Short- and long-term goals and objectives for students are listed explicitly on IEPs.
4. *Least-restrictive environment.* Students with disabilities are entitled to be educated with their nondisabled peers to the greatest extent possible.
5. *Due process.* Due process must be followed in all placement decisions and changes in placement. Records are to be kept confidential, and parents are to be involved in all aspects of the planning and placement process.
6. *Parent participation.* Schools must collaborate with parents in the design and implementation of special education services (Turnbull, Turnbull, Shank, & Leal, 1999).

In addition to these six common principles, several additions have been made to the original law:

1. *Transition services.* All 14-year-old students with disabilities must be provided with transition services on their IEP. These services are intended to facilitate the student's transition from school to community, vocational programs, college, or employment. The transition plan can involve professionals from other agencies, such as social or vocational services. Transition planning conferences are also specified for transition from infant and toddler programs to preschool programs.
2. *Early childhood education.* Amendments to the Education for All Handicapped Children Act (now IDEA) in 1986 and 1990 provided for services to infants, toddlers, and preschoolers with disabilities. Very young children (younger than 3) are entitled to an individualized family service plan (IFSP, which replaces the IEP), which takes family needs and responsibilities into account. Necessary components of the IFSP include (a) current statement of child's functioning levels; (b) current statement of the family's needs and strengths in relation to the child with special needs; (c) statement of the major expected outcomes, including a time line; (d) statement of the specific services to be provided to meet the special needs of the child and the family; (e) initiation and anticipated duration dates for services; (f) a case manager; and (g) statement of transition steps from infant early intervention services to preschool services.

For a listing of some of the most recent amendments to IDEA (105-17), see Figure 1.3.

States are required to take action to locate as many young children as possible, who may require special education services. Some recent amendments to IDEA are provided in Figure 1.3.

No Child Left Behind Act of 2001

The No Child Left Behind Act (NCLB) is a reauthorization of the Elementary and Secondary Education Act, and was not written specifically for students with disabilities. However, many aspects of the legislation have important implications for students with disabilities.

The law requires that all children be tested in grades 3 through 8, in reading and math, by tests developed by the states. Schools must demonstrate adequate yearly progress (AYP) toward the goal of 100% proficiency in reading, math, and science for all students within 12 years. Schools must demonstrate that students make progress in equal increments toward this goal, that is, that they are making steady, equivalent gains from year to year. Schools that fail to make AYP for two consecutive years must offer parents of the students the option to transfer to another public school, and the districts must pay the cost of transportation (if allowed under state law). The school district must provide technical assistance to the school. If schools fail to make AYP for more than two consecutive years, more

---

Some of the 1997 amendments to IDEA (PL 105-17) include the following:

Definitions. For children ages 3–9, "child with a disability" may include a child experiencing developmental delays and who needs special education and related services.

Least-restrictive environment. If states allocate funds to schools based on the type of setting in which the student is served, the funding procedures must not violate the requirements of the least-restrictive environment.

IEP participation. The general education teacher of the student is to participate, to the extent appropriate, in the development, review, and revision of the IEP. The parents of each student with a disability are to be members of any group that makes placement decisions regarding their child.

Transition services. Students' IEPs must include a statement of transition service needs that focus on the student's courses of study at age 14. Transition from infant and toddler programs to preschool programs must also be planned.

Assessments. All students with disabilities must participate in general state- and districtwide assessment programs. If students cannot participate in state- and districtwide assessments, guidelines for participation in alternative assessments must be developed.

Attorney fees. Attorney fees relating to any meeting of the IEP team are prohibited, unless the meeting is convened as a result of an administrative proceeding, judicial action, or mediation conducted before the complaint was filed.

Discipline. School personnel can order a change in the placement of a child with a disability to an appropriate interim alternative educational setting (IAES), an alternate setting, or to be suspended, for not more than 10 school days. Students with disabilities can be placed in an IAES, for no more than 45 days, for weapon or drug violations. Within 10 days, an IEP meeting must develop an assessment plan to address the problem behavior. If a hearing officer provides "substantial evidence" that the current placement may result in substantial injury to the child or to others, the student may be placed in an IAES for no more than 45 days. To find that a behavior was not a manifestation of a student's disability, the IEP team must determine that the student's IEP, placement, and services were appropriate, or that the student's disability did not impair the student's ability to judge the effect or consequences of the behavior, or impair the student's ability to control the behavior. Parents have the right to appeal this decision.

Infants and toddlers at risk for developmental delay. States are encouraged to expand opportunities for children younger than 3 who would be at substantial risk for developmental delays without early intervention services.

Figure 1.3
Some Recent Amendments to IDEA (PL 105-17)

corrective measures must be taken, including replacing staff, implementing different curricula, or ultimately a state takeover, hiring a private management contractor, or converting to a charter school (CEC, 2002). Other aspects of the law include compensatory education grants (Title I), bilingual and immigrant education programs, and standards and provisions for teacher training and recruitment.

The NCLB Act has several important implications for special education. If students with disabilities fail to meet adequate yearly progress toward reaching 100% proficiency in reading and math by 2012, the entire school will face a host of accountability measures, as described previously. Further, if students with disabilities receive accommodations for statewide tests, and those accommodations result in the scores being deemed unreliable or invalid, the students will not be considered to have participated in the assessment. If the overall participation rate does not meet the minimum requirement (possibly as high as 95%), the state can be considered out of compliance and subject to sanctions (CEC, 2002). Finally, NCLB requires that all teachers hold full state certification or licensure by 2005. In light of the present personnel shortages in special education, meeting these requirements will be a major undertaking (CEC, 2002).

One important feature of federal legislation is that it is constantly changing. Some technological approaches for keeping abreast of federal legislation are described in the Technology Highlight.

For updates on IDEA and for more information on NCLB and its implications for special education, check the Council for Exceptional Children and U.S. Department of Education websites on the Web Links module in the Companion Website for chapter 1.

Technology Highlight

Federal Government Updates

One way to keep abreast of the changes in federal legislation is to check the U.S. Department of Education website regularly (www.ed.gov). This website contains a wealth of information that is updated frequently and contains links to relevant research and legislation sites. For example, a link to *No Child Left Behind* (www.nclb.gov) provides an overview of the act that was signed in January 2002. The site contains an overview of the act; commonly asked questions and answers that are presented in a easy to understand format; links to your particular state level contacts; links for parents, educators, and policy makers; newsletter; and even slide presentations that emphasize key points.

Additional helpful websites linked to the U.S. Department of Education (U.S. DOE) page are directly relevant to special education initiatives. These sites are the U.S. Department of Education, Office of Special Education and Rehabilitative Services web site *http://www.ed.gov/offices/ OSERS/* and the Office of Special Education Programs *http://www.ed.gov/offices/OSERS/OSEP/*. These sites contain information such as recent special education initiatives including the recent IDEA legislation, possible changes in the identification of "learning disabilities," recent research findings from projects funded by U.S. DOE, funding opportunities for research, model programs, and personnel preparation and the annual reports to Congress indicating the status of special education programs across the country with respect to numbers of children served birth through 21.

Finally, the Council for Exceptional Children (CEC) has a *Discover IDEA CD 2002* available for easy searching of the Individuals with Disabilities Education Act (IDEA). The CD also contains print ready policy documents, an easy index for searching, and related links to important policy and practice findings. Check the CEC website for updates to his information. For a current list of relevant websites, CEC and others, check the Web Links module in chapter 1 of the Companion Website.

Models of Service Delivery

The Continuum of Services

The initial emphasis of legal actions was to provide access to educational services for students with disabilities. Once access was obtained, the focus shifted to the setting and placement of students with disabilities during education. Some of the earliest guidelines on placement emphasized availability of a range of services and program services, commonly referred to as a **continuum** (or "cascade") **of services** within the least-restrictive environment for students with disabilities (Deno, 1970). Least-restrictive environment was defined in IDEA as meaning that students with disabilities should be educated in a setting that as closely as possible resembles the general education program while simultaneously meeting the unique special needs for each individual with disabilities. For example, the basic model of a continuum of services ranges from full-time placement in the general education classroom to full-time placement in a nonpublic school facility, on a day or residential basis, based on student need. As the needs of the individual with disability increases, the least-restrictive environment may be further removed from the general education class on the continuum of services. Figure 1.4 presents a sample of the range of placement options.

Where Are Most Students with Disabilities Served?

Most students with disabilities are served in the public school with their nondisabled peers in Levels 1 through 5. In other words, these students receive their education in their local public school. Most students with mild disabilities, including those with learning disabilities, mild mental retardation, speech and language disabilities, and serious emotional disabilities are currently served in Levels 1 through 4. That is, these students spend some, if not all, of their day in the general education classroom along with students without disabilities. The general education teacher is responsible for their education for some, if not all, of the day, depending on the amount of time spent in that general education class. Table 1.1 on page 6 provides a listing of disability categories and the proportion currently served in general education classrooms.

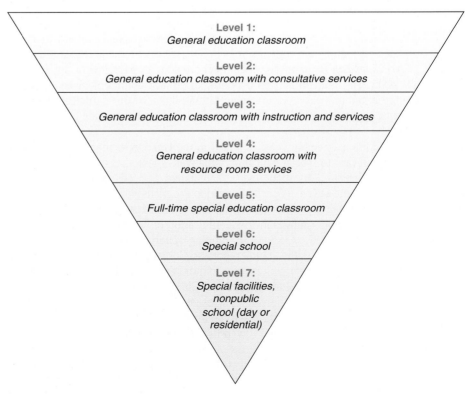

Level 1:
General education classroom

Level 2:
General education classroom with consultative services

Level 3:
General education classroom with instruction and services

Level 4:
General education classroom with resource room services

Level 5:
Full-time special education classroom

Level 6:
Special school

Level 7:
Special facilities, nonpublic school (day or residential)

Figure 1.4
Sample Continuum of Services, from Least Restrictive to Most Restrictive

What Are General Education Classroom and Consultation Services?

In some cases, students may be served in general education classes by general education teachers. Some special services may be provided by a **consultant** who works with individuals as needed. Special education teachers frequently provide consultative services to general education teachers. This consultation is intended to provide assistance and ideas for how to teach and work with the students with disabilities who are placed in general education classes. Although the special education teacher may not work directly with identified students, they may meet regularly with general education teachers, review assessment and progress data, and make specific recommendations for addressing special learning needs. These students would be receiving services on Levels 1 or 2 of the continuum of services model.

In other cases, special education teachers and classroom assistants (or paraprofessionals) may deliver instruction to students with special needs in the general education classroom. In these cases, students with disabilities still receive all their instruction in the general education classroom, but it may be delivered by different teachers or paraprofessionals. Teachers collaborate and share instructional responsibilities in one of several co-teaching models. For example, a special education teacher may lead instruction for small groups of elementary students with special needs during classroom reading instruction. On a secondary level, the special education teacher may co-teach with a general education teacher in a high school biology class. The two teachers share teaching responsibilities, with the special education teacher focusing on strategies for addressing special learning needs. These students would be receiving services on Level 3 of the continuum of services model. Co-teaching models are described further in chapter 2.

What Are Resource and Self-Contained Services?

Special education teachers also provide instruction in resource and self-contained classrooms within the public schools. In a resource room model, students with disabilities leave the general education class for a designated time period to visit the resource room and receive specialized instruction in areas such as language, reading, and math. For example, Kathi is a sixth grader who has been classified as having learning disabilities. Kathi is functioning intellectually within the average ability range, but she has reading, spelling, and written language skills on an upper third-grade level. The multidisciplinary team recommended that Kathi receive specialized instruction in reading, written communication, and spelling with a special education teacher 1.5 hours per day in her school's resource room. This means that Kathi would be receiving services on Level 4 of the continuum of services model.

Originally called the Education for All Handicapped Children's Act (PL 94-142), the Individuals with Disabilities Education Act (IDEA) provided that all children between the ages of 3 and 21, regardless of disability, are entitled to a free, appropriate public education.

Most of her school day would be in the least-restrictive environment of her general education class with Mrs. Gomez. Mrs. Gomez will be responsible for Kathi's instruction for the entire time that she is in the general education class. This might even include making some adaptations in instructional procedures and assignments to accommodate Kathi's special learning needs in the general education sixth-grade classroom. For example, during content area classes, Mrs. Gomez will need to provide adapted reading and study materials appropriate to Kathi's skill levels. During her 1.5 hours in the resource room, Kathi will receive instruction with Mr. Halleran, the special education teacher in the same school. This resource room arrangement represents the least-restrictive environment to meet Kathi's special needs in reading, written communication, and mathematics, while maintaining her placement in her general education class for the majority of the school day (see Wiederholt, Hammill, & Brown, 1993).

The resource model is often referred to as a "pull-out" model, indicating that students with disabilities are pulled out of the general education class for special education instruction. In a self-contained model of instruction (Level 5 of the continuum of services model), students with disabilities receive all or most of their classroom instruction from special education teachers. Even in these models, however, students with disabilities usually have opportunities to interact with their nondisabled peers during such activities as art, music, physical education, recess, lunch, and assemblies.

Special Schools and Special Facilities

In some cases, the need for specialized instruction is considered so pervasive that a special school or other special facility is considered necessary. In some cases, special public schools are established to focus specifically on the special needs of the students. In other cases, students are sent to nonpublic schools, either as special day schools or as residential schools. These students would be receiving services on Level 6 or 7 of the continuum of services model. The numbers of special schools or other special facilities have declined since the early years of IDEA, as traditional public schools have accommodated more students with disabilities and other special needs within their educational programs.

What Other Related Services Are Available?

Students with disabilities are also eligible to receive related services, if it is determined that the students require these services to benefit from special education. According to IDEA, related services may include parent counseling and training, physical therapy, occupational therapy, school health

Special educators working in resource rooms often provide individualized or small-group instruction for some students with disabilities.

services, or special transportation. This means that in addition to receiving special services along the continuum of services for a primary disability area, some students may also be eligible to receive additional related services. Related services may be delivered to individuals with disabilities in any of the setting options. Although described as "related" services, in many cases these services may be of critical importance in attending to the special needs of individual students. For example, Michael, a student with mental retardation, receives physical therapy in addition to his educational program to meet his special needs. Janice requires special transportation services to accommodate her wheelchair, and these are provided as related services.

The continuum of services and related services have been effectively applied throughout the history of IDEA. However, over this same time period there have been recommendations regarding how all or most students with disabilities could be more easily served entirely within the general education classroom. These movements have been referred to as the Regular Education Initiative and the full-inclusion movement.

Inclusion Movements

Regular Education Initiative

Following the initial promotion of mainstreaming, during the 1980s, a movement called the "Regular Education Initiative" (Will, 1986) was begun. This movement sought to educate students with disabilities—particularly those with mild and moderate disabilities—totally within the general education environment (see Kauffman, 1989, for a discussion). One example of a program developed to support the Regular Education Initiative was the Adaptive Learning Environments Model (ALEM)(Wang, Reynolds, & Zollers, 1990). Controversy surrounding this movement grew, however, because many educators questioned whether general education teachers wanted or felt qualified for increased responsibility for students with disabilities. In addition, it was argued that research evidence did not exist to support the elimination of special education classes and other services for students with disabilities (see Bryan, Bay, & Donahue, 1988; Bryan & Bryan, 1988; Fuchs & Fuchs, 1988a, 1988b; Lloyd, Repp, & Singh, 1991; Wang & Walberg, 1988). Nevertheless, the Regular Education Initiative did much to focus attention on the important issue of the best placement options for students with disabilities, and how such decisions should be made.

Full-Inclusion Movement

More recently, a movement referred to as inclusion, or full inclusion, has come to the forefront (Kauffman & Hallahan, 1995). Full inclusion has been referred to as placing and serving students with disabilities entirely within the general education classroom. This means, for example, that all students with disabilities, regardless of severity or type of disability, are placed in the general education class for the entire school day.

Consider the case of Kathi, our sixth-grader with learning disabilities. If Kathi were placed in a full-inclusion classroom, Mrs. Gomez, her general education teacher, would have Kathi in her room all day every day with all of the other sixth-grade students. Mrs. Gomez would be primarily responsible for all of Kathi's instruction, and for making adaptations appropriate for addressing Kathi's learning disabilities. In some full-inclusion models, Mr. Halleran, the special education teacher, would consult with Mrs. Gomez and provide ideas for her to use in teaching Kathi in her IEP need areas. In other full-inclusion models, Mr. Halleran might go into Mrs. Gomez's room and teach Kathi reading, spelling, and writing in that room. In this model, instruction with Mr. Halleran and Kathi may occur at a small table, perhaps with other students with special needs, while other groups of students meet for literacy activities. In still other full-inclusion models, Mr. Halleran may "team-teach" with Mrs. Gomez for part or all of the school day. During team-teaching, Mr. Halleran and Mrs. Gomez would work collaboratively on planning and implementing instruction for the entire class. In any of these full-inclusion models, however, Kathi remains in the general education class with her nondisabled peers all day.

As might be expected, considerable debate surrounds the issue of full inclusion (Fuchs & Fuchs, 1994; Kavale & Forness, 2000). It is important to remember that virtually all educational professionals recommend placement in general education classes for students with disabilities and other special needs; the disagreement usually centers on the *extent* to which students should be placed in general education settings (Mastropieri & Scruggs, 1997). Both proponents

More information on models of teacher collaboration is provided in chapter 2.

In full-inclusion classrooms, students with disabilities may spend the entire school day in the regular classroom setting.

of full inclusion and proponents of a continuum of services have articulated their positions, which are summarized in the following sections.

Arguments of Proponents of Full Inclusion

1. *Full inclusion is a civil right.* Proponents of full inclusion view full-time placement in the general education class as a civil right for all students with disabilities (Gartner & Lipsky, 1989; Stainback & Stainback, 1990b). These advocates state that students with disabilities have the right to be educated in the same classes alongside their nondisabled peers (Lipsky & Gartner, 1991). Proponents maintain that separate classes or schools are not equal to mainstream environments, and refer to the civil rights legislation of *Brown v. the Board of Education* (1954) as support for their position. Furthermore, full-inclusion advocates believe that students with disabilities learn more in integrated settings than in segregated settings (Stainback & Stainback, 1990a). They maintain that all students, including those with and without disabilities, develop better working relationships, communication skills, social interaction skills, and friendships when they are in fully inclusive environments (Stainback, Stainback, & Forest, 1989). Proponents argue that all students are better accepted and care more for others, and become more embracing of individual differences in full-inclusion environments.

2. *Full inclusion reduces stigma.* Proponents of full inclusion also state that students with disabilities are stigmatized when they are forced to be educated in a separate special school, special education class, or when they have to leave the general education classroom to receive services in a resource room (Kliewer & Biklen, 1996; Lilly, 1992). Such stigmatizing effects are seen to be harmful to the self-esteem of students with disabilities. It is suggested that nondisabled peers may ridicule and make fun of students identified as disabled in schools where students with disabilities are not fully included (Stainback & Stainback, 1990b).

3. *Full inclusion is more efficient.* Proponents say that students with disabilities lose valuable time from general education class activities during pull-out times in which students go to resource classes for specialized instruction. Some say that students with disabilities in pull-out programs, for example, might miss participating in content area instruction offered in general education settings (Affleck, Madge, Adams, & Lowenbraun, 1988). Often, if students are required to leave the classroom several times during the day for various support and related special services, the school day may become fragmented for them. This can lead to a lack of generalization of learning from the special to general education setting (Raynes, Snell, & Sailor, 1991). This position suggests that if students

are fully included, generalization will be less of a problem. It also has been argued that teaching approaches used in special education classes are not substantially different from those used in general education classes (Stainback & Stainback, 1984). Therefore, proponents of full inclusion maintain that all students should be instructed in the same general education classes.

4. *Full inclusion promotes equality.* Finally, Stainback and Stainback (1990a) maintained that inclusion deals with the basic value of equality:

> The most important reason to include all students in the mainstream is that it is the fair, ethical, and equitable thing to do. . . . It is discriminatory that some students, such as those "labeled" disabled, must earn the right to be in the regular education mainstream or have to wait for educational researchers to prove that they can profit from the mainstream, while other students are allowed unrestricted access simply because they have no label. No one should have to pass anyone's test or prove anything in a research study to live and learn in the mainstream of school and community life. This is a basic right, not something one has to earn. (pp. 6–7)

One position on full inclusion has been well articulated by The Association for Persons with Severe Handicaps (TASH), in their "Resolution on Inclusive Education." Many of the professional organizations' positions on inclusion are included in the appendix of Kauffman and Hallahan (1995) and on the organizations' respective Websites.

Arguments of Proponents for a Continuum of Services

1. *A continuum of service options is necessary.* Opponents of full inclusion maintain that a more cautious approach should be undertaken with respect to the full-time placement of students with disabilities in general education classes. A major argument is that the continuum of services, as implied by the least-restrictive environment clause of IDEA, needs to be maintained for the integrity of the service delivery system (Kauffman, 1995; Kauffman & Hallahan, 1995). Indeed, court decisions over the years regarding educational placements of students with disabilities have tended to place more emphasis on the "appropriate education" component of the law than the "least-restrictive environment" component (Johnson, 1986; Osborne, 1996). In fact, a Gallup Poll reported that the public tends to prefer the continuum of services model for educating students with disabilities (Elam & Rose, 1995).

2. *The regular classroom may also be stigmatizing.* Some types of services may draw attention to students' disabilities if teaching occurs in general education classes. For example, during speech therapy, students may feel stigmatized practicing articulation of speech sounds in the company of their peers. Other students may be uncomfortable undertaking physical therapy activities in the general education classroom. Still other students, particularly older students, may feel self-conscious if they have to practice reading out loud when the reading level materials are several grade levels below those of their peers. Vaughn, Elbaum, and Schumm (1996) reported that students with disabilities in inclusive placements were less accepted by peers, and declined even further in acceptance over time. Many students with reading disabilities have expressed a preference for receiving reading instruction in resource rooms, finding it a safer environment (Jenkins & Heinen, 1989; Klingner, Vaughn, Schumm, Cohen, & Forgan, 1998; Padeliadu & Zigmond, 1996; Vaughn & Klingner, 1998).

3. *General education teachers are not prepared for full inclusion.* Those favoring a more cautious approach to integration maintain that many general education teachers frequently report having inadequate training, time, and personnel resources for including students with disabilities in general education classes (Scruggs & Mastropieri, 1996a). Many states or teacher training preparation programs do not require that general education majors enroll in even a single special education class. This means that many teachers enter the workforce with no formal education about students with disabilities. This is likely to affect the quality of education teachers can provide to students with disabilities. Furthermore, teachers report that insufficient time is available to plan, design adaptations, and consult and collaborate with special education teachers (Boon & Mastropieri, 1999; Dev & Scruggs, 1997; Scruggs & Mastropieri, 1996a). Planning and collaboration time appear critical to the successful implementation of a full-inclusion model.

4. *General education classrooms may not have sufficient resources.* Proponents for a continuum of services further argue that many general education classes do not have sufficient resources available to include fully students with disabilities. For example, materials at varying readability levels

in science, social studies, and literature need to be readily accessible. Some students will also require access to adaptive equipment including Braillers, speech synthesizers, and specialized computers. General education teachers often have large classes and would find it difficult to include several students with disabilities full-time. Moreover, although some have argued that the same or similar instruction occurs in special and general education classes (Stainback & Stainback, 1984), others have identified clearly distinctive educational practices between general and special education classes. Special education classes are smaller and feature more cognitive-behavioral approaches toward instruction, different curriculum materials, strategy instruction, and more review and practice activities (Zigmond & Baker, 1994). Related to this issue is the concern of advocates for individuals with specific disabilities, including visual impairments (Bina, 1993), hearing impairments (Lane, 1995), autism (Rimland, 1993), and emotional disabilities (Diamond, 1993). Many of these individuals have expressed concern that the specialized needs of individuals with specific disabilities will not be met, and that the unique characteristics and culture of such individuals may be obscured in the general education setting.

5. *Research evidence does not support the superiority of full inclusion.* Finally, proponents of maintaining the continuum of services option argue that no research evidence exists to support the elimination of the continuum of services (Kavale & Forness, 2000). Further, it is argued that few data exist to demonstrate that students with disabilities who are fully included necessarily outperform students who receive special services in other settings. In fact, some evidence suggests that many students with disabilities perform better in resource room models or other special education settings (Carlberg & Kavale, 1980; Fuchs, Fuchs, & Fernstrom, 1993; Marston, 1987–1988). Further, research has suggested that many parents of students with learning disabilities are supportive of the resource room model and are reluctant to agree to have their children receive reading instruction in the regular classroom (Carr, 1993; Green & Shinn, 1995). Parents of students with severe disabilities can also be resistant to inclusive placements (Palmer, Fuller, Arora, & Nelson, 2001).

What Does This Debate Mean for Teachers?

Teachers need to be aware of the arguments for and against full inclusion. As the controversy continues, it is important to keep abreast of recent research documenting the efficacy of such procedures. Once aware of the positions, you can become acquainted with more of the details, especially whether the models are supported by research evidence and whether the legal obligations of IDEA are being met. You also must become familiar with your own legal responsibilities as a teacher. For example, what are general education classroom teachers' legal responsibilities with respect to the IEP when all instruction is implemented in the general education classroom? Other questions, although not necessarily legal in nature, may be relevant to the spirit of the law. Many professional organizations have published position statements regarding full inclusion, including the National Education Association (NEA), the American Federation of Teachers (AFT), and advocacy or special education organizations such as the Council for Exceptional Children (CEC), Council for Learning Disabilities (CLD), Division for Learning Disabilities (DLD), Council for Children with Behavioral Disorders (CCBD), The Association for Persons with Severe Handicaps (TASH), and the Consumer Action Network (CAN) of, by, and for Deaf and Hard of Hearing Americans. These position statements range from full support of full inclusion, to qualified support of full inclusion, to more negative views of full inclusion. Teachers should approach the issue in a practical way, with respect to their own school and district. Specific questions to ask about full inclusion include the following:

For information about TASH and the Divisions of the Council for Exceptional Children, go to the Web Links module in chapter 1 of the Companion Website.

- What are the school and districtwide policies and procedures regarding full inclusion?
- What are my obligations as a general educator with respect to the IEP, IEP meetings, case conferences, assessment procedures, annual review meetings, and meetings with parents?
- What types of modifications are expected, and is there a "reasonableness" standard associated with the number and types of modifications expected?
- Is this the best placement option for the student with special needs?
- How will we evaluate whether or not this placement and this set of accommodations are successful?
- What resources are available to assist me in working with the student with special needs?
- How can I receive necessary training for working with students in specific disability areas?
- What kinds of records and documentation should I maintain?

Answers to questions such as these can help determine the best placement options for students with disabilities and other special needs.

Teacher Attitudes

One of the most important determinants of inclusion success is the attitude of the general education teacher toward accommodating students with disabilities. The Research Highlight that follows presents the findings of a synthesis of studies on teacher attitudes toward inclusion. Teacher and administrator support for collaborative efforts in schools can also affect attitudes. Two scenarios help illustrate the initial implementation of inclusion in two different schools under very different circumstances.

Volunteerism

In a small rural school, Mrs. Lurgeon, the fourth-grade teacher, volunteered to take all the fourth-grade students with disabilities into her classroom. Because she worked well with Mrs. Goodrich, the special education teacher, she went to her principal and said, "Next year, I would like to have all five of the fourth-graders who have disabilities in my room. They can still go to the resource room for part of the day, but during science class and other content classes, I would like to have all of them. Also, Mrs. Goodrich and I would like to team-teach during science class when all five children are included."

That summer, Mrs. Lurgeon and Mrs. Goodrich met and discussed curriculum and planning issues for their science class. Mrs. Lurgeon was considered the "content expert," while Mrs. Goodrich was the "adaptation expert." When the school year began, they met at least one day a week after school to co-plan the activities for each science class. Mrs. Lurgeon and Mrs. Goodrich had a good working relationship that enabled them to solve problems as they arose. Because they planned together, they took turns presenting information and monitoring students during class. They were both enthusiastic and worked hard to design adaptations so the five students with disabilities could be active participants. They viewed science as an opportunity to have fun and their students appeared to really enjoy science.

Mandated Inclusion

In a suburban middle school, Mrs. Boon, the special education teacher, was told by her building principal two days before school began that she was going to implement inclusive instruction for one period a day during the coming year. She was told she would be going into Mrs. Toro's sixth period, seventh-grade history class on a daily basis. She was informed that three students with learning disabilities were in that social studies class.

General education and special education teachers are now more frequently expected to work together to adapt instruction to meet the educational needs of children with disabilities.

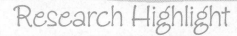

Teacher Attitudes Toward Inclusion

Scruggs and Mastropieri (1996a) summarized the results of 28 surveys of teacher attitudes toward including students with disabilities in their classrooms, conducted between 1958 and 1995 (e.g., Fulk & Hirth, 1994; Haring, Stern, & Cruickshank, 1958; Larrivee & Cook, 1979). They used quantitative synthesis procedures to combine the findings across similar questions from different surveys (Scruggs & Mastropieri, 1996b). They reported little change in teacher attitudes in past decades. Most teachers were in favor of some degree of inclusion, and most teachers were willing to accommodate students with disabilities in their classrooms. However, teachers were less positive about including students with more severe disabilities, and were less likely to agree that the general education classroom was always the best environment for all students with disabilities (i.e., full inclusion).

Although most teachers were generally supportive of some form of inclusion, many teachers did not believe they were given sufficient resources to implement inclusive education satisfactorily. Most teachers reported needing more support—in the form of more training, more personnel support, more materials support, more time for planning, and smaller class sizes—to make inclusion a success. When teachers do receive support, however, they usually become more positive about inclusive teaching. For example, Dev and Scruggs (1997) reported that teachers who had completed coursework in special education as part of their teacher training programs had more positive attitudes toward inclusive teaching than teachers who had not received such coursework (see also Chung, 1998).

For more information on teachers' attitudes toward students with disabilities, see Cook, Tankersley, Cook, and Landrum (2000).

Questions for Reflection

1. Why do you think teachers' attitudes have stayed stable over the years?
2. Why do you think teachers who had special education coursework had more positive attitudes?
3. What other factors may influence teacher attitudes?

Companion
Website

To answer these questions online, go to the Research Highlights feature in chapter 1 of the Companion Website.

Unfortunately, Mrs. Toro, the history teacher, had not been informed by the principal that Mrs. Boon was going to be team-teaching with her. When Mrs. Boon went to see Mrs. Toro, and explained the situation, Mrs. Toro appeared visibly shaken.

Now both teachers, who had never discussed the possibility of working together, felt awkward. Neither had thought about team-teaching previously, although neither was particularly opposed to the idea. Perhaps more important, the teachers did not have the same preparation periods free, which meant that any co-planning would have to take place before or after school. This would mean that Mrs. Boon and Mrs. Toro now had additional responsibilities they had not requested.

Neither teacher had a good understanding of the principal's expectations. They were also unsure how to execute the co-teaching. Mrs. Boon had expertise in special education and in making accommodations, and Mrs. Toro had content expertise in history, but now they had to figure out a way to blend their strengths during one period of instruction a day.

Although both teachers tried to be optimistic, there were so many ambiguities regarding their roles and expectations that initially they both experienced some discomfort with the situation. Mrs. Toro said she would continue to prepare and present information from the social studies textbook to the class and requested that Mrs. Boon circulate around the room during independent activities to provide assistance to anyone who needed it. Mrs. Boon agreed to this arrangement, but felt uncomfortable during class presentations, as she was unsure of what to do with herself. Both teachers tried to meet and plan, but something else always seemed to take a priority.

How Do These Situations Compare?

Compare and contrast the two teaching situations. What differences seem most likely to affect the success of inclusive instruction? What changes can you recommend? In the first example, inclusion during science appears successful. Both teachers volunteered for the team-teaching situation; they got along, worked in additional planning time, and enjoyed working together one period a day. In addition, all students seemed to enjoy science, and the students with disabilities were able to keep up with the learning of their peers during the team-taught content area class.

In the second case, however, neither teacher had been given adequate notice, nor had they volunteered for team-teaching, and several potential challenges existed before they even began. What options are available to Mrs. Boon and Mrs. Toro? How can they begin to monitor and evaluate their team-teaching? How can they overcome the barriers and make the experience successful for them and the students?

It can be seen that there are many considerations to be made in order for inclusive placements to be successful. These involve careful planning, and attention to the multiple perspectives of general education teachers, special education teachers, parents of students with and without disabilities, and, of course, the students themselves. However, with careful planning and appropriate programming, inclusive instruction can prove to be a successful and rewarding experience for everyone!

Summary

- In 1975, Public Law 94-142 (IDEA) was passed. This law, and its subsequent amendments, established the rights of students with disabilities to a free, appropriate public education. It further provided that this education would take place, to the maximum extent possible, in the least-restrictive environment. Before the passage of this law, students with special needs were routinely excluded from public school.
- IDEA provides for special services for disability areas including autism, deafness, hearing impairments, mental retardation, multiple disabilities, orthopedic impairments, other health impairments, emotional disturbance, specific learning disabilities, speech or language impairments, traumatic brain injury, visual impairments, and deaf-blindness. However, other groups of students may also require special adaptations by general education teachers, including students who are culturally or linguistically diverse, students at risk for school failure, and students with gifts or talents.
- Other court rulings and federal laws, such as Section 504 and the Americans with Disabilities Act, have provided for nondiscriminatory treatment of individuals with disabilities.

- Six important principles in IDEA are (1) zero reject, (2) nondiscriminatory testing, (3) free and appropriate education, (4) least-restrictive environment, (5) due process, and (6) parent participation.
- Current educational practice provides for a continuum of services for students with disabilities, from full-time placement in the regular education classroom, to special residential schools. Most students with disabilities today are served in regular education classrooms.

- Some controversy exists over the concept of "full inclusion," the full-time placement of students with disabilities in regular classrooms. Important points have been raised by concerned individuals on both sides of this issue.
- Most teachers favor some form of inclusion for their own classes. However, teachers report a need for sufficient time, training, and resources to teach effectively in inclusive classrooms. When these supports are provided, attitudes toward inclusive teaching also improve.

Council for Exceptional Children

Introduction to Inclusive Teaching

Information in this chapter links most directly to:

Standard 1—Foundations, particularly:

Knowledge:
- Models, theories, and philosophies that form the basis for special education practice.
- Laws, policies, and ethical principles regarding behavior management planning and implementation.
- Relationship of special education to the organization and function of educational agencies.
- Rights and responsibilities of students, parents, teachers, and other professionals, and schools related to exceptional learning needs.

- Issues in definition and identification of individuals with exceptional learning needs, including those from culturally and linguistically diverse backgrounds.
- Issues, assurances and due process rights related to assessment, eligibility, and placement within a continuum of services.
- Family systems and the role of families in the educational process.
- Historical points of view and contribution of culturally diverse groups.
- Impact of the dominant culture on shaping schools and the individuals who study and work in them.
- Potential impact of differences in values, languages, and customs that can exist between the home and school.

Inclusion Checklist
An Introduction to Inclusive Teaching

If you are uncertain of the issues surrounding inclusion and IDEA, are you familiar with the following concepts?

- ❏ The least-restrictive environment
- ❏ Mainstreaming and inclusion

Are you aware of the types of disabilities that students who are served by IDEA have?

- ❏ Autism
- ❏ Deaf-blindness
- ❏ Deafness
- ❏ Emotional disturbance
- ❏ Hearing impairment
- ❏ Mental retardation
- ❏ Multiple disabilities
- ❏ Orthopedic impairment
- ❏ Other health impairments
- ❏ Specific learning disabilities
- ❏ Speech and language disorders
- ❏ Traumatic brain injury
- ❏ Visual impairments

Are you familiar with other special needs not served under IDEA?

- ❏ Culturally and linguistically diverse groups
- ❏ At-risk
- ❏ Gifted and talented

Are you familiar with the legal foundations involving students with disabilities?

- ❏ Section 504
- ❏ Americans with Disabilities Act
- ❏ Individuals with Disabilities Education Act (IDEA)

Are you familiar with models of service delivery?

- ❏ Resource room and self-contained models
- ❏ General education models
- ❏ Related services

Chapter 2

Jesse Tessmer, 17
Wausau, Wisconsin
"The President Greets a King"

Collaboration
Partnerships and Procedures

Objectives

After studying this chapter, you should be able to:

- List and describe the six major steps involved in effective communication to establish collaboration.

- Describe the general education prereferral process, such as establishing timelines, intervention strategies, and consultations.

- Identify the educational evaluation or assessment steps as well as the key components comprising the case conference committee and IEP progam.

- Gain understanding of the importance of partnerships between special and general educators.

- Identify the benefits and potential barriers to co-teaching and research supporting the collaboration among educators.

- Understand the roles and responsibilities, background, and importance of communicating with paraprofessionals.

- Describe the importance of positive communication and collaboration with parents and families.

IDEA provides the legal rights for individuals with disabilities to receive free, appropriate public education. However, for the law to be effective, collaboration and constructive partnerships must be established among parents, teachers, school specialists, school administrators, and community agencies. Moreover, both the school and parents must accept certain basic responsibilities for the system to work effectively. Table 2.1 lists some of these responsibilities. To meet these responsibilities, parents and school personnel must engage in problem-solving strategies, working together to devise procedures necessary for identification, referral, assessment, and placement processes to accommodate students with exceptionalities and other at-risk students.

Collaboration—involving cooperation, effective communication, shared problem-solving, planning, and finding solutions—is the process for ensuring that all students receive the free, appropriate public education mandated by IDEA. The establishment of excellent working partnerships among all involved in working with students with disabilities is essential for constructive collaboration.

Professional roles, including teachers as collaborators, are topics on the Praxis *Special Education: Core Knowledge* Tests.

Table 2.1
School and Parent Responsibilities

School's Responsibilities	Parents' Responsibilities
Provide free and appropriate education through age 21.	Provide consent for educational evaluation and placement.
Provide an Individualized Education Program (IEP) for each student who requires special education and related services.	Participate in case conference committee, including development of IEP.
Assure testing, evaluation materials, procedures, and interpretations are non-biased.	Cooperate with school and teachers.
Educate students with disabilities in the least-restrictive environment.	Attend annual case review to ensure IEP remains appropriate.
Assure confidentiality of records for individuals with disabilities.	Reinforce procedures and policies (e.g., help with homework routines).
Conduct searches to identify and evaluate students with disabilities from birth through age 21.	Assist with any home-school behavioral contracting efforts.
Provide procedural due process rights for students and parents.	Help maintain open communication with school and teachers.

CLASSROOM SCENARIO

Debbie

Debbie is a tenth grader with physical disabilities and communication difficulties who has been experiencing problems completing her work within the typical school day. This morning, six of Debbie's teachers—her math teacher, Ms. Juarez; her English teacher, Mr. Mantizi; her science teacher, Mr. Stubbs; her history teacher, Ms. Blackman; her speech and language therapist, Ms. Ramirez; and her special education teacher, Mr. Graetz—are meeting with Ms. Meyer, Debbie's paraprofessional, in the small conference room near the front office. They are trying to determine what they can do to help Debbie be more successful in high school. Everyone at the meeting is sincere in their desire to brainstorm ways to arrange the school day so Debbie can learn successfully.

Mr. Graetz, the special education teacher, began the conversation by saying, "Thanks for agreeing to meet about Debbie this morning, as I know you are all so busy this time of year. I think we can look at what's been happening and try to come up with some solutions together. Recently, Debbie appears to be having a harder time completing her assignments and keeping up with all of her work. Her grades have started slipping below what we think she is capable of, and we thought that if we shared some ideas we might be able to help her keep up with everything."

Ms. Blackman, the history teacher, says, "I know that Debbie is excited about the topics we are studying in history because her eyes become animated during class discussions. I'm unsure how I can tap into that enthusiasm and allow her to express it more openly during class discussions. Maybe if I could get her to participate more actively she would feel better about school."

The speech therapist, Ms. Ramirez, suggests, "Have you tried allowing Debbie to type out her responses to questions on her notebook computer and then asking Ms. Meyer to read her answers to the class?"

"Hey, that's a good idea. I have time to do that while students are completing their lab work in science class," says the science teacher, Mr. Stubbs.

Ms. Juarez, the math teacher, adds, "I sometimes stop the discussion and allow extra time for Debbie to type her responses and have found that this provides additional thinking time for everyone in my math class. . . . "

And so the discussion continues. These teachers are collaborating by sharing suggestions in instructional modifications with the intention of trying something that will promote school success for Debbie.

Collaboration to Establish Need

Collaboration to decide how to best meet students' needs can occur among teachers and other school specialists during informal meetings, co-teaching, and formal meetings of prereferral teams and case conference committees. Collaboration also takes place with parents, siblings, guardians, and families—during parent conferences—as well as during day-to-day communication with parents regarding the progress of their children.

Shared Goals

Collaboration means working jointly with others; willingly cooperating with others; and sharing goal setting, problem solving, and the achievement of goals. Individuals involved in service delivery for students with disabilities work collaboratively toward the successful accomplishment of IEP goals for students with disabilities. For example, a special education teacher might have Marilyn, who is classified as mildly mentally retarded, for three periods a day, while the general education seventh-grade content area teachers in science, social studies, home economics, art, music, and physical education have her the remainder of the school day. General and special education teachers must collaborate effectively to implement the goals and objectives on Marilyn's IEP. For example, Marilyn's IEP specifies that general education teachers prioritize objectives, use positive reinforcement, adapt learning activities to reduce the amount of reading and writing required, adapt testing situations, and provide Marilyn with additional support as necessary. For these goals to be implemented consistently throughout the day for Marilyn, this team of teachers, including the content area and special education teachers, must work collaboratively and share ideas for best meeting Marilyn's needs.

For effective collaboration to happen, teachers must communicate effectively. This is most possible when collaborators hone their interpersonal skills and interject a positive attitude into the collaboration efforts.

Effective Communication

Interpersonal interactions revolve around communication. When communication is effective, several common elements are in place: active listening, depersonalizing situations, identifying common goals and solutions, and monitoring progress to achieve those goals (Gordon, 1987; see also Ginott, 1995).

Active Listening

It is not only important that you listen carefully to what someone has to say; it is also important that you convey to the speaker that you are listening carefully. Active listening is the way you demonstrate to the speaker that you are truly interested in the speaker's topic of conversation, and that you understand and appreciate what is being presented. Conveying interest and understanding improves communicaton and enhances interpersonal interactions. Active listening is demonstrated through both nonverbal and verbal actions. Nonverbally, you demonstrate active listening by maintaining direct eye contact, leaning toward the speaker, nodding your head in agreement or understanding, and demonstrating that you are devoting all of your attention to the

Effective collaboration depends on cooperation, shared goals, and shared problem solving.

speaker. Verbal components of active listening involve responding with affirmative words such as: "Yes," "Yes, I see," "I understand," and, "Can you tell me more?" An active listener is able to restate or summarize the major points of the conversation, and may do this during the course of the conversation with statements such as, "So, what you are telling me is. . . ." Teachers who use active listening techniques are more likely to maintain open communication and to avoid misunderstandings. Active listening is a way of informing the speaker that his or her views are important to you, and can be helpful in keeping interactions positive.

Depersonalize Situations

It is important to depersonalize individual situations and conversations as you orient collaborators toward possible solutions. Depersonalizing conversations avoids negative comments that may hurt an individual's character, and instead emphasizes a goal. For example, if a student, Lisa, has been remiss at turning in homework assignments, a "depersonalized" statement is, "Lisa, 7 out of the last 10 homework assignments are missing; what can we do to improve that?" A negative statement that might hinder finding a solution is, "Lisa, you obviously do not care enough about science to turn in your homework."

It is important to remember that if someone's character is attacked, as in the latter example with Lisa, further attempts at communication and problem solving may be hindered. Once Lisa is told that she does not care, she will be unlikely to continue the conversation in a productive manner. Lisa might think, "That's right! I don't care and my teacher thinks I'm a failure anyway, so what does it matter?" However, depersonalizing the situation will help Lisa focus on what "we" can do to help get the homework in. Depersonalizing conversations are beneficial when communicating with everyone, including students, other teachers, school specialists, administrators, parents, and professionals from community organizations.

Find Common Goals

It is important to restate and summarize conversations to identify common goals. Once common goals are found, conversations can be more positive and productive. Questions such as "Lisa, what do you want to do in science?" and "What are the barriers currently preventing Lisa from turning in her homework?" can help direct the conversations toward the identification of common goals. A positive and productive common goal among all teachers, the parents, and Lisa could be the following:

> We all want Lisa to succeed, and one way to help her succeed is to find ways to assist her in turning in her homework.

Once common goals are stated positively, it is easier to turn the entire conversation into productive problem solving toward goal attainment.

Brainstorm Possible Solutions

Effective communicators can use brainstorming techniques during meetings to help identify ways to achieve any common goals. During brainstorming, suggestions for solutions are compiled by participants, without passing judgment on any of them. The list of possible solutions can then be prioritized from those offering the most potential for success to the least. In Lisa's case, a brainstormed list created by her, her teachers, and her parents includes the following:

- serving detention for a month
- quitting her job
- keeping an assignment notebook
- having a place to complete homework at home
- having her parents check her homework nightly
- eliminating or restricing her television-watching
- staying after school once a week for homework assistance
- rewarding Lisa if she meets a certain criterion by the end of the quarter
- assigning a peer to work with her on completing her homework
- being grounded for a month

When all participants join in the creation of *possible alternatives* for helping Lisa succeed, they have more invested in reaching their goal.

Summarize Goals and Solutions

Summarizing the statement of goals and proposed solutions verbally (and perhaps in writing), before the end of the meeting, is beneficial for all participants. This prevents any misunderstandings and provides an opportunity for clarification. In our example the teacher summarizes the meeting by stating, "Let me summarize what we all agreed on. We all want Lisa to succeed in science. One way to have Lisa be more successful is to help her turn in all of her homework assignments. One thing Lisa will do is keep an assignment notebook in which she records her assignments and due dates, which she will show daily to her parents and teachers. Another step will be for Lisa and her parents to find a place at home for her to complete her homework. Her parents will assist her by asking regularly if she has completed her homework assignments. Finally, Lisa will attend after-school help sessions if she does not understand what to do to complete the assignments. We will meet and review Lisa's progress toward her goals within one month, at which time we will determine whether we need to modify any of the possible solutions."

Follow Up to Monitor Progress

Summarization makes the entire conversation positive and concrete. A goal statement is made, possible solutions are listed, one is selected for implementation and evaluation, and follow-up target dates are set for monitoring progress toward goal attainment.

All steps promote communication with everyone involved in educating students with disabilities. Review the following *In the Classroom* feature, which can be used to ensure decisions made by the group during problem solving are more easily executed. Whatever model of communication you use, note that practicing good communication skills enables you to be effective in the many roles associated with collaboration.

In the Classroom ...a feature for teachers

Communication Summary Sheet

For: _____   On: _____
      (Student's Name)   (Date)

Conversation Among (list participants):

_____   _____

_____   _____

_____   _____

Goals Identified:

1.

2.

3.

Solution Steps To-Be-Implemented (and by whom):

Solution Step   *Person Responsible*
1.
2.
3.

Progress toward goals will be reviewed on:

_____   _____
(Date)   (By Whom)

Collaboration and Communication for Intervention

Many types of collaboration occur in larger groups or "teams" within schools. One type of school-wide team is the general education **prereferral intervention team.** In many states the general education prereferral team meets before an actual referral for special education services. Depending on the school district, these teams may also be referred to as multidisciplinary teams, child study teams, general education assistance teams, prereferral assistance teams, or teacher assistance teams. No matter what the team is called, its function is to determine the need for educational interventions to assist individual students who are struggling to succeed at school. In addition, the teams' intervention strategies assist teachers who, after careful observation, are unsure whether a student needs special education services. Hence, the team's first purpose is to see if intervention strategies can make a difference for the student. The team convenes after a formal request is made to the building principal or other designated individual within a school.

General Education Prereferral Request

A formal prereferral request can be made by a teacher, school specialist, parent, school administrator, or the student. For example, a request might be made by a general education teacher who has worked with a student for a period of time and finds that all her efforts have not made the differences they should have in that child's educational success.

Additional information on implementing these and other collaboration skills are discussed in Walther-Thomas, Korinek, McLaughlin, and Williams (2000).

CLASSROOM SCENARIO

Omar

Mrs. Mayer is a second-grade teacher. In November, she began to worry about one of her students, Omar. At the beginning of the school year, Mrs. Mayer noticed that Omar seemed to be behind his classmates academically, but she attributed this to his forgetting over the summer. In September, several students in her class required additional review of first-grade material, and this was fairly typical for a proportion of students each academic year. Most students caught on quickly with the review and then progressed at a typical second-grade learning pace. Omar, however, continued to have problems with reading and writing tasks and had a hard time paying attention for any length of time.

When November arrived and Omar was still struggling, Mrs. Mayer decided that she and Omar needed some assistance. She contacted her school's general education prereferral intervention assistance team. The team members included a first-, third-, fourth-, and fifth-grade teacher, a school psychologist, the principal, and a special education teacher. The team scheduled a meeting to discuss the nature and severity of Omar's difficulties, and designed intervention strategies that Mrs. Mayer could implement and review within a specified timeline.

Documentation of observations, student work samples, test scores, and other relevant data often are submitted with a formal intervention request. It is important to reiterate that before Mrs. Mayer requested help from the intervention team she had taken a number of steps to address the problem. Often, these steps are sequential, in that each item checked should be undertaken before the next concern. Mrs. Mayer first reviewed Omar's records to verify that vision and hearing screenings had taken place. Parent conferences and student interviews were conducted to discuss the problem areas and consider possible solutions. She collected, analyzed, and filed samples of Omar's recent academic class work and evidence of disciplinary actions. She informally asked for advice from other

The prereferral process often begins when a classroom teacher recognizes that a student's classwork is well behind that of expected or typical performance.

The Inclusion Checklists at the end of each chapter contain more specific information and can be used to identify activities general education teachers may undertake to address problems.

teachers, school counselors, special education teachers, and mainstream assistance teams. Mrs. Mayer made available to the intervention team documentation of specific intervention strategies she had tried before asking the team for help. All of this information was useful to team members in deciding what other modifications, adaptations, or interventions might be tried to find the best educational program for Omar. For an illustration of all the steps in the referral process, see Figure 2.1.

The Intervention Process

The strategies addressed in the intervention process are designed, implemented, and evaluated before any formal referral for special education services. These are not special education procedures

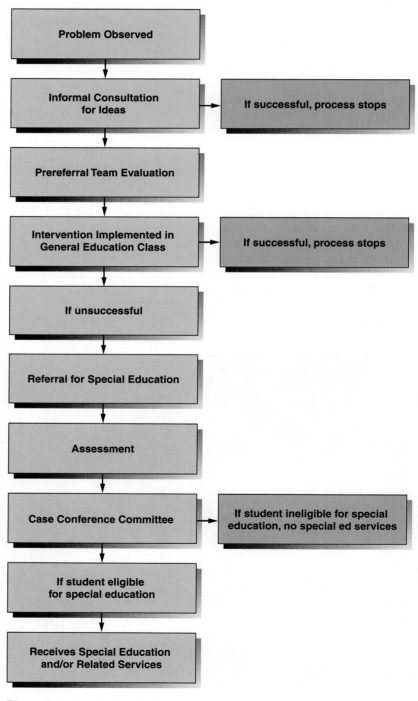

Figure 2.1
Steps in the Referral Process

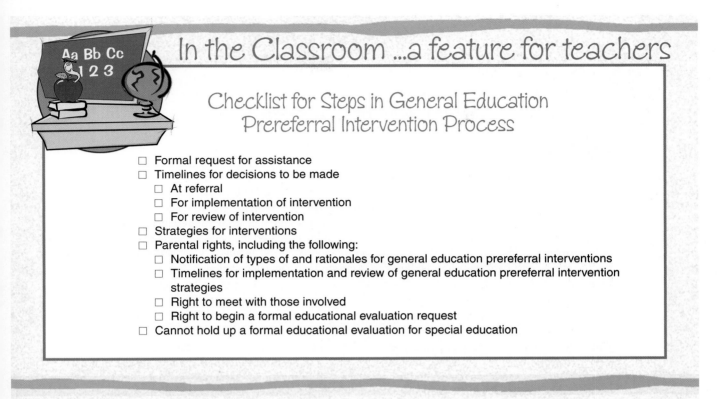

In the Classroom ...a feature for teachers

Checklist for Steps in General Education Prereferral Intervention Process

- ☐ Formal request for assistance
- ☐ Timelines for decisions to be made
  - ☐ At referral
  - ☐ For implementation of intervention
  - ☐ For review of intervention
- ☐ Strategies for interventions
- ☐ Parental rights, including the following:
  - ☐ Notification of types of and rationales for general education prereferral interventions
  - ☐ Timelines for implementation and review of general education prereferral intervention strategies
  - ☐ Right to meet with those involved
  - ☐ Right to begin a formal educational evaluation request
- ☐ Cannot hold up a formal educational evaluation for special education

but are part of the general education system required by some state special education legislation (see Indiana Department of Education, 2000). The *In the Classroom* feature above identifies a checklist of steps in a prereferral process.

Prereferral procedures are preventative in nature, intended to reduce inappropriate referrals and decrease the likelihood of future problems. Additionally, these procedures are meant to provide general education teachers and students with immediate assistance with classroom-related problems, including disciplinary issues. To determine whether the general education intervention is appropriate, team members may observe the student before the prereferral intervention takes place. At this point, parents may or may not have been notified that such observations are occurring, but it is a good idea to try to involve the parents whenever possible. However, before any general education intervention plan is implemented, parents must be notified in writing of the team's recommendation for intervention strategies and the rationale behind implementing them. Finally, the intervention is implemented.

Establishing Timelines. Once intervention strategies are developed, timelines are set to accompany the implementation and review of those strategies. In Mrs. Mayer's case, a strategy was designed to be implemented with Omar. In addition, a one-month timeline was established for her to implement, monitor, and evaluate Omar's progress. If adequate improvement is observed, the intervention will continue (or discontinue if it appears no longer necessary). However, if inadequate progress is noted, one of two steps may occur. First, the strategies may be redesigned along with new timelines, which Mrs. Mayer would then implement. Second, if the problem seems more severe or persistent than general classroom interventions can address, the team may decide to begin the referral process for special education services. At that point, Omar's parents will be contacted and asked to give permission for an educational evaluation for possible special education services. Omar's parents can request an educational evaluation for special education at any time during this process, and their request will be honored and not delayed due to the implementation of the general education intervention.

Intervention Strategies. Intervention strategies vary depending on the specific needs of the student, but may include modifications in (a) the curriculum, (b) instructional procedures, (c) classroom management, or (d) classroom environment. Curriculum modifications involve altering the curriculum or adapting the curriculum currently used, such as using materials at a lower

The prereferral process often begins when a classroom teacher recognizes that a student's classwork is well behind that of expected or typical performance.

Research Highlight

General Education Assistance Teams

Doug and Lynn Fuchs and their colleagues studied the effects of implementing teams within schools to assist with problems before referral to special education (Fuchs, Fuchs, Reeder, Gilman, Fernstrom, Bahr, & Moore, 1989). They demonstrated that successful general education assistance teams, composed of general and special education teachers and staff from Vanderbilt University, could design and implement interventions that successfully decreased the need for some special education referrals. In their model, behavioral consultation occurred between a general education teacher and a consultant regarding a difficult-to-teach student. The consultation included four major steps: (a) problem identification, (b) problem analysis, (c) implementation of a plan, and (d) evaluation of the problem.

During the first year of the project, the teacher and consultant completed all steps independently. However, findings from that year were equivocal—some were successful and some were not. Therefore, during the second and third years of the research project, staff from Vanderbilt identified specific interventions for teachers and students. The specific interventions included the use of student–teacher contracts and self-monitoring on the part of the individual students. If targeted behaviors were social–behavioral in nature, like talking out, out-of-seat, and so forth, then students were taught to monitor their behavior using an interval recording procedure and then to evaluate their behavior for the recording period.

If the problem was academic, students were taught to evaluate their completed product at the end of the session, and again provide a rating of "good" or "not good" for the product. After the initial two days of intervention, the students assumed the entire responsibility and monitored, recorded, evaluated, and provided themselves feedback. An example of self-talk taught to students is, "Did I stay on task today?" "Yes, I did great!" or, "No, but I'll do better tomorrow" (Fuchs et al., 1989, p. 28).

Important components of the prereferral interventions included the collection of pre- and post-intervention data to measure ultimate efficacy for targeted social–behavioral and academic objectives. This project was successful, and the majority of difficult-to-teach students were able to improve their targeted social and/or academic behaviors and to remain in the general education classes.

For more information on prereferral interventions, see Kovaleski, Gickling, Morrow, and Swank (1999). For information on prereferral practices for students from culturally and linguistically diverse backgrounds, see Craig, Hull, Haggart, and Perez-Selles (2000).

Questions for Reflection

1. How much prereferral intervention may be necessary before it is clear that students should be referred for special education services?
2. What other general interventions might be useful in a prereferral intervention program?
3. Could a student's response to prereferral interventions be useful as information to be used in identifying the student as having a disability?

Companion Website

To answer these questions online, go to the Research Highlights feature in chapter 2 of the Companion Website.

reading level. Modifications in instructional procedures include providing additional instruction or using different presentation formats, varying the types of practice activities, modifying task demands or testing procedures, or regrouping students within instructional activities. Modifying classroom management procedures involves intensifying behavioral monitoring for increasing attention to task, providing individual student behavioral contracts, or increasing reinforcement. Environmental modifications consist of rearranging the classroom desks, making the classroom more accessible, or changing seating positions. Finally, other resources available within the school and community may be used to assist in making general education interventions.

Self-monitoring and interval recording are described in chapters 8 and 10.

Prereferral Consultation

Several other types of prereferral intervention teams exist. Graden, Casey, and Bonstrom (1985a, 1985b) proposed a six-stage model for prereferral interventions. During the first four steps a consultant, typically a special educator, works closely with the general educator. The consultant helps to identify problems and potential solutions, and to implement and evaluate solutions. If the solutions prove effective, the case is essentially closed. If the problem persists, a referral to special education is made. The final steps include the referral for special education services. Preliminary findings indicated that referrals for special education decreased when the consultation model was in place effectively. The Research Highlight provides an example, and the following *In the Classroom* feature provides a sample contract.

Contact your state department of education for its specific guidelines for implementing federal and state special education policies.

In the Classroom ...a feature for teachers

Sample Contract

CONTRACT

This is an agreement between Tony Larsen and your teacher, Mr. Wallace. If you can turn in your homework every day during 4th period math class for two consecutive weeks (from 2/2 to 2/16), Mr. Wallace will give you 5 bonus points and a "no homework" pass for any day you choose! You can monitor your homework completion in your student log, which will be initialed by Mr. Wallace. This contract will begin on February 2, and will end February 14. At the end of this period, if you have turned in all your homework, we can negotiate for even more rewards, if you wish.

I agree with the Contract as specified above.

_____ Tony Larsen   _____ (date)

_____ Mr. Wallace   _____ (date)

Note: Adapted from *Mainstream Assistance Teams: A Handbook on Prereferral Intervention* (p. 30), by D. Fuchs et al., 1989, Nashville, TN: Peabody College of Vanderbilt University. Copyright 1989 by Peabody College of Vanderbilt University. Adapted with permission.

Date Received _____

Student Name _____ Sex _____ Birthdate _____

School _____ Grade _____ Teacher _____

Parent/Guardian _____ Primary Language _____

Address _____ Home Phone _____ Work Phone _____

Current Educational Program _____

Referring Person _____
                         (signature)   (title)   (date)

Principal/Designee's _____
                                (signature)   (date)

1. Please describe briefly the reason(s) for this referral.

2. Documentation of the general education intervention (attach copy of the GEI plan): What are effects of intervention?

    Comments from the remedial reading instructor, if applicable:

3. Documentation of support services such as counseling or psychological (non-testing) services provided by school or other agency.

    Comments and observations from the school counselor:

    Has a previous psychological evaluation been conducted?
    Yes _____   No _____   Date _____   Agency _____

Figure 2.2
Sample Referral Form

Collaboration for Referrals and Placements

The special education referral process can be initiated by almost anyone, including the student, although the student's teachers or parents usually make the referral. Each school has written referral procedures, designated staff for the various positions within the referral process, and accompanying forms.

Once the prereferral team determined that the strategies Mrs. Mayer had implemented on her own were insufficient to help Omar successfully perform in second grade, the referral process for educational evaluation began. Mrs. Mayer completed a "Referral Evaluation Form" from the school (see Figure 2.2 for a sample referral form). Once the referral form was completed, Omar's parents were contacted and asked to meet with school personnel. They were told that their son had been referred for an educational evaluation. They were told why he was referred and were asked to provide written permission to proceed. Omar's parents were informed about the evaluation procedures,

4. Documentation of conferences or attempts to conference, with the parent and appropriate school personnel concerning the student's specific problem(s).

5. Which of the disabilities/handicaps do you suspect?

_____ Autism _____ Communication disorders _____ Emotional disability

_____ Hearing impairment _____ Learning disability _____ Mental disability

_____ Orthopedic impairment _____ Other health impairment

_____ Traumatic brain injury _____ Visual impairment

6. In what subjects are the student's problems most apparent?

7. List schools previously attended and dates:

8. Comments from school nurse:

Current general health _____

Previous medical problems _____

Is the student taking medication? ___ If yes, specify _____

Vision: L _____ R _____ Correction _____

Date of vision screening _____ (must be done within a year)

9. Comments from speech, hearing, and language clinician:

Hearing: L _____ R _____ Correction _____

Date of hearing screening _____ (must be done within a year)

Is the student receiving speech and language therapy? In the past?

10. Copy and attach information from the student's education record:
   1. Previous achievement test results
   2. Grades earned since school entry
   3. Attendance record
   4. Summary of disciplinary actions

Complete and send all referral information to Special Services.

and told that a case conference committee meeting would be scheduled within 65 school days of the parent's signing the permission for testing. They were also told about how the school had already attempted to help Omar through the general education prereferral intervention.

All information should be presented verbally and in writing for the parents, and in the parent's native language. If parents speak Spanish, then school personnel must communicate with the parents using Spanish. Some school districts have developed handouts describing parents' rights. Figure 2.3 contains a handout used by the Crawfordsville Community School Corporation, based on Indiana state special education law.

The Educational Evaluation or Assessment Step

The educational evaluation for a referral to special education is much more comprehensive than the evaluation described for prereferrals by the general education teams. This evaluation provides extensive information on how the student learns best and the student's level of performance, and identifies strengths and potential need areas. The evaluation team includes a school psychologist and other school specialists as described briefly in Figure 2.4. For example, if a child is suspected of having a speech and language problem, then a speech and language therapist is a member of that evaluation team. In the case of Omar, who is suspected of having reading and writing problems that may be associated with learning disabilities, a teacher of students with learning disabilities will be a member of that team.

I. Educational evaluations and placement in special education programs cannot be done without written parental consent.

II. Parents have the right to inspect school records within a reasonable period of time of their request.

III. Parents have the right to have educational records explained to them by school personnel.

IV. Parents have the right to receive copies of the student's educational record.

V. Parents have the right to ask that records be amended if they believe that the information therein is incorrect.

VI. Tests during the evaluation should be valid, fair, and in the child's native language.

VII. The parent has the right to an independent educational evaluation at the school's expense if the parent disagrees with the findings of the evaluation completed by the school personnel.

VIII. The case conference committee must consider the results of independent evaluations obtained by parents.

IX. The parents must be notified in writing of an upcoming case conference. The conference should be set at a mutually agreeable time and place. The notice should be in the parents' native language and should include a list of those expected to participate in the conference.

X. The parent may bring any other individual to the conference including an advocate.

XI. The case conference committee must receive written parental consent before a child can be placed into any special education program. Parents must receive a copy of the educational evaluation, their parental rights, and the case conference summary.

XII. The public agency (school) must ensure that a child is placed with nondisabled peers to the maximum extent of his/her abilities.

XIII. A case conference must be scheduled at least once a year to review a child's educational program and placement.

XIV. A number of educational placements should be discussed at case conferences to ensure that children are placed in the least-restrictive environment.

XV. A parent, public agency (school), or state agency may initiate a due process hearing whenever any of these parties is concerned or dissatisfied with the educational evaluation, placement, or program of a student. This request must be made in writing.

XVI. Parents may bring legal counsel and individuals with training and knowledge in special education to a hearing.

XVII. Mediation may be sought when the parent and the school cannot through the case conference committee process agree on the student's identification, evaluation or educational placement.

XVIII. Complaints alleging the violations of these rights and the laws pertaining to special education may be submitted to the state Department of Education.

XIX. The public agency must appoint a surrogate parent whenever a child with a suspected disability is a ward of the state or whenever no parent is identified or can be located.

Figure 2.3
Summary of Parental Rights
Note: From "Parental Rights: Crawfordsville Community School Corporation." Reprinted with permission.

The education evaluation includes various activities, procedures, and tests. A physical examination, developmental history, and vision and hearing tests may be required. A battery of academic, intellectual, adaptive, and social–emotional tests are administered, depending on the specific referral reason. Observations of the student throughout the school day may be completed. The classroom teacher is asked to evaluate the student's classroom strengths and need areas.

All testing must be culturally unbiased, completed in the student's native language, and must consider cultural background and presumed disability, to provide the most accurate picture of the student's current level of functioning. This means, for example, that if a student's native language

General Education Teachers teach any grade level, any subject area, K–12; may be responsible for implementing part or all of a student's IEP.

Special Education Teachers teach any grade level, any disability area K–12; may teach in any of settings described for general education teachers; usually have primary responsibility for the implementation of the IEP.

School Psychologists or Diagnosticians take the lead on the educational evaluations, have major responsibilities administering, scoring, and interpreting tests; sometimes serve as behavioral consultant to teachers.

Counselors advise students; may conduct some social and emotional assessment; may deliver counseling sessions or advise teachers on how to deal with social–emotional needs for their students.

Speech/Language Therapists work with students who require assistance with any speech and or language needs.

Physical Therapists provide assessment and interventions in gross motor areas.

Occupational Therapists provide assessment and interventions for students in the fine motor areas.

School Nurses often provide medical histories, distribute medications to students; provide a link between families and other school personnel.

School Administrators provide administrative assistance among all involved; may include school principals, vice principals, directors of special education, directors of special services, special education coordinators.

Social Workers provide the link between families and schools; have similar roles to that of counselors.

Paraprofessionals provide assistance to teachers, special education teachers, and students with disabilities.

Other school specialists provide assistance in specialized ways, including adaptive physical education, sign language interpreting; bilingual special education; mobility specialists, psychometrists (complete educational testing), probation officers, and other consultants as necessary.

Figure 2.4
School Personnel as Team Members and Their Roles

is Spanish, then it may be important to administer tests in Spanish; otherwise, an inaccurate picture of the student's abilities may be obtained.

Parents, teachers, or other school personnel can request a reevaluation whenever one is deemed necessary. The educational evaluation is intended to collect sufficient valid and reliable information on the student's current level of functioning, strengths, and need areas.

Chapter 12 contains detailed information on assessment for eligibility and for instruction.

The Case Conference Committee

A **case conference committee** or multidisciplinary team is composed of all individuals concerned with a particular student. The 1997 amendments to IDEA require that general education teachers participate in the development, review, and revision of IEPs (*IDEA 1997: Let's make it work,* 1998). Moreover, the amendments require that parents be included as members of any group that makes educational decisions about their child. The members include the parents and their child; general and special education teachers; the school psychologist; school administrators, such as the building principal or special education director; and any other related personnel, such as the school nurse, counselor, and social worker, or specialists such as speech and language, physical, or occupational therapists.

A case conference committee meeting is convened after the educational evaluation is finished. The meeting is intended to determine whether the student is eligible for special education and related services. If so, then the IEP is developed and appropriate educational services decisions are made. Case conference committee meetings also take place during each annual review.

Ease the Concern of Parents and Students

During these meetings, all members of the committee should be made to feel welcome and comfortable, especially parents and students attending case conference committee meetings. Parents and students may feel overwhelmed, intimidated, or frightened by attending a meeting with so many school personnel. Prepare for meetings by thinking about how to present information in comprehensible ways for parents and students. It may be beneficial to practice with another teacher when describing classroom routines. For example, parents may be unfamiliar with terminology that is used so commonly among teachers (e.g., *decoding* is a term frequently used by teachers, but not necessarily by parents and children). Try to describe class activities, student performance, and behaviors using concrete, simple, direct language. Teachers frequently use abbreviations or acronyms when speaking with each other (e.g., saying "LD" instead of "learning disabilities"), and should avoid doing so when speaking at case conference committees, so that parents do not become lost in the "educational jargon." Teachers may want to secure brochures describing common disabilities that are described in ways suitable for parents and for students. Brochures can be distributed to parents at the case conference committee meetings. Important phone numbers, e-mail addresses, and Websites can also be printed on handouts for parents so they can contact school personnel later if questions arise.

When parents feel comfortable at the meeting, they will be more likely to share important information about their child. Parental input at the meeting can be invaluable. Parents have insight into their child's behaviors that no one at the school may have considered. They can provide input regarding the student's study habits at home and any difficulties encountered during homework. Such information, along with all of the other evaluation data that are presented by others at the meeting, is crucial in devising the IEP.

During the case conference committee, one member records the information on the case conference summary form. A copy of this is distributed to the parents at the end of the meeting. Figure 2.5 displays a sample case conference summary form. If the student does not qualify for special education, the student may still qualify for services under Section 504 of the Vocational Rehabilitation Act (see chapter 1). Figure 2.6 presents a flowchart of student needs considered under IDEA and under Section 504.

Related Services

Related services, if considered necessary by the case conference committee, are also identified on the IEP. Related services are other services that are necessary to help students with disabilities benefit from special education services. Related services may include physical therapy, occupational therapy, audiological services, counseling, rehabilitation counseling, social work services, parent counseling, psychological services, school health services, medical services, early identification, transportation, recreation services, or other services identified by the case conference committee. If a situation requires substantial mobility adaptations, the case conference committee might recommend bus routes with special or adapted vehicles, assign an aide as an assistant, or acquire special equipment like oxygen, ramps, or lifts.

The Individualized Education Program (IEP)

An IEP is written by the case conference committee when it is determined that a student is eligible for special education services. The IEP has several major components, including the following:

- Student's current level of educational functioning, including how the disability influences involvement and progress in the general educational curriculum
- Statement of long-term annual goals
- Statement of short-term objectives related to (a) meeting the disability needs to enable participation in the general education curriculum, and (b) meeting other educational needs resulting from the disability
- Statement of special and related services, any program modifications to be provided or support for school personnel required for meeting annual goals, and for involvement in academic and nonacademic activities with children with and without disabilities
- Statement explaining the extent to which a student may not be participating with children without disabilities
- Statement of any individual modifications in state- or districtwide assessment procedures, or alternative assessment measures
- Initiation dates of service delivery and the duration and frequency of services
- Statement of transition services for all students 14 years of age and older, including interagency responsibilities; and a statement informing children of their rights beginning a year before they reach that age

For IEP Websites that may be of interest, go to the Web Links module in chapter 2 of the Companion Website.

Delivery of services to students with disabilities, including placement and program issues are topics on the Praxis *Special Education: Core Knowledge* Tests.

CASE REVIEW CONFERENCE SUMMARY

Student's Name _____ DOB _____ School _____

Parents/Guardian _____ Address _____

Phone _____ Surrogate Parent _____

Committee Meeting: _____
              (date)   (time)   (location)

The Case Review Committee was composed of the following:

_____

Chairperson   Administrator

_____

Teacher   Teacher   Teacher

_____

Evaluation Team Member(s)

_____

Parent(s)   Student

_____

Others

The eligibility decision has been _____

Least-restrictive placement has been _____

Purpose of conference   _____ initial evaluation   _____ re-evaluation   _____ review of IEP

                             _____ transition planning   _____ new to district

Multidisciplinary report of present level of performance:

_____

_____

_____

_____

Based on the data presented, the following eligibility decision was made:
The student is

_____

Placement recommendation

_____

      Harmful effect considered: _____ yes

Options considered: _____

Reasons options were rejected: _____

Other factors relevant to the proposed placement _____

_____

Signatures of committee members with dissenting opinions:

     _____

     _____

     _____

Figure 2.5
Summary from Case Conference Committee Meeting

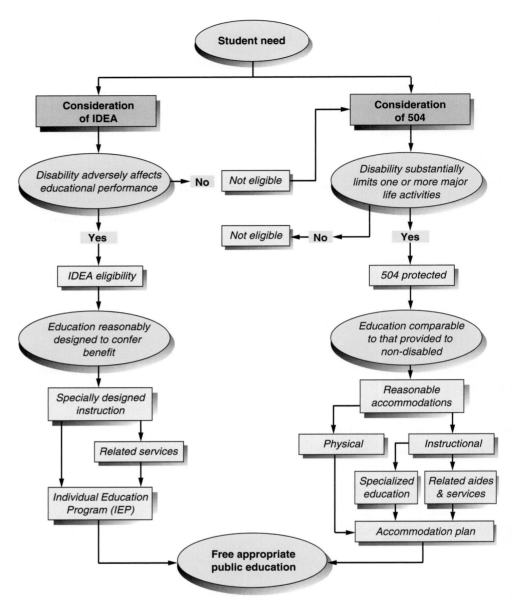

Figure 2.6
IDEA/504 Flow Chart
Note: Reprinted with permission from "Student Access: A Resource Guide for Educators," by Council of Administrators of Special Education, 1992, Council for Exceptional Children.

- Statement of how annual goals will be measured, how parents will be informed, and how progress will be monitored
- Objectives for parents to complete in the home in the case of early childhood special education

Moreover, when a special education student is placed in a general education setting, the IEP will contain modifications needed, including curriculum, instructional procedures, staffing, classroom organization, and special equipment, materials, or aides.

Although IEP formats used by school districts vary across the country, all must contain the required components. The Companion Website presents a sample IEP. Some computerized IEP programs are available commercially and are used to assist in developing the basic format of the IEPs (*The IEP Planner*, 1996). The Technology Highlight describes some additional technological applications.

School districts provide the parents with a written summary of the case conference committee meeting (see Figure 2.5), a copy of the IEP, and a copy of the parental rights (see Figure 2.3), and parents must provide written consent agreeing to the IEP before any services can begin.

Reviews of computerized software on IEPs can be found in the *Journal of Special Education Technology.*

Technology Highlight

IEP Software

Paperwork associated with special education can be reduced somewhat by using efficient systems for recording data, maintaining records, and communications. Advances in technology have assisted with saving teachers time. For example, the use of basic templates with school stationery for communications in a word processing program and databases containing frequently used names and addresses can help save valuable time. Such time saving programs are common features on most computers.

Recently, however, there have also been a large number of software programs commercially available to assist with writing Individual Education Plans (IEPs). Many of these programs share common features in that they work easily on both PC and Mac computer platforms. Many contain general templates of information that are required by law to be included in the IEPs. Some also contain banks of possible IEP objectives. Some programs available include: *IEP Planner, IEP Plus, IEP Ware, IEP Team Software*, and *Tera Systems IEP Manager.* A simple search using one of the widely available search engines such as google.com on the web will provide numerous commercially available programs.

Teachers can learn to use various forms of the software. Commercially available programs are usually advertised as highly relevant, time saving devices that help teachers produce high quality IEPs. Although this may be the case, teachers are cautioned to ensure that IEP objectives are not limited to what is available within individual software programs. As with any software, cautions are sometimes raised concerning hardware and or software malfunctions. For a list of relevant websites, go to the Web Links module in chapter 2 of the Companion Website.

Writing Goals and Objectives

A critical component of the IEP is the specification of the long-term annual goals and short-term objectives. Long-term annual goals are based upon the case conference committee's judgment of what the individual student should accomplish within a year. Annual goals can refer to academic functioning, such as reading grade-level textbooks at specific skill levels, or social behavior, such as exhibiting appropriate behavior in the cafeteria. In some cases, annual goals can refer to adaptive behavior or life skills, such as ordering independently in a restaurant or managing a personal bank account.

The best-written annual goals are measurable, positive, student-oriented, and relevant (Polloway, Patton, & Serna, 2001). Goals that are measurable can be more easily evaluated later. For example, "[Student] will read and comprehend grade-level reading materials," is much easier to measure at the end of the year than, "[Student] will improve reading." Positively written goals (e.g., "[Student] will use appropriate language in the classroom at all times") provide better implications for instruction than negatively written goals (e.g., "[Student] will stop swearing"). Student-oriented goals describe what the student will do (as in the previous examples), rather than what others will do (e.g., "[Student] will be given spelling worksheets"). Finally, relevant goals are not always limited to academic goals, but provide for the student's current and future needs, including social-emotional functioning, communication, and career-vocational areas when appropriate (Polloway, Patton, & Serna, 2001).

Short-term objectives are more limited and precise, and specify the steps to be taken to achieve long-term annual goals. For example, short-term objectives relevant to a long-term annual goal in reading should specify the subskills (e.g., letter identification, word recognition) that students will acquire on the way to meeting the long-term goal. Short-term objectives

For more information on preparing for due process hearings, see Ekstrand, Edmister, and Riggin (1989).

More information on writing goals and objectives is given in Mastropieri and Scruggs (2002).

Parent's input can be invaluable because of their insight about their children's behavior, habits, interest, and attitudes away from school.

For more information on writing IEPs, see Drasgow, Yell, and Robinson (2001).

should also be measurable, positive, student-oriented, and relevant. In addition, short-term objectives are usually best when they specify *conditions, behavior,* and *criteria.* As an example, consider the following objective: "In the lunchroom, [student] will use appropriate tone of voice at all times." In this case, "lunchroom" specifies the conditions, "appropriate tone of voice" specifies the behavior, and "at all times" (i.e., 100% of the time) specifies the criteria. Although long-term annual goals may also include these elements, they are sometimes more generally written. When objectives are specified in this way, they can be easily evaluated on the way toward meeting long-term goals.

Transition Services

Transition services are required to be written into IEPs when students turn 14, but in fact may be appropriate at younger ages (Ianacone & Stodden, 1987). IDEA 1997 also requires transitioning for preschoolers.

Often, transition services can be implemented the year before students begin to accumulate credits toward high school graduation. At the annual review meeting, when the student is in eighth grade or is of comparable age, the case conference committee may determine student educational, vocational, or employment training needs. Specific interagency linkages and responsibilities must be explicated in the **Individualized Transition Plan** (ITP), which is a supplement to the IEP. The Companion Website contains a sample ITP. The committee also determines whether students may require continual adult services upon completion of high school.

Monitoring IEPS

Legal safeguards are provided to ensure IEPs are monitored to reflect accurately the needs of individuals with disabilities. Regular reviews and evaluations of progress are required. Due process procedures are always available to resolve any disputes between the parents and the school district regarding the student's education.

Due Process. Due process is how conflicts are resolved between parents and schools regarding the student's education. Disagreements can arise in several areas: whether a student is eligible for special education, the outcome of an educational evaluation, the educational placement, the IEP, or some aspect of the "free, appropriate public education" (FAPE) guaranteed by IDEA.

Reviews of student IEPs need to be done regularly to assess student progress and create new goals as dictated by that progress.

Several alternatives exist for resolving these disagreements, some of which take place before a formal due process hearing. The simplest procedure for resolving conflicts is through informal meetings with parents and school personnel. Annual evaluations are required, but reevaluations can be requested anytime, and parents may request independent evaluations, after which another case conference committee must be scheduled to discuss any new evaluation data.

If conflicts remain unresolved during these meetings, mediation can be used to try to resolve the dispute. An independent person acts as a mediator between the parents and school district personnel to assist in resolving disputes (Ekstrand & Edmister, 1984). Mediation is a voluntary process that must be requested by both parties. After a formal mediation request is signed by both parties, the state selects a mediator, and schedules a hearing within 10 working days. Mediators should be trained in special education and mediation, possess excellent interpersonal skills, and serve as neutral facilitators. If mediation is successful, a written agreement is completed and forwarded to the case conference committee for its approval. Many conflicts can be resolved through mediation.

A request for a due process hearing is a formal request by either the parents or the school district to have the dispute arbitrated by an independent hearing officer. This process is more formal than mediation, and must take place within specific timelines as specified in the law. The case is presented to the independent hearing officer, who makes a decision based on evidence presented by both parties. Both parents and school district may be represented by legal counsel, present information pertaining to the case, bring forth relevant witnesses, and are entitled to see, at least five days before the hearing, any evidence the other party plans to introduce. Due process hearings can be open or closed to the public and the student may or may not be present. After listening to all the evidence, hearing officers produce a written decision. After the hearing decision, but within a specified number of days, the decision must be either executed, or appealed to the appropriate state board of special education by either party.

The appeal of the due process hearing decision must describe the parts of the decision that are objectionable and the associated rationale. The state board of special education is required to schedule another impartial review of the hearing and report on its decision. Its decision is considered final, unless either party appeals to the civil court within 30 calendar days. Throughout this process, the students remain in their current placement unless both parties agree to something else.

Special education departments in each school district have policies and procedures outlining teachers' roles and responsibilities should they become involved in these processes. The intent of the law is to best serve the student with disabilities, and these safeguards are in place to ensure that both parents and school district personnel are afforded due process rights.

Regulations associated with IDEA 1997 and a detailed discussion of transition services can be found in chapters 1 and 16.

Annual Reviews. Annual review meetings are conducted to monitor progress. During these meetings, teachers, parents, and other team members discuss the student's progress and make recommendations to amend, modify, or adjust the IEP as necessary. Changes in a student's educational placement to a more or less restrictive environment might be made based on the review.

Collaboration as Partnerships

Relationships develop among the many individuals working together as they collaborate to design optimal educational programs for students with disabilities. These partnerships grow as many of these relationships develop into shared decision making, shared planning, and even co-teaching relationships.

Partnerships Between Special and Regular Educators

Consultation exists when two individuals, such as special and general educators, work together to decide on intervention strategies for a specific student. During these meetings, which can be formal or informal, and verbal or in writing, effective communication procedures are critical.

For example, special education teachers may send weekly notes or e-mails to general education teachers to ask about the progress of specific students with disabilities. Teachers then describe any potentially difficult assignments with which they expect students with disabilities will require additional assistance, as in the following examples:

- A biology teacher indicates that a science fair project is being assigned next week. It will be due in a month, and students with disabilities may benefit from extra assistance.
- A history teacher indicates a test on a unit is approaching and students with disabilities may require additional studying assistance.

This information alerts special education teachers who can then help decide whether additional assistance is needed and then work with teachers in developing appropriate interventions as needed for students with disabilities.

Other special educators informally ask, during lunchtime, or before or after school, how students with disabilities are doing, and whether they are having any difficulties. In other cases, special educators schedule regular meetings with general educators. Ritter (1978) described a successful consultation project between a mental health worker and a general educator concerning educational strategies for an elementary-level student with learning and emotional problems. Likewise, Nelson and Stevens (1981) described successful consultation strategies for working more effectively with elementary-level students with learning and behavioral disorders. More recently, Kozleski and Jackson (1993) described consultation between special and general educators for designing inclusion strategies for a student named Taylor with severe mental retardation. Strategies included teaching students about friendships and including Taylor in an adapted version of the general education curriculum. The teachers worked together to implement the "Circle of Friends" strategy (Forest & Lusthaus, 1989) for increasing Taylor's social relationships. The key elements during the consultation process for these projects included the following:

1. Problem identification and clarification
2. Direct observations
3. Identification of intervention strategies
4. Implementation and evaluation of strategies
5. Increasing teacher knowledge of coping strategies for handling difficult situations

The Circle of Friends strategy is described in chapter 9.

Designing Adaptations

Another common type of consultation that occurs in middle and secondary schools is the discussion among content area teachers and special educators for designing adaptations for students with mild learning and behavioral difficulties. A history teacher, for example, requests assistance in providing additional study time and adapting worksheets for students with disabilities. An English teacher requests help designing alternative ways of assessing students' knowledge on literature assignments. A science teacher wants to know how to adapt lab materials to ensure success of

Refer to chapter 13 for strategies for adapting content area textbooks for students with reading difficulties.

- **One teacher and one assistant**. One person is clearly in charge of the classroom and has the major teaching responsibilities. The teacher has the traditional role of a teacher. The assistant helps students who are having difficulty, provides tutoring to those who require assistance, walks around the room, and observes the teacher and students.
- **Station teaching**. Students are divided into smaller groups and each of the two teachers is responsible for different components of instruction. Students may rotate around the room for instruction at the various stations within the class.
- **Parallel teaching**. Teachers teach the same information simultaneously to two smaller groups within the same classroom.
- **Alternative teaching**. Teachers teach similar content but may use different approaches depending on student needs.
- **Complementary instruction**. The general education teacher maintains responsibility for the content being taught, while the special education teacher maintains responsibility for the "academic survival skills necessary to acquire the subject content" (Bauwens et al., 1989, p. 19).
- **Supportive learning activities**. The general education teacher maintains responsibility for the content, while the special education teacher is responsible for developing and implementing supportive learning activities.
- **Team teaching**. During team teaching, teachers share equally in the responsibilities of teaching the class.

Figure 2.7
Co-Teaching Models
Note: Adapted from "Cooperative Teaching: A Model for General and Special Education Integration," by J. Bauwens, J. J. Hourcade, and M. Friend, 1989, *Remedial and Special Education, 10*(2), pp. 17–22. Also from "Co-Teaching: Guidelines for Effective Practices," by L. Cook and M. Friend, 1995, *Focus on Exceptional Children, 28*(3), pp. 1–16.

students with disabilities. Finally, many secondary content area teachers face the challenge of adapting content area textbooks for students who have lower reading levels.

Co-Teaching

Models of collaboration and co-teaching have been developed to meet the needs of diverse learners within a single classroom setting (Adams & Cesan, 1993; Dougherty, 1994). In some collaboration models, teachers meet with one another outside of the class teaching time (Hines, 1994). In some cases, both teachers are present during the actual teaching, but often only one teacher is present (Lundeen & Lundeen, 1993). In most co-teaching models, two teachers may or may not have the time to meet outside of class, but two teachers are present during the classroom teaching (Cook & Friend, 1995).

Cook and Friend (1995) described a number of co-teaching options currently in use: (a) one teacher and one assistant, (b) station teaching, (c) parallel teaching, (d) alternative teaching, and (e) team-teaching. They hypothesized that arrangements varied with respect to the amount of shared planning time available between the two teachers. Bauwens, Hourcade, and Friend (1989) described three teaching options within co-teaching: (a) complementary teaching, (b) team-teaching, and (c) supportive learning activities. Figure 2.7 describes some of the models and practices in place of collaboration and co-teaching.

Although many descriptions of co-teaching are provided, fewer models have been validated through empirical research evidence (for discussions, see Bauwens et al., 1989; Cook & Friend, 1995; Gately & Gately, 1993; and Reeve & Hallahan, 1994). Weiss and Brigham (2000) located 23 studies of co-teaching that provided supporting efficacy data; however, most investigated co-teaching at the elementary level. In order to ensure co-teaching is a productive and profitable undertaking, teachers should ask and answer specific questions before and during co-teaching:

(a) Why do we want to co-teach?
(b) How will we know whether our goals are being met?
(c) How will we communicate and document the collaboration?
(d) How will we share responsibility for the instruction of all students?
(e) How will we gain support from others? (Reinhiller, 1996, p. 46)

Team teaching is one model of co-teaching in which two teachers share the responsibility of one classroom, often with a great number of students or multiple students with special needs.

Another important consideration in co-teaching is building in sufficient planning time for the two teachers to work cooperatively to develop lessons to co-teach. In some co-teaching studies, planning time is built into the schedule. Try to include as much co-planning time as possible during the initial design. Finally, consider using the following guidelines when establishing co-teaching:

- Decide goals and objectives for co-teaching.
- Obtain support from the building and special education administration.
- Inform parents and request their support and permission, especially if co-teaching alters any IEP placement decisions that were made with parental consent.
- Build in sufficient planning time.
- Develop systematic measures to evaluate the effects of co-teaching on academic and social growth for students with and without disabilities.
- Determine student and teacher attitudes toward the co-teaching.
- Document how instructional responsibilities were shared during co-teaching, what instructional adaptations were made for students with disabilities, and how instruction changed over time.

Research Support

Although many models for co-teaching have been proposed, research has not yet identified a "most effective" model of co-teaching (see Reinhiller, 1996, for a review). Findings generally report positive attitudes from participating teachers (Friend & Cook, 1992; Harris, Harvey, Garcia, Innes, Lynn, Munoz, Sexton, & Stocia, 1987; Messersmith & Piantek, 1988; Nowacek, 1992; Pugach & Johnson, 1995; Weiss & Brigham, 2000). Qualitative and descriptive studies describe the evolving models of co-teaching and report on teachers and students' mostly positive attitudes toward the inclusive co-teaching. Reported benefits of co-teaching include improved instruction, increased enthusiasm for teaching, more communication, and more opportunities to generalize learned skills to the general education class environment (Reinhiller, 1996).

Challenges to effective co-teaching have also been identified (Reinhiller, 1996). These obstacles include budgetary constraints, lack of sufficient planning time, lack of cooperation, and increased teacher workloads. Other concerns include maintaining the full continuum of services for students, fear of losing services that are necessary for some students with disabilities, confronting negative attitudes toward individuals with disabilities, and confidentiality issues. The following three investigations help illustrate the practice of co-teaching, and the advantages and challenges associated with co-teaching.

Phillips, Sapona, and Lubie (1995) interviewed six general education teachers and four special education teachers at the end of the first year of co-teaching in an elementary school. Teachers initially expressed anxiety because of uncertainty about collaboration, and from fear of being evaluated by the other teacher. Successful co-teaching partners developed a definition of collaboration that was for the benefit of students, and developed a trusting relationship throughout the year. Some problems arose when a single special education teacher collaborated with more than one general education teacher, and when the numbers of special education students in inclusive classrooms seemed excessive. Teachers felt challenged negotiating roles and adapting to their co-teacher's style of interaction. In the beginning of the year, a great deal of time was spent in planning, but teachers became more efficient at organizing time and making plans later in the year. One pair of teachers had a more difficult time because of communication, anxiety, and different teaching styles, but overall the experience was viewed very positively by most teachers (Phillips et al., 1995; see also Weiss & Brigham, 2000).

Trent (1998) studied the experiences of an 11th grade U.S. history teacher who worked with two different special education co-teachers over two separate years. The first year, the two co-teachers shared compatible goals in trying to help special needs students succeed in the general education classroom. The general educator presented content, while the special educator monitored students, adapted curriculum, and taught organizational skills. Although the special education teacher expressed some concern for her role, both teachers noted benefits to the program, including increased awareness of the general education curriculum for the special education teacher, and learning how to adapt content for the general education teacher. In the second year, however, some communication problems arose with the second special education teacher. This situation evolved so that the general education teacher delivered content, while the special education teacher monitored behavior and performance. The relationship suffered to some extent from lack of planning time, and the perception of the teachers that their operational and communicative styles were not compatible.

Hardy (2001) observed two teachers co-teaching at the high school level, and reported that the biology teacher maintained her responsibilities as the content expert and the special educator assumed the role of adaptations and strategies expert. In this case, both teachers shared planning time and worked well together. Some of the modifications designed by the special educator included vocabulary study guides, video study guide sheets, and review and study sheets. She also made changes in formats, such as changing items in longer essay formats to fill-in-the blank responses, and inserted wider lines for responses on worksheets. A particularly useful adaptation during co-teaching included the use of visual aids, such as the use of an overhead projector to supplement information presented during lecture. The special educator reported during an interview:

> We were having a lab and Gwen [the general educator] was saying things like, "I want you to do this and I want you to do that," and it was all auditory. And the kids would be working on the lab and wouldn't hear, so I would get the overhead and start writing it out. (Hardy, 2001, p. 166)

Another major adaptation made by the special education teacher during the co-teaching was the use of small-group instruction to students who did not understand a concept taught to the entire class. The special education teacher reported:

> When I see that the students are confused, then I will work with a couple of tables at a time or have a little group back here . . . I will ask: "Who is still confused on this thing?" . . . And I will say: "OK, if you are confused and you have a question come back here." (Hardy, 2001, p. 171)

Hardy (2001) reported that the co-teaching was generally successful and appeared to benefit all students. However, the general educator indicated that she would not be able to implement modifications if the special educator were not working directly with her in a co-teaching situation. This finding suggests the great importance, in this case, of the special education co-teacher working directly in the classroom.

For a recent review of co-teaching research, see Murawski and Swanson (2001).

Collaboration with Paraprofessionals

Paraprofessionals, or specialized aides, are becoming more and more common in today's schools, working with teachers and students with disabilities (Katsiyannis, Hodge, & Lanford, 2000). Establishing effective communication with paraprofessionals is critical for designing optimal services for students with disabilities. If you supervise paraprofessionals, it is important to determine and implement district policies for supervision. Find out the roles, responsibilities, and the supervisory policies and share them with your paraprofessional to avoid any ambiguities in working relationships.

Background of Paraprofessionals

The backgrounds and experiences of paraprofessionals vary widely. Many paraprofessionals are certified teachers; some are enrolled in college. Some have degrees; others do not. Regardless of background, paraprofessionals must enjoy working directly with people and with students with disabilities.

Roles and Responsibilities of Paraprofessionals

Paraprofessionals may be aides to special education teachers, specialized aides for students with disabilities, or general aides for teachers within a school. Within those roles, paraprofessionals assume a variety of responsibilities, including recordkeeping, supervising, monitoring seatwork and classroom behavior, feeding and toileting, and providing instruction (French, 1998).

Very specialized responsibilities may be assigned to a paraprofessional. In the case of Jamal, a third-grader who uses a motorized wheelchair and has difficulties communicating and using his hands, a paraprofessional accompanies him throughout the school day. The paraprofessional functions as Jamal's assistant and accompanies him before, during, and after school in any activities, including helping him eat at lunch and dress appropriately for physical education and recess. The paraprofessional accompanies Jamal to all his classes. It may be a new experience for general education teachers to have another adult in their classrooms during instruction, but once teachers become familiar with the activities Jamal can accomplish independently, they will gain a better understanding of how to maximize the role of his paraprofessional. For example, activities the paraprofessional can help Jamal with include handling his class materials, reading tests out loud to him, writing down his responses, and assisting with mobility.

Communicating with Paraprofessionals

On occasion, teachers may feel overwhelmed with their responsibilities and find it difficult to know what to do with paraprofessionals. This may be especially true if paraprofessionals have strong personalities, are older, or have worked in schools longer than the teacher has. If a touchy situation arises, such as disagreeing on the amount of assistance necessary for a student, relations may become strained. To defuse these situations, use effective communication and problem-solving strategies to identify the problem and brainstorm potential solutions, as discussed earlier in the chapter. If you do not think you can handle the situation alone, seek the assistance of a more established teacher within your school. Often, simply discussing the situation makes everyone feel more comfortable.

Parents and Families as Partners

Building positive partnerships with parents yields important benefits to your students' education. Establish positive communication early in the school year and aim toward strengthening home–school cooperation. You will learn a great deal about your students from the parents' perspective of how they learn and interact in the home and outside of school.

Variability in Backgrounds and Family Structures

Parents represent the continuum of educational backgrounds, as well as racial or ethnic and socioeconomic status. Be sensitive to all individual parental needs and make all parents welcome in your classroom. Many parents feel intimidated by teachers, so be sure to let them know you share their goal of wanting the best for their child.

As mentioned before, avoid using educational jargon. State information in such a way that noneducators can understand what you are saying. If parents do not read or speak English, make the communications available in formats that are comprehensible to them. This may mean having foreign-language notes available for parents who do not read or speak English, or having interpreters

For more information on when and how to utilize paraprofessionals effectively, see Giangreco, Broer, and Edelman (1999).

Collaboration can also take place with community agencies such as rehabilitation services, mental health agencies, clergy, recreation agencies, and other legal services such as probation officers.

available for those with hearing impairments or who speak another language. In Fairfax County, Virginia, more than 100 languages are spoken by their students and families. Bilingual specialists in the school or from the community can assist in translating written documents and can attend meetings to translate communications effectively. Remember to have information read to parents who may not have prerequisite literacy skills themselves.

Families of today represent a wide array of configurations. Chances are the stereotypical family, consisting of a mother who stays at home taking care of children and a father who works outside of the home, may not be representative of your students' families. You may be working more closely with an individual who is not a parent, but rather is the legal guardian of your student. Or an older sibling might be the most direct communication link between the home and school. Some couples have reversed the traditional roles—the mother works outside the home while the father stays home with the children.

Positive Communication

A good way to initiate positive communication with parents is to send home introductory notes at the beginning of the school year. Ms. Susan Chung, an eighth-grade English teacher, sends home a short note stating the following:

> Hello Parents! I am your child's new eighth-grade English teacher. I am looking forward to getting to know your child, and meeting you. This year we will be working on many exciting reading and writing projects. There may be times during the year that I will ask for help from you with your child's work. Please feel free to contact me if I can answer any questions about your child or your child's performance in my class. I am looking forward to meeting you at our first open house on Tuesday, September 8th.
> Sincerely,
> Susan Chung, Eighth grade English teacher, Granby Middle School, phone: 555-4422.
> e-mail: schung@granby.edu

A positive first communication is especially important if a problem arises later and contact with home is necessary. Parents may be more likely to feel comfortable discussing sensitive issues concerning their child if you have contacted them earlier. If you only communicate when there is a problem, parents get the understandable impression that you only want to see them when something bad has happened, and they may become more reluctant to maintain communication with the school.

For Websites that may be of interest to parents and teachers of students with special needs, go to the Web Links module in chapter 2 of the Companion Website.

Maintaining a homework assignment notebook is one way to establish a line of communication between parents and teachers.

Many teachers also request parents' assistance regularly in their classes. This happens more frequently at elementary levels, but also occurs at the secondary levels. For example, letters may be sent home asking if any parents could volunteer in the class. Sometimes teachers specify what types of volunteer activity would be beneficial (e.g., making photocopies, cutting out pictures from magazines, or baking cookies for class parties). At other times, teachers might ask for help in obtaining specialized materials needed during specific units of instruction. But no matter what the request, it is important to emphasize that you realize it may be impossible for some parents to volunteer in class due to other responsibilities or to contribute financially to class activities. Be sure parents understand that neither of these limitations undermine the value of their roles in supporting the education of their children.

Sending home "happy notes" is another way to maintain positive communication with parents. Happy notes communicate positive things from school that day, week, or month. Ms. Halterman, a second-grade teacher, sends home one happy note every month with each of her students. Ms. Halterman also records in her grade book the dates that notes are sent home to preserve records and ensure positive contact is maintained regularly with all parents. Happy notes can also include reminders to parents of upcoming school functions. For example, before a class play, Ms. Halterman adds a section reminding parents that they are all invited to the play and reminds them of the day, date, and time.

Other examples of positive notes for parents are provided in chapter 7.

Communicating About Homework

Establish a "homework communication line" with parents. Some teachers have students maintain assignment notebooks in which daily homework assignments are recorded, including a listing of the materials necessary to complete assignments. When Mrs. Hesser, a fifth-grade teacher, assigned problem numbers 2 through 8 on page 27 in the math book, due Thursday, the students wrote down that information, along with the notation that they need to take home their math books to complete the assignment. If there is no assignment, students are required to write "No homework tonight" in the assignment book. Parents are shown assignment books nightly, and are asked to check and initial the book. This extra supervision keeps parents informed of assignments and provides opportunities for monitoring homework. Most parents welcome the idea of being more informed about assignments. Before Mrs. Hesser introduced the assignment notebook, many parents used to report that when they asked what their children had for homework, the children replied, "Nothing." Now the parents feel more informed in a less threatening way with their children. In some schools, "homework hotlines" have been established, in which parents can call a phone number, or check a Website, that informs them of their child's homework assignments.

Companion Website

Many schools are now using the World Wide Web and platforms such as "Blackboard" to facilitate communication among students, parents, administrators, and teachers. For more information on Blackboard, go to the Web Links module in chapter 2 of the Companion Website.

Parent Advisory Groups

Set up a parent advisory group in your school, to meet every month or two. This group can function as a liaison between parents and the school regarding class projects, special curriculum areas, or regular school functions and as a disseminator of information. Teachers can share information about special class projects with all parents at regular parent advisory group meetings. For example, these meetings might be a nice time for Mrs. Hesser to let parents know about the assignment notebooks. Mrs. Hesser could make sure that all the parents knew that during the upcoming parent advisory meeting she would be presenting that information and that she welcomed their comments regarding how they thought the process was working.

Other suitable topics include discussing the upcoming co-teaching planned by the sixth-grade and special education teachers, or discussing special education referral information. Again, these meetings afford extra opportunities for positive communication and collaboration efforts among family members and school personnel. Finally, teachers can ask the group to assist in identifying topics of interest to parents and specific presentations could be tailored to their needs.

Handling Disability Issues

It may be difficult for some parents to understand and accept that their child has a disability. In these cases, request assistance from the school social worker, counselor, or special education teacher. Parents may be frightened or feel overwhelmed trying to understand why their child has a disability, what needs to be done, and how they can help. It may be beneficial for parents to attend support groups for parents of children with specific disabilities. Use the expertise of the specialists within your school district to gather as much information as possible for the parents.

Disability Resources

Most schools have brochures and reference lists of sources suitable for parents to read concerning specific disability areas. Many parents appreciate knowing names of books or articles that describe additional information on their child's disability. Reference lists can identify where the materials can be located (e.g., the town library, the school library, the special parents' library). Professional organizations also maintain reference lists on specific disability areas. For example, the Council for Exceptional Children is the major special education organization, which not only maintains reference lists, but also has divisions specific to disability areas, such as the Division for Learning Disabilities and the Council for Children with Behavioral Disorders. Each division provides information pertaining to specific disability areas, including journals, newsletters, and Web pages.

Disagreements

On occasion, some parents may appear hostile toward teachers. In these cases, it is recommended that teachers obtain district assistance immediately. Some districts may recommend that specific documentation procedures be implemented; others may recommend that parent conferences be scheduled and attended by several teachers, including the building administrators. Understand that parent hostility might be due to a number of reasons, and assistance is available to help improve parental relations and ensure the best possible education for the student.

Summary

- Collaboration—involving cooperation, effective communication, shared problem solving, planning, and finding solutions—is the process for ensuring that all students receive the free, appropriate public education mandated by IDEA.
- Both schools and parents have responsibilities under IDEA. Partnerships can involve parents and professionals representing a variety of areas, including general and special education teachers, administrators, school psychologists, counselors, social workers, and community mental health agencies.
- Effective communication is critical for successful collaboration. Effective communication involves active listening, depersonalizing situations, finding common goals, brainstorming steps for achieving common goals, identifying possible solutions, and summarizing the conversation. These steps can be very helpful in solving problems.
- General education prereferral interventions are steps taken by schools to promote success in the regular classroom, before deciding on referral for special education. These actions can involve general and special education teachers, specialists, administrators, parents, and students.
- Effective communication and collaboration is particularly important in the referral and placement process. For case conference committees to perform successfully, effective communication is essential.
- Building effective collaborative partnerships is one of the most significant tasks of a successful inclusive teacher. With effective teamwork, solutions can be found to any number of problems.
- Collaboration can take the form of consultation, in which special education teachers work together to decide on intervention strategies for a specific student. Communication can take the form of notes, informal conversations, or scheduled meetings.
- Collaboration can also take the form of co-teaching, in which a general education and special education teacher teach together in an inclusive classroom setting. Some models are (a) one teacher and one assistant, (b) station teaching, (c) parallel teaching, (d) alternative teaching, and (e) team-teaching. Teachers should consider all models, and keep records of their own collaboration, to determine which best fits the needs of the students.
- Teachers must also collaborate effectively with paraprofessionals, to maximize the success of the

inclusive classroom. Teachers should carefully consider the background of the paraprofessional, outline roles and responsibilities, and communicate effectively at all times.

- Effective collaboration with parents is a key to effective inclusive teaching. Teachers should consider variability in family backgrounds and family structures, and maintain close, positive contacts with parents throughout the year.

Council for Exceptional Children

Collaboration: Partnerships and Procedures

Information in this chapter links most directly to:

Standard 10—Collaboration, particularly:

Knowledge:
- Models and strategies of consultation and collaboration.
- Roles of individuals with exceptional learning needs, families, and school and community personnel in planning of an individualized program.
- Concerns of families of individuals with exceptional learning needs and strategies to help address these concerns.
- Culturally responsive factors that promote effective communication and collaboration with individuals with exceptional learning needs, families, school personnel, and community members.

Skills:
- Maintain confidential communication about individuals with exceptional learning needs.
- Collaborate with families and others in assessment of individuals with exceptional learning needs.

- Foster respectful and beneficial relationships between families and professionals.
- Assist individuals with exceptional learning needs and their families in becoming active participants in the educational team.
- Plan and conduct collaborative conferences with individuals with exceptional learning needs and their families.
- Collaborate with school personnel and community members in integrating individuals with exceptional learning needs into various settings.
- Use group problem solving skills to develop, implement and evaluate collaborative activities.
- Model techniques and coach others in the use of instructional methods and accommodations.
- Communicate with school personnel about the characteristics and needs of individuals with exceptional learning needs.
- Communicate effectively with families of individuals with exceptional learning needs from diverse backgrounds.
- Observe, evaluate and provide feedback to paraeducators.

Inclusion Checklist

Collaboration: Partnerships and Procedures

If you would like to improve your communication skills, have you employed effective communication strategies, including the following?

- ❏ Active listening
- ❏ Depersonalizing situations
- ❏ Finding common goals
- ❏ Brainstorming ideas
- ❏ Summarizing the conversation

If a student is having persistent problems in your classroom, have you tried implementing general education prereferral intervention procedures?

If you would like to improve school teaming efforts, have you considered the following?

- ❏ Prereferral consultation
- ❏ General education assistance teams

If a student is having persistent problems in your classroom, have you implemented special education referral procedures?

If you would like to improve your co-teaching arrangements, have you considered the following?

- ❏ One teacher, one assistant
- ❏ Station teaching
- ❏ Parallel teaching
- ❏ Alternative teaching
- ❏ Complementary instruction
- ❏ Supportive learning activities
- ❏ Team-teaching
- ❏ Guidelines for co-teaching

If you would like to improve collaboration with paraprofessionals, have you considered the following?

- ❏ Background of paraprofessionals
- ❏ Roles and responsibilities of paraprofessionals

Have you considered improving collaboration with community agencies?

If you would like to improve collaboration with parents and families, have you considered the following?

- ❏ Variability in backgrounds
- ❏ Positive communication efforts
- ❏ Homework communication efforts
- ❏ Parent advisory groups
- ❏ Handling disability issues
- ❏ Disability resources

Chapter 3

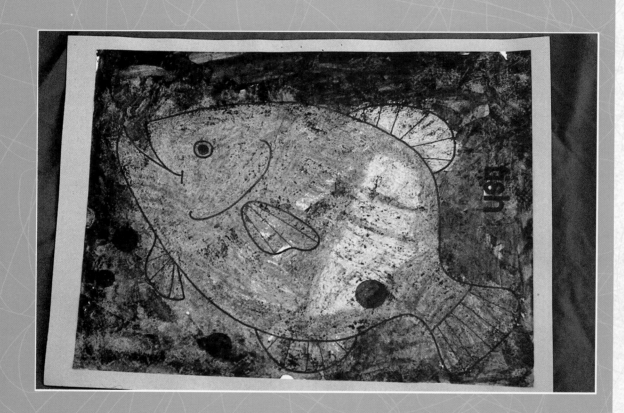

Justin Carrico, 11
Tallahassee, FL
"Fish"

Teaching Students with Higher-Incidence Disabilities

Objectives

After studying this chapter, you should be able to:

- Describe and discuss the prevalence and characteristics of students with communication disorders.
- Describe and discuss the prevalence and characteristics of students with learning disabilities.
- Describe and discuss the prevalence and characteristics of students with mental retardation.
- Describe and discuss the prevalence and characteristics of students with behavioral disorders and emotional disturbance.
- List, describe, and recommend adaptations and modifications to promote inclusion of students with higher-incidence disabilities.

Individuals who have higher-incidence disabilities—the disabilities that are most commonly seen in schools—include a wide range of abilities and disabilities, from mild to severe in intensity. Some higher-incidence disabilities are temporary, while others are lifelong conditions. Higher incidence disability areas include speech or language impairments, learning disabilities, mild or moderate mental retardation, and emotional or behavioral disorders. Together these disability areas make up about 90% of the total population of students ages 6–21 with disabilities served under IDEA (U.S. Department of Education, 2001). The percentages of students in each category are as follows:

Speech or language impairments—19.2%

Learning disabilities—50.5%

Mental retardation—10.8%

Emotional disturbance—8.3%

Although the mental retardation figure includes those with severe retardation, about 85% of the individuals in that group would be characterized as mildly or moderately mentally retarded. These disability areas are described in this chapter.

Speech or Language Impairments

Prevalence, Definitions, and Characteristics

Individuals classified with speech or language impairments make up 19.2% of all students ages 6–21 served under IDEA, and represent 1.7% of the school age population. **Speech** is the system of forming and producing sounds that are the basis of language, while **language** is considered the system of communicating ideas. Treatment is frequently provided by speech and language therapists (American Speech–Language Hearing Association, 1993). These therapists are excellent resource personnel for teachers and will provide guidelines for effective interactions with students with speech or language impairments (Costello & Holland, 1986).

Most students receiving speech and language therapy work individually or in small groups with a specialist for brief sessions several times a week and usually spend the remainder of their day in general education classes. In some schools, speech and language teachers may conduct therapy sessions in the general education classroom.

Some students with speech and language disorders may have another primary disability area, such as a learning disability, cerebral palsy, traumatic brain injury, or other severe disabilities. The latter groups are more likely to be using **alternative and augmentative communication** (AAC) devices to help them communicate.

Characteristics of students with disabilities are topics on the Praxis *Special Education: Core Knowledge* Tests.

Examples and Characteristics of Speech Disorders

Speech disorders may exist as voice, articulation, or fluency disorders. Voice disorders affect volume, pitch, and quality of voice and affect about 6% of the children with speech and language disorders. Examples of voice disorders include speech that is chronically strained, hoarse, breathy, or nasal. In the most severe instances, voice is not present at all. To be considered disordered, the student's voice should be significantly different from that of others of the same gender, age, or cultural background (Moore & Hicks, 1994).

Articulation disorders include difficulty pronouncing words, including omissions ("libary" for "library"), additions ("terribubble" for "terrible"), distortions (such as lisping), and substitutions (e.g., "tram" for "clam"). Articulation disorders represent the largest category (about 75%) of communication disorders (Hulit & Howard, 1993). A child with articulation problems might say, "a wabbit is a fuwwy animal." Younger children, and individuals with disabilities such as mental retardation and cerebral palsy, are more likely to exhibit articulation disorders. Articulation disorders can be treated with intensive speech therapy (Schwartz, 1994).

Fluency disorders are interruptions in the natural flow or rhythm of speech. A common fluency disorder is **stuttering,** "an involuntary repetition, prolongation or blockage of a word or part of a word that a person is trying to say" (Curlee, 1989, p. 8). Children who stutter know what they are trying to say, but seem to have difficulty getting words started, often at the beginning of sentences. They may repeat parts of words or prolong the initial sound of a word. Most people who stutter begin stuttering before age 5, but only after they have begun to speak in sentences (Curlee, 1989).

Examples and Characteristics of Language Disorders

Language disorders are problems in using or comprehending language, either expressive (using language) or receptive (understanding language of others). Language disorders may involve difficulties with phonology, morphology, syntax, semantics, or pragmatics. **Phonology** involves the ability to blend and segment the sounds that individual letters or groups of letters make to form words. For example, it may be difficult for students to hear the difference between the words *cap* and *cat* if they have a phonological problem. **Morphology** involves the meaningful structure of words, as expressed in **morphemes,** the smallest units of language that carry meaning or function. For example, the word *swimmer* contains two morphemes: a **free morpheme** (can stand alone as a word) (*swim*), and a **bound** morpheme (depends on other words) (*-er*). *Swim* signifies a type of aquatic locomotion, and *-er* represents that the word represents a noun meaning "one who swims." Other bound morphemes combine with words to form plurals and make various verb tenses. **Syntax** is the grammatical structure of language, and is concerned with such things as word order and noun-verb agreement. **Semantics** refers to the meanings of words used in language. For example, the sentence, "Walk can I take?" may convey a semantic meaning but is not correct syntactically.

Pragmatics refers to the use of language in the context of social situations. For example, students typically speak to teachers in a different manner than they would speak to classmates. Not understanding when to use more formal speech and when to use more informal speech represents a problem with pragmatics (see O'Grady, Dobrovolsky, & Aronoff, 1997).

One of the most severe language disorders is **aphasia,** which refers to difficulties speaking (expressive aphasia) or comprehending (receptive aphasia) language. Receptive aphasia is less common. Aphasia often accompanies brain injuries, and individuals may experience difficulty retrieving words that they knew before the injury. In cases of mild aphasia, students may simply need more time to retrieve words as they communicate. Students with more severe forms of aphasia may have extreme difficulty communicating (Benson & Alfredo, 1996).

In the most severe communication disorders, individuals cannot speak and must learn to rely on alternative and augmentative communication devices (Franklin & Beukelman, 1991). Sometimes these devices are used as supplements to communication when some speech is available; other times they are used for all communication (Lewis, 1993).

Causes of Speech or Language Impairments

In most cases, precise causes associated with specific speech and language disorders are unknown. Some children have severe language delays during early childhood development, but reasons for the delay are unknown. Voice disorders can be caused by growths, infections, or trauma to the **larynx** (structure containing the vocal cords); infections of the tonsils, adenoid glands, or sinuses; or physical disorders such as **cleft palate,** in which the upper part of the oral cavity is split (Moore & Hicks, 1994). The cause of stuttering is unknown, although it is currently thought to be the result of some slight brain dysfunction (Conture, 1989).

Speech and language disorders often accompany other coexisting disabilities. For example, if a child has a severe hearing loss or is deaf, then difficulties with speech and language almost certainly will be present. Individuals who have severe mental retardation also typically have speech and language difficulties. Additionally, physical problems such as cleft palate and neurological disorders such as cerebral palsy can contribute to speech and language disorders.

Parents and teachers are usually the first to recognize problems young children have with articulation or fluency of speech.

Issues in Identification and Assessment of Speech and Language Impairments

Parents and teachers are usually the first to identify a potential speech or language problem. Parents may become concerned when their 2-year-old has not begun to develop language. Primary school teachers may be the first to refer a child for a speech and language evaluation when they notice language delays; language comprehension difficulties; immature speech patterns, voice, articulation; or fluency disorders. Frequently administered tests include articulation tests, auditory discrimination tests, language development tests, vocabulary tests, and language samples from a variety of social contexts.

Classroom Adaptations for Students with Speech or Language Impairments

An open, accepting classroom environment is of utmost importance to promote acceptance, and decrease anxiety and opportunities for ridicule. Students with communication disorders may be subject to teasing by peers. Speak privately to students suspected of teasing and try to enlist their help and support. Punishing them for teasing may not be helpful (Stuttering Foundation of America, 1997).

Prepare general education students with information on the particular speech and language disorders that they may encounter among their classmates. Have speech and language specialists explain the disorders and provide examples of how peers can be supportive of students with communication difficulties. Tell students that they will have as much time as they need to answer questions, and that you are interested in having them take time to think through their answers.

Adapt the Physical Environment

Place students with communication disorders near the front of the room for easier listening. This will also enable easier access if they need help or if you have devised a special cueing system with them for responding orally in class. The following *In the Classroom* feature provides a checklist for considerations for adaptations in the physical environment.

Adapt Materials

Allow students to use any technology that may help them with their disability area. For example, perhaps they can prerecord responses on audiotapes, videotapes, or computers, and then play that recording for the class.

Use Alternative or Augmentative Communication. Adaptive communication methods are referred to as alternative and augmentative communication (AAC) techniques. AAC symbols and techniques fall into two broad categories—aided and unaided. Aided communication involves the use of some external device, such as simple handmade materials, a picture board, or more sophisticated computer-assisted devices. Unaided communication does not involve any apparatus other than the individual's own body. Examples include manual signing, making physical gestures, miming, pointing, and moving the eyes (Lloyd, Fuller, & Arvidson, 1997).

Alternative communication techniques involve the use of communication boards to assist communication. Communication boards contain pictures or words of commonly asked questions and responses to questions. When asking or responding to questions, students can point to the picture that communicates what they mean. When constructing communication boards, be sure to include words that the student is most likely to use. Specialized communication boards also can be developed that contain vocabulary associated with specific classes. Pointing devices that attach to the head can be used for students who have difficulty pointing with their hands or fingers. When the AAC user is unable to point, a communication partner can point to objects or symbols on the communication board, and the user can indicate by voice or gesture when the right symbol has been identified. Boards that include symbols for categories of items can facilitate this process. If the user's abilities are confined to eye-gaze, the board can be constructed on a sheet of clear acrylic and held up to the user. When the user looks directly at the intended picture or symbol, the communication partner can identify the focal point of the user's eyes. Some commercially available boards, such as the Touch Talker or LightTalker available from Prentke-Romich, produce speech output when the corresponding symbol or picture is touched (Lloyd, Fuller, & Arvidson, 1997).

For more information on alternative and augmentative communication, see chapter 4.

In the Classroom ...a feature for teachers

Sample Environmental Adaptation Considerations

Seating Position
_____ near teacher
_____ near peer assistant
_____ near paraprofessional
_____ near board
_____ near front of room
_____ alone
_____ quiet space
_____ other

Seating Planned for
_____ lunchroom
_____ assemblies
_____ bus
_____ all classes
_____ other

Rearrange Physical Space
_____ move desks
_____ move class displays
_____ other

Reduce Distractions
_____ visual
_____ auditory
_____ movement
_____ other

Provide Daily Structure
_____ first thing to do when
         entering class
_____ second thing
_____ third thing
_____ being prepared
_____ other

Provide Designated Places
_____ in boxes
_____ out boxes
_____ other

Provide Orderly Models
_____ organized desks
_____ organized lockers
_____ other

More recent advances in technology have also incorporated the use of synthesized speech sounds when using some alternative communication devices. Students can type information into computers, and computers will produce the speech output for them using a variety of tones.

Adapt Instruction

Effective teaching practices, including clear, well-organized presentations and activities, will help meet the needs of students with speech and language disorders in your classroom. Appropriate pace of instruction and maximized student engagement—including frequent questioning and feed-back—can help ensure academic success.

Facilitate Verbal Responding. Allow sufficient time for students with communication disorders to speak when responding. Do not impose time pressures on oral responses. When a student finishes, repeat the response for the entire class to hear. For example, in a seventh-grade class, Natalie had a severe speech and language disorder. Natalie spoke very slowly, and was difficult to understand. However, her math teacher, Mr. Lee, became adept at understanding Natalie's language. He made a point of trying to call on Natalie whenever he could, allowed her sufficient time to respond, and then repeated her comments so the entire class could hear them. He made comments like: "Thank you, Natalie, that was a good response. Natalie said, 'The numbers 11 and 23 are both prime numbers.'"

Some teachers have devised special plans to enable their students to know when they will be called on in class. For example, a high school history teacher, Mrs. Stobey, met at the beginning of the school year, after school, with Micky, a student who stuttered. Together they decided that if Micky raised his hand, then he felt comfortable trying to participate in the discussions and only then would Mrs. Stobey call on him to talk.

Communication boards can greatly improve learning and classroom interactions.

Initially, when students are getting used to your class, ask a student who stutters only questions that can be answered in a few words. If you are going to ask everyone in class to answer a question, call on the student who stutters relatively early. Because anxiety sometimes makes stuttering worse, answering sooner may allow less time for anxiety to develop (Stuttering Foundation of America, 1997).

Monitor your pace of instruction, especially with respect to the amount of new vocabulary introduced to students with receptive language disorders. Use language cards containing representational pictures and illustrations depicting the definitions of new terms. This will help reinforce understanding not only for students with language difficulties, but also for any student in your class for whom English is a second language. One third-grade teacher used pictorial language cards for all new vocabulary she introduced. She reported that all of her students enjoyed using the cards with pictures and that learning seemed to improve. Whenever possible, use concrete examples, rather than lengthy verbal descriptions, to illustrate new concepts for students with receptive language disorders.

Practice Oral Presentations. If oral presentations are mandatory, practice alone with students first and provide feedback. Some (but not all) students may feel especially frightened at standing up in front of peers to speak, thereby emphasizing their disability area. Consider allowing students to present with partners or in small groups, such that each group member has a different role during oral presentations.

Adapt Evaluation

Additional information about testing adaptations is provided in chapter 12.

Some students may require extended time periods to complete class tests. Others may require the assistance of readers, scribes, or communication boards and communication partners while taking tests.

Learning Disabilities

Prevalence and Definitions of Learning Disabilities

Learning disabilities (LD) is a general term describing a group of learning problems. Students with learning disabilities are very highly represented in general education classes, as learning disabilities is the largest single disability area. Approximately 4.5% of all school-age children are classified as having learning disabilities (U.S. Department of Education, 2001), or 50.5% of the children requir-

CLASSROOM SCENARIO

Maria

Maria is a 12-year-old girl of average intelligence and pleasant, cooperative disposition. She tries hard to succeed in school, but has great difficulty reading independently. She writes slowly, using simple statements and words that are easy for her to spell. Her writing is labored and does not accurately reflect her thinking.

Maria receives assistance with her reading and writing in the resource room, four days a week. She is making good progress, but still has difficulty with grade-level reading materials and writing tasks. Mr. Harrison, Maria's teacher, has prioritized Maria's class assignments. Mr. Harrison does not require that she read or write independently to participate in class activities. In social studies, for example, when the class is given an assignment to read parts of the textbook, Maria is allowed to read together with a classmate. The classmate reads questions from the assignments aloud, and Maria is allowed to write simple answers to the questions, or to dictate longer answers to her partner. Mr. Harrison uses clear, structured presentations to maximize Maria's understanding of the lessons. Finally, Maria's performance is systematically monitored, to ensure that she is learning adequately, and that the need for further adaptations is examined. By the second semester, Maria's reading and writing skills have improved enough that she is encouraged to complete reading and writing assignments independently when possible, but to ask a classmate or teacher for specific assistance when required.

To learn more about speech and language impairments and the American Speech–Language Hearing Association (ASHA), go to the Web Links module in chapter 3 of the Companion Website.

ing special education services in the schools. More males than females have learning disabilities, with some estimates ranging as high as four males to every one female.

Samuel Kirk coined the term *learning disabilities* at a parents' meeting in the early 1960s (Kirk, 1962) to describe the group of individuals who appeared "normal" in intellectual functioning, but had difficulties in some aspect of academic learning.

Learning disabilities is now used as an umbrella term to refer to a group of individuals with average or above average intelligence who nonetheless have difficulties with academic tasks such as reading, writing, processing information, spoken language, written language, or thinking abilities. The federal definition is given as follows:

> "Specific learning disability" means a disorder in one or more of the basic psychological processes involved in understanding or using language, spoken or written, which may manifest itself in an imperfect ability to listen, think, speak, read, write, spell, or to do mathematical calculations. The term includes such conditions as perceptual handicaps, brain injury, minimal brain dysfunction, dyslexia, and developmental aphasia. The term does not include children who have learning problems that are primarily the result of visual, hearing, or motor handicaps, of mental retardation, of emotional disturbance, or of environmental, cultural, or economic disadvantage. (*Federal Register,* 1977, p. 65083)

For more information on learning disabilities, go to the Web Links module in chapter 3 of the Companion Website.

Over the years many definitions of *learning disability* have been proposed by various task groups and professional organizations (Clements, 1966; Hammill, Leigh, McNutt, & Larsen, 1981; Haring, 1969; National Joint Committee on Learning Disabilities, 1989). Most definitions share components with the federal definition and include the following:

- possibly caused by irregular development or functioning of the central nervous system
- may be a lifelong condition
- affects academic areas including reading, writing, math, and language
- identified by an ability–achievement discrepancy
- incorporates an **exclusionary clause** (that is, a learning disability is not due to economic disadvantage or any other handicapping condition) (Kavale & Forness, 1995)

The exclusionary clause has often been the major force behind defining learning disabilities, in that it is frequently easier to describe what the learning disability is *not,* rather than name specific etiological factors (or causes) for the disability.

Most states require the presence of a *discrepancy* between ability and achievement to support identification of a learning disability. For example, Edward had a Full Scale IQ (Intelligence Quotient) score of 101 and a standard score of 85 on a test of reading achievement. This amounts to a discrepancy of 16 standard score points between ability (the IQ test) and achievement (the reading achievement test), where the Full Scale IQ is average (about the 50th percentile), and the reading achievement score is substantially lower (about the 15th percentile). In many states, this discrepancy would lend support to the overall case for learning disabilities (although discrepancy, by itself, does not demonstrate that a learning disability exists). Other evidence in support of the presence of learning disabilities is usually required, including relevant medical information, a social and developmental history, observational data on the student's academic performance in the general education classroom, or other evidence of learning problems (Lerner, 2000).

Many terms have been used to refer to problems associated with learning disabilities. Some of these labels include **dyslexia** (reading disability), minimal brain dysfunction, minimal brain damage, **dyscalculia** (math disability), **dysgraphia** (writing disability), word blindness, educational handicaps, perceptual handicaps, and attention deficit disorder with or without hyperactivity (Clements, 1966; Haring, 1969). Although many of these terms are still in use, the term *learning disability* has persisted and is most commonly used to refer to individuals who do not learn adequately, despite average or above average general ability and appropriate educational opportunity.

Causes of Learning Disabilities

The specific causes of learning disabilities remain unknown but are generally believed to be due to the way the brain functions. Three major factors—organic, genetic, and environmental—have been hypothesized as possible causes. Organic factors include indications of brain differences in size or

A discrepancy between student achievement and student ability may suggest the presence of a learning disability.

functioning perhaps due to differences during the development of the brain. Recent medical advances in detecting brain dysfunctions using electroencephalograms (EEGs), computerized axial tomographic (CAT) scans, magnetic resonance imaging (MRIs), and positron emission tomography (PET) scans have yielded evidence for a neurological basis that may be linked to possible causes of the learning disabilities (Hynd, Marshall, & Gonzalez, 1991). Genetic factors include evidence of heredity in the cause of learning disabilities, in that parents who experience reading difficulties have a higher risk of having children who experience similar difficulties learning to read (Olsen, Wise, Conners, Rack, & Fulker, 1989). Additionally, identical twins are more likely than fraternal twins to share learning disabilities (DeFries, Gillis, & Wadsworth, 1993). Finally, there is speculation that environmental factors such as poor diet and nutrition and exposure to toxins such as alcohol, smoke, and cocaine, either prenatally or postnatally, can contribute to causes of learning disabilities (Hallahan, Kauffman, & Lloyd, 1999). At this point, however, a single definitive cause associated with learning disabilities has yet to be discovered.

Issues in Identification and Assessment of Learning Disabilities

Some issues have been controversial regarding the assessment and identification of students with learning disabilities (Mather & Roberts, 1994; Scruggs & Mastropieri, 1994–1995). These issues include the specificity of differences between learning disabilities and general low achievement, and the use of ability–achievement discrepancy criteria in identification.

Specificity

One controversial issue involves whether students classified as learning disabled represent a truly specific category; that is, that they are distinguishable from students who are simply low achievers. Ysseldyke, Algozzine, Shinn, and McGue (1982) examined psychological and educational test scores of fourth-grade students who had been classified as having learning disabilities, or who had not been classified, but had scored below the 25th percentile on achievement tests. Ysseldyke et al. (1982) reported that "there were no psychometric differences in the performances of the two groups of students" (p. 83). Citing similar studies, Algozzine (1985) concluded "the learning disabilities category has outlived its usefulness" (p. 72).

These conclusions were challenged by Kavale, Fuchs, and Scruggs (1994), who reanalyzed the data presented by Ysseldyke et al. (1982), and reported that the data did in fact clearly identify differences between the two groups of individuals (for further discussion, see Algozzine, Ysseldyke, & McGue, 1995; Kavale, 1995). Similar research has revealed differences between students with learning disabilities and low achievers in areas of both academic and social functioning (Bursuck, 1989; Cleaver, Bear, & Juvonen, 1992; Donahoe & Zigmond, 1990; Fuchs, 1998; McLeskey & Waldron, 1990; Merrill, 1990; Shinn, Ysseldyke, Deno, & Tindal, 1986; Tur-Kaspa & Bryan, 1994; Wilson, 1985). More recently, Fuchs, Fuchs, Mathes, and Lipsey (2000) conducted a **meta-analysis** of 86 studies comparing students with learning disabilities and low-achieving students in reading and found that students with learning disabilities generally scored considerably lower than low-achieving students (see also Fuchs, Fuchs, Mathes, Lipsey, & Roberts, 2002).

Discrepancy

Although a discrepancy between intelligence and achievement is used in most states to help support the identification of learning disabilities, the use of discrepancy criteria has been controversial (Lyon et al., 2001; Scruggs & Mastropieri, 2002). Some research has revealed that different learning disabilities classifications could result depending on which discrepancy formula and which test data were used (Forness, Sinclair, & Guthrie, 1983; Kavale, 1987; Ysseldyke, Algozzine, & Epps, 1983). It has also been suggested that schools may not always apply discrepancy criteria correctly in identification procedures (MacMillan, Gresham, & Bocian, 1998). Misclassifications are dangerous and could result in incorrectly labeling individuals as learning disabled or overlooking individuals who truly are learning disabled (Mastropieri, 1987).

Further, it has been argued that discrepancy criteria are not conceptually sound (Algozzine, 1985), are vulnerable to measurement error (Wilson, 1987), and inhibit early identification of learning disabilities. Lyon et al. (2001) concluded, "the IQ–achievement discrepancy, when employed as the primary criterion for the identification of LD, may well harm more children than it helps" (p. 266).

However, some consideration of discrepancy does seem compatible with the overall conceptualization of learning disabilities; that is, students with learning disabilities are generally thought to have unexpected academic difficulties in spite of average or above-average general ability (Keogh, 1994; Mastropieri & Scruggs, 2002). And although some alternatives to discrepancy criteria have been suggested (e.g., deficits in some reading and language subskills, resistance to validated educational treatments, discrepancy between achievement and age–grade level, see Gresham, 2002; Lyon et al., 2001), none to date has received wide acceptance (Scruggs & Mastropieri, 2002).

Nevertheless, it does seem likely that some alternative to discrepancy criteria will soon be implemented. In a recent report sponsored by the U.S. Department of Education (2002), it was recommended that discrepancy criteria not be used for identification of learning disabilities, that renewed focus be placed on early identification, and that alternative procedures be explored. One highly recommended alternative was a response-to-intervention approach, where general education teachers implement scientifically based practices and use curriculum-based measurement (CBM; see chapter 12) to document student progress on a regular basis. Students who prove to be "treatment resisters" may be eligible for more intensive interventions, or referral to special education. It seems possible that criteria such as these may be employed in the near future.

Characteristics of Learning Disabilities

Individuals with learning disabilities possess a variety of characteristics that distinguish them from other students. However, not all individuals with learning disabilities have all the characteristics described in this section.

Language and Literacy

Many students with learning disabilities—as do many other students with high-incidence disabilities—experience difficulties with both expressive and receptive language. Language problems often encountered by students with learning disabilities include the following:

For the most recent developments in identification of learning disabilities, go to the Web Links module in chapter 3 of the Companion Website.

- Discriminating between sounds (e.g., mistakes "cat" for "cap")
- Understanding grammar (including use of certain pronouns and prepositions)
- Understanding subtleties in language
- "Word finding" abilities, or retrieving appropriate words when needed (Hallahan, Kauffman, & Lloyd, 1999; Kail & Leonard, 1986)

Most students with learning disabilities have significant reading problems (McLeskey & Waldron, 1990). Many students with learning disabilities lack **phonemic awareness**—the awareness that words are made up of individual speech sounds, each of which are represented by one or more letters (Liberman & Shankweiler, 1991). Reading problems result when such students are unsuccessful at learning the sound codes for the letters in the alphabet, and applying those codes for successful reading ("decoding")(Mather & Roberts, 1994). These individuals often have slow and labored oral reading abilities, are not inclined to read for pleasure, and lack any effective strategies for fluent reading. Rather, they often rely excessively on such things as context clues or pictures to compensate for their lack of word-reading skill. Some students may read as slowly as six or seven words per minute on grade-level texts. Reading comprehension difficulties frequently accompany decoding problems (Mastropieri, Scruggs, Bakken, & Whedon, 1996).

Other literacy problems encountered by students with learning disabilities include handwriting (Graham & Weintraub, 1996), spelling (Fulk & Stormont-Spurgin, 1995), and written composition (Graham & Harris, 1994). For example, Englert and Mariage (1996) described the journal entries of a second-grade student named John:

> [September 2 entry] I am a stopit (stupid).
> [September 6 entry] Lok (like) to play basball and I do triw (throw) it and ihitaball. (p. 165)

However, when students with learning disabilities receive phonemic awareness training and strategy instruction, their literacy skills can greatly improve (Fulk & Stormont-Spurgin, 1995; Harris & Graham, 1992; Mastropieri & Scruggs, 1997). For example, with the help of an effective writing in-structural program, John made outstanding gains in his writing by the end of the year, creating 150-word expository essays, with greatly improved spelling and syntax.

Mathematics

It is estimated that two-thirds of students with learning disabilities have mathematics disabilities (Cawley & Parmer, 1992). Students may exhibit difficulties in learning math facts, rules, procedures, or concepts, and in personal math such as managing money (Montague, 1995). Research indicates that students who are trained to use specific strategies improve their math problem-solving and computational abilities (Woodward, Baxter, & Scheel, 1997).

Attention and Memory

Many students with learning disabilities experience difficulties with sustaining attention to tasks (Riccio, Gonzalez, & Hynd, 1994). Some have serious problems referred to as **attention deficit disorder** (ADD) with **hyperactivity** (ADHD) or without hyperactivity (American Psychiatric Association [APA], 1994; Hallahan & Cottone, 1997). Many students who have a primary disability area such as learning disabilities, emotional disabilities, or mental retardation may also have ADHD.

Many students with learning disabilities have deficits in both long- and short-term memory, and memory for verbal information (**semantic memory**) (Ceci, 1986; Cooney & Swanson, 1987). Because most content areas in school introduce new vocabulary regularly and require factual recall for tests, students with memory difficulties may experience serious problems in school (Swanson, 1987). Memory problems can impede successful school performance unless students are provided with effective mnemonic (memory-enhancing) strategies to help compensate for such difficulties.

Swanson, Cooney, and O'Shaughnessy (1998) described problems that students with learning disabilities have in **working memory**—the ability to mentally operate on information in short-term memory. Problems in working memory may underline problems in higher-order cognitive processes, such as reading comprehension.

Thinking and Reasoning

Thinking and reasoning difficulties are apparent in many individuals with learning disabilities. Abstract reasoning may be especially problematic (Hollingsworth & Woodward, 1993; Mastropieri, Scruggs, & Butcher, 1997; Woodward, 1994). Individuals may take longer than others to learn new tasks and information. Other problems may include difficulties organizing thinking, drawing conclusions, over-rigidity in thinking, and general lack of effective strategies for solving problems.

Metacognitive Abilities, Including Study Skills, Learning Strategies, and Organizational Strategies

Metacognition refers to the knowledge about one's own learning and understanding. Students with well-developed metacognitive skills know how to study effectively, monitor their own understanding (**self-monitoring**), and plan and budget their time wisely. They are familiar with cognitive strategies that help them learn and remember more efficiently, and regulate their own strategy use (**self-regulation**). In contrast, many students with learning disabilities—as well as other students with high-incidence disabilities—lack metacognitive skills necessary to become successful, self-sufficient learners (Case, Mamlin, Harris, & Graham, 1995; Ceci, 1986). They may appear disorganized, and lack an understanding of what to do or how to proceed with academic tasks or assignments. Specific strategy training can increase students' performance on tasks requiring metacognitive abilities (Deshler, Ellis, & Lenz, 1996; Gaskins & Elliot, 1991; Lucangeli, Galderisi, & Cornoldi, 1995; Mastropieri & Scruggs, 1997).

Social-Emotional Functioning

As many as one-third to one-half of students with learning disabilities may also exhibit problems with social or emotional functioning (Bryan, 1994; Sullivan & Mastropieri, 1994; Tur-Kaspa & Bryan, 1994; Vaughn & Hogan, 1994). Social–emotional problems include social skill difficulties,

Additional information on attention deficit hyperactivity disorder is provided in chapter 5.

See chapter 10 for a discussion of the applications of mnemonic strategies.

Careful attention to seating arrangements can help promote attention and interest.

low self-esteem, low self-awareness and self-perception, low self-concept, weak self-confidence, anxiety, or depression (Heath, 1996; McPhail & Stone, 1995; Meltzer, 1996). Individuals with learning disabilities are more susceptible to adjudication than the population as a whole (Bryan, Pearl, & Herzog, 1989).

Sometimes the social-emotional functioning of students with learning disabilities is associated with academic functioning. For example, Centra (1990) interviewed high school students with learning disabilities about their school experiences. One student reported:

> Whenever we had to read in regular English class, I would refuse to do it. When the teacher would ask me to read, I would just say, "No." The teacher would keep going at me and I'd tell her no, and I'd even swear at her and everything. She'd make me so mad. I was thrown out of class and I didn't even care because when that happened then I didn't have to read. (p. 150)

Such reports underline the importance of teachers exhibiting kindness and understanding toward students with learning disabilities.

Generalization and Application

Most students with learning disabilities—as well as other high-incidence disability areas—have difficulty generalizing learned information to novel situations. Some students may master content area materials in special education settings, but fail to apply that information to the general education classroom or real-life settings (Scruggs & Mastropieri, 1984). For example, students who have learned basic division in school may not automatically apply this skill to dividing the cost of a pizza among four friends. While such **generalization** problems are also encountered among students without disabilities, they can be magnified in many students with disabilities. Many special education teachers attempt to build extensive generalization training into the educational programs of students with learning disabilities to help students apply what they have learned in different life situations.

Strategies for promoting generalization are described in chapter 6.

Classroom Adaptations for Students with Learning Disabilities

Teaching students with learning disabilities (like students from all disability areas) can be an exciting challenge. Most students with learning disabilities present unique problems that require collaboration, creative thinking, and problem-solving strategies. When teaching students with learning disabilities, consider the following adaptations:

Technology Highlight

AlphaSmart and Applet Software

Many students with high incidence disabilities can benefit from instruction using keyboarding and word processing. These skills can be taught when students are in the primary grades because they will continue to be useful throughout an individual's life. Various word processing programs and electronic devices are available. AlphaSmarts are one such relatively inexpensive device (low range is around $200) that consist of a small portable keyboard and screen that allows one to complete word processing, save programs, and upload and download information to computers and printers. AlphaSmarts are transportable and can be easily carried by young students to various locations in and out of school to take notes, compose, or write. Moreover, the functions for saving text are easy to learn. Applet or mini software programs that can be purchased separately that have increased the utility of the simple word processing features. For example, an *Inspiration* software applet is available that enables students to use the outlining and organizational features of the *Inspiration* software on the AlphaSmart and then upload the program to the full-featured *Inspiration* software program. (Inspiration software features are described in more detail in the study skills chapter.) Other applets include a quiz manager feature, Co: writer, a word prediction feature built into the word processing, and calculators. AlphaSmarts are also compatible with both MacIntoch and PCs.

Additional information on AlphaSmart and applet software is available from *http://www. alphasmart.com*

- **Adapt the physical environment:** Rearrange seating positions near students or personnel who can help students in the classroom and during school functions, and help them focus their attention.
- **Provide distraction-free environments:** Keep desks away from pencil sharpeners, open doorways, and windows to help reduce potentially troublesome extraneous visual and auditory stimulation. Arrange desks so they face away from any obvious distraction. When needed, arrange for a special quiet space within your classroom.
- **Model organization:** Designate specific locations for books, coats, lunch boxes, and so on. In addition, illustrate what organization looks like for desks, lockers, and notebooks.
- **Structure daily routines and schedules:** Clearly identify the first, second, and third thing done when you enter the class, and provide clear schedules for students to follow.
- **Adapt instructional materials:** This includes materials for reading and writing assignments, textbooks, work sheets, and organizational and study skill adaptations. These adaptations should make assignments more compatible for students with underdeveloped literacy skills, and are described in more detail in chapters 11 and 13. Some technological applications are described in the Technology Highlight feature.
- **Teach study skills:** These include keeping assignment notebooks, scheduling time, and using cognitive strategies. These skills are discussed in chapter 11.
- **Adapt instruction:** Instructional procedures can be modified to facilitate successful inclusion of students with disabilities. The use of the SCREAM variables (**s**tructure, **c**larity,

Chapter 6 provides further information on effective teaching strategies for inclusive classrooms, and chapter 9 describes strategies for keeping learning fun and exciting.

Facts:
The human body has more than 600 muscles.
These muscles make up nearly 50% of your body's total weight.
All muscles are made up of cells called muscle fibers.
After a weight-lifting workout, a person should wait 48 hours before lifting again.
Muscles grow when they are forced to put out more energy.

Positive results of weight training:
1. Improves health and physical fitness
2. Helps shape and sculpture your body
3. Relieves tensions of everyday life
4. Helps improve sports performance
5. Greatly improves your strength
6. Can be used to rehabilitate injuries

Positive results of aerobics:
1. More energy
2. Less tension
3. Heat rate lowered
4. Convert fat to muscle
5. Improves self image
6. Psychologically better

Terminology:
1. *Repetition*—(reps) one complete sequence of a single exercise.
   Example: To perform 10 repetitions at the bench press, you press the bar from your chest upward 10 times.
   Heavier weight—low reps increase muscle strength and bulk.
   Lower weight—higher reps increase muscle endurance and tone.
2. *Set*—a fixed number of repetitions. Example: To perform 3 sets of 10 repetitions at the bench press, you press up 10 times, rest a minute, press up 10 times, rest again, then press 10 more times.
3. *Range of motion*— the entire area that the muscle can move in.

Myths (or False Information):
1. Strong muscles make you muscle bound so you can't stretch and bend in games.
2. Muscles slow you down.

Figure 3.1

Modified Secondary-Level Class Notes on Weight Training and Aerobics
Note: Developed by Karen Yates, teacher, McCutcheon High School

redundancy, **e**nthusiasm, **a**ppropriate pace, and **m**aximized engagement, see chapter 6) can help students with disabilities learn more effectively in general education settings. Figure 3.1 shows a set of class notes adapted for students with special needs.

- **Vary presentation formats:** Use verbal information, visual aids, concrete manipulatives, field trips, computers, chalkboards, overhead projectors, audiotapes, and videotapes frequently.
- **Question students frequently:** Ask students to rephrase information in their own words, to ensure concepts are understood. Allow sufficient time for students to think after asking questions. Strategies for questioning and feedback are provided in chapter 6.
- **Provide clear directions and accessible goals:** Use short, succinct sentences, written copies of assignments for parental review, and shorter, more manageable assignment lengths. Remind students often of long-term assignments including due dates for completing interval parts of the assignment or project. Monitor students' progress to ensure success.

- **Teach students how to learn:** Model effective learning and metacognitive strategies when presenting new information—for example, how to use the attention and memory strategies described in chapter 10. Chapter 11 provides additional strategies for teaching metacognitive skills.
- **Use peer tutors:** Tutors can provide assistance or additional practice, as described in chapter 9.
- **Conduct periodic reviews:** Reviews of previously learned content reinforce learning and illustrate how reviewing can assist in learning new information.
- **Adapt evaluation procedures:** This will help ensure that you are obtaining a fair and accurate picture of what students with learning disabilities know, and whether they are meeting their objectives.

Mental Retardation

Prevalence and Definitions of Mental Retardation

Individuals classified as mentally retarded represent 10.8% of the students ages 6–21 served under IDEA (U.S. Department of Education, 2001) or about 1% of the population in general. Although this number includes all individuals with mental retardation served under IDEA, estimates indicate that as many as 85% represent those with mild or moderate mental retardation, as opposed to severe disabilities discussed in chapter 4 (Beirne-Smith, Ittenbach, & Patton, 2002).

Although *mental retardation* is commonly used, other terms are used to describe this condition, including *intellectual disability, cognitive disability, mental deficiency, mental subnormality, mentally handicapped,* or *intellectually challenged.* Mental retardation is also referred to as one type of the more general term, *developmental disability* (Beirne-Smith, Ittenbach, & Patton, 2002).

Criteria used to classify individuals with mental retardation have changed over the years. The American Association on Mental Retardation (AAMR) broadened its definition of *mental retardation* to include multifaceted intelligence, including conceptual intelligence, practical intelligence, and social intelligence (American Association on Mental Retardation, 1992). Other changes have included the lowering of the IQ (intelligence quotient) cutoff score, the inclusion of **adaptive behavior** measures, and the notion of "nonpermanence" for mild retardation (Schalock et al., 1994). Most educators agree with the IQ and the adaptive behavior components, and trends are continuing toward including the social and practical intelligence components as they become more precisely defined and measurable.

Mental retardation has been classified by degree of involvement. Mild mental retardation represents the upper range of functioning within the mental retardation classification with IQ scores between 55 to 70. Scores between 35 and 54 are considered moderate mental retardation, scores of 20 to 34 are severe, and less than 20 is considered profound retardation (Jacobson & Mulick, 1996).

The American Association on Mental Retardation (1992) has suggested that individuals could be classified according to the services or supports needed. These include *intermittent* support, to be delivered on an episodic or as-needed basis; and progressing to higher levels of support including *limited* support; *extensive* support; and *pervasive* support. These levels were intended to replace classifications of mild to severe mental retardation, although these latter terms are still widely used (Beirne-Smith, Ittenbach, & Patton, 2002).

Causes of Mental Retardation

The vast majority of causes of mental retardation are unknown, and some speculate that known causes account for only 10 to 15% of the cases of retardation (Beirne-Smith, Ittenbach, & Patton, 2002). The causes of mild mental retardation are more difficult to determine than causes for severe and profound mental retardation (Hallahan & Kauffman, 2003). Known causes can be classified into genetic factors, brain factors, and environmental factors (MacMillan, 1982).

Genetic Factors

Genetic disorders or damage to genetic matter can cause mental retardation. Disorders can include chromosomal abnormalities and genetic transmission of traits through families. **Down syndrome** is an example of a genetic disorder. It is sometimes referred to as Trisomy 21, because

For more information on mental retardation, go to the Web Links module in chapter 3 of the Companion Website.

See chapter 4 for more information on definitions of mental retardation and severe disabilities.

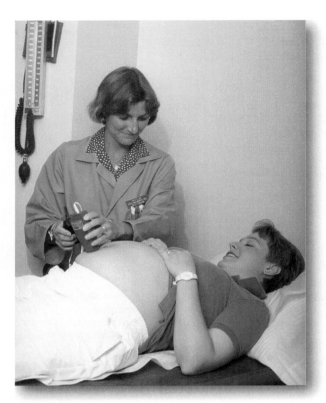

Genetic factors or exposure to teratogens or harmful substances, including alcohol, during pregnancy can cause mental retardation.

the 21st pair of chromosomes divides into three (trisomy) instead of a single pair of chromosomes. Down syndrome represents 5 to 6% of individuals with mental retardation, and is associated with some specific characteristics, including intellectual functioning in the mild to moderate ranges, short stature, upward slanting of the eyes, and a susceptibility to heart defects or upper respiratory infections. These characteristics vary greatly among individuals (Beirne-Smith, Ittenbach, & Patton, 2002).

Recent research into the hereditability of different traits, and other types of chromosomal abnormalities, have added to the knowledge base surrounding causes of some types of mental retardation (Blackman, 1983). Medical tests can detect the presence of some genetic abnormalities, including Down syndrome, during early pregnancy.

Brain Factors

Brain factors refer to defects in the brain, or central nervous system (MacMillian, 1982). These can occur during prenatal development, perinatally (during the birth process), or postnatally (after the baby is born). Brain factors may be congenital (present at birth), or may appear later in life. Prenatal factors include exposure to rubella (German measles) and syphilis (Beirne-Smith, Ittenbach, & Patton, 2002). Exposure to alcohol during prenatal development can lead to fetal alcohol syndrome (FAS), which may result in retardation (Hetherington & Parke, 1986; Jones, Smith, Ulleland, & Streissguth, 1973). Infections such as meningitis and encephalitis, which cause inflammations to the brain, may result in brain damage. Some forms of retardation are associated with cranial malformations that result in microcephaly or hydrocephaly. **Microcephaly** is associated with a very small skull, while **hydrocephaly** is often characterized by an enlarged head due to an interference in the flow of cerebral spinal fluid in the head (Beck, 1972; Wolraich, 1983). Finally, it is known that **anoxia,** or lack of oxygen to the brain, any time, including during birth, causes brain damage and may result in mental retardation, depending upon the extent of the damage (Graham, Ernhart, Thurston, & Craft, 1962).

Environmental Influences

Environmental influences refer to factors such as poor nutrition during prenatal development that can influence the development of the brain and result in retardation (Apgar & Beck, 1972). It has been seen that many premature and low birth-weight babies may have mental retardation. The ingestion of lead, often through lead-based paint, can also cause retardation. Although factors such as poverty and lack of early sensory stimulation are associated with retardation, it is more difficult to prove that such environmental factors always lead to mental retardation. Future research may uncover additional important factors related to causes and prevention of mental retardation (Beirne-Smith, Ittenbach, & Patton, 2002).

Issues in Identification and Assessment of Mental Retardation

Both intellectual functioning and adaptive behavior are assessed in making determinations regarding mental retardation. Individually administered intelligence tests are used in most states to assess intellectual functioning, and usually contain, for example, measures of vocabulary, common knowledge, short-term memory, and ability to solve mazes and jigsaw puzzles. Adaptive behavior scales assess how well individuals are able to perform daily living skills, self-help care, communication skills, and social skills. An individual should be functioning at least two standard deviations below average (approximately the 2nd percentile) on both measures to be classified as mentally retarded (Kavale & Forness, 1992). All measures administered are required to have strong reliability and validity, and to be free of cultural and linguistic bias.

Characteristics of Mental Retardation

The most common features associated with retardation include slower pace of learning, lack of age-appropriate adaptive behavior and social skills, and below-average language and academic skills. Many individuals with mental retardation exhibit poor motor coordination, which can be improved by working with occupational therapists, physical therapists, or adaptive physical educators (Gable & Warren, 1993). However, most students with mild and moderate mental retardation have the ability to learn to read, write, and do mathematics. The degree and extent of learning is usually directly associated with the severity of retardation and the existence of any coexisting disabilities (Scott & Perou, 1994). Although the pace at which these individuals learn is usually slower than that of their age peers (Ellis, 1979), many individuals with mild retardation can successfully learn academic skills up to the sixth-grade level, or higher in some cases. Following is an autobiographical statement written by Kirstin Palson, an individual with mental retardation who was institutionalized as a child. The statement was included in a book of poetry she wrote. Following her statement is one of her poems:

From "About the Author":

My name is Kirstin Ann Palson. I was born in Boston, Massachusetts, in 1952 with complications. My diagnosis was mental retardation plus cerebral palsy, due to brain damage at birth. It was difficult those early years. Because of my behavior problems, I was sent to the Wrentham State School when I was seven years old. Those were horrendous times. At the age of fourteen I came out of Wrentham. I have overcome my handicaps, graduated from High School at twenty-two, and worked as a volunteer library aid in two elementary schools. For two years after graduation, I had a struggle getting employment. Finally I got a full time job in a company and worked five years. The company moved out of town and I struggled with unemployment and job search for six and a half months. I have gained employment in another company full time. I got both jobs on my own.

I have a great love for words. When I was growing up, it was the reading of children's stories by Mom at bedtime which gave me the ability for reading and loving books. During the past years I have given books of my poetry to family members as gifts, especially at Christmas. My love for poetry is still with me and will remain forever more. K. A. P. (1986).

A Poem to the Mentally Retarded

Have sympathy for the mentally retarded.
For they are put in institutions.
People should have some programs started.
Living with families are a good solution.

Please let's stop discrimination.
Come on. Let's stop all this frustration.
Retarded citizens can't be isolated.
Don't say retarded are X-rated.

Stop this ridicule, labelling and abuse.
Because that is such poor excuse.
Remember they are God's children, too.
They need love and care like you.

Note: From *Essence of Kirstin* (p. 3), by K. Palson, 1986, Medfield, MA: Author. Copyright 1986 by K. Palson. Reprinted with permission.

Intellectual and Cognitive Functioning

Individuals with mental retardation, by definition, exhibit deficits in intellectual functioning. In addition, these individuals usually function substantially below their age peers in related areas, including metacognitive abilities, memory, attention, thinking, and problem-solving abilities (Ellis, 1970, 1979; Jensen, 1989; Spitz, 1979; Zeaman & House, 1963, 1979). Individuals with mental retardation may not draw the same inferences from information they encounter, and may require more direct explanations (Bos & Tierney, 1984). Like students with learning disabilities, individuals with mental retardation often have difficulty generalizing learned information to novel situations (Scott & Greenfield, 1992; Scruggs & Mastropieri, 1984). For example, students who have been taught a particular social skill, such as greeting or making eye contact with others, may not automatically apply this skill to real-life situations.

Research has indicated that systematic teaching in these important areas can be beneficial. It has been seen that teaching students to use cognitive and self-monitoring strategies, and carefully coaching students to think, can result in higher levels of performance on thinking, reasoning, and problem-solving tasks (Scruggs & Mastropieri, 1994, 1995a, 1995b; Scruggs, Mastropieri, & Wolfe, 1995; Whitman, 1990).

Social and Adaptive Behavior

By most definitions, individuals with mild mental retardation have less well-developed adaptive behavior than their peer counterparts, including such behavior as using the telephone or dressing appropriately (Korinek & Polloway, 1993; Margalit, 1993). They may appear socially immature, exhibit inappropriate social behavior, or have difficulty making and maintaining friendships. Some individuals may become easily frustrated when they experience difficulty, and then may act inappropriately, drawing negative attention to themselves (Gable & Warren, 1993). However, some individuals with mental retardation have particularly amiable dispositions, and are well liked by others.

Some individuals with mental retardation tend to have an external "locus of control," meaning they see their lives as being controlled and influenced by factors outside of themselves (e.g., fate, chance, other people). This external locus of control may hinder their development of self-reliance (Mercer & Snell, 1977). A related problem is "outerdirectness"; that is, looking to external cues, or modeling behavior of others rather than relying on their own judgments (Bybee & Zigler, 1992).

Language

Both receptive and expressive language are problem areas for individuals with mental retardation (Bricker & Bricker, 1972). There is usually a direct relationship with severity of retardation and all aspects of language development (Gable & Warren, 1993). Communication skills are typically less well-developed and can result in misunderstandings of directions (Martin, Boersma, & Bulgarella, 1968). Students may exhibit difficulties with comprehension of abstract vocabulary and concepts (Schiefelbusch & Lloyd, 1974).

Academic Skills

Individuals with mental retardation may have difficulty learning basic skills of reading, writing, and mathematics (Gable & Warren, 1993; Hendrickson & Frank, 1993). Performance in all academic skill areas is usually well below average for students' age. The rate of learning new information may be very slow, and students may require repetition, and concrete, meaningful examples on all learning activities. Instruction should proceed at a slower pace, include sufficient opportunities for guided and independent practice, and provide for repetition of previously learned information. Instruction that presents information in meaningful, concrete ways results in better understanding (Lloyd, Talbott, Tankersley, & Trent, 1993). With appropriate instruction, individuals with mild to moderate mental retardation are very capable of academic learning.

The World of Nigel Hunt is an autobiography written by an individual with Down syndrome who grew up in England. When it was written in 1967, individuals with Down syndrome were referred to as "Mongoloids."

The book provides some excellent examples of Nigel's abilities at thinking and writing. In addition, the preface of the book, written by Nigel's father, contains poignant instances of how both he and Nigel's mother continuously taught and supported Nigel. The positive results demonstrate how our greater understanding and expectations for students with mental retardation can make a difference in their academic growth and learning. Several excerpts from the preface follow.

From the Preface to *The World of Nigel Hunt* (1967):

This book is unique, using the word strictly in its most literal sense. It was written by a mongol—my son. No mongol has ever written a book before. In case you are not familiar with the term, a mongol—or mongoloid, to use the normal technical term—is a person born with a biological condition which involves a certain degree of mental retardation. All but the most enlightened of

The term "mongolism" was coined in 1866 by J. Langdon Down, based on Down's impression that individuals with this condition had facial similarities to Asians. Growing awareness that this syndrome is found in all racial groups led to the withdrawal of the term (Beirne-Smith, Ittenbach, & Patton, 2002).

Peers should be trained to avoid doing too much—or too little—for students with mental retardation.

the medical profession would hoot with laughter at the very idea that a mongoloid could write much more than his name, even after years of training. (Hunt, 1967, pp. 15–16)

How Nigel learned to read is a story of almost incredible patience and perseverance. Almost as soon as he could talk, Grace [his mother] started to spell short words to him phonetically. We have found this method far more successful than the "look and read" method, by which the child is shown a picture of every word. It is in any case only of use for concrete nouns . . . . When Nigel was not much more than five years old, we would throw a box of plastic letters on the floor and tell him to pick out a certain one. At first it would take him a fairly long time, but he would carefully reject the wrong ones and finally pick out the letter required. "That's right, Nigel," Grace would say. "That is an M. What does he say?" And Nigel would say "Mer.". . . Nigel was seated on the floor in front of the kitchen cupboard, from which he had extracted most of the tins and packets. This is what Grace heard: "Ker, O, ER, O Ker, O Er—Cocoa! You go in there," and the [cocoa] tin was replaced in the cupboard. . . . This was enough for Grace. She pounced on the lad and said, "Come on, Nigel—if you can read those labels, you can read your book"; and she presented him with a simple reader. With very little hesitation, Nigel read the book through. (pp. 24–25)

Classroom Adaptations for Students with Mental Retardation

Preparations

Careful preparation can greatly enhance the successful inclusion of students with mental retardation. First, have an open, accepting classroom environment so that students feel welcome as genuine class members. Provide students with the same materials—desks, lockers, mailboxes—as the other students. Involve students in daily activities. Meet with them privately and preteach the daily routine. Show them where materials are kept and how things in the class proceed. This will help build their confidence before they come in for the first time in front of the general education peers.

Prepare general education students for the arrival of students with mental retardation by asking a special educator to talk about mental retardation and explain strengths and limitations of individuals with mental retardation. Encourage students to ask questions and set a model of open acceptance. Tell them about their roles as possible peer tutors and helpers. Explain that all classmates can encourage students with mental retardation to be active participants and members of the class. Provide models of how peers can assist, but make clear that they should not try to do everything for students with mental retardation. For example, in one fifth-grade class, general education peers tended to complete all work sheet activities for a girl with mild mental retardation, even though the girl was able to complete many activities by herself. If peers do all the work, either out of expediency or good intentions, students with mental retardation may become more outerdirected, and may fail to develop self-reliance.

Monitor Peer Relationships

Although peers can be good friends and strong supporters of students with mental retardation, teachers also should be aware that some students may try to take advantage of students with mental retardation. For example, in one sixth-grade class, several boys bullied a boy with mental retardation and consistently took away part of his lunch. In another example, high school students who had been smoking cigarettes in the girls' restroom handed their cigarette to a girl with mental retardation when a teacher entered the restroom. Careful monitoring can decrease the likelihood of either negative situation occurring and increase the likelihood that peer relations will be positive and productive (see chapter 8).

Instructional Modifications

Many of the modifications described in the learning disabilities section may also be helpful for students with mental retardation. However, additional modifications probably will be required if the general education experience is to be successful.

- **Prioritize objectives** for students with mental retardation in general education classes, and teach directly to these prioritized objectives.
- **Adapt materials** to the needs of students, by reducing reading, writing, and language requirements and simplifying work sheets.
- **Adapt instruction** by employing clear, organized presentations; providing concrete, meaningful examples and activities; providing frequent reviews; and encouraging independent thinking.
- **Communicate with families,** to further your understanding and obtain additional information on how students work best (Thousand & Villa, 1990).
- **Adapt evaluation,** using individual testing, portfolio assessments, tape or video recordings, or other adaptations as described in chapter 12.
- **Use specialized curriculum** when necessary. Some students with mental retardation may require an alternative, more functional curriculum. Such a curriculum may include communication, community living, domestic skills, socialization, self-help, and vocational and leisure skills. Additionally, some students may benefit from a life-skills curriculum, which emphasizes transition to adulthood. This curriculum could include education in home and family, community involvement, employment, emotional-physical health, and personal responsibility and relationships (see Cronin & Patton, 1993; see also chapter 16). In these cases, work closely with special educators, identify special curriculum needs, and determine how that curriculum will be delivered in the general education classroom. Decide how relevant instruction will take place and who will provide it. Determine if a special education teacher or a paraprofessional will be in your room teaching those students, using a functional or life-skills curriculum.

Emotional Disturbance

Prevalence and Definitions

For the Website of the Council for Children with Behavioral Disorders, go to the Web Links module in chapter 3 of the Companion Website.

Individuals classified as having emotional disturbance (or behavioral disorders) represent 8.3% of all students ages 6–21 served under IDEA, or .7% of the school population (U.S. Department of Education, 2001). However, prevalence studies have suggested that the actual percentage may be much higher. Boys outnumber girls in this category as much as 5 to 1 (Kauffman, 2001).

Emotional disturbance refers to a number of different, but related, social-emotional disabilities. Individuals classified as emotionally disturbed meet one or more of several criteria established under IDEA, including the following:

- An inability to learn not due to intellectual, sensory, or health factors
- An inability to exhibit appropriate behavior under ordinary circumstances
- An inability to maintain relationships with peers or teachers
- An inappropriate affect such as depression or anxiety
- An inappropriate manifestation of physical symptoms or fears in response to school or personal difficulties

These characteristics must be manifested over an extended time period, and have a negative effect on school performance (Kauffman, 2001).

Individuals classified as emotionally disturbed represent a range of severity, and the disability itself may be temporary or permanent. Specific emotional disturbance areas include childhood **schizophrenia; selective mutism** (failure to speak in selected circumstances); seriously aggressive or acting-out behavior; conduct disorders; inappropriate affective disorders such as depression, social withdrawal, psychosomatic disorders, anxiety disorders, self-mutilating behaviors; and excessive fears (or phobias) (Kavale, Forness, & Duncan, 1996). Individuals characterized as socially maladjusted (e.g., juvenile delinquency) are not considered emotionally disturbed according to IDEA unless the social maladjustment is accompanied by emotional disturbance (Kauffman, 2001).

Causes of Emotional Disturbance

Most behavioral disorders or emotional disturbances have no known cause. However, in some cases, speculations about cause are made based on extensive case histories. As with the etiological factors associated with learning disabilities, several major factors have emerged from the literature indicating possible linkages. These areas include biological, family, school, and cultural factors (Hallahan & Kauffman, 2003; Kauffman, 2001).

Biological factors are genetic, biochemical, and neurological influences that interact and result in emotional disabilities. Schizophrenia, autism (see chapter 4), attention deficit hyperactivity disorders, and **Tourette syndrome**—a tic disorder characterized by involuntary muscular movements, vocalizations, and/or inappropriate verbal outbursts—all appear to have biological bases that interact with other factors and may contribute to emotional disturbances. However, Tourette syndrome is not necessarily associated with emotional disturbance. Family factors (such as domestic violence) are also considered to be strong contributing factors to emotional disturbance. School factors (such as failure to accommodate for individual needs, inappropriate expectations, or inconsistency) can also contribute to an emotional disability. Finally, certain cultural environmental factors (including peer group, urbanization, and neighborhood factors) interact with the individual, the home, and the school and may also contribute to emotional disabilities (Kauffman, 2001; Walker, Colvin, & Ramsey, 1995).

Issues in Identification and Assessment of Emotional Disturbance

Individuals with emotional disabilities are difficult to objectively identify and classify. Moreover, there appears to be a reluctance on the part of school personnel to label a child "emotionally disturbed" (Kauffman, 2001). Traditional measures to identify emotional or behavioral disabilities include teacher checklists, parental checklists, and classroom behavioral observations. Checklists are listings of frequently observed behaviors. Teachers and parents complete checklists by indicating the types and severity of problem behaviors. Direct observations are conducted during classes, on the playground, at lunch, and in other parts of the school. Individually administered tests of intelligence, achievement, and psychological status are also given.

Characteristics of Emotional Disturbance

As with most students with disabilities, not all individuals with emotional disturbance will exhibit all the characteristics described here. However, most display a sufficient number of characteristics to meet the specific classification requirements in their respective states and school districts.

Social Behavior

Most students with emotional disturbance have problems with their social behavior (Schoenwald, Thomas, & Henggeler, 1996), often manifested as less mature or inappropriate social skills. For example, some students may be particularly aggressive with peers and adults and cause harm when playing or interacting with others. These students act out in class, do not appear to respond appropriately to discipline from teachers, and may seem oblivious to class and school rules (Powers & Neel, 1997). Perhaps because of higher levels of impulsivity, some students with behavioral disorders are at higher risk for substance abuse (Steele, Forehand, Armistead, & Brody, 1995), and have

Schizophrenia is a disorder associated with detachment from reality, delusions, hallucinations, and distorted thought processes. For more information, go to the Web Links module in chapter 3 of the Companion Website.

Students with Tourette syndrome may receive services listed under the section Other Health Impairments (see chapter 4). For information on the Tourette Syndrome Association, go to the Web Links module in chapter 3 of the Companion Website.

To succeed, teachers working with students who have emotional and behavioral disorders need to provide positive comments, be patient and tolerant, and initiate behavior modification strategies.

been known to sniff items such as liquid white-out, glue, or felt-tip markers. Teachers, of course, should monitor the use of such classroom substances with all students.

Other students may exhibit social behavior similar to that of younger children and act socially immature. Some students may withdraw from others and appear socially isolated. Although withdrawn students may not call as much attention to themselves as conduct-disordered students, they nonetheless may require intensive interventions. These students may exhibit symptoms of depression. Social isolates do not interact with any peers or adults, and in the most severe cases may exhibit selective (or elective) mutism. Individuals with selective mutism have the physical ability to talk, but nevertheless do not speak in appropriate situations (Bauermeister & Jemail, 1975; Brigham & Cole, 1999). All of these emotional or behavioral disorders share the characteristic of an inability to interact appropriately with others, including peers, teachers, siblings, and parents, which negatively affects school performance (Kavale, Mathur, Forness, Rutherford, & Quinn, 1997; Talbott & Coe, 1997).

Students with emotional disturbance may also inappropriately attribute their behavioral or social problems to causes outside themselves, saying things such as, "Teachers are out to get me," or "Other kids always get me into trouble." By doing this, these students are able to avoid acknowledging or evaluating their own behavior, and their own role in behavior problems. Although an individual student's point of view should be listened to, it is also important that students come to attribute social consequences to behaviors that they can learn to control.

Affective Characteristics

Some students with emotional disturbances have serious affective disorders. Affective disorders can take many forms, but the most commonly recognized forms include depression, severe anxiety disorders, phobias, and psychosomatic disorders (Kauffman, 2001). Individuals with many of these disorders may be treated with different medications.

See chapter 4 for a listing of relevant medications.

Academic Characteristics

Often, students with emotional or behavioral disabilities are as far behind academically as students with learning disabilities. Research has indicated that students may function two or more years below grade level in reading, math, writing, and spelling (Epstein, Kinder, & Bursuck, 1989; Scruggs & Mastropieri, 1986). These deficiencies may be related to the emotional disabilities. For example, if students have severe anxieties, they may be unable to attend, listen, and learn in school.

Dropout Prevention for Youth with Disabilities

Students with learning and emotional or behavioral disabilities are at particular risk for dropping out of school (Marder & D'Amico, 1992). The time of transition from middle to high school can be particularly difficult, as students attempt to adapt to new situations and an increased focus on academics. Sinclair, Christenson, Evelo, and Hurley (1998) described the effects of an intervention to prevent school dropout as students made their transition from middle school to high school. The participants included 94 students with learning and emotional behavioral disabilities enrolled in public schools in an urban school district. All students received dropout prevention intervention in grades 7 and 8. At the end of eighth grade, students were randomly assigned to treatment and control conditions. The treatment condition students continued to receive intervention through the ninth grade.

The dropout prevention and intervention procedure was referred to as "Check and Connect." The Check component provided for continuous assessment of students' level of engagement with school, and monitored such variables as tardiness, skipping classes, absenteeism, disciplinary actions, and course failures. The Connect component was facilitated by a monitor assigned to individual students, who followed students as they changed schools. The monitor implemented two levels of intervention: basic and intensive. Basic interventions included sharing general information with the student about the system, providing regular feedback about educational progress, discussing the importance of staying in school, and problem solving with the student. The monitor's role was discussed with the student and the student's family at the beginning of the school year. At least monthly, students were guided through real or hypothetical problems using a Five-Step Plan based on materials developed by Braswell, Bloomquist, and Barkley (1991):

1. Stop. Think about the problem.
2. What are some choices?
3. Choose one.
4. Do it.
5. How did it work? (Sinclair et al., 1998, p. 11)

For students who displayed high risk for dropout, additional intensive interventions were employed, based on individual student needs. These included the following:

- More intensive problem-solving sessions, possibly involving social skills groups, family members, or school personnel
- Academic support, including work with mentors, teachers and school staff, and scheduling
- Recreation and community service exploration, such as assistance becoming involved with after-school activities, neighborhood and community programs, and summer employment or activities

Analysis of results revealed that the intervention had resulted in positive outcomes. By the end of ninth grade, 91% of students in the treatment condition were still enrolled in school, compared with only 70% of control condition students. Further, treatment condition students earned more credits toward graduation, and completed more class assignments than control condition students. Although all students had received dropout prevention interventions in grades 7 and 8, it appears that continued intervention was necessary to help maximize the number of students who stayed in school.

Continued

Noting that the monitors reported that many students appeared bored with a curriculum they often viewed as irrelevant, the authors encouraged "efforts to increase the relevancy of high school curriculum, geared toward a variety of postschool endeavors" (p. 19). They concluded, "interventions can retain youth with learning and behavioral challenges in school, but . . . comprehensive educational reform in conjunction with sustained dropout prevention efforts are needed to graduate students with desired skills and competencies" (p. 19).

For more information on dropout prevention, see the *Journal of At-Risk Issues,* published by the National Dropout Prevention Center, Clemson, SC. For Web links, go to the Web Links module of the Companion Website for chapter 3.

Questions for Reflection

1. In this investigation, what was the benefit of having two levels of intervention?
2. What was the overall purpose of the Five-Step Plan?
3. What steps could be taken to increase the relevance of curriculum for students with learning and behavioral disabilities?

Companion Website

To answer these questions online, go to the Research Highlights feature in chapter 3 of the Companion Website.

Some students lack social skills that are necessary for school success (Walker, Colvin, & Ramsey, 1995). Others may exhibit severe deficiencies in metacognitive skills, memory skills, and attention, which may in turn lead to academic underachievement (Montague, Fiore, Hocutt, McKinney, & Harris, 1996). Many students with emotional disturbances have impoverished knowledge bases in all academic areas from lack of sufficient active participation in school activities. Nevertheless, some students with emotional or behavioral disabilities attain average, or even above-average academic achievement.

Students with emotional disturbance are at risk for dropping out of school, hindering their future life possibilities. The Research Highlight on page 83 describes a program to reduce the dropout rate for students with learning and emotional-behavioral disabilities.

Classroom Adaptations for Students with Emotional Disturbance

General adaptations can facilitate the inclusion of students with emotional and behavioral disorders into general education classes. Many suggested modifications for students with learning disabilities and some accommodations for students with mental retardation may also prove helpful for these students. The following *In the Classroom* feature lists some examples. In addition, some specific adaptations are needed to promote successful inclusion.

Preparing the Class

Prepare your class for students with emotional disabilities. Set up models for tolerance and acceptance. Provide opportunities for students with emotional disabilities to assume class responsibilities, such as distributing papers. Give examples of ways general education peers can help students with emotional disabilities, such as how to ignore inappropriate behaviors. Some students may be able to serve as peer tutors or assistants to help support and reinforce appropriate behaviors from students with emotional disabilities. However, select peers carefully; not all peers would be good choices. Remember that sometimes emotionally disturbed students will do better working alone even when the rest of the class is working in small groups. At times, a group of "one" may be best. Chapter 8 provides additional information on using classroom peers.

In the Classroom ...a feature for teachers

General Accommodations for Students with Emotional Disabilities

- ☐ Establish open, accepting environment.
- ☐ Clearly state class rules and consequences.
- ☐ Emphasize positive behaviors and program for success.
- ☐ Reinforce positive behavior.
- ☐ Supply extra opportunities for success.
- ☐ Be tolerant.
- ☐ Use good judgment.
- ☐ Teach social skills.
- ☐ Teach self-control, self-monitoring, and conflict resolution.

- ☐ Teach academic survival skills.
- ☐ Teach positive attributions.
- ☐ Carefully select partners.
- ☐ Have alternative activities available.
- ☐ Design activity checklists.
- ☐ Use carefully selected peers as assistants.
- ☐ Have groups of "one."
- ☐ Use behavioral contracts.

Teaching Adaptations

Illustrate the rules with clear examples and specify rewards for following rules as well as consequences when rules are disobeyed. Be consistent when enforcing rules, but make sure the overall classroom atmosphere is positive, not punitive. Provide models of acceptable behaviors to avoid confusion or misinterpretation on the part of students:

> "Here's one thing you can say if you think another student is sitting too close to you . . . ." "Here is something you should *not* say . . . ."

Role-play examples with students:

> "Can someone give me an example of an appropriate tone of voice?"

Maintain a positive relationship with students with emotional disabilities by responding to them as human beings, rather than responding simply to their overt behavior, which often may be unpleasant. Use positive comments frequently to reinforce good behavior when you see it. Say things like the following:

- "Jeff, I appreciate the way you tried hard in class today. I know that math is not your favorite subject."
- "Richard, I think you had a great day today. Thanks for getting along well at lunch today."
- "Leslie, I am glad that you volunteered an answer in class today. Thank you for doing that."

Positive comments can be varied so they are suitable for either elementary-, middle-, or secondary-level students.

Supply additional occasions for success. For example, instead of reprimanding students for neglecting to proof a paper, return the paper and say, "Before you turn this in, think again and make sure you have double-checked everything."

Likewise, before reprimanding negative social behavior, say, "Stop and think about what you just did. What should you have done? Now, try to do it more appropriately."

Such procedures will allow students opportunities to think through what they did and practice doing it successfully. Reward students for successes on those second chances. Remember that students with emotional disabilities may suffer from severe anxieties, depression, and other problems, and may require more positive reinforcement than other students.

Chapter 7 provides specific suggestions on behavior management strategies.

More specific social skills instruction information is provided in chapter 7.

Chapter 9 presents more examples for promoting positive attributions.

Be tolerant, and use judgment in allocating times for enforcing compliance, times for cooling off, and times for allowing divergent responding. For example, one fifth-grade teacher, Mrs. Bahs, asked all students to move to the floor in the front of the room so she could show everyone a new class iguana. Tyler, a student with emotional disabilities, refused to move and remained at his desk. Mrs. Bahs sensed that Tyler was in a volatile mood and decided to let him stay at his desk, rather than start a confrontation by trying to make him move to the front of the room with the rest of the class. She de-escalated the situation by ignoring his refusal to move and allowing him to participate by watching at a distance from his desk. In this way, Mrs. Bahs was able to prevent a confrontation, and allow Tyler to participate in his own way.

Some students may have specific fears and anxieties, such as the dark, water, or getting dirty. Be aware of those fears by communicating with special education teachers, parents, and the students themselves. If class activities seem to bring out those fears in some students, have alternative activities available that they can work on independently.

Many students in your classes, especially students with emotional disturbance, can benefit from general social skills instruction. Social skills instruction can have a specific time slot within your daily schedule and be reviewed on the spot as appropriate occasions arise. For example, review more acceptable ways of asking and answering questions and more suitable ways of resolving conflicts at appropriate times. Role-play important social skills and teach students to stop and think before acting.

Teach students to monitor their own behavior and to make positive attributions. Teach students how to attribute their successes to positive strategies and effort on their part, rather than to luck or other external forces. Teach them likewise to attribute their failures to things under their control, like their own behavior, and not to external factors, such as, "The teacher hates me." Model effective positive attributions by saying, for example: "I used the 'stop and think' strategy before acting, so I stayed out of trouble!"

Use behavioral contracts with students with emotional disabilities. Behavioral contracts are individually negotiated contracts between the teacher and student. Specific behaviors students are expected to complete are listed along with designated rewards for the positively accomplished goals and are described in more detail in chapter 7.

Other Adaptations

Consider additional classroom adaptations, including the following:

- **Adapt the physical environment,** by considering seating arrangements and by keeping potentially harmful objects or substances away from easy access.
- **Adapt materials,** using the suggestions listed for students with learning disabilities and mental retardation. Devise self-monitoring checklists that students can use to check-off activities as they complete them. Break assignments into short segments to avoid overwhelming students.
- **Adapt instruction,** using the teacher effectiveness variables and teacher presentation variables to ensure that content is covered adequately. Teach the classroom social skills necessary for success.
- **Help students focus,** by teaching clearly and enthusiastically, providing additional review, and teaching self-monitoring for attention, as discussed in chapter 10.
- **Adapt evaluation,** by providing distraction-free environments for exams, providing extended time allocations during testing periods (Forness & Dvorak, 1982), and ensuring that students have the skills to take tests efficiently (Scruggs & Marsing, 1988).

Summary

- About 90% of the population of students with disabilities have learning disabilities, mental retardation, emotional disabilities, or communication disorders. Most students with higher-incidence disabilities are served in the general education classroom.
- In many cases, causes of these high-incidence disabilities are unknown, although a variety of biological and environmental explanations has been proposed.
- Students with communication disorders may exhibit problems with speech or language. Speech disorders may involve voice, articulation, or fluency; language disorders may involve difficulties with phonology, morphology, syntax, semantics, or pragmatics of language use.
- Students with learning disabilities make up about half of students with higher-incidence disabilities. These students may exhibit specific problems in basic academic skill areas, as well as areas such as language, attention, memory, and metacognition.
- Students with mental retardation exhibit deficiencies in intellectual functioning, and corresponding levels of adaptive behavior. These students also may exhibit learning problems related to language, social behavior, attention, reasoning, and problem solving.
- Students with behavioral disorders or serious emotional disturbance may exhibit problems in classroom behavior, social relations, or may exhibit disorders of affect, such as anxiety or depression.
- A variety of adaptations in the physical environment, instructional materials, instructional procedures, and evaluation procedures can make the general education classroom a positive learning experience for students with higher-incidence disabilities.

Council for
Exceptional
Children

Teaching Students with Higher-Incidence Disabilities

Information in this chapter links most directly to:

Standard 2—Development and Characteristics of Learners, particularly:

Knowledge:
- Educational implications of characteristics of various exceptionalities.
- Similarities and differences among individuals with exceptional learning needs.

Standard 3—Individual Learning Differences, particularly:

Knowledge:
- Effects an exceptional condition(s) can have on an individual's life.
- Impact of learners' academic and social abilities, attitudes, interests, and values on instruction and career development.

Standard 4—Instructional Strategies, particularly:

Skills:
- Use strategies to facilitate integration into various settings.
- Select, adapt, and use instructional strategies and materials according to characteristics of the individual with exceptional learning needs.

Inclusion Checklist

Teaching Students with Higher-Incidence Disabilities

If a student with higher-incidence disabilities is having difficulties in your classroom, have you tried the following?

Students with Speech or Language Impairments

- ❑ Consider the characteristics of the student
- ❑ General classroom adaptations for students with speech or language impairments
- ❑ Physical environment adaptations
- ❑ Instructional materials adaptations
- ❑ Instructional procedures adaptations
- ❑ Evaluation procedures adaptations

Students with Learning Disabilities

- ❑ Consider the characteristics of the student
- ❑ General classroom adaptations for students with learning disabilities
- ❑ Physical environment adaptations
- ❑ Instructional materials adaptations
- ❑ Instructional procedures adaptations
- ❑ Evaluation procedures adaptations

Students with Mental Retardation

- ❑ Consider the characteristics of the student
- ❑ General classroom adaptations for students with mental retardation
- ❑ Physical environment adaptations
- ❑ Instructional materials adaptations
- ❑ Instructional procedures adaptations
- ❑ Evaluation procedures adaptations

Students with Emotional Disturbance

- ❑ Consider the characteristics of the student
- ❑ General classroom adaptations for students with emotional disabilities
- ❑ Physical environment adaptations
- ❑ Instructional materials adaptations
- ❑ Instructional procedures adaptations
- ❑ Evaluation procedures adaptations

Chapter 4

Michael Cannon, 10
Tampa, FL
"Sailboat"

Teaching Students with Lower-Incidence Disabilities

Objectives

After studying this chapter, you should be able to:

- Describe and discuss the prevalence and characteristics of students with visual impairments.
- Describe and discuss the prevalence and characteristics of students with hearing impairments.
- Describe and discuss the prevalence and characteristics of students with physical disabilities and other health impairments.
- Describe and discuss the prevalence and characteristics of students with severe and multiple disabilities.
- Describe and discuss the prevalence and characteristics of students with autism.
- List, describe, and be able to recommend adaptations and modifications to promote inclusion of students with lower-incidence disabilities.

Individuals who have lower-incidence disabilities are far less commonly represented in schools than individuals with higher-incidence disabilities. Lower-incidence disabilities cover a wide range of disabilities, which can be present at birth (**congenital**) or acquired later in life (**adventitious**). Some lower-incidence disabilities are associated with very severe impairments; others involve only mild impairments. Some lower-incidence disabilities are temporary; others are permanent or even life-threatening. Lower-incidence disabilities include visual impairments, hearing impairments, physical and other health impairments, severe and multiple disabilities, and autism. It is exciting to see some of the creative adaptations that have been developed to help students with lower-incidence disabilities become more successful in inclusive classes.

Visual Impairments

Prevalence, Definitions, and Characteristics

Individuals with visual impairments, including blindness, make up one of the smallest disability areas, or about .04% of the school-age population and .5% of the students served under IDEA (U.S. Department of Education, 2001). Visual impairments range from mild to moderate to severe, and both legal and educational definitions exist. The legal definition includes acuity assessment information, and the educational definition is linked to learning to read. Individuals are classified as legally blind if their **visual acuity** is 20/200 or less even with corrective lenses and partially sighted if their visual acuity is 20/70. This means a person who is legally blind can see something at 20 feet that a person with normal vision can see at 200 feet; and a person who is partially sighted can see something at 20 feet that a person with normal vision can see at 70 feet. Legal classification qualifies individuals for tax advantages and some other legal benefits (Sacks, Rosen, & Gaylord-Ross, 1990).

Educational definitions are based more on the method necessary for learning to read. For example, many individuals classified as legally blind have some vision and can learn to read using enlarged print. These students are often referred to as students with low vision. Other individuals have such limited vision that they are referred to as totally blind and learn to read using the **Braille** system (raised dots that are read with fingertips), or by ear using audiotapes. The federal definition is "visual impairment including blindness means an impairment in vision that even with correction, adversely affects a child's educational performance. The term includes both partial sight and blindness" (U.S. Department of Education, 1999).

Visual impairments can be present at birth or acquired later in life. Common causes of visual impairments include the following:

- **Glaucoma**—excessive pressure on the eyeball
- **Cataracts**—clouding of the lens
- **Diabetic retinopathy**—lack of blood to the retina
- **Coloboma**—parts of the retina improperly formed
- **Retinitis pigmentosa**—degeneration of the retina
- **Retinopathy of prematurity**—excessive oxygen to premature infants

Muscle functioning disorders of the eye, such as strabismus (crossed eyes) and nystagmus (rapid involuntary eye movements), also may result in visual impairments.

Individuals with visual impairments can have one or more of a wide range of disabilities, from mild to severe. A common characteristic includes delayed language development due to the restriction of visual experiences (Warren, 1984). Students with severe visual impairments may rely on the tactile and auditory senses rather than the visual sense (Hull, 1990). These students need to hold and feel three-dimensional objects to obtain a sense of the phenomena. If entire objects are held at once, students obtain a complete **"synthetic touch"** of the article. If objects are too large to be held, however, different segments of the object must be touched sequentially. Using this **"analytic touch,"** the segmented touches must be recombined mentally to form "the whole." These skills are referred to as tactile learning, and some research indicates that strategies can be used to teach students with visual impairments how to use and improve their tactile sense of learning (Berla, 1981; Griffin & Gerber, 1982). Because these students may miss opportunities at learning incidentally from seeing everything in their environment, it is necessary to present this information in alternative formats.

Mobility skills vary among individuals with visual impairments depending on the age of onset, degree of severity, and the individual's spatial ability. Spatial ability appears to affect the mobility access of individuals with visual impairments (Bigelow, 1991). Some individuals with visual impairments learn to walk with canes, although the training can be lengthy and difficult. Some canes have light sensors near the tip that emit sounds when the amount of light changes, indicating shadows or objects in the path ahead. Some individuals learn to walk with human guides and Seeing Eye dogs, although the latter is not usually seen with children. The inclusion classroom teacher may need to obtain specialized instruction on proper ways of assisting students with visual impairments with their mobility needs.

Classroom Adaptations for Students with Visual Impairments

As you work closely with specialists, you will find a number of adaptations you can make in your classroom to accommodate students with visual disabilities. First, ensure that your classroom has clear, open walkways. Devise classroom procedures for responding to emergency situations, including fire and tornado drills. Be sure that students learn these procedures. Assign peers to assist students with visual impairments during emergency evacuations. Develop safety guidelines for using objects that are potentially harmful to students with visual impairments.

For a successful inclusion of students with visual disabilities, implement the following guidelines:

- Expect progress.
- Encourage independence.
- Make use of students' individual talents.
- Replace unseen visual cues with physical cues.
- Encourage finding alternative landmarks.
- Include multiple modalities (e.g., touch, sound, smell).
- Narrate what is happening in class using descriptive language.
- Use actual concrete objects and manipulatives during teaching to enable students to touch and feel the concepts.
- Teach socially acceptable behaviors when needed (Bigge, 1991).

The following scenario describes how one inappropriate behavior was eliminated.

CLASSROOM SCENARIO ━━━━━━━━━━━━

Crystal

Research on head-shaking behavior indicates that teaching students to touch their cheek as they begin head shaking appears to lessen the behavior (Ross & Koening, 1991). Based on research evidence like this, some teachers planned an intervention for Crystal, a student with visual impairments who had a tendency to shake her head back and forth during class. Because this behavior attracted negative attention from her peers, her fourth-grade teacher, Ms. Mendez, and her visual-disability teacher, Mr. Chung, brainstormed ideas to try to find a solution.

The teachers thought that if Crystal wore a bean-bag type hat that rested lightly on her head, she would feel it move every time she began to shake her head and would be able to control her movements. Mr. Chung worked with Crystal individually at first, emphasized the importance of good posture and told her that wearing the bean-bag hat would help alert her to when her head started to move inappropriately. Crystal said she felt comfortable with the idea and began to practice wearing the hat in Mr. Chung's class. Ms. Mendez told her other students that they were going to help Crystal implement a new plan that would help her. Students were asked to be supportive, provide positive feedback to Crystal, and to help her retrieve the bean-bag hat if it fell to the floor. The teachers continued to monitor her behavior and noted that within a week the amount of head-shaking behavior had decreased substantially, even when she was not wearing the hat.

The following list offers strategies you can use to make your classroom more inclusive for students with visual impairments.

- **Adapt the physical environment,** by keeping aisles clear, wide, and open. Familiarize students with the physical arrangement of the room and notify students if any changes are made. Extra space will be necessary to accommodate equipment for Braille and reading enlarged print materials.

The American Printing House for the Blind (1989) provides materials that are useful for students with visual impairments. Through a national network of cooperating libraries, National Library Service for the Blind and Physically Handicapped of the Library of Congress administers a free library program of Braille and audio materials that are circulated by postage-free mail. For relevant Websites, go to the Web Links module in chapter 4 of the Companion Website.

Refer to the chapters on assessment and reading for additional suggestions on adapting print materials for students with visual impairments.

Descriptive Video Service, WGBH, 125 Western Avenue, Boston, MA 02134; phone: (617) 300-2000, ext. 3490. For more information, go to the Web Links module in chapter 4 of the Companion Website.

- **Enlarge and enhance printed materials,** including dramatically increasing the size of fonts.

9 point example

15 point example

20 point example

30 point example

- **Increase visibility of materials,** which might include bold-lined paper, special lighting, and magnification lenses. Certain technology may be used, such as projection microscopes, closed-circuit television, scanners, and equipment to convert print to tactile formats (Bigge, 1991; Scadden, 1987).
- **Convert print to Braille formats,** using the Perkins Brailler or specialized computer programs such as Duxbury. Figure 4.1 shows examples of Braille.
- **Use oral output devices,** which produce speech, to enable students with visual impairments to participate in the same activities as their peers. These include the "Jaws" software program, the Kurzweil 1000 and 3000, and the Braille and Speak.
- **Use Descriptive Video Service,** provided on many public television broadcasts, to provide additional verbal descriptions of visual events (Cronin & King, 1990).
- **Use tactile and three-dimensional models** to enhance conceptual understanding.
- **Be explicit giving oral presentations.** Avoid vague phrases such as *over here, almost, this, that,* and use specific language such as *above your head, on your right,* and *the beaker in my hand.* Use time orientations such as "The model is on my desk at 2 o'clock." When walking with students, describe upcoming barriers, by saying, for example, "We are approaching an uphill ramp." When addressing students with visual impairments, always state their name first, so they know you are speaking to them, and speak in a normal tone of voice.

However you modify your instruction, provide sufficient time for students with visual impairments to complete class activities. Remember that reading enlarged print and Braille takes longer than reading regular print. Check with students to determine the optimal pace at which they are capable of working.

When assessing students with visual impairments, allocate sufficient time for students to complete tests. Extra time is required to transcribe responses from Braille to print formats or to use peer

Figure 4.1

Samples of Braille

Note: Reprinted with permission from the Division for the Blind and Physically Handicapped, Library of Congress, Washington, DC.

assistants. Many teachers report that students with visual impairments can perform optimally when allocated 150% to 200% of the regularly scheduled time.

During testing, consider using tape recorders for students to listen to questions and to record their responses. This adaptation may be sufficient to enable students to show what they know without interference of the testing format. When performance assessment is used, be sure that students have ample time to become familiar with the location and use of necessary apparatus before testing. Peer assistants can help facilitate the completion of performance-based items. Students with visual disabilities can direct peers to execute specific tasks for them and verbally report and record results.

Hearing Impairments

Prevalence, Definitions, and Characteristics

Individuals with hearing impairments make up .1% of the school-age population, and 1.3% of the students served under IDEA (U.S. Department of Education, 2001). Hearing impairments range in severity from mild to moderate to severe to profound, with the greatest educational distinctions occurring between hard of hearing and deaf. Individuals classified as hard of hearing can hear speech tones when wearing hearing aids, while persons who are deaf cannot hear even with hearing aids.

The age that a child loses hearing affects the degree of language delay and development. For example, children who are born with deafness have congenital hearing losses (**prelingual**) and more difficulty with language development than those who acquire deafness after age 2 (**postlingual**).

Print can be enlarged for individuals with low vision.

Pure tone audiometers are used to assess hearing ability. Tones with different pitches (or frequency measured in Hertz [Hz]) and volume (measured in decibels [dB]) are presented via headphones, and individuals raise their hand when they hear a sound. Levels of hearing impairment are classified along a continuum, with reference to zero dB indicating the quietest sound a person with normal hearing can detect. Individuals with slight hearing losses (27–40 dB) may not have difficulty in most school situations. Individuals with mild losses (41–55 dB) may miss up to 50% of classroom discussion if voices are faint or faces cannot be seen. Individuals with moderate losses (56–70 dB) can understand only loud speech, and may have limited vocabularies. Individuals with severe losses (71–90 dB) may be able to hear loud voices within one foot from the ear, and speech is likely to be impaired. Individuals with profound losses (> 90 dB) may hear some loud sounds, but are more likely to sense vibrations, and may rely on vision rather than hearing as a primary vehicle for communication (Heward, 1999). Assessment of students with hearing impairments is frequently difficult because traditional oral questioning and verbal response formats cannot be used. Reliable and valid specialized tests are needed to accurately assess the cognitive and academic functioning of individuals with hearing impairments (Paul & Quigley, 1990, 1994).

Causes of hearing impairments include heredity, prenatal infections such as maternal rubella, ear infections, meningitis, head trauma, prematurity, and oxygen deprivation. Impairments can be **conductive,** meaning the outer or middle ear along the passageway are damaged; **sensorineural,** referring to inner ear damage; or they can be a combination of the two (Heward, 1999).

Many children with hearing impairments have academic and cognitive deficiencies or developmental lags due to difficulties processing spoken and written language (Meadow-Orlans, 1990). Some children experience social–emotional functioning difficulties due to communication difficulties (Luterman, 1996).

Educational Programming

An ongoing debate exists over what should be considered the best approach for teaching individuals with severe hearing impairments. Some advocate "**total communication**" (Luterman, 1986), which involves using speech (lip reading), gestures, and sign language, or both oral and manual methods. Teachers using total communication rely on the structure of the English language, and speak while signing during communications with students who are deaf. Some advocate the use of only oral approaches, eliminating any manual components used in total communication. Teachers using only oral approaches rely heavily on parental and family involvement as well as auditory, visual, and tactile methods of presentation. Finally, others advocate using only sign language or manual approaches. These individuals advocate the exclusive use of sign language because they maintain that a unique "culture of the deaf" exists among those who communicate with sign language. They believe that when individuals with hearing impairments are taught only to speech read or use oral techniques, they are denied full participation in the culture of the deaf (Padden & Humphries, 1988; Paul & Quigley, 1990; Reagan, 1990). Individuals from this position say they are not disabled, but that they are part of another cultural group composed of individuals who are deaf. A 15-year-old deaf boy testified before the National Council on Disabilities to relay his positions on inclusion in the general classroom (Thomas, 1991) and stated that he felt more comfortable going to school with students who are all deaf rather than with hearing students. Teachers using this approach teach and use the American Sign Language system of signing.

An interesting and thought-provoking book, *Train Go Sorry: Inside a Deaf World* by Leah Hager Cohen (1994) describes attending a school for the deaf and provides a compassionate understanding for the culture of the deaf. In a chapter on the least-restrictive environment, she writes the following:

> Mainstreaming's proponents (many of whom are unfamiliar with the special circumstances of deafness but see special programs as a way of isolating and stigmatizing learning disabled and emotionally disturbed children) believe that the least-restrictive environment for all children is the same: regular public school. The goal of social integration must be achieved at any cost. As desirable as this outcome may be for many children, for some it amounts to bad pedagogy. For the deaf, it means dissolution of their culture. . . .
>
> Deaf people, unlike members of other disabled groups, have their own language. They have their own social clubs and athletic leagues, their own theater companies and television programs, their own university, their own periodicals, and their own international Olympics. Unlike members of ethnic minority groups, they do not receive their culture through their parents. Cultural transmission, formally and informally, has been carried out by schools for the deaf. In practice, few public schools can offer what most prelingually deaf children need: a visually oriented setting, community access to all activities, interaction with deaf peers and deaf adults, and at least minimal sign language fluency on the part of teachers and peers. And no public school can offer the richness and nurturance of a deaf cultural environment. (Cohen, 1994, pp. 53–56)

Although other perspectives have also been voiced, Cohen provides a unique and thought-provoking commentary on such issues as "least-restrictive environment" and the inclusion movement.

Several signing systems are in use today, including the American Sign Language (ASL), Fingerspelling, and Signing Exact English. All systems use manual signs made with the hands and fingers to represent words, concepts, and ideas. However, they are based on different systems. **The American Sign Language** (ASL) is a visual spatial language, is not phonologically based like English, and is the official language of the culture of the deaf in the United States. ASL has its own rules of semantics, syntax, pragmatics, and vocabulary (Paul & Quigley, 1990). Fingerspelling is a manual alphabet of 26 distinct hand positions used to represent each letter in the English alphabet. Fingerspelling is especially appropriate for unfamiliar words such as proper names. The following *In the Classroom* feature displays sample sign language positions and fingerspellings. Some teachers use Fingerspelling while speaking to students with hearing impairments. Signing Exact English is a system that employs components of ASL, but attempts to use correct English usage for facilitating the learning of reading and writing literacy skills in English for students who are deaf. No clear research evidence exists to promote one approach over the other in teaching students who are deaf. Therefore, it is likely that this debate will continue into the future.

Classroom Adaptations for Students with Hearing Impairments

Students with hearing impairments can benefit from instruction in general education classes if specific adaptations are made. Specific accommodations vary depending upon the degree of hearing impairment and whether students have interpreters to accompany them throughout the school day. If

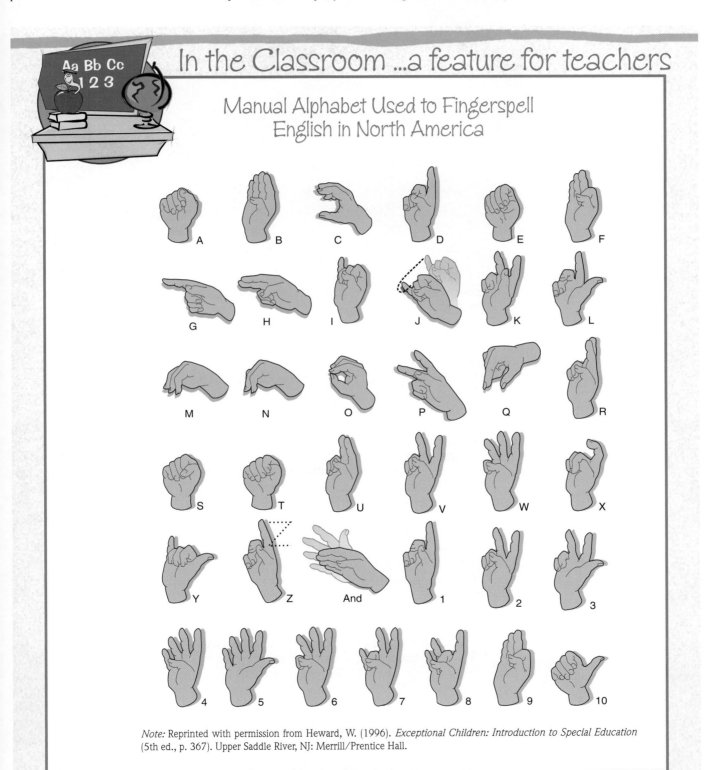

In the Classroom ...a feature for teachers

Manual Alphabet Used to Fingerspell English in North America

Note: Reprinted with permission from Heward, W. (1996). *Exceptional Children: Introduction to Special Education* (5th ed., p. 367). Upper Saddle River, NJ: Merrill/Prentice Hall.

Many students with hearing impairments communicate with sign language that employs its own unique rules of grammar.

you have a student with hearing impairments in your class, establish classroom emergency procedures for use during fire and tornado drills. Many fire alarms can be equipped with a light that flashes while the bell rings, alerting students with hearing impairments. Consider assigning a peer assistant who can pass along information that comes from the announcement system and who can be a buddy during any emergency situations. In addition to these guidelines, consider the following strategies:

- **Adapt the physical environment** so students are seated close enough to the front of the class to maximize their hearing and enable them to read speech (lip-read). They should also be able to turn to face other students while they are speaking. Because hearing aids are extra sound-sensitive, loud or irritating noises should be avoided. Consider choosing a room with carpeting and located away from noisy school areas, such as the cafeteria and gym.
- **Use technology,** including hearing aids, television captioning, adapted telephone equipment (TTY), computer-assisted instruction, and the Internet. When appropriate, use FM sound systems, which include cordless microphones for teachers, and receivers that attach to hearing aids for students. Pass your microphone to classmates who are speaking in a class discussion so they can also be heard.
- **Use visuals** such as illustrations, diagrams, pictures, and three-dimensional models to introduce vocabulary and concepts and enhance comprehension.
- **Use language cards** that contain vocabulary and illustrations of concepts and definitions that can accompany verbal presentations and be used to preteach. Encourage students to maintain personal dictionaries of their language cards.
- **Reiterate major points,** write out assignments, or write down questions on overhead transparencies or the chalkboard. Give students outlines or closing summaries as handouts. Repeat questions or answers that other students contribute, to enable hearing impaired students to fully participate in class. Sequence steps or procedures on written cards and place them in clear view.
- **Use hand signals or devise a signaling system** to denote transitions or allow students with hearing impairments or interpreters to review questions, answers, and concepts.
- **Alert students as to when to look or listen** and position yourself so students with hearing impairments can clearly see your face, without the reflection of glaring light.
- **Use a "listen, then look, then listen"** sequence of instruction, so students can focus on your face as you speak, then focus on the other aspects of the lesson separately, then

FM sound systems can help teachers communicate with students who have hearing impairments.

The Website of the National Association for the Deaf has links to sites that contain information about education for students who are deaf. For more information, go to the Web Links module in chapter 4 of the Companion Website.

focus on your face again. Say, for example, "Now, I'm going to pour the oil in with this water" (listen); then pour the oil (look), then say, "I poured the oil into the water. Who can tell me what happened?" (listen).

* **Repeat information** from the school public address system to ensure students have understood the announcements.
* **Plan for interpreters.** Interpreters often assist students who are deaf by translating lecture information, tutoring, and assisting special and regular education teachers (Salend & Longo, 1994). Extra space, including chairs or desks, may be required for interpreters to be near students with hearing impairments. Since interpreters are typically adults and taller than your students, check to see that all children have a clear view of important classroom information. Prepare your students for the interpreter and clearly explain the roles and functions the interpreter will have while in your classroom. Schedule time alone with the interpreter to discuss your typical classroom procedures, materials, and routines. Show any new or difficult vocabulary to the interpreter before introducing the words in class. Remember that an interpreter cannot proceed at the same pace as your verbal presentation, and you need to slow your rate of presentation accordingly. Use the effective instruction variables (see chapter 6) to help design, implement, and monitor your lessons.

For more information on teaching students with hearing impairments in specific content and curriculum areas, see Stewart and Kluwin (2001).

Adapt Evaluation

Testing and evaluation modifications for students with hearing impairments might include providing individual testing times in separate rooms, and extending the time limit as necessary. Remember to allow sufficient time for interpreters during oral testing situations. Allow students to draw illustrations of concepts. Use performance-based testing measures and identification formats whenever possible.

In performance-based testing, students can physically demonstrate, rather than write down, their understanding of relevant concepts. Refer to chapter 12 for additional information.

Physical Disabilities and Other Health Impairments

Prevalence, Definitions, and Characteristics

Physical disabilities and other health impairments include many types of disabilities that range from mild to moderate to severe, and from temporary to permanent or life-threatening. Approximately .5% of the school-age population has a physical or other health-related disability, or 5.8%

of the students served under IDEA (U.S. Department of Education, 2001). Physical disabilities are often described as either orthopedic or neurological impairments (Bleck & Nagel, 1975; Harder, 1996; Haslam & Valletutti, 1996). **Orthopedic impairments** involve damage to the skeletal system, while **neurological impairments** involve damage to the nervous system (Bleck, 1975a). Frequently physical disabilities are referred to by the affected parts of the body. For example, **quadriplegia** means both arms and legs are impaired, **paraplegia** means the legs are impaired, **hemiplegia** means either the left or right side of the body is involved, and **diplegia** means both legs are involved more than the arms (Clayman, 1994; Leppert & Capute, 1996). Common physical disabilities include cerebral palsy, epilepsy, spina bifida, muscular dystrophy, rheumatoid arthritis, scoliosis, osteogenesis imperfecta, and athrogyrposis (Bleck & Nagel, 1975).

Other health impairments include physical or medical conditions resulting from diseases or illnesses (Haslam & Valletutti, 1996). Great variability exists in severity level of impairment. Some health impairments improve over time while others do not (Valletutti, 1996). Major health conditions include cancer, acquired immune deficiency syndrome (AIDS), allergies, asthma, and fetal alcohol syndrome (Clayman, 1994; Haslam & Valletutti, 1996) and are discussed next. Other conditions are presented in Figure 4.2. School-related difficulties due to physical disabilities and other health impairments are covered by the provision of "special education services" under IDEA 97. Sometimes physical disabilities or other health impairments do not lead to difficulties in academic or intellectual functioning.

Cystic Fibrosis. Cystic fibrosis is an inherited disease in which upper respiratory and digestive problems are chronic due to the inability of the pancreas to produce digestive enzymes (Kelly, 1996). Glands in the bronchial tubes also malfunction and produce thick mucous that stagnates in the bronchial tubes. Treatments include special diets and intensive respiratory therapy (Kelly, 1996). Work closely with medical staff to monitor the condition.

Hemophilia. Hemophilia is an inherited sex-linked disorder in which the blood does not clot properly and excessive bleeding may occur with minor cuts or injuries (Kelly, 1996). Know relevant first aid information. Internal bleeding is very serious. Watch for falls at recess or during physical education classes. Avoid dangerous situations in which cuts are possible. Follow safety guidelines when using sharp objects or cutting tools.

Rheumatic fever. Rheumatic fever usually begins with a throat infection that may lead to painful swelling in the joints that can spread to the heart or brain and result in severe damage. Consult with medical personnel and your student's family to design optimal interventions.

Cancer. Cancer is a group of diseases in which the normal process of cell production malfunctions. Cell growth is uncontrolled, becomes malignant, and damages healthy tissues (Clayman, 1994). Individuals with cancer may require special supports for both social-emotional well-being and for accommodating less energy and pain during school activities. Based on advice from treating physicians and multidisciplinary team members, many school activities may need to be restricted in time and scope (Harder, 1996). Reduce assignments commensurate with your student's energy level. Arrange for peers to take notes for these students when they are absent due to their medical needs (Valletutti, 1996). Moreover, as with all health impairments, provide the necessary psychosocial support for students and prepare classmates for helping the student with cancer.

Tuberculosis. Tuberculosis is a disease in which bacteria infect the lungs, and may spread to the brain, kidneys, or bones.

Nephrosis and nephritis. Nephrosis and nephritis are disorders of the kidneys. These disorders, if left untreated, can result in kidney failure.

Sickle-cell anemia. Sickle-cell anemia is an inherited disease in which an abnormal red hemoglobin is formed (Kelly, 1996). This results in less oxygen in the body and the malformed cells may move improperly through the bloodstream resulting in additional complications. Students with sickle-cell anemia may tire more easily and need accommodations with reduced assignments commensurate with their energy-ability levels.

Figure 4.2
Other Health-Related Disorders

CLASSROOM SCENARIO

Nicole

Nicole is an 11-year-old girl in a fourth-grade classroom. She has athetoid cerebral palsy. She is severely limited in controlled movements; however, she does have some use of her right hand and can manipulate lightweight objects (i.e., computer disks, paper, name stamp). She can also access a computer keyboard with one finger. Nicole has difficulty reading text in a book and following along in workbooks and on work sheets due to the extraneous movements of her body and head. She continually loses her place and loses time trying to find it again.

Nicole is provided with several pieces of equipment that encourage independent functioning. These include the following:

1. An adapted desk with baskets and caddies attached to access materials and work space.
2. [A computer] with a printer. The computer is placed on a fitted computer table with castors. The size is fitted to accommodate Nicole's electric wheelchair and gives her a proper position while working. The castors allow the computer table to be moved within the room and to another classroom if necessary.
3. A heavy-duty swing-arm book stand is attached to the computer table to hold papers and textbooks.
4. A special keyguard with an armrest to reduce uncontrolled arm movements. It also has a lock feature that holds down the OPEN-APPLE and CONTROL key so Nicole can touch RESET and boot up her own programs.

Nicole's primary instruction occurs in the regular classroom and is taught by the regular fourth-grade teacher. Behind the scenes, supporting this teacher, is a teacher of students who have physical disabilities (PH) and a management aide. It is the PH teacher who evaluates and determines the key components of each lesson, step 1 in the process. With the understanding of Nicole's limitations, she modifies the lesson to enable Nicole to independently participate in it along with her classmates. It is the paraprofessional, under the direction of the PH teacher, that actually prepares materials prior to the time in which the lesson is presented to the class. This may include enlarging text, cutting and pasting workbook materials to make them visually accessible, preprogramming math facts or spelling words into the computer, or preparing written language materials. (pp. 364, 367)

Reprinted with permission from J. L. Bigge (1991). *Teaching individuals with physical and multiple disabilities* (3 ed.). New York: MacMillan, pp. 364, 367.

Physical and Health-Related Impairments

Cerebral Palsy

Cerebral palsy is the most common physical disability, with about 1.5 occurrences in every 1,000 births (Bigge, 1991). It is a neurological disorder that causes permanent disorders of movement and positions. Cerebral palsy is not progressive in nature, which means it does not worsen over time. It does, however, range in impairment levels from mild to moderate to severe (Bleck, 1975a). Individuals with cerebral palsy may or may not have coexisting difficulties in language, communication, vision, hearing, psychosocial, self-help, and intellectual development (Leppert & Capute, 1996).

Many individuals with cerebral palsy use wheelchairs or other motorized vehicles to assist with mobility, or use other adaptive devices to assist with fine motor control and speech and language difficulties (Leppert & Capute, 1996). **Alternative and augmentative communication** techniques used with some individuals with cerebral palsy include communication boards containing pictures or words of commonly asked questions and responses to questions, and computerized devices using synthesized speech. The Technology Highlight feature describes uses of technology to improve communication, News-2-You and Boardmaker.

The classroom scenario (Bigge, 1991) describes adaptations made for Nicole, a student with cerebral palsy.

The NORD Manual, available on CD, contains information and Internet links to more than 1,100 rare and uncommon disorders. For more information, go to the Web Links module in chapter 4 of the Companion Website.

For more information from the United Cerebral Palsy Association, go to the Web Links module in chapter 4 of the Companion Website.

Technology Highlight

Alternative and Augmentative Communication, News-2-You and Boardmaker

Many students with low-incidence disabilities require some adaptations in literacy materials that will aid their ability to communicate. Several examples of alternative and augmentative communication devices are widely available and range from high-tech to low-tech options. This means that some use very little technology, while others are reliant on more complex technological systems for delivery. One alternative and augmentative version of a newspaper that is available is *News-2-You* (*http://www.news-2-you.com*). *News-2-You* is published weekly during the school year and available for a subscription fee. The newspaper features relevant newsworthy stories printed using visual symbols that represent words. Each paper includes four to five pages of weekly current event news stories, a recipe, a joke, a game page, a sports story, and a weekly quiz based on the paper. The paper also includes sample communication boards as downloads that can be used as part of *Boardmaker,* a software program that contains graphics that can be used to develop and design communication displays or word documents (for those who do not have access to *Boardmaker*). The newspaper provides an excellent vehicle for access to news for many students who might otherwise be unable to read a paper. Since the paper is available online on a weekly basis, a teacher can select to have students read it online, from a saved online version on a computer, or in a printed hard copy format. The newspaper provides an excellent tool for working on reading comprehension skills with the short quizzes that accompany the weekly papers. Teachers can also decide to make their own versions of newspapers and reading materials using similar formats.

For example, teachers who like the format of *News-2-You* will most likely want to obtain the software *Boardmaker* that can be used to develop a wide range of displays using the over 3,000 graphic picture communication symbols and over 100 templates for calendars, schedules, and other formats. Pictures can be sized to meet your needs and *Boardmaker* for Windows comes with 19 languages including English, Spanish, German, Portuguese, Vietnamese, Russian, and Turkish, but has space for over 150 languages. The software is available from Mayer-Johnson Inc. (*http://www.mayer-johnson.com*). *Boardmaker* can also be combined with *Speaking Dynamically Pro* to include the speech capabilities. This way, the symbols can be used as overlays and can be heard aloud for students who require hearing the symbols in addition to looking at them.

A sample page from *News-2-You* showing a restaurant review questionnaire is presented.

Source: Reprinted with permission: Dave and Jackie Clark, News-2-You, Inc.

Restaurant Review   By _____

Restaurant _____

What did you eat?

Main Dish _____

Side Dish _____

Dessert _____

Drink _____

How was the food?

☆☆☆   ☆☆   ☆

Great   OK   Bad

Spina Bifida

Spina bifida is caused during fetal development when the vertebrae do not properly enclose the spinal cord, causing the nerves that control muscles in the lower body to develop incorrectly. Spina bifida occurs in 1 in about 2,000 births. Resulting motor impairment can range from mild to severe and include loss of sensation to paralysis in the lower body. Spina bifida is often associated with hydrocephalus, a condition in which cerebrospinal fluid collects in the brain tissues (Clayman, 1994). If left untreated, swelling can cause severe brain damage and result in mental retardation, attention difficulties, and learning problems (Mitchell, 1983). Shunts, or one-way valves, are inserted surgically to drain the fluid from the brain to reduce the risk of pressure on the brain and possible resulting brain damage. Shunts need to be replaced as children grow. Be aware of warning signs or changes in a student's behavior, as sudden changes may indicate shunt blockage or infections. Alert parents immediately of any changes.

Individuals with spina bifida—and other physical disabilities—may lack bladder and bowel movement control due to paralysis of the lower body (Bleck, 1975b). Most children use a catheter, or bag to collect their urine. Many children are taught to use a procedure called "clean intermittent catheterization." Request assistance from school nurses or other educational team members to learn how to assist a child with this procedure. Plan rest-room breaks to accommodate these students' specialized toileting needs.

Many children with spina bifida walk with braces or crutches, relying on wheelchairs for longer distances. In these cases, maintain classroom space to ensure clear, wide, and open walkways for students with mobility difficulties. Arrange storage for crutches or removable braces near students for easy access. Physical therapists can provide suggestions for accommodating the physical needs of these students.

For more information from the **Spina Bifida Association of America**, go to the Web Links module in chapter 4 of the Companion Website.

Muscular Dystrophy

Muscular dystrophy refers to a group of diseases that weaken and progressively destroy muscle tissue. Muscular dystrophy occurs in about 1 in 3,500 births. No known cure exists. Some forms of muscular dystrophy are fatal, but other forms are not life-threatening (Clayman, 1994). At birth children appear normal; however, between the ages of 2 and 6 they begin to experience motor difficulties, which increase with age. Often by the ages of 10 to 14 children lose the ability to walk. Children with muscular dystrophy should be lifted only by those with explicit training, as their limbs are easily dislocated. Because the disease is often progressive, it is important to learn what types of muscular difficulties may be expected throughout an academic year. Physical therapists and physicians can provide important information for classroom teachers pertaining to mobility and physical needs. For example, these students may tire more easily than peers and may require rest breaks throughout the school day (Kelly, 1996).

For more information from the **Muscular Dystrophy Association**, go to the Web Links module in chapter 4 of the Companion Website.

Traumatic Brain Injury

Traumatic brain injury (TBI), although now a separate category of exceptionality under IDEA, represents a type of physical and cognitive disability (Caldwell, Sirvis, Todaro, & Accouloumre, 1991). Traumatic brain injury is the result of an external injury that impedes learning along the continuum from mild to severe disabilities, and may result in physical, cognitive, attention, memory, problem-solving, sensory, and psychosocial difficulties. The resulting disabilities may be temporary or permanent. Often traumatic brain injuries are caused from falls or motor vehicle accidents (Haslam, 1996). The National Head Injury Foundation (1985) defined *traumatic brain injury (TBI)* this way:

> (TBI) is an insult to the brain, not of degenerative or congenital nature but caused by an external force, that may produce a diminished or altered state of consciousness, which results in impairment of cognitive abilities or physical functioning. These impairments may be either temporary or permanent and cause partial or functional disability or psychosocial maladjustment. (p. 1)

Estimates of the number of traumatic brain injuries are difficult to determine, but some have speculated that each year 200,000 injuries are sustained by children (Pipitone, 1992), most of which are from motor vehicle, bicycle, and other sporting accidents. The Federal Interagency Head Injury Task Force (1990) reported that more than 2 million head injuries occur annually, with 70,000 to 90,000 individuals sustaining physical, intellectual, and psychological disabilities. Head injuries occur most often in the warmer spring and summer months, on weekends and afternoons,

For more information from the **Brain Injury Association of America**, go to the Web Links module in chapter 4 of the Companion Website.

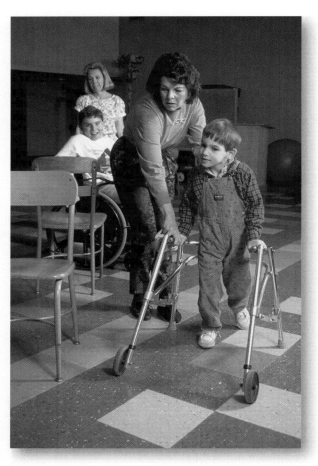

Some physical or health impairments—such as muscular dystrophy—have obvious physical limitations; other conditions— such as asthma, diabetes, and epilepsy—are not as obvious.

when children are most likely to be playing outside, or riding in cars (Michaud, Duhaime, & Lazar, 1997). Special education services are provided for the resulting difficulties in school learning. Teachers can play an important preventative role by encouraging students to take safety precautions, such as wearing helmets when riding bicycles.

A significant role of the classroom teacher is in assisting successfully with the transitions the individual has to make from the hospital to rehabilitation to the classroom. Successful transition planning includes preparing peers of the changes in the behavior of the affected classmate. IEPs may need to be adjusted and modified more frequently due to changing conditions in students with a traumatic brain injury.

Students with TBI who recover adequate intellectual functioning but who continue to exhibit difficulties in learning may resemble students with learning disabilities in some respects. However, students with TBI also may differ in several ways. Students may continue to change neurologically, even months after their readmission to school. Achievement test scores may be misleading because they may reflect knowledge or skills acquired prior to the injury. Further, psychosocial problems may emerge as a consequence of coping with challenges associated with TBI. Unpredictable difficulty could occur even years after the injury, if parts of the brain were injured that are needed for later maturation (Ylvisaker & Feeney, 1998).

Initial school adaptations may include a shortened school day due to extreme tiring and shortened attention spans on the part of the recovering student. Cohen, Joyce, Rhoades, and Welks (1987) listed learning criteria that can be used to determine whether students with TBI are ready for more academics. These criteria include determining whether students can (a) attend for 15 minutes, (b) sit in a class for 30 minutes, (c) work with a group of two students, (d) engage in conversations, and (e) follow directions. Initial accommodations may also include the need to reduce significantly the amount of homework and class work.

For more information from the Epilepsy Foundation of America, go to the Web Links module in chapter 4 of the Companion Website.

Epilepsy

A seizure is caused when abnormal electrical energy is released in the brain that can cause a loss of consciousness and lack of motor control (Haslam, 1996). The effects can be minimal or severe, depending on the amount of energy released and the number of brain cells affected. The precise cause of seizures is not always known (Engel, 1995), but some are due to brain damage from physical trauma or infections.

Any child may have a seizure. Individuals may experience a single seizure associated with a head injury or high fever, and never have one again. About half of those with seizure disorders also have mental retardation. Repeated seizures are indicative of epilepsy. No matter what the physical condition that leads to a seizure, be aware that seizures vary in duration, frequency, onset, movements, causes, associated disabilities, and control.

Seizure disorders can be treated with antiepileptic drugs (such as phenobarbital), special diets, and surgery (Brown, 1997). Because of the chance of body injury or brain damage, it is wise to learn about the correct handling of seizures and to educate all students about seizures and their treatment.

Arthritis

Arthritis, or juvenile rheumatoid arthritis, is a disease in which the muscles and joints are affected. Arthritis can be painful and can severely impede the mobility of an individual. Physical exercise and anti-inflammatory drugs may help relieve some of the symptoms, but no known cause or cure exists. Because mobility may be hindered, some children with severe arthritis use canes or braces while walking. Be aware that these students will have good days and bad days and build in extra rest periods during more painful days. Students may experience great difficulty trying to grip a pencil. Writing may be extremely tedious and painful. Reduce writing demands by allowing students to use tape recorders or other students as "scribes." Provide extended time for written assignments.

Asthma and Allergies

Asthma is a respiratory condition associated with breathing difficulties that can be exacerbated during exercise. Children with severe asthma often require restricted athletic activities and may need to be reminded to take appropriate medication (Feldman, 1996; Kelly, 1996). Physicians can provide relevant information on particular adaptations for individual cases.

Allergies are conditions in which elements in the environment cause allergic reactions in some individuals. Exposure to pollens, molds, dusts, animal dander, and carpet fibers can cause reactions such as congestion in the nose, chest, and eyes. Allergic reactions to certain foods like milk, fish, or nuts can cause skin rashes and more serious mouth and throat reactions. Still other reactions are caused from insect bites like honey bee stings, and can result in anaphylactic shock, a condition that can be fatal if not treated immediately (Feldman, 1996). Many individuals who know they have these conditions carry emergency kits with them. Be sure to have plans in place for dealing with such medical emergencies, including the quickest ways to seek medical assistance.

Know which of your students have asthma and allergies, the associated allergens, the preventative medications, first aid, and the specific nature of the allergic reactions. In some cases, it may be necessary to maintain a dust and animal dander-free environment to avoid allergic reactions. In other cases, teachers or other school staff can monitor food consumption during lunchtime and class parties (Valletutti, 1996).

Diabetes

Diabetes is an inherited condition in which sugar is not metabolized correctly due to insufficient production of insulin in the pancreas (Christiansen, 1975; Clayman, 1994). Individuals with diabetes have strict diets and special schedules for administering medication that needs close monitoring. Learn the warning signs of diabetic shock and be ready to administer first aid (Daneman & Frank, 1996). The school nurse can usually provide relevant information for classroom teachers who can share information with all students. Monitor dietary needs during the school day for students with diabetes (or create a plan for an aide to do so), especially if extra food or physical activities are added to the regular schedule. Careful planning with the family and other health-care providers is necessary to ensure safety during daily class activities, and especially for special events like field trips or overnight trips (Daneman & Frank, 1996).

Fetal Alcohol Syndrome and Other Disorders

Fetal alcohol syndrome (FAS) results when pregnant mothers consume alcohol that damages the developing fetus (Jones, Smith, Ulleland, & Streissguth, 1973). This places a child at risk for a variety of developmental disabilities, including mental retardation, learning disabilities, and physical disabilities (Jones & Lopez, 1988). Students with fetal alcohol syndrome can have additional problems with attention and impulsivity (Burgess & Streissguth, 1992). Moreover, women who abuse drugs and alcohol frequently have concomitant difficulties including inadequate nutrition, prenatal care, housing, and psychosocial problems, and may be less responsive to their newborns (Vincent, Poulsen, Cole, Woodruff, & Griffith, 1991). Exposure to substances during the first trimester is likely to cause neurological and structural damage to the developing fetus (Briggs, 2001; Ryan, Ehrlich, & Finnegan, 1987). Effective service delivery for infants born under these conditions comes from personnel from health, social services, mental health, children's services, education, and drug and alcohol programs who must collaborate to work effectively with the family.

Some adaptations developed for students with cerebral palsy who have gripping difficulties may also be suitable for students with arthritis.

JayJo Books (P.O. Box 213, St. Louis, MO 63088-0213; or call 1-800-801-0159) is a publisher of books for teaching elementary school children about their classmates or others who may be living with a chronic disease. Titles include *Taking Diabetes to School*, *Taking Asthma to School*, and *Taking Seizure Disorders to School*.

Companion Website

For more information from the American Diabetes Association, go to the Web Links module in chapter 4 of the Companion Website.

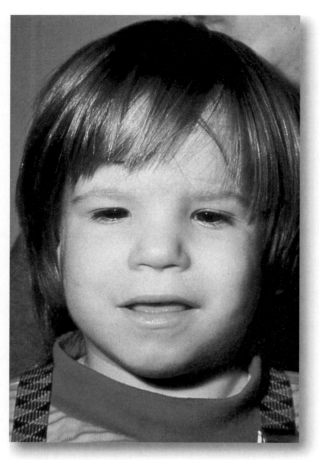

Fetal alcohol syndrome places a child at risk for a variety of developmental disabilities. (Streissguth, A. P., Landesman-Dwyer, S., Martin, J. C., & Smith, D. W. (1980). Teratogenic effects of alcohol in humans and laboratory animals. "Science, 209", 353–361.)

For more information on AIDS, go to the Web Links module in chapter 4 of the Companion Website.

Acquired Immune Deficiency Syndrome

Acquired immune deficiency syndrome (AIDS) is caused by the human immunodeficiency virus (HIV), which destroys a form of white blood cells, weakening the immune system. HIV can be transmitted to an unborn fetus during pregnancy, or during childbirth to an infant, or through infected breast milk during nursing (Byrom & Katz, 1991). Children with AIDS may have coexisting disabilities such as mental retardation, emotional disorders, seizures, and cerebral palsy (Rudigier, Crocker, & Cohen, 1990).

AIDS and HIV can also be spread through sharing drug needles, sexual intercourse, and contact with blood (Byrom & Katz, 1991). Education regarding optimal ways to interact with children with AIDS should be ongoing. Professional organizations, such as the Council for Exceptional Children (CEC), have published policy statements and resolutions regarding AIDS, education of students with AIDS, and prevention policies (Byrom & Katz, 1991). Determine your local school policies and procedures for handling students with AIDS and for educating all students about AIDS. Guidelines published by CEC provide basic information about the virus and procedures for handling blood and other bodily fluids in schools. Byrom and Katz (1991) provide a sample AIDS curriculum guide for kindergarten through grade 12. Finally, maintain the district's confidentiality policies for all students with disabilities, especially for those with AIDS.

Classroom Adaptations for Students with Physical Disabilities and Other Health Impairments

Although each individual and disability area may require specific adaptations, the following guidelines can help you develop adaptations for accommodating individuals with physical and other health impairments.

Medical Guidelines

Medical needs are of primary concern. Devise checklists containing reminder steps for general class and emergency procedures specific to the medical conditions of students. For example, a medical checklist could include the following items:

- Check medication schedule.
- Monitor medication effects.
- Monitor medication side effects.
- Monitor first aid procedures.
- Communicate with parents.
- Monitor classroom emergency procedures.

Maintain careful records of student behavior (such as lethargy or fatigue) and communicate clearly any changes in your student's behavior.

Be aware of medications. An awareness of the types of medications, specific uses, and potential side effects is also necessary.

Table 4.1 presents background information on some of the most commonly prescribed medications for individuals with disabilities. Careful monitoring of students' behaviors while on and off medication (for example, with observational records) can provide valuable educational insights for you, and for prescribing physicians.

A school nurse or other designated school official distributes medications to students from a centralized location in the school, usually the nurse's office. Be sure that students obtain their medication at the scheduled times and that they ingest the medication when administered. Some students feign taking their medication and attempt to give or sell it to other individuals. Parents have reported that

Table 4.1
Some Commonly Prescribed Medications

Psychostimulants

- *Medications:* Adderall, Concerta (methylphenidate), Cylert (pemoline), Dexedrine (dextroamphetamine), Ritalin (methlyphenidate)
- *Benefits*: Used as a treatment for Attention Deficit Hyperactivity Disorder (ADHD), inattention, impulsivity, or hyperactivity.
- *Common side effects*: All medications can decrease appetite, cause gastro-intestinal (GI) upset; may cause tics, headaches, insomnia.

Selective Serotonin Reuptake Inhibitors (SSRI)

- *Medications:* Celexa (citalopram), Luvox (fluvoxamine), Paxil (paroxetine), Prozac (fluoxetine), Zoloft (sertraline)
- *Benefits:* Used for treatment of anxiety disorders, depression, and pervasive developmental disorders (PDD).
- *Common side effects:* All medications can cause GI upset, insomnia or sedation, activation, headaches, or sexual dysfunction (adolescents).

Trycyclic Antidepressants

- *Medications:* Anafranil (clomipramine), Elavil (amitriptyline), Norpramin (desipramine), Pamelor (nortriptyline), Tofranil (imipramine)
- *Benefits:* Used for treatment of ADHD, depression, anxiety, and enuresis. Anafranil is used for treatment of obsessive-compulsive disorder.
- *Common side effects:* All medications can cause GI upset, constipation, sedation, headache, dry mouth, blurry vision, urinary retention, EKG changes, or orthostatic hypotension (decrease in blood pressure when moving from a supine to a standing position).

Antipsychotic medications

- *Medications:* Haldol (haloperidol), Mellaril (thioridazine), Orap (pimozide), Prolixin (fluphenazine)
- *Benefits:* Used in treatment of psychosis, aggression, tics, bipolar disorder, and pervasive developmental disorder.
- *Common side effects:* All medications can cause sedation, movement disorders, weight gain, orthostatic hypotension, cognitive blunting, Parkinsons-like symptoms, and decreased seizure threshold.

Mood Stabilizers

- *Medications:* Depakote (valproic acid), Lithium, Neurontin (gabapentin), Tegretol (carbamazepine)
- *Benefits:* Used for treatment of aggression and bipolar disorder; Lithium can be used to augment other medications.
- *Common side effects:* All medications can cause GI upset, dizziness, weight gain, enuresis, tremor, or sedation. Lithium can cause acne, polyuria (passage of a large volume of urine), polydipsia (excessive thirst), or thyroid dysfunction. Depakote can cause polycystic ovary disease.

*Drug Class is given in bold, brand name is capitalized, and generic name is given in parenthesis.
Note: Adapted with permission from "Guide to psychiatric medications for children and adolescents," by S. Hack and B. Klee, Retrieved April 26, 2003, from *http://www.AboutOurKids.org/articles/guidetopsychmeds.html,* and "Psychopharmacologic medication: What teachers need to know," by S.R. Forness, D.P. Sweeney, and K.Toy, 1996, *Beyond Behavior,* 7(2), pp. 4-11. For more information, see American Academy of Child and Adolescent Psychiatry (2000); Griffith and Moore (2002); Hack & Klee (2001).

For more information on commonly used medications, go to the Web Links module in chapter 4 of the Companion website.

children may pretend to take their medication, hide it under their pillow, and share it later with their siblings. This is a serious problem that can become troublesome or dangerous if not monitored closely.

Plan for Fatigue. Students with physical disabilities or other health impairments may tire more easily than other students. If so, schedule frequent rest breaks throughout a day, prioritize daily schedules, and schedule break periods in the nurse's office if needed. If students lack the strength to carry necessary materials from class to class and to and from school, obtain duplicate sets of books and materials. Some students may require a shortened school day while they recuperate from illnesses. Reduce assignments, prioritize to ensure that students receive the most critical information, and assign peers to share class notes and materials.

Establish Emergency Procedures. All classes containing students with physical and other health impairments may require specialized classroom procedures for emergencies such as fire or tornadoes. For example, assistance may be required moving adaptive equipment along with the student. Also, depending on the position of the individual in the class when the emergency alarm sounds, students may need assistance into their wheelchairs, braces, or other adaptive mobility devices. During fire drills, students often proceed to an athletic field adjacent to the school and mobility across the uneven grass may be especially difficult for some students with physical disabilities. Others tire easily and cannot walk quickly enough to maintain the speed of evacuation with the rest of the class.

Pair students with and without disabilities for evacuation efforts during emergencies. It may be helpful to have more than one student assigned to assist each student with disabilities. You can add the names of peer assistants to the overall listing of procedures on your "emergency chart." Be prepared: Outline emergency procedures in advance and practice them many times so that if an actual emergency situation occurs all students are well-prepared for any evacuation procedures.

Plan for Seizures. Know which of your students are likely to have seizures and what first aid treatment is appropriate. Since seizures range in severity from very minor to very intense and severe, consult your student's family and physician for precise medical treatment. If a seizure does occur, stay calm. You are a model for your students and if you stay calm, so will they. Help the student to the floor. Gently tilt the head to the side so the child does not choke. In any seizure, do not attempt to restrain movements of the individual or place anything in between the teeth or in the mouth of the affected person. Clear all harmful objects out of the way, and place a blanket or pillow under the student's head to minimize the potential for injury.

Try to remember all of the distinctive features associated with the seizure to record on monitoring sheets and share with parents and attending physicians later. If it is the student's first seizure, contact a physician immediately. Moreover, if seizures persist more than 5 minutes, immediate medical attention should be sought. Notify parents when seizures have occurred (Spiegel, Cutler, & Yetter, 1996).

Learn how to handle a student who has just recovered from a seizure. Some students may feel tired and disoriented after a seizure and may want to lie down and rest. Others may feel fine and simply want to continue with the class activity. Still others may feel embarrassed and may need time outside of the class to regain self-control and self-respect. It is also important to redirect the attention of peers away from the students with the seizure. The individual having seizures should not be made to feel self-conscious. Do anything necessary to make the student feel comfortable. Provide all students with relevant information about seizures and proper ways of handling situations emotionally during and after seizures (Spiegel, Cutler, & Yetter, 1996).

When you document the details of the seizures, record the date and time of the seizure as well as the behavior exhibited before, during, and after the seizure. Note the student's and peer reactions to the seizure, and any other information that seems relevant (Michael, 1992).

Moving and Positioning Students. Determine what special procedures are required for moving, lifting, or transferring body positions of students with special needs. Some students, for example those with "brittle bone disease" (osteogenesis imperfecta), should be lifted only by people with specialized knowledge about how to lift and position the individual. Physical therapists, who often work directly with these students, can provide valuable information to you and your students.

1.   2.   3.

Figure 4.3

Alternatives to Allow Change of Position throughout the Day: (1) Sidelyer, (2) Wedge, (3) Tricycle with Built-up Back and Pedals. Adult Three-wheeled Bikes are Available for Older Children.

Note: From *Teaching Individuals with Physical and Multiple Disabilities* (p. 137), by J. L. Bigge, 1991, Upper Saddle River, NJ: Merrill/Prentice Hall. Reprinted by permission.

Find out whether students feel more comfortable in some positions than others. Periodically check their positions throughout the school day. Some types of positioning devices, such as braces and wedges, help improve personal comfort, control muscle movements, and position students to more easily communicate or complete schoolwork. Figure 4.3 shows examples of positioning devices.

Adapt for Chronic Medical Conditions. If students in your class have chronic medical conditions, you should know how to accommodate them. Consult with medical personnel to learn to recognize the signs and symptoms of relevant medical problems, and any modifications you can make. Limiting physical activity, administering medications, providing diet and fluid supplements as needed, and providing easy access to bathrooms are among the modifications you can make, depending on the condition.

Dealing with Terminal Illness. Health-care and mental-health professionals are good sources of information about dealing with terminally ill students, as are the students' parents. Ask how you should interact with the terminally ill student and the student's classmates (Obiakor, Mehring, & Schwenn, 1997). Mental-health professionals sometimes provide extra guidance and counseling sessions to small groups of students to address their questions about interacting with a terminally ill student. If the student dies, request assistance from the school's crisis intervention team and mental-health professionals. Some professionals speculate that different age-related reactions result when a death occurs (Petersen & Straub, 1992). For example, children ages 6 to 10 may have reduced attention spans, display out-of-character behavior, and lose trust in adults. Children ages 10 to 14 may show anger or psychosomatic illnesses. Adolescents may be suspicious, develop sleeping or eating disorders, lose impulse control, or turn to alcohol and drug abuse (Obiakor, Mehring, & Schwenn, 1997).

Prepare the Class

Prepare the class for students with disabilities who are about to enter the class. Describe the students' special needs, and the roles of classroom peers in supporting the inclusive classroom. One way to enhance disability awareness in students is by using classroom simulation activities and demonstrations using adaptive devices (Hallenbeck & McMaster, 1991). Simulations can be designed for almost any disability area. For example, having students keep one of their hands behind their backs while attempting to perform regular class activities lets them experience the challenges encountered daily by other students. Similarly, allowing students to try out wheelchairs or use walkers, braces, or canes will enable them to appreciate the challenges encountered in simple tasks such as getting a drink from a water fountain or getting to and from the playground. Simulations for cognitive impairments can also be designed, such as having students try to read a foreign language, or write with their eyes closed. Discussions with all students

See Caldwell, Todaro, and Gates (1991) and Caldwell, Sirvis, Todaro, and Accouloumre (1991) for more information about health-care supports in the school.

Find out your school's crisis intervention plan for dealing with the death of a student. Refer to Obiakor, Mehring, and Schwenn (1997).

For more information on terminal illness from the Hospice Foundation of America, go to the Web Links module in chapter 4 of the Companion Website.

While simulation activities can be beneficial, students should be reminded that having disabilities involves a great deal more than is represented in the simulation activities.

following simulation activities can help increase their awareness of the frustrations that may be encountered by students with disabilities.

Adapt the Physical Environment

Check with your principal and special education administrators regarding confidentiality issues, before identifying students with disabilities to peers.

Arrange the classroom to meet the mobility requirements of students with physical disabilities. Provide sufficiently wide aisles to accommodate wheelchairs, walkers, three-wheel motorized wheelchairs, crutches, canes, braces, or other adaptive devices. Most wheelchairs require passages at least 32" wide for one wheelchair to pass. Keep aisles clear of debris and monitor regularly to ensure that no books, book bags, backpacks, toys, or other objects impede mobility. Verify that the height of door knobs, water fountains, sinks, and cabinets are accessible for students with physical disabilities. If not, perhaps minor adaptations can be made to ensure equal accessibility.

Examine the type of floor in your classroom, with respect to whether carpeting or tile is used, and the extent to which surfaces either facilitate or impede mobility of individuals with physical disabilities. For example, carpeted floors can decrease slippage, but may also impede mobility of some adaptive devices. Conversely, tile surfaces may be dangerously slippery, especially after washing and waxing.

Adapt Instructional Materials

Commercially available materials include communication boards, computers to assist with voice synthesizer production, specially designed hand grippers, head pointers, keyboards, touch screens to assist with computer usage, and speech reading or word prediction software to minimize difficulty producing output for assignments. Other adaptive devices including flap switches and reaches that can be added to pencils or dowels to extend the grasp of individuals are available from the Prentke Romich Company.

Some teachers use "page puffs" to assist students with fine motor difficulties in turning book pages (Bigge, 1991). Page puffs are small pieces of sponge glued behind pages that make it easier to grasp and turn the pages. A book stand can be designed to hold instructional materials at an appropriate height and distance for easy viewing for students with restricted mobility. Choose books that are larger and easier to manipulate. Anchor materials in place by using clipboards or magnets to help stabilize papers.

Enlarge the gripping area of pencils by attaching spongelike material, plastic tubing, or plastic golf balls around pencils and pens. Use felt tip pens, which require less pressure than some other

Specially designed adaptive devices give some students the ability to be more independent.

writing tools. Specialized rubber stamps with large handles that contain commonly written items, such as names, *yes, no, rest room,* and *hungry,* also can help students communicate.

Larger paper with extra space between lines helps accommodate writing needs for some students. When class activities involve charting or graphing, provide larger graphs, stickers, or magnets for students to place on graphs rather than using smaller paper-and-pencil versions. Felt boards and pieces of felt are easier for some students to manipulate. Place vocabulary words or other content inside clear picture photograph cubes. Put clear plastic folders or sheet protectors on paper handouts. These are easier to grip than a single sheet of paper and can be held together with a clip. The coating also protects the papers from spills. Use calculators with large numbers that are easier to touch and read.

Stabilize instructional materials with Velcro. Slatted trays or trays with built-in dividers can be used to hold small objects that need to be manipulated during activities. Place a detachable bag or backpack onto the wheelchair for carrying books and other materials. Notes or tape-recorded messages to parents can be placed in the bag before students leave school. Often simple modifications such as these can allow students with physical disabilities to participate more independently.

Some students with physical disabilities may also have the assistance of an animal, such as a specially trained dog, that accompanies them throughout the school day. Teachers need to know how they and their students in the class and throughout the school should interact with the animal (Hallahan & Kauffman, 2003). Usually, no one is allowed to pet or interact with the animal other than the individual with disabilities. The student's family can provide detailed information on how to interact appropriately with these animals.

Adapt Instruction

Schedule extra reading, studying, and instructional support time when needed. Students who have difficulty speaking require extra time to respond to teacher questions. When calling on an individual during class discussions, provide sufficient wait time and make students feel comfortable and not rushed while responding.

Consider assigning a peer assistant to work with individuals with physical disabilities or health impairments. Peer assistants can enable the student to be a more active participant during class activities. In some cases, paraprofessionals are assigned to accompany students throughout the school day. Work closely with paraprofessionals to design effective modifications.

Adapt Evaluation

Testing and assessment modifications are necessary for students with physical disabilities and other health impairments. Because many of these students have difficulty reading and writing independently, schedule their tests when a special education teacher, paraprofessional, aide, peer assistant, or tutor can read the test items and record responses. These individualized sessions may require more time than the regularly scheduled exam time slots. Use communication boards during testing situations and record responses when students point to response sheets.

See chapter 12 for additional suggestions on modifying tests and testing situations.

Severe and Multiple Disabilities

Depending on the needs of the student, parental concerns, school or district policies, and multidisciplinary team recommendations, you may have a student with severe or multiple disabilities included in your class. The guidelines described in the following pages discuss the responsibilities such inclusion might entail.

Prevalence, Definitions, and Characteristics

Many individuals with severe disabilities have severe and profound mental retardation. Some individuals with moderate mental retardation may also be included in this group (Beirne-Smith, Ittenbach, & Patton, 2001). Some individuals with severe impairments usually have several coexisting disabilities (for example, sensory or physical disabilities). Moderate mental retardation is classified according to an IQ test score continuum of 35 to 54; severe retardation is represented by scores between 20 and 34; while profound retardation is classified as any score less than 20. The American Association on Mental Retardation proposed a new classification scheme for mental retardation established on a hierarchy of level of support for independent living, with severe and profound retardation requiring more extensive and pervasive support (AAMR Ad Hoc Committee on Terminology and Classification, 1992).

Individuals with moderate, severe, and profound mental retardation represent about 15% of all individuals with mental retardation, or about .15% of the school-age population and 1.6% of the students served under IDEA. Students with multiple disabilities represent about .18% of the school-age population, and about 2.0% of the students served under IDEA (Beirne-Smith, Ittenbach, & Patton, 2001; U.S. Department of Education, 2001).

The Association for Persons with Severe Handicaps (TASH) has defined severe disabilities as:

> Individuals of all ages who require extensive ongoing support in more than one major life activity in order to participate in integrated community settings and to enjoy a quality of life that is available to citizens with fewer or no disabilities. Support may be required for life activities such as mobility, communication, self-care, and learning, as necessary for independent living, employment and self-sufficiency. (Lindley, 1990, p. 1)

Educational Placement Considerations

The optimal educational placement and the design of effective instruction for students with severe and multiple disabilities are usually determined by the case conference team. The priorities vary depending on the age, severity level, and needs of the individual. Priorities come from family, medical, school, leisure, transitional, vocational, and peer support concern areas and are designed to match each student's needs and strengths. Sailor, Gee, and Karasoff (1993) recommend the following steps for designing programs for individuals with severe disabilities:

- Assemble a case conference team.
- Set priorities after compiling a student profile of strengths and needs for school, home, and the community.
- Design action and integration plans.
- Conduct assessments including contextual, skill, performance, and curricular domains.
- Evaluate needs from the classroom and other school-based and community-based areas and balance needs across areas.
- Design educational objectives and strategies to teach objectives.
- Train staff for instructional delivery.
- Facilitate friendships, peer supports, and after-school activities with peers.
- Evaluate program implementation continuously.

Students with severe and multiple disabilities generally have severe cognitive and adaptive behavior difficulties and require instruction in self-help skills, communication skills, functional academic skills, daily living skills, community awareness, and recreation, social, and vocational education skills. These students benefit greatly from positive social interactions with their general education peers. The creation of peer support networks, friendship circles, social circles, and participation in after-school activities is strongly advocated for individuals with severe disabilities (Sailor, Gee, & Karasoff, 1993; Snell, 1993).

Structure specific procedures within an educational day to provide interaction between students with and without disabilities. For example, provide peers with information on how to be problem-solving supports for their classmates with disabilities. Arrange peer tutoring or cooperative learning group experiences during which time students with and without disabilities interact on academic-related activities (Forest & Lusthaus, 1989a, 1989b; Stainback & Stainback, 1992). Provide opportunities for peers to initiate and respond to students with severe disabilities in after-school activities. Turnbull and Morningstar (1993) described a student with severe disabilities who assumed the position of manager of the school football team. This allowed additional interaction between students with and without disabilities after school hours, and according to the parents, greatly improved the school experience for their child.

For more information on severe disabilities, go to the Web Links module in chapter 4 of the Companion Website.

Classroom Adaptations for Students with Severe Disabilities

Because of the nature of severe and multiple disabilities, most students require special education and related services from many educational team members, including physical therapists, occupational therapists, speech and language therapists, adaptive physical education specialists, special educators, and paraprofessionals. Establish good working relationships with these partners and arrange the classroom for easy access by these specialists. Specialists may include their activities along with general education instruction. For example, specialists can assist with positioning and grasping techniques during classes involving art activities or computer applications. Arrange a special place in the classroom for specialists to work with the students with severe disabilities within the general education classroom. This should be done in a way that neither draws unnecessary attention to students with severe disabilities nor distracts the rest of the class.

Establish Good Working Relationships with Paraprofessionals

Paraprofessionals are often assigned to accompany students with severe disabilities for the entire school day. This means general education teachers will have another adult in the classroom whenever the student with severe disabilities is present. Because many teachers are used to being alone in their classrooms, having another adult in their room while teaching may require some adjustment (Downing, Ryndak, & Clark, 2000; Frith, 1982). The benefits can far outweigh the disadvantages because paraprofessionals can assist in many instructional and administrative responsibilities, as well as self-help care (Giangreco, Broer, & Edelman, 1999). These might include the following:

- Adapting materials under the direction of the teacher or special education teacher
- Administering tests individually to students with severe disabilities
- Reviewing and practicing materials already covered in class
- Presenting adapted materials to students
- Taking notes for students
- Assisting teachers during a class presentation
- Promoting peer cooperation during class
- Helping to arrange the classroom environment to accommodate activity needs
- Grading papers and assisting with recordkeeping
- Assisting with duplicating or laminating class materials
- Attending case conferences or team meetings as necessary
- Assisting with feeding and toileting
- Assisting with dressing before and after recess
- Supervising during recess
- Assisting with mobility during class changing time periods including going to lunch, and before and after school

Additional information on working effectively with paraprofessionals is described in chapter 2.

Increase Disability Awareness

Prepare your students for the arrival of a student with severe disabilities. Information regarding the strengths and needs of the individuals can be conveyed using a variety of formats and you play an important role in educating students' awareness of disability-related issues (Sapon-Shevin, 1992). One method of presenting information is to have guest speakers present information on specific disability-related issues pertaining to the student who will be included within the class. Special education teachers, parents of students with disabilities, speech–language therapists, physicians, school psychologists, or local disability organizations such as the Council for Exceptional Children (CEC) or the Association for Retarded Citizens (ARC) can present relevant information (see Plumb & Brown, 1990).

Paula Billingsley, a first-grade teacher at Strong Elementary School (Texas), described how her students began to express their natural curiosity about "Lisa," and she used their curiosity to provide a teaching moment:

> One of the advantages of teaching first grade is that the children are totally honest. After about a week of having Lisa with us and watching her communicate with sign language, and using her book with symbols, the children began to ask questions about how Lisa was learning. We seized the moment and began answering questions about Lisa. They were so concerned and interested in their fellow classmate. How did she learn, can she see them (she tends to hold her head sideways and

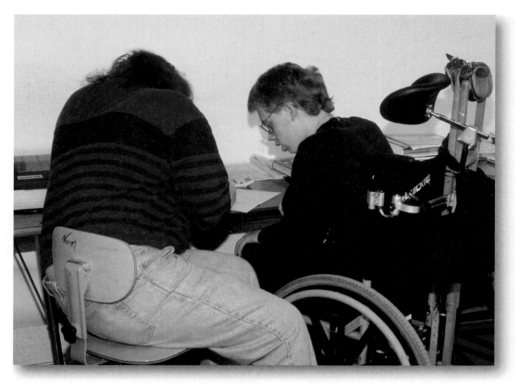

Paraprofessionals assist teachers with many administrative and instructional responsibilities.

be involved in her own world), would she ever go to college, could they help her learn, could they learn to talk with her, and where did she go when she was not with us? I listened to their questions with tears in my eyes as I realized they had a genuine interest in her and wanted to be a part of her learning experience. Aren't children wonderful with their nonjudgmental behavior!

Conceptualize Inclusive Instruction

Several authors have suggested a variety of ways to begin to conceptualize the inclusion of students with severe disabilities into general education classes (Giangreco, Cloninger, & Iverson, 1990; Giangreco, Edelman, & Dennis, 1991; Snell & Brown, 1993). These include the following:

- Focus on activities that can be engaged in by all students, without modification, such as homeroom or music class.
- Use "multilevel curriculum instruction," such as having a student in a wheelchair work on different muscle control while the rest of the class does exercises on floor mats during physical education class.
- Engage in "curriculum overlapping," such as having the student with severe disabilities work on communication skills while working on another academic area, such as mathematics (Snell & Brown, 1993, pp. 102–103).

Adapt Instructional Delivery Systems

A variety of instructional delivery systems is of primary importance during the inclusion of students with severe and multiple disabilities. This means that different personnel may at times be the supporting instructor for individuals with severe disabilities including teachers, students, and peers. For example, a special education teacher may be present in the general education classroom and be teaching and working directly with the students with severe disabilities. At other times, a paraprofessional may be delivering the instruction. At still other times, teachers may involve general education peers who are trained to assist students with severe disabilities.

Parents and other family members can be an important source of information and support for meeting the needs of individual students.

Consider Special Health-Care Needs

Many students with severe disabilities have coexisting medical needs and require special health-care adaptations and accommodations. Some students may be medically fragile, have infectious diseases, or simply have coexisting severe medical needs. Caldwell, Todaro, and Gates (1991) describe the possibility of accommodations that students with special medical needs may require in the general education classroom.

Consider writing daily health-care plans for individuals with severe medical needs. Health plans, written with input from the student's health-care provider, can detail information pertaining to the condition itself, restrictions in activities or precautions to be considered, the independence of the student in health care, medication schedules, whether students can recognize signs or symptoms of their own disorders, toileting schedules, and emergency plans for medical or other emergency situations (such as procedures for contacting medical assistance and parental notification).

Some students need assistance from medical technology such as respirator support, intravenous or nutritional support, alternative bowel and bladder assistance, breathing support with the use of ventilators, suctioning to remove mucous—especially for those with tracheostomies, and continuous feedings provided by pumps. The establishment of good, open lines of communication with health-care professionals and parents will enable general education teachers to better accommodate individuals requiring such assistance in their classes (Bigge, 1991; Caldwell, Sirvis, Todaro, & Accouloumre, 1991).

Classroom Adaptations

While not all students with severe disabilities have physical disabilities, many students do have coexisting physical disabilities. In these cases, adaptations to the physical environment and instructional materials—such as those detailed in the students with physical disabilities section described earlier—will be required.

In addition, many of the adaptations described for students with mental retardation in chapter 3 may be beneficial. Prioritize the educational and social objectives for the time spent in the general education class. Once the goals are prioritized, you will be in a better position to design and implement any necessary adaptations.

Primary adaptations for students with severe and multiple disabilities may involve devising procedures for communication systems, handling instructional materials, allowing additional time to complete activities, and devising activities that appear instructionally relevant and meaningful for students.

Work closely with the special education teacher to develop an appropriate and effective manner of interacting with students with severe disabilities. Because many students with severe disabilities have limited language skills, make certain that all your communications are clear and understandable.

In some cases, students with severe disabilities may exhibit inappropriate behavior in the classroom. These problem behaviors may be addressed by assessment of the classroom curriculum and environment and communication training, as described in the following Research Highlight.

Students with severe disabilities may be learning different things than other students in the classroom, and therefore will have different learning objectives. Make certain that you are familiar with all the IEP objectives for students with severe (or any other) disabilities. All objectives should be stated in a way that progress can be directly observed and recorded. For example, if one of a student's objectives involves interacting more positively with other students, be certain you know exactly what is meant by positive interaction (e.g., more direct eye contact, friendly expression, positive statements or gestures), and monitor progress on this objective.

Autism

Prevalence, Definitions, and Characteristics

Autism is a disorder characterized by severe impairments of social, emotional, and intellectual functioning (Kanner, 1943). Children with autism are often described as having great difficulty communicating and interacting with and responding to other people. Many individuals with autism also exhibit stereotypic behavior such as self-stimulating behaviors; bizarre speech patterns such as repeating words over and over again; and disruptive behavior, sometimes including self-injury (Lovaas

Improving Problem Behavior at School

Umbreit and Blair (1996) described an intervention to improve the behavior of an 11-year-old boy, Reggie, who had moderate to severe retardation, seizures, and behavior disorders. Reggie had been in a full-inclusion program the previous year, but his behaviors were such a problem that school officials were considering removing him from the program. Reggie's behaviors included emitting a loud, high-pitch "Eee!", hitting other people and objects, lying on the floor, biting, and spitting.

This problem behavior occurred in all the settings Reggie attended, including the regular classroom, the gym, the cafeteria, the playground, the library, and the self-contained inclusion support room. Through observations, hypothesis development, and hypothesis testing, it was determined that Reggie's behavior was most appropriate when he was engaging in *preferred activities* (such as those involving movement or computers) rather than nonpreferred activities (such as looking at books or writing letters); when he *chose his activities* (from among three preferred or three nonpreferred activities); and when he received frequent (every 30 seconds) rather than infrequent (every 2–3 minutes) *social attention* from the teacher. In addition, interviews revealed that every respondent believed Reggie's limited skills were related to his problem behavior.

An intervention was planned for Reggie based on the assessments. Reggie was taught needed skills as much as possible through preferred activities he had chosen. When nonpreferred activities were necessary, Reggie was allowed to choose which of the nonpreferred activities he would do. In both types of activities, frequent teacher attention was given whenever Reggie behaved appropriately. Finally, additional communication training with language cards was undertaken so that Reggie could communicate more effectively (e.g., ask for help rather than behave inappropriately).

According to the authors,

> The intervention virtually eliminated all problem behavior and resulted in appropriate behavior nearly all of the time. In addition, the effect occurred immediately, lasted for at least several months, and generalized to three non-targeted (generalization) problem behaviors (Umbreit & Blair, 1996, p. 151).

Additionally, the intervention received high ratings from the staff, in contrast to previously employed methods, including time-out, prompting, and redirection.

For additional information on problem behavior see chapter 7; Kerr and Nelson (2002).

Questions for Reflection

1. Why do you think this intervention was so successful?
2. Even though the present investigation employed only a single student as a participant, how could the results be used to support inclusive education for all students?
3. What modifications could be made in cases in which teachers or other staff were not always available to give such frequent attention?
4. What similarities can you identify between Reggie's case and those of students with higher-incidence disabilities?

Companion Website

To answer these questions online, go to the Research Highlights feature in chapter 4 of the Companion Website.

& Newsom, 1976; Ritvo & Freeman, 1978). Children with autism are typically identified before the age of 3. Frequently, parents are the first ones to become concerned when their infants do not respond positively to being touched and held closely, and when language does not develop along the common developmental milestones.

Individuals with autism make up approximately .09% of the school-age population, or 1% of the students served under IDEA (U.S. Department of Education, 2001). The prevalence of autism appears to be increasing in recent years, although the reasons for this are not completely clear (Simpson & Zionts, 2000). Diagnostic categories of autism include autism, pervasive developmental disorder, Asperger's syndrome, Rett's disorder, and childhood disintegrative disorder (American Psychiatric Association, *Diagnostic and Statistical Manual—Fourth Edition,* 1994). The current diagnoses indicate that individuals with autism may function along a continuum of severe to mild disabilities, and that educational accommodations vary according to an individual's functioning level. Individuals with severe autism may have limited to no expressive and receptive language, while individuals with milder forms of autism may have developed more sophisticated communication as in the case of those with Asperger's syndrome. Although symptoms and severity level vary among individuals with autism, communication and social competence are typically the two greatest challenges. Some individuals—perhaps as many as 75% of those with autism—also have mental retardation (McDougle, 1998). Individuals with Asperger's syndrome, however, are often very intelligent.

Temple Grandin (Grandin, 1995; Grandin & Scariano, 1986) has written extensively about her autism. She has a Ph.D. in animal science and is also an expert in the design and construction of livestock handling facilities. Grandin describes her life growing up as a child with autism and recounts the difficulties she encountered getting along in life. Some have classified her autism as Asperger's syndrome. These types of autistic individuals may excel intellectually and have high language abilities; however, they also possess the characteristics that make interacting with individuals and some forms of sensory information extremely difficult. Grandin describes autism as follows: "A defect in the systems which process incoming sensory information causes the child to over-react to some stimuli and under-react to others. The autistic child often withdraws from her environment and the people in it to block out an onslaught of incoming stimulation" (Grandin & Scariano, 1986, p. 13). In describing her past she states, "I was a 'bizarre kid.' I didn't even talk until I was three and a half years old. Until that time, screaming, peeping, humming were my means of communication" (Grandin & Scariano, 1986, p. 12).

Other cases of autism include individuals who have outstanding abilities at unusual tasks, in spite of their other difficulties. In the past, some have referred to this group of individuals as "savants," meaning a learned person in some area. For example, an Italian boy with autism, who functioned at low academic and social levels, had extraordinary abilities when it came to figuring out future dates. For example, given the question, "Tell me what day of the week July 4, 2007, will be?" the boy could provide a correct response almost instantly. Oliver Sacks (1993–1994) also described several individuals with autism who had outstanding abilities in unique areas, including an accomplished artist, a family of gifted people with autism, as well as Temple Grandin. Such individuals are the exception rather than the rule, however; it is more common to encounter individuals with autism who do not possess such unique abilities.

Classroom Adaptations for Students with Autism

Classroom adaptations for individuals with autism can be classified into adaptations for those with severe autism and for those with mild autism. Individuals with severe autism may function similarly to those individuals with severe disabilities, and it is recommended that you try the suggested adaptations for individuals with severe disabilities. Conversely, individuals with milder forms of autism may be included more frequently into general education classes, and you may wish to consider using modifications recommended for students with mild disabilities, including learning disabilities and behavior disorders. In both cases, work closely with special education teachers and parents. This collaboration ensures that IEP goals and objectives are being addressed, and that you have assistance in interacting with students. The following adaptations are also helpful for including students with autism in general education classes.

Establish Effective Communication

Discuss optimal communication patterns and design communication strategies with special education teachers, parents, and peers. Strategies might include sign language or alternative and augmentative communication (AAC) methods. For example, in the following scenario, Mark is a young

It has been estimated that 50% of individuals with autism never develop language (McDougle, 1998).

For more information on autism go to the Web Links module in chapter 4 of the Companion Website.

boy with autism who does not have language, but does communicate with an AAC procedure referred to as the Picture Exchange Communication System (PECS) (Bondy, 1996). PECS teaches students to use pictures and symbols to initiate and respond to communication from others (Schwartz, Billingsley, & McBride, 1998).

CLASSROOM SCENARIO

Mark

Mark, a young boy with autism, is sitting at the art center with several of his classmates. He is using PECS to request the materials he needs. His favorite painting utensil is Dot Art paints. He looks around and sees that Mary, who is typically developing and new to the class, has the Dot Art by her. He builds the sentence, "I want Dot Art paint," with his symbols and extends his sentence strip to her.

Ben, who has been in Mark's class for the past year, sees that Mark is trying to communicate with Mary, but Mary is intent on her painting and does not notice. Ben turns to Mary and says, "Mary, Mark is talking to you. Take the sentence from him and see what he wants." Mary looks up and reaches for Mark's sentence strip, looks at the picture, and gives Mark what he requested. Ben then says to Mary, "If you want it back you can just ask Mark for it. We have to share in our class."[1]

For a discussion of communication of individuals with autism, see Ogletree (1998).

Figure 4.4 presents examples of commonly used symbols in different communication systems.

Facilitated Communication. Some programs use a procedure called "facilitated communication," a controversial technique that has been largely discredited by research, but still can be found in some schools. Facilitated communication relies on the use of a facilitator, who places a guiding hand on the wrist or arm of the individual with autism, and then assists the individual with autism type out responses on a "communicator" or a small technological device. The device is usually a Cannon communicator, and contains a small keyboard that produces a strip of the typed letters, words, and sentences. Initially, some thought that individuals with autism were able to read and type large amounts of information with the assistance of their facilitators. Unfortunately, research indicates that the "thinking" behind the reading and typing generally comes from the facilitators, not the individuals with autism (Braman, Brady, Linehan, & Williams, 1995; Myles, Simpson, & Smith, 1996; Rimland, 1992a, 1992b, 1993a; Simpson & Myles, 1995, 1998; Simpson & Zionts, 2000; for another point of view, see Biklen, 1990). Given the research evidence to date, if facilitated communication is used, evidence should be collected on each individual child to validate that the communication is authentic and generated by the student.

Develop Social Competence

Unless you make a point to design behavior plans with the student's IEP team and implement these plans systematically, you may find it easy to become overwhelmed by the student's challenging behaviors (e.g., aggression, self-injury, hyperactivity, compulsive behaviors, self-stimulatory behaviors, or running away) (Ruble & Dalrymple, 1996). Teach students to wait their turn, share materials, and know when they need to be quiet and when they can talk. Teach them to use socially appropriate behaviors throughout the school day to help promote generalization of appropriate social behavior. Reward successive approximations, and work toward having students become more independent. Develop behavior management plans based on an analysis of student preferences and classroom dynamics, such as that devised for Reggie in the Research Highlight.

Additional information on social competence can be found in chapter 7.

---

1 *Note:* From "Including Children with Autism in Preschools: Strategies That Work," by I. S. Schwartz, F. F. Billingsley, and B. M. McBride, 1998, *Young Exceptional Children, 1*(2), pp. 19–26. Reprinted by permission.

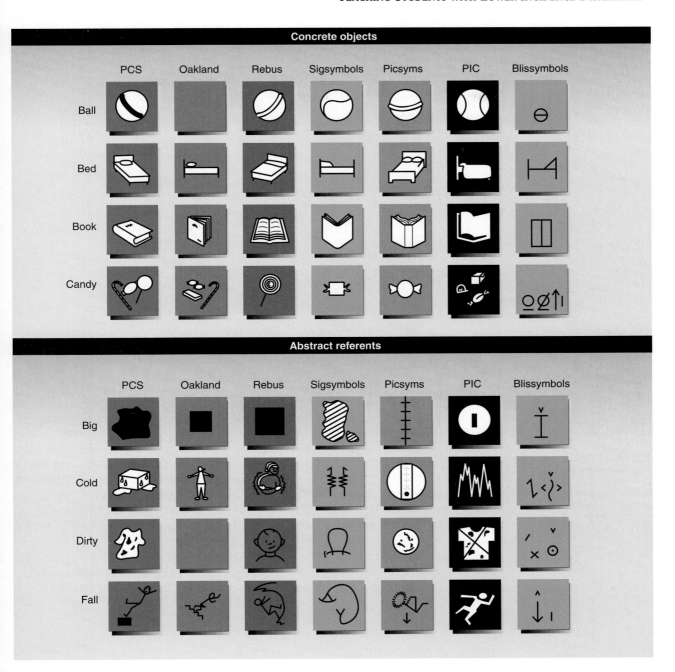

Figure 4.4
Sample Communication Board Symbols
Note: Reprinted with permission from "Non-speech Modes and Systems," by G. C. Vanderheiden and L. L. Lloyd, 1986, in S. W. Blackstone (Ed.), *Augmentative Communication* (pp. 48–161), Rockville, MD: American Speech–Language Hearing Association.

Create a learning environment in which the student with autism feels comfortable, including a predictable schedule of daily activities, a pattern of events, and class routines. Use pictures to list the sequence of activities if the student is a nonreader, and allow the student to order the sequence if possible. If you change the class routine, prepare the student ahead of time to avoid undue stress.

One promising technique for improving social behavior is the use of social stories (Gray & Garand, 1993). A social story is written for an individual student, as a small book, to address a specific behavior, such as behavior in the cafeteria, or waiting one's turn. Social stories use simple sentences and pictures to demonstrate the desired social behavior and the feelings and reactions of

Students with autism often withdraw from any kind of physical contact with others.

More information on social stories is provided in chapter 7.

Peers can alert you to sudden behavioral changes in students with autism.

others, such as, "When I return my tray after I have finished eating, my teacher is happy." Although more research is needed, results to date suggest that use of social stories is a promising technique for improving social behavior (Graetz, 2003).

Enlist the help of peers to reinforce socially appropriate behavior. Group students with autism with higher functioning students. Students with autism can be included successfully in cooperative learning groups when paired with partners who have been taught to communicate effectively with them in reading and science (Kamps, Leonard, Potucek, & Garrison-Harrell, 1995).

Watch for signs that the student is becoming stressed. Students with autism may react aggressively or withdraw completely under novel or stressful situations. Try to predict when the class demands might become stressful and attempt to eliminate that source of stress.

Finally, establish and maintain effective communication with all individuals who are in contact with students with autism. Communicate regularly with parents. Send home weekly or daily notes, short audiotaped messages, or a journal that travels back and forth from you to parents.

Summary

- Lower-incidence disabilities occur less frequently in the general population than other disability areas. Lower-incidence disabilities include visual impairments, hearing impairments, physical disabilities, other health impairments, severe and multiple disabilities, and autism.
- Individuals with visual impairments represent the smallest category of exceptionality. Students may have very low vision to no vision. These students may have difficulty learning unless adaptations are made such as arranging the physical environment for easy accessibility, enhancing printed materials, using Braille and oral formats, and using concrete tactile and three-dimensional examples.
- Students with hearing impairments have mild to severe hearing losses. Individuals with mild to

moderate hearing impairments usually wear hearing aids, while individuals who are deaf use sign language, total communication, or some aural techniques for communication. Students may require specific language, communication, and social skills instruction.

- Students with physical disabilities may exhibit difficulties using their arms, legs, or both arms and legs. Some of these students may exhibit problems with communication. Specific adaptations for increasing mobility, assisting with fine motor control, and improving communication skills help students become more independent and successful.
- Students with other health impairments may have serious medical needs that require special attention and that restrict their learning in school. Coordination with medical professionals while monitoring health and educational needs helps these students with school success.

- Some students with severe disabilities have severe mental retardation and exhibit difficulties in cognition, adaptive behavior, academic, social, self-help, problem-solving, attention, and memory areas.
- Students with autism may have mild to severe difficulties, but usually have serious difficulties with social behavior. Students with more severe autism have difficulties with language, communication, cognitive, attention, memory, and basic skills.
- Arrange special classroom procedures for emergency situations for classrooms containing individuals with lower-incidence disabilities. These individuals may miss the usual safety alert systems, tire more easily, or have special medical or mobility needs that require special preparation.
- A variety of adaptations in the physical environment, instructional materials, instructional procedures, and evaluation procedures make the general education classroom a positive learning experience for students with lower-incidence disabilities.

Council for Exceptional Children

Teaching Students with Lower-Incidence Disabilities

Information in this chapter links most directly to:

Standard 2—Development and Characteristics of Learners, particularly:

Knowledge:
- Educational implications of characteristics of various exceptionalities.
- Similarities and differences among individuals with exceptional learning needs.
- Effects of various medications on individuals with exceptional learning needs.

Standard 3—Individual Learning Differences, particularly:

Knowledge:
- Effects an exceptional condition(s) can have on an individual's life.
- Impact of learners' academic and social abilities, attitudes, interests, and values on instruction and career development.

Standard 4—Instructional Strategies, particularly:

Skills:
- Use strategies to facilitate integration into various settings.
- Select, adapt, and use instructional strategies and materials according to characteristics of the individual with exceptional learning needs.

Inclusion Checklist
Lower-Incidence Disabilities

If a student with lower-incidence disabilities is having difficulties in your classroom, have you tried the following?

Students with Visual Impairments

- ❏ Consider student characteristics
- ❏ General classroom adaptations for students with visual impairments
- ❏ Physical environment adaptations
- ❏ Instructional materials adaptations
- ❏ Instructional procedures adaptations, including modifications for oral presentations

Students with Hearing Impairments

- ❏ Consider student characteristics
- ❏ General classroom adaptations for students with hearing impairments
- ❏ Physical environment adaptations
- ❏ Instructional materials adaptations
- ❏ Instructional procedures adaptations
- ❏ Evaluation adaptations

Students with Physical Disabilities and Other Health Impairments

- ❏ Consider characteristics of students with physical disabilities and other health impairments
- ❏ General classroom adaptations for students with physical and other health impairments

- ❏ Medical guidelines
- ❏ Plan for emergencies
- ❏ Use moving and positioning strategies when needed
- ❏ Prepare the class
- ❏ Prepare the physical environment
- ❏ Adapt instructional procedures and materials
- ❏ Adapt evaluation

Students with Severe and Multiple Disabilities

- ❏ Consider student characteristics
- ❏ Educational placement considerations
- ❏ General classroom adaptations for students with severe and multiple disabilities
- ❏ Working with paraprofessionals
- ❏ Instructional delivery system adaptations
- ❏ Medical and special health care needs
- ❏ Physical environment adaptations
- ❏ Instructional materials and procedures adaptations

Students with Autism

- ❏ Consider the characteristics of the student with autism
- ❏ General classroom adaptations for students with autism
- ❏ Develop communication skills
- ❏ Develop social competence

Chapter 5

Zachary Briley, 9
Tallahassee, FL
"Boats at Sea"

Teaching Students with Other Special Learning Needs

Objectives

After studying this chapter, you should be able to:

- Describe and discuss the prevalence and characteristics of students with attention deficit disorder (ADD) and attention deficit hyperactivity disorder (ADHD).
- Describe and discuss the prevalence and characteristics for students who are gifted, creative, or talented.
- Describe and discuss the prevalence and characteristics of students from culturally and linguistically diverse backgrounds.
- Describe and discuss the prevalence and characteristics of students at risk for school failure.
- List, describe, and be able to recommend adaptations and modifications to promote inclusion of students with other diverse learning needs.
- Describe the prevalence, characteristics, causes, issues in identification, and general classroom adaptations for students with ADD and ADHD.
- Analyze the prevalence, characteristics, issues in identification, and general classroom adaptations for students who are gifted, creative, and talented.
- Discuss the prevalence, characteristics, issues in identification, and general classroom adaptations for students from culturally and linguistically diverse backgrounds.
- Describe the prevalence, characteristics, issues in identification, and general classroom adaptations for at risk students.

Not all individuals with diverse or special learning needs are classified as disabled. Students with other special learning needs represent a wide range of abilities and include (a) students from different cultural and linguistic backgrounds, (b) students with attention deficits, (c) students who are gifted and talented, and (d) students who may be considered at risk for school failure because of poverty, abuse or neglect, substance abuse, truancy, pregnancy, homelessness, or depression. These students belong to an increasing population in schools and are served in general education classes. Rather than being served under IDEA, some individuals with diverse learning needs are served under Section 504 of the Rehabilitation Act.

Students Served Under Section 504

Students with attention deficit disorder (ADD) or attention deficit hyperactivity disorder (ADHD), who do not meet eligibility requirements under the Other Health Impaired category, or who do not have a coexisting disability that qualifies them for services under IDEA, may still qualify under Section 504 of the Vocational Rehabilitation Act of 1973. Students with other health impairments, including asthma, AIDS, tuberculosis, diabetes, drug or alcohol addiction, or behavioral problems, might not qualify for services under IDEA, but may qualify under Section 504.

Definitions, Prevalence, and Characteristics of Attention Deficit Hyperactivity Disorder

Spitzer, Gibbon, Skodol, Williams, and First (1994) provided some excellent case studies and analyses of students with ADHD.

Robert has an attention deficit hyperactivity disorder and both his family and teacher could benefit from suggestions as to how to best work with him. Robert's disruptive behaviors and his inability to sustain attention will put Robert at risk for failing in school (Maag & Reid, 1994). Attention deficit hyperactivity disorder (ADHD) refers to a "persistent pattern of inattention and/or hyperactivity-impulsivity that is more frequent and severe than is typically observed in individuals at a comparable level of development" (American Psychiatric Association, 1994, p. 78). Observations made in the classroom will identify these students as those who often say "Huh, what?" immediately following directions; often appear to be daydreaming; act before they think; blurt out answers; interrupt; and constantly fidget, wiggle, and move around. Table 5.1 compares the sharp contrast between commonly noted behaviors on elementary school report cards with students with ADHD.

CLASSROOM SCENARIO

Robert Black

Robert Black had so much energy that he drove everyone around him crazy including his parents; his teacher, Ms. Moore; and his classmates. When he arrived at school everything around him appeared to get caught in a whirlwind of activity: Papers flew to the floor, books were dropped, toys were broken, classmates were annoyed, and teachers threw their hands up in dismay. Robert was a nice 8-year-old boy, but he could not focus on one thing at a time. He seemed mesmerized by everything, moving from activity to activity with limitless energy. When someone spoke, he would interrupt and start talking about something that popped into his head. If he saw something that interested him, he would immediately take it in his hands. His feet, hands, and eyes seemed to be moving constantly. He seemed unable to sit still. Ms. Moore was frustrated and unsure of how to handle Robert in the class, so she called Mr. and Mrs. Black and asked them to come in for a conference. What became immediately evident at the parent conference was that Mr. and Mrs. Black were experiencing similar problems and frustrations at home with Robert—and had been since he was 2 years of age.

See chapter 1 for more details pertaining to legislation protecting individuals with disabilities and chapter 2 for procedures for qualifying for services under Section 504.

From 1.35 to 2.25 million children—3% to 5% of all school-age children—may have attention deficit hyperactivity disorder (or ADHD) [American Psychiatric Association (APA), 1994; Barkley, 1998; Council for Exceptional Children (CEC), 1992]. Most students with ADHD are served full time in general education classrooms, with only about half of them qualifying for special education services under IDEA. In other words, nearly half of the ADHD school-age population is not receiving any special education services (CEC, 1992). More important, however, this group of individuals with ADHD is considered at risk for school failure due to the disorder.

The *Diagnostic and Statistical Manual–IV* (DSM–IV) of the American Psychiatric Association (APA, 1994) describes criteria for classification as ADHD. The symptomatic behaviors must be maladaptive and must be present for a minimum of 6 months to warrant a classification as either inattentive ADHD or hyperactivity-impulsivity ADHD. Some symptoms should have been present before 7 years of age. Furthermore, a child must display a minimum number of identifying charac-

Table 5.1
Elementary School Report Cards and Commonly Observed Statements Describing Students with ADHD

	Typical Behaviors on Report Cards	Observed Statements Describing ADHD Students
Compliance	• Follows directions • Obeys rules	• Frequently ignores directions • Talks continuously
Self-Control	• Waits turn • Tolerates frustration	• Impatient • Gives up easily
Social Development	• Polite, courteous • Keeps hands to self	• Often interrupts • Touches everything
Attention	• Stays on task • Makes efficient use of time	• Rarely finishes work • Frequently fidgeting

Note: Adapted from *Rethinking attention deficit disorders* (p. 126), by M. Cherkes-Julkowski, S. Sharp, and J. Stolzenberg, 1997, Cambridge, MA: Brookline Books. Copyright 1997 by Brookline Books. Adapted with permission.

teristics before ADHD is diagnosed. For example, students must meet six of nine characteristics under Inattention, or six of nine characteristics under Hyperactivity/Impulsivity. Figure 5.1 presents these criteria. There also must be evidence of impairment in social, occupational, or academic functioning, and some impairment from the symptoms must be present in at least two settings.

Any inattentiveness, impulsivity, and hyperactivity must be observed across settings (APA, 1994). Or, as in the case of Robert, the teacher and parents must observe similar behavior patterns at school and at home. Although some symptoms change over time, ADHD is now considered a lifelong disorder (APA, 1994). Males outnumber females about 3 to 1 in the disorder (Barkley, 1998; Bender, 1997).

Students with ADHD are thought to be more likely to have a learning disability than other children. In a sample of students with ADHD, Barkley (1990) identified 21% with disabilities in reading, 26% in spelling, and 28% in math. In a sample of normally functioning students, the proportions were 0%, 2.9%, and 2.9%, respectively (see also Barkley, 1998).

Students with ADHD can demonstrate substantial fluctuations among settings, time, and caregivers. Differences between students with ADHD and other students may be most evident in academic classes such as reading and math, and less evident in nonacademic periods such as lunch and physical education. Some research has suggested that behavior is substantially better in the mornings than in the afternoons (Barkley, 1998).

Causes of ADHD

Precise causes of ADHD are unknown; however, it is thought that many factors contribute to it (Riccio, Hynd, & Cohen, 1997). These factors include genetic, nongenetic, psychosocial, and neurobiological bases. Genetic evidence is based on research with families who have ADHD. Some researchers estimate that as many as 32% of children with ADHD have parents or siblings with ADHD (Biederman et al., 1992), and concordance of ADHD has been seen to be much higher in identical (monozygotic) twins than in fraternal (dizygotic) twins, suggesting a genetic component (Barkley, 1998). Nongenetic factors include prenatal and perinatal factors, food additives and sugar, allergies, and thyroid disorders (Riccio, Hynd, & Cohen, 1997). Although both the food additives (Feingold, 1975) and sugar (Smith, 1975) hypotheses have received a great deal of publicity in the popular media, research has not substantiated these as plausible causes of ADHD (Barkley, 2000; Connors, 1980; Wolraich, Milich, Stumbo, & Schultz, 1985). Barkley (2000) also lists hormomes, motion sickness, yeast, bad parenting, or too much television as factors that have been claimed to cause ADHD, but are lacking in research support. Other research has investigated the psychosocial and neurological correlates associated with ADHD, with evidence growing in support of neurological indicators (Riccio, Hynd, & Cohen, 1997). To date, however, as with many disorders, no definitive single etiological factor has been uncovered. At present, it seems that ADHD appears to be

Inattention:

1. Often fails to pay attention to details or makes careless mistakes in schoolwork, work, or other activities.
2. Often has difficulty sustaining attention in tasks or play activities.
3. Often does not seem to listen when spoken to directly.
4. Often does not follow through on instructions and fails to finish schoolwork, chores, or duties in the workplace (not due to oppositional behavior).
5. Often has difficulty organizing tasks and activities.
6. Often avoids, dislikes, or is reluctant to engage in tasks that require sustained mental effort.
7. Often loses things necessary for tasks and activities.
8. Is often easily distracted by extraneous stimuli.
9. Is often forgetful in daily activities.

Hyperactivity:

1. Often fidgets with hands or feet or squirms in seat.
2. Often leaves seat in classroom or in other situations in which remaining seated is expected.
3. Often runs about or climbs excessively in situations in which it is inappropriate.
4. Often has difficulty playing or engaging in leisure activities quietly.
5. Often on the go or acts as if driven by a motor.
6. Often talks excessively.

Impulsivity:

1. Often blurts out answers before questions have been completed.
2. Often has difficulty waiting turn.
3. Often interrupts or intrudes on others.

Figure 5.1
DSM—IV Diagnostic Criteria for ADHD

Note: From *Diagnostic and Statistical Manual of Mental Disorders, Fourth Edition, Tex Revision.* Copyright 1994 American Psychiatric Association. Reprinted by permission.

more influenced by neurological and genetic factors than by social or environmental factors (Barkley, 1998).

Issues in Identification and Assessment of ADHD

Many experts recommend a two-step approach to the assessment of ADHD. The first step is to determine whether ADHD exists and the second step is to determine whether the student's educational progress is adversely affected by it (CEC, 1992). During the first step the following information is collected:

1. Observations of the individual's behavior throughout the day
2. Medical history
3. Family information
4. School information
5. Social-emotional functioning
6. Cognitive-academic functioning (CEC, 1992; Schwanz & Kamphaus, 1997)

Rating scales of the individual's behavior are usually completed by the child's parents and teachers as part of this evaluation process.

See Schwanz and Kamphaus (1997) for a comprehensive listing of behavior rating scales.

A student who displays maladaptive, inattentive behavior for a period of six months or more may have attention deficit hyperactivity disorder (ADHD) and be served under Section 504 of the Vocational Rehabilitation Act of 1973.

If it is concluded that a child has ADHD, then it is necessary to collect information to determine the extent to which academic performance is hindered (CEC, 1992). Teachers can supply samples of class work, class grades in various subject areas, and additional observational and rating scale data. Much of this data may have been collected during the first part of the evaluation. To qualify for special education services in the "other health impairment" category of IDEA, it must be documented that the ADHD has an adverse effect on educational performance. To qualify for special services under Section 504 of the Vocational Rehabilitation Act, it must be documented that the ADHD substantially limits learning. If either of these requirements are met, an intervention plan is designed and implemented as either part of the IEP in compliance with IDEA or the accommodation plan for compliance with Section 504. In the event that students with ADHD do not meet criteria for either IDEA or Section 504, no special accommodations are designed as part of any legally mandated system. However, these students with ADHD also frequently benefit from some of the general classroom adaptations described in this text and listed in the following section.

General Classroom Adaptations for Students with ADHD

Many adaptations described for students with higher-incidence disabilities (chapter 3) are appropriate for students with ADHD, as are strategies described in chapter 10. The following *In the Classroom* feature provides some suggestions for accommodations that can add to classroom success. In addition, you might review several books that are devoted entirely to the topic of ADHD and contain teaching suggestions (Barkley, 2000; Bender, 1997; Jones, 1991; Markel & Greenbaum, 1996).

Behavioral Interventions

Behavioral interventions are strategies that use the principles of consistent behavior management (see chapter 7 for additional information). Students' behaviors are first analyzed with respect to **antecedent** and **consequent** events (that is, what happened before and after the undesirable behavior occurred). Strategies are then implemented systematically based on that analysis. For example, a teacher observed that every time a worksheet was distributed in class, Max got out of his seat to sharpen his pencils, got a drink of water, and bothered several classmates. After this, the teacher would reprimand Max, which would make Max feel sullen and resentful. After analyzing this behavior, it seemed likely that Max was reacting to the difficulty or interest level of

Companion Website

For additional information on ADHD, contact the Council for Exceptional Children, 1110 North Glebe Road, Suite 300, Arlington, Virginia 22201-5704; Children with Attention Deficit Disorders (CHADD), 499 NW 70th Avenue, Suite 308, Plantation, FL 33317; and Learning Disabilities Association of America (LDA), 4156 Library Road, Pittsburgh, PA 15234. For a listing of organization Websites, go to the Web Links module in chapter 5 of the Companion Website.

In the Classroom ...a feature for teachers

Accommodation Suggestions for Students with ADHD

For Beginning Activities
Give small amounts of work
Provide signals to begin
Use timers and encourage self-monitoring
Use verbal and written directions
Provide additional structure (e.g., large-lined paper)
Highlight directions using larger fonts or colors

For Keeping on Task
Increase frequency of positive reinforcement
Use peer assistants
Make tasks interesting
Break tasks into smaller "manageable" units
Allow breaks
Use hands-on activities

For Listening
Teach note taking and encourage use of notebook organizers
Use positive reinforcement
Allow doodling
Allow standing

For Excessive Activity
Use activity as rewards (errands, wash boards, move desks)
Allow standing during class
Encourage active participation
Reward sitting

For Impulsive Behavior
Provide acceptable alternatives
Encourage trying to continue with another part of the assignment before interrupting the teacher
Recommend note taking during lectures
Recommend writing down questions and answers before blurting out
Teach acceptable social behavior for conversations, for class behavior, and for interacting with peers
Reward listening and appropriate behaviors

For Working Independently
Ensure tasks match ability levels
Provide brief directions
Use brief tasks
Use checklists for self-monitoring
Use positive reinforcement

For Following Class Rules
Keep rules simple
Post and review class rules
Model and role-play following rules
Be consistent with enforcement of rules
Provide students with copies of rules

---

the task, and his own predisposition toward physical activity. The teacher decided to have Max sharpen his pencils and get a drink of water before class every day. In addition, the teacher would praise Max for remaining in his seat and leaving classmates alone after the worksheets were passed out. The teacher also monitored the content of the academic activities, to make sure they were of the appropriate difficulty level and held some interest for Max. She also provided opportunities for Max to leave his seat under teacher supervision, so he could engage in some physical movement when needed. Such strategies can be effective when they are designed to meet the specific needs of problem behaviors. More examples of effective behavioral strategies are discussed in detail in chapter 7.

Cognitive-Behavioral Interventions

Cognitive-behavioral interventions use the same principles of behavior management just described, but in addition, add a **self-instruction and self-monitoring** component to the intervention. For example, Max could be taught to keep daily records of (a) how often he remembered to sharpen his pencils and get a drink of water before class, and (b) whether he was able to stay in his seat once the worksheet was handed out. Specific rewards might even be paired with how well he monitored his own behavior. Other commonly used cognitive-behavioral interventions involve the use of self-monitoring for on-task and task completion. Strategies such as these have been particularly successful with students with ADHD. More specific details on implementing cognitive-behavioral strategies are provided in chapters 7 and 9.

Medications

Many students with ADHD take psychostimulant medications, such as Ritalin or Cylert, to help control their attention and hyperactivity. The number of children taking medications for ADHD has risen significantly in recent years. The table in the *In the Classroom* feature in chapter 4 describes the major types of medications prescribed for ADHD. If students are taking medications, teachers must keep thorough records of behavior to help monitor the effects of medications. Reviews of research on the effects of stimulant medication generally indicate positive benefits (Kavale, 1982), in that attention to task increases and hyperactivity decreases (Hallahan & Cottone, 1997). However, the practice of administering medications has remained controversial. Some educators and physicians argue that the side effects of medications can be harmful and that no students should be given medications to control their classroom behavior. Barkley (1998) suggested that some organizations overstated the dangers of medications in an attempt to influence public opinion. Other opponents contend that when students are taking medication they still need to be taught how to control their own behaviors (as in the cognitive-behavioral interventions described previously). However, teachers may not always undertake cognitive-behavioral instruction when students are medicated, perhaps because students appear under control.

Proponents contend that medication enables students to maximize their potential in school. Some parents have also reported that when their children began taking medication they were able for the first time to sit and read to their children. The following Research Highlight describes the findings from 115 studies evaluating the effects of medication on students with ADHD.

Combinations of Behavioral, Cognitive-Behavioral, and Medications

Most educators take a more pragmatic view toward interventions for students with ADHD and contend that a combination of approaches works best to help students maintain successful performance in school (Hallahan & Cottone, 1997; Montague, Fiore, Hocutt, McKinney, & Harris, 1996). For example, in Max's situation, the cognitive-behavioral strategy described earlier would be taught to Max even if medication were prescribed. The logic behind this strategy should be clear. Max, like other students with ADHD, needs to learn how to monitor his own behavior with and without the benefits of medication. In any case, students with ADHD need to learn how to control their behaviors, and educators, parents, and physicians need to monitor carefully all the effects of medications.

See chapter 4 for further information on medications and monitoring behaviors while under the effects of medications.

A meta-analysis combines the effects of studies on similar topics by converting the results of individual studies into a single number, called an effect size. An effect size of .25 to .30 is often considered educationally meaningful.

Gifted, Creative, and Talented

Definitions, Prevalence, and Characteristics of Gifted, Creative, and Talented

Individuals with special gifts and talents come from all cultural and ethnic backgrounds and may be extraordinary in intelligence, specialized academic areas, music, or the arts (Genshaft, Bireley, & Hollinger, 1995). Although gifted, creative, and talented individuals are not included in IDEA, these students have unique needs that require special attention and accommodations for them to succeed in school. Various definitions of *gifted, creative,* and *talented* exist in the literature, but there is little agreement on the best definition. Early definitions relied heavily on the use of IQ scores for identifying gifted individuals. The Gifted and Talented Act, passed in 1978 (PL 95-561, Title IX, sec. 902), included creative capabilities or high performance in the performing arts. In 1993, the U.S. Department of Education (1993) proposed a new definition:

> Children and youth with outstanding talent perform or show the potential for performing at remarkably high levels of accomplishment when compared with others their age, experience, or environment. These children and youth exhibit high performance capability in intellectual,

Research Highlight

The Effects of Stimulant Medication on ADHD

Crenshaw, Kavale, Forness, and Reeve (1999) synthesized the results of 115 studies published from 1985 through 1995 that examined the effects of stimulant medication for students with attention deficit hyperactivity disorder (ADHD). About 3,300 students with ADHD with an average age of 9.4 years and an average IQ of 99.2 participated in the studies included in the synthesis. The types of stimulant medications tested were methylphenidate (Ritalin) (103 studies), dextroamphetamine (Dexedrine) (10 studies), and pemoline (Cyclert) (2 studies). The average intervention length was 5.7 weeks.

The overall effect size for students receiving stimulant medication was .673, which indicates that drug intervention changed the average student with ADHD from the 50th to the 75th percentile. This large gain suggests that the average student with ADHD taking stimulant medication would be expected to be better off than 75% of students with ADHD not taking stimulant medication.

When behavior measures such as on-task and attention were analyzed, the effects of stimulant medication were slightly greater, yielding a .743 effect size. Unfortunately, fewer studies examined the effects of the medication on academic achievement. Effects from those 36 studies were somewhat lower, yielding an effect size of .399. However, even this effect translates into an 18th percentile rank gain on academic measures. The authors concluded that this synthesis provided not only a more optimistic outlook on the positive benefits of stimulant medication for students with ADHD, but also generated additional questions about the effects of stimulant medication. Such questions are "whether the positive findings for classroom-type measures translate into longer-term academic gains" and examining "the role of possible mitigating factors (e.g., family functioning, presence of other difficulties, and use of multimodal treatments) that might increase or decrease the chances of longer positive gains" (Crenshaw et al., 1999, p. 160). In addition, the issue of monitoring students closely for any potential side effects should be continually addressed.

For additional information on medications for ADHD, see Barkley, 2000.

Questions for Reflection

1. Why do you think the effects for on-task and attention were higher than those for academic achievement?
2. Why do you think academic achievement was not studied as much as behavioral measures?
3. What considerations other than on-task behavior, attention, and achievement are important to take into account?
4. How do the results of this investigation fit within the debate about prescribing stimulant medication?

Companion Website

To answer these questions online, go to the Research Highlights feature in chapter 5 of the Companion Website.

creative, and/or artistic areas, possess an unusual leadership capacity, or excel in specific academic fields. They require services or activities not ordinarily provided in the schools. Outstanding talents are present in children and youth from all cultural groups, across all economic strata, and in all areas of human endeavor. (U.S. Department of Education, 1993, p. 3)

These federal definitions highlight the areas of giftedness, talent, and creativity, and are more representative of recent trends in gifted education (Genshaft, Bireley, & Hollinger, 1995). Other conceptualizations of giftedness continue to broaden the single intelligence notion (Maker, 1993). The following are examples of broadened definitions for gifted, creative, and talented youth: (a) three-trait definition, including above-average ability, task commitment, and creativity (Renzulli, 1978); (b) especially high aptitude, potential, or ability (Feldhusen, 1992; Feldhusen & Moon, 1995); (c) synthetic, analytic, and practical intelligence (Sternberg, 1991); and (d) multiple intelligences (Gardner & Hatch, 1989). All proposed models include more than a single intelligence quotient as criteria, most include talents as critical components, and many recommend advice on counseling gifted and talented youth (Van Tassel-Baska, 1990).

In one of the most complex conceptualizations of giftedness, Howard Gardner (Gardner, 1983, 1999; Gardner & Hatch, 1989) proposed that eight specific intelligences exist, which have been observed across cultures and societies. These areas include musical, bodily kinesthetic, logical-mathematical, linguistic, interpersonal, intrapersonal, naturalist, and spatial. Each area is associated with different characteristics and different early indicators. Although this conceptualization differs from the federal definitions, it nonetheless acknowledges that outstanding ability can be evidenced in a variety of domains, and that it is prudent to avoid being overly narrow in conceptualizing giftedness.

Given the variety of definitions, it is not surprising that little consensus exists on the actual number of gifted and talented youth. Many reports indicate that 3% to 5% of the population is gifted and talented (Hallahan & Kauffman, 2003); others believe the figures are much higher. For example, Renzulli (1982) reported that 15% to 25% of the population have the potential to be gifted and talented. Great variability also exists in how individual states classify and implement programs for gifted and talented youth, which results in some states having high prevalence rates and others having very low prevalence rates in comparison.

Students who are gifted and talented might be easily identified from the products they create or might remain unidentified because they are underachieving.

Agreement usually converges on the notion that several major types of gifted and talented youth exist, including those with intellectual gifts, those with creative talents, and those with hidden gifts and talents. Because great variability exists within the gifted and talented group, not all individuals exhibit all characteristics described.

Intellectually Gifted

Intellectually gifted students are those who have scored very high on standardized tests and usually excel in school. They are frequently very highly skilled verbally and have outstanding memories and literacy abilities—especially in reading and writing—compared with their typical age peers. They also tend to have outstanding critical-thinking and problem-solving abilities and insatiable curiosities (Bireley, 1995). Intellectually gifted youth acquire, retain, and manipulate large amounts of information and appear to learn in intuitive leaps (Gallagher & Gallagher, 1994; Maker, 1993; Silverman, 1995).

Creative and Talented

The definitions of *creative* and *talented* are widely varied, but consensus usually converges on the identification of individuals with exceptional talents in particular areas (Davis, 1995). Creatively gifted and talented youth often excel in the visual or performing arts. These students typically show outstanding abilities at young ages in particular areas. Davis (1995) listed the following 12 categories as representative of creative individuals: original, independent, risk taking, aware of creativeness, energetic, curious, has a sense of humor, attracted to complexity, artistic, open-minded, needs time alone, and intuitive. Several major tests of creative thinking exist, and based on an analysis of those tests, Davis generated a listing of creative abilities including analogical thinking and the ability to define problems and predict outcomes.

Hidden Gifted, Creative, and Talented

Many students who are gifted and talented remain unidentified or hidden. This may be due to a number of factors. First, they might be underachievers and consequently their scores fall below the cutoff scores for classifying gifted students. Second, intelligence tests and standardized tests may be biased against some students due to cultural or linguistic diversity (Davis & Rimm, 1989; Patton, 1997; Plummer, 1995). Third, girls who may be gifted and talented are often underidentified (Hollinger, 1995). It is speculated this may be because of underachievement in science and math, as well as declining achievement in adolescent years, although precise reasons are unknown. Finally, some students may not be identified due to existing disabilities in other areas (learning or physical disabilities). Special attention during classification and screening efforts at identifying gifted and talented youth can help eliminate underidentification of these individuals. Gregory, Starnes, and Blaylock (1988), and Patton (1997) provide some specific suggestions for finding and nurturing potential giftedness among Hispanic and African American students. Their suggestions include the following:

- Develop a "belief system" in school that culturally and linguistically diverse students can be and are gifted and talented.
- Develop an identification process that reflects appreciation of the culture, language, values, and world views of culturally and linguistically diverse students and their families.
- Be alert and responsive to differences within culturally and linguistically diverse groups (e.g., Asian Americans).
- Employ a multidimensional assessment process that includes qualitative as well as quantitative measures.
- Develop programs to educate the public in ways giftedness may be manifested (and sometimes concealed) in different cultures. Collaborate with people knowledgeable in the particular culture for assistance and support.
- Ensure that insights gained in the identification and assessment process are incorporated into the instructional program.

Issues in Identification and Assessment of Gifted, Creative, and Talented

CLASSROOM SCENARIO

Lucy

Lucy, a seventh grader, lived on a reservation 30 miles outside a large metropolitan area and attended a school on the reservation. The school was composed almost entirely of other Native American children from the same tribe as Lucy. Lucy's academic achievement as measured by her grades in school and her performance on standardized achievement tests was below her grade level. She was polite and quiet during class discussions, had some friends, and seemed to get along well in school.

Lucy lived with her grandmother, Mrs. Springwater, who seemed to think Lucy had more potential than officials from Lucy's school believed. During the last parent conference, Lucy's grandmother told the science teacher, Ms. Chee, that she thought Lucy was not working up to her potential. Upon reflection, Ms. Chee agreed. She noted that although Lucy never participated much during class discussions, whenever she called on her specifically she knew the answers or came up with thought-provoking questions. Ms. Chee asked Mrs. Springwater to suggest ways she could help Lucy meet her potential and assured Lucy's grandmother that she would pursue this as well.

Ms. Chee contacted her school guidance counselors and found that a local university offered testing to determine whether children qualified for extra assistance programs, including programs for the academically precocious, or gifted and talented. Lucy went for testing and when the results were returned Mrs. Springwater's intuitions were confirmed—Lucy's intelligence testing score was 140, or within the top 1st to 2nd percentile for children her age! Lucy was immediately enrolled in one of the after-school university programs during the school year and a summer program to help her maximize her potential. Lucy's grandmother had helped the teacher recognize that Lucy's abilities were currently untapped.

Several approaches exist for identifying gifted and talented children and youth. Common approaches include nomination methods, standardized test scores, talent pool searches, and a multiple measures–multiple criteria approach. Nomination approaches consist of distributing nomination forms to teachers and parents. Schools often implement an approach by which parents, teachers, peers, and students are provided nomination forms in which they detail reasons for nominating a student (or self) for the gifted and talented program. Clark (2001) detailed a series of questions that can be used as guidelines for identifying students with gifts or talents. Questions include, "Does the student show an unusual ability in some area? Have a vivid imagination? Seem to pick up skills in the arts with no instruction? Invent new techniques?" The *In the Classroom* feature on page 137 presents a sample nomination form for a gifted program.

Standardized test score approaches include the use of intelligence and achievement test scores. These tests may be individually or group administered. Cutoff scores to qualify students as gifted and talented are usually designated to identify which students score in the top 8% (Renzulli & Reiss, 1991). This approach is usually combined with some other approach, in that standardized test scores alone are seldom the only criteria considered.

Universities around the country conduct talent pool searches to identify gifted and talented youth (Renzulli & Reiss, 1991). For example, Duke University advertises that students in the junior high school can register to take the Scholastic Aptitude Tests (SATs) early. Performance on the SATs is used to determine whether individuals qualify for various gifted and talented programs around the country. (SATs are typically taken in the junior year of high school.) Many universities run programs during the summers and academic years for students with gifts or talents, or who are academically precocious.

Finally, a multiple measures–multiple criteria approach is implemented in many schools (Davis & Rimm, 1989). This approach combines many of the pieces of evidence collected in the approaches previously discussed, but may also include detailed family histories, student work samples and inventories of interests, and discussion of all evidence by a gifted-and-talented screening committee. Feldhusen (1992) has recommended attempting to identify as many students as possible who are precocious and have potential, which would necessarily abandon most of the methods relying on a single method or approach.

General Classroom Accommodations for Students Who Are Gifted, Creative, and Talented

Several educational approaches exist for programming curriculum and classes for gifted and talented youth. These include acceleration and enrichment, and are provided in regular classes, resource classes, self-contained classes, university classes, and through mentoring programs (Genshaft, Bireley, & Hollinger, 1995). Many of these program recommendations are challenging for teachers to implement within the general education class setting, but effective teaching practices can be used to help address important learning objectives. Careful pretesting identifies skills and information that gifted students have and can be used to place them in a more ability-appropriate curriculum.

Acceleration

Acceleration refers to moving students through the curriculum at a faster pace than general education students (Gallagher & Gallagher, 1994). Acceleration can mean admitting a child to school early, skipping grades, providing level-appropriate curriculum, or testing out of classes. Advancing students places them in grades that match their achievement levels. For example, a fourth-grader who is working at a sixth-grade level academically might be advanced to the sixth-grade class. Another example is maintaining students in the age-appropriate class, but providing them with the appropriate-level curriculum (sixth-grade level, in this example). It might also mean advancing students several grade levels only in specific academic classes. For example, if seventh-grade students were gifted mathematically, they might be placed with juniors in the Algebra II class, but remain with their age peers for other subjects. Universities also may allow students who are gifted or talented to enroll in college-level courses when prerequisite criteria are met. This is done during the summers or during the academic year if students live close to university settings. Students who are gifted or talented frequently take advanced placement tests for college, which enables them to skip college-level courses. Finally, many students are admitted early to colleges and universities.

Acceleration is controversial, with proponents arguing strenuously for and opponents arguing strenuously against acceleration programs (Jones & Southern, 1991). Proponents claim students need acceleration to maintain interest in school and to be challenged adequately. Opponents claim that acceleration harms the social-emotional development of gifted students. Unfortunately, research results are ambiguous and yield no clear definitive answers (Jones & Southern, 1991).

Enrichment

Numerous models of enrichment exist (Clark, 2001). The common element across enrichment programs is the expansion upon the curriculum. In other words, students are allowed and encouraged to study topics in depth that extend beyond the scope of the general education curriculum. The goals behind enrichment activities are to allow opportunities for critical thinking and problem solving through in-depth analyses of specific content areas. This is often accomplished by having students work independently on projects within general education classes. However, enrichment may also take place in off-campus settings. For example, students may be assigned to work with mentors in business and industry, or in university settings. In either case, general education teachers can facilitate coordination of programming for students who are gifted or talented.

Adapt Instructional Materials

In the case of either acceleration or enrichment, it may be necessary for general educators to adapt curriculum materials to better meet the needs of students who are gifted or talented. Prioritize objectives for students and carefully complete pretesting of content to be covered. When students have demonstrated mastery of content, be prepared to move them ahead in the curriculum or design suitable enrichment activities that enable them to study more in depth in that area. Seek

Information on using the teacher effectiveness variables to accommodate student diversity in the classroom is provided in chapter 6.

For a listing of Websites that contain information on gifted and talented, go to the Web Links module in chapter 5 of the Companion Website.

In the Classroom ...a feature for teachers

Sample Nomination Form for a Gifted Program

Name of student being nominated _____

Grade _____ Teacher(s) _____

Individual nominating _____

1. Provide a brief rationale for the nomination.

2. Describe areas of gifted, creative, and talented abilities.

3. List the student's current academic levels and compare the student's academic abilities with those of age peers.

     Reading _____

     Math _____

     Language Arts _____

     Science _____

     Social Studies _____

     Art _____

     Music _____

     Spanish _____

     Other _____

4. List student's major interests, activities, and special projects.

5. Describe why you think the student's educational needs are not being met in the regular education program.

Note: From *Teaching Young Children in Multicultural Classrooms: Issues, Concepts, and Strategies* (p. 217), by W. R. de Melendez and V. Ostertag, 1997, New York: Delmar. Copyright 1997 by Delmar. Reprinted with permission.

assistance from teachers who work with students who are gifted or talented and from guidance counselors, as well as from the families of the students.

Adapt Instructional and Evaluation Procedures

Be prepared to adapt your instructional procedures for students who are gifted or talented. They may not require intensive or explicit instruction on new content. You may be able to meet with them independently and briefly explain new concepts and content, thus allowing more time for either acceleration or enrichment activities. Students who are gifted or talented may also be able to provide tutorial assistance to age peers. Be aware that some gifted and talented youth may also require explicit instruction in study and organizational skills when work demands increase for them. Finally, evaluation methods can be modified to allow for assessment of enrichment and acceleration activities. More performance-based measures may need to be devised to obtain true indicators of students' abilities on such tasks.

Students Who Are Culturally and Linguistically Diverse

Prevalence, Definitions, and Characteristics of Cultural and Linguistic Diversity

Some refer to Caucasians or White Americans as European Americans because their ancestors immigrated here from Europe (Grossman, 1995).

Evidence exists that many students from culturally and linguistically diverse backgrounds are at a higher risk for school failure than students from European American backgrounds (Stephens & Price, 1992; Stephens, Varble, & Taitt, 1993). Furthermore, the prevalence rates for students with disabilities are higher than expected in some culturally and linguistically diverse groups (Separate and Unequal, 1993). For example, Table 5.2 presents data from the U.S. Department of Education (USDOE, 2001) on special education classification by disability categories for American Indian/Alaska Native, Asian/Pacific Islander, Black, Hispanic, and White students. Data for percent of the racial-ethnic group in each category are provided, as well as percent of each category by group. This means, for

Table 5.2

Data from U.S. Department of Education (2001) Shown by Percentage of Group by Racial-Ethnic Category and by Percentage of Category by Group for All Disability Categories

Disability	American Indian/ Alaska Native % of group	% of category	Asian/ Pacific Islander % of group	% of category	Black (non-Hispanic) % of group	% of category	Hispanic % of group	% of category	White (non-Hispanic) % of group	% of category
Specific Learning Disabilities	6.36	1.41	1.66	1.53	5.46	18.21	5.05	17.39	4.12	61.45
Speech/Language Impairments	1.99	1.15	1.02	2.43	1.85	16.01	1.49	13.19	1.74	67.22
Mental Retardation	1.02	1.03	.41	1.73	2.20	33.49	.60	11.09	.77	52.66
Emotional Disturbance	.83	1.14	.21	1.16	1.33	27.23	.44	9.04	.67	61.43
Multiple Disabilities	.24	1.43	.09	2.26	.22	19.76	.13	12.51	.16	64.03
Hearing Impairments	.14	1.24	.12	4.53	.12	16.20	.14	18.91	.10	59.12
Orthopedic Impairments	.09	.081	.08	2.98	.11	14.54	.11	15.40	.11	66.27
Other Health Impairments	.42	1.06	.13	1.39	.39	14.83	.21	8.45	.43	74.26
Visual Impairments	.04	1.05	.03	3.39	.05	18.20	.04	15.65	.04	61.71
Autism	.07	0.65	.12	4.77	.14	20.35	.06	9.77	.10	64.46
Deaf-Blindness	.01	1.94	.01	7.38	.00	24.25	.00	12.71	.00	53.72
Traumatic Brain Injury	.03	1.60	.01	2.43	.02	16.88	.02	10.76	.02	68.32
Developmental Delay	.03	0.87	.01	0.82	.06	30.51	.01	4.05	.03	63.71
All Disabilities	11.26	1.48	3.90	1.86	11.96	20.08	8.30	14.55	8.30	62.30
Resident Population		.96		3.84		14.52		16.23		64.45

example, that during the 1999–2000 school year, 2.20% of Black or African American students were classified as mildly mentally retarded (% of group); but also that 33.49% of the students classified mildly mentally retarded were African American (% of category). This constitutes overrepresentation because only 14.52% of the student population were African American students.

Harry (1992, 1994) provided an analysis of special education classification by race that yielded similar figures regarding the disproportionate number of African Americans from inner-city schools being identified as mentally retarded. Her data indicated that African Americans account for 35% and 27% of mildly and moderately mentally retarded, respectively, and 27% of students with emotional disabilities, but represent only 16% of the school population in general. Harry's data also indicate that Hispanics (Latinos) were not overrepresented in special education classes, but that Asian Americans were underrepresented. A similar pattern of findings was reported by Chinn and Hughes over a decade ago (1987). This indicates that little has changed with respect to over- and underrepresentation issues by racial or ethnic group in past decades.

Although exact reasons for observed overrepresentation of some racial-ethnic backgrounds are unknown, several reasons are hypothesized. Some speculate that there are insufficient successful role models in schools and society for students from culturally and linguistically diverse backgrounds. Others suggest that cultural and linguistic differences often are inaccurately perceived as detriments (Harry, 1992, 1994), while others suggest that students from these underrepresented groups are discriminated against because educational methods, traditional assessment, and grading procedures do not accommodate students from various cultural and linguistic groups (Patton, 1998). It has also been suggested that percentages of some minority populations in special education are relatively high due to low income and resulting disabilities associated with poverty (U.S. Department of Education, 1998), or that representation in special education reflects the larger issue of representation in other remedial or compensatory programs such as Title I (MacMillan & Reschly, 1998).

The National Research Council issued a report on representation of minority groups in special and gifted education that noted overrepresentation (and underrepresentation) of some minority groups in special education (Donovan & Cross, 2002), and underrepresentation of some minority groups in gifted education. They suggested that minority children are more likely to be poor, and that poverty is associated with higher rates of exposure to harmful toxins (such as lead, alcohol, and tobacco) in early developmental stages. Children in poverty are also associated with low birth weight, poorer nutrition, and are more likely to be raised in households with less support for positive cognitive and emotional development. However, the National Research Council report also noted that students from minority groups are less likely to attend schools with high-quality instructional and classroom management practices, and therefore may not have received the benefits of such supports before being placed in special education programs or screened for gifted programs (Donovan & Cross, 2002).

Whatever the theory, however, the fact of overrepresentation of students who are culturally and linguistically diverse in special education is evidence that schools must pay greater attention to issues of cultural diversity. It is of critical importance that assessment instruments and procedures be nondiscriminatory and free of bias, and administered in the student's native language (Winzer & Mazurek, 1998). The National Research Council has suggested that students be considered eligible for special education only when a student differs markedly from typical performance in specific academic or social-emotional domains, and with evidence that the student has not responded to high-quality interventions in these specific domains of functioning (Donovan & Cross, 2002).

See chapter 1 for a discussion of legal issues in nondiscriminatory testing; and see chapter 12 for testing modifications.

Cultural Diversity

Two major philosophical approaches toward education of culturally diverse populations are prevalent. One is assimilation and the other is cultural pluralism (Kitano, 1991). Assimilation refers to having students from diverse ethnic and cultural groups assimilate into the dominant cultural group and essentially leave their own culture behind (Kitano, 1991). Conversely, cultural pluralism refers to encouraging students from diverse ethnic and cultural groups to retain their own culture while succeeding in school. Rueda and Prieto (1979) used the term *cultural pluralism* to describe the fostering of different cultural groups within school settings.

The concept of cultural pluralism becomes increasingly important as the number of individuals from diverse cultural and ethnic groups increases. This means that greater attention is needed to increase respect of all cultural and ethnic diversity in U.S. schools. Many proactive approaches can be implemented in schools to increase appreciation and awareness of cultural and ethnic differences

The European American culture has been the majority throughout U.S. history, but it has been estimated that by 2010, 37% of U.S. students will be from diverse cultural and/or language backgrounds, and 46% in 2020 (Baca & Cervantes, 1998).

For a listing of resources and links relevant to race and ethnicity, go to the Web Links module in chapter 5 of the Companion Website.

(Grossman, 1995). This approach is sometimes referred to as **multicultural education** because cultural pluralism is endorsed, which means appreciation of all cultures is taught and fostered.

It is difficult to increase respect of all cultural groups without having some knowledge about differences among groups. However, it must be remembered that it is dangerous to generalize from cultural groups to individuals. As Lynch (1992) stated:

> Culture is only one of the characteristics that determine individuals' and families' attitudes, values, beliefs, and ways of behaving. . . . Assuming that culture-specific information. . . applies to all individuals from the cultural group is not only inaccurate but also dangerous—it can lead to stereotyping that diminishes rather than enhances cross-cultural competence. When applying cultural-specific information to an individual or family, it is wise to proceed with caution. (p. 44)

Just as students with a particular disability may lack all of the characteristics associated with a disability area, the same is true of someone from a particular culture. An individual representing a particular ethnic or cultural group may not be "representative" of that cultural group. However, when teaching and learning about cultures, some general characteristics can serve as guidelines for learning about the various cultural groups. Suggestions for teaching toward a more proactive culturally pluralistic approach and away from a biased, monocultural approach are described in the following list.

- *Eliminate teacher bias.* Increase awareness of prejudices and decrease prejudices and stereotypes.
- *Eliminate curriculum bias.* Select curriculum to reflect diversity of all cultural groups; avoid stereotyping and overgeneralizations of cultural groups.
- *Teach about prejudice.* Discuss racism and discrimination; have students examine news for instances of racism; invite guest speakers; eliminate stereotypes.
- *Improve group relations and help resolve conflicts.* Use case studies and teach problem solving.

Recognize the Needs of Students from Multiracial Families. There is also an increasing trend in the number of multiracial and multicultural families in the United States (Grossman, 1997). It has been estimated that 1 in 39 marriages currently cross races and ethnic groups, a 350% increase from a quarter of a century ago (Grossman, 1997). Moreover, multiracial marriages have resulted

Assess the special needs of students from culturally and linguistically different backgrounds using test instruments that avoid cultural bias.

in more than a million multiracial children being born in the United States. Many of these children defy being classified as only one part of their heritage. For example, Dorothy Adams, a 36-year-old whose father is African American and mother is Japanese American, stated:

> I'm for the multiracial category. When I was a kid, the first time I paid attention to the race box was on a Social Security form. It was a problem to check one box, so I checked black and Japanese. The teacher said to check only one box, so I checked 'Other,' then wrote in 'black and Japanese.' I've never gone back to see how I'm listed with Social Security. (Grossman, 1997, p. 13)

Philip Vernon, age 34, whose father is African American and mother is Norwegian American, declined an award of Outstanding Black Athlete when he graduated from high school because he refused to distinguish one part of his background from the other. He offered the following opinion of being multiracial:

> We don't just try to understand the other person's point of view. We live that understanding. Bi- and multiracial people should be used as arbitrators or bridges between races. It's the blends that will define the future of our nation. No other country has attempted it. The multirace category reflects reality. It'll take two to three generations to catch on. . . . Human history shows nations and tribes have always been commingling. Why should we be different? (Grossman, 1997, p. 15)

Be aware that many people who represent a variety of racial and ethnic backgrounds wish to be treated as individuals rather than as members of particular racial groups.

Develop a Plan to Address Linguistic Diversity

Linguistic diversity is also an increasing issue within public schools in the United States. Currently, as many as 8 million children in the United States have a non-English background, either because they were born in another country, or because they grew up in a U.S. household where English is not spoken (Grossman, 1995). Spanish is currently the second most commonly spoken language in the schools, but it has been reported that as many as 72 languages are spoken in some schools. Some estimates indicate that as many as 8 million students in U.S. schools have a language other than English as their primary language (Winzer & Mazurek, 1998). Inner-city schools have higher proportions of students with limited English proficiency (U.S. Department of Education, 1998). Moreover, it has been reported that the majority of students with limited English proficiency reside in California, Texas, and New York. The Technology Highlight feature describes the use of multilingual translators.

These data indicate that difficulties with learning are likely because students may not have acquired the necessary English language skills for success in English-speaking schools (Cummins, 1984). In addition, it is more challenging to establish effective communication between families and the school when common languages are unknown. It is necessary to enlist the assistance of interpreters who can translate communications, schoolwork, notes, papers, and materials between school and home settings.

Linguistic diversity is not limited to different languages. Some students may speak a dialect of English, rather than a different language. For example, many African American students may speak a Black dialect or Black English rather than standard English. Using a dialect in school may present some communication difficulties, especially with respect to written language assignments (Bryen, 1974; Winzer & Mazurek, 1998).

Several approaches to bilingual education exist, and controversy exists regarding the optimal approach. It is a matter of debate whether children should be "immersed" in English-speaking classrooms (with English instruction also provided by teachers of English as a second language), or whether English and non-English languages should be combined within classroom instruction. Furthermore, even if different languages are used during instruction, it is unclear how this can best be done to optimize performance and learning of all students. It has been suggested that students may acquire practical, conversational skills in English much sooner than academic skills, and that it may be useful to support students in academic learning in their native language for several years until English skills are maximized (Ovando & Collier, 1998). It is important to note that virtually all concerned professionals agree that some level of support is needed for students who are not fluent in English.

Bilingual Special Education.
Bilingual special education refers to services provided for students with limited English proficiency who also have a disability. It is estimated that "5% of students with disabilities from inner city districts have limited English proficiency" (U.S. Department of Education,

Technology Highlight

Multilingual Pocket Translators

Students for whom English is a second language may benefit from having the use of a multi-lingual pocket translator to use in classes. Multilingual translators can be small pocket-sized electronic devices that contain a keyboard and a small screen. Students can enter text in one language, press a key, and have the text translated into another language. The devices are small enough to be carried from class to class in an unobtrusive fashion. They can provide valuable assistance and allow students to participate in class more frequently and to perform more optimally on class assignments and tests. In some schools students are allowed to use these during the school day and even during statewide competency testing situations. Such devices would also be beneficial for teachers to have to enhance their communication with students and families of individuals for whom English is a Second Language.

The functions of the various devices range from that of a dictionary, to phrases and idioms, to calculator, to data storage functions, to speech output. Some devices, such as the Language Teacher Pocket Translator, have built in synthesizers that produce a voice output as well. Many models have software available that can be loaded onto notebook computers or other hand held devices including palm pilots. More information on these devices can be obtained from *http://www.translation.net* (Language Teacher Pocket Translator) and *http://www.franklin.com* (Franklin electronic publishers) who also produce the Franklin Language masters and Spell checkers.

1998). Students who are bilingual who are also referred to special education are in need of both types of services and may be particularly at risk for inappropriate classification due to the difficulties communicating in English (Ortiz & Garcia, 1988). Bilingual special education teachers deliver services to those students who require bilingual education and special education services (Diaz-Rico & Weed, 1995; Winzer & Mazurek, 1998).

Issues in Identification and Assessment

IDEA provides stipulations for evaluations and assessment that are free of cultural and linguistic bias. It is especially important to monitor testing and assessment procedures to ensure this right for students from culturally and linguistically diverse backgrounds. Special precautions should be taken to ensure that ethnicity or cultural differences are not misinterpreted. For example, students in some cultures may tend to avoid direct eye contact with adults, a practice that may be misinterpreted by some teachers unfamiliar with cultural differences.

Overrepresentation in large part may be attributed to inappropriate identification and assessment procedures (Artiles & Trent, 1994; Artiles & Zamora-Durán, 1997; Chinn & Hughes, 1987; Rueda, 1997). For example, African American students may be mistakenly referred for classification as having emotional or behavioral disabilities because of cultural misunderstandings (Anderson & Webb-Johnson, 1995). Likewise, research has shown that some students who are bilingual exhibit behaviors that may be interpreted as behaviors similar to students with learning disabilities, or behavioral disabilities (Ortiz & Yates, 1983). When students cannot understand the spoken language in class, they may appear uninterested or confused, or act inappropriately. Because these are some of the distinguishing characteristics of students with higher-incidence disabilities, general education teachers may misinterpret those behaviors and overrefer these students for special education services. Ortiz and Garcia (1988) described a prereferral system for preventing inappropriate referrals for students who are bilingual, including assessing students in their dominant language.

Research has indicated that children with language disabilities perform better when tested by familiar examiners (Fuchs & Fuchs, 1984, 1989), with higher performance differences found for students with learning disabilities, but with no differential effects found for students with mental retardation (Fuchs, 1987). This does not mean that every referral and placement for students from culturally and linguistically diverse groups is inappropriate. However, it does suggest that evaluation procedures need to be closely monitored to ensure appropriate tests, testing situations, and familiar examiners are provided for those individuals. For example, students who do not speak and understand English fluently should not be placed into special education classes based on their performance on tests administered in English. Because many parents of students from diverse cultural and linguistic backgrounds speak only their native language fluently, have translators available to help facilitate communication efforts between families and schools when language barriers exist.

English as a second language (ESL) teachers who are bilingual specialists can provide valuable information on students who are beginning to learn English as a second language (Baca & Almanza, 1991). They can provide suggestions to facilitate comprehension during classes. Bilingual teachers may provide academic instruction in students' native language (Baca & Almanza, 1991; Bennett, 1999). They may also work with special education teachers to ensure that instruction is sufficiently adapted to meet any specific disability needs. Use these specialists to help understand how to better serve students from different linguistic backgrounds. Bilingual special education teachers assume responsibility for the implementation of IEPs and provide English as second language and special education instruction for students with both needs (Winzer & Mazurek, 1998). These specialists work closely with general educators in inclusive models and coordinate instruction and instructional approaches to ensure IEP goals are met. Finally, consider the following:

- Test scores are only single indicators of performance.
- Include multiple observations of students' behaviors.
- Testing by itself is insufficient for special education classification.
- Obtain assistance from bilingual and cultural diversity experts.
- Work closely with the families of students who are culturally and linguistically diverse, to obtain the most valid and relevant information (Harry, 1995).

For links for multicultural curriculum resources go to the Web Links module in chapter 5 of the Companion Website.

General Classroom Adaptations for Students from Culturally and Linguistically Diverse Backgrounds

Many of the adaptations described for students with disabilities may be beneficial for accommodating students from diverse cultural and linguistic backgrounds.

- *Create an open, accepting classroom environment to ensure that students from all cultural and linguistic backgrounds feel comfortable in classes.* Make all students and their families feel welcome in your class. Model acceptance and tolerance of individual differences. Teach students that we are alike and different, and that immigrants from all parts of the world have historically settled in the United States and contributed to its development (de Melendez & Ostertag, 1997).
- *Complete a needs assessment to determine the ethnic, cultural, and linguistic background of the school, students, and community.* The following *In the Classroom* feature presents one suggested by de Melendez and Ostertag (1997). Information obtained can be used to plan activities that address all cultural and linguistic backgrounds.
- *Include books and stories in your curriculum to enhance understanding of other cultures.* Kollar (1993) and Ramirez and Ramirez (1994) have developed an annotated bibliography of multicultural literature. Some recommended books from this bibliography are presented in Figure 5.2.
- *Teach about sensitivity and acceptance issues.* Role-play scenarios that are concrete and meaningful to students. Examine curriculum materials to ensure they eliminate stereotypes. Examine your teaching style and practices to ensure all students are treated equally and offered chances of success. Monitor the pace of instruction to ensure

In the Classroom ...a feature for teachers

A Needs Assessment for an Educational Setting

Sample Questionnaire

A. The Community
1. What is the cultural and ethnic makeup of the community?
2. What languages are spoken?
3. What are the immediate priorities of the community?
4. What are the main community issues?
5. How do the community members feel toward the school, toward my classroom?

B. The School
1. What is the cultural and ethnic makeup of the school?
2. What is the diversity profile of the school?
3. What attitudes do teachers and staff have toward diversity?
4. Is anyone engaged in a multicultural program? What approaches are they following?
5. Are multicultural programs among the school's priorities?
6. Would the faculty, administrators, and staff support my efforts?

C. Children and Families
1. What are the families like? Socioeconomically, how are they defined?
2. What elements of diversity are reflected in these families?
3. What are some of the essential needs of families?
4. What are their religious affiliations?
5. Can I address those needs in my classroom?
6. What are the traits that, ethnically and culturally, characterize children in my classroom?
7. What diversity issues are unclear to my students? (For example, language differences, equality, interracial relations)
8. How do children see me?

D. The Classroom
1. What are the ethnic and cultural origins of the children in this classroom?
2. What opportunities do they have for dealing with diversity at the school?
3. Generally, how do children interact in this classroom?
4. Have there been any incidents because of racial or cultural differences?
5. Are there children who tend to use racial slurs or pejorative terms against others?
6. How do they respond when a person with given cultural characteristics comes into the classroom?

Note: From *Teaching Young Children in Multicultural Classrooms: Issues, Concepts, and Strategies* (p. 217), by W. R. de Melendez and V. Ostertag, 1997, New York: Delmar. Copyright 1997 by Delmar. Reprinted with permission.

students with limited English proficiency are succeeding. Use concrete examples as frequently as possible when describing new concepts. Provide hands-on activities to ensure active involvement and active learning for all students (Baca & Almanza, 1991). By using many modalities when teaching, you will help clarify language and provide multiple examples for developing new vocabulary words. Help students relate any prior knowledge to new concepts you present. Figure 5.3 provides suggestions to increase appreciation of others.

- *Adapt the physical environment, instructional materials, and evaluation procedures as needed to ensure success for students from diverse cultural and linguistic backgrounds.*

Title	Subject
Best Loved Folktales of the World (J. Cole, Doubleday, 1982)	Anthology that provides stories from cultures from all over the world (K–2).
The Chinese Mirror (M. Ginsburg, Harcourt Brace Jovanovich, 1988)	An adaptation of a Korean folktale (K–2).
The Day of Ahmed's Secret (F. Heide & J. Gilliland, Lothrop, Lee, & Shepard, 1990)	Story of a boy in modern-day Cairo (K–2).
Diego (J. Winter, Knopf, 1991)	Biography of the famous Mexican muralist Diego Rivera (3–5).
Ellis Island: New Hope in a New Land (W. Jacobs, Scribner's, 1990)	An account of Ellis Island, and its role in American immigration (3–5).
The Flute Player: An Apache Folktale (J. Lacapa, Northland, 1990)	Folktale of an Apache boy who learns to play the flute for a girl that has captured his heart (3–5).
Children of Promise: African-American Literature and Art for Young People (C. Sullivan, ed., Harry N. Abrams, 1991)	This book contains a variety of stories, poems, plays, speeches, and documents that describe the African American experience (6–8).
Shabanu: Daughter of the Wind (S. Staples, Knopf, 1989)	Story of a girl from Pakistan's Cholistan desert (6–8).
Look What We've Brought You from Mexico: Crafts, Games, Recipes, Stories, and Other Cultural Activities from Mexican–Americans (P. Shalant, Julian Messner, 1992)	Describes the many contributions to the United States from Mexican culture (6–8).

Figure 5.2
Books to Promote Multicultural Awareness

Students at Risk

Definitions, Prevalence, and Characteristics of Students at Risk

Students at risk for school failure come from diverse environments and represent all racial, ethnic, and linguistic backgrounds. They also span all socioeconomic classes, although students coming from severe poverty may tend to be at a higher risk than others. At-risk students may ultimately fail or drop out of school and experience difficulties later in life. These students are usually found in general education classes, may require additional assistance from teachers, and may benefit from classroom modifications similar to those suggested for students with higher-incidence disabilities. Many educators have identified factors associated with at-risk students (Gardner, 1983; Slavin, Karweit, & Madden, 1989; Stephens & Price, 1992). These factors are listed in Figure 5.4, and describe a variety of situations.

Abused and Neglected Children

Child abuse and neglect has devastating emotional, physical, cognitive, social, and intellectual effects on children and reported cases have been increasing in the United States (Garbarino, 1987). Federal legislation, the Child Abuse Prevention and Treatment Act of 1974 and its subsequent amendments—PL 93–247; PL 100–294; PL 98–457—defined child abuse and neglect as maltreatment, sexual abuse or exploitation, mental or physical injury, withholding medical treatment for life-threatening conditions, or negligent treatment of children younger than 18 by persons responsible for the child (Warger, Tewey, & Megivern, 1991). In some cases, child abuse has been linked to causing disabilities in children. For example, severe shaking of infants has been linked to brain injury (Klein & Stern, 1971); some cases of abuse have been related to cerebral palsy (Diamond & Jaudes, 1983); other cases have been linked to mental retardation and learning disabilities (Caplan & Dinardo, 1986). Table 5.3 presents behavioral and physical indicators of child abuse and neglect.

For additional information and resources for students at risk, go to the Web Links module in chapter 5 of the Companion Website.

For Younger Students	For Older Students
Share children's literature and stories about many cultures.	Complete a class, school, and community cultural and linguistic diversity profile.
Make a classroom "quilt."	Teach about inequity and individuals who have fought to combat inequitable practices.
Develop a class family cookbook.	
Discuss foods eaten at meals by different cultural groups.	Teach about cultural contributions: The arts, folk art, music, dances, literature, and crafts
Prepare, cook, and eat ethnic foods.	Traditions, holidays, festivals, myths
Dress in ethnic clothing.	Distinguished individuals and their accomplishments
Wear ethnic jewelry and accessories.	
Play ethnic music.	Prepare, cook, and eat ethnic foods.
Teach ethnic dances.	Dress in ethnic clothing.
Teach words and phrases from different languages.	Play ethnic music.
Invite parents in to share family traditions.	Teach ethnic dances.
Make illustrated family histories and post them in the classroom.	Teach words and phrases from different languages.
	Bring in international newspapers or newspapers written in a language other than English.

Figure 5.3
Classroom Practices to Increase Appreciation for Others

Schools and teachers have the responsibility to report any signs of child abuse or neglect as per state and local definitions and guidelines. A sample reporting form can be found in Figure 5.5. Determine state definitions and local procedures for reporting any cases and adhere to those policies and procedures upon noticing any cases of child abuse or neglect (Garbarino, Brookhouser, & Authier, 1987).

Homeless Children

The term *homeless* refers to individuals who lack a nighttime home, cannot afford housing, live in provided public or private shelters, cars, or elsewhere (Heflin & Rudy, 1991). The number of homeless individuals in the United States is rapidly growing, and includes an increasing number of families with children from infants to teenagers (Rossi, 1990). Some estimates indicate that 90% of the homeless families are single mothers with an average of two to three children (Bassuk & Rubin, 1987; Stronge & Tenhouse, 1990). The U.S. Department of Education has estimated that 272,773 homeless school-age children exist (Cavazos, 1990), while homeless rates of children reported by the Children's Defense Fund range as high as 1.6 million (Burns, 1991). Burns (1991) indicates that the number may be even greater if counting the "hidden homeless"—individuals who live with friends or relatives because they cannot afford housing.

It is important to realize that homeless children have to confront many barriers to succeed in school and in life. Issues for homeless children include transportation problems; social barriers due to transience; lack of money for food, clothing, and shelter; appearance; acceptance by peers; legal barriers; family problems; and excessive absenteeism. Even more important are issues surrounding their self-esteem, security, safety, and trust. Some schools with high rates of homeless children have modeled examples of safe, comfortable environments by:

- maintaining a super clean environment.
- arranging "living room" areas with rugs, chairs, and carpets in all classrooms.
- filling the school with homey things such as plants and pictures.
- maintaining an emphasis on building self-esteem.

- Children with poor academic performance (Knapp & Turnbull, 1991)
- Children who are born exposed to alcohol and other narcotic substances (Vincent, Poulsen, Cole, Woodruff, & Griffith, 1991)
- Children who abuse alcohol and drugs (Leone, 1991)
- Abused and neglected children (Warger, Tewey, & Megivern, 1991)
- Children living in poverty conditions (Wagner, Blackorby, Cameto, & Newman, 1993)
- Children suffering from depression and suicidal tendencies (Guetzloe, 1991)
- Students who are pregnant and parents (Muccigrosso, Scavarda, Simpson-Brown, & Thalacker, 1991)
- Homeless children and children who move excessively (Heflin & Rudy, 1991; Lombardi, Odell, & Novotny, 1990)
- Children with excessive absenteeism (Knapp & Turnbull, 1991)
- Students who have been suspended two times within a year (Lombardi, Odell, & Novotny, 1990)
- Students who drop out of school (MacMillan, 1991)
- Children who are slow learners (Watson & Rangel, 1989)
- Students who have experienced traumatic events such as death of someone close to them (Germinario, Cervalli, & Ogden, 1992)
- Children whose parents are alcoholics or drugs abusers (Lombardi, Odell, & Novotny, 1990)
- Students who are older than their grade level peers due to retention (Lombardi, Odell, & Novotny, 1990)
- Children who may be from urban, suburban, or rural settings (Helge, 1991)
- Children who are angry or socially alienated

Figure 5.4
Major At-Risk Factors

Table 5.3
Physical and Behavioral Indicators of Child Abuse and Neglect

Type of Abuse or Neglect	Physical Indicators	Behavioral Indicators
Physical Abuse	Unexplained injuries: • Bruises • Burns • Fractures • Abrasions	• Apprehensive of adult contacts • Frightened of parents • Behavioral extremes
Physical Neglect	• Hungry • Poor hygiene • Unattended medical needs • Lack of supervision	• Stealing food • Always tired • Delinquency • Substance abuse
Sexual Abuse	• Difficulty walking or sitting • Venereal disease • Pregnancy	• Unwilling to take gym or change for gym class • Withdrawn, poor peer relations

Note: From *Abuse and Neglect of Exceptional Children* (pp. 15–16), by C. L. Warger, S. Tewey, and M. Megivern, 1991, Reston, VA: Council for Exceptional Children. Copyright 1991 by CEC. Adapted by permission.

Child Abuse–Neglect Reporting Form

Oral report made to principal or designee: Date: _____   Time: _____

Child's name _____ / _____ / _____
                    Last name (legal)   First   Middle

Age _____   Birthday _____

Child's address _____

Names and addresses of parents or other person(s) responsible for the
child's care.

Father _____   Mother _____

Guardian or caretaker _____

Address _____   Telephone _____

Observations leading to the suspicion that the child is a victim of abuse or neglect.
Supply time and date of observation(s).

Additional information. Interview with the child and name of other school employees
involved.

Written report made to principal or designee: Date: _____   Time: _____

Signature _____   Signature _____
              Initiator of the report   Observer of the Interview

To be filled out by the principal or designee:

Oral report made to: Written report made to:

Local City Police   _____   Local City Police   _____
County Sheriff   _____   County Sheriff   _____
Division of Family Services _____   Division of Family Services _____

Date: _____   Time: _____   Date: _____   Time: _____

Principal's signature _____

Distribute copies: 1. Mail to agency receiving the oral report.
                            2. Mail to the district's pupil personnel office.
                            3. Place in principal's child abuse–neglect file.
                                (Not to be placed in child's personal file.)

Figure 5.5
Sample Child Abuse–Neglect Reporting Form
Note: From *Child Abuse and Neglect: A Primer for School Personnel* (p. 34), by D. F. Kline, 1977, Reston VA: Council for
Exceptional Children. Copyright 1977 by CEC. Reprinted with permission.

Some students who are homeless have been known to save parts of their free lunch for younger siblings at home and to cry before leaving school because they didn't know if they would be able to come back the next day. You can help your students feel safe and comfortable in school by creating an open and accepting environment.

Alcohol and Substance Abuse

Students who use alcohol and other narcotics illegally are at a higher risk for failing in school and life. Reports indicate that 36% of all high school seniors have used illegal drugs (Leone, 1991). This figure is distressing, but even more alarming are the reports that indicate that children in elementary schools are using drugs. These students are at a greater risk for failing. Students may become more withdrawn and act irrationally. Moreover, many may become involved in stealing and other illegal activities to maintain their drug habits.

Miksic (1987; see also Kauffman, 2001) described elements of a successful substance abuse education program. These elements include a clear, well-defined school policy regarding how teachers and administrators will deal with drug use and possession; a basic drug education classroom curriculum; increasing teacher awareness; a supportive atmosphere for teacher training in dealing with drug abuse problems; involving families as well as students; teacher self-evaluation; use of peer-group approaches; and promoting understanding that emotional concerns, such as self-esteem, are often associated with substance abuse.

Drug abuse is not appropriately treated in the classroom; however, teachers should know whom to contact if a drug-related emergency occurs. It is also appropriate to make referrals when drug use has been established, particularly when it is associated with disruptive classroom behavior or problems in academic functioning (Kerr & Nelson, 2002). Leone (1991) provides a treatment checklist as a guideline for selecting optimal treatment for adolescents who have been using illegal drugs.

Family Poverty

It has been well documented that children living in poverty are at high risk for failing in school and life (U.S. Department of Education, 1996). Poverty complicates life success and places children at risk for failure for a variety of complex reasons. First, prenatal care may be nonexistent for those in low-income families. This alone may result in low birth-weight infants who are at higher risk for ill health. Second, drug use is high among people from impoverished conditions. Children born of substance abusers are at a greater risk for health-related problems (Vincent, Poulsen, Cole, Woodruff, & Griffith, 1991). Third, statistically, children born of teenage mothers are high among students from impoverished conditions (additional information on risk factors associated with teen pregnancies will be presented in the next section). And last, continued poor nutrition, lack of health care, and the low educational achievement of parents are factors associated with poverty that can perpetuate failure in school. In addition, families in poverty are less able to provide the educational materials, computers, or travel experiences that can enrich students' backgrounds and provide support for school learning. Children from families in poverty are more likely to be obligated to work to contribute to family income; these responsibilities may detract from schoolwork. Vincent et al. (1991) provide suggestions for educators in dealing with some of these high-risk factors. These are summarized in Figure 5.6.

Young, Pregnant, and Parents

Teenagers who are pregnant or become parents are at risk for failing in school and present a high at-risk factor for their unborn child (Muccigrosso, Scavarda, Simpson-Brown, & Thalacker, 1991). Teenage pregnancy is found across all racial, ethnic, and socioeconomic strata. Many teenagers lack appropriate educational backgrounds, have poor prenatal care, and have babies who are also at very high risk for failing in school and life. Educational programs providing information about pregnancy, as well as information about abstinence, venereal disease, and AIDS, are needed on a widespread basis to inform youth about the consequences of teenage pregnancy. More programs are needed to

Figure 5.6

Suggestions for Educators for Dealing with High-Risk Students

Note: From *Born Substance Exposed, Educationally Vulnerable* (pp. 18–22), by L. J. Vincent, M. K. Poulsen, C. K. Cole, G. Woodruff, & D. R. Griffith, 1991, Reston, VA: Council for Exceptional Children. Copyright 1991 by CEC. Adapted with permission.

- Develop trust
- Plan predictable, secure, and stable environments
- Build in mutual respect between teachers and students
- Accept students' feelings
- Establish home–school partnerships
- Allow student decision making
- Coordinate activities with family and school

Homelessness and poverty can provide social, financial, and other barriers that preclude student success at school.

Companion Website

For a guide to safe schools, read the U.S. Department of Education's Early Warning, Timely Response: A Guide to Safe Schools, accessible on the Web Links module in chapter 5 of the Companion Website.

provide child care for teenagers with babies to help them complete their high school requirements and pursue advanced degree training.

At-risk factors are not all-inclusive, but highlight the variety of conditions that contribute to making students vulnerable for school failure. Be aware of these conditions, but realize that a single factor may or may not place students at risk. Upon noticing students who may be associated with at-risk factors, alert school guidance counselors, other school support personnel, and families to determine optimal plans of action to counteract any at-risk factors.

Warning Signs for Suicide or Violence

Many students in today's schools are at risk for suicide or violence, so it is important to be alert for warning signs. According to Guetzloe (1991), suicide warning signs include: (a) an inability to recover from loss, such as a death in the family or loss of a friendship; (b) obvious changes in sleeping patterns, weight, or personality; (c) dramatic changes in school behavior including academic performance; (d) neglect of personal appearance; and (e) an increase in use of drugs or alcohol. In addition, students may give away prized personal possessions or make overt threats of suicide. If you encounter a student who threatens suicide, stay with the student, and speak in a calm and nonthreatening manner. Introduce yourself if you do not know the student, and let the student know you are there to help. Try to get the student to talk, and acknowledge the student's feelings. Try to reinforce statements that describe alternatives to suicide, and ask the student to discard potentially harmful objects or substances. Remind the student that others care and would like to help (Guetzloe, 1991). Teachers should take all threats of violence, to self or others, seriously, and report them promptly to parents, co-teachers, counselors, and building administrators.

Issues in Identification and Assessment of Students at Risk

Contact support personnel immediately within your school and determine policies and procedures for assisting students at risk. A number of at-risk factors are critically serious and affect the lives of children involved. Do not delay in requesting immediate assistance. It is better to request assistance and then not need any help, than to delay and be too late. Because these difficulties are complex and varied, be prepared to seek aid from a variety of sources, including families, school administrators, special education personnel, psychologists, social workers, mental health agencies, police, and probation officers.

Compensatory Education

Schools may qualify for federal funding for compensatory education under Title I (previously, Chapter I) of the Elementary and Secondary Education Act (ESEA) if they have concentrations of students from low-income and/or immigrant families. Funds may be provided for additional teachers, paraprofessionals, and supplies, so that additional remedial instruction can be applied. If students are receiving additional assistance in basic skills from Title I, it is important that these programs are well coordinated with other types of instruction the student may be receiving. Information on effective collaboration strategies is provided in chapter 2.

General Classroom Adaptations for Students at Risk

Students at risk for failure represent a wide and varied range of problems and potential difficulties. Most important is to maintain an open, accepting classroom environment and let your students know they are welcome in your room. Seek assistance from other school support personnel and students' families. Be considerate of students' needs, maintain realistic but high expectations, and encourage them to succeed in class. Provide additional opportunities for them to be successful in school. Model enthusiasm toward learning, encourage active participation, make students feel comfortable, and be ready to do the following:

- Remediate basic skills when needed, by providing for additional instruction with paraprofessionals or tutors, so that students can apply themselves on higher-order academic tasks.
- Help coordinate services among social services agencies among the community, school, and parents, to maximize the effectiveness of service delivery.
- Inform parents about all services available, including free meals, education, healthcare, and mental-health services. Many parents are simply unaware of services available to them.
- Provide assistance in obtaining support services of counseling and social work, when needed.
- Help arrange before and after school care and activities for students that may lack supervision outside of school hours.
- Arrange for awareness training for personnel in your school for children at risk and at-risk factors (Heflin & Rudy, 1991).
- Consider using the adaptations suggested for students with higher- and lower-incidence disabilities for students considered at risk for school failure. These include adapting the physical environment, instructional materials, instructional procedures, and evaluation procedures. Most importantly, do not hesitate to seek assistance from school administrators or other personnel when uncertain.

Students at risk for school failure present some unique and special challenges for educators. Nevertheless, successfully adapting instructional practices to help a student succeed, who might otherwise have failed, can be one of the most rewarding experiences you can have as a teacher.

Summary

- Students with diverse learning needs other than specific disability areas also are found in general education classes and can benefit greatly from teacher assistance and attention.
- Students with diverse learning needs include those with attention deficit disorder and attention deficit hyperactivity disorder; those who are gifted, talented, and creative; those from cultural and linguistically diverse backgrounds; and those at risk due to factors such as poverty, drug use, homelessness, teenage pregnancy, and child abuse and neglect.
- Students with attention deficit disorder and attention deficit hyperactivity disorder may be served under Section 504 or IDEA. Adaptations for this group of individuals may include behavioral approaches, cognitive-behavioral training, medication, or a combination of the three.

- Students who are gifted, talented, or creative may be identified by a variety of methods, including test scores, behavioral descriptions, and qualitative-descriptive methods. Students who are gifted, talented, or creative may be served by acceleration programs, enrichment programs, or a combination of approaches.
- Students who are culturally or linguistically diverse may also present some special learning needs. Teachers should adopt a culturally sensitive, pluralistic approach that incorporates an awareness of cultural differences, and their implications for learning.

- Because students who are culturally or linguistically diverse are often overrepresented in special education placements, teachers should be particularly careful when considering referral for special education. Unbiased testing, culturally sensitive behavioral expectations, and prereferral intervention strategies can help address this important issue.
- Factors that may place students at risk for school failure include poverty, drug use, homelessness, teenage pregnancy, and child abuse and neglect. Contact and communication with students in question, their families, relevant school personnel, and community agencies can help address risk factors.

Council for Exceptional Children

CEC Standards Link: Teaching Students with Other Special Learning Needs

Information in this chapter links most directly to:

Standard 2—Development and Characteristics of Learners, particularly:

Knowledge:
- Characteristics and effects of the cultural and environmental milieu of the individual with exceptional learning needs and the family.
- Family systems and the role of families in supporting development.

Standard 3—Individual Learning Differences, particularly:

Knowledge:
- Impact of learners' academic and social abilities, attitudes, interests, and values on instruction and career development.
- Variations in beliefs, traditions, and values across and within cultures and their effects on relationships among individuals with exceptional learning needs, family, and schooling.
- Cultural perspectives influencing the relationships among families, schools, and communities as related to instruction.

- Differing ways of learning of individuals with exceptional learning needs including those from culturally diverse backgrounds and strategies for addressing these differences.

Standard 4—Instructional Strategies, particularly:

Skills:
- Use strategies to facilitate integration into various settings.
- Select, adapt, and use instructional strategies and materials according to characteristics of the individual with exceptional learning needs.

Standard 6—Language

Knowledge:
- Effects of cultural and linguistic differences on growth and development.
- Characerics of one's own culture and use of language and the ways in which these can differ from other cultures and uses of languages.
- Ways of behavior and communicating among cultures that can lead to misinterpretation and misunderstanding.

Inclusion Checklist
Teaching Students with Other Special Learning Needs

If a student with other diverse learning needs is having difficulties in your classroom, have you tried the following?

Students with Attention Deficit Disorder or Attention Deficit Hyperactivity Disorder

- ❏ Consider the characteristics of the student, including inattention, hyperactivity, and impulsivity
- ❏ Provide general classroom adaptations for students with ADD or ADHD
    - ❏ Behavioral interventions
    - ❏ Cognitive behavioral interventions
    - ❏ Monitoring medications

Students Who Are Gifted, Creative, and Talented

- ❏ Consider the characteristics of the student, and the variety of domains in which outstanding potential may be observed
- ❏ Provide general classroom adaptations for students who are gifted, talented, and creative
    - ❏ Acceleration and enrichment
    - ❏ Instructional materials adaptations
    - ❏ Instructional procedures adaptations
    - ❏ Evaluation procedures adaptations

Students from Cultural and Linguistically Diverse Backgrounds

- ❏ Consider the characteristics of the student, and specific cultural needs
- ❏ Consider the issues associated with overrepresentation of some minority groups in special education
- ❏ Provide a proactive, culturally pluralistic approach and avoid monocultural bias
- ❏ Recognize the needs of students from multiracial families
- ❏ Develop a plan to address linguistic diversity
- ❏ Provide fair and unbiased identification and assessment techniques
- ❏ Provide general classroom adaptations for students from culturally and linguistically diverse backgrounds

Students with Special At-Risk Factors

- ❏ Consider the characteristics of the student with at-risk factors, including abused and neglected children, homeless children, alcohol and substance abuse factors, family poverty, teenage pregnancy, and warning signs for suicide or violence
- ❏ General classroom adaptations for students with at-risk factors
    - ❏ Remediate basic skills
    - ❏ Coordinate support services
    - ❏ Involve families
    - ❏ Adapt the physical environment, instructional materials and procedures, and evaluation procedures

Chapter 6

Brooke Clayton, 18
Crawfordsville, Indiana
"Dinner in the Red Room"

Effective Instruction
for All Students

Objectives

After studying this chapter, you should be able to:

- Describe the effective teaching variables, including planning for content coverage and delivering instruction.
- Identify the various types and levels of learning occurring across content areas.
- Identify strategies for maximizing academic engagement (time-on-task).
- Describe the teacher presentation (SCREAM) variables.
- Compare and contrast higher-level and lower-level questioning.
- Describe the use of practice activities to reinforce recall and comprehension.
- Describe the uses of formative evaluation and contrast with summative evaluation.
- Describe the PASS variables and their application to effective instruction in inclusive settings.

To be an effective inclusive classroom teacher, you must first be an effective teacher. You must employ the skills that enable you to expect, and receive, the very best in learning and achievement from your students. This chapter describes the variables most important for maximizing student learning, and ways you can implement these variables in your classroom. As you learn to apply these strategies consistently and systematically, you will see the learning, achievement, and attitudes of all of your students increase dramatically.

Overview of Effective Instruction

The teaching behaviors most important to classroom achievement have not always been widely known. Since World War II, educational researchers have studied what "effective teaching" means, but they have not always examined the variables that were the most critical. The earliest research on teacher effectiveness examined a number of *personal characteristics,* such as teacher appearance or personality, which turned out to have little systematic effect on teaching. Later research examined the role of *curriculum* in determining student learning. Numerous comparisons were made between, for example, phonics versus look-say approaches to reading. Although curriculum has been found to be an important educational consideration (as we will see in Part III of this book), curriculum alone has not been a consistent predictor of student achievement.

See Wittrock, 1986, for several comprehensive reviews of teacher effectiveness research, including Biddle and Anderson, 1986; Brophy and Good, 1986; Doyle, 1986; Rosenshine and Stevens, 1986; Walberg, 1986.

See also Englert, 1983, 1984; Larrivee, 1985; Leinhardt, Zigmond, and Cooley, 1981; Mastropieri, 1989; and Sindelar, Smith, Harriman, Hale, and Wilson, 1986, for research directly relevant to special and inclusive education.

Charlotte Danielson relied heavily on the teacher effectiveness research literature in providing support for her Framework for Teaching (Danielson, 1996).

During the 1970s and 1980s, educational researchers became interested in learning about specific teaching behaviors—the things teachers actually do—and how these teaching behaviors were related to student achievement. Through the efforts of such researchers as Jere Brophy and Thomas Good (1986), variables consistently related to student learning have been identified, and became known as the "effective instruction" variables. The variables were described as "alterable," because they included things that teachers could alter in themselves to become more effective, rather than static, "nonalterable" variables such as age, race, or gender.

Some of this research has been criticized (see Pressley & McCormick, 1995, for a discussion), for its supposed emphasis on teacher-driven (rather than student-generated) curricula, knowledge transmission by direct instruction (rather than by student discovery and inquiry), and an overemphasis on achievement test scores as outcomes (rather than affective measures, classroom tests, performance tests, or portfolio assessments; see chapter 12). However, we suggest that the "effective instruction" variables are extremely important regardless of the type of teaching, learning, or assessment that is being undertaken.

Research has consistently shown that teachers who are most effective at including students with disabilities and other diverse learning needs are also generally effective classroom teachers (Larrivee, 1985; Mastropieri, Scruggs, & Bohs, 1994; Mastropieri et al., 1998; Scruggs & Mastropieri, 1994a). Overall, this research has been critically important in identifying the things teachers should do and not do to maximize learning for all students. In this chapter, we summarize much of what has been learned from this research (see also Mastropieri & Scruggs, 1987, 2002).

The important effective teaching variables that will be considered in this chapter include planning for content coverage (including scope and sequence, objectives, curriculum, and pacing), and delivering instruction (including academic engaged time, teacher presentation, practice activities, review, and formative evaluation). Making effective use of these variables will help maximize the performance of all students, including those with diverse learning needs.

Planning for Content Coverage

The importance of content coverage is obvious, in that students will almost certainly not learn content that has not been covered. However, the amount of content covered must be appropriate to the preskills and abilities of the students learning the content. Careful planning of content coverage can help ensure that learning will be maximized for all students. Several important considerations to make when planning content coverage include objectives, scope and sequence, curriculum, and pacing.

Objectives

All content to be covered should be based on specific instructional objectives. Objectives state the outcomes of instruction in ways that allow you to find out whether your instruction was successful. Objectives specify (a) the content of the objective (what is being taught), (b) the conditions under which a student's performance will be assessed (e.g., in writing, verbal responding), and (c) the criteria for acceptable performance (level of achievement). For example, consider the following objective: "The student will write five precipitating causes of the Civil War with 100% accuracy." The content of the objective is the causes of the Civil War; the conditions specify that students will write; and the criterion for acceptable performance is 100% accuracy. Another example of an objective is as follows: "The student will read 3 pages from the grade-level reading materials at a rate of 120 words per minute with 95% of words read correctly." This objective also specifies the content, the conditions, and the criteria to be achieved. Another objective could state, "After silent reading of a grade-level reading assignment, the student will verbally restate the setting, main characters, problem and resolution with 100% accuracy."

Because the content of instruction is based on objectives, it is important to include as many objectives as necessary to maximize content coverage. This is particularly important for students who receive special education services, because their IEPs (see chapter 2) are based on objectives. An effective inclusive teacher specifies objectives and translates IEP objectives into relevant methods and materials, with the assistance of the special education teacher.

Scope and Sequence

Scope and sequence refer to the breadth and depth of content that will be presented in school (scope) and the order in which the content will be presented (sequence). All areas of instruction should be presented with respect to an overriding scope and sequence of instructional objectives. Scope and sequence allow for long-term planning and evaluation of instruction, and provide implications for time allocations, and the overall pace of instruction. Most states have published their state's curriculum guidelines that contain scope and sequence for all subject areas across grade levels. Established scope and sequence of instruction help prevent redundancy in learning, and can help ensure that new learning is based on previously acquired knowledge and relevant preskills.

Reasonable modifications in scope and sequence can be helpful in enhancing learning for all students. For example, if content coverage seems excessive for some students, perhaps it may be considered appropriate for them to focus on more essential aspects of the curriculum (e.g., mathematical word problem solving), and spending less time on aspects considered less necessary (e.g., Roman numerals). Of course, any changes in the overall scope and sequence should be communicated to the teacher of the subsequent grade level, so that misunderstandings do not occur.

Curriculum

The curriculum not only includes the instructional materials used for learning, but also refers to the course of study for each discipline and the scope and sequence within each grade level necessary to build conceptual understanding. Curriculum serves as an interface between the student and the learning objectives. Curriculum issues are discussed in detail in Part III.

Overall, it is important to consider that curriculum materials do not *determine* instructional objectives, but, appropriately employed, should *support* and *enhance* the learning of instructional objectives. That is, if a teacher says, "This week we are studying chapter 12, and will take the chapter test at the end of the week," the teacher is not specifying instructional objectives, but merely specifying the instructional materials that will be used.

However, as will be discussed in Part III of this book, curriculum decisions can play an important role in inclusive schooling. The following *In the Classroom* feature shows a checklist of curriculum materials being considered to maximize learning for all students. When serving on curriculum adoption committees, or making a choice from existing school materials, be certain to consider those points, to ensure maximized learning for all students.

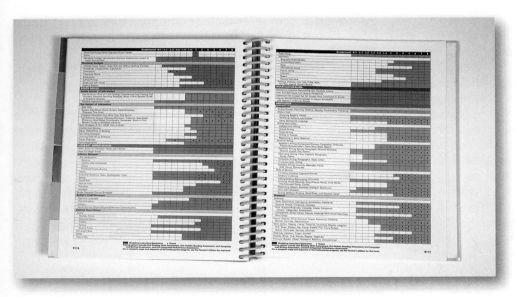

A scope and sequence usually found in any teacher's edition provides the parameters for concepts that need to be covered in sequential grade levels. (From Treasury of Literature: A Place to Dream *[Teacher's Ed., Level 3-1, pp. R116–R117], Orlando, FL: Harcourt Brace & Co., 1995. Copyright 1995 by Harcourt Brace and Company. Reprinted by permission.)*

In the Classroom ...a feature for teachers

Checklist for Curriculum Materials for Inclusive Environments

_____ Do the materials provide sufficient opportunity for *active student involvement,* or do they simply provide verbal information to be recalled?

_____ Are the materials written on a level that is *most comprehensible to all students,* or do they include unnecessary complexity or an overabundance of unnecessary vocabulary?

_____ Do the materials lend themselves to use by *cooperative learning groups* or other peer interactive activities?

_____ Do the materials allow for *sufficient practice* of key concepts before moving on to other content?

_____ Do the materials provide simple means for frequent *evaluation of learner progress* toward prespecified goals and objectives?

_____ Do the materials include examples of individuals from *culturally diverse backgrounds,* and people of *diverse learning abilities?*

_____ Do the materials provide recommendations for *modifications* for students with disabilities or other special needs?

_____ Do the materials provide *validity data,* that demonstrate that positive learning gains can be realized from use of the materials?

Pacing

Pacing refers to the rate at which teachers and students proceed through the curriculum. Pacing is not simply how fast a teacher speaks, but is rather the amount of content covered in a given unit of time. How teachers pace their instruction throughout the year establishes to a large extent the amount of content covered that year. Many high school teachers fail to "finish the book" by the end of the school year, possibly because they felt that additional time was needed to master topics earlier in the text, or possibly because the pacing of instruction was not planned as efficiently as it might have been. Unless the content at the end of the text is judged to be of less value than other content, however, more efficient planning produces better content coverage.

One of the most significant problems teachers encounter in inclusive settings is adjusting the pace of instruction to diverse learning needs. While some students appear to master new content almost as soon as they are exposed to it, other students require substantially more instructional time to learn the same content. In classes that include students with disabilities, adaptations are necessary to ensure that all students receive appropriate opportunities to learn. Students who have learned certain concepts should not be held back, but could be engaged in learning more in-depth knowledge about a concept, or learning about related concepts. While addressing different needs, focus most on the objectives with the highest priority; increase learning time with teachers, aides, parents, or peers; and consider adopting curricula that emphasize depth of understanding over breadth of content.

Planning for Learning

When planning for student learning, consider specifically *what* will be taught, and to *what level of proficiency.* These considerations have been referred to as types and levels of learning (Mastropieri & Scruggs, 2002). Knowing what types and levels of learning are desired provides implications for planning instruction.

Types of Learning

Different types of learning occur in school, across all different subject areas. These types include discriminations, facts, rules, procedures, concepts, and problem solving and critical thinking. Although there can be much overlap on school tasks, it is helpful to examine some of the distinctions among the categories, particularly when planning effective instruction.

Discrimination Learning. **Discrimination** often occurs early in learning and involves determining how one stimulus is either the same or different from another stimulus. In learning the alphabet, numbers, colors, shapes, math concepts, plants, or foreign languages, for example, learning to discriminate among stimuli may be difficult for students with disabilities. Some very young students, or students with reading disabilities, for example, may have difficulty discriminating between the letters "p" and "q" (or "b" and "d") because they differ in orientation in space rather than in shape. Careful attention to the relevant and irrelevant distinctions between various stimuli can help improve discrimination learning for students with disabilities. For example, the critical feature that distinguishes "p" from "q" is the relative placement of the round part of the letter. The critical feature that distinguishes squares from triangles is the number of sides. Repeated practice that emphasizes comprehension of the distinctions promotes learning.

Factual Learning. **Factual learning** is a common aspect of school learning and includes vocabulary words and their definitions, names of famous people and their accomplishments, dates and causes of historical events, addition facts, sight words, and names of rivers or mountain ranges. Some factual learning is in the form of **paired associates,** where one thing is paired with another (e.g., Ulan Bator = Capital of Mongolia; or the Italian word *mela* = "apple"). Other factual learning is in the form of a **serial list** (e.g., "a–b–c–d–e–f–g. . . ."; or, "2–4–6–8–10. . . ."), where information is learned with respect to a specific sequence. Because many students with disabilities have difficulties with memory, learning factual information can be problematic for them. Special attention to the design of instruction emphasizing factual learning can help many of these students overcome memory problems. Appropriate strategies include redundancy, drill and practice, enhancing meaningfulness, and use of elaborations or other memory-enhancing techniques (see chapter 10).

Learning factual information can be difficult for some students with disabilities.

Rule Learning. **Rules** are also pervasive in school, and many students with disabilities and other special needs have difficulties learning these rules. Examples of rule learning include social behavior rules (e.g., "Always raise your hand before speaking in class."), phonics rules (e.g., "*i* before *e* except after *c*"), math rules (e.g., "When dividing fractions, invert the divisor and multiply."). Rules often include discriminations and facts, and appropriate circumstances for use of those rules. For example, students might need to know that the rules for speaking in class are different in Mr. Halleran's class than they are in Ms. Butcher's class, and that they need to learn to apply the rules appropriately in each class. In Mr. Halleran's class, students are required to raise their hands and wait until called on before speaking. However, in Ms. Butcher's class, students are free to speak out whenever they think they have something relevant to say.

Procedural Learning. Procedural learning involves the sequential execution of multiple steps, and is found frequently in school tasks. Remembering and executing the steps involved in going through the cafeteria lunch line is one example of **procedural learning.** More academic examples include reading comprehension strategies (e.g., determine the purpose, survey the material, read, recite, review), math algorithms (e.g., learning to execute the steps in solving long division problems), or learning the procedures involved in math problem-solving strategies, note-taking strategies, organizational strategies, and study strategies. Students with disabilities frequently require extensive explicit instruction in the execution of procedures. This can involve describing or listing the steps in the procedure, modeling or demonstrating the application of the procedure, or prompting students to execute the steps of the procedure. Procedural learning requires that students (a) recognize when a specific procedure is called for (e.g., in learning a list of spelling words), (b) retrieve the steps in the procedure (C–C–C, or Cover, Copy, and Compare), and (c) correctly execute the procedure (use the strategy correctly to learn the list).

Conceptual Learning. Most tasks involve some conceptual learning, which can be taught using procedures similar to discrimination, factual, and rule-learning paradigms. **Concepts** are completely learned only when the concept can be applied to a new instance. For example, students do not know the concept of "dog" if they can only identify their own household pet as a dog—they must be able to identify dogs they have never seen before. When a child riding in a car points to a horse in a field and says, "Doggie," this suggests that only part of the concept has been acquired: that dogs are four-legged animals. Further refinement through experience and instruction can develop this concept further.

Concepts can range from simple ("red") to more complex ("radial symmetry," "nonpolar covalent bonding"). Some students with disabilities or other special needs experience difficulties learning new concepts. Conceptual learning can be enhanced by the use of examples (e.g., of radial symmetry or the color red), provision of non-instances ("this is not an example of a carnivore"), and statement of and application of rules ("Insects have six legs; how many legs does this specimen have?").

Problem Solving and Critical Thinking. **Problem solving** refers to determining solutions when no specific strategy for solving the problem is known. Similarly, **critical thinking** involves using active reasoning to acquire novel concepts, ideas, or solutions. These types of learning are commonly found in science and mathematics curriculum (e.g., geometric proofs), but could also be found in any other area (e.g., solving a social problem in social studies). Problem solving and critical thinking are important goals in education, but also present some of the greatest challenges for students with disabilities. They can be enhanced by the use of careful coaching techniques, described elsewhere in this chapter, as well as in chapters 14 and 15.

Levels of Learning

Levels of learning refer to the level of proficiency attained by the student for any of the types of learning. These levels include—in order of complexity—initial acquisition, fluency, application, and generalization behaviors.

Acquisition and Fluency. **Acquisition** refers to a simple accuracy level criteria such as 9 out of 10 correct responses to listing 10 letters of the alphabet. Accuracy criteria are important in the initial stages of learning. **Fluency** combines the accuracy criteria with a specified amount of time.

Concrete experiences can help students develop an understanding of concepts. Students can see and handle objects that are one color; older students can experience how simple objects can represent levers.

For example, 90% accuracy within 2 minutes, or 90 out of 100 letters correct in 5 minutes. Fluency is particularly important when tasks need to become automatic, such as in basic literacy and math skills.

Application and Generalization. **Application** refers to applying learned skills or content to relevant contexts, and **generalization** is the ability to transfer previous learning to novel situations. For example, applying a social skill learned in a lesson in the special education setting to a role-play activity is an example of the application level. An example of generalization could be employing appropriately a social skill learned in the special education classroom in an inclusive regular education setting.

Application and generalization levels of learning can be difficult for some students with disabilities to reach (Scruggs & Mastropieri, 1984, 1994a). Simply because a student has learned a particular skill in one situation, it does not necessarily mean the student can now apply or generalize that skill to every appropriate situation. It has frequently been seen, for example, that students who have learned particular skills in special education settings have failed, at least initially, to generalize those skills when in regular classroom settings. Inclusive teaching provides opportunities for students with disabilities to generalize. Application and generalization levels of learning can be promoted by a variety of learning activities, including the following (see also Alberto, Troutman, & Feagin, 2002; Stokes & Baer, 1977):

- *Train loosely,* avoiding overly rigid presentations, so that students become familiar with employing the concept or skill in a variety of situations and contexts.
- Use "*indiscriminable contingencies*" that sometimes, but not always, reward students for applying and generalizing behavior—students are more likely to apply newly acquired behaviors (e.g., saying "please" and "thank you") when they do not know when they will be rewarded for using them.
- Use *modeling* and *role-play,* by demonstrating the behavior yourself, and having students practice in simulation situations (e.g., riding a bus or asking directions).
- Use *peer mediation,* where classroom peers help remind the student to apply or generalize learned skills.
- Teach *self-monitoring,* where students learn to systematically monitor their behavior in different situations.
- *Retrain* skills in generalization situations, for example, retrain job-related social skills in the vocational education setting.

Identification versus Production

These criteria can apply to any level of learning and refer to the type of responding that will be expected from students. Students can either identify or produce information learned at the acquisition, fluency, application, or generalization levels.

Identification includes such responses as pointing to the correct answer (e.g., on a communication board); responding to matching, multiple-choice, or true-false test formats; and are usually learned more readily. At first, examples and nonexamples should include very different stimuli until learning appears. Describe relevant and irrelevant attributes, highlighting important attributes during initial learning. Slowly add more distractors or nonexamples for students to select the correct example from during the acquisition stage of learning.

Production responses may be required after the mastery of identification responses and include writing, saying, doing (e.g., executing procedures), computing, orally reading, orally spelling, and exhibiting appropriate behavior. When planning instruction, consider whether students will be required to identify or produce correct responses. For example, if students are required to produce correct responses (such as spelling words), it is important that they practice producing, rather than simply identifying, correctly spelled words during instruction.

Addressing Learning Problems

To best address special learning needs, first, determine where the problems lie. For example, Mario is exhibiting great difficulty with multiplication and division of fractions. He can identify correct answers on a multiple-choice test (if the choices are not too similar) but he is expected to produce the correct answer for assignments and tests. If the problem is on the accuracy level, Mario cannot compute any answers (or very few), even with additional time. In this case, drill and practice may be necessary on multiplication and division facts or on relevant procedures (e.g., invert the divisor and multiply for division). Problems on the fluency level mean that Mario can compute answers accurately, but not quickly or efficiently. Additional independent practice and timed tests may be helpful. Problems on the application level may mean that Mario can multiply and divide fractions on worksheets, but has difficulty using different print formats, or applying these procedures on word problems. In these cases, practice with new formats, application of rules, and self-monitoring sheets may be helpful. Problems on the generalization level may mean that Mario can compute fractions correctly in the resource room, but not in the regular classroom, or in the "real world," such as a pizza parlor. In these cases, it may be appropriate to directly reteach the procedures in the different settings, use self-monitoring sheets, or point out similarities in calculating with fractions in different situations. In any case, it can be seen that "problems with multiplication and division of fractions" can refer to many different aspects of learning, and can imply many different teaching strategies for addressing these problems.

Once clear objectives are established that take into consideration the appropriate level and type of learning, instructional strategies best suited for each objective can be selected. Research has documented that certain strategies are clearly effective for teaching students with disabilities specific types of learning. Tables 6.1 and 6.2 present suggested instructional strategies to accompany specific levels and types of learning. Remember that many different strategies may be successful and that in teaching, identification and production formats can be considered with any of the other levels and types of learning.

Table 6.1
Instructional Strategies for Specific Levels and Types of Learning

Type of Learning	Instructional Strategies
Discrimination	Present examples and nonexamples; use models, prompts, and feedback, instruction on the relevant dimensions, mnemonics (e.g., "This is purple. This is not purple. Is this purple?"; "This is the letter 'b'. Notice that the bubble at the bottom faces toward the right.").
Factual	Repetition, rehearsal, practice using drill procedures (e.g., "*Dorado* means fish. What does *dorado* mean?"); chunking pieces of information together, elaborating on information to enhance meaningfulness (e.g., with labeled pictures of fish); using mnemonic strategies ("*Dorado* means fish. *Dorado* sounds like door. Think of a fish on a door").
Rule	Practice using the rules, repetition, making up meaningful "sayings" using the rules, drill and practice with the rules, modeling applications of the rules (e.g., "Remember, 'i before e except after c' is the rule to use to check your spelling." "Everyone, repeat the rule for recess: 'stay on the grass.' ").
Procedure	Model use of procedures, cue cards with steps of procedures written out as reminders, drill and practice, practice with applications using the procedures, mnemonics involving acronyms, feedback on recall of steps and accurate use of steps (e.g., "First we get our materials. Second, we write our names on the papers. And third, we complete the task." "Remember that SQ3R stands for Survey, Question, Read, Recite, and Review.").
Concept	Use procedures for teaching rules and discriminations, examples and nonexamples, model, prompt, feedback, use "if–then" scenarios to demonstrate instances and noninstances of concepts, use coaching questioning procedures, application activities, use elaborations to enhance meaningfulness (e.g., "if an insect has 6 legs and 3 body parts, then, is this [show picture] an insect?").
Problem solving	Use modeling, coaching, prompting, demonstrate examples of successful problem solving, show how to activate prior knowledge and use that to solve problems (e.g., "Why do anteaters have long front claws? I don't know, but what else do I know about anteaters? What do they eat? Where do they live? Now do I know why they might have long front claws?").

For Assistive Technology considerations for all types of instruction, contact the Technology and Media Division of the Council for Exceptional Children. Go to the Web Links Module in chapter 6 of the Companion Website.

Table 6.2
Instructional Strategies for Specific Levels of Learning

Levels of Learning	Instructional Strategies
Acquisition	Slower pace of instruction, model, demonstrations, lots of reinforcement for accurate responding, show examples and nonexamples, direct questions (both lower-level and higher-level depending upon the nature of the content) (e.g., "An ecosystem is a place where living and nonliving things affect and depend on each other. Look at our terrarium, here are some examples of living and nonliving things. . . . How do they affect and depend upon each other? . . . So what is the definition of an *ecosystem*?").
Fluency	Faster pace of instruction; reinforce more rapid, accurate responding; graphing performance and goal-setting; vary schedules of reinforcement; vary types of reinforcers (e.g., "Let's see how quickly and accurately we can complete our math problem solving today . . . I'll set the clock . . . ready . . . go.").
Application	Several instances and application problems, model procedures and directions, provide demonstrations, make examples concrete and meaningful, active coaching with questioning to prompt correct responding (e.g., "Remember how we did . . . , This is just like it, only now. . . .").
Generalization	Ensure students have mastered relevant skills; train and retrain in "real-world" settings and situations; train loosely, using multiple examples of stimuli; use peer assistance; use indiscriminable contingencies; train self-monitoring; use modeling and role-play; reinforce generalization; practice skills ("When we go to the store, we are going to use the *polite behaviors* that we practiced in class. What are we going to do? If you need help, how will you ask? Is this a good way?").

Using Effective Teaching Strategies

Maximizing Academic Engagement (Time-on-Task)

Research has consistently supported the idea that the more time students devote to a particular subject or skill—time on task—the more likely they are to master it. This is true whether the area is reading, science, creative writing, archery, music, or debate: More time effectively engaged in learning leads to more (and better) learning outcomes.

Implementation of curriculum and instruction, including teaching strategies, are topics on the Praxis *Special Education: Core Knowledge* Tests.

CLASSROOM SCENARIO

Jimmy

Jimmy is a 10-year-old fifth grader who was having trouble succeeding academically in school. His teacher, Ms. Merkle, believed that Jimmy had the overall ability to succeed in her classroom, but he rarely completed his work, often failed to turn in assignments, and performed poorly on his tests. As a result, he was falling far behind the other students in the class.

To try to help Jimmy succeed in school, Ms. Merkle began to pay more attention to how Jimmy was spending his time. She found that he was often the last student to take his books, paper, and pencil from his desk and begin working. During this period, he also spent more time than other students going to the pencil sharpener, asking to get a drink of water, daydreaming, or playing with pencils or rulers in his desk. On some occasions he tried to talk to students seated nearby. When Ms. Merkle recorded his behavior at the end of every minute over a 30-minute period, she found that Jimmy was actually working on his assignment only 10 of the 30 times she sampled his behavior. Clearly, if Jimmy was going to make acceptable progress in school, he was going to have to find a way to increase the amount of time he put into his schoolwork.

Students who understand the concepts they are learning are able to identify how to apply what they learn.

It seems clear that Jimmy's learning will not improve as desired until he can begin to increase the amount of time spent on his work. Although most teachers **allocate** appropriate time for learning a certain subject (by, for example, scheduling a specific amount of time per day to reading instruction), a far smaller number of teachers consistently ensure that students are actually **engaged** in learning, to the greatest extent possible, during this allocated time. This distinction between allocated and engaged academic time is critical for student learning. For example, research has suggested that, in some classrooms, less than 50% of the allocated time is actually spent engaged on relevant learning activities (e.g., Haynes & Jenkins, 1986). In these cases, teachers may be able to double the amount of classroom learning simply by increasing student engagement rates throughout the allocated time period.

Academic "On-Task" Behavior

But how can academic engaged time be maximized? The first step is to determine what is meant by academic engaged time, or "on-task" behavior. Students can be considered to be on-task academically when they are directly engaged—physically, mentally, or both—in the instructional methods or materials. It is impossible to know for certain what students are thinking at a given moment, but it is possible to observe what they are doing. Activities that are logically related to thinking and learning are more closely associated with learning success.

On-Task Student Behavior. What do on-task behaviors of students include? They vary depending on the grade level of the students, the curriculum, the type of lesson, the learning activities, and the behavior of the teacher. However, in general, students are considered on-task when they are doing such things as actively looking at or otherwise attending to the teacher, instructional materials, or other students who are actively engaged. Giving direct answers to relevant teacher questions or asking relevant questions are also considered on-task. During teacher presentations, examples of on-task student behavior include actively listening, taking notes, outlining, and asking for clarification. Likewise, being appropriately engaged in science experiments, or math manipulatives, or engaging in relevant debate in social studies can also be considered on-task. Overall, student behavior is usually considered on-task if it is logically related to instructional activities.

Some students with disabilities may be engaged in different ways. For example, some students with visual impairments, and some students with emotional handicaps, may not be actively watching the teacher, but nonetheless provide other signs that they are actively attending. Students with physical disabilities may interact differently with educational materials, but nonetheless be observed to be interacting. Students with hearing disabilities may need to watch the interpreter rather than the teacher. Some students with learning disabilities are unable to listen and take notes simultaneously, but may be on-task. Careful consideration of the special needs and abilities of different learners will reveal how different students may display appropriate on-task behavior.

However, off-task behavior is behavior that is not logically related to academic learning. Off-task behavior can include tardiness, daydreaming, attending to inappropriate material, asking irrelevant questions or making irrelevant statements, or interacting inappropriately with peers or instructional materials. These activities are negatively related to learning; in other words, the more off-task behavior that occurs in a classroom, the less learning takes place.

On-Task Teacher Behavior.   Your on-task behaviors as a teacher influence how much students learn. These include statements made directly relevant to the lesson, questioning and feedback directly relevant to the lesson, and demonstrations and modeling relevant to the lesson. These are important for lecture presentations, group discussions, and group activities and are discussed in the teacher presentation and feedback sections that follow.

Teachers may be off-task, and this behavior can impede student achievement. One example of off-task behavior is making unnecessary digressions, such as talking about personal experiences or current events that are irrelevant to the lesson. Students with special learning needs may find it especially difficult to follow teachers when they are making irrelevant digressions. During practice activities, teachers can be off-task by being unprepared with student materials, or by speaking loudly to an individual student and disrupting other students. Teachers can also be off-task by not returning promptly after breaks, allowing longer than necessary transition times, and by being unprepared for lecture presentations. In the following Research Highlight, Larrivee (1985) demonstrated how effective use of time-on-task, along with other teacher effectiveness variables, was positively related to achievement of special education students included in general education classes (see also Brophy & Good, 1986).

Effective teaching means that no matter what teaching strategy you use, you consciously think about your goals for the lesson and stay on-task with those goals.

Research Highlight

Teacher Effectiveness in Inclusive Settings

Larrivee (1985) described an investigation of 118 elementary classrooms that included a special education student (usually a student with learning disabilities) for literacy activities. Each classroom was observed on four occasions, using four different classroom assessment measures. Particular attention was paid to the student with learning disabilities and certain other targeted students. Larrivee reported that the special education students demonstrated the greatest academic achievement in classrooms where the teacher:

- made efficient use of time.
- had good relationships with students.
- provided substantial amounts of positive feedback.
- maintained a high success rate.
- provided supportive responses to students in general.
- offered supportive responses to low-ability students.

The lowest student achievement was observed in classrooms with higher levels of the following:

- Off-task behavior
- Time lost in transitions
- Punitive or critical responses
- Frequent interventions on behavior problems

Larrivee concluded that the variables consistently correlated with success of students with disabilities could be organized into four categories:

1. **Classroom management and discipline** (including efficient transitions, limited negative responses, maximized engagement rates)
2. **Feedback during instruction** (including providing positive feedback, avoiding criticism)
3. **Instructional appropriateness** (including appropriate task difficulty, high rate of correct responses)
4. **Supportive environment** (including using supportive interventions, responding supportively to problems, using punishment infrequently)

For additional information on the teacher effectiveness variables and their application in inclusive settings, see Mastropieri and Scruggs, 2002.

Questions for Reflection

1. Do you think these findings would be the same for all types of disability?
2. What differences might be found in secondary-level classrooms, and how might these be addressed?
3. Do you think Larrivee would have had different findings if classes other than literacy had been studied (e.g., science, physical education)?

Companion Website

To answer these questions online, go to the Research Highlights feature in chapter 6 of the Companion Website.

Technology Highlight

Managing Time with the Time Timer™

Many students have difficulties with understanding the concept of time, especially when told they need to keep working for a specified amount of time. Other students have difficulties with transition periods and changing from one activity to the next. One technological device called the time timer may help students visually see the amount of time left as they work and help them comprehend in a more concrete fashion the amount of time left for work or the amount of time left for one activity before moving to the next activity. The visual timer is a timer—a clock that comes in various sizes. One standard version is approximately 8 inches square and has a 60-minute timer. Another smaller 3-inch square version is also available that can be clipped to a student's belt. When setting a specified amount of time, say 15 minutes, that amount of time appears in red. A red disk actually shows on the timer when a time is set. As the time passes, the red disk disappears, such that when time is up, the red disk is gone. When this happens, students can visually see the red disk disappearing as time passes and obtain a better picture of the amount of time left. Such a device may help students feel more comfortable with the concept of time because it makes the concept more concrete for them.

For additional information on the time timers contact *www.timetimer.com* or contact 877–771–TIME.

Photograph reprinted with permission from Time Timer.

Maximize Academic Engaged Time

Research suggests that much **academic engaged time** is lost for a number of reasons including inefficient transition activities, inappropriate verbalizations, and inappropriate social behavior.

Streamline Transition Activities. **Transition activities** involve students moving from one location, subject, or group to another. Academic engaged time can be lost during transitions, through such activities as going to the rest room, sharpening pencils, and unnecessary socializing. Students with disabilities can lose time going between the regular classroom and the resource room. Smooth and effective transitions may be even more important for students with disabilities, who may require additional time for transition, and who may not adjust as easily to different activities. In addition, learning to make smooth and efficient transitions can be an important educational experience for students who can benefit from learning how to regulate their behavior more efficiently.

One way to maximize transition efficiency is to set time limits, and reinforce adherence to those limits. For example, if classes begin at the sound of a bell, let students know exactly what is expected of them when the bell rings. Typically, students should be in their places and prepared with their materials at this time. Any time lost after the bell—for example, sharpening pencils or finding workbooks or other materials—takes away from instructional time. Likewise, at the end of the class, if materials are not put away before students leave, time may be lost at some other point in the day. If your students are transitioning to a resource room, you should document the time they left the classroom, and report the time to the resource teacher. Similarly, the resource teacher should inform you when students have left the resource room to return to your class.

One obvious way to promote efficient transitions is to inform students that time lost in transition will be made up during free time, in after-school detention, or during other student activities. However, teachers can also reinforce prompt transitioning more positively by awarding points, stickers, or tokens (see chapter 7), or simply by responding positively to students when they make smooth transitions.

You can make efficient transitions by being prepared ahead of time with materials for the next activity, and not losing time looking for instructional materials, organizing supplies, or inefficiently passing out student materials. By setting a good model for transitions, you can promote good transitions in your students.

Students also have been known to delay deliberately in transition to lessons or other activities that they do not enjoy. In these cases, try to make the lessons more interesting and enjoyable, as described in chapter 9.

Reduce Inappropriate Verbalizations. Academic engaged time is lost when class discussions drift away from the point of the lesson. Teachers may find themselves wandering, and students may also wander by raising irrelevant issues. Some students deliberately attempt to keep teachers off-task to avoid getting to homework, tests, or other undesired activities.

One way to monitor inappropriate verbalizations is to audiotape or videotape individual lessons, and review them in reference to the purpose of the lesson and the appropriateness of teacher and student verbalizations. This can allow you to determine how often inappropriate verbalizations occur, when they occur, who is most likely to initiate inappropriate verbalizations (the teacher or the students), and what responses are made when they occur. This can provide you with important information on how to reduce the number of inappropriate verbalizations.

At times, however, digressions from the purpose of the lesson may reflect genuine curiosity or interest on the part of students, or a developing understanding of the concepts addressed in the lesson. In these cases, you may find it wiser to alter the lesson to accommodate student interest, as long as the digression will meet learning goals equivalent to those originally undertaken, and that enhanced student interest will make the digression a better learning experience. When this happens, acknowledge that the lesson objective has changed, and evaluate it with respect to the changes that were made. Alternatively, you can inform students that they will talk about those other important ideas after the class finishes the present activity.

Minimize Inappropriate Social Behavior. Inappropriate social behavior, including passing notes, teasing, arguing, and fighting, is one of the greatest threats to academic engaged time. When students behave inappropriately, they inhibit their own learning and often the learning of other students. Valuable class time can be lost dealing with this behavior. Inappropriate social behavior can cause much off-task behavior of students who have emotional disabilities.

Handle inappropriate social behavior quickly and efficiently, so that as little instructional time as possible is lost. Punitive classroom environments that include long-winded lectures on social behavior are not as effective (or as time-efficient) as positive learning environments where good behavior is expected and rewarded, and misbehavior is dealt with efficiently. Strategies for reducing inappropriate classroom behavior are discussed in detail in chapter 7.

Use Strategies for Individual Cases. Many classrooms contain one or more students who seem to spend far less time on schoolwork than other students. Frequently, these are the very students who need to spend more time on their schoolwork, such as Jimmy in the earlier scenario. In such cases, try to increase the students' amount of engaged time-on-task. Following are some procedures that may be helpful:

1. *Be certain the student can do the work.* Many students become "off-task" if they cannot (or believe they cannot) do the assigned work. Talk to individual students privately, and give them samples of the work to do. Ask about the difficulty of the work. If the work is considered too difficult, assign work that is more compatible with the students' abilities, or modify assignments so that they can be completed. Also, consider pairing students with peer tutors or have them work in small groups. In some cases, the special educator may be able to provide instructional support for specific subjects.
2. *Try simple strategies, such as direct appeal and proximity.* Speak to students individually, and tell them you would like to see them working harder on schoolwork. Tell individual students that you will send a signal when they are getting off-task by approaching student desks. When students return to work, walk away.

Handling inappropriate social behavior quickly and subtly can keep the class on-task.

3. *Provide simple rewards or consequences.* Students can be offered stickers, free time for a preferred activity, or other rewards for completing all work in a specified time period. Additionally, students can be required to make up work they have not completed during more desired periods such as recess.

4. *Notify parents or guardians.* Contact parents or guardians to elicit their suggestions or support for increasing on-task behavior. Perhaps arrangements can be made to link home privileges or rewards to assignment completion in school. In some cases, simply communicating the idea that parents and teachers are interested in the student's academic progress can make an important difference.

Making Effective Teacher Presentations

The teacher presentation variables describe how you can best interact and communicate with students. Although some earlier teacher effectiveness research described teacher presentation more within the context of a "knowledge transmission" model of teaching, effective teacher presentation variables are important for any model of instruction. Above all, communicate effectively with all of your students in classroom situations. This can be accomplished by employing the teacher presentation variables, known also as the SCREAM variables: structure, clarity, redundancy, enthusiasm, appropriate rate, and maximizing engagement through questioning and feedback (Mastropieri & Scruggs, 1997, 2002; Scruggs & Mastropieri, 1995).

Structure

Structure refers to the organization of the components of the lesson. Structure does not necessarily mean that the content of your lesson will be teacher-driven or that your students sit in rows doing worksheets. Rather, lessons are structured when you (a) communicate to students the overall organization and purpose of the lesson, (b) display outlines of the lesson and indicate transition points, (c) emphasize the critical points of the lesson, and (d) summarize and review throughout the lesson. Following is an example of structure in teacher dialogue, taken from a fourth-grade science lesson on ecosystems. Although the format is activities-based and inquiry-oriented, the teacher still provides a structured presentation so that all students know what they are expected to do:

> The first thing—and Mrs. (name of special education teacher), if you would like to write this on the board—the first thing you're going to do is get your supplies and aquarium. . . . The second

Some lesson activities are done in groups.

thing that I want you to do is put your gravel in, which is step number 2 . . . [repeats] . . . . The third thing that's going to happen is that you are going to fill out parts of your activity sheet. . . . (Mastropieri et al., 1998, p. 18)

Structure is particularly helpful when students who have difficulty sustaining attention, or who exhibit difficulties in language comprehension, are included in general education classrooms. Structure refers not only to providing an overall organizational framework for the lesson, but also to ensuring that students understand this organization. This can be done by telling students, writing the outline on the board or on an overhead transparency projected in front of the class, or using illustrations to indicate the lesson's sequence. For example, suppose a lesson on writing begins with students meeting in small groups to discuss writing ideas, followed by students writing individually, and then gathering in small groups to compare stories. Armed with ideas for revision, students then work independently to revise their work before a final meeting to share their completed stories. To share this process with students you could provide a series of pictures depicting students first working in groups, then one student working alone, students in groups again, and so on. Each picture could be accompanied by sentence strips that identify the main focus of each part of the writing process such as brainstorming, writing, comparing, revising, and sharing. Variations of those procedures can be used depending upon the ability levels of students and considerations of needs for students with disabilities included in the classroom.

Clarity

A teacher exhibits clarity when he or she speaks clearly and directly to the point of the objective, avoids unclear or vague language or terminology, and provide concrete, explicit examples of the content being covered. Clear presentations address only one objective at a time, and are directed explicitly to the lesson objective.

Select vocabulary and syntax that are familiar to all students in the class. If you use words that are unfamiliar to all students, take a minute to practice the word meaning:

Teacher:	Class, at 1:30, we're going to go out in the corridor—what's another word for *corridor*, Marcy?
Marcy:	Hall.
Teacher:	Good! What's another way to say "go out in the corridor," Ravi?
Ravi:	"Go out in the hall?"
Teacher:	Good! Go out in the hall; go out in the corridor . . . .

Sentence strips can be purchased at teacher stores. They are made of oaktag and are set up for teachers to use to teach writing skills.

Choose language that is comprehensible to all students, including those with disabilities and those from cultural and linguistically diverse backgrounds. For example, if students with disabilities for whom English is a second language are included in the class, use illustrations, physical modeling, or hand gestures to accompany verbally provided directions. These procedures are also beneficial for communicating with students with hearing impairments who have language difficulties, and students with learning disabilities who have language comprehension difficulties. When employing co-teaching, as described in chapter 2, the special education teacher can assume the role of promoting clarity and understanding in students whose language comprehension skills are less well developed.

To teach with clarity, it is important to eliminate vagueness in your presentations (Brophy & Good, 1986). Smith and Land (1981) reported that vague terms added to teacher presentations consistently lowered achievement. These terms are highlighted in the following teacher presentation:

> This mathematics lesson *might* enable you to understand a *little more* about *some things* we *usually* call number patterns. *Maybe* before we get to *probably* the main idea of the lesson, you should review *a few* prerequisite concepts. *Actually*, the first concept you need to review is positive integers. *As you know*, a positive integer is any whole number greater than zero. (Smith & Land, 1981, p. 38)

Clarity is also impeded by "mazes," which include confusing word patterns, false starts, and unnecessary or irrelevant repetition (Brophy & Good, 1986). The following excerpt of teacher dialogue highlights a maze that inhibits student understanding and achievement:

> This mathematics lesson *will enab*. . . will get you to understand *number, uh,* number patterns. Before we get to the *main idea of the,* main idea of the lesson, you need to review *four cond*. . . four prerequisite concepts. The first *idea, I mean, uh,* concept you need to review is positive integers. A positive *number*. . . integer, is any whole *integer, uh,* number greater than zero. (Smith & Land, 1981, p. 38)

Smith (1977) reported that lower student achievement was found in classrooms where teachers said "uh" frequently. Clarity in presentation is particularly important in inclusive settings, where students may vary in their facility for comprehending spoken language. It is important not only when lecturing, but also when providing directions for group activities, directing seat work, or leading and summarizing group discussions. Clarity can be particularly important when restating comments made by individual students, so that they will be more understandable to all students.

Redundancy

Redundancy increases learning by emphasizing and reinforcing the most important aspects of lessons. Unlike unnecessary and irrelevant repetition of words described previously, continued reemphasis of key concepts, procedures, and rules is critical to the success of the lesson. Redundancy is especially helpful in lecture formats; however, redundancy is also helpful in other contexts.

Many students with disabilities require additional opportunities to hear, see, and practice lessons before mastering the objectives. It is unnecessary for components of the lesson to be identical to provide redundancy for students. In fact, opportunities for applying and generalizing learned information to novel situations are excellent ways to incorporate redundancy within lessons. Additionally, opportunities for extra practice can be established to help provide redundancy for selected students. For example, supplemental practice times can be arranged for students either before or after school, or during lunch and study hall periods. Peers who have mastered the topics can be asked to provide assistance during these additional practice periods. Finally, some teachers schedule extra help sessions, during which times critical information is presented again, to ensure that all students can master the required objectives (see the section on pacing, described earlier in this chapter).

Enthusiasm

Students consistently learn more and appreciate the content more when teachers display enthusiasm in their teaching. Enthusiasm also creates higher levels of student engagement with the lesson, increasing academic learning time (Bettencourt, Gillett, Gall, & Hull, 1983; Brigham, Scruggs, & Mastropieri, 1992). Enthusiastic teachers create exciting learning environments, in which students perceive that learning is fun, challenges are great, curiosity is enhanced, and thinking is encouraged. Enthusiastic teachers also make learning meaningful and concrete for learners, and assist learners in becoming more motivated to learn. Enthusiastic teaching can be especially helpful for students who have histories of academic failure and are poorly motivated to succeed in school. For example, some students with learning disabilities are used to performing poorly in classes and have little motivation to attempt to succeed; however, an enthusiastic teaching style can provide the necessary excitement and encouragement to motivate such students to be successful. More detailed information about the effects of teacher enthusiasm on student motivation and affect is provided in chapter 9.

Appropriate Rate

Effective teachers deliver instruction at the optimal rate. Generally, a brisk rate of presentation throughout the lesson, and a brisk rate of interacting with students, interacts well with enthusiasm variables and helps keep lessons interesting and motivating. During basic skills instruction, a fast pace may be important in increasing learning (Carnine, 1976; Gleason, Carnine, & Vala, 1991). However, an excessively rapid rate of presentation may not be related to increased learning. When learning outcomes are not being met, changing the overall rate of presentation may allow information to be better understood by all students.

Rate of presentation is integrally related to the redundancy variable and is particularly important for students with disabilities who may require a slower rate to master information. It is important to use any continuous assessment data and make appropriate instructional decisions based on the formative data. For example, if all students in the class, including the students with disabilities, are mastering the information with the current rate, then perhaps the rate is fine or could even be increased. If, however, several students are not keeping up with the current rate of instruction, you can choose one of several instructional options, such as (a) slow the rate of presentation for the entire class, (b) provide additional "redundant" lessons for selected students, (c) provide extra opportunities for practicing the information either before or after school or during study halls, or (d) split the class in half, and have students tutor each other until mastery occurs.

Maximized Engagement

Teachers can maximize learning by maximizing the engagement of students with instruction and instructional materials. This is done by selecting materials that are at the correct level of difficulty and that are motivating and interesting for students; by careful planning, monitoring, and rewarding high rates of engagement, such as in the scenario about Jimmy; and by careful implementation of questioning, praise, and feedback, described in the following sections.

Questioning. Teachers must be effective at questioning students. Generally, the more questions asked that are directly relevant to the lesson, the more students learn from the lesson. Questioning has several purposes. First, questioning allows teachers to monitor students' understanding of the content being presented. In inclusive classrooms, questioning can be particularly helpful in determining whether all students understand the content being presented. When breakdowns in understanding are revealed through questioning, teachers can modify and adjust their instruction (considering such things as rate of presentation, choice of vocabulary, and use of examples) to address students' learning needs more effectively.

Second, questioning allows students to actively practice the information being covered. In this way, repeated questioning related to the same concept can provide redundancy necessary for information to be learned and remembered:

Teacher: In Boston, in 1770, what was one of the major concerns of the colonists, Marcia?
Marcia: Taxation without representation.
Teacher: Taxation without representation. What's another way of saying that, Dan?
Dan: That, uh, you have to pay taxes, but you don't have someone to represent you in the government.
Teacher: You pay taxes, but don't have a representative, good!

Questioning can be delivered to individuals or groups. When addressed to individuals, it may be helpful to state the question first, before calling on a particular student. If a student's name is given first, other students may be less likely to carefully consider an answer. For example, ask, "Why do you think Germany would strengthen its relation to Mexico during the first years of World War I? Frederick, why do you think this happened?" Rather than, "Frederick, why do you think Germany . . . ?"

Effective questioning in inclusive classrooms means providing students with extra time to answer.

When addressing the question to groups, it may be possible to promote "covert" responding on the part of all students, which will maximize student engagement. For example, "Now I want everyone to think about this problem, and make a prediction: If I add weight to this pendulum, will it swing more rapidly? Everyone think (pause), now, thumbs up for yes, thumbs down for no." Alternatively, ask students to write down answers to questions individually, to be read back later. For example, "Everybody, write down a definition of *metonomy,* and give an example. When you're done, we'll compare answers."

There are also different types of questioning, including lower-level questioning and higher-level questioning. Lower-level questioning usually involves repetition or restatement of previously covered information, and is often used in basic skills instruction, or in early stages of learning. For basic skills and basic facts, questioning should be fast-paced and require simple, direct answers (examples: "What is the silent *e* rule?" "What is the Pythagorean Theorem?" "What are the three branches of government?"). For this type of questioning, teachers should aim for 80% to 100% correct responding. This type of questioning is frequently used when building fluency with responding, such as when practicing math facts or vocabulary definitions using flashcards.

Higher-level questioning requires more in-depth thinking. For higher-level responses requiring thinking and reflection, questioning should proceed at a slower rate and may not require simple, direct answers. For example, "Why do you think a type of mossy algae is usually found on the north side of trees? Would this be true all over the world?" In this example, students could consider the general position of the sun in the northern hemisphere, and conclude the south side of trees may often be drier. Considering the characteristics of mossy algae, students may conclude that they may more frequently—but not always—grow on the north side of trees. This, of course, would not be generally true in the southern hemisphere. With such questioning, you should consider that students will need more time for reflection, and may need additional questioning to direct their thinking (e.g., "What conditions are favorable for mossy algae?").

Students with disabilities may need extra thinking time to respond to higher-level questions. Research has documented that when students with mild disabilities have been "coached" to answer higher-level questions they can be successful (Scruggs, Mastropieri, & Sullivan, 1944; Sullivan, Mastropieri, & Scruggs, 1995). Some recent research has documented the critical need for coaching students with disabilities. Guided and structured coaching may enable students with disabilities to answer the same questions that nondisabled students can answer without coach-

Experimenter: Anteaters have long claws on their front feet. Why does this make sense?

Student: I don't know.

Experimenter: Well, let's think. What do you know about anteaters? For example, what do they eat?

Student: Anteaters eat ants.

Experimenter: Good. And where do ants live?

Student: They live in holes in the ground.

Experimenter: Now, if anteaters eat ants, and ants live in holes in the ground, why do you think that anteaters have long claws on their front feet?

Student: To dig for ants.

Experimenter: Good. To dig for ants.

Figure 6.1
Coaching Dialogue
Note: From "L'instruzione Mnemonica e L'interrogazione Elaborativa: Strategie per Ricordarsi e per Pensare," by M. A. Mastropieri, 1995. In C. Cornoldi & R. Vianello (Eds.), *Handicap e Apprendimento: Ricerche e Proposte di Intervento* (pp. 117–124). Bergamo, Italy: Juvenilia. Copyright 1995 by Juvenilia. Reprinted with permission.

ing. For example, consider the coaching dialogue in Figure 6.1 used with students with learning disabilities and mild mental retardation to promote thinking about animals. This type of explicit coaching provides the structure and support students need to promote reasoning, but still allows them to come up with their own answers.

Some questions—some may say the most important questions—do not have simple answers with which everyone would agree. These include such questions as "Who was the United States' most important president?", "Should we go to school 12 months a year?", or "Does life exist on other planets?" Some students may have difficulty answering questions like this. When presenting this type of question, inform students that a specific answer is not required, but rather an answer that reflects both knowledge of the subject and careful thought about the answer. Give students models of good possible answers. Ask students to consider subquestions, such as "What qualities are considered important in a president?", "What things would be gained, and lost, in a 12-month school year?", or "What conditions appear necessary for life to develop? What is the likelihood that these conditions exist elsewhere in the universe?"

Feedback. How teachers respond to student answers is as important as how the questions are asked. Appropriate feedback can be helpful in informing students of their level of understanding, providing redundancy, and encouraging students to continue to learn. Feedback should be clear and overt, so that there is no ambiguity about the teacher's evaluation of the answer. When appropriate, it should provide the entire class with information on the correctness of the response of an individual student.

During rapid questioning, drill and practice of skills, or review of previously learned material, feedback may be simple and brief. In some cases, the fact that the teacher has continued with the lesson imparts the information that the previous answer was correct (e.g., multiplication facts prompted by flashcards). At other times, feedback may be more substantive.

The type of feedback delivered depends to some extent on the response that has been given (Rosenshine & Stevens, 1986). If a student does not respond right away, you should try to elicit some type of response, to determine the level of student understanding. It is important to consider whether the question is a lower-level question that should require only a short response latency (time for responding) or a higher-level question that requires a longer response latency. It is also important to determine whether the answer is unknown, the question was unclear, or whether the student simply did not hear the question. You should also determine whether students can answer the question with additional coaching or prompting. Teachers should not appear to "badger" students who clearly do not know how to respond. However, it is important to retest students later in the lesson.

See Rosenshine and Stevens (1986) for a review of research on teacher feedback.

For completely incorrect responses, a simple, tactful statement that the answer was incorrect may be sufficient. Simply state the correct answer, provide the student with a prompt or additional information and restate the question, or call on another student for the answer, as seen in the following classroom dialogue:

Teacher:	OK, let's review. What is the capital of the state of Washington, Markeisha?
Markeisha:	Salem.
Teacher:	Well, Salem is a capital but not of Washington. Danielle, do you know the name of the capital of Washington State?
Danielle:	Olympia.
Teacher:	Olympia, good! Markeisha, what is the capital of Washington?
Markeisha:	Olympia.
Teacher:	Good, Olympia is the capital of Washington. Salem is the capital of . . . ?
Markeisha:	Oregon.
Teacher:	Oregon, that's right. Good.

If an answer is partially correct, first acknowledge the part of the answer that was correct, then provide additional prompts or restate the question to elicit the rest of the answer, or call on another student. For any answer that was incorrectly answered, partially or completely, teachers should make an effort to return to the question with individual students later in the lesson to ensure that the material was learned:

Teacher:	[writes "1/4 of 1/2" on blackboard] Can anyone give me the answer? Jeri?
Jeri:	1/6?
Teacher:	No, not quite. The numerator 1 is correct, but not the denominator, 6. Anyone else want to try? George?
George:	1/8.
Teacher:	1/8, good. Do you see what George did, Jeri? He multiplied 1×1 in the numerator, like you did, but the product of the denominators, 2×4, is . . . ?
Jeri:	8.
Teacher:	8, correct.

See chapter 9 for more discussion of the best uses of praise.

If the question was correctly answered, acknowledge the correctness of the answer and move on in the lesson:

Teacher:	Now, which astronomer first determined that the planets travel in an elliptical pattern? Juanita?
Juanita:	Kepler.
Teacher:	Kepler, correct.

Praise. Praise can be an important motivator for students. When the situation warrants it, actively praise your students for paying attention to the lesson, carefully considering teacher questions, and providing answers that are correct, or at least reasonable and thoughtful. Although many teachers are concerned about delivering too much praise to students, this should not be a concern if it is delivered systematically and effectively. Effusive or overelaborate praise may not be helpful in many instances, because it may interrupt the flow of the lesson, or embarrass students (particularly on the secondary level). However, most teachers deliver too little praise to students. Praise may be particularly important to help students with disabilities or special learning needs persist in their efforts to learn.

Monitoring Practice Activities

Practice activities are intended to reinforce memory and comprehension of information that was gained in the lesson. If the lesson involves the teaching of skills, such as how to write the letters "p," "d," and "q" in cursive, practice activities are used to promote application and skill develop-

Reviewing information—opportunities for overlearning—promotes application and generalization of concepts.

ment, and to ensure the skills learned will be remembered. If the lesson involves the acquisition of content information, such as the causes of the War of 1812, practice activities promote recall, comprehension, and application objectives. If the lesson involves an activity in which small groups of students study principles of buoyancy, practice activities can enhance recall, comprehension, application, and generalization objectives.

Practice activities are particularly helpful for students with special needs, as they provide more engaged time to ensure relevant concepts are fully understood. Often, practice activities are taken from work sheets or workbooks, but practice activities can take other forms as well, such as practice with tutors or classroom peers, flashcards, computer software, or group problem solving or application tasks using relevant materials. Table 6.3 provides examples of appropriate practice activities.

Practice activities can be divided into *guided* and *independent* practice (Rosenshine & Stevens, 1986). Guided practice takes place under teacher supervision, and is most appropriate immediately after presentation of the initial concept. Students' rates of correct responding may be lower, and more teacher supervision is needed. Independent practice is done with indirect teacher supervision (some independent practice activities can be done as homework), and is undertaken when students' rates of correct responding are very high, and students can correct themselves by proofreading and checking their work.

Both types of practice are necessary to ensure that concepts are mastered and remembered, and that learning is complete for all students. Request assistance from special educators for devising supplemental practice activities and assigning when and where the extra practice can occur. For example, special educators may be able to find time to work with the students with disabilities during other school periods. Some high schools schedule students with disabilities for a supervised study hall, during which support teachers are available to provide additional study and practice assistance. Other middle schools schedule extended homeroom periods several days a week, during which students with disabilities can obtain extra practice

Table 6.3
Appropriate Practice Activities

Lesson	Practice Activity
Writing CVC words in cursive for handwriting practice.	*Guided:* Dictation by teacher, work checked after every sentence.
	Independent: Students write from manuscript models, check each others' work at the end of the period.
Solving quadratic equations from a formula.	*Guided:* Students solve problems one at a time, while the teacher monitors their execution of each step.
	Independent: Students solve a set of problems independently, corrected by the teacher at the end of the activity.

from teachers. Some schools have established regular study partners who have scheduled times to work together. Finally, some teachers have established excellent working relationships with parents and siblings at home, and enlist their help when extra practice is needed (see chapter 9 for more information).

Any successful practice activity must meet several criteria. First, it must be directly relevant to the objective of the lesson. Practice activities that do not allow students to practice the learning objectives, or are only indirectly related to the objective, will not improve student learning. Second, practice activities must be used to enhance learning that occurred during the earlier part of the lesson; practice activities usually are not intended to introduce new information or skills. Students with disabilities or other special learning needs are particularly unlikely to learn new information from work-sheet-type activities. Therefore, select practice activities that enhance and augment learning that has already occurred.

Practice activities also must be at an appropriate level of difficulty. If they are too difficult, students will not be able to work on them independently. If they are too easy, student learning will not be enhanced. Finally, it must be remembered that students soon tire of repetitive work-sheet-type activities. Keep the pace and enthusiasm level as high as possible during guided practice (e.g., "Everyone who thinks they have the answer, put your thumbs up!"). During independent practice, teachers should reinforce prompt, accurate, and neat responding, and should keep the activity moving at an efficient pace.

Homework can often be considered a type of independent practice activity, undertaken outside the classroom. Because teachers are less likely to be available to answer questions when homework assignments are being completed, it is necessary that students completely understand assignments before taking them home. It may be helpful to complete the first part of the homework assignment in class, as a guided practice activity, to be certain every student knows how to complete the assignment. Homework completion can be facilitated by having students meet in groups at the beginning of class, under the direction of rotating group leaders, to record and provide peer feedback on homework assignments.

Review

Near the end of a lesson, it is important to summarize what has been learned, and review this information with students. It is also important to review information weekly and monthly, to ensure that previously learned information is not forgotten, and that students understand the relation between previous and current learning. Although frequent review is helpful for all students, it is particularly important for students with disabilities, who are more likely to forget or not understand the relevance of previously learned material. This extra review may be especially helpful before exams. As discussed in the redundancy section, students with disabilities not only benefit from review, but may require more review to be successful. In these cases, ad-

Companion Website

Using a digital camera and scanner, you and your students can create Websites that contain their journals and portfolios. Sunburst's school version of Web Workshop contains many easy-to-use templates. For relevant Websites, go to the Web Links module in chapter 6 of the Companion Website.

ditional review can be helpful in "overlearning" information, which can help promote application and generalization.

Special education teachers can assist in either providing additional review for students with disabilities or brainstorming ideas for collecting or developing materials to be used for review. If planned initially, review sessions may be easier to schedule. For example, you could make videotapes of the class engaged in activities during the instructional unit, and then show them to students who may benefit from extra review of the information. Students can make "descriptive video scripts" (narrations describing everything in the video) to accompany the videos either on paper or on tape recorders. The Public Broadcasting System (PBS) originated descriptive video (DV) for individuals with visual impairments. Descriptive video augments the dialogue on broadcasts by inserting narrations that describe the action taking place on screens. This extra narration provides individuals with visual impairments with verbal details of the action on the screen. This technique can be used to highlight important features of classroom videos to assist students with disabilities in reviewing the important features of activities.

A variety of student journals or logs can be completed during instruction to document daily activities. Later, these journals can be used for review. Photographs of students participating in class activities can be included in the journals and students can include written captions emphasizing important concepts. The photo journals can be used for review to prompt memory of previous activities. Vocabulary journals can be maintained that include all terms used during specific classes. Personalized journals can be illustrated either with student artwork and products or with cutouts from magazines and can also be helpful as review materials. Finally, portfolios of student work can be maintained and used as review of previously learned information.

Formative Evaluation

Formative evaluation refers to the frequent and systematic monitoring of learner progress toward prespecified goals and objectives. It is different from summative evaluation, in which, for example, tests are given at the end of a school year to determine how much was learned during the year. Teachers who use formative evaluation monitor student progress continuously throughout the school year, and do not wait until the end of the year to determine whether learning took place. Students with special needs may not always learn in the same way as other students in the class, and formative evaluation provides you with information regarding whether such students are benefiting from your instruction. If not, you can modify and adjust your instruction to accommodate learning differences.

Research has suggested that formative evaluation works best when it is used at least twice a week. In some cases, student learning can be recorded on a chart or graph, so that learning outcomes can be predicted throughout the year. An example of this would be in one-minute timings of a sample of end-of-year reading selections that students administer to each other regularly in groups of two. Number of words read correctly per minute can be recorded for individuals, and for the class as a whole. This allows you to determine whether adequate progress is being made in reading fluency, and to make adjustments (e.g., increase academic engaged time) when indicated. Students could also be asked to restate, describe, infer from, or sequence the passages they read to determine whether specific comprehension skills are improving.

In other cases, student progress may be more difficult to place on a chart, but progress can still be monitored. One example might be handwriting, where weekly samples are collected in student folders. Qualitative evaluation of these products over time can provide teachers with important information regarding the adequacy of students' progress. Similarly, writing samples that portray students' writing expressiveness and creativity can be collected and compared over time; and tape recordings of oral reading can be evaluated over time for verbal expression.

Components of a Model Lesson

The teacher effectiveness variables that appear to be most closely related to high achievement have been described. But how do these variables appear in a real lesson? As you review the structure of a model lesson, observe how teacher effectiveness variables fit into a lesson sequence as indicated in Figure 6.2.

Daily Review
- Begins with a review of previous learning.
- Provides teacher with information on how much was learned and retained from previous lessons.
- An example of daily review:
  "We have been studying ecosystems. Hold up your hand if you can tell me what an ecosystem is [calls on individual students]. Yesterday, we said that ecosystems have nonliving and living parts. We listed several nonliving parts of ecosystems. Write down on your paper three nonliving parts of an ecosystem. [The teacher waits for a minute or two, walking around the classroom to encourage students to think and write answers.] Now, who can tell me what you wrote . . . ."

Statement of Purpose
- State the main objective of the current lesson in language meaningful to students.
- An example stated clearly and simply is the following:
  "Today we are going to learn about the living parts of ecosystems, and how they may interact with the nonliving parts."

Presentation of Information
- Present the content of the lesson using a variety of instructional materials, depending on the purpose and objectives of the lesson.
- Use the teacher presentation or SCREAM variables. That is, deliver content or procedures with structure, clarity, redundancy, enthusiasm, appropriate rate, and maximized engagement using questioning, feedback, and praise.

Guided Practice
- Practice newly acquired content, skills, or concepts with teacher guidance.
- Carefully monitor students and provide corrective feedback, as necessary.

Independent Practice
- Provide opportunities for students to repeat, apply, and extend information from the lesson more independently.

Formative Evaluation
- Evaluate students' independent performance.
- An example could take the form of a brief quiz: "See if you can solve the following problems independently."
- Results provide the basis for decisions about the adequacy of student progress and can be considered in planning future lessons.

Figure 6.2
Putting the Components into a Model Lesson

Promoting Effective Inclusive Instruction: The PASS Variables

To maximize the success of students with special needs in inclusive settings, we recommend using the **PASS** variables (Mastropieri & Scruggs, 1997, 2002; Scruggs & Mastropieri, 1995). PASS represents a way of thinking and approaching instruction for including students with disabilities in general education classes. PASS stands for:

Prioritize objectives.
Adapt instruction, materials, or the environment.
Use **S**ystematic instruction (SCREAM) variables during instruction.
Implement **S**ystematic evaluation procedures (Mastropieri & Scruggs, 2002)

Prioritize Objectives

Prioritizing objectives means examining all instructional objectives, determining which are the most important for students with disabilities who are included in general education classes, and eliminating objectives that are unnecessary for those students. For example, Cliff, a fourth grader with physical disabilities, is going to be included in Mr. Masoodi's science class. Cliff has severe arthritis and has a great deal of difficulty using a pencil or completing tasks that require much fine motor control. He uses canes to assist with mobility when he needs them. Any motor tasks usually require more time for Cliff to complete than the other fourth-grade students. Mr. Masoodi uses hands-on approaches to science instruction. Most class objectives revolve around active participation in the science activities and students are assessed on their participation as well as performance. To accommodate Cliff's needs, Mr. Masoodi first reprioritized his class objectives. He examined the content and selected the most important activities for Cliff to focus on specifically. Because handwriting was not a priority for that class, any assignment that required unnecessary handwriting for Cliff was eliminated. Cliff was placed in a group with other students who assisted him as needed. For example, peers often recorded Cliff's notes for him or executed the steps to manipulative activities according to Cliff's directions when he was unable to do so by himself. Cliff was then able to complete many of the activities. By first examining all the class objectives and then reviewing the instructional needs of this student with disabilities, Mr. Masoodi was able to make wise instructional decisions. This meant emphasizing the most important instructional objectives for Cliff.

Adapt Instruction, Materials, or the Environment

Once the instructional objectives have been prioritized, the instruction, materials, or environment can be adapted to accommodate more completely the needs of the students with disabilities. Adaptations can take many forms. For example, Mr. Masoodi allocated one period a day for the completion of the science activities. However, when it became apparent that Cliff needed additional time to complete many activities, he decided to keep the materials arranged on a table in the back of the room, so that Cliff could work on the science activities at other times during the school day. Mr. Masoodi also began to acquire some materials that were larger and easier for Cliff to handle. For example, the hand-lenses that came with his rocks and minerals unit were tiny and difficult for Cliff to manipulate. Mr. Masoodi acquired some hand-lenses that were larger and easier to handle, and found that Cliff was able to complete more activities with the larger hand-lens. Because there was frequent movement around the room during science class, and Cliff often needed to use his canes for mobility, Mr. Masoodi rearranged desks to create more aisle space for Cliff and his two canes. It also was obvious that Mr. Masoodi would have to pay particular attention to maintaining clear, open pathways for Cliff. To accomplish this, he enlisted the help of the other students. Each week a different student was assigned the role of monitoring the room to maintain clear, sufficiently wide spaces between rows.

Some adaptations involve changing the instructional procedures. Others may involve acquiring adaptive curriculum materials and equipment. Others may involve rearranging the classroom environment. It may be that combinations of all possible adaptations become the key to successful inclusion. Brainstorming adaptations with other teachers, especially the special education teacher, can usually result in a variety of possibilities. It is recommended that the adaptation that requires the least amount of teacher effort be tried first.

Systematic Teaching, or the SCREAM Variables

Systematic teaching refers to the use of the effective teacher presentation (SCREAM) variables, as described earlier in this chapter. As mentioned previously these variables include structure, clarity, redundancy, enthusiasm, appropriate rate, and maximizing engagement through questioning and feedback. If these variables are considered along with the specific needs of students with disabilities during instruction, all students may be more successfully included, and overall classroom achievement will improve.

Systematic Evaluation

The last S in PASS stands for systematic evaluation. Systematic evaluation means frequently measuring students' progress toward meeting the instructional objectives of the class, as well as IEP objectives, using the formative evaluation procedures described previously and in chapter 12. If students are not seen to be progressing adequately, additional modifications may be necessary.

The PASS variables can be used as a guideline for planning, delivering, and evaluating effective inclusive instruction for specific students with special needs. The *In the Classroom* feature

In the Classroom ...a feature for teachers

Sample Working Adaptation Sheet

1. Identify unit title or name.
2. Identify specific activity within unit.
3. Summarize the major goals and objectives for the unit and for individual lessons.
4. List any potential difficulties students with disabilities may encounter.
5. **P**rioritize the objectives for the students with disabilities. (HINT: Eliminate any unnecessary objectives, or make some objectives less of a priority for those individuals.)
6. **A**dapt the materials, instruction, or environment for the students with disabilities as necessary. (HINT: Describe any modifications that might be necessary for these individuals.)
7. Utilize **S**ystematic teaching strategies including <u>s</u>tructure, <u>c</u>larity, <u>r</u>edundancy, <u>e</u>nthusiasm, an <u>a</u>ppropriate pace, and a way to <u>m</u>aximize engagement. Think about how you could incorporate the teacher presentation variables into the unit. (HINT: Are there any ways of adding redundancy so individuals with disabilities may be allowed to complete variations of the activities several times?)
8. Develop **S**ystematic evaluation measures for individuals with disabilities. (HINT: Adapt any evaluation procedures to ensure you are obtaining accurate measures of student performance.)

provides a sample working adaptation sheet that can be used to modify instruction using the PASS variables. Using these variables and other information from this chapter, you can deliver effective instruction to all your students.

Summary

- Effective instruction variables are variables that have been shown to exert a positive effect on student achievement. These variables include planning for content coverage and using effective teaching strategies. Effective instruction variables have been demonstrated to be positively associated with achievement of all students in inclusive settings.
- Planning for content coverage is a critical component of teacher effectiveness. Teachers must consider carefully the role of objectives, scope and sequence, curriculum, pacing, and types and levels of learning.
- Types of learning include discrimination, factual, procedural, rule, conceptual, problem solving and critical thinking. Levels of learning include acquisition, fluency, application, and

generalization. Students can provide either identification or production responses. Consideration of types and levels of learning can be beneficial when planning instructional strategies.
- Effective teaching strategies include maximizing academic time-on-task, making effective teacher presentations, monitoring practice activities, review, and formative evaluation. All are critical components of effective teaching for all students.
- Effective teacher presentations use the SCREAM variables, including structure, clarity, redundancy, enthusiasm, appropriate rate, and maximized engagement. Additionally, effectively used questioning, feedback, and praise are all important contributors to student learning.

- Practice activities provide opportunities for students to solidify and apply their learning. Practice activities can include guided practice, in which teachers closely monitor student responding, and independent practice, in which students work more independently. Frequent review allows for long-term learning.
- Formative evaluation refers to collecting student performance data throughout the course of instructional units, so that instructional decisions can be made—such as, increasing academic engaged time—while instruction is still ongoing.
- A sample model of a lesson based on teacher effectiveness variables includes daily review,

statement of objective, presentation of information, guided practice, independent practice, and formative evaluation. Model lessons are based on careful consideration of objectives, scope and sequence of instruction, pacing, curriculum materials, and types or levels of learning expected for successful achievement of all students.
- The PASS variables stand for: Prioritize instruction; Adapt instruction, materials, or the environment; Systematic teaching using the SCREAM variables; and Systematic evaluation. The PASS variables provide a model for planning and delivering effective instruction in inclusive settings.

Council for Exceptional Children

Effective Instruction for All Students
Information in this chapter links most directly to:

Standard 4—Instructional Strategies, particularly:

Skills:
- Use strategies to facilitate integration into various settings.
- Select, adapt, and use instructional strategies and materials according to characteristics of the individual with exceptional learning needs.
- Use strategies to facilitate maintenance and generalization of skills across learning environments.

Standard 6—Instructional Planning

Knowledge:
- Theories and research that form the basis of curriculum development and instructional practice.
- Scope and sequences of general and special curricula.

Skills:
- Identify and prioritize areas of the general curriculum and accommodations for individuals with exceptional learning needs.
- Use task analysis.
- Sequence, implement, and evaluate individualized learning objectives.
- Prepare lesson plans
- Prepare and organize materials to implement daily lesson plans
- Use instructional time effectively.
- Make responsive adjustments to instruction based on continual observations.

Inclusion Checklist
Effective Instruction for All Students

If you are having problems with classroom or individual academic achievement, have you examined the following?

- ❏ Instructional objectives
- ❏ The district scope and sequence
- ❏ The curriculum materials
- ❏ The scope and sequence with the adopted curriculum
- ❏ The instructional pace
- ❏ Instructional strategies to match the level and types of learning

Have you used effective teaching strategies by:

- ❏ Maximizing academic engaged time by:
  - ❏ maximizing student on-task behavior
  - ❏ maximizing teacher on-task behavior
  - ❏ minimizing transition times
  - ❏ reducing inappropriate verbalizations
  - ❏ reducing inappropriate social behavior
  - ❏ increasing time-on-task in individual cases
  - ❏ checking difficulty of material
  - ❏ using direct appeal and proximity
  - ❏ providing simple rewards or consequences
  - ❏ notifying parents or guardians
- ❏ Maximizing effectiveness of teacher presentations by:
  - ❏ improving structure in lessons
  - ❏ increasing the clarity of presentations for all students
  - ❏ presenting sufficient redundancy

- ❏ teaching enthusiastically
- ❏ teaching at an appropriate rate
- ❏ using questioning procedures appropriately
- ❏ using lower-level questioning effectively
- ❏ using higher-level questioning effectively
- ❏ questioning when there are no obvious answers
- ❏ using feedback and praise effectively
- ❏ varying the types of feedback according to students' responses
- ❏ using praise effectively
- ❏ varying the types of praise statements
- ❏ employing appropriate practice activities
- ❏ employing sufficient review
- ❏ employing formative evaluation
- ❏ Employing all teacher effectiveness variables in model lesson format by:
  - ❏ daily review
  - ❏ statement of objective
  - ❏ presentation of information
  - ❏ guided practice
  - ❏ independent practice
  - ❏ formative evaluation
- ❏ Employing the PASS variables:
  - ❏ prioritize objectives
  - ❏ adapt instruction, materials, or the environment
  - ❏ systematic teaching using the SCREAM variables
  - ❏ systematic evaluation

Chapter 7

Kevin Krouse, 10
Galloway, Ohio
"Untitled"

Improving Classroom Behavior and Social Skills

Objectives

After studying this chapter, you should be able to:

- Describe how to observe, record, and manage classroom behaviors.
- Identify effective classroom management strategies.
- Discuss less-intensive classroom behavior strategies as well as more formal management systems, and their implications for classroom management.
- Compare and contrast different methods of assessing social skills.
- Describe interventions to improve social skills.
- Discuss and evaluate important considerations of social skills training.

All students must know how to interact with others appropriately in group learning experiences, how to engage in classroom discussion, and how to distinguish between active classroom behavior that promotes learning and active classroom behavior that disrupts learning. Classrooms are well managed when students stay on-task academically, but also feel free to actively participate in classroom activities, take risks, and interact positively with others. By attending to two important components of the classroom social environment—classroom behavior and social skills—you can dramatically improve the success of your classroom.

Managing Classroom Behavior

Cambone (1992) documented the behavior management problems of Anne, a teacher of primary-grade students with behavioral disorders. In the following scenario, Cambone describes Anne's difficulty controlling the class during a science lesson.

CLASSROOM SCENARIO

Anne

Steve has been continually thwarted by Paul's misbehavior and when Paul, perpetual motion on the bench, bounces around the bench toward Steve, Steve punches him in the side—not hard, just enough. Paul hits him back. Anne is firm, calm. "Now Steve and Paul, each of you has three minutes to sit quietly and we're not going to go on until you're finished." The room bursts into pandemonium.

Anne's mind races to meet the crisis. . . .

Paul leaps up to run from the room but Cathy [Anne's aide] grabs him. Samuel starts rocking back and forth, head like a rag doll. Paul is yelling [obscenities]. "Paul, you have to the count of three to be back on your bench or you will leave the classroom. One, two . . . " Paul stops screaming and cursing, smiles at his classmates, cocky. Samuel gets quiet but then laughs and seems like a willing participant in the misbehavior. "Now the whole group is going to sit." When they hear this, the room bursts into chaos again. Paul grabs [himself] and starts shouting suggestive words. Samuel laughs hysterically. Paul lifts his shirt and displays his stomach provocatively to Samuel, sing-songing, "BELLYBUTTON!!" Anne takes his arm and starts to remove him. . . . (Cambone, 1992, p. 358)

This scenario describes a teacher losing control of her classroom. Although Anne began to gain more control of her class as the year continued, maintaining positive behavior in the classroom causes great anxiety for most teachers. Understanding the factors that cause and maintain problem behavior can help you improve your students' behavior.

Understanding Behavior Problems

Why do some students work hard and behave well in school, while others seem angry, disruptive, or noncompliant? A variety of explanations exists for these diverse responses. Dreikurs and Cassel (1992) believe that all students essentially want to be liked and accepted by others, but that they might have *mistaken goals* that problem behavior will get them the acceptance they want. These mistaken goals include the following:

1. Gaining attention
2. Concealing inadequacy
3. Gaining power or control over people or situations
4. Exacting retribution or revenge from real or perceived injuries

According to Dreikurs and Cassel, teachers can identify these mistaken goals and replace them with more appropriate and positive goals.

Canter and Canter (1993) suggest that many students get into antagonistic relationships with teachers and other school personnel because they lack trust in adults. For a variety of reasons, they may not believe the adult is necessarily acting in their interest, and may be reluctant to comply with even simple classroom directions. Intervention then, for Canter and Canter, should focus on reestablishing trust between students and adults.

Observing and documenting student behavior is the first step in determining an appropriate intervention strategy to help the student control future behavior.

Student behavior is also a response to the environment, which includes the teacher, peers, other school personnel, and even the physical environment (Kerr & Nelson, 2002). In all cases, an important key to effectively managing classroom behavior—and controlling the negative behaviors of some individual students—lies in establishing positive, caring relationships with all students in your class, implementing and consistently enforcing effective rules for classroom behavior, and helping students learn to make positive choices that increase their level of success in school.

One problem teachers frequently have is precisely describing the problem behavior that they would like the student to change. While it may be true from the teacher's point of view that a student "misbehaves" or "has a bad attitude," such terms do not specify the behavior problem so that strategies for changing the behavior can be easily implemented and evaluated. Before effective interventions can be implemented, you must first carefully define classroom behavior, so it can be easily observed and recorded.

Observe and Record Classroom Behavior

Define Behavior

Before interventions on classroom behavior can be carried out, carefully observe and document those behaviors. This process allows you to determine precisely what behaviors need to be changed, and to evaluate whether progress is occurring after interventions. Several observation systems can be employed to accomplish this.

The first step in observing and recording behavior is to *operationally define* the behavior in question. This means that you describe the behavior so that another person knows exactly what is meant. For example, if you describe a student as "has a bad attitude," it may be difficult to know exactly what you mean. However, if you use specific behavioral descriptions, such as "late to class 70% of the time," or "takes at least 10 minutes after the assignment has been given to become actively engaged, 50% of the time," it is much easier to know what is meant. It is also much easier to specify how the behavior is to change, and to know whether it has changed. For example, if "late to class less than 20% of the time" is specified as a behavioral objective, it will not be difficult to determine whether this objective has been met. Many students with disabilities have behavioral objectives such as these included on their IEPs.

Following are some examples of **operational definitions** (other definitions of the same behaviors are possible and may be more appropriate in particular situations):

- **On-task.** Student's eyes are directed toward the teacher (or classmate, if making a relevant contribution) or instructional materials (e.g., books, pencil, paper, laboratory materials), and manually engaged with instructional materials when appropriate.
- **In-seat.** Student in direct, physical contact with the seat, facing forward, sitting upright, with feet on the floor.
- **Teasing.** Student makes inappropriate, unsolicited remarks to another student, apparently intended to hurt or offend the other student; or, student stares provocatively, gestures inappropriately, or makes inappropriate facial expressions to another student.

When you use operationalized behaviors, it is easier to create a behavioral objective (see chapter 6), specifying (a) the content of the objective, (b) the conditions under which a student's performance will be assessed, and (c) the criteria for acceptable performance. For example, an objective for on-task behavior could be: "The student will exhibit on-task behavior in social studies class, to a criterion of 85%, for four out of five consecutive days." This behavior can then be recorded, in baseline (pre-intervention) or intervention conditions, to determine whether it has improved.

Use Observation and Recording Systems

Table 7.1 provides some examples of observation and recording systems. These can be used to record specific behaviors, depending on the type of target behavior, and the circumstances under which it is exhibited (e.g., Alberto, Troutman, & Feagin 2002; Martin & Pear, 2002).

Observing and recording behaviors are much more difficult with large numbers of students. Some strategies for observing with large classes include enlisting the assistance of an aide, enlisting peer assistance, or observing a small number of students at a time. When observing the whole class, try using seating charts, and time sampling at longer intervals—for example, at the end of every 10-minute interval, make a checkmark on the square representing the desk of every student who is off-task.

Determine the Context of Behavior

One good strategy for determining the dynamics of classroom behavior is to use an "A-B-C" chart (Bijou, Peterson, & Ault, 1968; Zirpoly & Melloy, 1997). The teacher creates a chart with three columns: **A**ntecedent, **B**ehavior, and **C**onsequence (see Figure 7.1 for an example). The target behavior to be observed is noted in the middle column, but the events that occurred immediately before the behavior (antecedent) are also noted, as well as the consequence, or what happened following the behavior. For example, you may find that peer attention was almost always a consequence of the behavior, or that independent work assignments usually were the antecedent (Zirpoly & Melloy, 1997). Such analysis can help provide insights into classroom factors, including mistaken goals, that help establish and maintain specific behaviors. These insights are helpful in planning interventions. Consider a case in which Sean typically acts out in socially immature ways when given written assignments. This gains the attention of some students in the class, which appears to reinforce Sean. You may decide to examine the assignments to determine whether they are (or Sean perceives them to be) too difficult or uninteresting. If so, you could reduce the difficulty level of the assignments, increase the interest level, and provide positive support of some kind for Sean's assignment completion. Further, you could arrange an intervention in which you support other students for ignoring Sean when he acts out. Although these strategies are likely to work, they may not—to be more certain of their effectiveness, graphically present data on Sean's behavior both before and after intervention.

Table 7.1
Observation and Recording Systems

Name	Description
Event Recording	Observer tallies the number of times a particular behavior occurs. This procedure is best when documenting behaviors that are discreet, such as talk-outs, tardiness, or tantruming. If the duration of these behaviors is always similar, or irrelevant, the observer simply records the number of events.
Duration Recording	Observer records (e.g., with a stopwatch) the cumulative amount of time during which the behavior occurs. This system is appropriate when the length, or duration, is of concern. For example, a teacher may wish to record the total amount of time a socially withdrawn student engages in solitary play activities during recess. The observer starts the stopwatch when the socially isolate play begins, and stops it when the child begins interacting with others. The recording resumes when the child returns to isolate play.
Interval Recording	The observer sets an interval, say, 1 minute, and documents whether a particular behavior has occurred at any time during that interval. For example, if talking to classmates is the target behavior, the observer records for each 1-minute interval whether the behavior has occurred. At the end of the period in question (e.g., a 50-minute class period), the number of intervals in which the behavior has occurred is divided by the number of intervals (e.g., 50). Therefore, if talking to classmates was recorded for 10 intervals, then the amount of talking for the time period could be recorded as $^{10}/_{50} = 20\%$.
Time Sampling	At a specific point of time, the observer records whether a behavior is occurring. For example, a recorded "beep" goes off in an observer's headset every minute. At that instant the observer records whether the behavior (e.g., on-task) is being exhibited. At the end of the period, as with interval recording, the observer can divide the number of times a target behavior has occurred with the number of times that were sampled.

Student's name: __Marcie__   Observer: __Mrs. Wilson__

Setting: __Cafeteria__   Date: __April 7, 2004__

Observation time period: __Lunch, 12:15 – 12:45__

Antecedent Events	Behaviors Observed	Consequent Events
12:22: Marcie approaches a table in the lunchroom where several students are seated.	Shawna told Marcie, "You can't sit here!"	Marcie sits at another table.
12:28: Students seated at lunch table.	Shawna calls out to Marcie, "Marcie, you stay over there."	Marcie makes a face at Shawna.
12:45: Students are leaving the lunch area.	Shawna steps in front of Marcie, ostentatiously.	Marcie pushes Shawna, and says, "You get away from me!"

Figure 7.1
Example Record Form for an ABC Analysis

Figure 7.2
Recording On-Task Behavior

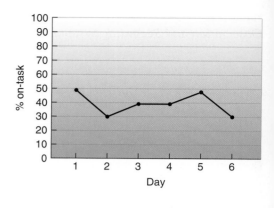

Figure 7.3
Recording an Intervention on On-Task Behavior

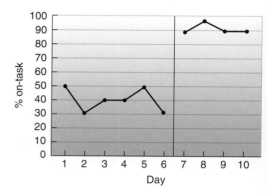

Make Graphic Presentations of Data

Behavior is much easier to evaluate over time if it is presented in some type of chart or other graphic display (Martin & Pear, 2002; Scruggs, 1992). For example, suppose the percent of time-on-task during math class is recorded for that week. Usually the amount of behavior exhibited is recorded on the vertical axis, and the time (e.g., days) is recorded on the horizontal axis, as shown in Figure 7.2.

In this figure, the vertical axis records the percent of on-task behavior for each day, and the horizontal axis records the days when the behavior was measured. On-task behavior is *stable* (does not appear to be going up or down, over time), but is lower than desirable. If an intervention is planned, such as praise for on-task behavior and for task completion, the effectiveness of this intervention can be evaluated, as illustrated in Figure 7.3.

From the data in Figure 7.3, it appears that the intervention is having a positive effect on the behavior, at least initially. For the most positive behavioral effects, use effective classroom management strategies.

Use Effective Classroom Management Strategies

Establish a Positive Classroom Atmosphere

The first and most important step in effective classroom management is establishing and maintaining a positive, supportive classroom atmosphere. Students are more likely to follow directions, work hard, and exhibit positive classroom behavior when they feel wanted and appreciated by the teacher. You can influence the classroom atmosphere, and should make the classroom warm and accepting of all students (Scruggs & Mastropieri, 1994b). If individual students perceive that you like them and are on their side, they will feel more like working hard and behaving well for you. This may be especially true of particularly difficult students, who may not trust adults, and who may feel that most teachers are "out to get" them.

Project a Feeling, Caring Persona. Convince students that you like them (even though you might not always like their behaviors). Take time to greet students at the door when they first come into the classroom. Address students by name, and express an interest in their activities. If you learn of a student about to enter your class who appears to need special encouragement, or who may

More information on graphic presentation of data is provided in chapter 12. For information on more complex recording systems for establishing validity of an intervention, see Martin and Pear, 2002.

Structuring and managing the learning environment are topics on the Praxis *Special Education: Core Knowledge* Tests.

need special help, call the student at home before the class begins, to welcome the student into your class. Build up a store of positive comments to individual students, so that if later you must deliver negative feedback, it is not the first evaluation you have made of the student. Use social praise whenever possible, but praise difficult or limit-seeking students discreetly. Above all, try to assure all students that you genuinely like them, and you have their best interests in mind. Even though you will have both positive and negative reactions to their specific behaviors, you nevertheless always value them as individuals.

Teach with Sincerity and Enthusiasm.   Use interesting and motivational activities, and avoid long-winded lectures and lengthy independent work-sheet activities (Brigham, Scruggs, & Mastropieri, 1992). Vary the classroom activities, and avoid a tedious sameness in classroom routine. Prolonged boredom in classrooms promotes alienation, indifference, and ultimately, behavior problems. If students enjoy your class and are interested in the subject, they will be less likely to misbehave.

Try to maintain a very high rate of correct student responding to your questions, to build student confidence (see chapter 6 for details). Ask insecure or withdrawn students questions to which you are certain they know the answer; or give them a hint before class that you may be asking them a particular question. Tape record yourself during class and review the tape to determine whether you are being as positive as you would like to be. Think of some of your own favorite teachers from when you were in school, and try to emulate some of their positive behaviors.

If you find a student in your class who exhibits hostile or aggressive behaviors, it is particularly important that you establish relations that are as positive as possible. This is true even if the student is rarely or never positive with you. You must enforce rules fairly and consistently, and you must not give in to student attempts to control the classroom agenda; nevertheless, you should always remain calm and polite, reminding difficult students that you simply wish to see them make good decisions (Canter & Canter, 1993).

Use Less Intensive Strategies

Rules.   An important early consideration for effective classroom management is familiarizing all students with your classroom rules. For younger students, post the classroom rules in a place where all students can observe them. Write them as positively as possible. When rules are first posted, describe them carefully to the class, model the behaviors covered by the rules, and ask students to give their own examples. Discuss instances and noninstances of following the rule. For example:

Teacher: One rule we have says "Respect other people." That means that I don't do anything hurtful or inconsiderate to any other person. For example, if I am a student and I take another student's eraser without asking to borrow it, is that respecting other people?

Class: No.

Teacher: No, it's not. If I tease another student on the playground, is that respecting others?

Class: No.

Teacher: No, teasing isn't respecting others. Who can give me a good example of what you could do to respect others? James?

James: You could move over and make room for them when we do group work.

Refer to these rules often when discussing classroom behavior. Keep the rules simple, and list only a few. Ultimately, rules will be followed to the extent that they are consistently enforced; however, at first it is important that all students consider carefully the meaning of class rules. Rules for junior or senior high school could be similar to the rules described previously; however, it may be better to pass them out with other student materials rather than posting them in the classroom, and asking students to come to you if they have questions. If you have students with special needs who you think might not understand some rules, it may be helpful to meet with them independently before or after school.

Praise and Ignoring.   Posting and discussing classroom rules can help orient students to classroom expectations. However, simply posting rules is unlikely to lead to improved classroom behavior. Madsen, Becker, and Thomas (1968) reported that posting rules alone had little effect, but that

On the elementary level, try using a "hot seat" activity as described in chapter 9.

Strategies intended to promote interest and motivation in the classroom are in chapter 9.

ignoring inappropriate behavior and praising appropriate behavior can positively influence classroom behavior. While potentially dangerous disruptive behavior must be attended to, many inappropriate behaviors can be effectively attended to by ignoring and pointing out positive models. For example, if a particular student is not getting books and materials ready for a new lesson, the teacher could acknowledge a positive example of a student seated nearby and say, "I like the way Melissa has put away her spelling book and taken out her reading book. She has all her materials ready and is ready to start class. Thank you, Melissa."

Such comments show well-behaved students that their efforts are appreciated and provide a model for other students. Ignoring inappropriate behavior and focusing attention on productive behaviors has been found to substantially improve behavior in elementary classrooms (Becker, Madsen, & Arnold, 1967).

Peers can help to ignore inappropriate social behavior. Carlson, Arnold, Becker, and Madsen (1968) described the case of an 8-year-old girl who threw tantrums in class. To not reinforce this behavior by removing the student from the class, the teacher rewarded the rest of the class for ignoring her. Later, the girl was given the opportunity to earn a treat for the rest of the class by not throwing a tantrum. This procedure was found to be more effective than removing her from class.

In most cases, teachers praise their students far too little. Although any intervention can be overdone, if praise is genuine and sincere (see chapter 9), most students will respond positively to a great deal of praise.

Proximity. Physical **proximity** has long been recommended as one simple strategy for promoting more positive classroom behavior (Redl & Wineman, 1965). Effective teachers do not remain seated at their desks, but establish a more dynamic presence in the classroom, attracting student attention by moving around the classroom. Moving closer to students who are beginning to demonstrate off-task or disruptive behavior can, in many instances, help to minimize classroom behavior problems. Werts, Zigmond, and Leeper (2001) demonstrated that proximity of paraprofessionals greatly improved the on-task behavior of primary grade students.

Direct Appeals. Often overlooked as a behavior management strategy, **direct appeals** can be effective. Students can simply be asked personally to follow class rules more carefully; alternately, a more systematic procedure can be used (Redl & Wineman, 1965). Mary, an eighth grader in Ms. Simms' math class, frequently whispered and giggled with her neighboring classmate during whole-class activities. During an independent seatwork activity, Ms. Simms asked to speak to Mary privately:

> Mary, you're a good student, and I appreciate the good work you do in class. But I have a problem. Often, when I try to speak to the whole class, or do an activity with the whole class, I notice you talking to your friend Shawna. I know you try to keep your voice down, but it makes it very difficult for me to concentrate on teaching when I know you are talking to someone else. Also I think you and other students are distracted by your talking and don't learn as much as they should. So what I want you to do for me is talk to Shawna during recess, or break, or lunch, but please not during class. Do you think you can do that?

Ms. Simms also related that if she saw Mary talking again, she would prompt her to stop by moving toward Mary's desk (proximity). After this conversation, Mary's talking decreased substantially, and after a few prompts, remained in control throughout the school year.

Another example of direct appeal to promote attending is given in chapter 10.

Use Reprimands Judiciously. Although positive responses to positive behavior are among the best overall methods of classroom management, negative feedback in the form of reprimands is sometimes necessary to help students succeed in your class. Overall, reprimands are best viewed as direct feedback that the student's behavior is inappropriate. If they are provided in a way that indicates concern for the student's well-being, they can be effective in improving behavior. Reprimands are less effective when viewed as punishment—that is, that criticism and scorn, or a negative, aggressive, or hostile tone of voice are expected to prevent the student from repeating the inappropriate behavior. Delivered in this way, reprimands may sometimes be effective in the short run, but are likely to create resentment and lack of trust in the long run.

Kerr and Nelson (2002) reviewed research on reprimands (e.g., Van Houten, Nau, MacKenzie-Keating, Sameoto, & Colavecchia, 1982), and the *In the Classroom* feature on page 196 offers a list of their recommended guidelines for using reprimands. It is also important that teachers link repri-

For some students, correcting inappropriate behavior can be done with a direct appeal in a one-on-one conversation.

mands directly to class rules, and avoid warnings, threats, sarcasm, or ridicule that may further alienate the student. However, avoid allowing students to argue with you, by saying, for example:

- "For what? What'd I do?"
- "I didn't do anything!"
- "You let Fredericka do it!"
- "James started it!"

In some instances excessive warnings have been known to increase the amount of inappropriate behavior (e.g., Twyman, Johnson, Buie, & Nelson, 1994). If your reprimand is ineffective, and the behavior persists, avoid making additional reprimands. Instead, a more intensive, prearranged contingency should be enforced (e.g., the student loses a privilege, or a call is made to the student's home). If a student repeatedly argues with you, it may be helpful to set "arguing" as a personal target for that student to work on.

Validate the Student's Feelings.   Sometimes when faced with a reprimand, students accuse teachers of unfair treatment: "It doesn't matter what I do, you're always picking on me!" This type of accusation often results in a defensive statement from the teacher: "I am not picking on you," or "I treat everyone in this class the same."

Instead of making a defensive comment, try validating the student's feelings by asking for specifics: "I really don't want you to think I am always picking on you. If you give me specific examples, maybe we can solve this problem." Such an approach not only avoids a confrontation, it also validates the student's expressed feeling (whether "true" or not), as well as subtly challenging the student to document "always" being picked on. It also openly attempts to keep the lines of communication open (Canter & Canter, 1993).

Use More Formal Management Systems

Informal management systems can be helpful; however, when problems continue, more formal management systems may be necessary.

Reinforce Positive Behavior.   Praise is an effective method of promoting a positive classroom atmosphere and positive social behavior. However, sometimes more tangible reinforcement is required. Tangible reinforcement includes such things as stickers, stars, or "primary reinforcers" such as snacks or drinks. Some teachers disapprove of tangible reinforcers because they believe students should learn to work for the satisfaction of doing well in school. However, for some students, more

In the Classroom ...a feature for teachers

A Summary of Research on Reprimands

- Reprimand students privately, not publicly, to avoid humiliating or embarrassing the student.

- Stand near the student you are reprimanding. This allows you to use a more confidential tone of voice. However, remaining one leg length away respects the student's personal space.

- Use a normal tone of voice. Students can become desensitized over time to raised voices, and may be less inclined to respond defensively to a calm tone.

- Look at the student while you are speaking, but do not insist that the student return your eye contact. Forced eye contact can be viewed as hostile and aggressive, and in some cases can violate some cultural norms.

- Do not point your finger at the student you are reprimanding, as this again conveys aggression and hostility.

- Do not insist on having the last word. This may be particularly true when dealing with adolescents. The final goal of your reprimand is increased student compliance with class rules, and if this goal is achieved in the long run (e.g., the student ultimately returns to work, or stops bothering a classmate), a little face-saving posturing may be allowable.

Source: Adapted and reprinted with permission from Kerr, M. M., & Nelson, C. M. (2002). *Strategies for Managing Behavior Problems in the Classroom* (4th ed., pp. 209–210). Upper Saddle River, NJ: Merrill/Prentice Hall.

---

tangible rewards may be necessary to help them make the transition to the general education classroom. Survey students or keep personal records to determine what sort of reinforcers appeal to your students. Check out teacher stores that carry stickers, pencils, or other supplies that could be used as rewards. Rewards should be applied consistently, for following specific rules or meeting specific academic or behavioral objectives.

Sometimes a student with special needs may require rewards for doing things for which other students in the classroom do not require rewards. For example, Larry is a student with mental retardation who is newly enrolled in a general education sixth-grade classroom, and exhibits a great deal of difficulty sustaining attention on academic tasks. Larry does not respond well to reprimands, but he loves animal crackers. His special education teacher, Ms. Wills, told the general education teacher, Mrs. Leinart, that Larry would work for prolonged periods of time (with prompting) for a reward of a small number of animal crackers. With the approval of Larry's mother, Mrs. Leinart made an arrangement with Larry that if he continued working on his assignments for 5 minutes he would receive 1 point. After he collected 25 points, he could receive an animal cracker to eat at lunch. She made a point sheet, and let Larry know after every 5-minute period whether he had earned a point.

Sometimes individual rewards can be combined with group rewards. If students feel "left out" that students with special needs are receiving rewards while they do not, allow the class to have some group reward if the students with special needs meet their goals. This allows students to help and encourage the students, rather than feeling left out. Emphasize that some students need to be treated a little differently to succeed in school, and that fairness has more to do with meeting people's needs than with everyone being treated exactly the same.

Use Punishment Judiciously. Punishment involves providing negative consequences to inappropriate behavior. Punishment is less effective in the long run than positive reinforcement, but is sometimes necessary to maintain order and provide a safe environment for all students. Canter and Canter (1993) recommend posting a Discipline Hierarchy so that students are informed about the consequences for violating a rule. Another advantage of posting rules and consequences is that the teacher can assume the role of enforcer or arbiter of class rules, rather than the role of a dictator who administers rewards and punishments at whim. If rules are consistently enforced, the teacher can merely state, "I'm sorry you broke the rules, too, but you were aware of the consequences. I will try to help you follow the rules better in the future."

The following *In the Classroom* feature shows a sample Discipline Hierarchy for grades 4–6, recommended by Canter and Canter (1993). The severe clause refers to any severe breach of class rules, such as vandalism or fighting and it replaces the routine sequence of the Discipline Hierarchy. That is, if a student disrupts the entire class, or endangers the safety of other students, the student is sent to the principal, regardless of whether it is the first, second, or third violation of a rule.

A Think Sheet documents that the student is well aware of the rule that was broken, why the rule was broken, the consequences of breaking the rule, and that the student has a strategy for dealing with the same situation more appropriately in the future. A Think Sheet is presented in the *In the Classroom . . . for sharing with students* feature, which can be found in the Companion Website.

Some students are able to convince their parents that the teacher is simply picking on them, and that they did not really do anything wrong. In these situations, place a tape recorder near the student, and inform the student that you will be tape recording for the remainder of the period. Then play the tape later for the parents. This in itself may help control the behavior. If the inappropriate behavior is more physical, consider placing a videotape recorder in the classroom (where school policy permits) to monitor classroom behavior.

Other more severe types of punishment are also sometimes used. **Overcorrection** refers to requiring the student to compensate beyond the effects of the misbehavior. For example, if a student deliberately made a mess at the lunch table, the student could be required to clean not only the one table, but all the tables in the cafeteria. *Suspension* involves not allowing the student to return to school for a specified time period. Some schools use *in-school suspension,* in which the student must attend a specific suspension room in the school, but is not allowed in the regularly assigned classroom. Removing the student from school usually involves a group decision of teachers and administrators.

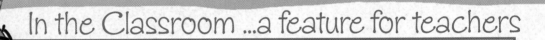

In the Classroom ...a feature for teachers

Sample Discipline Hierarchy for Grades 4–6

First time a student breaks a rule:	Warning
Second time:	10 minutes working away from the group
Third time:	15 minutes working away from the group plus fill out a Think Sheet
Fourth time:	Call parents
Fifth time:	Send to principal
Severe clause:	Send to principal

Note: From *Succeeding with Difficult Students: New Strategies for Reaching Your Most Challenging Students* (p. 138), by L. Canter and M. Canter, 1993, Santa Monica, CA: Lee Canter & Associates. Copyright 1993 by author. Reprinted with permission.

Many states limit the number of days a student with disabilities may be suspended (e.g., 10 days) until it is considered a change of placement, and requires a formal placement decision of the multidisciplinary team. It is also important to consider whether the behavior for which the student is being suspended is a consequence of the disability. If so, suspension may be considered a type of denial of school services because of the student's disability—which, of course, is inappropriate.

Some states also allow teachers or administrators to administer **corporal punishment,** such as paddling or some other method of inflicting physical pain. Such treatment is almost never more effective than alternatives, and is almost certain to promote resentment and anger in the student. The Council for Children with Behavioral Disorders (CCBD) (1990) has issued a position statement on punishment generally, arguing that some punishment procedures may sometimes be needed, but that corporal punishment should not be used to manage problem behavior of students with or without disabilities.

> It is especially unfortunate that use of corporal punishment continues in face of the considerable evidence that other behavior reduction procedures are probably more effective. (CCBD, 1990, pp. 252–253)

Reward Students with Token Systems. **Token systems,** or token "economies," can be used with individual students, small groups of students, or entire classrooms. In a token system, students who follow class rules are awarded points at the end of specified time periods, such as class periods. The positive benefits of token systems have long been observed (Jenkins & Gorrafa, 1974; McLaughlin & Malaby, 1976). Remember Larry and how tokens for animal crackers were used as a reward for increased on-task behavior? His tokens were offered in shorter increments of time because this met his special need. For other situations, however, you may want to award bonus points for unusually hard work or cooperative behavior. A sample chart that can be used to record tokens awarded to individual students is presented in Figure 7.4.

In this figure, students receive a star if they follow a classroom rule throughout a particular time period. In some cases, the period can be the entire school day. For younger students or stu-

Class Rules

1. Always respect other people.
2. Raise your hand before speaking.
3. Remain in your seat.
4. Ask for help when you need it.
5. Complete all assignments.

Student	Rule 1	2	3	4	5
Marybeth	*	*	*	*	*
Bill	*	*	*	*	
Shawna		*	*		*
Michelle	*	*	*	*	*
Arnold	*	*	*	*	
James	*	*	*	*	*
Dustin	*	*	*	*	*
Chico		*	*	*	*
Kelly	*			*	*
Pam	*	*	*	*	*

Figure 7.4
Sample Recording Chart for Token System

dents with special needs, it may be more appropriate to evaluate behavior after each period. Students can accumulate stars, or points, and exchange these later for small prizes (such as stickers or school supplies) or privileges. Entire classrooms can be awarded points after each period, depending on the behavior of all students, and thus accumulate points toward group rewards, such as a popcorn party, or a longer recess break. Teachers can also post a "menu" of prizes or privileges that can be exchanged for tokens, and the corresponding "price" of each. For older students, try holding an "auction" of possible prizes that students can bid on. Students can be surveyed ahead of time on their preferences for prizes.

Like all behavior management systems, token systems are most effective when they are used primarily to reward positive behavior. In many cases, not earning positive points can motivate students to exhibit appropriate behavior. However, when necessary, token systems can also be used as punishment for seriously inappropriate behavior, such as deliberately endangering the safety of classmates. In a procedure also known as **response cost** (Buchard & Barrera, 1972), previously earned points are withdrawn for serious misbehavior. If using response cost, be certain that students have been informed of this consequence ahead of time.

Some educators object to token systems (and other reward-based systems) as attempts to bribe students for behavior they should exhibit without rewards (see also chapter 9). Certainly, token systems are inappropriate in situations in which less-intensive treatments are effective. Also remember that token systems alone are unlikely to be effective if no other alterations of the classroom environment are made. That is, if you have not established a positive classroom atmosphere, and have not gained the respect and trust of your students, a token system is unlikely to be effective (Kuypers, Becker, & O'Leary, 1968).

Train Positive Attributions. Many students with problem behaviors make **negative attributions;** that is, they attribute things that happen to them to forces outside of their own control. For example, Nick is an eighth grader who had been classified as having behavioral disorders because of his oppositional and disruptive behaviors with teachers and peers. When interviewed about his behavior problems, Nick attributed his behavior problems to, first, a teacher's unexplained prejudice, and second, to the unexplained influence of the passage of time:

- Like I had this teacher and, uh, I didn't really like her. She was rude to me; she always picked on me. Like, someone would be doing something, they'd get in trouble, and she'd be all furious, and she'd come and take it out on me.
- Well, I'm doing better this year. . . . It's like, every other year, I'm good or I'm bad. Last year I was bad so supposedly this year I'm going to be good (Snapshots 2, 1997).

Tokens awarded for good behavior can be accumulated and redeemed for a greater reward or privilege.

In each instance, Nick explained his behavior as being under the control of other people or other events, and not under his own control. This type of explanation not only provides an excuse for inappropriate behavior, it absolves Nick of responsibility for this behavior. According to these explanations, it is provoked or caused by outside forces.

Nick could simply be informed of more appropriate attributions after each incident of misbehavior, for example:

> Nick, the reason you got in trouble is not that the teacher doesn't like you—the reason you got in trouble is that you threw your book and swore in class.

Nevertheless, Nick probably will make more **positive attributions** only after he has internalized the relevance and importance of these attributions, and begins to believe that refocusing attributions is really in his own interest. Negative attributions can be resistant to change, because they serve to both excuse the individual from blame or criticism and to justify inappropriate behaviors. To make positive attributions, students must begin to take responsibility for their behavior. Retraining in more appropriate attributions usually takes considerable time, and requires frequent review of appropriate attributions for positive outcomes . . .

> The reason you got to come with us to the zoo today was that you tried very hard to control your talk-outs this week. Good job!

. . . as well as negative outcomes:

> The reason you got detention today is that you didn't do your work and you argued with your teacher. Let's talk about some ways to keep out of detention in the future.

Your students are also much more likely to change their negative attributions in an atmosphere of trust and caring. If students do not trust you, or do not believe you are looking out for their best interest, they are more likely to cling to negative attributions, for example, that teachers simply do not like them. Other examples of training positive attributions are given in the Think Sheet provided in the Companion Website, and debriefing activities (discussed elsewhere in this chapter), which require students to describe their own behavior and the consequences of the behavioral choices they make. The most important effect of these procedures is in helping students learn that making good choices about their own behavior is in their own best interest.

Post Positive Behavior. Public posting of students' behaviors has also been seen to reduce behavior problems (Kerr & Nelson, 2002). In one instance, public posting of daily quiz scores where behavior had been a problem improved both behavior and quiz scores (Jones & Van Houten, 1985). The daily quiz scores were displayed on laminated pieces of poster board, and were recorded for 5-day periods. In other variations, student's behavior can be evaluated and recorded on a publicly posted chart. Students who follow all class rules can be given a star next to their name for each class period, day, or other appropriate length of time.

Use Timeout for Specific Behavior Problems. **Timeout** refers to some type of separation of the student from the routine classroom environment, usually for a violation of class rules. Timeout originally stood for "time out from positive reinforcement" (Alberto, Troutman, & Feagin 2002; Allison & Allison, 1971). This meant that the procedure was not punishment as much as it was a removal from a potentially rewarding situation. This interpretation may be literally true, however, only if the class activity from which the student is being removed is truly considered rewarding by the student. Timeout procedures have been used frequently in classrooms of elementary-level students with more serious behavior problems, and less frequently in resource rooms, or with secondary-level students (Zabel, 1986).

Timeout can be useful to help students cool down after a volatile situation, or provide them time to quietly reflect on their behavior. In other cases, timeout may serve as tangible feedback about their classroom behavior. Overall, timeout is most effective when classroom activities the students are excluded from are enjoyable and rewarding, and the students do not feel reinforced for the attention they receive when placed in timeout (Kerr & Nelson, 2002). Behaviors that result in timeout, such as specific disruptive events, should be posted and discussed with the class before implementation of the procedure.

Use Appropriate Levels of Timeout. Many different levels of timeout have been applied in practice (Nelson & Rutherford, 1983). The mildest form of timeout involves the systematic ignoring of a student for a specific period of time. Students may be asked to place their head on the desk and refrain from participating in the activity or interacting with any other person (Martin & Pear, 2002). "Timeout ribbons" (Foxx & Shapiro, 1978) have been used on the elementary level, where all students wear ribbons on their arm and receive considerable positive reinforcement and attention from teachers and aides. When misbehavior occurs, the timeout ribbon is removed, and the student's behavior is ignored while the ribbon is off.

The timeout ribbon procedure also can be applied to small groups of students. A ribbon for each group is placed at the front of the class, and students can earn tokens for prizes during the time the ribbon is up for their group. If any student in the group breaks a rule during this time, the ribbon is removed for the entire group, and only returned when group members have behaved appropriately for a specified time period. Students can earn tokens to be redeemed later for small rewards and privileges, such as stickers, brain teasers, or time on the computer (Salend & Gordon, 1987). The advantage of this type of group contingency is that it encourages students to promote the good behavior of the entire group.

A more restrictive version is **contingent observation** timeout, in which students who misbehave must sit away from classroom activities and not participate, but are able to observe the activities from which they have been excluded. In another variation, a student is seated well away from the rest of the class, or even outside of the room, with adult supervision. Finally, in some cases, students can be put in "timeout rooms," small enclosures where students are to remain for the duration of their timeout, usually no more than 5 minutes. Timeout rooms can be a quiet area for students to "cool off" and consider their behavior. However, the procedure should be supervised, the door should remain unlocked, and the light should remain on. Timeout rooms should not be considered a form of incarceration.

Use Debriefing Procedures after Timeout. Regardless of the type of timeout, students need to be debriefed before returning to full status in the classroom. This is a form of attribution training and serves to ensure that students are aware of the behavior that resulted in the timeout and how they could handle a similar situation better in the future.

Notice that in the beginning of the following debriefing procedure, Marie attempts to attribute her behavior to another student's teasing.* It may be helpful to consider the events that led to the student misbehavior (i.e., Sheri's teasing), but to plan better ways of handling such situations, it is critical that a direct link be made between the student's behavior and the consequence. Such debriefing procedures can be helpful for any type of punishment, including withdrawal of rewards or privileges.

Teacher:	Marie, the time for your timeout is over. But before you join the other students, I want you to tell me what happened. Why did you get sent to timeout?
Marie:	I don't know.
Teacher:	Well, can you tell me what happened?
Marie:	'Cause Sheri was talking about me and laughing at me. So I knocked her books over.
Teacher:	Did you have to go to timeout because Sheri was talking about you?
Marie:	No.
Teacher:	No. You were sent to timeout because you threw Sheri's books.
Marie:	I know.
Teacher:	Do you know why we have a class rule about throwing things?
Marie:	So somebody doesn't get hurt.
Teacher:	That's right. So our class will be a safe place for all of us. Now, what can you do the next time you think Sheri is teasing you?
Marie:	Just don't pay any attention to her.

*From M. A. Mastropieri & T. E. Scruggs (2002). *Effective instruction for special education* (3rd ed.), p. 80. Austin, TX: Pro-Ed. Reprinted by permission.

A timeout chair or location enables students who have been excluded to observe activities they miss because of inappropriate behavior.

Teacher:	That's right. If you ignore her, she will probably stop. What else can you do, if you think you are not going to be able to ignore her?
Marie:	Tell you.
Teacher:	If you tell me, I will try to help so that you don't get in trouble and also so that no one teases you. Can you try to do that next time?
Marie:	Yeah.
Teacher:	You don't have to throw things. Ignore it or come and tell me if you're having a problem. You need to control your behavior better, but I like you and I want you to do really well in my class. Can you?
Marie:	Yeah.
Teacher:	Good. Now let's go back and see how well you can do.

Implement Level Systems. **Level systems** involve assigning to students specific classroom privileges based on previous and current behavior, and have frequently been used in classrooms where inappropriate behavior is a problem (Bauer & Shea, 1988; Bauer, Shea, & Keppler, 1986). In a level system, all students are assigned a level (e.g., red, green, blue, gray; or I, II, III, IV; and so on) that is associated with specific privileges and responsibilities. For example, students assigned to the "red" (lowest) level must be in their seat at all times, always raise their hand before speaking, and be prepared for class. If they complete an assignment before the end of the period, they are allowed to read a book of their own choosing at their seat. On the "gray" (highest) level, students must be prepared for class. They are allowed to study in a group and talk with other students on the same level, may leave the room independently for restroom break, and may negotiate with the teacher for other privileges (Mastropieri & Scruggs, 2002). In an investigation by Mastropieri, Jenne, and Scruggs (1988), students remained on each level for one week, and at the end of the week submitted their requests to the class for a level change. If the majority of the student's classmates voted in favor of the student's request, and the student had maintained an accuracy level of 85% on classroom assignments that week, the level change was allowed. Mastropieri et al. (1988) reported that talkouts decreased from an average of 4.5 per minute to .11 per minute, and, in a second implementation, students improved considerably in accuracy and completion of classroom assignments. Students also reported that the level system had been successful in improving their behavior. One advantage of level systems is that they allow the students

In the Classroom ...a feature for teachers

PALS Level System

Level	Sample Expectations	Privileges/Program Changes
0	Promptness; no sleeping in class; no abusive or vulgar language; comply with group rules; weekly group counseling.	
I.	Personal goal; daily journal; complete 65% of assignments; participate in group counseling; 20 days of stable attendance.	In-school field trips; one cafeteria pass weekly; one outside lunch with teacher.
II.	Personal review of goals with teacher; complete 75% of assignments; document helping others; 30 consecutive days of attendance.	Food privileges; two cafeteria passes weekly; two off-campus lunches with teacher; in-school field trips.
III.	Weekly log; complete 85% of assignments; integration into 4 classes and PE; 60 days of consecutive attendance; passing all classes; 100% attendance.	Three cafeteria passes weekly; up to four outside lunches with teacher; food privileges; in-school field trip; outside field trips.
IV.	All general education classes; daily or weekly check in; meet with social worker to review goals.	Regular education.
V.	Passing all classes; after 20 days, review for termination of special services.	Regular education.

Note: From "Level Systems: A Framework for the Individualization of Behavior Management," by A. M. Bauer, T. M. Shea, and R. Keppler, 1986, *Behavioral Disorders, 12,* pp. 28–35. Reprinted with permission.

to take more responsibility for their own behavior, and to receive privileges for demonstrating behavioral self-control.

Level systems can also be employed to improve transitions between special education classrooms to general education classrooms. The Hinsdale, Illinois, South High School used a Personal Adjustment Level System (PALS) to facilitate entry of students with behavioral disorders into general education classrooms (Bauer, Shea, & Keppler, 1986). As students gained further control over their behaviors, they participated independently to an increasing extent in general education classes. Students on the first four levels were required to attend group counseling sessions. The second-highest level in this system involved full-time placement in general education classrooms, while the highest level included a review for termination of special services and special education classification. The *In the Classroom* feature above shows the expectations and privileges associated with each level. Although in this case regular class placement should not be considered a "reward" to be earned, it does demonstrate how students can gain control over their behavior sequentially, to the point that full-time placement in the general education classroom, and even removal of special education classification, is appropriate.

Use the Good Behavior Game. Researchers including Harris and Sherman (1973) have described a behavior management technique referred to as the Good Behavior Game. Using this procedure, the teacher divides the class into two or more groups. During an instructional period, each disruptive or noncompliant behavior counts as a point for the team of the offending student. Rules such as the following are set: "(a) raise your hand before talking; (b) sit in your seat properly; (c) pay attention; (d) keep your hands to yourself; and (e) stay in your seat" (Brigham et al., 1992, p. 7). At the end of a designated time period, the team with the fewest points is declared the winner, and may be provided with a group reward.

Set Up Student Contracting. Behavioral **contracting** involves the establishment of a written agreement that formalizes the behaviors a student agrees to exhibit, and the positive consequences that will result from the fulfillment of the contract. Often, the negative consequences of not fulfilling the contract are also specified. For example, Morris has been erratic in turning in his homework for math class. Sometimes he completes his homework assignments and turns them in promptly; other times he does not turn in his homework and acts defensive and belligerent when questioned about it.

Morris has been trying to talk his parents into taking him to a favorite amusement park during the school's spring break, which will occur in two months. His parents had planned either to stay at home, or to visit relatives during that time. As a result of a conversation with the math teacher, however, they agreed to complete a behavioral contract with Morris. They agreed to take Morris to the amusement park for 2 days if he turns in all of his homework assignments in math for the next 2 months, with no more than two lapses. However, if he misses more than two homework assignments in the next 2 months, he will lose some of his television privileges, according to the severity of his lapses.

Promote Self-Monitoring. **Self-monitoring** strategies involve teaching students to monitor and evaluate their own classroom behavior (DiGangi & Maag, 1992; Hughes, Ruhl, & Misra, 1989; Maag, 1999). In some cases, students may be asked to monitor their general on-task behavior. In other cases, students may monitor themselves for a specific behavior, such as teasing. Before implementing self-monitoring interventions, meet individually and discuss with the students the purpose and importance of classroom behavior, and how they will benefit personally from better classroom behavior. The students should be made to understand that the intervention is in their best interest.

To implement a self-monitoring system for a target behavior, such as teasing, provide the student with a self-monitoring sheet for the target behavior. The behavior should be operationalized, so that it is very clear what constitutes teasing and what does not. These definitions will depend on the particular student's behavior. For example, teasing could in some cases include making statements such as "Cornelius is a stupid jerk." Teasing in other cases could involve making faces at another student, staring at another student, or scratching the head with the middle finger while looking at another student. The *In the Classroom . . . for sharing with students* feature, available on the Companion Website, provides an example of a self-monitoring sheet for teasing. The student is familiarized with the self-monitoring sheet and how to use it. After each specified time interval (e.g., 5 or 10 minutes), prompt the student, or play a timed and tape-recorded "beep" or ask the student to take responsibility for monitoring the clock. The student then checks the appropriate column for "teasing," or "not teasing." At the end of a class period, or the end of a day, you and the student compare notes. Students may not only receive rewards or consequences for behavior, but also receive rewards for matching your recording of teasing. The purpose is to make students conscious of their behavior, so they have more control of their actions. Self-monitoring sheets could be used with several students at a time, to record several different target behaviors.

Another type of self-recording system can be used to monitor on-task or other ongoing behaviors by delivering randomly spaced "beeps" on a tape recorder. When students hear the beeps, they record whether they were on-task or off-task at the moment the beep sounded. This procedure could be used with an entire class at once. If some students have hearing impairments that prevent them from hearing the beep, pair the sound with a light stimulus, use a visual timer as described in the technology feature, or ask a peer to provide a visual or tactual cue to the student.

Self-monitoring can be used to facilitate students' entry into a general education classroom (Prater, 1992). If students are taught how to monitor their own behavior in a special education setting, these same techniques can be transferred to the general education setting, to promote appropriate behavioral standards to the general education classroom.

Teach Students Self-Instruction Strategies. **Self-instruction** training involves teaching students to employ self-directed statements that guide social problem solving. Questions can involve

Refer to chapter 2 for a sample contract.

Self-monitoring for attention is described in detail in chapter 10.

Technology Highlight

From Beep Tape to Vibrating Watch to Assist with Self-Monitoring of Attention

Self-monitoring attention can be successfully implemented with many students with attention difficulties at many age levels. Several types of self-monitoring procedures have proven effective. Key elements in the self-monitoring system include (a) precisely defined behaviors to be monitored; (b) a recording sheet or system that is easy to use; (c) a predetermined system for knowing when to monitor the behaviors. Once these elements are established, many students are very successful at improving their attention to school-related tasks.

In defining the appropriate behaviors, work closely with the student to describe exactly what is meant by paying attention or by staying on-task during class. Specific examples of the behaviors using instances and noninstances are usually helpful at first. A simple recording sheet that contains two columns, one for on-task and one for off-task, on which students are taught to place a check mark if they are on- or off-task is also a good starting place.

Finally, a system for helping students monitor their behaviors must be designed. One way is to make what has been referred to as a beep tape. This is an audiotape that teachers or parents can make that contains a "pencil tap" or other distinctive noise at random intervals on the audiotape. Initially, on the tape the "taps" should be recorded closely together giving the students many opportunities at practicing recording the behavior. Each time the tape "taps" or beeps students are required to check off whether they were on-task or off-task. Initially, teachers want to check students' recording behaviors with their own recording to ensure accuracy by students. As students improve at monitoring their behaviors, the "taps" can be at larger intervals. Often students can use earphones to listen to the audiotape so that the tape is unheard by classmates.

One criticism of this method has been the lack of portability into the inclusive class due to the potential obtrusive nature of a cassette tape and beeps or taps. Recent technological advances have provided another alternative for students. Watches that provide a vibrating sensation on the wrist have been developed and can be used to self-monitor behaviors as well. These watches will be completely unobtrusive and yet provide students with the feedback they might need to monitor their attention in classes in the form of a small vibration to the wrist. Some watch models can switch from audible to vibrating systems. Additional information on one type of vibrating watch can be found at *http://dynamic-living.com/vibrating_watch.htm.*

---

defining the situation, thinking through possible solutions, and choosing the best option (see also Mastropieri & Scruggs, 2002, pp. 80–82). Following is a possible example:

Check each step, and think before you act!

1. What happened?
2. What are all possible solutions?
3. What is my goal for right now?
4. What is the best thing for me to do?
5. Did I make the best choice?

Teachers should model and role-play these thought processes. For example, the teacher should say: **What happened** is that Kimberly is making faces at me. The **possible solutions** are that I could make faces back at her, I could tell the teacher, or I could try to ignore her and finish my work. **My goal for right now** is just to finish this assignment, so I think the best thing to do is try to ignore her, and see if she stops. If she doesn't, I tell the teacher. . . . Well, she stopped making faces at me (or if she didn't, I didn't notice), so I think I made the best choice.

Have students talk through similar scenarios, while you continue to prompt this type of self-instruction in the classroom. Provide students with examples in which they can identify when these strategies should be used.

Train for Generalization. Most positive social behaviors are of limited use unless they can be shown to generalize to appropriate situations outside the training context (Maag, 1999). It is particularly important that students in inclusive settings are able to generalize all the positive social behaviors they have learned in other settings; however, students with special needs often demonstrate problems in generalizing learned behavior (Scruggs & Mastropieri, 1984). As important social behaviors are learned, make a list of all the settings and situations into which the behavior must generalize, and all the individuals who will observe the generalized behavior. Then, create a plan to promote generalization across all these settings and individuals.

There are several strategies available for promoting generalization, some of which have already been described. Self-monitoring and self-instruction are strategies very relevant in promoting generalization, through the use of cognitive routines. Students can use self-monitoring techniques to evaluate and modify their behavior in different contexts, such as the teasing example described previously. In addition, strive to teach behaviors that will be reinforced in natural settings, such as positive social responding. In other occasions, be sure that all relevant teachers and staff are aware of the behavior and reinforce it whenever it occurs. Classroom peers can also be very helpful in ensuring that target behavior maintains over time and generalizes by, for example, providing positive attention when students exhibit target behaviors. Train "loosely," so that students are provided with a variety of situations and a number of possible responses. Be ready to reinforce any unprompted generalization of a learned behavior. Finally, when needed, retrain positive behaviors in several appropriate contexts; for example, retrain appropriate sitting in all relevant contexts, such as classroom, resource room, homeroom, assemblies, and school bus. By using a variety of possible strategies and monitoring their effectiveness, students will be much more likely to generalize their positive behaviors (Maag, 1999; Scruggs & Mastropieri, 1994a; Stokes & Baer, 1977).

More information on generalization is provided in the social skills portion of this chapter.

Handling Confrontations

One of the things that frightens teachers most is direct confrontations by students. Confrontations can directly challenge the teacher's authority, and can, depending on how they are handled, have a profound effect on the classroom environment.

Canter and Canter (1993) have described the problems of confrontations in detail as seen in the following dialogue:

CLASSROOM SCENARIO

Jason

Teacher: Class, please take out your notebooks and begin writing the answers to the questions on the board. This is an open-book quiz, so you may use your textbook.

The teacher scans the room as students begin to get out their materials and start to work. After a few moments she sees that Jason, a difficult student in her class, hasn't made a move to get started.

Teacher: Jason, it's time to get to work.

Jason sullenly looks up at her.

Jason: I don't feel like it today. Just stay off my case, okay?

Angered by the hostile response, the teacher reacts instantly to Jason's words.

Teacher: I didn't ask you if you feel like it or not, Jason. Take your notebook out and get started.

Jason:	*(with increased hostility)* Back off. I told you I don't want to.
Teacher:	*(angrier)* I heard what you said. Now you hear what I say. Get your notebook out and start writing. Everyone else seems to be able to get to work. I think you can, too.
Jason:	*(mumbling under his breath)* You want it done so bad, do it yourself.
Teacher:	What did you say?
Jason:	I didn't say anything *(looking around the class for support)*. Nobody said anything, right? Maybe you're hearing things.

Other kids laugh along with him. As other students become involved, the teacher's anxiety increases.

Teacher:	That's it, Jason. I've had enough of this. Keep this up and you won't be out of detention till the end of the year.
Jason:	Yeah? Well the end of the year is now. I'm out of here.

Jason gets up and storms out of the classroom. *

*Canter & Canter, 1993, pp. 159–160. Reprinted with permission.

Jason has placed himself in a situation where his anger and anxiety can only escalate. The teacher, by also being confrontational, has helped place Jason in this position. The teacher has reacted emotionally, and this emotional reaction has fed into Jason's desire to control the situation. A difficult situation has become more difficult, the teacher's relationship with Jason has deteriorated, and now the entire class is off-task. Some students, such as Jason, may not believe that teachers can be trusted to act in the students' best interest, and may feel compelled to fight teachers in these situations.

Canter and Canter (1993) recommend several steps for dealing with this type of confrontation. The most important thing to remember is to *remain calm.* Count to 3, 4, 5, or 10 if necessary. Control your breathing by taking long, slow breaths. Take yourself out of the situation by depersonalizing it. In Jason's case, if you have been doing your job as a teacher, he is probably responding to his own past experiences, lack of trust, and his own needs at the moment. *Don't take it personally.* Remind yourself,

Confrontations must be handled effectively to maintain a productive classroom atmosphere.

"This is not about me!" If you are able to remain calm, you will have more control of the situation. Your calmness and task-orientation in the face of hostility can go far toward resolving the situation.

The most effective approach would be not to escalate the situation in the first place by making loud reprimands and threats. Remain calm, restate your desire privately to Jason that he return to work, and restate your personal interest in his succeeding in your classroom:

Teacher: *(quietly and calmly)* I understand you're upset, Jason, but I really need you to go back to work just now. I know you can do well on this.

If necessary, move Jason away from his peers, and speak to him privately—preferably with Jason seated with his back to the class. Then, if Jason is still upset, give him a little time and space to make a positive choice.

If necessary, speak to the student later. Ultimately, of course, your rules must be enforced. However, keep in mind the bigger picture of establishing trust and helping Jason fit into the classroom environment. Do not behave in such a way that Jason feels heroic by standing up to your raised voice and threatening manner. Make Jason believe that you wish him to get started simply because you don't want to see him get a failing grade on the quiz, and you want him to succeed in school. Do not feel that you must have the last word in the dialogue. If Jason returns to work, even while grumbling and rolling his eyes, you have achieved your purpose for the moment, and you have prevented an unpleasant situation from escalating.

Consider removing your entire class, except the problem student, to another room when a confrontation has occurred and you know a student will refuse to back down because he does not want to lose face in front of his peers. For example, work out ahead of time with a teacher in a nearby room that your entire class may stop in for a few moments if this ever becomes necessary.

If a student's behavior seems very much out of character, it may be wise to ignore the behavior for the moment, and then later speak about the problem when the student has calmed down somewhat. It may also be necessary to back off for a certain period of time, if the student's behavior appears particularly volatile or threatening, or if a student refuses to leave the peer group. If you believe that situations such as this are possible in your classroom, find out ahead of time how to call for support (Canter & Canter, 1993).

Life Space Interviewing/Life Space Crisis Intervention

Life Space Interviewing (LSI) was first proposed by Fritz Redl and colleagues (e.g., Redl & Wineman, 1965) as a clinical therapeutic tool to serve the needs of students who displayed severely disturbed, aggressive behavior. This perspective views a student crisis not as a disaster to be avoided, but rather as an opportunity for affecting real change (Merritt-Petrashek, 1996). As a humanistic, nonjudgmental approach, the clinical staff employing LSI serve as the student's advocate to help him or her to understand patterns of behavior, to accept responsibility for behavior, and to learn more appropriate social skills. The assumption is that life events influence behavior, and that appropriate verbal mediation can make a crisis event a positive experience in the long term (Rosenberg, Wilson, Maheady, & Sindelar, 1997). LSI techniques include short-term procedures, such as draining off frustration, support for managing emotions, and maintaining communication. Long-term strategies seek to link current behavioral problems to similar past experiences to lead the student to better understand patterns of behavior and develop more effective behaviors (Rosenberg et al., 1997).

More recently, LSI procedures were modified to make them easier to understand and more adaptable to educational settings (Merritt-Petrashek, 1996). These procedures, known as Life Space Crisis Intervention (LSCI), include the following:

- *Stage One: Student Crisis Stage and Staff's De-escalation Skills.* This stage provides support for students during periods of intense emotion, and employs techniques to de-escalate intensity and maintain communication.
- *Stage Two: Student Timeline Stage and Staff's Relationship Skills.* This stage assists the student in recounting and reflecting on the incident. Staff interpret and summarize the student's comments.
- *Stage Three: Student Central-Issue Stage and Staff's Differential Diagnosis Skills.* During this stage educational or clinical staff attempt to identify the central issue, assess the student's insight and motivation to change, and select an appropriate therapeutic goal.

- *Stage Four: Student Insight Stage and Staff's Clinical Skills.* In this stage, staff carry out the appropriate intervention, which should lead to some insight on the part of the student regarding his or her self-defeating behavior, and to learn more appropriate social skills. Although a number of different intervention situations are specified (see Merritt-Petrashek, 1996), staff generally attempt to identify a student's perceptions (e.g., "No one understands me!" "Everyone is so unfair!"), and replace them with new insights that better reflect the entire problem and the student's own role. Staff also strive to get a commitment from the student for positive problem solution.
- *Stage Five: Student New-Skill Stage and Staff's Empowering Skills.* During this stage, staff rehearse the new behaviors with the student using role-play, discuss the application of the new behavior and its possible less-than-desired consequences, and affirm the potential benefits of the new skill.
- *Stage Six: Student Transfer-of-Training Stage and Staff's Follow-up Skills.* In this final stage, the student is prepared for return to the peer group, and the student is assisted in attempting new more positive behaviors.

It can be seen that many of the components of LSI or LSCI are similar to those described previously, including debriefing procedures and attribution retraining. The emphasis of this model is more on individual student insight through dialogue as a means of affecting more permanent and general behavior change. Nevertheless, the effectiveness of LSI or LSCI techniques can be monitored using the same techniques for observation and recording of behavior described earlier in this chapter.

For more information on Life Space Interviewing and Life Space Crisis Intervention, and their applications in school settings, see Long and Morse, 1996; and Long, Wood, and Fecser, 2001.

Schoolwide Discipline Systems

An obvious advantage of schoolwide discipline systems is that the same rules are enforced in the same way throughout the school, and the structured consistency can be beneficial to limit-seeking students, as well as to students who have difficulty adjusting to different standards or rules being enforced in different classrooms. Some disadvantages to schoolwide discipline systems are that they may not effectively address the needs of all individual students, and that, if misapplied, they can promote an overall punitive atmosphere throughout the school. Any behavior management system must be as positive and supportive to the needs of students as possible, as schools that are perceived as punitive or oppressive will be resented and may actually encourage noncompliance and vandalism (Mayer, Nafpaktitis, Butterworth, & Hollingsworth, 1987).

Employing Assertive Discipline

Assertive Discipline is a schoolwide system developed by Lee Canter (e.g., 1979, 1992). In this system, all students are first apprised of the rules, which include (a) following directions, (b) remaining seated, (c) keeping hands and feet to self, (d) not speaking without raising hand and being called on, and (e) refraining from swearing or teasing. The discipline plan is then provided, which could be similar to the Discipline Hierarchy described previously. That is, the first infraction is a warning, which results in the student's name being written on the chalkboard; the second infraction results in a checkmark being placed after the student's name, then the student must stay 15 minutes after school; and so on. This plan is intended to be administered in an overall positive environment, marked by verbal praise for appropriate behavior, positive contact with parents or guardians, and other rewards determined by school personnel. Students who exhibit behavior problems for several teachers may be given a "discipline card," on which all infractions made throughout the day are noted by each teacher. This program is expected to be implemented schoolwide, which means that all school personnel must agree to support this program. It is also important that parents and guardians are informed and support the program. Schools that wish to implement Assertive Discipline should acquire all the relevant training materials (see Canter, 1990). Additionally, schools may wish to develop their own schoolwide discipline system, and monitor its implementation and effectiveness. It is important that any schoolwide system be built upon an overall foundation of positive support and encouragement, so that it does not appear overly punitive to students.

Positive Behavioral Supports

Positive behavioral supports (PBS), or Positive Behavioral Interventions and Supports (PBIS, Gagnon & Leone, 2002) rely on behavioral principles to produce socially important outcomes with procedures that are socially and culturally appropriate (Horner & Sugai, 1999). Behavioral support is not viewed simply as a way of reducing or eliminating inappropriate social behavior through punishment or extinction, but rather as a process of assisting students in being successful within a social or educational context. It involves a functional behavioral assessment (FBA) to determine the nature of problem behavior, and how it is maintained within a social system. Based on the FBA, a behavioral support plan can be developed that focuses on (a) altering the environment so that problem behaviors become irrelevant, (b) teaching new skills to students to supplant previous counterproductive behaviors, and (c) establishing consequences that make inappropriate behaviors less effective (Horner & Sugai, 1999).

Nelson and Sugai (1999) described the schoolwide application of PBS as a four-stage process, undertaken by a rotating committee of eight (or fewer) members representative of the entire school staff. During Stage One, the committee defines and identifies the problems to be addressed by the schoolwide PBS program. This can be accomplished by surveys and interviews, direct observations, and archival school data. During Stage Two, the committee undertakes a site analysis to determine the extent aspects of PBS are in place. In the third stage, the committee works to develop and implement the PBS programs in four systems: schoolwide, for all staff, students, and settings; specific setting or nonclassroom systems (e.g., rest rooms, cafeterias); classroom systems; and systems for support of individual students, usually those with serious and chronic problem behavior. The program is developed and revised through a multi-step consensus-building process. As the programs are implemented, progress is monitored in Stage Four with respect to baseline data collected during needs assessment. Findings of the evaluation are shared with all staff members on a regular basis, and the programs are adjusted as needed, based on the results of the evaluation.

Positive behavioral supports have been successfully employed in schools. According to Gagnon and Leone, "results of the PBIS model are promising, with a reduction in office referrals ranging from 30 percent to 68 percent. Furthermore, these results have been maintained over several years with continued implementation" (2002, p. 107).

For more information on positive behavioral supports and related strategies, see Gagnon and Leone (2002).

Teaching Social Skills

Appropriate behavior from students is often limited because some students lack adequate knowledge of certain **social skills.** Social skills are the behaviors we use to work and socialize with other people. Walker et al. (1988) defined social skills as having three elements—social responses and skills that:

1. Allow one to initiate and maintain positive relationships with others,
2. Contribute to peer acceptance and to a successful classroom adjustment, and
3. Allow one to cope effectively and adaptively with the social environment (p. 1).

Working collaboratively and sharing are important social skills.

Many students referred for special education services exhibit deficits in social skills (e.g., Kavale & Forness, 1995; Sullivan & Mastropieri, 1994), and are less accepted by their peers (Goodman, Gottlieb, & Harrison, 1972; Parker & Asher, 1987), at least partly because of their lack of social skills. Good, or at least adequate, social skills are necessary for successful functioning in school and later in life. Beyond the classroom, effective social skills are necessary for success in job interviews, and once employed, in maintaining employment (Salzberg, Lignugaris/Kraft, & McCuller, 1988).

Many different types of behaviors or responses can qualify as social skills. In fact, it could be argued that specific social skills are required for any social act a person engages in throughout life. Skills commonly defined as social skills and studied by researchers are listed in Table 7.2.

Table 7.2
Specific Social Skills

Content Area	Component Skills
Conversation skills	Joining a conversation Interrupting a conversation Starting a conversation Maintaining a conversation Ending a conversation Use of appropriate tone of voice Use of appropriate distance and eye contact
Assertiveness skills	Asking for clarifications Making requests Denying requests Negotiating requests Exhibiting politeness
"Play" interaction skills (e.g., making friends)	Sharing with others Inviting others to play Encouraging others Praising others
Problem-solving and coping skills	Staying calm and relaxed Listing possible solutions Choosing the best solution Taking responsibility for self Handling name calling and teasing Staying out of trouble
Self-help skills	Good grooming (clean, neat) Good dressing (wearing clothes that fit) Good table manners Good eating behaviors
Classroom task-related behaviors	On-task behavior Attending to tasks Completing tasks Following directions Trying your best
Self-related behaviors	Giving positive feedback to self Expressing feelings Accepting negative feedback Accepting consequences
Job interview skills	Being prepared (dress, attitude, etc.) Being attentive Listening skills Asking for clarification Thinking prior to speaking

Note: From *Effective Instruction for Special Education* (3rd ed., p. 252), by M. A. Mastropieri & T. E. Scruggs, 2002, Austin, TX: Pro-Ed. Copyright 2002 by Pro-Ed. Reprinted with permission.

It may be useful to distinguish among the factors that apparently control particular social skills deficits. For example, Dale is an affectionate boy with mental retardation who is disposed to hug nearly anyone he encounters. Dale continues to hug people even though he receives subtle (and sometimes not so subtle) feedback that his hugging is not always welcome. This behavior also is considered "weird" by Dale's classmates. Dale's behavior is apparently controlled by the social satisfaction he gains from hugging, as well as his seeming inability to distinguish when his hugging is welcome and when it is not.

For a different example, Kyle is a student with emotional-behavioral disorders who is often verbally abusive to other students and teachers. Kyle is aware that his behavior is not appreciated by others, and he is able to distinguish between socially appropriate and socially inappropriate speech. When Kyle believes it is in his direct interest, his speech is positive and appropriate. Kyle's behavior, however, is apparently controlled by the reinforcement he seems to receive from upsetting others with his speech.

In both cases, students exhibit inappropriate social skills. In both cases, students are unaware that it is in their own long-term interest to improve their social behavior. However, Dale does not seem to be fully aware of the effects of his social behavior, while Kyle does appear to be aware of the social consequences of his behavior. For both Dale and Kyle, social skills training is necessary.

Social Skills Assessment

Several methods are available for assessing social skills and social acceptance of students in your classroom. One method involves the use of a **sociometric measure.** In this measure, you can ask students to write down their most favorite and least favorite students:

> *Sociometric Survey*
>
> Please keep all information confidential!
> Write down the names of your three favorite classmates:
> 1.
> 2.
> 3.
> Now, write down the names of your three least favorite classmates:
> 1.
> 2.
> 3.

Any given student's score is simply the number of "nominations" received by classmates; this could be either the number of positive nominations or the number of negative nominations. For younger students, you need to record shared, confidential verbal responses. Also determine the students who receive neither positive nor negative nominations. Other possible sociometric surveys could include rating all students on a Likert-type scale (e.g., 1 to 5, where 1 = like to play with a lot, and 5 = don't like to play with at all). Of course, with all such ratings, it is important to keep the results confidential.

Sociometric ratings can help provide a sense of how well liked individual students are; however, they are not a direct measure of social skills. For students who receive many negative ratings, it may be necessary later to determine exactly what the particular student does that is not positively valued by others, so that these behaviors can be changed.

Teacher rating scales are another method of determining individual strengths and weaknesses in social skills. Some social skills curriculum include teacher checklists that can be linked directly to the curriculum. The ACCEPTS program (Walker et al., 1988), for example, has questions as part of its screening checklist, to determine whether placement in the program is appropriate, as shown in Figure 7.5.

The ACCEPTS program also includes a placement test with items such as "The student takes initiative to assist others when they need help" (Walker et al., 1988, p. 138). Teachers respond to this item on a 5-point scale, where 1 = not descriptive or true, and 5 = very descriptive or true.

The *Job-Related Social Skills* curriculum (Montague & Lund, 1991) also includes teacher surveys of particular social skills, in which items are rated from 1 (never) to 5 (always). Sample items include "Is the student confident in knowing where to get information?" and "Can the student handle other people's complaints graciously?" (p. 35). Each item is linked to specific lessons in the curriculum.

Section I. Classroom Behavior

1. Does the child *fail to listen* to instructions
   and directions?   _____ Yes   _____ No   _____ Unsure

4. Is the child *noncompliant* to the
   instructionsand directions of adults?   _____ Yes   _____ No   _____ Unsure

Section II. Social Behavior

2. Does the child *talk less* than peers?   _____ Yes   _____ No   _____ Unsure

6. Is the child *teased* or *picked on* more
   than peers?   _____ Yes   _____ No   _____ Unsure

Figure 7.5

Sample Questions from Social Skills Screening Checklist

Note: From *The Walker Social Skills Curriculum: The ACCEPTS Program* (p. 132), by H. M. Walker, S. McConnell, D. Holmes, B. Todis, J. Walker, and N. Golden, Austin, TX: Pro-Ed. Copyright 1988 by Pro-Ed. Reprinted with permission.

Role-play tests can also be developed by teachers to determine how students may respond (or believe they would respond) to particular social situations. For example, a teacher could say "You are going to go out to play softball with the team for the first time. You go out in the field with the others, but you are not certain what to do. Pretend I am another student. Show me what you would do, and tell me what you would say."

The type of responses students give could provide you with information on the students' understandings of different social situations, and their understanding of the options available. Because role-play activities reveal only how students function in contrived scenarios, however, it is best to combine results with other sources of information (e.g., how the student has behaved in similar situations).

Probably the best overall method of assessing social skills is by direct observation of social behavior in naturalistic settings, using observational procedures such as event recording, described previously. These observations, based on operationalized behaviors, can determine the specific levels of the behavior being exhibited (or not being exhibited), and can be used later to determine whether any interventions appear to be positively influencing behavior. For example, you could observe a particular student and record the number of positive versus negative comments made to others during a cooperative learning activity. When an intervention on the student's social skills is implemented, further observations could determine whether the intervention was effective.

Train Students to Improve Social Skills

Many different interventions to improve social skills have been undertaken (McIntosh, Vaughn, & Zaragosa, 1991; Zaragosa, Vaughn, & McIntosh, 1991). These have included both teacher- or researcher-developed training, or commercially available curriculum materials (e.g., *Getting Along with Others,* Jackson, Jackson, & Monroe, 1983). However, most social skills training procedures are classified into four categories: (a) modeling, (b) shaping, (c) coaching, and (d) modeling--reinforcement (Kavale & Forness, 1995). Modeling involves demonstrating the appropriate social behavior and allowing students to observe. Shaping involves the use of positive reinforcement to promote the use of a social skill. Coaching requires the use of verbal cues to improve target behaviors, and modeling–reinforcement employs a combination of observation and shaping techniques.

Social skills training often begins with a definition and discussion of the target social skill. The teacher models positive and negative examples of the social skill (e.g., inviting others to play), and asks students to identify these examples. Then the teacher may describe some scenarios for role-playing guided practice activities, and students offer suggestions or demonstrate examples of appropriate behavior. Students may be given independent practice activities, in which they are asked to record their own social behavior in relevant social situations outside of class. Formative evaluation is used to determine whether the purposes of the lessons have been accomplished. In this way, social skills instruction parallels the components of academic instruction described in chapter 6, including review, statement of objective, presentation of information, guided practice, independent practice, and formative evaluation.

For example, in the ACCEPTS program (Walker et al., 1988), Skill #1 (Using Polite Words) in Area III (Getting Along) involves the teaching of the use of polite words in appropriate circumstances.

Other commercially available social skills curriculum materials include the ACCESS program (for adolescents) (Walker, Todis, Holmes, & Horton, 1988); *ASSET: A Social Skills Program for Adolescents* (Hazel, Schumaker, Sherman, & Sheldon, 1995); *Skillstreaming in Early Childhood* (McGinnis & Goldstein, 1990), and *Teaching Social Skills: A Practical Instructional Approach* (Rutherford, Chipman, DiGangi, & Anderson, 1992).

Software published by Exceptional Innovations (P.O. Box 6085, Ann Arbor, MI 48106) includes *Teaching Social Skills* and *The Job Planner: Social Skills*.

After the review of the previous day's skill, the teacher defines polite words and gives examples (e.g., "please," "thank you," "I'm sorry"). Students are then provided with opportunities to identify the polite words in teacher-provided examples, and later to produce polite words in appropriate situations. The teacher provides positive and negative examples (e.g., bumping into someone's chair and saying or not saying "excuse me"), and asks students to identify the examples. Students respond to teacher modeling, and then produce their own polite words in response to teacher scenarios (e.g., ". . . you need to borrow a pencil. What polite word do you use?", p. 65).

For another example, Rosenthal-Malek and Yoshida (1994) employed a metacognitive training procedure to improve the social behavior of students with moderate mental retardation (ages 9–14) during free-play periods. During 10-minute instructional sessions that preceded free-play, students were taught to use a metacognitive strategy (see also Brown, 1987), which included six self-interrogation questions:

1. Stop and think!
2. What (or who) do I want to play with?
3. What will happen if I do _____?
4. How do I feel (happy, sad, angry)?
5. How does my friend feel (happy, sad, angry)?
6. What (or who) else could I play with? (Rosenthal-Malek & Yoshida, p. 216)

The self-questions were introduced cumulatively during instruction at a rate of one per week, and were practiced and applied throughout the 10-minute lesson. The interventions involved students planning, predicting, monitoring, checking, and evaluating their own performances. During the free-play periods that followed each lesson, self-interrogation was reinforced whenever the student demonstrated the lack of a targeted skill (e.g., someone upset the student, the student needed help, the student wanted to play with a group or another child).

The Research Highlight describes an intervention by Moore, Cartledge, and Heckaman (1994) to improve social skills in game-playing activities. Self-monitoring of social behavior can positively influence generalization, although treatment effects may decline after the self-monitoring procedures are eliminated (Hughes, Ruhl, & Misra, 1989).

One important consideration of social skills training in general education settings is that many general education students may not need to be trained in many of the same social skills as students with disabilities or other special needs. In these cases, it may not be efficient to teach social skills to the whole class. Following are some recommendations for teaching social skills to a smaller number of students:

- Invite the special educator to present lessons in social skills to smaller groups of students in your class.
- Train an aide in teaching specific social skills, or in using one of the social skills curriculum materials, and ask the aide to teach these lessons in small groups in your class.
- Support social skills training the students may be receiving from special educators, and work with them to promote generalization to the general education classroom.
- Employ a peer-mediation strategy, in which specific social skills are modeled, prompted, and reinforced by classroom peers (see chapter 8).

Choose Curriculum Materials Thoughtfully

A variety of curriculum materials exist for teaching social skills, and several of these are listed at the end of this chapter. In selecting a particular curriculum material, ask yourself several questions to ensure that a particular material will meet your needs. The *In the Classroom* feature on page 217 lists these factors (see also the curriculum checklist in chapter 6). If the material you are considering does not address one or more of these elements, determine whether it can be appropriately adapted, or whether you should consider selecting a different program.

Conduct On-the-Spot Training

It is also important to monitor appropriate social skills outside of your training situations. If specific social skills have been targeted and practiced with particular students, prompt and reinforce those skills throughout the day. For example, Colin has a habit of taking things that he needs from classmates and teachers without asking permission. Even though he has learned and practiced more ap-

Social Skills Instruction for Game Playing

Moore, Cartledge, and Heckaman (1994) implemented a social skills training program for three inner-city adolescents with emotional or behavioral disorders, all of whom had been characterized as "disruptive" and "aggressive," and who had exhibited problems with perceived peer provocations and exhibiting good sportsmanship when participating in games, such as checkers or team sports. Six specific behaviors were operationalized and targeted for intervention, both to decrease inappropriate behaviors and to increase appropriate behaviors:

1. Inappropriate peer-reactive behaviors, such as spitting, kicking, tripping, and name-calling
2. Appropriate peer-reactive behaviors, such as ignoring the situation, walking away from the situation, or seeking help from an authority figure
3. Inappropriate reactions-to-losing behaviors, such as refusing to shake hands after the game, verbally abusing the opponent, or making other aggressive facial or physical gestures
4. Appropriate reactions-to-losing behaviors, such as congratulating and thanking the opponent
5. Inappropriate reactions-to-winning behaviors, such as taunting the loser
6. Appropriate reactions-to-winning behaviors, such as making positive statements to the loser, shaking hands, and offering a rematch.

Students were given training in appropriate social skills 4–5 days a week for a 5½-week period. Then students' behavior was observed both during a 30-minute classroom game activity immediately after the training session, and during a 20-minute regular gym period.

Students were taught social skills using five steps:

Step 1: Providing a rationale for exhibiting appropriate social skills, by providing scenarios and discussing them.

Step 2: Modeling appropriate ways of handling each skill.

Step 3: Having students use role-play activities to practice the target skills, either with prepared scripts or student-written scripts. For example, a situation is described in which Carlos becomes angry when Shawn fouls him and throws the basketball at Shawn:

Carlos: Hey, Shawn, you fouled me. You made me miss my shot. (*throwing the ball at Shawn*)

Shawn: (*dodging the ball*) I didn't mean to foul you, I was only trying to get the rebound.

Carlos: Well, I'm going to foul you when you try to get your shot.

Shawn: If I fouled you, take another shot. If we can't play fair, I don't want to play. (p. 257)

Step 4: Having students describe their own experiences, and perform role-play to practice more appropriate behaviors.

Step 5: Giving students homework assignments, in which they are encouraged to try the new skill outside the class and record the outcome on a supplemental work sheet.

Beginning on the third week of intervention and continuing until the end of the school year, students completed self-monitoring forms, where they recorded the number of times they did or did not perform target skills. Students recorded their behavior during the classroom play activity and after the gym period. Verbal praise was given to students whose forms closely followed the recording forms of the researcher.

Results of this investigation revealed that all students, as a result of training, began to exhibit more appropriate social behaviors in both the classroom and gym, although the behavior appeared to improve more in the classroom setting than in the generalization (gym) setting. For example,

(Continued)

inappropriate peer-reactive behaviors declined by an average of 4.3 per 30-minute class period. The authors concluded the following:

> Results showed that these interventions had a positive effect on the targeted behaviors in both treatment and generalization settings for three ninth-grade male students with [emotional and behavior disabilities]. (p. 263)

For more information on social skills training, with particular reference to cultural diversity, see Cartledge (1996).

Questions for Reflection

1. How can you design "homework" activities for specific social skills? How could you monitor that they had been completed?
2. Why do you think the behavior improved more in the classroom than in the gym setting?
3. For what other social skills would this intervention be beneficial?
4. Do you think an intervention like this could be effective for much younger students?

Companion Website

To answer these questions online, go to the Research Highlights feature in chapter 7 of the Companion Website.

propriate ways of interacting with others, he may still benefit from additional practice whenever this behavior reoccurs. If he takes a pencil without asking during math class, you could correct his behavior by pointing out the social skills training:

Teacher: Colin, what have you been practicing to do when you want something from others?

Colin: Ask politely.

Teacher: Ask politely, good! So how could you ask me politely for a pencil?

Colin: May I please have a pencil?

Teacher: Good job, Colin! That's just right! (*gives pencil*).

Train for Generalization

In most cases, trained social skills are of limited use if these skills do not generalize to other social situations. Generalization of social skills, like other behaviors described previously, must be specifically programmed (Alberto, Troutman, & Feagin 2002; Stokes & Baer, 1977). Programming for generalization of social skills could include the following strategies (see also Elksnin, 1994):

- Make certain students have mastered the skills they are to generalize. Students will not generalize behaviors they have not learned adequately in the first place. For example, a conversation skill that is not completely learned is not likely to generalize to other settings.
- Make the training as realistic as possible, so students can recognize situations for which generalization is appropriate. For example, when training job interview skills, make the situation as much like a real job interview as possible.
- Teach behaviors that will maximize students' social success and minimize their failures. This will make students want to generalize and maintain their behavior.
- Use real-life homework assignments for application of learned social skills (see Moore, Cartledge, & Heckaman, 1994). For example, have students apply their skills in maintaining a conversation outside of class, and report on their success the next day.
- Enlist the help of peers, parents, and school personnel with prompting and reinforcing the social skills. Teach others what social skills to prompt or watch for, and how they can be appropriately rewarded.

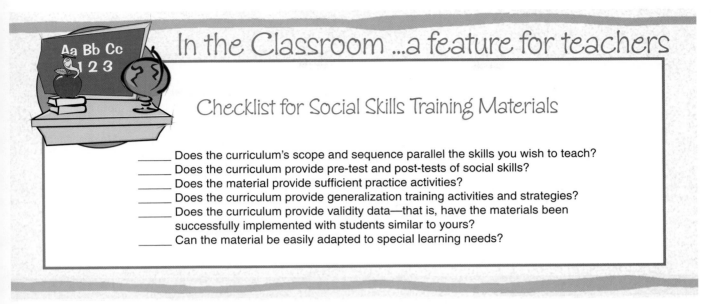

In the Classroom ...a feature for teachers

Checklist for Social Skills Training Materials

_____ Does the curriculum's scope and sequence parallel the skills you wish to teach?
_____ Does the curriculum provide pre-test and post-tests of social skills?
_____ Does the material provide sufficient practice activities?
_____ Does the curriculum provide generalization training activities and strategies?
_____ Does the curriculum provide validity data—that is, have the materials been successfully implemented with students similar to yours?
_____ Can the material be easily adapted to special learning needs?

- If necessary, initially accompany the student into the generalization setting or situation and prompt and reinforce there.
- Teach self-management skills, so students learn to recognize appropriate situations for generalizing a social skill, and monitor their success.
- Use periodic retraining and reminders of social skills (e.g., "Remember how we practiced accepting feedback?").

It is also important to use frequent reminders of the effectiveness of particular social skills. In their investigation of social play training with students with moderate mental retardation described previously, Rosenthal-Malek and Yoshida (1994) used the following statements to students to promote generalization of self-interrogation questions:

1. Look how well these questions are working for you.
2. You can see these questions can help you get what you want.
3. You can use these questions when you are in other places (i.e., gym, playground).
4. You are doing great! See how these questions can help you.
5. Using these questions really helps you to plan what you are doing (p. 216).

Validate Treatments

Recent comprehensive reviews of research on social skills training (e.g., Forness & Kavale, 1996; Gresham, 1998; Kavale, Mathur, Forness, Rutherford, & Quinn, 1997) have revealed that, overall, the effects of social skills training on different aspects of social behavior have been positive, but modest in scale—especially compared with behavioral treatments such as reinforcement, token systems, and timeout (Skiba & Casey, 1985). Nevertheless, there is no doubt that many students lack important social skills and that many students benefit from social skills training. Carefully document the effectiveness of your training to ensure that social skills instruction is having the maximum impact in improving social skills (see also Vaughn, McIntosh, & Hogan, 1990).

First, operationalize the target social skill (e.g., smiling, asking permission, being a "good sport"). Be sure that the target social behavior is one that is specific enough to demonstrate a response to treatment. Then take baseline measures, in which you record how much of the behavior is currently being exhibited. After the intervention begins, continue to monitor the behavior to ensure the treatment is working. Be sure you have chosen a behavior that is closely matched to the targeted social skill. If the behavior does not change, make a change in the intervention, and try again. Positive social-behavioral changes come with persistence of effort and creative problem solving. These may be among the most important skills that you teach.

Summary

- Students misbehave for a variety of reasons, such as gaining attention, gaining control, gaining retribution, or because of distrust of others.
- Much of student behavior is controlled by the classroom environment.
- Classroom behaviors can be better observed, managed, and evaluated if they are operationalized and monitored by formal observation and recording systems, such as event recording, duration recording, time sampling, and interval recording.
- Establishing a positive classroom atmosphere is an important key to effective behavior management.
- Less-intensive strategies, such as establishing rules, praise and ignoring, proximity, direct appeals, and reprimands, are helpful in maintaining appropriate classroom behavior.
- More formal management systems for effective behavior management include positive reinforcement, punishment, token systems, attribution training, public posting, timeout and level systems, the Good Behavior Game, and contracting.

- Self-monitoring and self-instruction training is helpful in allowing students to become more aware and take more control of their own behavior.
- A variety of strategies can be used to deal effectively with confrontations, and to prevent them from escalating.
- Schoolwide discipline systems have been effective in managing classroom behavior across entire school environments.
- Several methods exist for assessing social skills, including surveys, checklists, role-play, and direct observation.
- Social skills are usually taught by modeling, reinforcement, shaping, and modeling–reinforcement. Several strategies can be effective in promoting generalization of social skills.
- The effectiveness of social skills training, like other academic and behavioral interventions, should be monitored and validated in individual cases.

Council for Exceptional Children

CEC Standards Link: Improving Classroom Behavior and Social Skills

Information in this chapter links most directly to:

Standard 4—Instructional Strategies, particularly:

Skills:
- Use strategies to facilitate integration into various settings.
- Use strategies to facilitate maintenance and generalization of skills across learning environments.
- Use procedures to increase the individual's self-awareness, self-management, self-control, self-reliance, and self-esteem.

Standard 5—Learning Environments and Social Interactions, particularly:

Knowledge:
- Demands of learning environments.
- Basic classroom management theories and strategies for individuals with exceptional learning needs.
- Effective management of teaching and learning.
- Teacher attitudes and behaviors that influence behavior of individuals with exceptional learning needs.

- Social skills needed for educational and other environment.
- Strategies for crisis prevention and intervention.
- Strategies for preparing individuals to live harmoniously and productively in a culturally diverse world.

Skills:
- Create a safe, equitable, positive, and supportive learning environment in which diversities are valued.
- Identify realistic expectations for personal and social behavior in various settings.
- Identify supports needed for integration into various program placements.
- Design learning environments that encourage active participation in individual and group activities.
- Modify the learning environment to manage behaviors.
- Use performance data and information from all stakeholders to make or suggest modifications in learning environments.
- Use effective and varied behavior management strategies.
- Use the least intensive behavior management strategy consistent with the needs of the individual with exceptional learning needs.
- Design and manage daily routines.
- Organize, develop, and sustain learning environments that support positive intracultural and intercultural experiences.
- Use universal precautions.

✓ Inclusion Checklist
Improving Classroom Behavior and Social Skills

If you are experiencing classroom behavior problems, have you considered the following?

- ❏ Understanding the reason for some problem behaviors
- ❏ Carefully defining, observing, and recording classroom behavior problems
- ❏ Using classroom behavior management techniques, including the following:
  - ❏ Establishing a positive classroom atmosphere
- ❏ Using less-intensive strategies, including the following:
  - ❏ Rules
  - ❏ Praise and ignoring
  - ❏ Proximity
  - ❏ Direct appeals
  - ❏ Reprimands
  - ❏ Validating the student's feelings
- ❏ Using more formal management systems, including the following:
  - ❏ Positive reinforcement
  - ❏ Punishment

- ❏ Token systems
- ❏ Attributions
- ❏ Public posting
- ❏ Timeout
- ❏ Level systems
- ❏ Good Behavior Game
- ❏ Contracting
- ❏ Self-monitoring
- ❏ Self-instruction
- ❏ Using strategies for dealing with confrontations
- ❏ Using schoolwide discipline systems, such as Assertive Discipline and positive behavioral supports
- ❏ Teaching social skills
  - ❏ Assessing problems in social skills
  - ❏ Using appropriate social skills training procedures
  - ❏ Using on-the-spot training procedures
  - ❏ Training for generalization
  - ❏ Validating treatments

Chapter 8

Binta Johnson, 16
Washington, D.C.
"Lily Pond"

Promoting Inclusion with Classroom Peers

Objectives

After studying this chapter, you should be able to:

- Gain understanding of the advantages and potential limitations of cooperative learning.
- Compare the various types of cooperative group arrangements and activities.
- Compare and contrast the uses and features of cooperative learning and peer tutoring.
- Describe important teacher functions when employing cooperative learning.
- Gain understanding of peer tutoring and the benefits to tutors and tutees.
- Describe and evaluate different types of peer-tutoring programs (cross-age, same-age, and classwide).
- Describe the procedures for effectively employing a peer-tutoring program.
- Compare and contrast peer assistance and peer tutoring.

Your general education classroom students can facilitate successful inclusion of students with special needs by making them feel welcome in the classroom and building friendships with them. More importantly, you and your students set the stage for celebrating diversity within your class by openly accepting all students as equal members of the class. These actions build a foundation for having a true community of learners within your class. Within this community, an accepting atmosphere is established in which all students help and encourage one another to reach their own potential. You can assist your students by teaching them several strategies for working more effectively with classmates who have special needs. These strategies help promote acceptance of all students and teach students how to support one another using peer assistance, peer tutoring, and cooperative learning. All of these strategies can be implemented during academic and nonacademic situations and will help you and your students maintain a helpful, positive class environment.

Promoting Social Acceptance

Classroom peers can become involved in accepting students with special needs from their first placement in a general education classroom. Describe the new students before they arrive in class, remind the class what it feels like to enter a new classroom environment, and ask them to brainstorm strategies to help the new students feel more accepted (Stainback & Stainback, 1990). Then select one or more of these strategies that seem promising and ask for volunteers to implement them. For example, some students may volunteer to create a poster welcoming the new students into the classroom. Other students may volunteer to offer personal words of encouragement and support. Still other students may offer to help the new students orient to the new classroom, or offer to telephone them at home.

When you help students with special needs become true members of your class, you will help prevent them from being ostracized or rejected by classroom peers (Goodman, Gottlieb, & Harrison, 1972; Iano, Ayers, Heller, McGettigan, & Walker, 1974). In many ways, classroom peers are the key to social acceptance, and under the right circumstances can provide necessary assistance for helping students with disabilities be more accepted in the classroom.

Circle of Friends

In the **Circle of Friends** activity (Forest & Lusthaus, 1989), you distribute papers with four concentric circles drawn, and a stick figure in the middle. Students are told to write in the first circle the most important people in their lives, such as family members. In the second circle, they are to put their best friends, and in the third circle, they are to put other people they enjoy playing with or interacting with. In the fourth circle are people who are paid to be in their lives, such as doctors and dentists. When students have filled out the circles, ask the class how they would feel if they only had their mother in the first circle and no one in the second and third circles. After students share their feelings (e.g., "I would hate myself," or "I would be unhappy all the time"), inform the class that the new student might not have very many people in the second and third circles. The point of the activity is to demon-

Before identifying any student with special needs to the rest of the class, you must have permission from the parents. Ask your principal and director of special education for your district policies regarding confidentiality and then follow those procedures.

See chapter 7 for more information on helping students acquire appropriate social skills.

Classroom peers can help establish a welcoming environment for students with special needs.

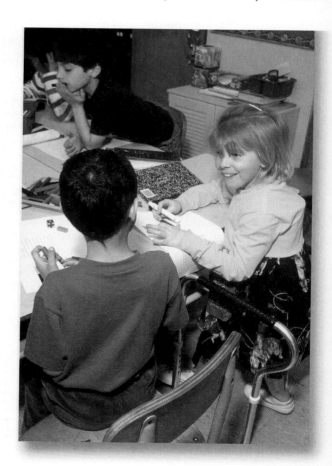

strate that everyone needs "circles" of friends, with people in every circle. Not everyone needs to be the student's best friend, but all can be friendly and interact well with the student.

Special Friends

Cole, Vandercook, and Rynders (1988) described a **Special Friends** program in which upper elementary students were trained to interact with students with severe disabilities. The training sessions, which covered rules, procedures, and disability awareness, are described in Table 8.1. The students then interacted with their Special Friends 2 to 4 times per week, 15 minutes per session, for 8 weeks. Students enrolled in this program enjoyed the interactions with their Special Friends, and maintained their contact with them after the sessions ended.

Another positive classroom activity to promote social acceptance involves dividing all students into pairs based on shared interest areas and asking them to complete a joint project on a subject they are both interested in. Or divide students into pairs and ask each student to complete a list of positive attributes of the other student (Stainback & Stainback, 1990). These lists can then be read to the class.

Table 8.1

Content of Special Friends Training Sessions

Session	Topic of Session	Activities
1	*Rules and Roles of Special Friends*	Play with your friend with some fun toys and activities.
2	*How Do We Play Together?*	Demonstrate a model play interaction, followed by a discussion about giving your friend a choice, helping only if necessary, taking turns, praising, and being enthusiastic.
3	*How Do We Communicate?*	Discuss nonverbal communication and guidelines for communicating (eye contact, talk, allow time for response, try another way if your friend does not understand you, and don't give up).
4	*What Is a Disability?*	Students experience various simulated disabilities, followed by a discussion of their feelings and perceptions of people with disabilities.
5	*What Is a Prothesis?*	Discuss the use of tools that people need to do tasks they would not be able to do or do as well without them. Show examples of protheses.
6	*How Does a Person with Disabilities Live?*	Invite a person with disabilities to talk with the students. Provide opportunity for the students to ask questions.
7	*What Is a Friend?*	Discuss friendship in general and then ask students to contemplate similarities and differences in their relationships with a Special Friend and with a best friend.
8	*Why Integration?*	Discuss the SF program, what are the benefits for them? Discuss the positive and negative aspects of having a friend in their lunchroom, recess, and classes.

Note: From "Comparison of Two Peer Interaction Programs: Children With and Without Severe Disabilities," by D. A. Cole, T. Vandercook, & J. Rynders, 1988, *American Educational Research Journal, 25*, pp. 415–439. Copyright 1988 by American Educational Research Association. Reprinted with permission.

Peer Assistance

What Is Peer Assistance?

Peer assistance refers to pairing students for the purpose of having one student available to assist another student when necessary. Peer assistance from a buddy can be helpful in promoting success in inclusive classrooms. However, peers should lend assistance only when help is required. For example, some students may need directions read to them; others may need assistance getting materials to their desks; and others may require help transcribing lecture notes. But when help is unnecessary, students with disabilities should be encouraged to perform tasks as independently as possible.

Peer assistance need not be arduous or time consuming for the helpers. Many of the activities are tasks the peer assistant is performing anyway, and helping their buddies usually does not take much extra time. Peers can share responsibilities with peer assistants. Overall, however, it is important to consider that peer assistance can be beneficial for the student helper, promoting such positive attributes as awareness of the needs of others and social responsibility.

Peer Training

Peer assistance programs should be set up in a systematic manner. The following *In the Classroom* feature offers a checklist for implementing peer assistance programs. The first consideration is to determine the precise nature of the situation that requires peer assistance. It is insufficient, for example, to think, "Mario has a visual impairment. I must assign a peer assistant to help Mario." Rather, consider the specific need that you believe peer assistance can address and how it can be addressed. For example, you may think, "Mario has a visual impairment, and sometimes needs someone to read information to him that is written on the blackboard."

Next, identify the student or students who can serve as peer assistants. In selecting peer assistants, teachers must exercise their best judgment based on their knowledge of the students in their class. In the past, teachers usually considered only the most responsible students, those who exhibited qualities of academic responsibility and conscientiousness as peer assistants. However, it may be as beneficial to consider less-obvious students, such as those who are shy or who at times have minor difficulties themselves with classroom assignments. These students usually are not only very capable of assuming the responsibilities, but also may flourish when given the opportunity to be a peer assistant.

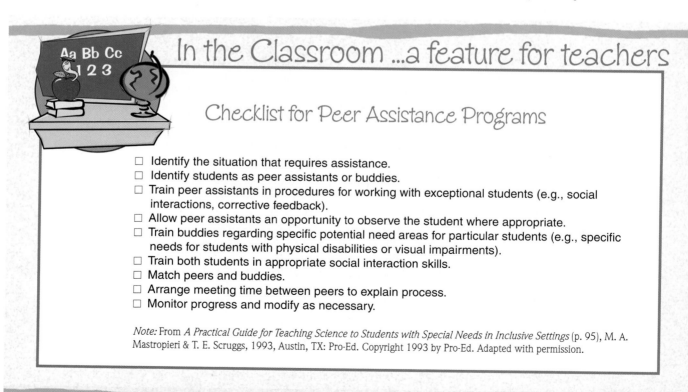

In the Classroom ...a feature for teachers

Checklist for Peer Assistance Programs

- ☐ Identify the situation that requires assistance.
- ☐ Identify students as peer assistants or buddies.
- ☐ Train peer assistants in procedures for working with exceptional students (e.g., social interactions, corrective feedback).
- ☐ Allow peer assistants an opportunity to observe the student where appropriate.
- ☐ Train buddies regarding specific potential need areas for particular students (e.g., specific needs for students with physical disabilities or visual impairments).
- ☐ Train both students in appropriate social interaction skills.
- ☐ Match peers and buddies.
- ☐ Arrange meeting time between peers to explain process.
- ☐ Monitor progress and modify as necessary.

Note: From *A Practical Guide for Teaching Science to Students with Special Needs in Inclusive Settings* (p. 95), M. A. Mastropieri & T. E. Scruggs, 1993, Austin, TX: Pro-Ed. Copyright 1993 by Pro-Ed. Adapted with permission.

Provide advanced training to both students before starting the peer assistance. Inform students exactly what the relationship will entail. For example, Kimberly may have volunteered to assist Mario. In this case, both Kimberly and Mario are made aware that Kimberly is undertaking the specific role of assisting Mario with reading, or repeating, what has been written on the board. Then let both students know what the procedures of this peer assistance will be. Kimberly will be taught how to recognize when information on the board should be presented to Mario and how to present this information to him. Mario will be taught to ask Kimberly a question when he needs clarification. When the procedures are clear to both participants, role-play a few practice sessions and then implement the peer assistance program. Finally, monitor the program to determine that it is meeting its objective. Following are some situations in which peer assistance may be appropriate.

Working with Students with Different Types of Disabilities

Peers can assume the role of assistant with any student. Table 8.2 provides some tasks and strategies that peer assistants can engage in with students with disabilities. Although some tasks appear very disability-specific, others are more general and extend across disability areas. For example, during emergency situations it is essential that specific students have been designated to assist students with disabilities who may require special assistance. Monitor closely all emergency-related procedures.

Another important way peer assistants can help address safety issues includes the handling of potentially dangerous materials such as materials that are breakable, sharp, or hot that may be used in laboratory activities. Peers can describe proper handling of materials that may be dangerous for

Consider using technological advances by having a peer assistant take notes on a computer and provide the computer disk to the student with hearing impairments. The notes can be printed or examined on the computer monitor.

Table 8.2

Suggestions for Use of Peer Assistants by Specific Disability and Task/Situation Area

Disability Area	Tasks/Situations	Strategies for Peer Assistants
All disabilities	Classroom activities	Answer questions and provide examples.
All disabilities	Emergencies (fire or tornado drills)	Provide assistance in exiting rapidly and safely.
Visual impairments	Mobility in unfamiliar places or rearranged rooms	Describe verbally the layouts of the rooms; guide students around new places.
Visual impairments	Written materials that are not enlarged print or Braille	Read orally.
Visual impairments	Videotapes that are not in descriptive video format	Provide additional verbal descriptions.
Hearing impairments	Lectures or films without closed captioning	Provide supplemental verbal or written information.
Hearing impairments	Abstract materials	Provide concrete models or descriptions.
Physical disabilities	Mobility	Provide assistance as necessary.
Physical disabilities	Fine motor tasks such as writing	Turn book pages, hold objects, take notes, act as scribe, provide copies of own notes.
Attention deficit hyperactivity disabilities	Attending	Reward student for on-task behavior and prompt student to get back to task.
Behavioral disabilities	Social skills	Provide appropriate social model.
Learning and cognitive disabilities	Writing	Act as scribe, take notes, share copies of notes.
Learning and cognitive disabilities	Reading	Read orally and provide summaries of materials.

Maintaining constant attention to speechread a lesson taught through direct instruction can tire a student with a hearing impairment. Thus, a peer assistant can provide a concrete visual model to demonstrate the concepts or assignments that students are to do.

someone with vision or fine motor difficulties. Peers can also help conduct portions of the activities involving those materials for students with visual impairments or fine motor difficulties.

When classroom activities are to be undertaken, peer assistants can provide concrete visual models to demonstrate what students are to do. When extensive listening is required, such as during teacher presentations, peer assistants can make copies of their notes so that students with hearing impairments or writing difficulties can focus their attention on the speaker or interpreter. Peers can also assist with speaking tasks if students with communication difficulties lack the stamina to complete a classroom presentation. For any kind of oral assignment a peer assistant could share some of the speaking responsibilities.

Peer assistants can assist with physical mobility by moving obstructions or collecting classroom materials. Peers can also assist students with classroom organization skills. They can help remind students what materials are necessary for each class when they take trips to their lockers. They can help students remember to complete and turn in their assignments and how to keep their notebooks organized. If special materials are needed for school, peers can telephone or e-mail students at home the night before to remind them to bring the required materials.

Peers can also promote appropriate social behavior by providing explicit models of positive classroom behavior and subtle prompts when appropriate. Such assistance should be monitored by the teacher; nevertheless, some students with behavioral disorders would rather receive feedback from specific classroom peers, if it is done appropriately, than from the teacher.

Peer assistants can also help students with mental retardation, who may occasionally need activities explained and modeled. Assistants also can help orient the students and supervise their movement through environments outside the classroom, such as libraries or museums. Peer assistance in promoting social acceptance by encouraging social initiations of students with disabilities is discussed in the following section.

Peer Social Initiation

Peer social initiation refers to procedures intended to enlist peer assistance in promoting social interaction with withdrawn or "isolate" children (Kerr & Nelson, 2002). This is done by such acts as asking the isolate student to play, giving or sharing a desired toy, or assisting the student in using a particular material. This technique has been used successfully with students (often, preschool or primary-grade students) from a variety of disability areas, including nondisabled students who exhibit some social withdrawal (e.g., Mastropieri & Scruggs, 1985–1986; Ragland, Kerr, & Strain, 1978). These procedures can also be used with any shy child. Very young peer assistants, and even assistants with moderate mental retardation, have been successfully trained at initiating social interactions (Young & Kerr, 1979).

In the Classroom ...a feature for teachers

Peer Social Initiation Procedure

1. Set aside at least 6 minutes for each target individual during the play session.
2. Try to use the same free-play area with the play materials suggested each day.
3. Before each intervention session, review with the peer trainer the activities that are most likely to succeed.
4. Remind the peer trainer before each session that the pupils may not respond at first but to keep trying.
5. Remind the peer trainer to play with only one target individual at a time. It helps if the adult in the session reminds the peer trainer when to change to and when to begin play with another student.
6. Reinforce the peer trainer for attempting to play with the withdrawn individuals. If the session is going slowly, you may wish to reinforce the peer trainer during the session. Otherwise, provide the peer trainer with some form of reinforcement at the end of the session.

Note: From *Strategies for Addressing Behavior Problems in the Classroom* (4th ed., p. 266), by M. M. Kerr and C. M. Nelson, 2002, Upper Saddle River, NJ: Merrill/Prentice Hall. Copyright 2002 by Merrill/Prentice Hall. Reprinted with permission.

According to Kerr and Nelson (2002), teachers should choose peer assistants who (a) attend school regularly, (b) consistently exhibit appropriate social skills with peers, (c) follow instructions reliably, and (d) can maintain concentration on the task for at least 10 minutes per session.

The first step in training is to explain to the peer assistant what will be expected (e.g., "Try to get Chris to play a game with you"). Assistants should be prepared for rejection and teachers can role-play ignoring a positive social gesture from the peer assistant. Tell the student not to give up, but to keep trying. If toys are being used to initiate social interaction, point out the target students' favorite toys, or provide cue cards to prompt the peer assistant. Continue to role-play until the student becomes skilled at persisting to prompt appropriate interaction; this may require at least four 20-minute sessions. Be sure the peer assistant is reinforced and supported for her efforts, and understands the importance of this intervention.

The peer-mediated social initiation procedure is then undertaken, as described in the *In the Classroom* feature above. Adaptations of this procedure can also be used to train peer assistants to facilitate interaction between two other students. The student plays with the two other students, modeling and prompting appropriate play (Kerr & Nelson, 2002).

Overall, classroom peers can be used in many ways to facilitate social acceptance. By considering the great potential of peer assistance in promoting social acceptance, assisting with academic tasks, and planning strategies, you and your students can create positive and accepting social environments.

Peer Tutoring

Why Use Peer Tutoring?

Peer tutoring is one of the most widely studied interventions in education, and many positive effects of tutoring have been noted. All reviews to date suggest tutoring can be a powerful tool in improving classroom performance (Fuchs & Fuchs, 1992; Topping & Ehly, 1998). Figure 8.1 highlights reactions to tutoring programs and the following scenario discusses the benefits of peer tutoring.

Implementation of curriculum and instruction, including peer tutoring and cooperative learning, are topics on the Praxis *Special Education: Core Knowledge* Tests.

I enjoy tutoring a lot. I really look forward to it. It's my favorite part of the day. Some mornings I'll wake up and not want to go to school. Then I'll remember, David gets to start a new book today, or something like that, and I'll be excited all day!
Karen Mylerberg, sixth-grade tutor, Franklin School.

Kara, a sixth grader, tutored Michael, a third grader, in reading. Kara's parents reported that she commented daily on Michael and his reading lesson. "She talks about her job all the time." Michael must also talk about Kara, for at Christmas, Michael made "candy sundaes" for Kara and his resource room teacher. Expressions of caring such as these are not uncommon.
LMJ, special education resource teacher.

My children like working with their tutors more than anything else! P.E., music, and other activities which are usually favorites with children don't have as much appeal for them as the one-to-one companionship with their tutors.
Mary Davis, second-grade teacher, Audubon School, Redmond, Washington.

Scott, a fourth-grade youngster 2½ years behind in reading, was being tutored by the special education resource room teacher. Due to scheduling problems he had to be tutored during his lunch recess two times a week. Scott was not terribly enthusiastic about missing lunch recess and his teacher had to "find" him on those days. Later, as part of a cross-age tutoring program, Scott was assigned a fifth-grade girl, Kelly. With Kelly as his tutor, Scott always came to the resource room voluntarily. Scott and Kelly formed a good relationship and both gave up more recess time to make a "sticker poster for good work," which was hung in the resource room. In fact, Scott enjoyed being tutored by Kelly more than by the teacher. His own involvement in planning his lesson, and his perception of Kelly's commitment toward his learning to read, made noon recess an acceptable sacrifice.
LMJ.

Figure 8.1

Comments About Tutoring Programs

Note: From *Cross Age and Peer Tutoring: Help for Students with Learning Problems.* J. R. Jenkins and L. M. Jenkins, 1981, Reston, VA: Council for Exceptional Children. Copyright 1981 by CEC. Reprinted with permission.

CLASSROOM SCENARIO

Peer Tutoring in Seventh-Grade History

This year Mr. Easton, the seventh-grade history teacher, began giving weekly quizzes on important people, events, and geographic locations from readings in the textbook. Students with learning disabilities had a difficult time learning and remembering this information. The overall performance of his students on the weekly quizzes was very poor, and Mr. Easton was beginning to wonder whether some of the students belonged in his class.

"Why should they be in my class if they cannot keep up with the work?" he asked Mrs. Canevaro, the seventh-grade special education teacher. Mrs. Canevaro knew something had to be done soon. She knew that her students with learning disabilities needed additional practice learning information from their general education social studies class.

After meeting with Mr. Easton, and examining the students' schedules, she decided that she could set up a 25-minute peer-tutoring program 3 days a week during seventh-period study hall when most of the students could practice studying and reviewing history with one another. Her first step was to determine exactly what Mr. Easton wanted the students to know. Her second step included developing plans for tutoring sessions and training the students to become tutors and tutees. After that, she would begin the tutoring program. Finally, she would evaluate the tutoring program by recording the performance of the students on weekly tests, and asking the students how they felt about the tutoring program.

Step 1: *Determine the Content for Tutoring Material*

Mrs. Canevaro met with Mr. Easton weekly and generated a list of the most important information from each social studies chapter. For example, some of the information on the World War I chapter included the following:

- Woodrow Wilson was the president of the United States.
- William Jennings Bryan, a pacifist, was secretary of state.
- Definition of alliance system, and how military alliances contributed to the start of World War I.
- Names of countries in the Central Powers and in the Allied Powers.
- Initial U.S. position was neutrality.
- Incidents leading up to the U.S. involvement in World War I, including the Zimmermann Note and the sinking of the Lusitania.
- Famous individuals of the era and their accomplishments, including flying ace Eddie Rickenbacker and songwriter George M. Cohan.

Step 2: *Devise a Tutoring Plan*

Mrs. Canevaro designed a plan for tutoring that included specific procedures for students to use while tutoring each other, and rules for appropriate behavior during tutoring sessions. In her program, students would serve as both tutors and tutees during sessions, because they all needed review and practice in history. She decided that the best way to practice learning the information would be to have the students quiz each other on the content. She put the questions and answers on index cards, to be used as the tutoring materials. Questions would be on one side, with answers on the reverse side. For example, one card read on one side: "Who was Eddie Rickenbacker, and what was he famous for?" The other side held the answer: "Eddie Rickenbacker was a flying 'ace,' who shot down 26 enemy aircraft."

Mrs. Canevaro established guidelines for the tutoring session, which she posted on the wall:

1. Be nice to your partner, and sit facing each other.
2. Decide who will be the tutor first. The first tutor will go through the cards, asking each question in order. When the tutee responds, the tutor will verify the answer. If it was answered correctly, the tutor will place it in the "correct" pile. If answered incorrectly, the tutor will correct the tutee, ask the question again, and after it is answered correctly, will place it in the "incorrect" pile. The cards in the "incorrect" pile are asked again after the set of cards is completed. After 10 minutes, a timer rings, and students reverse roles.
3. Speak in a pleasant tone when asking questions or when responding.
4. Encourage your partner by using statements like, "Great job, good answer," or "Can you think of anything else?" For incorrect answers, the tutor can state, "No, the answer is _____. What (who) is _____?"
5. At the end of the two tutoring periods, students should quiz each other on the entire list, and record the number of correct answers.

[For a list of rules for tutoring and for correcting mistakes, see the *In the Classroom. . . for sharing with students* feature in the Companion Website.]

Step 3: *Tutor Roles and Behaviors*

Next, Mrs. Canevaro planned a couple of sessions to review the tutoring roles and behaviors. She presented the guidelines and modeled both the tutor and tutee's roles for the students. She then provided them with opportunities to practice both roles and provided feedback. When students had mastered the tutoring behaviors and understood their roles, she began the tutoring sessions.

Step 4: *Monitor Performance*

During the tutoring sessions, Mrs. Canevaro collected systematic data on the efficacy of the tutoring. She wanted to know whether tutoring improved students' scores on their weekly quizzes in Mr. Easton's history class and if students enjoyed the tutoring. She began to collect students' weekly quiz scores and charted them. She also devised a questionnaire for students to answer periodically. Sample questions included the following:

Do you like being a tutor?

Do you like being a tutee?

Do you think tutoring helps you perform better on social studies quizzes?

Do you like history class better since you've been in the tutoring program?

After a month of tutoring and collecting data, Mrs. Canevaro was able to state that students' quiz scores had increased an average of 30 points, and that nearly all students reported enjoying being both tutors and tutees. Nearly all students reported that they did better on the weekly quizzes as a result of the tutoring sessions.

Step 5: *Collaborate with the History Teacher*

Mr. Easton also observed that many of the students were doing much better on the weekly quizzes. He considered the tutoring program successful, and believed that there were many other students in his class who could benefit from tutoring sessions. With Mrs. Canevaro's help, he began implementing 15-minute sessions in his own class 3 days per week. Under this new tutoring program, all students in his class benefited. Mrs. Canevaro was able to reduce the students' tutoring sessions to one day per week, arranging for additional tutoring sessions only before major tests.

Tutoring to Improve Academic Skills and Attitudes

Tutoring can also be helpful in addressing diverse learning needs in inclusive classrooms. However, tutoring, just like any educational strategy, should not be considered a panacea. Topping (1988) noted:

Peer tutoring *can* work and is unequivocally supported by research evidence. However, the evidence also shows that peer tutoring can *fail* to work, and failure you cannot afford. Careful planning is necessary to ensure that you are successful. (p. 27)

Benefits to Tutees

The most consistent benefits reported are to those students receiving tutoring. With careful planning of sessions and choice of materials, tutees are likely to improve academically in the area being tutored. If tutoring roles are alternated, with tutor and tutee changing places periodically, all students can benefit (e.g., Scruggs & Osguthorpe, 1986). Most evidence to date suggests that tutors function better in basic skills areas, such as spelling words, math facts, phonics and reading fluency, and basic facts and vocabulary in content areas such as science and social studies. Effects have been less reliable in areas involving concept acquisition, comprehension, or learning strategies. When programs in these areas are more successful, they have involved more extensive training procedures. Students involved as tutees have also reported better attitudes toward the subject area being tutored.

Although tutoring is often effective, those effects often depend on what other potential instructional strategies are available. For example, in learning spelling words, a well-implemented independent study strategy may be as effective as peer tutoring (Higgins, 1982). Tutoring also may not be more effective than small-group, teacher-led instruction (e.g., Kane & Alley, 1980; Sindelar, 1982). However, tutoring is likely to be quite useful when individual teacher assistance is not available and when students lack effective independent study skills.

Benefits to Tutors

Students serving as tutors also usually benefit from tutoring, but the benefits are not as reliable as those for tutees. Students with special needs can also benefit from being tutors, either in alternating tutor–tutee roles, or as tutors of less-able students (Cook, Scruggs, Mastropieri, & Casto, 1985–1986; Osguthorpe & Scruggs, 1986). Tutors with behavioral disorders have also been helpful in academic interventions (Gable & Kerr, 1980). Tutors usually benefit academically from tutoring in areas in which they have gained some initial competence, but could stand to benefit in fluency building and comprehension (Scruggs, Mastropieri, & Richter, 1985). For example, Singh

(1982) reported that tutees with learning disabilities improved in math computation and math concepts or applications tests, while tutors made relative gains on concepts or applications tests, but not on computation tests. Tutors can expect to improve academically if they tutor in areas in which they have not achieved complete mastery. For example, older tutors can gain reading skills (Scruggs & Osguthorpe, 1986), but may not benefit academically from tutoring in basic language acquisition areas (Scruggs, Mastropieri, Veit, & Osguthorpe, 1986; Scruggs & Richter, 1988).

Although it is often reported that students can improve in self-esteem from tutoring, these benefits are unreliable (Cook et al., 1985–1986; Sharpley, Irvine, & Sharpley, 1983). Students serving as tutors have rarely been observed to improve in global self-esteem measures. Nevertheless, tutors frequently benefit in attitude toward their tutoring partner, attitude toward the content being tutored, and in some cases, attitude toward school. Students in tutoring programs often report making new friends, suggesting that tutoring programs may help students with disabilities become more accepted within a classroom (Scruggs & Mastropieri, 1998). Some research evidence suggests that classwide peer tutoring can improve the social standing of students with learning disabilities (Fuchs, Fuchs, Mathes, & Martinez, 2002).

However, tutoring programs do not guarantee improved socialization. In one case, on the first day of a new tutoring program in an elementary classroom, one prospective tutoring partner commented, "I don't want to sit next to him—he stinks!" As stated earlier, students must be trained how to interact appropriately during tutoring sessions, and their behavior should be carefully monitored. Krouse, Gerber, and Kauffman (1981) cautioned, "Although it has been demonstrated that academic and social gains are frequently obtained by the tutor, this in itself is not sufficient justification for the child to be a tutor. Instead it must be shown that by being a tutor specific needs are being met" (p. 112).

Implementing a Tutoring Program

Tutoring programs must be carefully planned and systematically implemented. The following *In the Classroom* feature presents some suggestions for planning and implementing tutoring programs. For some possible rules for a tutoring program, including procedures for correcting mistakes, see the *In the Classroom. . . for sharing with students* feature in the Companion Website. Remember also that students serving as tutors often model their teacher's behavior—so be sure that your own teaching style is a good model for your classroom tutors.

Cross-Age Tutoring

In **cross-age tutoring,** older students serve as tutors for younger, lower-functioning students. The roles of tutor and tutee are clearly established, and do not alternate. An example of cross-age tutoring would be students from a nearby high school volunteering to tutor elementary school students who are having difficulty in school. The volunteers can schedule their time with the classroom tutor, be assigned a tutee, and be given explicit directions on their roles and responsibilities. It is also a good idea to have the tutors keep a notebook that details the dates and times of each session, the material tutored, and a report of the student's progress. Tutees can learn much from such partnerships, and volunteer tutors can gain valuable experiences, especially if they are considering a career in education or child care.

Same-Age Tutoring

Students can also tutor students of the same age. In some cases of **same-age tutoring,** students who are more skilled in a particular area can tutor less-skilled students. In other cases, pairs of students can alternate roles. This alternating role tutoring can work particularly well when students drill one another with flashcards. In this way, the tutor does not need to know the correct answer because it is printed on the back of the card.

Classwide Peer Tutoring

One of the most highly recommended strategies for promoting achievement among diverse groups of learners is **classwide peer tutoring** (Delquadri, Greenwood, Whorton, Carta, & Hall, 1986). All students in the class are divided into pairs of students, who then alternate roles of tutor and tutee to master basic academic skills. The most significant feature of classwide peer tutoring is the dramatic increase in engaged time on task and opportunities to respond (Hall, Delquadri, Greenwood,

In the Classroom ...a feature for teachers

Planning and Implementing a Tutoring Program

1. Clarify the specific objectives of the tutoring program, including both academic and social objectives when appropriate.
2. List objectives in a form that can be easily measured. For example:
   "Students serving as tutees will improve reading fluency by 30% on classroom reading materials in the next 12 weeks."
   "Performance of all students on weekly spelling tests will improve to an average of 85%; no student will score lower than 60%."
   "Within 8 weeks, students involved in tutoring will report that math is at least their third-favorite class."
3. Choose tutoring partners carefully. No firm conclusions can be drawn to direct tutoring choices; nevertheless, several considerations should be taken into account. Some teachers have recommended choosing students as tutors who are conscientious in class, and who generally have to work for their grades. These teachers have believed that the brightest students may have less empathy for students who do not learn easily (Jenkins & Jenkins, 1981), although exceptions to this are commonly found. Other considerations include the compatibility of the tutoring pair. Teachers should find pairs who will work together well; however, they should also encourage pairing students who are different in gender, race, or socioeconomic status whenever possible, and not exclusively support established social groupings.
4. Establish rules and procedures for the tutoring program. These rules should cover how students are to interact with each other, and specify the type of interactions that are not acceptable. Procedures should specify the times and dates of tutoring, the materials to be used, and the specific activities to be undertaken.
5. Implement the tutoring program, monitor it carefully, and be consistent in enforcing the rules and procedures. Modify rules and procedures as necessary.
6. Evaluate the program frequently, and do not wait for the end of the program to determine whether it was effective. Collect information throughout the program, and predict whether it will be successful. If progress is not being made, modify the program.

& Thurston, 1982). For example, consider a 45-minute, fifth-grade reading class of 30, in which one student is called on to read aloud at a time. In this class then, each student will read aloud for an average of no more than 1.5 minutes per class. In a classwide peer tutoring program, however, students in this same class could read aloud for an average of as much as 22.5 minutes per class, an increase of 1,500%! As described in chapter 6, increasing engaged time-on-task—or "maximizing engagement"—is closely linked to academic success. Research has continuously documented the positive benefits of classwide peer tutoring (Fuchs, Fuchs, Mathes, & Simmons, in press; Greenwood, Delquadri, & Hall, 1989; Mathes & Fuchs, 1994). Teachers today are more likely to need a justification for *not* employing classwide peer tutoring than for using it. Successful classwide peer-tutoring programs have been established in reading (Mathes, Fuchs, Fuchs, Henley, & Sanders, 1994), math (Fuchs, Fuchs, Karns, & Phillips, 1995; Fuchs, Fuchs, Phillips, Hamlett, & Karns, 1995), and spelling (Maheady & Harper, 1987). Following is a summary of classwide peer tutoring in reading (Fuchs & Fuchs, 1992; Fuchs, Mathes, & Fuchs, 1995; Mathes, Fuchs, Fuchs, Henley, & Sanders, 1994).

Peer tutoring can mutually improve the academic performance of the tutee and tutor.

Peabody Classwide Peer Tutoring in Reading

In the Peabody College classwide peer-tutoring program, all students are first paired with a partner (Fuchs & Fuchs, 1992). After the teacher announces the reading selection and tells the class to start, the stronger reader reads the passage aloud to the partner for 5 minutes. The roles are then reversed, and the weaker reader reads for 5 minutes. During oral reading, the partner follows along and corrects reading errors. After the 10-minute total reading session is a 2-minute "Retell" session, in which the weaker reader is prompted to answer:

- What did you learn first?
- What did you learn next?

The partner provides feedback on the answers. In the third segment, "Paragraph Shrinking," the weaker student is asked by the partner to provide the following information for each paragraph:

- Name the "who" or "what."
- State the most important thing about the who or what.
- Say the main idea in 10 words or less.

If an error is made, the partners are told to say, "No, that's not quite correct," and encourage the student to skim the passage for the answer. The last segment is the "Prediction Relay," and is composed of four segments:

Predict	_____	What do you predict will happen next?
Read	_____	Read half a page.
Check	_____	Did the prediction come true?
Summarize	_____	Name the who or what.
	_____	Tell the most important thing about the who or what.
	_____	Say the main idea in 10 words or less (Mathes et al., 1994, p. 46).

Students are given prompt cards that contain this information to assist them in questioning their partners.

More information on the teaching of strategies for improving reading comprehension, such as summarizing, sequencing, and predicting, is presented in chapter 13.

Every four weeks, tutoring pairs are rearranged, and the entire class is divided into two teams (e.g., a "Red" team and a "Blue" team). During classwide peer-tutoring sessions, students are given a score card, on which points are tallied for good reading and good tutoring skills. At the end of a four-week session, all individual score cards are tallied, and the winning team is congratulated by the teacher and classmates. The second team is also congratulated. Then, two new teams are formed and students again begin earning and accumulating points.

Recommendations

Mathes et al. (1994) have made several recommendations for implementing classwide peer tutoring, based on several years' experience in research and practice. These recommendations include the following:

Tutoring Materials. Teachers have reported using a variety of reading materials in classwide peer-tutoring programs, including basal readers, novels, library books, and content-area textbooks. It is not necessary for all pairs to read from the same book; both members of a tutoring pair are encouraged to read from the less capable reader's book to ensure that both students receive practice reading. If a weaker reader is compelled to read from a text that is too difficult, the tutoring experience may become ineffective and frustrating.

Other materials include a timer or stopwatch for timing sessions, and a calculator for adding up team points. Student materials include, in addition to the reading materials, a prompt card, a score card, and pencils.

Scheduling. Mathes et al. (1994) recommended scheduling tutoring sessions 3 days per week, 35 minutes per day, for 15 weeks. They also recommended scheduling the reading class when all members of the class are present (i.e., none, or as few as possible are attending resource programs or other special services).

Training. Mathes et al. (1994) suggested that teachers devote one 45-minute session to teaching students how to use the materials correctly, and how to be a helpful partner. Further, they have found that teachers should spend about two sessions for teaching each of the three reading activities, and that they teach only one activity at a time. That is, teachers could train and practice Retelling for the first week. The second week, they could train Paragraph Shrinking, and the third week, practice Retelling and Paragraph Shrinking together. The fourth week, they could add Prediction Relay, and begin to practice all three activities together.

Mathes et al. (1994) also reported that students need time and practice acquiring the skills of sequencing, skimming, summarizing, main idea, and predicting. They found main idea and summarizing the most difficult concepts to teach, and recommended the use of pictures to promote the idea of most important "who or what" before transferring the concept to reading.

Interpersonal Skills. Along with other researchers, Mathes et al. (1994) found that "many students left to their own devices may become bossy, impatient, or disrespectful toward their tutoring partner. . . . Giving positive feedback and rewards is not a natural behavior for most children" (p. 47). They recommend teaching students specific words and gestures for reinforcing partners, and emphasizing good sportsmanship and cooperative behavior. Additionally, close monitoring of interpersonal skills by teachers is recommended in keeping students positive toward one another.

Secondary Applications

In several investigations, Maheady and colleagues (Maheady, Harper, & Sacca, 1988; Maheady, Sacca, & Harper, 1988) implemented classwide peer tutoring in secondary-level classes for students with disabilities. In these studies, students tutored one another on important facts from high school social studies classes. They reported that when students with disabilities participated in classwide peer tutoring, their content area test scores improved, for example over 20 percentage points on weekly tests in the Maheady, Sacca, and Harper (1988) investigation. More recently, classwide peer tutoring has been employed to improve achievement in middle school English classes that included students with learning disabilities and mild mental retardation (Mastropieri, Scruggs,

Mohler et al., 2001). Spencer, Scruggs, and Mastropieri (2003) demonstrated that middle school students with emotional-behavioral disorders could participate effectively in classwide peer tutoring in social studies, and increased in achievement and on-task behavior when they did so.

Mastropieri, Scruggs, Spencer, and Fontana, (2003) employed classwide peer tutoring in world history classes with students with learning disabilities, emotional disturbance, or mild mental retardation. Students were divided into stronger and weaker readers. At the beginning of tutoring, "admirals" read one paragraph while "generals" listened and then students reversed roles, reading the same paragraph a second time. Immediately after oral reading, students employed summarization strategies to promote reading comprehension. Students asked each other after reading each paragraph, "What is the most important what or who in the text?" followed by "What is the most important thing about the what or who in the text?" and "What is the summary sentence?" similar to previous applications (e.g., Fuchs & Fuchs, 1992; Spencer, Scruggs, & Mastropieri, 2003). After the tutoring session, the teacher provided a whole-class review session by placing a blank summarization sheet on the overhead projector, and asking students to answer the questions. Differing responses were discussed and students were encouraged to alter their own responses to reflect information based on the class discussion. Compared to students receiving more traditional instruction, students who participated in classwide peer tutoring scored much higher on chapter tests, unit tests, and an end-of-year cumulative exam.

Peer tutoring has also been employed in inclusive high school chemistry classes (Mastropieri, Scruggs, Graetz et al., 2002). Student tutoring pairs received materials with which they questioned each other on important target content (e.g., "What is nonpolar covalent bonding?") as well as broader elaborations of that content ("What else is important to know about nonpolar covalent bonding?"). Tutoring was used as a supplement to regular instruction (about 15–20 minutes of a 90-minute class) to help ensure that students mastered basic facts and concepts in chemistry.

Cooperative Learning

Cooperative learning has been widely recommended as a technique to promote inclusive education of diverse learners (Johnson & Johnson, 1986). It has frequently been demonstrated to result in increased achievement (Johnson, Maruyama, Johnson, Nelson, & Skon, 1981), and improved attitude toward the subject matter (Slavin & Karweit, 1985). In cooperative learning, students are

Cooperative learning improves classroom learning while enhancing socialization among diverse learners.

Research Highlight

Cooperative Learning in Math

Slavin, Madden, and Leavey (1984) investigated the effectiveness of Team-Assisted Individualization (TAI) on the math achievement of both students with disabilities and normally achieving students. The study was conducted for 24 weeks, and included 113 students with disabilities and 113 normally achieving students in grades 3–5. Students were first assigned to teams. On the basis of pretests, all students were placed in an individualized, structured math curriculum. Before students began to work within their assigned teams they were taught explicitly how to work collaboratively. The student teams met daily and during their sessions the students worked individually on their assignments and helped other team members whenever necessary. In a whole-class session later in the day, teachers reviewed the content. Throughout the study points were awarded to teams based on each student's progress. Groups were presented with awards, based on the average number of problems solved correctly, and the average number of units completed by each student.

At the end of the 24-week program, students were given an achievement test in math. Compared with control students, who were given more traditional, whole-class instruction, TAI condition students scored significantly higher on the computation and on the concepts or applications subtests of the mathematics achievement tests. Further, students with disabilities outperformed their counterparts in the control classes on both measures of math achievement.

For more information on research on cooperative learning, see McMaster and Fuchs (2002).

Questions for Reflection

1. Why does cooperative learning often result in such positive achievement gains?
2. Why is cooperative learning sometimes not entirely effective?
3. Why do you think students might prefer cooperative learning to more traditional models of instruction?
4. Why do you think some teachers might resist using cooperative learning?

Companion Website

To answer these questions online, go to the Research Highlights feature in chapter 8 of the Companion Website.

assigned to small groups and work collaboratively to complete group activities. Cooperative learning programs can be configured in many ways. Johnson and Johnson (1986) have described some important overall elements in implementing cooperative learning programs, which are described in the Research Highlight. These major sets of strategies are summarized in the *In the Classroom* feature.

Important Teacher Functions in Implementing Cooperative Learning
Create Objectives

Teachers should carefully specify both the academic objectives to be accomplished, and the collaborative skills objective, which describes the interpersonal skills and small-group skills that will be

In the Classroom ...a feature for teachers

Five Major Strategies for Cooperative Learning

- Specify clearly the objectives for the lesson.
- Make a number of decisions about placing students in learning groups before the lesson is taught.
- Explain clearly the task, the positive interdependence, and the learning activity to the students.
- Monitor the effectiveness of cooperative learning groups and intervene to provide task assistance (such as answering questions and teaching task skills) or to increase students' interpersonal and group skills.
- Evaluate the students' achievement and help students discuss how well they collaborated with each other.

Note: From "Mainstreaming and Cooperative Learning Strategies," by D. W. Johnson and R. T. Johnson, 1986, *Exceptional Children, 52,* 553–561. Copyright 1986 by CEC. Adapted by permission.

addressed. Whenever you implement a cooperative learning activity, you should specify the collaborative skills that will be necessary to complete the activity successfully. According to Johnson and Johnson (1986), "These collaborative skills have to be taught just as purposefully and precisely as academic skills" (p. 555).

Determine Group Parameters

Cooperative learning groups usually range from two to six students. The groups should be larger when materials are scarce, or when limited time is available to complete the activities. If students are younger or inexperienced with cooperative learning activities, the group size should be smaller. Students should not work in groups of four or more if they have not mastered the preskills of group work.

It is also important to plan carefully whether students should be in homogeneous or heterogeneous groupings. While it is helpful to have groups that work well together, it is also important to mix groups by gender, race or ethnicity, and ability level. Sometimes random assignment to groups is effective. Teachers should also consider how long they want groups to operate together. For example, for a longer project in plant growth and development, it may be necessary for groups to remain intact throughout the activity. For other projects, groups can be changed more frequently. When absenteeism is a problem in the school, group assignments may need to be made daily.

Also consider the physical arrangement of the groups. Ideally, groups sit around a circular table that is small enough to provide close proximity, and large enough to accommodate relevant materials. However, teachers usually must cope with the best furniture available. Just be sure that groups are arranged so you can easily move from one to another. When distributing materials, try to arrange for cooperation. One way to do this is to only provide one set of materials that must be shared efficiently for the task to be completed.

Another important decision involves the roles that students will assume during the cooperative learning activity. Usually it is helpful to assign specific duties to individual students to promote teamwork and cooperation. These roles might include a summarizer (who restates the conclusions, consensus, or final products of the group), a checker (who ensures that all students have understanding of the activity objectives), an accuracy coach (who corrects or verifies other students' responses), and an elaboration seeker (who attempts to relate learning of the present activity to other

Table 8.3

Student Cooperative Learning Roles in the Full Option Science System

Role	Responsibility
Reader	**Reader** reads all print instructions, ensures that all students in the group understand the task, and summarizes the activity.
Recorder	**Recorder** is responsible for recording all the data, including observations, predictions, and estimations. This involves using pens, pencils, and the appropriate chart and graph paper.
Getter	**Getter** is responsible for getting all the necessary materials and for returning them at the end of the activity. This involves walking and carrying equipment, such as trays, microscopes, water, slides, pans, and eye droppers.
Starter	**Starter** begins the manipulations of the materials, supervises the assembly of materials, and ensures that all group members have equal opportunity at using the hands-on materials.

Note: From *A Practical Guide for Teaching Science to Students with Special Needs in Inclusive Settings* (p. 78), by M. A. Mastropieri and T. E. Scruggs, 1993, Austin, TX: P-E. Reprinted with permission.

situations) (Johnson & Johnson, 1986). Of course, individual students are also responsible for all other aspects of the assigned tasks. Another, more procedural set of roles, involving groups of four students, is recommended in the *Full Option Science System* (Britannica, 1991) materials, and is described in Table 8.3.

Explain Goals, Rules, and Procedures

Before group activities begin, be sure that all students understand both the assignment, and the purpose of the activity. Group goals and rewards should be carefully explained to all group members, for example, bonus points for completing the task within a certain time period. Overall, students should be aware that they are responsible for (a) their own learning, (b) the learning of the group, and (c) the learning of the entire class, in that order. The criteria for success should be explained to the students. Individual accountability within the group structure is necessary (Stevens & Slavin, 1991), and should be clearly specified. Also, when appropriate, students could be informed that they can assist other groups if they have finished their own assignment first.

Because cooperative learning activities are different from many other classroom activities, particularly independent seatwork, students need to be informed what is and is not appropriate in cooperative learning exercises. One method of conveying expectations is by use of a **T-Chart** (Johnson, Johnson, & Holubec, 1991), which employs two columns in the shape of a T. The T-Chart specifies what the room will look like (e.g., "All students participating") and sound like (e.g., "Low voices from students in groups"), if the rule is being followed. An example of a T-Chart is given in the *In the Classroom. . . for sharing with students* feature that can be found on the Companion Website. Other classroom rules for cooperative learning that could be displayed on a T-Chart include "Everyone shares with others" or "Students encourage each other."

Monitor Group Activities

When cooperative groups begin working, your role differs dramatically from more traditional instruction. Many teachers begin by presenting information to the class as a whole and then break students into their groups. Instead of directly presenting information or demonstrating procedures to the whole class for the entire period, the teacher's role involves moving around and monitoring group activities. Ensure that students remain on-task, and interact appropriately. When necessary you may assist with the task or demonstrate procedures. When students are interacting inappropriately, intervene to model, demonstrate, and teach collaborative skills necessary for the task to be accomplished. Finally, when the activities are completed (or allocated time expires), you must provide closure to the lesson by restating the objectives, summarizing the major points,

Technology Highlights

Working with Peers on Computers

Computers provide ideal opportunities for peers to work collaboratively. Students enjoy the motivating aspects of working with computers, and working collaboratively on projects involving computers can be a rewarding experience for all students. For example, students who are working on developing multimedia projects can assist one another in activities including: finding appropriate sources from the Internet, downloading multimedia files, and editing pictures and other multimedia to include in their projects. One student can be designated as the official computer operator and the other as a co-navigator. Roles can be reversed during the project after specified amounts of time. Before assigning partners, students can be ranked according to their computer expertise along a continuum of expert to novice. This information can be used to pair so that computer experts are paired with novices. The models suggested for implementing peer-tutoring and cooperative learning in other subject areas can be applied to computer use during either peer-tutoring or cooperative learning scenarios.

Several researchers have successfully involved collaborative group work using multimedia projects and using computers to write essays. In an investigation by Ferretti, MacArthur, and Okolo (2001), students with learning disabilities and typically achieving partners worked collaboratively in small groups on developing multimedia technology-based projects in social studies. Students worked collaboratively and all students gained in the social studies content being studied, although students with learning disabilities learned less than their typically achieving peers.

Consider pairing students to prepare presentations made on the computer. For example, many teachers have successfully taught students to use PowerPoint™ software to develop multimedia presentations. Some of the presentations can be simple using only text, while more complex presentations can involve pictures, graphs, animation, and sounds. Pairing students to develop these projects can help all students gain the technological expertise necessary to function independently.

having students provide ideas or examples, and answering any final questions. Because cooperative learning activities are less formally structured than more traditional methods, summarizing and providing closure are critically important. Group activities can easily overrun the allotted time, so plan carefully to ensure that enough time remains for closure and summaries at the end of the activity.

Evaluate Individual and Group Efforts

Evaluation needs to occur throughout the cooperative learning process and include any individual and group products. You can evaluate the process for students with special needs by observing them while they are working in their groups. The following *In the Classroom* feature lists some ideas for evaluating the process. Group efforts should be considered, and students should be individually evaluated for their learning and their contributions to the group process. Finally, teachers and students should both evaluate how well the groups functioned and consider how the group could function better in the future.

In the Classroom ...a feature for teachers

Evaluation Checklist for Cooperative Learning

Process Evaluation Component
- ☐ Is the student working with the group members?
- ☐ Does the student appear to understand what to do?
- ☐ Is the student capable of doing the assigned tasks?
- ☐ Do the group members encourage independent work when appropriate?
- ☐ Are all group members actively engaged in the activity?
- ☐ Do the group members appear to be getting along?
- ☐ Do the students exhibit appropriate social behavior?
- ☐ Do the group members share materials appropriately?
- ☐ Do the group members speak in a pleasant, quiet tone of voice?
- ☐ Does the group start and finish activities on time?

Product Evaluation Component
- ☐ Did the student complete the activity?
- ☐ Does it appear that the work completed meets the objective for the learning component of cooperative learning?
- ☐ When given a performance-based assessment covering the objectives, do students demonstrate mastery of their prioritized objectives?
- ☐ When questioned, can students with disabilities explain what they did or show you what they learned?

Integrating Students with Special Needs into Cooperative Groups

Prepare Students with Special Needs

Cooperative learning is frequently described as an important inclusion strategy because it enables students with special needs to receive additional attention and assistance from peers, while making their own contributions to the group (Scruggs & Mastropieri, 1994). Nevertheless, students with disabilities may be fearful or anxious about joining a cooperative learning group. It is important to explain procedures and roles carefully, so students will understand the expectations. It may be helpful to role-play the role the students will assume before the activity. Present them with a role in the group that is appropriate for their skill levels. For example, if a student does not read at the appropriate grade level, provide a role of organizing, summarizing, or restating what others have reported. If the student lacks some specific social or academic skill that is important for group functioning, see if the special education teacher can teach some of these skills before the student joins the group.

Prepare Students without Disabilities

As stated earlier, classroom peers play an integral role in the integration of students with disabilities and other special needs into general education classrooms. However, students must be taught how to interact appropriately, and how to accept individual differences in learning. Positive peer interactions should be prompted and carefully monitored. As an example of unproductive interactions on a group learning task, O'Connor and Jenkins (1996) provided the following observation:

> Toby, a fifth-grade boy with [learning disabilities], rarely received productive help from his partners, although he frequently requested it. By this point in our observation, Toby's partner had long since ceased to follow Toby's reading or correct his errors. Toby stopped reading and an-

nounced, "I need help." The partner supplied a word, but it was not the word in the text. Toby used it anyway, and they both laughed. This game escalated until each time Toby needed decoding help, his partner said, "I'm a dumbo," which Toby inserted into the sentence. . . . Eventually, Toby tired of the game. "I need help," he said again, but from this partner he would not receive it. (p. 36)

Some students may need particular types of assistance in cooperative group situations, such as help turning pages or understanding directions. The special education teacher may be able to meet with relevant cooperative groups and explain how best to interact with the student with special needs. Many students with special needs will need particularly to be made to feel welcome, and students can be taught how to be appropriately welcoming and encouraging.

When students are working to earn group points or rewards, sometimes they are concerned that having a student with a disability will impair the group's chances to succeed. In these cases, consider varying the group criteria for different members, or the amount of material each student is expected to master. For example, in a group spelling activity, an individual with learning disabilities may be expected to learn only the easier spelling words from the list. These students can also be evaluated with respect to how much they improved over the previous time period, rather than how much they learned in a particular activity. Individual students can be given different assignments, lists, or problems appropriate to their abilities, and can be evaluated on the percent correctly completed. Finally, consider awarding bonus points for groups that include students with disabilities. This may make group members more receptive to including students with special needs.

Types of Cooperative Group Arrangements

Cooperative learning activities can be arranged in many ways, and many types of tasks can be adapted for cooperative learning. Johnson, Johnson, and Holubec (1991) listed several, including the following intended to help teachers get started with cooperative group activities:

1. Discuss a lesson with your neighbor for 3 to 5 minutes, asking questions and clarifying.
2. Reading groups, in which three students serve as reader, recorder, and checker, in reading material and answering questions.
3. Have students meet in small groups and check homework assignments, discussing and resolving any questions that were answered differently.
4. Students meet in groups to proofread and critique each other's papers, and meet again to respond to revisions.
5. Students work in small groups to prepare for specific tests (pp. 1:19–1:22).

Slavin (1991) described several types of more formal cooperative learning arrangements and activities. These groups included the following:

1. *Student Teams-Achievement Divisions* (STAD): After the teacher has presented a lesson, students meet in heterogeneous groups to study the material. After the study session, students take a quiz, and are graded with respect to how much improvement was made over the previous test. The winning group is recognized in a class newsletter.

2. *Team-Assisted Individualization* (TAI): In this procedure, described previously in the Research Highlight, students are given pretests on an academic area, and placed in a structured curriculum based on their score. Students are then placed in heterogeneous groups and help each other complete their assignments. Rewards are based on the number of activities completed and on percentage correct.

3. *Cooperative Integrated Reading and Composition* (CIRC): Students work in cooperative groups on reading and writing assignments. For part of the instruction, teachers lead the instruction. Then students work cooperatively on decoding, vocabulary, writing, spelling, and comprehension activities, and prepare each other for tests.

4. *Jigsaw*: This is a popular cooperative learning strategy, in which each student learns a particular piece of information and then contributes it to the group. Students are tested individually on their learning of all the material. In another version of Jigsaw, each student contributes a particular component of a larger task and then the larger task is presented to the entire

class. For instance, one group could be preparing a presentation on Dr. Martin Luther King. One student could prepare information on King's early life; another could prepare information on King and the Civil Rights movement; another could gather material from King's speeches; and a fourth could collect information about King's assassination. The group then meets and cooperatively compiles the entire presentation, with each student informing the group what she has learned.

5. *Group Investigation*: Group investigation requires the most independence on the part of cooperative groups. In this method, students decide how they will learn the material, how they will go about organizing the group to best facilitate learning, and how they will communicate their results to the other students in the class.

While some activities are intended to be undertaken throughout the year, for example, in science or mathematics, other cooperative group activities can be designed for a single lesson. Teachers should consider their own classroom needs to design the best arrangement for cooperative group learning.

Conflict Resolution

In some cases, peer mediation strategies have been used to manage conflict situations that occur among peers. Johnson, Johnson, Dudley, Ward, and Magnuson (1995) trained students how to identify conflicts, how to negotiate, and how to mediate to better resolve peer conflicts. The negotiation procedure had five parts:

1. Jointly define the conflict.
2. Exchange positions and interests.
3. Reverse perspectives.
4. Invent at least three optional agreements for mutual gain.
5. Reach an integrative agreement.

After 12 45-minute training sessions, Johnson et al. (1995) reported that the training had a significant effect on the strategies students used and the resulting resolutions of conflicts.

Peer mediators trained in resolution strategies can help manage peer conflicts.

Advantages and Limitations of Cooperative Learning

Advantages

It has been reported that cooperative learning is an effective strategy for improving achievement, group interactions, social learning, and improving the learning of students with disabilities and other special learning needs (Johnson, Johnson, & Holubec, 1991; Slavin, 1991). With cooperative learning, students with disabilities can be included in—and contribute to—activities that they otherwise may not be able to participate in individually (Mastropieri, Scruggs, Mantzicopoulos et al., 1998). Johnson and Johnson (1986) concluded the following:

> In both competitive and individualistic learning situations teachers try to keep students away from each other. "Do not copy," "Move your desks apart," and "I want to see how well you can do, not your neighbor" are all phrases that teachers commonly use in their classrooms. Students are repeatedly told, "Do not care about the other students in this class. Take care of yourself!". . . Cooperative learning, however, should be used whenever teachers want students to learn more, like school better, like each other better, have higher self-esteem, and learn more effective social skills. (p. 554)

Potential Limitations

In spite of the benefits of cooperative learning, some potential limitations also exist that teachers should consider. Tateyama-Sniezek (1990) reviewed literature on cooperative learning in research in which students with disabilities were participants, and in which their achievement was examined separately from students without disabilities. She concluded that students with disabilities often did not learn significantly more than if they participated in alternative learning conditions. Stevens and Slavin (1991) responded that the effects for students with disabilities were generally positive, even if they were not always statistically significant. McMaster and Fuchs (2002) conducted a review of more recent research, and concluded that outcomes were variable for students with learning disabilities. However, cooperative learning programs that combined individual accountability and group rewards appeared more successful. It should be noted that positive effects for students with disabilities are often, but not always, realized in cooperative learning interventions, and that teachers should plan and monitor the interventions carefully to ensure they are having the desired effect.

Other potential limitations that have sometimes been mentioned by teachers include increased teacher preparation time, increased transition time, increased allocated time for lessons, and anxieties on the part of both students with and without disabilities regarding working together and teaching one another. Additionally, dominant students may monopolize groups, passive students may become disengaged from the activity, assignments may not always be at the appropriate level for all students, higher noise levels are found in the classroom, and all students may not learn unless individual accountability systems are enforced (Mastropieri & Scruggs, 1993). Plan ahead to effectively address these issues.

However, many of these potential concerns may occur with other instructional arrangements, and strategies for dealing with many of these limitations have been presented earlier in the chapter. As with any educational intervention, teachers must assure that they have maximized the positive benefits while addressing possible limitations. Overall, cooperative learning can be an effective strategy for promoting inclusive instruction. For example, Mastropieri, Scruggs, Mantzicopoulos et al. (1998) employed cooperative learning to promote learning in a hands-on elementary science class, which included five students with disabilities, including learning disabilities, emotional disturbance, mild mental retardation, and physical disabilities. Not only did students in this class greatly outperform students in comparison classes that employed traditional textbook-based instruction, the students with disabilities scored at about the middle of the class! Appropriately employed, cooperative learning can be an important strategy for many classroom situations.

Summary

- Peers can be taught a variety of strategies that involve students helping each other during classroom and school activities.
- Peer assistance can be used to promote inclusion of students with a variety of special needs.
- Circle of Friends and Special Friends are training programs that can promote classroom acceptance of students with disabilities or other special needs.
- Peer assistance refers to pairing students for the purpose of having one student available to assist another student when necessary.
- It is important to identify the situations that require peer assistance, appropriately train students, match peer assistants and buddies carefully, and monitor progress and modify as necessary.
- Tutoring is a powerful tool in improving classroom performance, which can also be very helpful in addressing diverse learning needs in inclusive classrooms.

- Tutors and tutees both can gain academically and socially from tutoring interventions, although the procedures and outcomes should be carefully monitored.
- Classwide peer tutoring is one of the most highly recommended strategies for promoting achievement among diverse groups of learners.
- Cooperative learning is another strategy that can improve achievement and social integration of diverse learners.
- Cooperative learning interventions require specifying objectives, making placement decisions, explaining the task, monitoring effectiveness, and evaluating student achievement.
- A variety of formal and informal procedures for cooperative learning can be employed to address a variety of classroom situations.

Council for Exceptional Children

Promoting Inclusion with Classroom Peers

Information in this chapter links most directly to:

Standard 4—Instructional Strategies, particularly:

Skills:
- Use strategies to facilitate integration into various settings.
- Select, adapt, and use instructional strategies and materials according to characteristics of the individual with exceptional learning needs.

Inclusion Checklist
Promoting Inclusion with Classroom Peers

If you are planning to integrate students with disabilities or other special needs into your class, have you considered the following?

- ❏ Using peer assistance for students with lower-incidence disabilities
- ❏ Using peer assistance for students with higher-incidence disabilities
- ❏ Using peer assistance strategies for promoting social acceptance of students with disabilities or other special needs

If you wish to increase academic achievement and attitudes in your inclusive classroom, have you considered the following?

- ❏ Cross-age tutoring
- ❏ Same-age tutoring
- ❏ Classwide peer tutoring

If you want to increase achievement and promote cooperation and collaboration in your classroom, have you considered the following?

- ❏ Implementing cooperative learning programs
- ❏ Integrating students with special needs into cooperative learning groups
- ❏ Selecting from a variety of cooperative learning group arrangements and activities
- ❏ Addressing potential advantages and limitations of cooperative learning

Chapter 9

Ernestine Glidden, 14
Portland, Maine
"Untitled"

Enhancing Motivation and Affect

Objectives

After studying this chapter, you should be able to:

- Describe the preconditions to improving motivation and affect in the classroom.
- Identify techniques for improving and enhancing student motivation and affect.
- Describe strategies for increasing self-efficacy.
- Demonstrate the uses of goal setting and attribution training.
- Discuss strategies for increasing students' personal investment in shared decision making in the classroom.
- Identify and implement strategies to make learning more fun, exciting, and meaningful.
- Describe the uses of praise and reward to reinforce students' success in the classroom.
- Compare and contrast tangible and intangible rewards.

It has been said that three "horses"—ability, motivation, and affect—pull the "chariot of learning" (Paris & Cross, 1983). All are necessary components for successful learning to occur. Students may have the ability or skills necessary to succeed in school, but may still fail if not properly motivated. Likewise, if students have ability and general motivation, but are depressed or anxious, they may not achieve their potential.

Because of their combined effect on student learning, motivation and affect may be the most important topics in this book. While motivation and affect overlap to some extent, they are used to represent important, separate aspects of school functioning. **Motivation** refers to the degree to which students desire to succeed in school, while **affect** refers to the students' emotional mood and personal feelings. **Intrinsic motivation** refers to participation in an activity purely out of curiosity, desire to succeed, or desire to contribute. **Extrinsic motivation,** however, refers to participation in an activity in anticipation of an external reward (Dev, 1997). Martin Ford (1995) has argued that motivation "is the single most important factor in long-term competence development" (p. 72).

Given that instruction is adequate, high levels of motivation and positive affect provide students opportunities to master the learning tasks set before them. However, at one time or other, students—particularly those with disabilities and other special needs—can lack motivation and positive affect (e.g., Carlson, Booth, Shin, & Canu, 2002). Students who lack a life history of success may be more likely to quit working on a task because they believe they have little chance of succeeding (Licht, 1992). According to Pressley and McCormick (1995):

> Learning-disabled children often are caught in a terrible cycle. Because they have done poorly in school, they begin to think of themselves as academic failures—they begin to believe they are stupid. Such a belief does nothing to motivate academic effort, which results in additional failure, which, if anything, strengthens the perception of low ability. (p. 599)

In other words, many students with disabilities are more likely to fail at academic tasks and to attribute such failure to personal inadequacies rather than to lack of effort. Finally, students with disabilities and other special needs may be more at risk for affective problems such as depression and low self-esteem (Harter, Whitesell, & Junkin, 1998; Heath, 1996) as in the case of Danny, described in the following scenario.

CLASSROOM SCENARIO

Danny

Danny is enrolled in a ninth-grade mathematics class. In fifth grade, he was classified as learning disabled in reading, and he attends the resource room for four 50-minute periods per week for help with his reading. He is interested in basketball and has many friends. In math class (pre-algebra), however, his manner is anything but cheerful. He received a failing grade the first semester, and seems to be headed for another at the end of the next grading period. During lecture or class discussion, Danny seems to simply stare off into space. When given classroom assignments, he makes a modest effort to complete them, but it is clear from his manner that he is just waiting for the bell to ring. He turns in only about half of his homework assignments—and most of these are either incomplete or incorrect. Clearly, mathematics is neither an academic strength nor an interest area for Danny; nevertheless, it seems likely that he could produce much higher quality work if he applied himself more and developed a more positive attitude toward math. However, when his math teacher Mr. Hamilton spoke with him about his attitude, Danny seemed to believe his problem was hopeless. "What's the use?" he said. "You know I'll just fail anyway."

The best way to handle motivational and affective problems of students with disabilities, and all others, is to start by making the classroom a positive and motivating experience for all students.

Preconditions for Improving Motivation and Affect

Before any attempt to improve motivation and affect will succeed, several preconditions must exist (Brophy, 1987). These are not motivational strategies in themselves, but they set the stage for the development of motivation and positive classroom affect. When these preconditions are in place, motivation and positive affect will be much easier to promote. These preconditions include the following:

- A supportive, organized classroom environment
- Instructional materials that are at an appropriate difficulty level
- Meaningful and relevant instructional tasks

It is also important for the classroom environment to be task-oriented rather than ego-oriented (Nicholls, 1989). Making decisions to create the most ideal conditions for motivating students, and increasing positive affect, is within your control as a teacher, and can make an enormous difference in classroom atmosphere and student achievement.

Create a Supportive, Organized Classroom Environment

The first decision a teacher must make is how to organize the classroom so that *all* students feel welcome and accepted. A classroom that is managed and structured well, that has clear expectations, and that provides a sense of safety and support to every student creates an ideal environment for the use of motivation strategies and positive affective learning. However, a disorganized or punitive classroom is unlikely to promote motivation and affect. A positive and motivating classroom can contribute greatly to success for all students, including those with special needs (Murray, 2002; Murray & Greenberg, 2001).

Elicit Positive Peer Support

Teachers can encourage peers to help create supportive, accepting classroom environments. In one such activity, a student from the class sits in the "hot seat," which may be a special chair designed for that activity. All other classmates take turns contributing only positive comments about the student in the hot seat. One fourth-grade teacher, Mrs. Ramirez, uses this activity regularly (about twice a week). Initially, the teacher sat in the hot seat and modeled types of comments that students should make. She said, for example, "Everyone has to think of nice things to say about me. Would this be a nice comment? 'Ms. Ramirez has a nice smile.' Would this be a nice statement? 'Ms. Ramirez is wearing an ugly dress.'" After the students appeared to understand the rules and types of appropriate comments for the activity, Ms. Ramirez selected a student to sit in the hot seat. She monitored the comments students made, and determined how long to continue the activity.

If you use this activity as a teacher, randomly select students or devise a systematic schedule to ensure that all students have opportunities to sit in the hot seat. Throughout the remainder of the day, week, month, and school year, use the positive comments that are said about students to reinforce the concept of an open, accepting environment for all students.

Use Statements That Promote Acceptance

Another important way for teachers to create supportive classrooms is through the use of statements that demonstrate that all students are accepted. For example, before a classroom activity in which students are about to break into small groups, you might say, "Remember that everybody is good at something, and that we should all get to practice something we are good at during our group work.

An effective teacher provides a classroom environment that is supportive and safe for all students.

Who is good at coloring? Who is good at reading? Who is good at writing? Now remember, when you go to your groups, practice something you can do well!"

Any statements you make carry a lot of weight with your students, so emphasize statements that indicate how each student in your class is an important contributing member. This attitude helps your students not only to accept the divergent responses of others, but also encourages other students to make positive contributions to the class. For example, one teacher said the following to her class on the value of diversity to her class:

> We're all different in some ways. Even [name] wears glasses. And the twins, they are different, aren't they, even from one another? You have to expect that kind of difference; it's sometimes fun and happy to work with someone who is a little different. You don't always have to work with the same kinds of people, do you? It makes life more exciting to work with different kinds of people. (Scruggs & Mastropieri, 1994b, p. 796)

Consider surveying students' feelings about being in the classroom. A classroom survey can provide important feedback on how the classroom environment is perceived. An example of a classroom survey is available in the *In the Classroom . . . for sharing with students* feature in the Companion Website. You can use this feedback to improve the atmosphere in your classroom.

Ensure Materials Are of an Appropriate Difficulty Level

The second precondition for improving motivation and affect is to ensure that curriculum content is taught at the appropriate difficulty level. If students are provided with content that consistently is too easy, they quickly lose interest in the tasks and take little satisfaction in successful task completion. However, if the content is too difficult, students are less likely to persist in their efforts to master it and may begin to display negative attitudes toward the content. The content must be at the difficulty level at which students are likely to succeed if they apply a reasonable amount of effort. Questioning students and frequently monitoring their progress should help you determine the appropriateness of the difficulty level. In inclusive settings, devote extra attention to students with special needs to ensure that activities are the correct level for the class as a whole, but are not too difficult for them. Conversely, gifted students may need more challenging tasks than those provided to other students.

A variety of techniques has been implemented to modify the difficulty level of materials for students with disabilities in general education classes. One technique involves the use of materials that contain several readability levels. The Mesa, Arizona, elementary science curriculum materials, for example, have different readability level passages within each grade level's materials. The lower readability level materials have the same appearance as the rest of the materials, but are designed for students who have serious reading difficulties. Even though teachers select lower readability level passages for specific students to read out loud, they are assured that all students are reading from the same material. For example, in a unit on Mexico, one paragraph reads as follows:

> The low, flat Yucatan Peninsula goes out into the Gulf of Mexico. Hurricanes start in the Gulf and many of them sweep over this peninsula. This peninsula gets a lot of rain each year and it is always hot. Most of the peninsula is covered by a jungle, called a rainforest. The soil is very thin over the rock and is not very good for farming. Tropical fruits, such as bananas and some citrus, are grown there. There is fishing in the Gulf of Mexico.

In the same reading passage is a much shorter paragraph, using more familiar words:

> Perhaps your family's car is using gasoline that has come from Mexico. Oil sales are an important source of income for Mexico.

Although some words are similar in length to the previous passage, their familiarity (family, gasoline, Mexico; rather than Yucatan, hurricane, peninsula) should make them easier to read. Further, in the Mesa materials, a picture of a car is placed alongside the paragraph, which provides a semantic cue to the passage and makes the paragraph look longer.

Other modifications to help balance the difficulty levels of content include the availability of audiotapes or computerized sound versions of texts, guided notes, and the use of peer assistants.

For more specific information about adapting print materials to meet individual needs, see chapters 11 and 13. Chapters 14 and 15 provide additional information on accommodating diverse learning needs in specific academic areas.

Ensure That Tasks Are Meaningful

A third precondition for improving motivation and affect is that the learning tasks are seen by students as meaningful and worth learning. Students must consider the information or skills they are learning to be personally interesting, relevant, or helpful in their lives, or likely to prove useful in their future. This is accomplished, first, by you as a teacher assessing the content for importance. Second, take time to point out to students the importance and worth of the information being learned. Third, behave as though the content being learned is important by modeling enthusiasm and interest in the content. Students will more likely see the value of the lesson if the instructional materials and student-assigned tasks reflect the worth of the content. An endless series of worksheets, or lists of uninteresting material to be memorized, are likely to have a negative effect on motivation. The choice of instructional materials and the meaningful presentation of them, making them explicitly or implicitly relevant to your students' lives, promote motivation. For example, students who participate in classroom activities on democracy are more likely to appreciate relevant concepts than students who simply read about democracy.

Keep in mind that many students with special needs may not immediately understand the worth of an academic activity, so monitoring students' understanding of the relevance of schoolwork is important. When students begin to think that learning is meaningful to them, motivation will increase. Ways to make learning more worthwhile and meaningful to students include the following:

- Select topics that reflect students' interests.
- Relate the content being studied to local issues or problems that are familiar and important to students.
- Allow students to select their assignment from a list of options; for example, students may choose to write a paper or draw and label illustrations to complete a task demonstrating their knowledge of the migration patterns of birds.
- Begin and conclude classes with statements such as: "This is an important topic because . . . " and "Why was this an important topic for us to learn about?"

Create Task-Oriented, Not Ego-Oriented Classrooms

The overall orientation of the classroom environment is also an important condition for enhancing motivation and affect. Nicholls (1989) described important differences between what he characterized as **ego-oriented** and **task-oriented classrooms.** In ego-oriented classrooms, students function in an overall competitive environment with each other. Success for individual students is defined

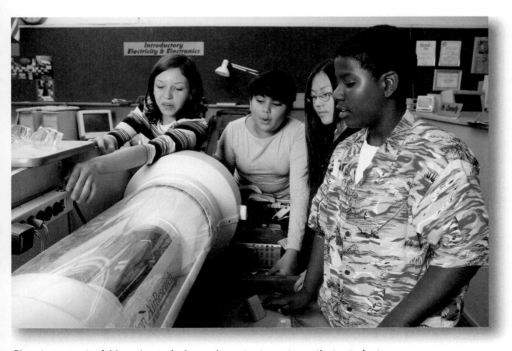

Planning meaningful learning tasks is one important way to motivate students.

Table 9.1
Ego-Oriented Versus Task-Oriented Classrooms

Classroom Orientation	Representative Teacher Comments
Ego-Oriented	"Marcy, you're the smartest student in the class!"
	"Class, look at how smart Fredrica is, to have figured this out!"
	"Richard, why can't you be more like Bernie?"
Task-Oriented	"Marcy, this is your best work yet!"
	"Fredrica must have worked very hard to have figured this out!"
	"Richard, I know you can do much better on this assignment if you use the strategies we practiced and put more effort into it."

with respect to the performance of other students and is associated with high academic capacity (e.g., that successful students are "smart," outperforming other students). Failure, or doing worse than other students, is associated with low capacity (e.g., that unsuccessful students are "dumb," and perform more poorly than other students). In such classrooms, students are graded on the "curve" (i.e., relative to each other), percentile ranks on standardized achievement tests are emphasized, and all grades may be publicly posted. Ego-oriented classrooms may be viewed positively by the top few students who think they are likely to achieve at the highest level. However, such classrooms may actually decrease motivation for the majority of students who think they are not "smart" and therefore have little chance of achieving at the highest level. If students think they have low (or not sufficiently high) capacity for learning, they will be less likely to try their best in the future.

Task-oriented classrooms provide a very different atmosphere. Students are led to believe that success is not defined as their "capacity" but rather is determined by a combination of factors that they can control. These factors include interest and a sincere effort to learn. Students are evaluated with respect to their previous performance and not against the performance of others. They are acknowledged for persistence of effort and a positive attitude toward learning. With student permission, products are publicly posted when they demonstrate an impressive display of effort. Even top students can benefit from the task-oriented classroom, because they learn that only substantial efforts are rewarded. Sample teacher comments characteristic of ego-oriented and task-oriented classrooms are given in Table 9.1.

Students with special needs can benefit greatly from the atmosphere provided by task-oriented classrooms. Most students with disabilities are very much aware that they perform academically far below most students without disabilities. Thus, in ego-oriented, competitive classrooms, many students with disabilities soon realize they cannot effectively compete with other students and stop trying. However, in task-oriented classrooms, even though students may perform at different levels of competence, all students have an equal chance at making an effort to learn. When best efforts are rewarded, rather than supposedly "fixed" abilities such as intelligence, leadership, or creativity, all students can benefit.

Techniques for Improving Motivation and Affect

Once the important preconditions have been met to create a positive classroom atmosphere, you can turn to several categories of techniques to enhance motivation and affect both in individual students and in your class as a whole:

- Improving **self-esteem** and **self-efficacy**
- Increasing a personal investment in learning
- Making learning fun and enjoyable
- Using praise and rewards

Raising Students' Self-Esteem

Self-esteem is a general term for the regard in which individuals hold themselves. Generally, students who feel good about who they are and what they can do are more successful than students who do not feel good about themselves. Self-esteem has been found to differ among boys and girls, Caucasian and minority students, and students with and without disabilities (e.g., Harter, Whitesell, & Junkin, 1998; Scruggs & Mastropieri, 1983). However, self-esteem has also been seen to be quite variable within all these groups. That is, some students with disabilities exhibit very high self-esteem and some highly competent students exhibit low self-esteem.

Students with disabilities may be particularly vulnerable to beliefs that they do not compare favorably with their classmates. In fact, some students with disabilities have reported higher self-esteem when in classes with other students with disabilities than when in inclusive classes (Battle & Blowers, 1982). This fact by itself does not mean that students should not be in regular classrooms—it may be, for example, that students with disabilities lack socialization skills that could be enhanced in an inclusive setting. It does suggest, however, that students with disabilities should be carefully monitored for such affective characteristics as self-esteem. It also suggests that the key to enhancing the self-esteem of students with disabilities in inclusive settings is to promote the student's sense of worth and efficacy. This can be accomplished by providing students with tasks at which they can succeed, and providing positive feedback and rewards for their success. Be sure that students with special needs know that they have an important role to play in the classroom by providing roles in which they can assume responsibility and ownership, such as care of classroom pets, distributing materials, or collecting papers. Such assignments, as well as public statements of support, can convince students with special needs that their presence is valued. Classroom peers can also assist in helping other students feel better about themselves (see chapter 8).

Provide Opportunities to Increase Self-Efficacy

Students are motivated to persist on tasks at which they believe they will succeed. They are more apt to think they will succeed on future tasks if they have succeeded on previous tasks. In this situation, students believe they have the knowledge and the skills to ensure their attainment of the goal. This confidence in one's own abilities has been referred to as *self-efficacy* (Zimmerman, Bandura, & Martinez-Pons, 1986). You can improve self-efficacy by structuring academic tasks that can be accomplished with a reasonable effort and high rate of success. Classroom activities benefit all students—especially students with disabilities—when they provide additional practice, continually assess understanding, make connections to prior learning, organize learning in advance of instruction, recognize good social models, and offer support for learning.

Provide Additional Practice to Reinforce Prior Knowledge

Learning is more likely to occur when previous learning was successful. The time you spend making sure that previous material has been completely learned is valuable. Initiate regular reviews and **overlearning** (additional practice after goals have been achieved) to reinforce any knowledge previously presented. This is especially important for students with special needs. Additional practice could be provided by the special education teacher or by a parent, volunteer, or aide.

Use Ongoing Assessment Strategies

First, be sure your instructional presentations are clear and effective. As you go through the lesson, monitor students' comprehension by asking frequent questions. Carefully supervise guided practice activities, so students do not undertake activities they do not fully understand. Finally, provide independent practice only after you are certain students can be successful independently. If independent practice is not successful, go back immediately to guided practice or review the lesson concepts in a new way. If this structure is carefully followed and necessary adjustments are made in the curriculum materials, students will learn to expect success in the classroom.

Motivating students to persist on tasks in which they can succeed can increase their self-efficacy.

Point Out Appropriate Social Models

Social models also can increase self-efficacy. Students may believe they can be successful—even if they have no experience with a task—if they observe students like themselves succeeding at the task. When using this strategy, try pointing out appropriate social models and offering assurances that students can do what the social models have done. Say, for example, "Hey, James couldn't do this either last week. James worked hard and learned to do this, so I'm sure you can learn to do it, too!"

Provide Positive Support

Direct encouragement from teachers can help students' self-efficacy. Saying, "I really believe you will be able to do this if you give it a try!" provides positive support for effort, rather than criticism for failure, and can demonstrate your confidence in individual students. It will also provide evidence that success is possible.

Demonstration of genuine teacher interest at appropriate times can also improve student motivation and attitude toward schoolwork, as shown in the continuation of Danny's scenario.

CLASSROOM SCENARIO

Danny

Mr. Hamilton arranged for a meeting with Danny. During this meeting, Mr. Hamilton expressed his concern about Danny's progress in math, and his hope that he could improve. Danny seemed pleased with the extra attention from Mr. Hamilton, but indicated his overall pessimistic attitude: "I appreciate you trying to help me, Mr. Hamilton, but it's no use. I'll never learn this math." Mr. Hamilton replied, "Danny, I think you're just not giving yourself a chance."

Mr. Hamilton arranged to edit Danny's homework assignments so that he could spend more time on a smaller number of problems within Danny's current skill level. He would discuss the problems briefly with Danny in the few minutes before the class started; he would also arrange for a peer to help Danny during class exercises. Mr. Hamilton also began to privately praise Danny when he made an effort and completed his assignments: "You see? I told you, you would begin to catch on if you made this kind of effort!" When Danny's assignments were not completed, Mr. Hamilton acted disappointed, but hopeful that the next assignment would be done correctly: "Danny, we both know from before that you can do better than this—I hope to see something really impressive on your next assignment!"

By the end of the second quarter, Danny's grades had improved from an F to a D+. On the last test of the semester, Danny earned a C+. Mr. Hamilton wrote a note to Danny's parents stating that he was the most improved student in his class. With additional prompting, Danny continued to perform successfully throughout the second semester. Danny concluded, "At first I thought I could never do it. But math's really not that bad, if you put your mind to it!"

Avoid Counterproductive Statements

One well-meaning strategy that is often counterproductive is characterizing a particular task as "easy," saying, for example:

- "You can do this. It's easy!"
- "Anybody should be able to do this!"

Such statements are often intended to convince students that a task is doable and within their reach, but the effects of such statements can be very different. Because teachers rarely need to encourage a student to accomplish "easy" tasks, the use of this strategy has often been used with tasks that the student considers difficult. However, the strategy can undermine motivation: Little satisfaction is gained from accomplishing an "easy" task; shame and embarrassment result from failing at a task that is considered "easy."

Also, remember that if students express satisfaction in their performance by stating that a particular task was easy, use prudence in agreeing completely with the student. As discussed later in this chapter, students need to learn to attribute their success on academic tasks to effort, rather than the ease of the task. You could say something like, "It may have been easy for you because you worked hard to learn it, but I don't think it was really that easy!"

Teach Students to Set Goals

Once students believe they are capable of accomplishing a task, involving them in goal setting can increase their motivation to complete that task. Research has found that students often increase their achievement when they help set their own goals (Locke & Latham, 1990). Students involved in setting their own goals and in monitoring their own progress will be more likely to see learning goals as meaningful and personal—more so than if they are simply imposed by the teacher. Motivation can be maximized when goals meet the standard of "optimal challenge"—that is, the goal is difficult for the student to attain, but can be achieved with vigorous or persistent effort (Ford, 1995).

Establish Goals and Monitor Progress

Realistic, but high, goals should be set and progress toward goal attainment monitored on graphs or charts (e.g., Fuchs, Fuchs, & Deno, 1985). Daily goals can be established and progress can be charted. For example, students can select goals for solving a certain number of math problems, reading a specific number of pages in the social studies text daily, for getting 90% correct on weekly spelling tests, or for getting 80% or higher on biology unit tests. Goals also can be set for a specific amount of time-on-task. For instance, 30 minutes can be established as a daily goal for working on math problem solving, reading assignments, or practicing spelling words. The charts and graphs can track progress toward attaining those goals (see Fuchs, Fuchs, Reeder, Gilman, Fernstrom, Bahr, & Moore, 1989, for additional examples). A sample goal sheet is depicted in Figure 9.1.

Teachers can combine aspects of goal setting with self-efficacy and have students predict the amount of time they will work successfully. Self-monitoring charts can be developed to monitor

GOAL SHEET

Student name _____

Dates _____

Class _____

# of daily math problems	Monday	Tuesday	Wednesday	Thursday	Friday
Daily Goal:	20	20	20	25	25
Accuracy Goal:	18	19	20	20	22
Number Completed	16	19			
Number Correct	16	19			
Teacher Comment	Good work; try working faster	Super job!			

Figure 9.1
Sample Goal-Setting Sheet

progress toward goal attainment. For an example of a self-monitoring chart, see the *In the Classroom . . . for sharing with students* feature in the Companion Website. For example, have students complete the statement goal, such as "I will work hard by trying my best and not getting out of my seat for 5-minute segments. When the bell rings, if I have been working hard, I can place a checkmark in the YES column. If I have not been working hard when the bell rings, I will place a checkmark in the NO column."

Promote Effort with Contracts

Individual contracts can promote effort on the part of individual students by helping them set and meet personal goals. A contract is a written agreement between you and a student that specifies (a) goals that the student is expected to meet, (b) when the student is expected to meet them, and (c) the rewards the student will receive when the goals are met. The contract is discussed extensively in a private meeting with the student and is signed by you and the student. It can also involve the parents or guardians and be signed by them. For example, the contract may specify that the student will receive a trip to an amusement park, sponsored by the parents, if all assignments are completed by the end of the marking period. The contract could also specify that the student will receive a special privilege for coming to class on time for three consecutive weeks. Contracts can be particularly helpful in increasing the motivation of individual students.

See chapter 8 for sample contracts.

Encourage Parent or Family Involvement

Parents are usually the primary advocates for their children and can be an invaluable source for promoting self-efficacy and supporting the continued efforts of students. This is particularly true for students with special needs. Communicate frequently with parents to share your expectations for the student and ask for parents' help in meeting these goals. Parents often will agree to participate in a reinforcement system, through which the student is rewarded at home for positive effort made during school. Parents can also be a positive source of support in reaffirming the value of school learning.

Train Students to Use Positive Attributions

Attribution training is another important strategy teachers can use to increase motivation and positive affect, and raise self-esteem. With this technique, students are taught to attribute success to their own efforts and academic strategies and to attribute failure to their lack of effort or failure to use appropriate strategies. Students who learn to attribute success and failure to things they con-

Table 9.2
Student Attributions for Success or Failure

Positive Attributions	Negative Attributions
Success	*Success*
"I succeeded on the spelling test because I used the spelling strategy I learned."	"I succeeded on the spelling test because I got lucky."
"I got an 'A' on my science project because I started early and used my time effectively."	"I got an 'A' on my science project because my teacher likes me."
Failure	*Failure*
"I failed the math test because I put off studying until the last minute, and then I fell asleep. Next time I'll start earlier."	"I failed the math test because I'm stupid at math."
"I didn't do as well as I could have on the test because I didn't study for an essay test. Next time I'll practice writing essay answers when I study."	"I didn't do well on the test because the teacher doesn't grade fairly."

trol are more likely to try hard and succeed in the future than those who do not (Fulk & Mastropieri, 1990).

Attribution is related to **locus of control;** that is, a student with an **internal** locus of control implies that the student feels personally in control of his or her own successes and failures, while an **external** locus of control suggests external forces are responsible (Lawrence & Winschel, 1975).

Attributions that correctly attribute success or failure to student behavior—things a student does or could do—are called positive attributions. Negative attributions, however, attribute success or failure to such things as inherent ability or teacher prejudices. Examples of positive and negative attributions are given in Table 9.2.

All students should be made aware that blaming their failures on others or on their own personal traits is not acceptable. When students fail, they should be reminded of choices they made themselves that contributed to that failure. When students are successful, they should be reminded of the positive things they did that brought on that success (Fulk & Montgomery–Grimes, 1994).

As a teacher, you should be alert to the development of negative attributions, particularly for students with special needs. To counter these kinds of attributions, first make certain that all assignments are within the ability of the student. Then simply do not accept negative statements such as "I'm stupid" or "I'm handicapped." These declarations should not be allowed to justify failure. You can reply to such attributions with statements such as "No, the reason you failed is that you gave up too soon," or "No, the reason you failed is that you didn't use the strategies you practiced for that test."

Students with disabilities, perhaps more than other students, need to be reminded of the important role of personal commitment and effort. Reinforcing positive efforts students make can be voiced by saying something like "That was difficult, but you worked hard and finished it anyway!"

The combination of attribution and strategy training (i.e., training in a specific academic strategy, such as a summarization strategy for reading comprehension) is a powerful tool for success. For example, Borkowski, Weyhing, and Carr (1988) taught students with learning disabilities to use specific summarization strategies and specific attribution strategies. Some of the important attribution statements were "I need to try and use the [e.g., summarization strategy]," while actually using the strategy. In addition, a cartoon character described by the caption, "I tried hard, used the strategy, and did well," was used to emphasize the role of effort (p. 49).

Although students with disabilities often do not exhibit positive attributions or internal locus of control, it would be a mistake to assume that all students with disabilities have problems in these areas (Mamlin, Harris, & Case, 2001). Before initiating attribution training, be certain that students have a specific need for such training. Nevertheless, it may always be useful in classroom instruction to remind students of the relationship between effort or strategy use and academic success.

Arrange Counseling Interventions When Needed

Counseling interventions have been designed to increase self-esteem of individuals and may involve a number of techniques. Relaxation techniques (Amerikaner & Summerlin, 1982), rational emotive educational procedures (Lo, 1985), and group counseling involving variations of psychotherapy (Mishna, 1996) have all been helpful in increasing self-esteem in students with learning disabilities (Mastropieri, Scruggs, & Butcher, 1997). Counseling research studies have been conducted for students with disabilities and have yielded positive findings on measures of increased relaxation, decreased school truancy, increased self-esteem and self-concept, and general well-being. Positive benefits were reported after relatively short interventions consisting of weekly sessions for 6 to 10 weeks. Such information indicates that after a relatively small number of group-counseling sessions, some students with difficulties may experience positive benefits in social-emotional functioning.

Counselors use a variety of techniques that enhance confidence and self-esteem. During relaxation counseling, students are taught to identify the signs of tension by listening to relaxation tapes while viewing photographs of relaxing scenes, and by developing positive self-talk and positive self-therapy during counseling sessions (Omizo & Omizo, 1987). During rational emotive therapy sessions, students are taught to identify, challenge, and replace inappropriate thoughts with appropriate beliefs (see also Knaus & McKeever, 1977). Psychotherapy through group counseling employs group dynamics to help students express their feelings about themselves and others, and to promote mutual support (Mishna, 1996). Improvements in students' self-esteem often occur after students have participated in counseling. One such example is in the following Research Highlight.

Exercise Care When Handling Serious Affective Disorders

Some disorders of affect are very serious and may not be substantially improved with the application of the strategies described in this chapter. If you encounter students with serious affective problems, obtain outside professional help and contact the parents. Special education teachers, counselors, or school psychologists may help or refer you to other professionals if you have a student who appears to exhibit signs of severe depression, anxiety, or suicidal behavior.

Issues related to suicide prevention are discussed in chapter 5.

Increase Students' Personal Investment in the Classroom

Students who believe they have some ownership in what is happening in your classroom are also more likely to make an effort to help the classroom be successful. If they have had some input in classroom decision making, students are also more likely to identify positively with classroom activities. Conversely, students who think they have no influence in how classroom business is conducted are more likely to lose motivation and interest. In some extreme cases, such perceived disenfranchisement can lead to more serious antisocial acts.

Share Decision Making for Classroom Procedures

Students may feel more involved with the classroom if they play some role in the decisions that affect how the classroom functions. For example, we have observed teachers who allow students to decide what the seating arrangement of the class would be even when this arrangement was different from traditional seating arrangements (Scruggs & Mastropieri, 1994d). If modifications were necessary, as in improving access for students with physical disabilities, students were understanding when the situation was explained to them.

Students can also be involved in decisions such as the sequence in which daily lessons are presented. For example, elementary students may have opinions about what activities they would like to do first thing in the morning, or immediately after recess periods. You also can solicit students' input in developing academic grading standards and rules for classroom behavior. Of course, as the teacher, you would have the final word on standards, but students will appreciate the opportunity to provide input. Provided that at least some of the student input is acceptable to you, standards can be said to be collective decisions, rather than edicts imposed by you on your students. You will probably be surprised by the standards students recommend. Students can be quite strict

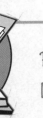

Raising Self-Esteem by Challenging Irrational Beliefs

Lo (1985) provided a detailed discussion of an A-B-C-D-E process for challenging irrational beliefs and replacing them with rational beliefs that he implemented with students with learning disabilities. Sixty 12-year-old students with learning disabilities were randomly assigned to either the rational emotive education (REE) therapy group or a control group that viewed films. Counselor-led group sessions took place twice a week for 30–45 minutes each for a period of 11 weeks. The REE program included training students to identify irrational beliefs and replace them with more appropriate beliefs. The specific training procedures involved the following:

"'A' [stands for] the *activating* event or 'What happened.'

'B' is the *belief* system or 'What I believed.'

'C' is the emotional or behavioral *consequence,* or 'What I felt and what I did.'" (Lo, p. 80)

'D' is introduced later as standing for *disputing* the irrational belief by problem solving and asking self-questions.

'E' stands for the *effects* of thinking on reduction of negative thoughts and beliefs and is introduced after mastery of the B-C-D components of therapy.

Students who participated in Lo's training increased significantly on self-esteem and self-concept measures.

> For instance, when you become sad and drink a large amount of alcohol, you would become intoxicated, may be argumentative and quarrel with your boyfriend/girlfriend and you may drive your car risking an accident. You also do harm to your health. All of these behaviors are potentially harmful, dangerous, and in the long run, self-defeating. The next time you feel sad and have irrational thoughts about yourself and others but then start asking yourself questions about your irrational beliefs, you are disputing. If you ask yourself, "How will getting drunk make me feel and get better?" you are challenging your irrational beliefs. If you decide not to drink when you feel bad and replace the irrational thinking with rational, you are changing your thoughts and behavior. (p. 90)

School counselors may be helpful in arranging sessions with individuals or groups of students, including students with disabilities, who might benefit from increased self-esteem. Counseling or certainly professional advice and contact with the parents will be needed to get help for students with serious affective disorders.

For more information, see Mastropieri, Scruggs, and Butcher (1997).

Questions for Reflection

1. What other services do you think counselors might provide to students?
2. How can you determine whether a problem is one for which a counselor's advice should be sought?
3. What strategies similar to the one described above would be appropriate for you to employ as a teacher?

Companion Website

To answer these questions online, go to the Research Highlights feature in chapter 9 of the Companion Website.

Getting students involved in decision making can allow students to see their role in carrying out fair and acceptable classroom procedures.

in their opinions about academic and behavioral standards, and you might feel compelled to argue for more lenient criteria! Where differences of opinion between you and your students exist, identify the differences and the reasons you have to enact different standards or choose not to enact certain standards students put forth. Such actions demonstrate to students that their ideas are important, even if they are not always implemented.

Another potential problem with student-established standards is that they may indirectly promote the "tyranny of the majority." That is, standards that are not obtainable by all students are nonetheless imposed on the class as a whole, because they are within the reach of most students. It is important that students know, when providing input on classroom standards, that standards must be reasonable for all students.

Solicit Student Feedback

Finally, you may wish to provide students an opportunity to give input anonymously. One way of doing this is by providing a survey of student opinions about things they think are fair or unfair in your class. An example of such a survey can be found in the *In the Classroom . . . for sharing with students* feature in the Companion Website. Students might feel more comfortable providing information about their opinions and attitudes on a questionnaire. Sometimes, teachers are surprised to discover that policies they thought were popular are in fact unpopular with students. Other teachers have a suggestion box in which students can place anonymous comments and feedback. These techniques may also uncover information that students would not volunteer for fear of being accused of "tattling." If you are able to modify the way you manage the classroom in response to student opinion, students are likely to appreciate the consideration they receive. In addition, they are more likely to feel that they are an important part of the classroom.

When soliciting student feedback, be certain to consider minority opinion. Some rules may affect different students in different ways. For example, a cooperative learning feature may not be positively received by some students with special needs, because they may think they are not being treated fairly or respectfully by other students when you are unavailable to supervise the group. You could use this feedback to find better ways to teach students how to behave in groups and better ways to monitor student interactions. Use all survey feedback to enhance learning for all students and to make students feel important as classroom decision makers.

Make Learning More Fun and Enjoyable

Techniques that increase self-esteem and self-efficacy encourage positive attributions, and sharing classroom decision making should indicate to students that effective learning requires effort and persistence. However, the classroom should not focus solely on work; teachers should do what they can to make learning experiences as fun and enjoyable as possible. Motivation and positive affect will improve when students have more than a day of drudgery to look forward to each morning. The classroom can be made much more enjoyable if students catch the enthusiasm of teachers and the interest level of tasks is heightened.

Make Tasks More Interesting

A number of strategies are at your disposal to make learning more interesting and fun (Mastropieri & Scruggs, 2002).

Prepare More Concrete, Meaningful Lessons. Students are more motivated to learn information that is concrete and personally meaningful. Include as many examples as possible of how the concepts being learned are relevant to the students' personal lives. For example, when presenting information on the branches of government, you can discuss executive, legislative, and judicial actions that are undertaken in school, on the athletic field, and in the home, and the reasons these actions are necessary. For secondary students, if the level of concepts go beyond what they encounter in daily life, provide examples of how the skills being taught can be used in their jobs, careers, or independent living.

Concreteness and meaningfulness can also be enhanced by classroom exhibits and demonstrations. Hands-on science curriculum materials provide students concrete experiences to help them better form science conceptions. Hands-on activities illustrate the nature of science more easily than written words only. Such materials are particularly helpful for students with special needs, because they lessen the need to study abstractions from the text. If science curriculum materials are not available, consider bringing interesting classroom demonstrations to class. For example, one teacher greatly increased classroom excitement by bringing her pet iguana to class (Mastropieri, Scruggs, & Bohs, 1994).

Illustrations can bring concreteness and greater meaning for some students who are visually oriented. The construction of murals, posters, bulletin boards, or three-dimensional projects all can promote learning. Creating portfolios of students' work, rather than consistently relying on paper-and-pencil tests, also can make the content more meaningful for learners.

More information on hands-on science methods is provided in chapter 15.

Portfolios are described in more detail in chapter 12.

Create Cognitive Conflict. Interest in learning can be aroused by discussion or demonstration of situations that promote **cognitive conflict,** situations that are not easily predictable or explainable at first. The presentation of discrepant events can create cognitive conflict in students. A discrepant event is an event (often in science) whereby things behave differently than expected. Some examples of discrepant events include "dancing" raisins, whereby raisins appear to be suspended mystically in a soft drink. Further observation and deduction reveals that the raisins are suspended by the carbon dioxide rising in the soft drink. Another example is an electric repulsion coil, which dramatically repels, rather than attracts, objects. Discrepant events enhance curiosity and interest and increase motivation to learn (Wright & Govindarajan, 1995).

Additional activities presented in other subject areas can have the same effect. Discussion of equivocal moral or political issues—such as whether carrying concealed weapons should be prohibited, or the idea that overpopulation of Canada geese in a community park might lead to their extermination—may raise students' level of interest as it raises their concern about issues. The more personally relevant the issues are, the more involved students are apt to become.

Before beginning any cognitive conflict activities, students need to be reassured that any guesses they make to explain discrepant events, or opinions they may have on moral or social issues, will be accepted with tolerance and respect. If you establish a safe risk-taking environment within the class, more students will be encouraged to participate.

For more information on "off-beat" learning features or other fun and interesting information for students, go to the Web Links module in chapter 9 of the Companion Website.

Songs by Bob Blue (tapes and music books from Bob Blue, 77 Belchertown Rd., Amherst, MA 01002) and the Banana Slug String Band (from Carolina Biological Supply) are excellent classroom additions.

Ask for assistance and take appropriate safety measures for novel science demonstrations.

Use Novel Ways to Engage Students. Students also tend to respond to novelty in the classroom. Sometimes students begin to lose motivation simply because instruction has become stale and predictable. In this case, interest may be restored by incorporating new and novel ways of doing things. Changing the order of classroom routines, reallocating classroom responsibilities, and rearranging classroom seating are all ways to increase novelty.

You also can provide variety in the way instruction is delivered. Here are some suggestions:

- Use different media, such as tape recordings, songs, videos, and newspaper articles.
- Invite guest speakers known to be knowledgeable or "expert" on a specific topic.
- Direct students to prepare their own presentations on topics, either individually or in small groups.
- Use computer applications to allow students to review or practice, using tutorial or simulation activities that reinforce content.
- Pose questions, such as "Does gum weigh more or less after chewing? How could we find out?"
- Modify the way you ask for assignments to be done, creatively alter homework routines, and alternate the use of group and individual assignments when appropriate.

Although novelty alone may not consistently improve motivation and affect, it can be useful when combined with other techniques described in this chapter.

One concern should be mentioned with the use of novelty in classrooms that include students from some disability areas. Some students with autism, or some forms of mental retardation or other disabilities, may find it very difficult to deviate from established classroom routines. Sometimes, simply being included in a "regular" classroom may constitute as much novelty as some students can easily accommodate. If students who prefer "sameness" in their environments are placed in your inclusive class, school psychologists and special educators can provide specific information for dealing with novelty situations.

Develop Competitive and Gamelike Activities. Competition that pits students against one another, and for which students may not perceive an equal chance of winning, may be detrimental to a motivating classroom; such competition is more characteristic of ego-oriented classrooms. How-

Challenging students cognitively or engaging them in novel activities can create a motivating classroom environment.

Technology Highlight

Advancing Technologies Are Motivating!

Advancing technologies are especially motivating tools for students with disabilities. Classrooms containing computers with or without Internet access can be used as motivation and rewards (although Internet access is ideal, many of the technological advances can be used without accessing the Internet). Students will have more ownership of their learning during instruction when they are encouraged to use computers to find answers to questions that arise in the classroom.

Encourage students to find answers on electronic encyclopedias that are multimedia and available on CD-ROM. Entries may not only have photographs and illustrations, but also interactive media with video and audio components that add to the excitement of finding answers to classroom discussions. Many encyclopedia programs are relatively inexpensive, including *World Book, Britannica,* and *Encarta,* and many encyclopedia programs can now be accessed online.

Online access broadens the amount of information available and includes the use of the various Internet search engines such as Yahoo and Google and others directed more specifically to your students' age group. Surfing using these search engines opens the world to students. Technology enables students to access more information in less time than ever before. Some Websites encourage students to submit homework questions!

Arrange pen pals via e-mail for your students to share their school experiences with other students from across the country and the world. Websites exist that help arrange pen pals and contain bulletin boards for student resources as well as resources for teachers. Refer to the Companion Website for chapter 9 for links to these sites.

Encourage students to search and find answers to their questions! Allowing these activities demonstrates that students have active roles in their own learning and will help to increase their ownership in their learning and serve to help motivate them to continue to succeed in school.

---

ever, when students believe they have a fair chance of winning, and when the same small group of students does not always win, competition and gamelike activities can provide a high degree of motivation and interest in the class.

The following is an example of small-group competition in a practice activity: First, divide students randomly into several small groups. Then direct one individual student from each group to take turns answering questions about the topic being studied. Allow the selected students to accept suggestions from other students in their group but let them know that they each must decide on the answer individually. When an answer is correct, the group receives a point. At the end of the activity, the group with the most points is the "winner." In some cases, the winning group may be given a reward or privileges of some kind, but students may find it sufficiently rewarding simply to be on the winning team. Each time the game is played, assign students to different groups.

Students with special needs can be easily included in activities such as the one described, because they are able to contribute fully to the activity. This cooperative aspect makes such activities more fair and increases chances of success for students with disabilities.

Make Use of Cooperative Learning. Cooperative learning strategies can also be used to enhance student interest, affect, and motivation (see chapter 8). Students often enjoy working together on projects, and these opportunities may make learning more enjoyable for them. Group projects, group participation in science activities, group studying, guided-practice activities, and group competition in gamelike activities described in the previous section are helpful in enhancing student interest. However, monitor group activity carefully to ensure that all students are being treated fairly and that all students are participating equally and learning adequately from the activities (McMaster & Fuchs, 2002).

Don't Overdo Motivational Attempts. As in many other areas of promoting student motivation and positive affect, teachers can appear to be trying too hard to make activities interesting and enjoyable. If students see such efforts as contrived and artificial, your efforts may fail. Ongoing feedback from students, surveys of student interest in different activities, and direct questioning and prompting when needed can provide important information on whether teacher attempts to make the class more interesting are actually succeeding.

Be Enthusiastic! As described in chapter 6, enthusiasm is one of the teacher presentation variables that helps to develop student interest and make learning more fun. Enthusiastic teachers enhance motivation by modeling interest in the subject being learned and the amount of enjoyment that can be attained when learning occurs. Enthusiastic teachers also are more interesting presenters, so students are more likely to pay attention to what is being presented.

Teaching with enthusiasm involves the use of several techniques, described by researchers (Bettencourt, Gillett, Gall, & Hull, 1983; Brigham, Scruggs, & Mastropieri, 1992) and listed in the following *In the Classroom* feature. These techniques demonstrate that enthusiasm is something that teachers *do,* not something that teachers *are.* It is clear that teachers can change the amount of enthusiasm they display and improve student motivation and affect when they do so. A teacher in one study deliberately manipulated his level of enthusiasm and positively influenced student achievement (Brigham et al., 1992).

Enthusiasm is an attribute that you can vary within your own teaching. And although it may make you a little self-conscious at first, you can practice being enthusiastic simply by raising and lowering the intonation of your voice and by using your hands and arms when you talk to students to explain or elaborate on a point. Statements made enthusiastically can gain students' attention. For example, one fourth-grade teacher used the following statement to gain attention and to control transitions within her classroom during an ecosystems science activity: "Class, when I say 'Ecosystems are a blast!' everyone go to your science groups!"

Enthusiastic teaching can also help encourage open acceptance of student contributions. This is of critical importance for students with special needs, because such students often believe their contributions may not be welcome. In the case of disabilities such as communication disorders or hearing impairments, it may take longer to communicate ideas to the class. In other cases, the ideas, answers, or suggestions may seem less sophisticated than those of some other students. In these instances, it is particularly important for teachers to demonstrate enthusiastically that ideas and input from all students are welcome. One fourth-grade teacher noted:

I have a difficult time saying any of my "kids" have behavior problems. I view each child in my class as a challenge and rarely do they have problems I can't "get at" through my teaching approach. My main focus at *all* times is to be upbeat, fast-paced, and in a great mood!! This alleviates many "problems." (Mastropieri et al., 1994, p. 142)

Can enthusiasm be overdone? Possibly. But one essential element of enthusiasm is that it be (or appear to be) sincere. If students regard teachers' enthusiasm as genuine, they will probably welcome and appreciate very high levels of enthusiasm. However, if the enthusiasm seems forced or insincere, students will be less likely to appreciate it. Overall, however, our experiences (and research evidence) have convinced us that teacher enthusiasm promotes motivation and positive affect; and that enthusiasm is often underused but rarely overused.

Your enthusiasm in teaching a lesson will be contagious.

In the Classroom ...a feature for teachers

Teacher Enthusiasm Variables

- *Rapid speaking rate, varied inflection, uplifting vocal delivery.* This prevents teacher dialogue from sounding redundant, monotonous, or boring.
- *Animated, wide-open eyes.* Animated eyes model a state of alertness and interest in the classroom activity.
- *Physical gestures that emphasize what is being said.* Teacher can help emphasize the interest level and importance of what is being covered with demonstrative physical gestures.
- *Dramatic and varied body movements.* Dramatic body movements attract student visual attention, which in turn can lead to more positive attending.
- *Facial expressions that are animated and emotive.* Facial expressiveness conveys positive attitude toward, and interest in, the subject.
- *A varied choice of words.* Variation in language usage prevents dialogue from sounding boring and predictable.
- *Active and open acceptance of ideas or suggestions made by students.* Open acceptance of student ideas, input, and thinking conveys that teachers are secure with their own knowledge, and anxious to hear other ideas.
- *General demonstration of a high energy level.* This variable suggests that enthusiasm is not simply the sum of several individual components. Enthusiasm is conveyed through the entirety of teachers' overall manner.

Note: From "Effects of Teacher Enthusiasm Training on Student On-Task Behavior and Achievement," by E. M. Bettencourt, M. H. Gillett, M. D. Gall, & R. E. Hull, 1983, in *American Educational Research Journal, 20,* pp. 435–450. Copyright 1983 by American Educational Research Journal. Adapted with permission.

Praise Students and Reward Their Efforts

Praise and concrete rewards are often the first things people think of when considering ways to increase motivation and affect. Naturally, most people (including teachers!) feel more valued and more motivated when they are praised and positively rewarded for their achievements.

Praise Student Effort

The effective use of praise is of paramount importance to enhancing motivation and affect, and, appropriately employed, closely conforms to the idea of a task-oriented classroom. Praise is highly motivating to students because it provides encouraging feedback for student efforts, and demonstrates that their work is being appreciated.

Jere Brophy (1981) has investigated the appropriate uses of teacher praise. A summary of his conclusions is presented in Figure 9.2. Overall, praise that is vague or that describes general traits of students has not been successful in promoting motivation and positive affect. This includes praise that conveys to students that they have some "trait" that the teacher considers valuable (e.g., "You are very bright.") Praise such as this—comments that give students the message that they are praiseworthy without making any particular effort—usually does not motivate students.

Conversely, effective praise is based on truly meritorious work, positive student efforts to meet specific criteria, and tangible improvement from previous work. This kind of praise clearly

- Praise should be used to reinforce **specific student behaviors.** It should specify exactly what the student did to warrant praise. It should not be random or vague (e.g., "You are a good student.").
- Praise should sound **sincere and genuine.** It should not sound unconvincing or mechanical.
- Praise should **specify the criteria** being met (e.g., "You had no spelling errors") and **relate the achievement to previous work** (e.g., "This is one of your best papers yet!").
- Praise should be delivered when the student has made a **noteworthy effort** (that is, noteworthy for that student; e.g., "You really worked hard to complete this assignment so well!"). It should not be given for indifferent or routine efforts.
- Praise should indicate the **relation between student effort and achievement** (e.g., "You worked really hard to earn this grade!"). It should not suggest that the student was "lucky" or the task was easy.
- Praise should **promote personal satisfaction** on the part of the student (e.g., "You should be very proud of the job you did on this!"). It should imply that the student enjoyed accomplishing the task, or that the student wanted to accomplish the outcome that was praised.
- Praise should suggest that **similar efforts will be met with success in the future** (e.g., "If you keep working this well, you will get an A on all your assignments!").

Figure 9.2

Effective Uses of Praise

Note: From "Teacher Praise: A Functional Analysis," by J. Brophy, 1981, in *Review of Educational Research, 51,* pp. 5–32. Copyright 1981 by American Educational Research Journal. Adapted with permission.

links accomplishment with effort, and suggests strongly that similar efforts in the future also will be praiseworthy. In this way, students receive the message that hard work, effective study strategies, and persistence of effort—variables under student control—are truly valuable.

Reasons for giving praise can be combined with praise statements. For example, "That's great! I like how neat your work is!" combines a praise statement with the action that deserves the praise. This combination of statements informs students why they are being praised. These statements work well with students with and without disabilities. It might be particularly important to point out to students with disabilities the reason that praise is being given. Students usually enjoy being praised and will often work harder to obtain more praise from teachers. Although praise works well with all grade levels of students, consider the appropriateness of particular statements selected for targeted grade levels. Table 9.3 presents sample praise statements with corresponding reasons for both elementary- and secondary-level students.

It has been noted by many teachers that all students at all age and grade levels desire praise from their teachers and that many statements can be used successfully with all age levels. Remember to vary the praise statements. For example, when one phrase or word is used repeatedly (e.g., "Good"), it may lose its effect. The following *In the Classroom* feature provides some adjectives that can be used for praising students and corresponding behaviors that can be combined with them to create many alternatives to "Good!"

Students usually enjoy public praise. Comments that praise students' persistence of effort can be publicly announced or posted on a banner or sign in the classroom. Some schools have weekly assemblies during which "Student of the Day," "Student of the Week," or "Class of the Week" awards are distributed in front of the entire student body. This action rewards individuals publicly and promotes the idea that the school is appreciative of motivation and effort.

Good work, effort, and behavior can also be praised by sending positive notes home regularly. This communication with parents helps maintain a good relationship between school and home. Notes can be designed for elementary, middle, or secondary school levels and for any subject area.

Students with special needs particularly need praise, because they may face greater limitations in the quantity and quality of work they produce. To reassure them that their efforts to attain specific goals are highly valued, praise their accomplishments. If the overall atmosphere of the class is

Table 9.3
Praise Statements and Reasons for Praise

Elementary-Level Examples	Secondary-Level Examples
• That's wonderful! You showed me how to write your name!	• That's a great observation! You understand how a pendulum works!
• Super! I can tell you are trying your very best!	• Terrific paper! Your writing has really improved.
• I like the way you are working!	• Keep up the hard work! Your compositions are really improving!
• Exactly right! You completed all the problems!	• Good work! I know you worked very hard to complete the project!
• Good job! You seem to understand how to answer those questions.	• Great sentences! Will you share your paper with the class?
• Great work! I like the way you tried to read all the words!	• Nice going! Can you repeat the phrase in Spanish again?
• Super duper! You showed me that you can proof your paper!	• That's definitely A+ work! I liked the way you drew an illustration to explain your answer!
• Great! You did a nice job in math class today!	• Much better! Your history test grade is improved!
• I'm proud of you! You completed all of the writing assignment!	

Note: In reality, many statements could be used with either elementary or secondary students.

In the Classroom ...a feature for teachers

Alternative Statements for Praise

Use any of the below praise words and match them with a variety of behavior words:

<u>Adjectives:</u>

Amazing, Astonishing, Fantastic, Super, Beautiful, Lovely, Fine, Gorgeous, Splendid, Wonderful, Terrific, Stunning, Striking, Magnificent, Extraordinary, Great, Much Better, Super Duper, I like the way you are _____, Fabulous, Incredible, Remarkable, Marvelous, Neat, Keep it up, Very impressive

<u>Behaviors:</u>

Work, Job, Performance, Thinking, Reflection, Judgment, Paper, Assignment, Reading, Homework, Exercise, Lesson, Practice activity, Worksheet, Sitting, Problem solving, Paying attention, Complying with the class rules, Completing math problems, Writing, Composing papers, Proofing your work

<u>Combinations of Adjectives and Behaviors:</u>

Amazing work, Amazing job, Amazing performance, Astonishing thinking, Astonishing reflection, Fantastic judgment, Fantastic paper, Super assignment, Super reading, Beautiful homework, Lovely exercise, Fine lesson, Terrific practice activity, Splendid worksheet, Wonderful sitting, Wonderful problem solving, Terrific paying attention, Terrific complying with the class rules, Stunning completing math problems, Magnificent writing, Great composing papers, Much better proofing your work!

task-oriented, and all students are praised for their efforts, students with special needs will be less likely to consider themselves outsiders who need to be treated differently from everyone else.

Use Rewards to Reinforce Student Success

In previous decades, when behavioral models of teaching were more widespread, motivation was sometimes referred to as little more than the strength of the reinforcer being used (e.g., Martin & Pear, 1978). We chose to include a discussion of rewards later, rather than earlier, in this chapter because we wanted to emphasize the idea that enhancing motivation and positive affect can involve much more than simply providing rewards for desired behavior. Nevertheless, we do not wish to understate the powerful effects of rewards in promoting learning and positive social behavior.

Avoid the Overjustification Effect. Some researchers have suggested that rewards—as extrinsic, or external motivation—can undermine intrinsic motivation, the internal desire to achieve. Lepper and Hodell (1989) cited research suggesting that (a) when interest in the activity is already high, and (b) when the reward is so tangible that it can be considered a "bribe," rewarded students can feel less satisfied with their performance and less likely to undertake the same activity than students who do not receive rewards. This outcome is referred to as the **overjustification effect.** Therefore, if you have applied strategies described previously in this chapter, and find that students are already very interested in the activity, it may be prudent to avoid direct, tangible rewards. In these cases, however, praise for positive effort and task completion may still be appropriate.

Distinguish Between Rewards and "Bribes." Rewards may often be condemned as "bribes," and irresponsible use of rewards may indeed have such an effect. However, since you as a teacher expect to be rewarded by receiving your paycheck, it does not seem surprising that often students also work toward rewards! In our pragmatic view, rewards should be considered as a potent tool when used under the right conditions. Another consideration in the rewards-versus-bribes argument was recently voiced by Susan Lucas, a special education professional in Indiana, who said, "Bribes, to me, are payments made for illegal actions, and I never do this with students. I reward my students for honest, hard work."

Set Up Conditions for Rewards. Many school tasks, in spite of a teacher's best efforts, may not be considered intrinsically interesting to students. When the initial task interest is low, rewards can provide students with reasons to persist and persevere on tasks that will be helpful to them at a later date. For example, learning to play the scales on the piano, learning specific skills during batting practice, learning spelling words, or memorizing and practicing foreign language vocabulary and grammar are tasks that are important prerequisites of accomplishment, but nonetheless are unlikely to be considered enjoyable or motivating in and of themselves. You can do much to increase persistence of effort on such tasks by the appropriate use of rewards. Because the learning of many basic skills areas, such as spelling, fall into this category, and students with disabilities typically exhibit difficulties mastering basic skills, rewards may play an important role in inclusive settings. It should also be noted that reinforcement has been demonstrated to be effective with students with special needs, and that the strength of the learning outcome has been seen to be associated with strength of the reward (Scruggs & Mastropieri, 1994a).

Set Up Performance Criteria. Rewards should be given in response to previously stated performance criteria. Rewards should reflect perseverance and hard work, and generally all students should have an equal opportunity to receive rewards. The relation between the reward and the behaviors that led to the reward should be made clear. Also note that if the effort exhibited is praiseworthy, future efforts could result in further rewards.

Develop Appropriate Performance Criteria for Students with Special Needs. Several techniques allow students to perceive an equal opportunity for rewards when they are aware that they differ with respect to academic abilities. One way is to set performance standards that reflect improvement over previous efforts, rather than standards that compare students with other students. Rewards can be provided for aspects of tasks at which all students have an opportunity to succeed. For example, in small reading groups, individual students could be directed at random intervals to read (e.g., using a spinner). Students could be awarded one point for knowing where to begin read-

Read Katz (1997) *On Playing a Poor Hand Well* for more ideas on helping students overcome challenges.

ing when they are called on. Such a system rewards paying close attention to the reading task, something at which all students have a reasonable chance of succeeding.

Use Tangible and Intangible Rewards. Tangible rewards are desired objects given to students upon completion of specific academic or behavioral standards. These rewards can include prizes (such as stickers, pencils, erasers, decals, or bookmarks) or consumables (such as crackers, cookies, or juice). In a "token system," tokens such as chips, stars, or checkmarks in a book are awarded for specific positive academic or social behaviors, such as accuracy, homework completion, or positive classroom behavior. Specific numbers of these tokens are later exchanged for desirable rewards or classroom privileges. Tangible rewards can be effective in increasing persistence of effort, particularly for students with special needs (Lovitt, 1995). Nevertheless, these are the types of rewards that are most often condemned as "bribes," so be judicious with them.

Intangible rewards can also promote motivation and positive affect. Besides teacher praise, which has been described, you can reward students by publicly posting their name as, for example, "Student of the Week." You may also try providing desired free-time activities, such as a favorite game—or privileges, such as the right to be out of seat without permission. Intangible rewards are less costly and appear less like bribes. The following *In the Classroom* feature provides possible tangible and intangible rewards for a token system.

You can also provide group rewards to promote positive social and academic performance of the entire class. If, for example, the class is completing an activity in small groups (and the groups are equally constituted), a group reward such as a desired activity can be awarded to the first group that finishes or to the group that provides the best product. Alternatively, the reward could be presented to the class as a whole, if the class meets a specific standard over a period of time. For example, provide bonus recess time to the class if all assignments are turned in on time for that week. Such rewards allow students to help or encourage other students to meet class criteria. However, they may also encourage group sanction of individual students whose behavior may have cost rewards for the entire class, so monitor the consequences carefully.

In the Classroom ...a feature for teachers

A Token System

Tokens are received by:

1. Being in seat and prepared for class when the bell rings (1 token).
2. Turning in class assignments on time (1 token).
3. Improving over previous quiz (1 token).
4. Working hard on class activities, decided by teacher (1 token).

Tokens can be redeemed for:

1. Pencils (5 tokens).
2. Stickers (10 tokens).
3. Free time (20 tokens).
4. Release from one homework assignment (20 tokens).
5. Eat lunch with teacher (25 tokens).
6. Caretaker of class pets for a week (30 tokens).

More information about rewards for behavior management is provided in chapter 8.

In some circumstances, individual students can be used to distribute group rewards. This can lead to greater acceptance of individual students by the entire class and greater confidence and self-esteem on the part of the student. In one example, distribution of group rewards was used to help one student overcome "elective mutism," an emotional disorder in which an individual does not speak. After the student began distributing weekly rewards to the class for good class behavior, the student began speaking more in class.

At several times throughout the school year, survey students to determine their preferences for rewards. Their responses can be used in developing any possible reward systems. A sample inventory of student preferences is provided in the *In the Classroom . . . for sharing with students* feature in the Companion Website.

Surveys can be designed for students at any age level. We recommend that you continue to monitor the use of specific rewards after they are selected and implemented. If the same reward is used repeatedly, it may lose its reinforcing values and it may mean it is time to survey students again for additional ideas.

Justify Fairness When Necessary. The final consideration for rewards is that some students with disabilities may have a greater need for reinforcement than other students do, to ensure continued persistence of effort. Although it may be necessary for some students to receive rewards to exhibit the same efforts that other students give without rewards, it is sometimes difficult to explain this to the class. If one student is rewarded for working hard on a particular task, should not all other students who work hard be similarly rewarded? Not always. One possibility in such cases (as appropriate) is to provide rewards discreetly, such as after class or during visits with the special education teacher. Another possibility is simply to explain the situation to the class in a businesslike fashion and make little ceremony about it. Another possibility is to reward all students in some fashion for continued efforts on tasks, but to award more substantial rewards to students who seem to require this, and to offer more intangible rewards to others.

One final possibility is to explain to the class how "fairness" in life may mean different things for different individuals. The excellent illustration by Richard LaVoie (1996) in the videotape *How Difficult Can This Be: FAT (Frustration, Anxiety, Tension) City* could be shown to the class as an example. In the videotape, LaVoie explains how, if a member of the class had a heart attack and needed CPR, it would be absurd to say, "I cannot give [student's name] CPR, because if I did I would have to give CPR to everybody!" The belief that *fairness means sameness for everyone* is disputed. *Fairness* is then described as meaning that each individual receives what he or she needs, and not that each individual receives the same.

Summary

- Motivation and affect are extremely important variables that can make the difference between success and failure in the classroom. Many students with special needs may benefit particularly from strategies to enhance motivation and affect.
- Before implementing specific strategies to enhance motivation and affect, ensure that the necessary preconditions have been met. These preconditions include creating a supportive, well-organized classroom environment; assigning tasks that are meaningful, concrete, relevant, and of the appropriate difficulty level; and creating task-oriented, rather than ego-oriented, classrooms, in which students are rewarded for effort and improvement, rather than static variables such as "ability."
- Motivation and affect can be improved by engaging in practices to improve students' self-esteem, such as providing positive statements, assigning classroom responsibilities, and use of classroom peers.

- Self-efficacy is an important determiner of positive motivation and affect. Students succeed, and believe they will be successful, when provided with additional practice, advance organizers, appropriate social models, and positive support.
- Students' motivation and affect improves when they participate in setting goals for themselves, and assist in monitoring their progress toward meeting these goals. Contracts and parent involvement can also contribute to personal goal setting.
- Students feel more in control when they learn to attribute their classroom successes or failures to their own behaviors, such as appropriate effort, attitude, or use of academic or behavioral strategies. Students can appropriately take credit when they succeed, and identify strategies for improvement when they fail, when they make appropriate attributions.
- Students feel more ownership in the classroom when they participate in decision making involving classroom rules and procedures. Use a variety of techniques to receive input from students, and implement positive and helpful suggestions whenever possible.
- Students are more motivated to learn when learning is fun and interesting. Use a variety of approaches, media, gamelike activities, and peer interactions to prevent classroom learning from becoming monotonous and routine. Express personal enthusiasm in the subjects being covered, and teach with enthusiasm!
- Students are motivated to learn when their accomplishments are acknowledged and rewarded. Use positive feedback and praise frequently to demonstrate your positive regard for students' accomplishments. Use rewards, in the form of prizes, privileges, or tokens, when needed to acknowledge achievement and maintain persistence of effort.

Council for Exceptional Children

Enhancing Motivation and Affect

Information in this chapter links most directly to:

Standard 4—Instructional Strategies, particularly:

Skills:
- Use strategies to facilitate integration into various settings.
- Select, adapt, and use instructional strategies and materials according to characteristics of the individual with exceptional learning needs.

Standard 7—Instructional Planning

- Integrate affective, social, and life skills with academic curricula.

Inclusion Checklist
Enhancing Motivation and Affect

If you are having problems with student motivation or affect, have you considered the following?

- ❑ Met preconditions for improving motivation and affect by:
  - ❑ Creating a supportive, organized classroom environment
  - ❑ Eliciting positive peer support
  - ❑ Using statements that promote acceptance
  - ❑ Ensuring that materials are of an appropriate difficulty level
  - ❑ Ensuring the tasks are meaningful
  - ❑ Creating task-oriented classrooms
- ❑ Employed techniques for improving motivation and affect by:
  - ❑ Raising students' self-esteem
  - ❑ Providing opportunities to increase self-efficacy, by:
    - ❑ Providing additional practice to reinforce prior knowledge
    - ❑ Using ongoing assessment strategies
    - ❑ Pointing out appropriate social models
    - ❑ Providing positive support
    - ❑ Avoiding counterproductive statements
  - ❑ Teaching students to set goals, by:
    - ❑ Establishing goals and monitoring progress
    - ❑ Promoting effort with contracts
    - ❑ Encouraging parental involvement

- ❑ Training students to use positive attributions
- ❑ Arranging counseling interventions when needed
- ❑ Exercising care when handling serious affective disorders
- ❑ Increasing students' personal investment in the classroom by:
  - ❑ Sharing decision making for classroom operations
  - ❑ Soliciting student feedback
- ❑ Making learning more fun and enjoyable by:
  - ❑ Preparing more concrete, meaningful lessons
  - ❑ Creating cognitive conflict
  - ❑ Using novel ways to engage students
  - ❑ Developing gamelike activities
  - ❑ Using cooperative learning
  - ❑ Avoiding overdoing motivational attempts
  - ❑ Teaching enthusiastically
- ❑ Praising students and rewarding their efforts, by:
  - ❑ Effectively praising student effort
  - ❑ Using rewards appropriately to reinforce students' success

Chapter 10

Justin Carrico, 10
Bradenton, Florida
"Fall Leaves"

Improving Attention and Memory

Objectives

After studying this chapter, you should be able to:

- Describe preconditions for improving attention in the classroom.
- Describe and analyze extreme cases of attention deficits and the effects of stimulant medications.
- Understand the importance of memory and attention for students with special needs to school success.
- Describe preconditions and the various strategies to improve memory for students with special needs.
- Design and implement strategies to enhance meaning and concreteness of instruction.
- Understand various ways to promote active learning and increase practice through clustering, organization, and elaboration.
- Describe, create, and apply mnemonic strategies (keyword, pegword, and letter strategies) to improve and enhance memory.

"My experience," wrote William James in his 1890 masterpiece, *Principles of Psychology,* "is what I agree to attend to. Only those items I *notice* shape my mind—without selective interest, experience is utter chaos" (p. 260).

Attention and memory are two fundamental psychological processes necessary for learning to occur. It is easy to understand that instruction, however well presented, is of little value if it is not remembered. Conversely, memory is only possible for those things to which we have paid attention in the first place!

In this chapter, we describe the problems students may have with attention, and strategies you can use in your teaching to improve the length of students' attention. Next we describe the problems students may have in remembering information they encounter in the classroom, and describe a number of strategies you can use to improve your students' memory.

Attention

Attention and Students with Special Needs

All students exhibit lapses in attention at times, either because of a lack of interest in a subject, boredom, fatigue, or from being distracted by temporary anxieties or concerns. However, many students with special needs exhibit difficulties with attention and memory. For example, poor attention and concentration are commonly reported characteristics of students with learning disabilities (Lerner, 1993). Students with mental retardation may exhibit difficulties attending to the appropriate stimulus in a lesson, such as focusing on the shape of the hands of a clock rather than the position of the hands in a lesson on telling time (Beirne-Smith, Ittenbach, & Patton, 2001; Scruggs & Mastropieri, 1995).

Some students with physical or sensory impairments also have difficulty sustaining attention when attending to particular tasks that interact with disability areas. For example, some students with cerebral palsy have difficulty keeping their heads aligned and eyes focused on a class demonstration; some students with hearing impairments tire from lengthy intervals of speechreading (Heward, 2000).

Serious problems with attention can severely impede learning. A variety of teaching strategies can be useful in improving student attention.

> Some students with attention deficit disorder and attention deficit disorder with hyperactivity may receive services under IDEA or Section 504 (see chapter 5).

CLASSROOM SCENARIO

Ana

Ana is a fifth-grader with average academic abilities and a positive disposition. However, she has difficulty sustaining her attention to school tasks for more than about 3 minutes at a time. When prompted, she returns to task, but within a few minutes, she is again off-task, looking out the window, playing with her pencils, or doodling on her paper. This happens during teacher presentations, on seatwork activities, and sometimes during group activities. As a consequence, her grades have been falling, especially in math.

Strategies for Improving Attention

Preconditions

It is inappropriate for teachers to target individual students for special interventions to improve attention without first doing everything possible to make their classrooms interesting and engaging for all students. For example, if you lecture day after day using the same presentation style, it would not be surprising if the attention of many of your students began to wander.

If getting and holding students' attention is a problem, first consider whether you are using the teacher planning and presentation variables consistently (see chapter 6). If each lesson does not contain elements such as structure, clarity, redundancy, and enthusiasm, it is unlikely to sustain student attention. Determine, for example, whether you have done as much as you can to teach enthusiastically:

- Have you used dramatic changes in volume and tone of voice when emphasizing important points?
- Have you offered extremely positive responses to student contributions?
- Have you demonstrated a strong willingness to laugh with the class, and to model excitement about the subject being taught?

How much enthusiasm to demonstrate for best effect differs from class to class, and particularly for different grade levels.

A huge part of teaching effectively and thus maintaining student attention (and memory) is using interesting and motivating examples to enhance lessons. Such examples allow teachers to personalize instruction and make the subject appear more meaningful and useful to students.

Teaching effectively requires maintaining students' attention.

Finally, consider whether you are using attention-getting demonstrations. Demonstrations can include the use of "real" objects in teaching mathematical operations; showing artifacts in lessons on the Civil War; demonstrating, rather than describing, the effects of certain chemical interactions; or dressing in historical clothing and acting out life from different geographic regions and time periods. Pictures and illustrations can also be helpful when actual demonstrations are not possible.

Use of the teacher presentation variables, interesting examples, and attention-getting demonstrations are all strategies that provide a more effective means for getting and sustaining attention. You should be employing them regularly before making any decisions about attention deficits of individual students. However, if some students continue to have difficulty sustaining attention, try the following strategies.

Direct Appeal

Direct appeal is a simple strategy that has been recommended for behavior and attention problems (Redl, 1952; see also chapter 7). To use direct appeal, simply find a quiet time and place to speak to students individually. Explain the problem as explicitly as possible, including the effect of the problem on you and other students as well as the target students. Then make a direct request to the students to improve their behavior. This strategy will be effective when students recognize they are not paying attention. An example of direct appeal is given in Figure 10.1.

Proximity

Proximity is another simple strategy that is sometimes effective in promoting attention (Zirpoli & Melloy, 1997). Simply move toward or stand near a student who is beginning to lose attention. This can prompt the student to refocus attention. Once this strategy has been established, it may be possible in time to fade it to a direct glance or a gesture that the student can easily interpret as a prompt to refocus attention. It also may be helpful to move the student or rearrange the classroom to accommodate teacher proximity.

> *Teacher:* Christine, may I speak with you privately for a minute?
>
> *Christine:* OK.
>
> *Teacher:* I think you're having a problem in my class. Do you know what I think it is?
>
> *Christine:* No.
>
> *Teacher:* Sometimes in class, I think you are having problems paying attention.
>
> *Christine:* Oh.
>
> *Teacher:* I think that because sometimes I see you just looking out the window, or doodling with your pencil, or wearing a blank expression on your face, as if you're daydreaming. Do you think that happens sometimes?
>
> *Christine:* Yeah, I guess so. I guess I'm just not that interested in history.
>
> *Teacher:* Well, I'm afraid that when that happens, it makes class harder for me, because I think I'm not getting through to you. Also, I think other students notice you and it makes them more likely to not pay attention.
>
> *Christine:* Oh.
>
> *Teacher:* But here's what I'd like to suggest. You daydream in class because you aren't interested in history. But if you think about what we're discussing a little more, and you raise your hand in class more often, I guarantee that you will begin to find class more interesting. You will also find that the time passes much more quickly. And most important—and this is what I want—you will find that you will get a much better grade in my class. So what do you say? Will you give it a try?
>
> *Christine:* OK, I'll try.

Figure 10.1
Example of Direct Appeal

Break up Activities

Some students may be able to sit still and concentrate on a task for a certain number of minutes. Attention spans vary with the age and maturity of students. In general, however, rather than giving a student the full length of time to complete a relatively lengthy assignment, divide the task into 10 subtasks of, say, 3 minutes each. At the end of each subtask, the student's progress could be checked, recorded, and praised by you or an assigned classroom peer. Dividing tasks into smaller segments is a great strategy for accommodating students with limited abilities to stay focused.

Allow Sufficient Movement

In some cases, especially in the elementary grades, students begin to lose concentration if they have been made to sit still for a long time. Recording when student attention begins to fade is a way to determine when periods of student inactivity are too long. If students regularly begin to lose attention after extended periods of sitting, consider rearranging the classroom schedule (e.g., recess periods) to allow for more movement (Kerr & Nelson, 2001). Adjust the amount of time spent on each discipline and consider alternating between quiet sit-down activities and more actively involved learning activities. If your schedule cannot be easily changed, try giving students a minute to stand, stretch, reach up to the ceiling, take a deep breath and let it out slowly, and march in place. Brief movement intervals and including student movement in lessons can also be helpful in promoting student attention.

Provide Student Activities

Students are much more likely to pay attention when they are asked to complete activities than when they are asked to listen to someone talk. Providing relevant activities can be an excellent way of promoting attention. For example, instead of asking students to listen to a verbal presentation on how a telegraph works, students could work in small groups to construct their own telegraphs, and then send and decode messages to one another. Such activities help to focus student attention and make learning concepts more meaningful.

Use Classroom Peers to Promote Attention

Classroom peers also can be effective in working with students who have attention problems (Montague, Fiore, Hocutt, McKinney, & Harris, 1996). Peer interventions can be set up through group activities or working one on one. Peers could be asked to work in pairs with students who have some difficulty sustaining attention. Such collaborative sharing of activities can help students with attention problems by providing ongoing prompts for students to attend only to relevant tasks.

Peers seated near target students can also prompt attention. Peers can be trained to provide subtle cues to students (e.g., lightly touching the student's back) when lapses in attention are observed; they can be asked to report inattending to you only when these more subtle prompts are disregarded. Before you use this kind of strategy, be sure everyone involved is amenable to trying to use peer intervention strategies. Be sensitive to the needs of the students you are trying to help. Choose peer assistants wisely, perhaps using those students who appear to have strong interpersonal skills.

Training procedures for implementing peer assistance, peer tutoring, and cooperative learning are described in chapter 8.

Provide Reinforcement for Attention

You can increase attention in individual students by measuring and reinforcing it (Crossairt, Hall, & Hopkins, 1973; Hallahan & Cottone, 1997; Walker & Buckley, 1968). Set an egg timer, alarm clock, wristwatch alarm, vibrating watch, or tape recorder to sound at random intervals (the length of the interval depends on the frequency prompts the student needs). Whenever the alarm sounds, determine whether the target students were paying attention at that instant. If so, they can be rewarded with verbal praise, points on a check sheet, or tokens that can be accumulated and exchanged at a later date for desired objects, privileges, or activities. For example, a student who earns 90% of possible tokens over a 2-week period might be entitled to take an extra recess with another class, go out for an ice cream, or have a special break with you. If other students appear to resent this arrangement, consider including the rest of the class in some reward scheme for good behavior such as a pizza party or game time. Allow the target student to work for a class reward or privilege, such as bonus recess time, or a favored activity. In this way, the class can share responsibility for the target student's success or failure, as in the continuation of Ana's scenario.

For information on "beep tapes" and vibrating watches, see the Technology Highlight in chapter 7.

CLASSROOM SCENARIO

Ana

Ana's teacher, Mrs. Lawson, asked a responsible student to sit behind Ana and prompt Ana when her attention wandered for more than a few seconds. This seemed to help, but Ana still seemed to need frequent reminders to maintain her concentration. Mrs. Lawson determined from talking to Ana and other students that Ana liked to please her classmates. Mrs. Lawson told Ana that she could help do something nice for the class. The peer that was monitoring Ana's inattention would tally each time Ana was prompted. If the number of prompts declined by half by the end of the week, Mrs. Lawson would allow her to distribute animal crackers to everyone in the class. Almost immediately, Ana began to pay more attention. After 3 weeks, Ana appeared to need only minimal prompting to stay attentive.

Punishment, in the form of mild corrections or reprimands, has also been found effective for students with attention problems (Abramowitz, O'Leary, & Futtersak, 1988; Abramowitz, O'Leary, & Rosen, 1987). Generally, short reprimands have been found to be more effective than long reprimands, and immediate reprimands have been found to be more effective than delayed reprimands (Montague et al., 1996). Saying something like, "When you pay attention in class, the teacher is very happy with you. When you don't pay attention, your grades will suffer," reminds students of

Record any student's success at paying attention over a period of time and reinforce that behavior with positive recognition or rewards.

the rule, their responsibilities, and the consequences, without placing too much emphasis on the reprimand component. Remember that reprimands lose their effectiveness if they are used too often (see chapter 7).

Teach Self-Recording Strategies

Self-recording strategies are useful in teaching students how to monitor and evaluate their own attention (Harris, Graham, Reid, McElroy, & Hamby, 1994; Kendall & Braswell, 1985; Lloyd, Hallahan, Kosiewicz, & Kneedler, 1982; Lloyd & Landrum, 1990; Prater, Joy, Chilman, Temple, & Miller, 1991). Special educators often teach self-monitoring strategies in their classrooms, and therefore many students with special needs may have already learned how to use self-recording strategies. Self-monitoring skills learned in a resource setting have been observed to improve student attention in the regular classroom (Rooney, Hallahan, & Lloyd, 1984). With systematic communication between the regular and special education teachers, problems with attention can be improved.

To start a self-recording system, set up a procedure for delivering randomly spaced beeps, as described in the previous section. (If the sounds are distracting to other students, use a vibrating watch, or prerecord randomly spaced beeps on a tape recorder and have the target student listen with earphones.) The cueing interval can be set between 1 and 5 minutes at first and expanded as attention improves. This procedure could be used with several students at a time. If students have hearing impairments that prevent them from hearing an auditory cue, pair the sound with a light stimulus, or provide the signal to a peer who then provides a visual or tactual cue to the target student.

When the cue sounds, the target students should indicate whether they were paying attention by placing a checkmark on a self-monitoring sheet. The self-monitoring sheet should have two columns. At the head of the first column is "Was I paying attention?" including examples such as "Looking at teacher," and "Reading textbook." At the head of the second column is "Was I **not** paying attention?" including examples such as "Looking out the window," and "Daydreaming." Under each column is a numbered underline (or box) where students can record their level of attending after each cue.

At first, you should also make your own record of student attending, and compare the two records at the end of the period. Students can be reinforced for recording at all appropriate times, and for approximating the results obtained by you. For example, if you record 70% paying atten-

Companion Website

An example of a self-monitoring sheet is provided in the *In the Classroom . . . for sharing with students* feature in the Companion Website.

tion, the student should be rewarded for recording something between 60% and 80%. As the recording becomes reliable, create a graph of student attending, and look for progress over time.

Before beginning a self-recording intervention, meet individually with the students, discuss why paying attention in class is important, and explain how the students will benefit from attending better. The students need to understand that the self-recording is in their best interest and that they will benefit as a result. It might be helpful to involve parents to support this intervention.

As students improve in monitoring their attention, you can set timers so that they sound less frequently. However, serious attending problems are unlikely to disappear in a short time. Consistency on your part is helpful in effecting long-term improvements in attention. Continue to give frequent and regular feedback to students on their ability to attend, and on their consistent self-monitoring of their own attention.

Researchers have considered whether it is better to train students to monitor their own attending or their actual academic performance on tasks where attention is required. The Research Highlight describes a study designed to compare self-monitoring of attention and self-monitoring of performance.

See chapter 5 for information describing some more intensive interventions for students with more serious attending difficulties.

Basic Skills Problems

Many students with special needs do not read or write as well as other students in the class. These students may appear less attentive because paying attention requires reading from a text or writing notes that are beyond their skill level. For these students, find other means for them to acquire relevant information. Strategies for addressing these problems are provided in chapters 11 and 13.

Other adaptations could be similar to what Mrs. Montgomery, a fourth-grade teacher, tried with Jeannie, her student with basic skill and attention difficulties. Because Jeannie struggled to stay on task during math seatwork and worked very slowly, Mrs. Montgomery reduced the number of math problems assigned to Jeannie during seatwork. In addition, Jeannie became overwhelmed when looking at a page covered with math problems, so Mrs. Montgomery constructed a "window" cut out of the middle of a 4-by-6-inch card. When she placed the window over her math worksheet, Jeannie could see only one math problem at a time. The task then didn't seem as overwhelming to Jeannie and she sustained attention long enough to complete her assignment.

In other cases, students may not process oral language as fast as it is spoken. When this happens, try to find ways to reduce the rate of speaking, increase redundancy, provide "advance organizers," or find other means to present information. Mr. Davis, an eighth-grade social studies teacher, displayed charts containing the organizational framework of units during the entire month-long units. Students said the charts helped them refer back to major points during classes and helped promote a better understanding of everything in the unit. Mrs. Fluke, a fourth-grade teacher, placed language cards containing pictures illustrating the concepts of new vocabulary on a bulletin board. She encouraged her students to make versions of the cards for their personal picture dictionaries.

Additional strategies for making language more comprehensible for students from culturally and linguistically diverse backgrounds are described in chapters 5 and 13.

Extreme Cases of Attention Deficits

Some extreme cases of attention problems are challenging to address in a general education classroom without intensive assistance from special educators. These students may appear so distractible that they cannot reasonably be expected to attend appropriately for more than a few minutes at a time. For example, a 14-year-old described his severe attention problem as follows: "I'll tell you just what my head is like. It's like a television set. Only one thing: It's got no channel selector. You see, all the programs keep coming over my screen at the same time" (Lerner, 1993, p. 277).

Intensive Teacher-Led Instruction

For this student and others like him, brief, intensive teacher-led instructional sessions may be the most realistic teaching strategy. These sessions can be delivered either one on one or in small groups with a great deal of teacher–student interaction; novel, interesting, age-appropriate tasks; and frequent reinforcement including preferred activities (Kerr & Nelson, 2001). Because your time is often limited, this kind of intensive instruction may have to be accomplished by the special education teacher or a closely supervised aide.

Stimulant Medication

Another alternative used more frequently in recent years is the administration (under medical supervision) of stimulant drugs to help students focus attention more appropriately. Although

Research Highlight

Self-Monitoring of Attention and Performance Compared

Harris et al. (1994) designed an investigation to determine whether it was more effective for students to monitor their attention or their academic performance. Four students in the fourth and fifth grade with learning disabilities were trained to record their own attention during a 15-minute independent study of their weekly spelling words. At the sound of a taped tone that occurred at random intervals averaging about 45 seconds, they recorded whether they were attending to task. These students were also trained to record their performance—how often the spelling words were practiced correctly—at the end of every session. Attention-monitoring conditions and performance-monitoring conditions were alternated, so that the treatment orders were different for different students.

During the baseline (no treatment) study sessions, the students were attending to task about 30% of the time, and practiced their spelling words correctly about 30% of the time. Students in the self-monitoring of attention (SMA) phase, however, attended to task 70% to 90% of the time. Results were similar during the self-monitoring of performance (SMP) phase. Academic performance also improved substantially, whether students were in the SMA or the SMP phase. During a third phase, students were allowed to choose their self-monitoring system. Most chose self-monitoring of performance, and their attending and performance scores maintained their high levels.

In a second experiment, Harris et al. (1994) again compared SMA and SMP, this time with fifth- and sixth-grade students with learning disabilities on writing tasks. Again, students gained substantially over baseline on on-task behavior and number of words written, whether the SMA or the SMP procedure was employed. Additionally, students greatly improved on holistic ratings of writing quality. Again, most students chose the SMP condition during the choice phase, and continued their previous gains in attention and performance. Harris et al. concluded that both SMA and SMP were effective interventions, and that:

> Regardless of the self-monitoring chosen, the procedures need to be parsimonious, minimally obtrusive or laborious, appropriate to the target behavior, enjoyable for the student, and relevant to the student's needs and goals. (p. 138)

For more information, see Barkley (1998).

Questions for Reflection

1. What type of student do you think would be most likely to benefit from self-monitoring interventions?
2. Which procedure, self-monitoring of attention or self-monitoring of performance, do you prefer? Why?
3. Can you think of some applictions of self-monitoring other than independent study?
4. How could self-monitoring procedures be modified for use in group learning activities?
5. How could you ensure that students maintain the gains they made using self-recording?

Companion Website

To answer these questions online, go to the Research Highlight module in chapter 10 of the Companion Website.

medication has certainly been helpful in many cases (about 75% of children with attention deficit hyperactivity disorder respond favorably), concern has been expressed that it has been overprescribed in recent years. Stimulant medication generally affects behavior and attention more than higher-order skills, learning, or achievement (Montague et al., 1996). Side effects can include insomnia, decreased appetite, irritability, weight loss, abdominal pain, and headaches (Hallahan & Cottone, 1997). If relevant and qualified professionals agree that stimulant medication is indicated for a specific student, your job as a teacher should be to collect formative data that identify how the medication affects the student's behavior both positively and negatively.

In some cases, stimulant medication used in conjunction with cognitive-behavioral training can be effective (Montague et al., 1996). In addition, parent training of cognitive/behavioral interventions and communication strategies has sometimes been effective in managing noncompliant behavior, reducing stress, and improving the quality of family relationships (Hallahan & Cottone, 1997).

Autism

Some students with autism have severe attention problems. Autistic students may attend little or not at all to teachers, even though they can be demonstrated to have adequate hearing (Scruggs, Prieto, & Zucker, 1981). Students with such severe attention deficits may benefit from one-to-one instruction, direct provision of tangible or edible reinforcers for attending and responding appropriately, and ongoing supervision. Parents and special educators may be able to provide more specific information on the needs of individual students. Educational placement in the general education classroom is possible if special educators or highly trained aides are available to provide individual attention.

Chapter 4 provides detailed information on some of the more commonly prescribed medications and their side effects. The Research Highlight summarizes these findings.

See chapter 4 for more information on autism.

CLASSROOM SCENARIO

James

James was classified as having learning disabilities. With extra practice and resource room assistance, he was able to cope with the reading demands of his seventh-grade class; however, he continued to have difficulty remembering information for tests. A major concern of his was a test of states and capitals that was coming up in 4 weeks, and which was considered a test that all seventh graders must pass. He had studied on his own and even with classmates, but he had a difficult time remembering more than a few states and capitals at a time. He asked his resource teacher, Mr. Pearl, for help.

Memory

Memory is a psychological process that is critically important for school learning. Analysis of tests given by junior and senior high school teachers indicate that the great majority of test items require students to remember specific facts relevant to the content area (Putnam, 1992). Even when teachers devote more of their test questions to such higher-order tasks as analysis, synthesis, and evaluation, students must first *remember* relevant information before they can reason effectively with this information. Effective memory is a necessary requirement for school success.

Aspects of Memory

Two types of memory that are considered important for school success are **semantic** and **episodic memory** (Tulving, 1972; 1983; see also Pressley & McCormick, 1995). Semantic memory is memory (usually verbally based) of facts and concepts about the world, known independently of one's personal experiences. Remembering the location of Botswana, the climate of Newfoundland, the isochronism of pendulum movement, an image of the American bison, or the Italian word for *rabbit*

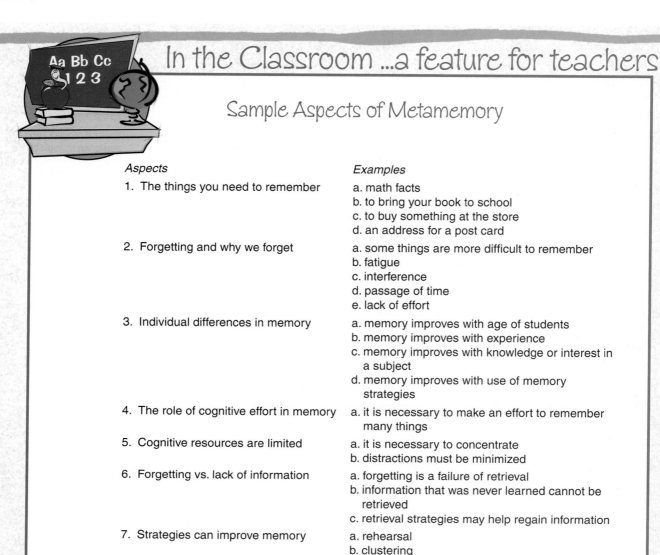

In the Classroom ...a feature for teachers

Sample Aspects of Metamemory

Aspects	Examples
1. The things you need to remember	a. math facts b. to bring your book to school c. to buy something at the store d. an address for a post card
2. Forgetting and why we forget	a. some things are more difficult to remember b. fatigue c. interference d. passage of time e. lack of effort
3. Individual differences in memory	a. memory improves with age of students b. memory improves with experience c. memory improves with knowledge or interest in a subject d. memory improves with use of memory strategies
4. The role of cognitive effort in memory	a. it is necessary to make an effort to remember many things
5. Cognitive resources are limited	a. it is necessary to concentrate b. distractions must be minimized
6. Forgetting vs. lack of information	a. forgetting is a failure of retrieval b. information that was never learned cannot be retrieved c. retrieval strategies may help regain information
7. Strategies can improve memory	a. rehearsal b. clustering c. semantic organization d. keyword, pegword, and letter strategies

are examples of semantic memory. This information is at the heart of much of school learning, and therefore good semantic memory is critical to school success.

Episodic memory is memory for events that students have personally experienced, and include memories of friends and relatives, school events in which students participated, and summer vacations. Examples of episodic memories are trips made to Mexico or Newfoundland, experiments conducted with pendulums, or personal interactions with bison at national parks. These memories may not entail knowledge of the phenomena (e.g., bison) experienced apart from the experience itself.

Memory researchers also frequently distinguish between **long-term memory** and **short-term memory** (Atkinson & Shiffrin, 1971; Shiffrin & Schneider, 1980). *Long-term memory* is thought to be virtually limitless, assuming that the information has been correctly encoded (put in) and stored. *Short-term memory* refers to new information that can be held in the consciousness only briefly (e.g., a telephone number) while it is used, placed in long-term memory (e.g., by rehearsal), or forgotten. When information is being actively processed in short-term memory (for example, in solving a two-part math problem), this capacity is sometimes referred to as **working memory** (Ashbaker & Swanson, 1996).

Memory and Students with Special Needs

Many students with special needs exhibit difficulties with semantic memory (Baker, Ceci, & Herrmann, 1987), short- and long-term memory, and working memory (Kavale & Forness, 1992; Swanson, 1994). Certain strategies, however, have been seen to be effective in enhancing memory for all students.

Preconditions for Improving Memory

Before describing memory strategies that may prove to be extremely effective in helping your students remember important school content, consider the preconditions that must be in place for learning and memory to occur. One critical precondition is ensuring that all students are attending appropriately to instruction. Increase attention by maintaining a well-organized and distraction-free classroom (see chapter 7) and by trying the strategies discussed in the first part of this chapter.

> Adequate time-on-task and content coverage are also important preconditions for memory. See chapter 6.

Next, keep students motivated to learn. Even if they are paying attention, students will learn and recall little if they are not interested in or do not see the value of the content, or do not believe they can succeed. Similarly, students are unlikely to remember information if they do not have a positive affective response to the content presented; that is, if they have indifferent or negative feelings toward the subject, or if their morale is low. Finally, learning will be minimized if lessons appear boring and monotonous. Once the preconditions for good memory have been met, implementation of the following suggestions should improve students' memory.

Strategies for Improving Memory

Develop "Metamemory"

Metamemory is the metacognitive process of knowing about memory. Specifically, metamemory is the process of knowing when, where, and how to remember (Brown, 1978). For example, knowing that you may remember less when you are tired or knowing that rehearsal can improve your recall are components of metamemory. Metamemory develops as students grow older (Flavell & Wellman, 1977); however, some students have more highly developed metamemory than other students. Research has shown that some students with special needs, such as students with learning disabilities or mental retardation, have less metacognitive awareness of memory (Cornoldi & Vianello, 1992). Fortunately, some aspects of metamemory can be trained (Lucangeli, Galderisi, & Cornoldi, 1995). The *In the Classroom* feature lists aspects of metamemory that can be incorporated in classroom lessons (Cornoldi & Caponi, 1993).

> Strategies for improving motivation and affect are discussed in chapter 9.

Cornoldi and Caponi (1993) developed a program for training metamemory that was successfully implemented in Italy with students with and without disabilities. This training program, which involved several lessons in each of 17 areas, improved metacognitive awareness of memory and also improved performance on memory tasks, compared with untrained control groups (Cornoldi & Vianello, 1992; Lucangeli et al., 1995). Figure 10.2 provides a sample lesson from these materials.

Many students, especially in the elementary grades, are unaware of the nature of memory, and how they can learn to remember better. Activities and class discussions on memory and how it functions could help many students learn how to remember more efficiently.

Use External Memory

External memory refers to the use of devices to increase memory. For example, the Pima Indians once used "calendar sticks," sticks carved with notches and other markings to prompt the recall of historical events that were related by the narrator (Russell, 1975). In schools, external memory can be used to remember homework assignments, locker numbers, important school dates, and to remind you to bring relevant materials home (or back to school). External memory examples include writing things down in notebooks, appointment books, or language cards; placing things to be remembered in places where they will be seen (e.g., putting homework by the outside door); and physical prompts (e.g., attaching a note to clothing or backpack). Although external memory is not permissible in all situations (e.g., most written tests), students can be informed about appropriate times to use external memory to improve school functioning.

Enhance Meaningfulness

It is known that we remember meaningful information better than nonmeaningful information (Underwood, 1983). You can make learning more meaningful by providing specific examples that are directly relevant to your students' experiences. For example, in a presentation about how each of

---

Lesson 11.2: Wanted: Secret Agents!

The Italian Counterespionage Agency is seeking persons of **courage** (like a lion), **strength** (like a tiger), and **cunning** (like a fox) to undertake a special mission.
If you think you would make a good secret agent, take the following test of your skills!

The Telephone

Imagine that you must make a telephone call to a new friend, whose phone number consists of seven digits.

How many digits do you think you can remember immediately after you first hear them?

_____ the first 2   _____ the last 2   _____ all   _____ 3 or 4

Now try it. The number is 9216548.
Was your prediction correct?

_____ YES   _____ NO

Have you passed this first test? Don't think that being a secret agent will be easy! You will need to follow a special course.
Would you like to try? Now, quickly dictate a number with nine digits to a friend. How did he do? Did he remember all the numbers?

Figure 10.2

Lessons from Memoria e Metacognizione

Note: From *Memoria e Metacognizione: Attivita Didattiche per Imparare a Ricordare* [*Memory and Metacognition: Teaching Activities for Learning How to Remember* (pp. 137, 141), by C. Cornoldi and B. Caponi, 1993, Trento, Italy: Erickson. Copyright 1993 by Erickson. Reprinted by permission.

the three branches of government—legislative, executive, and judiciary—functions, use examples that are directly relevant to schools and how these examples affect students. That is, legislative bodies establish specific laws for the establishment and operation of schools, the executive branch is responsible for enforcing these laws, and the judicial branch adjudicates and interprets these laws. Students can study and discuss how the actions of each of these branches affect their own lives personally with respect to school policy.

Use Concrete Examples, Pictures, or Imagery

Concrete information is better remembered than abstract information. You can enhance the concreteness of relevant content by bringing in examples of the topics being studied. For example, the study of trilobites (prehistoric marine animals) can be made more concrete by bringing in fossil specimens of trilobites. Such specimens can provide demonstrations of the "three lobes" that give trilobites their name. They can also spur discussion on how trilobites may have moved or behaved, or what they may have eaten. Ask students to design modern-day trilobites using illustrations or three-dimensional models using the historical information. Such enriched thought, activity, and discussion can greatly improve memory of the content.

Video Presentations. When specific examples cannot be brought to class, for example, because of their size, cost, or limited availability, consider enhancing visual images through CD, videotape, or pictures. For example, science CDs can provide excellent recordings of things students might not ordinarily have an opportunity to see, such as tornadoes, vacuum chambers, or space flight. Videotapes or CDs can provide interesting visual coverage of such things as Mayan architecture, insect life, or microorganisms. When selecting video presentations, be certain that they assist directly in enhancing the concreteness of specific information to be remembered. View the presentation selectively, to focus specifically on instructional objectives (example: focusing on Doric, Ionic, and Corinthian columns—an instructional objective—in a videotape on ancient Greek architecture). Finally, do not be afraid to provide redundancy in viewing, to help enhance the specific facts or concepts to be remembered. Students can describe what they believe will appear next in a video presentation, and then confirm after viewing whether they were accurate. For students with visual impairments, descriptive video may be available or can be created (see chapter 4).

Illustrations. Using pictures, illustrations, or graphics enhances the concreteness of information. Pictures are frequently provided in student textbooks, or in overhead transparencies included in instructors' materials. However, sometimes these are included more for decorative or marketing purposes than for meeting specific objectives. Try to locate pictures that seem directly relevant to instructional objectives, for example, illustrations that document clearly the physical characteristics of insects, or the living conditions of American pioneers. The World Wide Web is an excellent place to begin looking for all types of pictures. Ask your students to pay attention to specific aspects of the

Some knowledge that students need requires memorization.

A visual presentation of information can facilitate learning and remembering over a long period of time.

picture that are directly relevant to your instructional objectives (e.g., "Jackie, point out the thorax of the insect in the picture" or "Bill, show me on the picture the things that make you know that it is a picture of a beetle"). Reading through diagrams carefully with students, and questioning them frequently helps ensure that diagrams are understood (e.g., "Darryl, show me where the switch is in this electrical diagram"). After pictures and diagrams have been studied, question your students about the illustrations with their books closed, or the overhead projector turned off, so they continue to practice studying the mental image of the illustration. Ask students to draw and label their own pictures. Peers may assist students with visual impairments with the careful description of pictures, diagrams, or illustrations. Additionally, tactual representations of pictures can be created, as described in chapter 4.

Imagery. If you cannot locate relevant pictures, and if you feel unable to draw pictures yourself, you can encourage students to use their mental imagery to create pictures. For example, to help understand that whales are the largest animals on Earth, encourage students to imagine an enormous whale next to a much smaller elephant. Students should be encouraged to create details of the image, and discuss them with the class for accuracy. For example, you could suggest that students imagine a very large whale, and an elephant standing next to the whale that is only about as large as the whale is from its eye to the tip of its mouth. Students could then be asked other questions ("Which way is the elephant facing?") to make the image more permanent. Later, when students are asked this information ("What is the largest animal?"), they can also be asked to report how they remembered that fact. With practice, students can improve their ability to use imagery.

You can help students with imagery by providing activities that enable them to remember images. For example, one teacher had students cut adding machine tape in the lengths of different animals, then attach them to the walls in the hall where they could compare animal lengths. Sometimes students would use lengths of yarn or string and work in pairs, with each partner holding one end of their "animal." Other teachers have completed similar activities for estimating distances from town to town, state to state, to various countries, and even to the planets and stars. Try to videotape these class activities and show them for review and to reinforce images.

Another way to improve the concreteness of a subject is through field trips to relevant zoos, museums, or nature areas. As with videotape presentations, focus your students' attention on the specific objectives to be met during field trips, and monitor that students are meeting these objectives. When appropriate, call ahead so that necessary preparations for specific students with disabilities can be made.

Minimize Interfering Information

Sometimes students forget information because the emphasis on the targeted content was insufficient to promote good memory. This can happen in many ways. For example, only part of a videotape presentation may be relevant to a particular objective to be remembered; without specific emphasis by the teacher on the most important information, students may not filter and remember the targeted information. Consider a videotape about Greece, which emphasizes the contemporary landscape and culture, but makes only passing reference to ancient Greek architecture, the real objective of the lesson. If you do not specifically highlight the portions of the videotape dealing with architecture, the objective may be lost in the confusion of competing stimuli.

Teachers can inadvertently provide interfering information if they digress from the presentation, provide unnecessary elaboration or examples that are not directly relevant, or frequently interrupt presentations with lectures about social behavior. In general, consider that information is more likely to be remembered when it is presented clearly, directly, and without unnecessary embellishment.

Use Enactments and Manipulation

Information is better remembered when students actually carry out the relevant actions rather than merely reciting them (Cohen, 1989). For example, in experimental studies, students who enact a sequence of steps (e.g., drink from a cup, pick up a pencil, sit in a chair) remember this information better than students who merely practice saying the steps. Enactments may be helpful because they occur at the intersection between semantic memory and episodic memory, allowing actual experience to enhance recall of academic content.

Students can benefit from role play activities as in this mock trial preparation activity.

Enactments may explain much of the positive effects typically found for hands-on science activities, in general education (Bredderman, 1983), in special education (Scruggs, Mastropieri, Bakken, & Brigham, 1993), and in inclusive settings (Mastropieri, Scruggs, Mantzicopoulos, Sturgeon, Goodwin, & Chung, 1998). For example, students who have studied first-hand the effects of weak acid on the mineral calcite are more likely to remember these effects (the calcite begins to deteriorate) than if they simply read about the subject.

Symbolic Enactments. Sometimes teachers are tempted to have students enact symbolic representations of the concepts being studied. These enactments are less likely to enhance memory, unless the students understand exactly what is being enacted. For example, students are enacting symbolic roles when they play the roles of electrons moving in a circuit, or water traveling as capillary action through a plant, or various parts of a hand loom. In such cases, there is a danger that the physical enactment will be remembered, but the concept being represented will not (or was not clearly understood in the first place). There is also a danger that individual students will remember their particular role (e.g., the shuttle in the loom), but will lose sight of the entire process. If symbolic enactments are used, you should be sure that students fully understand the role they are playing and the meaning of that role, and that they understand all relevant aspects of the concept. You could assign students different roles during these activities so that they are responsible at some point for describing what happens as the activity is reenacted. Careful summaries and questioning at the end of the activity may be helpful in determining that relevant information will be remembered.

Promote Active Learning

Information is better remembered if students actively participate in the learning process, particularly by actively reasoning through the content. Craik and Lockhart (1972) referred to "depth of processing" as an important learning variable and demonstrated that information is learned and remembered better if learners actively think about the meaning of what is being studied.

Answering any type of relevant question usually promotes better memory of a topic than passive listening to teacher lectures. Answering factual questions helps focus attention on the significant components of the content (e.g., "Who were the major U.S. novelists of the first half of the nineteenth century? Jeff?"). Answering questions that require reasoning can also help improve memory (e.g., "What do you think Hawthorne is trying to say about medical science in *Rappacini's Daughter*? Brigham?"). However, some students with special needs may require additional coaching to assist them in thinking through a problem systematically. For example, elementary-level students with learning disabilities and mild mental retardation were taught facts about animals, as well as the explanations for those facts (Scruggs, Mastropieri, & Sullivan, 1994; Sullivan, Mastropieri, & Scruggs, 1995). In the experimental ("elaborative interrogation") condition, students were not directly provided with the explanations for the facts, but were coached to reason through the information actively, as shown in the following dialogue:

Teacher:	The camel has a double row of eyelashes for each eye. Why does this make sense?
Student:	I don't know.
Teacher:	Well, let's think. What do you know about camels? For example, where do they live?
Student:	In the desert.
Teacher:	In the desert, good. And what is it like in the desert?
Student:	Hot and dry.
Teacher:	Good, what else can you think of about deserts?
Student:	Um, it's sandy. And windy.
Teacher:	Good, sandy and windy. So why would it make sense that camels would have two rows of eyelashes?
Student:	Oh! To keep the sand from blowing in their eyes.
Teacher:	To keep the sand out of their eyes, good!

Results indicated that students taught with these "elaborative interrogation" strategies remembered and understood more information than students in other conditions who had been directly provided with the same information (e.g., "The camel has a double row of eyelashes for each eye, to keep out the blowing sand. What do camels have? Why do they have them?").

Students will remember information that is logically connected if they are encouraged to reason through it actively. However, remember that many students who have memory problems (e.g., many students with learning disabilities or mild mental retardation) also have problems with tasks that require insight on the part of the learner (Mastropieri, Scruggs, & Butcher, 1997). Thus, although active reasoning is a helpful strategy for promoting comprehension and memory, you may need to meet independently with some individual students to provide appropriate instructional support.

Increase Practice

Information is better remembered if it is practiced or rehearsed. Rehearsal or repetition has frequently been demonstrated to improve recall among students of all ages and ability groups. This is an important component of the "redundancy" variable discussed in chapter 6. To increase the effects of practice, you should first target the information that is most important to be remembered. Then provide as much practice as possible in individual lessons by questioning. Questioning and practice after learning has been achieved is referred to as **overlearning,** and can be an effective strategy for promoting long-term memory.

Many students with special needs may need more practice than their peers. This can be accomplished in several ways. First, if students are capable of studying information independently, they can complete self-practice activities at home or at special allocated times during the day. For example, if they have mastered the "C-C-C" (cover, copy, compare) spelling strategy (see chapter 11), all that is needed is a list of the spelling words to be mastered and the opportunity for study. If the students are not completely independent in their study skills, extra practice could be provided with other students (see chapter 8), special education teachers, instructional aides, or parents. Practice activities can be with flashcards, practice lists, or tutorial computer programs. Clearly state practice objectives and monitor progress (e.g., how many cumulative sight words are read correctly each day).

Increased practice can also be given during a classwide tutoring activity. You might be surprised to discover how much more information your students can learn in brief (e.g., 10–15 minutes), fast-paced daily sessions in which pairs of students question each other on the significant parts of lessons to be remembered, such as multiplication facts, spelling words, key facts and concepts in a geography unit, or parts of speech. You can feel even more confident about student success if you pair students with special needs with students who have demonstrated that they can be effective partners.

Clustering and Organization

Information is better remembered if it is organized in some meaningful way. For example, when students are asked to remember experimental lists of common items—such as *frog, dress, chair, sofa, cat, belt, table*—they remember better if they **cluster,** or arrange information by category and then rehearse the information (Gelzheiser, 1984). In the current instance, students remember the list better if they cluster the names into categories of animals, clothes, and furniture, and rehearse the categories—that is: *frog, cat; dress, belt;* and *chair, sofa, table.* In classroom applications, this may take the form of clustering similar information. For example, products produced and exported by a country could be grouped as agricultural, industrial, and mining products before students practice remembering the list (Gelzheiser, 1984).

Another organizational strategy is the use of organizational charts, visual displays, **semantic maps,** or **relationship charts** (Bos & Anders, 1990). These displays present a spatially organized, as well as semantically organized, representation of the topic. For example, in a unit on Argentina, a visual display can be created that organizes the different areas of study in the unit, such as land features, climate, people, way of life, and government (Figure 10.3).

Use of spatially organized charts and displays are described in more detail in chapter 11.

Elaboration

Information is better remembered if it is elaborated (Scruggs & Mastropieri, 1985). For example, Jensen and Rohwer (1963) found that adults with mental retardation remembered experimental word pairs (e.g., FROG-POCKET) better if they created an elaborative sentence that linked the two (e.g., "The FROG jumped into the POCKET"). With new, unfamiliar, or nonmeaningful words (e.g., MEARDON-ZUMAP), Scruggs and Cohn (1983) reported that learners who created an elaboration of parts of the new words with information that was familiar (e.g., "Meardon is on zee MAP") remembered better than students who simply rehearsed the words (see also Scruggs & Mastropieri, 1985). Similarly, you can provide simple elaborations that can help students remember the new word (e.g., "To remember the meaning of *precipitation,* think of the 'sip' sound in 'precipitation:' Animals can 'sip' from puddles left from precipitation"). To promote elaboration, ask students to think of everything they can about a topic (e.g., "What else does buoyancy remind you of?" "How does a *buoy* remind you of *buoyancy*?"). More complex forms of elaboration are known as "mnemonics."

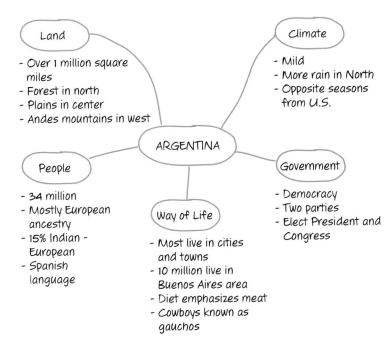

Figure 10.3
Organizational Display

Improve Memory with Mnemonic Techniques

Mnemonic strategies have been used since the times of the ancient Greeks to remember information (Yates, 1966). Although some people disregard mnemonic strategies as no more than "tricks" to aid mindless memorizing, in fact, the principles of mnemonic strategies are strongly supported by psychological theory and research (Scruggs & Mastropieri, 1990).

Everyone remembers using specific mnemonic techniques to remember some declarative (semantic) information. For example, most people remember using the word-acronym *HOMES* to remember the names of the Great Lakes. Many also remember the traditional rhyme "In fourteen hundred ninety-two, Columbus sailed the ocean blue" to remember the year that Columbus first sailed to America. What many people do not know is that mnemonic strategies are versatile and can be used in hundreds, or even thousands, of situations to improve memory.

Another interesting research finding is that mnemonic strategies are powerful. Learning gains of as much as 2-to-1, or even 3-to-1, are common in mnemonic strategy research with students with disabilities. In a meta-analysis of mnemonic strategy research on students with disabilities, Mastropieri and Scruggs (1989a) reported a mean "effect size" of 1.62 standard deviations, an effect that was reported to be the overall most powerful effect of any type of special education intervention to date (Forness & Kavale, 1997).

Nevertheless, mnemonic strategies, like any other teaching or learning strategies, have their limitations. Mnemonic techniques are most effective when they are:

- used to reinforce objectives to remember specific content.
- directly taught and practiced.
- combined with comprehension instruction.
- included with application activities.

Three specific types of mnemonic strategies—the **keyword method,** the **pegword method,** and **letter strategies**—have been successful in enhancing memory for students with memory difficulties, typically, students with learning disabilities, mild mental retardation, and emotional disorders (Mastropieri & Scruggs, 1991; Mastropieri, Scruggs, Whittaker, & Bakken, 1994). They are also useful for students without disabilities, including gifted students (Scruggs, Mastropieri, Jorgensen, & Monson, 1986).

We have not experienced a population that could not benefit from some type of mnemonic strategy. However, most mnemonic research has been conducted with students with learning disabilities, emotional-behavioral disorders, and mild mental retardation. We have found that students with mild mental retardation benefit most from simple, concrete mnemonics. Also, some students with mild mental retardation may have difficulty learning rhymes (Scott & Perou, 1994), and may need additional time learning rhyming mnemonics such as pegwords. Students with visual impairments may benefit less from mnemonic pictures, and more from verbal elaborations (Paivio & Okovita, 1971). However, some visually impaired students perform similarly to nondisabled students on visual imagery tasks (Zimler & Keenan, 1983). Finally, some students with hearing impairments may be less likely to benefit from mnemonics, although verbal elaborations have been helpful in some cases, and using pictures may be beneficial mnemonics for learning sign language. Students with hearing impairments may not differ with respect to elaborative strategy use on verbal learning tasks (Dickens, 1977). Finally, pronounceability is an important determinant of verbal learning for all categories of deafness (Chen, 1973).

Keyword Strategies

The keyword method was first studied experimentally by Atkinson (1975), although earlier versions of this strategy are far older (Yates, 1966). The keyword method is used to strengthen the connection between a new word and its associated information. For example, the Italian word *strada* means *road* (Figure 10.4). To strengthen this association, the learner is first provided a "keyword" for the new word, *strada.* A keyword is a word that is familiar to the learner, but that *sounds like* the new word and is easily pictured. In the case of *strada,* a good keyword is *straw,* because it sounds like *strada* and is easy to picture. Next, a picture (or image) is created of the associates interacting together. Again, in the case of *strada,* the interactive picture could be a picture of straw lying on a road. This picture then is shown to the student, while the teacher says the accompanying dialogue.

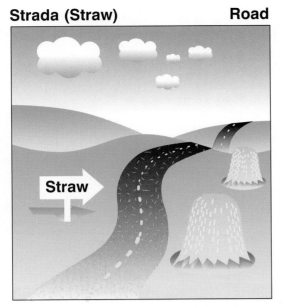

Strada (Straw)   Road

Straw

The Italian word *strada* means road. The keyword for strada is *straw* [show picture]. Remember this picture of straw lying on a road. Remember this picture of what? Good, straw lying on a road. Now, when I ask you for the meaning of *strada*, think first of the keyword, *straw*. Then think back to the picture with the straw in it, remember that the straw was on a road, and then retrieve the answer, *strada* means road. Now, what does *strada* mean? Good, *strada* means road. And, how did you remember that? Good, you thought of the keyword, *straw*, and remembered the picture of the *straw* on the road.

Figure 10.4

***Keyword Mnemonic Strategy for* Strada = Road**

Note: From Mastropieri, M. A. (1993). "Uso Della Mnemotechnica Nell'insegnamento a Studenti con Distubi di Apprendimento." In R. Vianello and C. Cornoldi (Eds.), *Disturbi di Apprendimento: Proposte di Intervento, Congresso Internazionale CNIS* (pp. 15–32). Bergamo, Italia: Juvenilia. Reprinted with permission.

Keyword strategies have been successfully used to teach the following:

- Foreign language vocabulary
- Scientific terms such as *ranidae* (Figure 10.5)
- English vocabulary (e.g., *barrister* is a lawyer, provide a picture of a bear, keyword for barrister pleading a case in a court room)
- People and their accomplishments, such as Zimmerman, the German foreign minister, who sent the coded "Zimmerman note" to Mexico that precipitated U.S. entry into World War I (Figure 10.6)
- Map locations for Revolutionary War battles (Brigham, Scruggs, & Mastropieri, 1995)
- States and capitals[*] (Mastropieri, Scruggs, Bakken, & Brigham, 1992)

State (keyword)	Capital (keyword)	Mnemonic Picture
Kentucky (kennel)	Frankfort (frankfurter)	Dogs in a kennel eating frankfurters.
Tennessee (tennis)	Nashville (cash)	Playing tennis for cash.
Nebraska (new brass)	Lincoln (Abe Lincoln)	Abe Lincoln polishing new brass.
California (calf horn)	Sacramento (sack of mint)	A sack of mint on a calf's horn.
Florida (flower)	Tallahassee (television)	A flower on a television set.
Arkansas (ark)	Little Rock (little rock)	Noah's Ark landing on a little rock.

[*]*Note:* From *Teaching Students Ways to Remember: Strategies for Learning Mnemonically,* by M. A. Mastropieri and T. E. Scruggs, 1991, Cambridge, MA: Brookline. Copyright 1991 by Brookline. Reprinted with permission.

Figure 10.5

Keyword Mnemonic Strategy for* Ranidae = *common frogs

Note: From "Mnemonic Vocabulary Instruction for Learning Disabled Students," by M. A. Mastropieri, T. E. Scruggs, J. R. Levin, J. Gaffney, and B. McLoone, 1985, *Learning Disability Quarterly,* 8, 57–63. Copyright 1985 by Council for Learning Disabilities. Reprinted with permission.

Ranidae (Rain)   **Frog**

Figure 10.6

Keyword Mnemonic Strategy for* Zimmerman = *Sent a Coded Note to Mexico

Note: From "Constructing More Meaningful Relationships: Mnemonic Instruction for Special Populations," by M. A. Mastropieri and T. E. Scruggs, 1989, *Educational Psychology Review,* 1(2), pp. 83–111. Reprinted with permission.

Zimmerman (Swimmer)   Note to Mexico to fight U.S.

These strategies can be helpful for students who need assistance remembering long lists of information for school, as seen in the second part of James's scenario.

CLASSROOM SCENARIO

James

Mr. Pearl, James's resource teacher, told James that he thought he had the solution to James's problem. He constructed keywords and simple pictures for all the states and capitals information, such as those in the previous illustration. He spent one period with James, explaining the keyword method and how it could be used to remember states and capitals. He demonstrated by teaching James capitals for six states. First, they practiced state names and their keywords (e.g., Arkansas—ark). Next they practiced capital names and their keywords (e.g., Little Rock—a little rock). Then he went over the six pictures of states and capitals and practiced the strategies, as follows:

Mr. Pearl:	The capital of Arkansas is Little Rock. The keyword for Arkansas is . . . ?
James:	Ark.
Mr. Pearl:	Good, and the keyword for Little Rock is . . . ?
James:	A little rock.
Mr. Pearl:	Good! Now, remember this picture [shows picture] of Noah's Ark landing on a little rock. Remember this picture of what?

James: Noah's Ark landing on a little rock.
Mr. Pearl: [turns over the picture] And the capital of Arkansas is . . . ?
James: Little Rock.
Mr. Pearl: Little Rock, good.

When James was certain he knew how the strategies worked, Mr. Pearl told him to study no more than six pictures at a time, and test himself frequently on the information he had accumulated. Mr. Pearl tested him periodically, and encouraged him to keep studying.

When the time for the states and capitals test came, James received one of the highest scores in the class! The seventh-grade teacher, Mrs. Sullivan, was so impressed that she asked James how he was able to do so well. James showed her the mnemonic pictures, and Mrs. Sullivan asked Mr. Pearl if she could use the strategy with her entire class the following year.

———

Uberti, Scruggs, and Mastropieri (2003) used mnemonic keyword strategies to improve learning and recall of new vocabulary words prior to a story-reading activity in inclusive third-grade classes (e.g., *ionosphere, fjords, jettison*). Although the keyword strategies improved all students' recall of word meanings over alternative vocabulary learning conditions, students with learning disabilities benefited the most from the keyword method, learning 2 to 3 times the number learned under alternative conditions.

Terrill (2002) created keyword mnemonic strategies to help her high school students with learning disabilities learn important vocabulary words in preparation for the SAT. For example, for the vocabulary word *palatable,* the keyword was *table,* and a picture was shown of people sitting at a table enjoying a meal. A sentence under the picture stated, "All the food on the **table** tasted very good." Students learned and remembered 92% of the words they learned mnemonically and only 49% of the words they learned using more traditional activities, such as drill and worksheet activities.

"Reconstructive Elaborations." **Reconstructive elaborations** refers to procedures for reconstructing information into more meaningful and memorable forms. Three types of reconstructions include acoustic (or keyword) reconstructions, symbolic reconstructions, and mimetic reconstructions (Scruggs & Mastropieri, 1989).

The **keyword** method (or **acoustic reconstructions**) is best used when the information to be learned is unfamiliar. Such terms as *saprophytic, nepenthe,* or *carnelian* are excellent candidates for the keyword method because they are unfamiliar, and similar-sounding keywords (acoustic reconstructions) can easily be created (Mastropieri, Scruggs, & Fulk, 1990). Unfamiliar proper names (e.g., *Modigliani, Volga*) also fit into this category.

Some information is familiar to students, but is more *abstract* and difficult to picture. In such cases, teachers can use **symbolic reconstructions,** in which the information is reconstructed into a symbolic picture, rather than a representational (mimetic) or keyword (acoustic) picture. For example, to demonstrate the U.S. policy of neutrality before World War I, a picture could be shown of Uncle Sam (symbol for U.S. policy) watching the war in Europe and exclaiming, "It's not my fight!"

Some information is familiar and concrete, and does not need to be transformed into familiar forms. In these cases **pictorial or mimetic reconstructions** work best. For example, a U.S. history text states that World War I soldiers stationed in unhealthy trenches were more likely to die from disease than from battle wounds. To remember this information, it is not necessary to create keywords; rather, simply picture *sick soldiers* in *trenches* to demonstrate the relation. Students can simply think back to the picture and retrieve the answer. To help students remember that sponges grow on the ocean floor, simply show a picture of sponges growing on the ocean floor (Scruggs & Mastropieri, 1989, 1992).

Reconstructive elaborations refers to a method for classifying important information in terms of familiarity and concreteness, and developing appropriate strategies. This method can be useful in planning and developing mnemonic strategies across larger units of content.

For mnemonic strategies for learning hundreds of secondary level vocabulary words, see Burchers, Burchers, and Burchers (1997, 2000).

Number	Pegword	Number	Pegword
one	bun, sun, or gun	fifty	gifty
two	shoe	sixty	witchy
three	tree	seventy	heavenly
four	door or floor	eleven	lever
five	hive	twelve	elf
six	sticks	thirteen	thirsting
seven	heaven	fourteen	forking
eight	gate	fifteen	fixing
nine	vine or lion	sixteen	sitting
ten	hen	seventeen	severing
twenty	twin	eighteen	aiding
thirty	dirty or thirsty	nineteen	knighting
forty	party		

Figure 10.7
Pegwords

Pegword Strategies

Pegwords are rhyming words for numbers, and are useful in learning numbered or ordered information. Commonly used pegwords are provided in Figure 10.7 (see also Browning, 1983; Willott, 1982). For example, to remember that insects have six legs, picture an insect crawling on *sticks* (pegword for six). To remember that spiders have eight legs, picture a spider spinning a web on a *gate* (pegword for eight).

Pegwords can be helpful in remembering the three classes of levers (based on the arrangement of fulcrum, load, and force). For example, an oar is an example of a first-class lever, because it has the fulcrum at the middle and the force and load at opposite ends. To remember that an oar is an example of a first-class lever, provide a picture of an oar with a *bun* (pegword for one) at the fulcrum. To remember that a wheelbarrow is an example of a second-class level (with the fulcrum at one end and the force at the other), provide a picture of a wheelbarrow on a *shoe* (pegword for two). Finally, to remember that a rake is an example of a third-class lever (with the fulcrum at one end and the force at the middle), provide a picture of a rake leaning against a *tree* (pegword for three). These examples are shown in Figure 10.8.

Pegwords can also be used to remember lists of information, such as the following:

- possible reasons (ranked by plausibility) that dinosaurs might have become extinct (Veit, Scruggs, & Mastropieri, 1986).
- the hardness levels of minerals (pegwords can also be combined with keywords for this) (Scruggs, Mastropieri, Levin, & Gaffney, 1985).
- the order of U.S. presidents (Mastropieri, Scruggs, & Whedon, 1997).
- multiplication tables (pegwords can be used with other pegwords) (Willott, 1982).

Letter Strategies

Letter strategies can be useful for remembering lists of things. For example, the HOMES strategy prompts recall of the names of the Great Lakes (H—Huron; O—Ontario, etc.). However, this strategy will only be effective if students are familiar enough with the names of the Great Lakes that thinking of a single letter will prompt the entire name. That is, if students are not familiar with the name Ontario, the letter "O" will not be enough to help them remember it. To ensure letter strategies are effective, ask students to rehearse the names represented by the letters.

The HOMES strategy is an example of an **acronym.** An acronym is a word formed from the first letters of the list to be remembered. Another example of an acronym is "FARM-B," which is used to remember the names of the classes of vertebrate animals (F—fish, A—amphibian, R—reptile,

Mnemonic strategies for mathematics learning are discussed in detail in chapter 14.

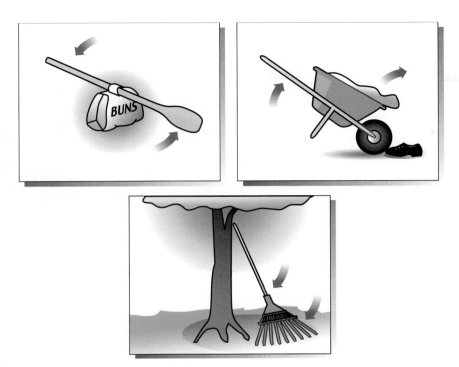

Figure 10.8

Pegword Mnemonic Strategy for Classes of Levers: Oar = 1st class, wheelbarrow = 2nd class, rake = 3rd class

Note: From *A Practical Guide for Teaching Science to Students with Special Needs in Inclusive Settings* (p. 154), by M. A. Mastropieri and T. E. Scruggs, 1993, Austin, TX: PRO-ED. Copyright 1993 by Purdue Research Foundation. Reprinted with permission.

M—mammal, B—bird). A picture showing vertebrate animals on a farm can help enforce this concept. In this strategy, the "B" serves no particular purpose—it is just left over after "farm" is spelled. Students need to practice this to remember it is FARM-B, and not some other letter.

In spite of their success and popularity, acronyms are relatively rare as mnemonics. The reason for this is that many lists of things to be remembered do not contain first letters that can easily be combined into words. For example, the first letters of the planets in the solar system (M, V, E, M, J, S, N, U, P), cannot be easily combined into an acronym, mostly because the list contains seven consonants and only two vowels. Also, it seems important to create a mnemonic that preserves the order of the planets from the sun. To accomplish this, an **acrostic** can be used instead. To form an acrostic, a word is created from each first letter, and the words are arranged to make a sentence. To remember the planets, a good acrostic is, "My very educated mother just served us nine pizzas." The first letter of each of the words in this sentence represents the planets in order of their distance from the sun. Another example of an acrostic is "My Dear Aunt Sally," which reminds students to *M*ultiply and *D*ivide before they *A*dd and *S*ubtract in a math sentence (see chapter 14).

Acrostics are more versatile than acronyms, and therefore can be more frequently used. However, acrostics are somewhat more difficult to remember than acronyms, because the word order of an acrostic is less certain than the letter order of an acronym. That is, while the letters in HOMES are invariant, if the acrostic is spelled correctly, the words in "My very educated mother . . . " are more arbitrary. Whose educated mother? Did she serve us, buy us, or give us nine pizzas? How many pizzas did we get? And so on. Acrostics can be helpful, but more practice will probably be necessary for them to be effective. It is also important to remember that many acrostics, like acronyms, rely only on the first letter of the word to be remembered, so it is important that each word is familiar and easy to retrieve, given the first letter.

Finally, letter strategies can be combined with keywords or pegwords. For example, to promote recall of three countries in the Central Powers during World War I, provide a picture of children playing tag in Central Park. *Central Park* is a keyword for Central Powers, and *TAG* is an acronym for Turkey, Austria–Hungary, and Germany (Figure 10.9). To help students remember freedoms guaranteed by the First Amendment to the Constitution, provide a picture of a rap singer who

Figure 10.9

Mnemonic Strategy for **Central Powers**

Note: From *Teaching Students Ways to Remember: Strategies for Learning Mnemonically* (p. 119), by M. A. Mastropieri and T. E. Scruggs (1991), Cambridge, MA: Brookline Books.

Central Powers (Central Park)

Turkey
Austria Hungary
Germany

raps about *buns. Buns* is a pegword for one, or first, amendment, and *RAPS* is an acronym for the freedoms of religion, assembly, press, and speech.

Creating Mnemonic Pictures

Some teachers feel that they cannot use mnemonic strategies because they are not artistically inclined, and feel unable to draw good mnemonic pictures. However, it is not necessary that the pictures be "artistic," rather it is only important that they are recognizable. You can use stick figures or cut-outs from magazines to create pictures. Some teachers have enlisted the assistance of an artistic student to help. Most recently, clip art has become available that can easily be combined to create excellent mnemonic pictures. Clip art on disks containing literally hundreds of thousands of pictures are now available commercially. As an alternative, a great deal of clip art is available on the World Wide Web, and can be located by typing in "clip art" followed by the picture being sought (e.g., "clip art frog") on a search engine. Mnemonic pictures are not difficult to create, and once created, can be used again and again to improve students' memory of important content. The Technology Highlight describes methods for using the Internet to help develop and produce mnemonic strategies.

Combining Mnemonic Strategies with Other Classroom Activities

Mnemonic strategies are not only powerful tools for improving memory, they are very versatile, and can be incorporated with other means of instruction. The keyword method has been used to improve recall of important vocabulary for hands-on science learning (e.g., predator-prey; parasite-host; Mastropieri et al., 1998). In this case, students used the keyword method to help remember important vocabulary, while they engaged in hands-on activities to enhance their understanding of important scientific concepts (e.g., how plants and animals affect and depend on each other in an ecosystem).

Mnemonic strategies have also been employed in peer tutoring configurations in high school chemistry classes. Mastropieri, Scruggs, Graetz, et al. (in press) combined mnemonic strategies for recall of important vocabulary with peer tutoring with content elaboration questioning to develop recall and comprehension of important science content. For example, to learn that a *mole* is the atomic weight of a substance in grams, students were shown a picture of a mole sitting on a scale, getting its weight in grams. Students tutored each other on their recall of the fact and strategy. However, students also questioned each other on additional information about moles, for instance, what is important to know about moles, and examples of moles and how they are calculated. Figure 10.10 provides an example of these materials.

Other Types of Mnemonics

Other types of mnemonic strategies are also seen in school learning. An example is the use of "musical mnemonics," where students are asked to learn information in the form of a song (Scruggs & Brigham, 1991). Although sometimes beneficial (e.g., Cade & Gunter, 2002), such mnemonics can be idiosyncratic in their effects—some might be helpful only to the individual who created the

Creating mnemonic strategies as a study skill is described in chapter 11; many more examples of mnemonic strategies are provided by Mastropieri and Scruggs (1991).

What is a mole?

Your weight in grams is. . .

Atomic weight in grams of an element or compound

If your partner is correct, go to ⇒
If your partner doesn't know the answer, review the strategy.

Strategy: Think of the word *mole*. Then, think of this picture of a mole on a scale, looking at his weight in grams, to help you remember that a mole is the atomic weight in grams of an element.

Then ask: *What is the strategy to remember mole?*

Then ask again: *What is a mole?*

⇒ Then ask: *What else is important about moles?* [Answers include: The mole serves as a bridge between the invisible world of atoms and the macroscopic world of materials and objects.]

Then ask: *What is an example of a mole?* [Answers include: O (oxygen) is atomic weight 16, so 1 mole O = 16 grams O.]

Figure 10.10
What Is a Mole?
From Scruggs, T. E. and Mastropieri, M. A. (2002). *Teaching tutorial: Mnemonics instruction.* TeachingLD.org, copyright 2002 by TeachingLD.org, Division for Learning Disabilities. Reprinted with permission.

Technology Highlight

Using the Internet for Memory Sites

Access to the Internet has increased dramatically the number of available sources for improving memory. Many Websites are devoted to teaching strategies to assist students' memory of school-related information. Go to a search engine like google.com or yahoo.com and **type in mnemonics and you will**

(continued)

find numerous sites containing mnemonics for various school-related activities. Carefully examine any Websites before giving them to your students because some mnemonics may contain X-rated or "politically incorrect" material that should not be used with your students.

Free clip art that can be used to develop mnemonic illustrations can be downloaded from the Internet. Clip art can eliminate the need for an artist in developing mnemonic illustrations. Several clip art illustrations can be successfully combined to create interactive illustrations such as the ones described in this chapter. For example, if the concept of molar weight is going to be taught mnemonically, look for pictures of "moles" to use in developing a mnemonic illustration. To find some clip art examples, go to a search engine and type in "clip art moles" or "clip art chemistry" or "clip art" (name of desired object). Many relevant sites will appear. Search through the sites and select the clip art that best meets your needs and download it to a disk or your computer's hard drive. Then use the clip art to develop the interactive illustrations necessary to create your mnemonics pictures.

Next are some of the sites that may assist students. (Please note that Websites do change so these sites may need to be updated when you search for them. Refer to the chapter 10 Companion Website for additional relevant links.)

- *http://www.medicalmnemonics.com/* Contains a database of all mnemonics for medical terms. The site can be searched. You can rate the mnemonics provided and you can even add mnemonics to the database. You can download the files into various formats including zip files or even files for your palm pilot.

- *http://www.frii.com/~geomanda/mnemonics.html* Contains a listing of mnemonics collected by the author and organized by subject area, including arithmetic, astronomy, calendars, geography, and physics, among many others. Many of the mnemonics are first letter strategies and can be helpful as long as students know the responses required. The first letter strategy helps in organizing and retrieving the information. One arithmetic example included is: "Please Excuse My Dear Aunt Sally" for the order of operations in algebra: Parentheses, Exponents, Multiplication, Division, Addition, Subtraction. One auto mechanics example for tightening screws is: "Righty tighty, lefty loosie." One geography example is: "I Am A Person" to help remember the four oceans (Indian, Arctic, Atlantic, Pacific).

- *http://www.demon.co.uk/mindtool/memory.html* Contains an introduction to mnemonics and examples of various mnemonic systems including the link system, systems using numbers, and memory for exams, for lists, for people's names, for dates, and for telephone numbers. For example, to assist in remembering a person's name, the site recommends attending carefully to the physical characteristics of the individual's face and making an association with the name and those characteristics. The site also recommends rehearsing that association in order to facilitate recall.

- *http://lever.cs.ucla.edu/geoff/mnemonics.html* Contains information to help learn boating terminology including the many aspects associated with lights, buoys, and sounds.

- *http://www.mindtools.com/* Contains a general overview of mnemonic techniques as well as some specific ones including remembering lists, places, studying for exams, and learning a foreign language.

- *http://www.1000plus.com/BirdSong/* Contains many examples for learning bird songs by bird and by song. The site lists a verbal description of the sounds made by various birds.

- *http://www.premiumhealth.com/memory/* Contains tutorials to assist with remembering of basic school-related information. Describes association principles, learning lists, and learning with numbers, among others.

See how many mnemonic Websites you can find. Identify a mnemonic strategy you would like to use, find clip art on the Web, and make an interactive illustration using that clip art.

mnemonic. Furthermore, mnemonics that have been proven to be useful in some circumstances may not be useful for all students. Always monitor the effectiveness of any mnemonic strategies you use, especially when they differ substantially from the keyword, pegword, and letter strategies discussed in this chapter.

Summary

- Attention and memory are two important psychological processes necessary for success in school. Being able to attend to and remember academic content is often a problem for many students with special needs. However, research has uncovered many successful strategies for enhancing attention and memory.
- Effective teaching, including using the teacher planning and presentation variables, can help all students pay more attention in class.
- Simple strategies for increasing attention include asking students directly to try to pay attention better, or moving closer to the student who struggles to attend.
- Breaking activities into smaller segments, alternating among various types of class activities, allowing opportunities for movement, using reinforcement, and teaching self-recording may also help improve attending.

- Peer assistance can be used to promote attention of students with a variety of special needs. Reinforcement of attention and teaching self-recording strategies can also be effective.
- Meeting the preconditions for improving memory may help many students remember better. These preconditions include promoting attention, motivation, and positive attitudes.
- Teaching students metacognitive awareness strategies helps promote better memory strategies for all students.
- Using pictures, enhancing meaningfulness, using activities, providing sufficient practice, and promoting active learning all help promote better memory skills for students with disabilities.
- Using mnemonic strategies such as the keyword method, the pegword method, and letter strategies helps promote learning of unfamiliar content.

Council for Exceptional Children

Improving Attention and Memory

Information in this chapter links most directly to:

Standard 4—Instructional Strategies, particularly:

Skills:
- Use strategies to facilitate integration into various settings.
- Select, adapt, and use instructional strategies and materials according to characteristics of the individual with exceptional learning needs.

Standard 7—Instructional Planning

- Incorporate and implement instructional and assistive technology into the educational program.
- Prepare and organize materials to implement daily lesson plans.

✓ Inclusion Checklist
Improving Attention and Memory

If students are having problems with attention:

- ❑ Have you met the preconditions for improving attention, by:
  - ❑ using the teacher presentation variables in your teaching
  - ❑ using interesting and motivating examples
  - ❑ using attention-getting demonstrations
- ❑ Have you used direct appeal
- ❑ Have you used proximity
- ❑ Have you broken up activities into smaller segments
- ❑ Have you allowed students sufficient movement
- ❑ Have you provided student activities
- ❑ Have you used classroom peers to promote attention
- ❑ Have you provided reinforcement for attention
- ❑ Have you taught self-recording strategies

If students are having problems with memory:

- ❑ Have you met the preconditions for improving memory, by:
  - ❑ ensuring students are paying attention
  - ❑ ensuring students are properly motivated
  - ❑ ensuring students have positive affect
- ❑ Have you taught metacognitive awareness of memory ("metamemory")
- ❑ Have you enhanced meaningfulness
- ❑ Have you used pictures or imagery
- ❑ Have you minimized interfering information
- ❑ Have you used enactments and manipulation
- ❑ Have you promoted active learning
- ❑ Have you increased practice
- ❑ Have you used mnemonic techniques, including the following:
  - ❑ keyword strategies
  - ❑ pegword strategies
  - ❑ letter strategies

Chapter 11

Alita Vaughn, 10
Dallas, TX
"Bugs"

Teaching Study Skills

Objectives

After studying this chapter, you should be able to:

- Demonstrate understanding of tools to develop independent learners and develop personal organizational skills.
- Identify ways to clearly state class expectations toward doing and successful completion of homework.
- Define the purpose, requisite skills, and various strategies to practice effective listening skills.
- Identify and demonstrate understanding of various note-taking skills and strategies.
- Demonstrate familiarity with various library resources and reference skills necessary to successfully complete a report or project.
- Describe and apply strategies for assisting students with disabilities to prepare reports and projects.

Good study skills are necessary for success in school. Although some general education students appear to develop excellent organization and study skills independently, most students with disabilities and students at risk for failure in school can benefit from explicit instruction in organizing themselves for studying and completing assignments in a timely fashion. Research has demonstrated that individuals who are trained to use efficient study and organizational strategies perform better and are more likely to succeed in school (Deshler, Ellis, & Lenz, 1996).

CLASSROOM SCENARIO

Ravi

When Ravi, a ninth grader with learning disabilities, entered Mr. Ford's room, he was holding a stack of books with papers sticking out from all angles. Some of the papers were bent, some were folded, some were slightly torn, but all books had been covered with brightly colored paper. As he approached the desks, his glasses were sliding down toward the end of his nose and he slightly bumped the edge of one of the tables. Before you could blink your eyes, everything that had been in his arms was strewn all over the floor. Ravi smiled sheepishly as he began to pick up his belongings.

Somewhere in that pile of books and papers there was evidence of Ravi's attempts at completing his homework. Unfortunately, however, the homework was torn and tattered and Ravi was unable to find it. When Mr. Ford asked him about it, Ravi said, "I've done some of the homework, but I can't seem to find it at the moment. . . ." This was a typical day for Ravi. Although he usually attempted his assignments, often he did not hand them in because he could not find them. Other times, he would forget about his homework and appear confused when asked about it—almost as if it were the first time he had heard of the assignment.

Learning strategies help all students study more effectively (Wood, Woloshyn, & Willoughby, 1995). This chapter provides you with information on how to help your students become more personally organized and efficient at planning for homework, develop effective listening and note-taking skills, and learn to use outlining and guided notes. In addition, strategies are presented for using libraries, writing reports, completing long-term assignments and projects, and studying for later retrieval.

Tools to Develop Independent Learners

Study skills are tools for learning, behaviors necessary to enable learners to become self-sufficient at studying. Several excellent study skills books are available (e.g., Carman & Adams, 1984; Carter, Bishop, Kravits, & Bucher, 2002; Devine, 1987; Gall, Gall, Jacobsen, & Bullock, 1990; Gaskins & Elliot, 1991; Luckie & Smethurst, 1997; Wood, Woloshyn, & Willoughby, 1995). Most study skills textbooks present a number of study skills and strategies with the expectation that students will master all strategies with minimal instruction. Students with disabilities, however, typically do not have good study and learning strategies and experience difficulties when trying to use these strategies independently. These students may require extensive explicit instruction in learning strategies, controlled practice, and feedback before they are able to execute them successfully independently (Deshler, Schumaker, & Lenz, 1984). Teaching students to become independent learners and thinkers includes providing "tools for learners" in self-instruction, self-monitoring, self-questioning, and self-reinforcement (Deshler, Ellis, & Lenz, 1996).

Many of these studying and learning strategies are described here. Other strategies are described in chapter 15.

Help Students Develop Personal Organizational Skills

Personal organizational skills include using time schedules; understanding class and school schedules; using a daily, weekly, and monthly planner; and being organized for completing homework assignments (Gall et al., 1990). These skills are what some experts call good self-management skills. Other organizational skills include knowing how to analyze tasks required for assignments and optimizing performance and studying time (Devine, 1987). Try to arrange small groups of students who need instruction in study skills. Special education teachers can work with you and provide instruction in these strategies to those who need it. Finally, you may decide to team-teach groups of students who need to learn these strategies. However you present them, building study and organizational skills will reap huge benefits in student performance.

8:00–8:10	Get ready for the school day (sharpen pencils, use restrooms)
8:10–8:15	Complete scrambled sentence activity
8:15–9:15	Reading
9:15–9:40	Recess and restroom breaks
9:40–10:40	Mathematics
10:40–11:15	Writing and Language Arts
11:15–12:15	Lunch and Recess
12:15–1:15	Science
1:15–2:15	Social Studies
2:15–2:45	Physical Education (Tues–Thurs)

BRING SHORTS and SNEAKERS for GYM Tomorrow!!!

Music (Mon)

Art (Wed–Fri)

Figure 11.1
Sample Elementary School Daily Agenda

Post and Review Class and Time Schedules

All grade levels follow systematic schedules. Present the schedules to students with disabilities in clear, comprehensible language to ensure they are prepared for each segment of the school day.

Many elementary teachers write daily agendas or schedules on the board that contain all daily class activities, such as the one shown in Figure 11.1. The list can include reminders to bring specific materials for various classes and brief descriptions of homework assignments. Future events also can be highlighted. For example, highlighting special classes such as art, music, and physical education can help students remember to bring sneakers and shorts for gym class or instruments for music class. Although many students may not require these reminders, students who do need them will not be "singled out" when you make the information available to all.

Secondary schools require students to see many teachers throughout the school day. Some schools have a constant number of daily periods throughout the week, while other schools have rotating schedules—referred to as block scheduling—that alternate daily. Although they allow longer class periods, block systems can be confusing to students with disabilities. Some classes do not meet daily, so students must follow different schedules from day to day. This means that students have to become efficient at learning their schedules and planning their time to complete assignments and study for exams on correct days. You may need infinite patience and creative abilities to review and re-review schedules with some students. Figure 11.2 shows an example of a block schedule.

How to Start. At the beginning of a new year or semester you may need to describe for students how to locate rooms within the school. This is especially important in very large buildings, where one floor looks similar to another. One idea might be to make yourself, a peer, or an aide available to meet students before or after school to go over their class schedules and walk it with them. Follow up by meeting students, especially students with disabilities after each class, and walk with them to the next class until students demonstrate confidence about where they are and where they need to be at what time. Often students with disabilities have keen perceptions. They want to appear as competent as their peers seem to be and, although they might be confused about building layouts and schedules, they will not want to risk embarrassing themselves by asking for help. Your awareness and subtle ways of keying in to students' needs can enhance students' self-perceptions.

Don't Forget Lockers. As students move from class to class, they may need to visit their lockers for books or materials. This can be particularly challenging for some students with disabilities because the use of lockers requires extra time and mental and physical challenges. Combination locks can be troublesome for even the most capable students, so seeking ways to accommodate opening them is important.

Start by privately asking students to open their lockers in front of you. If students have trouble remembering the combination, suggest they write the combination on a wallet-size card for easy access until they master the information.

Provide extra time and instructions for opening lockers. Extra practice can build students' confidence and help them get to class on time. Some students have been known to carry everything (all

Parents might be willing to have these wallet-size cards laminated. Many copy centers have the equipment to accomplish this.

Black Day Schedule	
Daily Order	Period
1. First	1. English, room 204
2. Second	2. Phys. Ed, gym
3. Third	3. Algebra I, room 105
4. Fourth	4. Study Hall, cafeteria

Red Day Schedule	
Daily Order	Period
1. First	5. Biology, room 209
2. Second	6. U.S. Government, room 115
3. Third	7. Band, music room
4. Fourth	8. Spanish, room 215

Figure 11.2
Sample Secondary School Schedule

In large school buildings, practicing finding the rooms where classes will take place is an essential "beginning-of-the-year" activity for secondary students with disabilities.

books, notebooks, lunch, and coats) around all day simply because they could not open their lockers. Another student pretended she hated physical education and refused to participate in gym, when she actually did not know how to open her locker that contained her gym clothing. Finally, note the accessibility of lockers. Lockers or locks that are placed too high or low can cause unnecessary frustrations. This is also true for younger students who cannot easily reach their storage cubicles.

Clearly Post and Review Schedule Changes. Some students do not handle changes well, but if they are prepared ahead of time, they will be more likely to adjust to the changes. For example, explain what will happen if you are absent from school and a substitute teacher is assigned to take over the class. Believe it or not, some students with emotional disabilities may be very upset when you are absent! These changes may be particularly difficult for some students if you are gone for a long period of time, such as for an extended medical or maternity leave. When students are informed ahead of time, these transitions can be handled more smoothly. In addition, students should be prepared for the arrival of student teachers or practicum students. Enlist the support of special education teachers to provide extra guidance and assistance during any major transitions.

At the middle and secondary levels it is common for students to have different teachers for each subject. Each teacher may establish different class routines and expectations. Many students with disabilities require extra help learning the routines that are used in each teacher's classroom (Mastropieri & Scruggs, 2002). For example, some teachers may require students to be seated when the class bell rings, while others may require that students only be inside the room when the bell rings. Some teachers may require students to bring pencils to class; others may lend students necessary class materials. Encourage students to write down any specific expectations and routines for each class and teacher. Take care to show students your own class expectations, schedules, and routines and provide support for them while they are learning all of the new routines simultaneously. A little role-playing or memory game might help. For example, say the name of a teacher to a group of students and ask them to quickly tell you the unique expectations that teacher has.

Daily, Weekly, Monthly Planners, and Planning

Many adults use daily planner calendars that contain space for weekly and monthly entries. These planners are ideally suited to keeping track of both long-term and short-term school assignments. Show students a variety of planner formats and have them select one that meets their needs. Show them how most effective people in all disciplines use some type of planner to help keep organized. Ask other teachers, the principal, parents, and business people from the community to visit your class and share the way they plan and schedule events.

Explain the differences between long- and short-term planning. Provide examples of how studying time needs to be divided among subject areas and across types of assignments (Rafoth, Leal, & DeFabo, 1993). Provide examples of "to-do" lists and show students how to prioritize them. Some people like to do the easiest thing on the list first; others prefer to get the hardest item out of the way first. Figure 11.3 shows a sample planner and to-do list that might work for individual content

Student _____				_____ Quarter	
Subject	To do	Assigned on	Due date	Turned in on	Parent initials

Figure 11.3
Sample Planner and To-Do List

areas. Encourage students to discuss optimal ways of proceeding for themselves. The goal is to encourage organizational skills that are effective for each student—you should realize that some students may develop procedures that are idiosyncratic but nevertheless effective. Students with disabilities may need specific examples of each step spelled out for them. For example, general education students with good study habits: (a) review their assignment notebooks, (b) prioritize what needs to get accomplished, (c) set goals of finishing tasks for themselves, and (d) work hard to accomplish those goals. Conversely, students with disabilities may be forgetful and may not deliberately plan their activities. Some may need teachers to complete sample planners for them and take them step by step through the thinking involved in figuring out what to do.

Consider teaching your students a set of general strategies for completing tasks. Preparing students to manage their time wisely will help them be more successful in your class and in life. Model good organizational behaviors and demonstrate how effective time management helps your class run more smoothly, too.

Task Analysis

Task analysis is another skill that helps many students and is an extension of long-range planning. Task analysis is the process of taking a large task or assignment and breaking it into subcomponent smaller tasks, estimating task completion time for each subcomponent. Teaching students to write out the assignment, decide what must be done, sequence the steps of what must be done, and estimate the amount of time necessary to complete each step is one of the most valuable skills you can teach them. For example, a biology teacher may make an assignment that students read pages 264–277 in the textbook, write a summary paragraph, and answer questions 13–21 at the end of the chapter. A task analysis may reveal that the student must:

- locate the textbook and a quiet area to work;
- find the relevant text pages and read carefully, highlighting or taking notes;
- write a summary paragraph based on reading and notes;
- locate the relevant questions at the end of the chapter;
- answer all questions, referring to text and notes; and
- check all work and be certain all components of the assignment are completed.

A self-instruction sheet your students can use for organizing and analyzing an assignment is provided in the *In the Classroom . . . for sharing with students* feature in the Companion Website. Figure 11.4 has a planning task sequence for preparing a book report.

Model and demonstrate how task analysis can be applied to long- and short-term projects at any grade level. Provide practice with partially completed task analyses and have students estimate the time necessary for each step. Show how these subcomponent steps can be written into students' calendar planners. Reinforce how this planning results in completing tasks on time.

Homework

Homework is assigned at virtually all grade levels, but increases in regularity and complexity with each grade level (Polloway, Epstein, Bursuck, Jayanthi, & Cumblad, 1994; Polloway, Foley, & Epstein, 1992). Homework provides opportunities for students to develop fluency with the information being taught and to develop organizational and self-study skills. For example, when learning new vocabulary words, students should review the definitions frequently to become fluent with the new words and their meanings.

Some homework assignments may need to be reduced in size and scope for students with disabilities because these students often require more time to process and complete the same activities. Polloway et al. (1992) reported that students with learning disabilities had more than 2½ times more difficulties completing homework than their peers did. Because many teachers consider homework grades in computing grades for semesters, you might want to modify the amount and type of homework or the grading procedures for students with disabilities (Polloway, Epstein, Bursuck, Jayanthi, & Cumblad, 1994). Figure 11.5 lists some assignments and possible adaptations.

Most students with disabilities find it helpful to record their assignments in an assignment notebook. Include spaces for teachers and parents' signatures to help ensure that your students asked someone to verify whether assignments were completed accurately. This also keeps parents informed so they can monitor homework progress daily.

Task analysis is an important component of special education teaching, and is a useful strategy to employ whenever a student exhibits difficulty with academic skills. For more information, see Mastropieri and Scruggs (2002).

	Sun	Mon	Tues	Wed	Thurs	Fri	Sat
Week 1							
Week 2							
Week 3							
Week 4							

Assigned Date _____ Due Date _____ Time Available _____ days

1. Go to library and select book. (1 day)
2. Count chapters or pages in book and determine the number of chapters or pages that should be read daily (e.g., 13 chapters or 208 pages). Adjust according to your reading rate and the number of days available. For example, if you can read 1 chapter per day you will need 13 days. If you can read 16 pages a day, you will need 13 days to read the book.
3. Brainstorm book report outline. (1 day)
4. Organize outline from brainstorming activity. (1 day)
5. Fill in details on outline. (1 day)
6. Write draft book report using outline. (2 days)
7. Proof and revise first draft of book report. (2 days)
8. Write final version and proof carefully. (2 days)

Total number of nights necessary to complete assignment—20

	Sun	Mon	Tues	Wed	Thurs	Fri	Sat
Week 1		Go to library and select book	Count pages and chapters and figure out how much to read daily	Read	Read	Read	Read
Week 2	Read	Read	Read	Read	Read	Read	
Week 3	Read	Read	Read	Brainstorm book report outline	Organize outline from brainstorming	Fill in outline details
Week 4	Write first draft	Write first draft	Write first draft	Write final draft	Edit and proof final version	Proof final version

Figure 11.4
Task Planning for a Book Report

Some simple homework arranging plans can be communicated to parents and established at home to help students finish their homework successfully. For example, parents likely would appreciate a letter requesting their assistance in establishing homework procedures and arranging an environment conducive to studying at home (see Figure 11.6).

When assigning students homework, provide good, clear instructions, and always explain the purpose of the assignment. Say something like "This homework assignment will help you understand the concepts we are learning in science class so that when we begin our lab on Thursday, you will have a better understanding of what we are doing." Try to write the assignment clearly on the board or overhead projector. Some teachers wisely write assignments in the same location daily so that students can find them easily and copy them accurately into their assignment notebooks.

Such predictable, consistent practices can help students establish patterns that promote success.

Subject	Assignment	Adapted Assignment
Spelling	Study 20 words.	Study 10 prioritized words.
Math	Complete 30 word problems.	Complete 15 prioritized word problems.
Reading	Read 2 chapters and write a summary.	Read 1 chapter and tape record a summary of the information; or listen to an audiotape recording of the 2 chapters and tape a summary of both chapters.
Social Studies	Read section 3 in chapter 4 and answer the 20 questions at the end of the section.	Read section 3 in chapter 4 and answer the even-numbered questions at the end of the section (half the questions).
Science	Write a summary of the experiment completed during today's lab.	Tape record a summary of the experiment completed in today's lab.

Figure 11.5
Homework Assignments and Possible Adaptations

Several teaching practices can help students complete their homework successfully:

- Give clear, concise directions for completing assignments; establish due dates that are reasonable and clearly communicated so your students perceive that you are fair and well organized.
- Describe any materials necessary to complete each assignment. For example, will students need to take their textbooks home with them? Will they need to go to the library and sign out materials before they can complete the work? Will they need to bring materials to class such as glue and markers to work on an in-school project?
- Repeat or explain the directions. If you provide a sample of the homework assignment, complete it together as a class, be specific, and ensure that students understand what they are to do by asking two or three students to repeat or explain the directions. Encourage students to ask questions concerning completing the task independently.
- Anticipate any areas of difficulty with an assignment and attempt to provide extra clarification.
- Explain how students can get help if they confront problems. Perhaps some students could be trained as "telephone homework assistants" who could be contacted in the evenings until 8 o'clock. Distribute a list of names and phone numbers of these homework assistants.
- Establish a regular time for collecting and distributing assignments. Students will become familiar with these procedures and know that completing and turning in homework is taken seriously. Some teachers have special locations arranged for dropping off and picking up completed and corrected assignments. For example, "in" and "out" boxes on your desk or a table near the front of the room may work well. Telling students to drop off completed work at the beginning of class, rather than at the end of the class period, helps ensure that students come with their work completed.
- Consistently collect, grade, and return assigned work. When teachers neglect to collect or return graded assignments, some students take away the message that homework is unimportant to them.
- Coordinate assignments with other teachers. If you teach at the middle school level or above you may be a team member and can more easily coordinate assignments, especially longer-term projects and tests. Your students with disabilities will benefit greatly from any shared planning you do with your co-teachers to avoid scheduling several exams on a single day or overlapping longer-term assignments.

Refer to chapter 8 for suggestions on providing training to peer assistants.

Date _____

Dear Parent,

As we begin this school year I want you to know how delighted I am to have your child, _____, in my class. I am looking forward to meeting you at our first Open House. Please try to come and bring any questions you may have about this school year with you.

I would like to explain to you some of the procedures and requirements of my class so you will have a better understanding of what is expected of your child. I usually assign homework nightly. Most nights the assignments are rather short and can be completed within 20 minutes. A few times throughout the year, however, I assign longer-term projects that will require your child to work a little bit each night over a period of about a month to complete the project. Examples of the longer-term projects include the following:

- Book reports
- Library research projects
- Models of inventions
- Science fair projects
- Interviews with business people from the community

I would like to request some assistance from you to ensure that your child successfully completes his/her assignments. Every afternoon or evening, **please ask your son or daughter to show you the assignment notebook.** Ideally your child should take the initiative and bring the notebook to you. Please initial and date that day's assignments. That will let me know that you have seen the assignment and ensure that it has been successfully completed or that an honest attempt was made to complete it. Some of you may want to see the assignment book and completed assignment, while others of you may wish to see only the assignment notebook.

Second, it would be most helpful if you could establish a **regular space** for your child to complete his or her assignments. That way, when he or she arrives home from school, all necessary school materials can be placed in a specific location and kept all together. Establishing a regular place also helps ensure that the materials are together and will not be forgotten when leaving for school the next morning.

Third, it would be beneficial to **establish a regular time for your child to do his or her homework.** I realize that this can be difficult because of extra-curricular activities. However, establishing regular homework times on Mondays, Tuesdays, Wednesdays, Thursdays, and Saturdays or Sundays can help illustrate the importance of maintaining responsibility for completing homework.

Finally, please feel free to add notes to the assignment notebook if you wish to communicate any information to me. If you have questions concerning your child's performance or understanding of the assignments I will do my best to help.

If students don't complete or turn in assignments, they will lose points from their grade and be given after-school detention after missing three assignments.

Thanks so much for your help with this important matter. Please feel free to contact me by telephone or e-mail.

Regards,

Figure 11.6
Homework Procedures: Request for Home/School Cooperation

- Arrange classroom incentives for completing and turning in homework. Some teachers establish either individual or class rewards to encourage timely completion of homework.
- Provide students with feedback on their homework. Giving corrective feedback and having students keep records of their performance helps them see the importance of accuracy and timeliness.
- Remember to assign projects that are within the capability levels of all students. Homework is an opportunity to practice previously acquired skills, practice for fluency, and practice applying skills.

Clearly State Class Expectations. Provide students with specific expectations for completed work. Give clear models of what the headings for assignments should look like. Explain how you intend to evaluate work and provide examples of what you consider to be "model" assignments and insufficiently completed assignments. Provide samples of completed assignments, especially for longer-term projects, but also for daily assignments. Is it acceptable, for example, to turn in a page torn from a spiral notebook?

May assignments be completed in pencil? In manuscript format? Will you accept incomplete assignments or will those be returned with the grade of "F"? Clarify, for example, whether the paper must be lined and whether assignments must be completed by hand or by word processor. Creating a checklist for students to keep in their notebooks would be helpful. For younger students, post a short list of expectations in large bold letters so students can refer to them throughout the year. A checklist and a self-monitoring sheet for sample class expectations for younger and older students, respectively, are provided in the *In the Classroom . . . for sharing with students* feature in the Companion Website.

Plan for Special Problems. Students with disabilities and other students at risk for school failure may have trouble completing homework not only because of difficulty levels but also because they may forget to do it or forget *how* to do it (Polloway, Epstein, Bursuck, Jayanthi, & Cumblad, 1994). You can attempt to circumvent these problems in several ways. Implement the previously described assignment notebook suggestion. Work with special education teachers to coordinate assignments and use any assignment book across subject areas. Special education teachers frequently sign assignment notebooks and may be able to provide assistance with suggestions for the best way of monitoring the home-school coordination.

Ask individual students with disabilities to summarize or re-explain assignments in their own words. This could be done just after the whole class explanations and can demonstrate to you if they really understand what to do. If at all possible, present a completed model problem on the homework sheet for them and allow them to start the assignment in class. If students experience difficulties with the first problem, additional explanation and teaching can be provided before sending the work home for them to undertake independently. Remember: *Homework should be something that can be done independently* or something for which students already possess the skills and knowledge to complete without your assistance. A completed example refreshes their memory when they are at home alone and unable to request assistance from you. The completed example also provides sufficient information to parents who can sometimes answer their children's questions if necessary. However, remember that many parents may be unable to complete all the tasks that have been sent home as homework, so allow flexibility in task completion. If parents include a note explaining that their child could not figure out how to complete the work independently, but that they tried for a sufficient amount of time, do not penalize students for incomplete homework.

Go through the PASS variables with the homework assignment.

- *Prioritize.* Determine the objectives of the assignments and then *prioritize* them for students with disabilities. Are all of the homework objectives priorities for students with disabilities, too?
- *Adapt.* Do the materials need to be adapted? For example, can a lower-level reading book be used to obtain most of the information? Do the instructions need additional clarification? Can the number of problems be reduced? Is the assignment too difficult or inappropriate for students with disabilities? Can another assignment be substituted with similar results?
- *Systematic Instruction and Systematic Assessment.* Has systematic instruction and evaluation taken place so the student knows what to do and can do the assignment independently?

After assessing the assignment using the PASS variables, make any necessary modifications and give that assignment to those students.

Set up individual behavioral contracts with students who need extra supervision and assistance in executing assignments independently (Kerr & Nelson, 2002). It may be especially difficult for students with disabilities to complete long-term assignments, such as science fair projects. During these projects, arrange shorter intervals during which you check to see if students with disabilities are making sufficient progress independently. For example, arrange weekly check periods in which students must turn in what has been completed to date. This enables you not only to determine whether sufficient progress is being made but also to check whether progress is adequate. Corrective feedback can then be provided before it is too late. Work with parents to design rewards on the contract so that home-school cooperation is enhanced. Sometimes parents will want to deliver the reward at home, while other times the reward may be designed for school. In either case, consistent monitoring of progress toward completion of the long-term project is essential to ensure successful completion of the project.

Cooperative Homework Teams. O'Melia and Rosenberg (1994) created Cooperative Homework Teams (CHT) to help middle-school students with learning and behavioral disabilities com-

Chapter 2 displays a sample contract. More information on designing contracts is presented in chapter 7.

plete their mathematics homework more frequently and more accurately. Students in CHT classes were assigned into three- and four-member heterogeneous cooperative homework teams. During the first period of class, immediately after the opening activity, the teams met, and a "checker" who had been assigned to each team on a rotating basis graded the assignments for the day, using teacher-made answer sheets. The grades are recorded, and the homework is returned to the students with corrections. Team members were encouraged to assist each other. Checkers then turned in all the corrected homework. After eight weeks of this intervention, results indicated that students who had participated in Cooperative Homework Teams had a 74% rate of homework completion, compared to a 55% rate in comparison classes. Further, CHT condition students were 30% more accurate in the assignments they did complete.

Assignment Completion Strategy. Hughes, Ruhl, Schumaker, and Deshler (2002) successfully taught middle-school students with learning disabilities an assignment completion strategy that was successfully used in their inclusive general education classes. The strategy was taught using the mnemonic "PROJECT," which represented the following steps:

- P = Prepare your forms, including monthly planner, weekly study schedule, and assignment sheet
- R = Record and ask, in which students record assignments on the assignment sheet and ask for clarification
- O = Organize the assignment, subdivided into BEST—Break assignment into parts, Estimate the number of study sessions, Schedule your sessions, Take materials home
- J = Jump into it, in which students overcome task avoidance, prepare necessary materials, affirm the quality of the work to be done, and check requirements
- E = Engage in the work, in which students complete the assignments and enlist assistance from parents or a "study buddy" when needed
- C = Check your work, in which students evaluate the quality of the work, make corrections, and assign a "quality grade" on the assignment sheet
- T = Turn in your work, in which students place the assignment folder where it can be located easily, checks the monthly planner and assignment sheets, and turns in the assignment on time (Hughes et al., 2002)

Students were taught how to implement the strategy using assignment notebooks over an extended time period. Results appear very promising for assisting many students for becoming more independent and successful at completing and turning in homework assignments.

Promote Listening Skills

Define the Purpose

Listening skills are critical for school success (Devine, 1987). Because teachers provide oral directions and instructions continually throughout the school day, students who have good listening skills can follow along, understand what is expected of them, and be successful in school. Many students, however, especially younger elementary-age children and students with disabilities and attention deficit disorders, lack good listening skills. This hinders their ability to succeed in classes (Deshler, Ellis, & Lenz, 1996).

Requisite Listening Skills

Verify whether students have the appropriate requisite skills for listening by using the teacher checklist in the following *In the Classroom* feature. First, determine if students can hear the speaker adequately. Judge whether the student's position in the classroom interferes with hearing abilities. Evaluate when students appear to have difficulties listening. For example, does the problem exist when information is presented over the loudspeaker, or during audiovisual presentations? Does it exist during teacher presentations in the classroom, in large-group sessions in auditoriums, or outdoors at recess? Analyze the situations during which listening is required and pinpoint any problems. Difficulties in hearing in any of these environments may indicate that a referral is needed for a hearing test. Specific plans can be devised to assist students, providing them with various seating positions to meet listening needs. Have students sit near audiovisual equipment or near the front of large auditoriums, or ask peer assistants to help by repeating directions given outdoors.

In the Classroom ...a feature for teachers

Checklist for Effective Listening Skills

Does the student:
- ☐ Hear the speaker
  - ☐ Teacher's voice
  - ☐ Loud speaker
  - ☐ Audiovisual presentations
  - ☐ Auditorium presentations
  - ☐ Outdoors at recess or field trips
- ☐ Attend to the speaker
  - ☐ Come to attention
  - ☐ Sustain attention
- ☐ Understand the speaker
- ☐ Understand the vocabulary
- ☐ Recognize and select important points
- ☐ Follow a sequence of ideas
- ☐ Understand organizational cues (*first, then*)
- ☐ Attend to transitional statements ("Next I will. . . ")
- ☐ Understand verbal emphasis cues ("This is important.")
- ☐ Understand nonverbal cues (moves to the front of the room)

Adaptations for ADD and ADHD can be found in chapter 10.

Second, determine whether an attention problem exists. Some students have difficulties coming to attention at the beginning of class or lectures. Other students, such as students with attention deficit hyperactivity disorder (ADHD), might exhibit problems sustaining attention throughout listening activities.

To help students come to attention and to encourage active listening from the start, try pairing a visual cue with the beginning of the listening activity. For example, flip the light switch in the room or on the overhead projector to alert students the presentation is about to begin. Pair a teacher movement, such as walking and standing still in the front of the room for a few seconds, with the beginning of new lectures. If sustaining attention is problematic, encourage active listening by calling on students for group responses several times through lectures. Questions can be used as review of the information presented, and also involve students more and help them maintain attention to lectures. Distribute small chalk or dry-erase boards and have students write answers to questions and hold up their boards to show answers to you or their neighbors. Another strategy that often works well is to move and stand by students who are not paying attention and call them by name before you share the new information. This subtle movement lets them know that you want their attention.

Third, determine if students understand the speaker. Unfamiliar accents or dialects can be difficult to understand or the vocabulary and sentence structure may be beyond the lexicon level of the students with disabilities. Ask students to repeat what was just said in their own words. If they say "I don't know," repeat the information and ask again. Ask them if they understand any unfamiliar accent. When vocabulary is too difficult, you may need to teach some vocabulary and concepts before students can benefit from certain lecture activities.

Fourth, judge whether students can recognize and select important points from lectures or presentations. Can they follow the sequence of ideas? Do they understand organizational cues used during a lecture, such as *first, second, third, next,* and *then*? Teach students that important points are often introduced at the beginning of lectures and then explained and elaborated on separately after organizational cue statements.

Decide whether students recognize and know what certain types of statements given during lectures mean. For example, do they recognize transitional statements like "Moving right along now" or "One other important thing to remember is. . . ." are cues used by teachers to emphasize that certain information should be noted by students? Phrases such as "This is important," "This will be on the test," and "I want you to remember" are also cues for a listener. Finally, do students understand nonverbal cues used by teachers, such as silent long pauses, extra loud speech, or exaggerated hand movements? Role-playing or some other simple instructional practice on verbal and nonverbal cues enables students to become better listeners.

Teach Listening Skills

Some students require extra practice in learning how to listen (Gall et al., 1990). Use the teacher effectiveness variables discussed in chapter 6 and design some fun lessons in which students are motivated to learn to listen. Keep the activities short and try the following:

- Explain the purpose of a listening activity to students, present information, and have older students repeat what was presented in their own words. Have younger students act out the sequence of events.
- Model and demonstrate the use of keywords and phrases, such as *first, second, third,* and *next.*
- Have students identify any important phrases and ask them to tell you when they hear relevant sequences or specific details in the presentations.
- Demonstrate how certain verbal and nonverbal cues can highlight important information.
- Have students act out or tell their neighbors the listening cues they hear during a presentation.
- Give students cards containing cue words like *first* and *second* and direct them to raise the appropriate cards when they hear them.
- Use topics that are interesting and motivating and include favorite characters from shows, musicians, words from songs, or interviews with famous athletes.
- Give students advance organizers of talks and have them generate questions they would like answered about the upcoming talk.
- Give students several questions before the presentation and have them try to figure out answers to the questions during the talk.
- Ask students to relate the presentation to their own knowledge by asking them what else this talk reminded them of or what else they know about the topic.
- Give outlines or partially completed outlines and study guides to students before listening activities.
- Have students follow along and teach them to try to listen for "missing" information.
- Segment your presentation into three or four smaller parts. Stop after each segment and have students summarize the major points from each segment and summarize the entire presentation at the conclusion.

When practicing listening skills, emphasize how it is important to try to remember the most important information and the sequence of events. Have students generate questions to use as listening guides. For example, "What is the purpose of this lecture?" "What should I remember from this presentation?" These activities will prepare students for taking notes during lectures. There are, however, some ways you can adjust any lecture or use direct instruction for lower grade levels to effect better listening.

Adjust Lectures.
You can include simple techniques during lectures to help facilitate listening and note taking for students (Devine, 1987).

- Begin presentations by stating the overall objectives such as "Today I will be talking about a, b, and c."
- Include key words and emphasize their use during the presentations, saying in a louder voice, "This is *very* important," or "Here are the three major points," "Listen to this and see if you can _____," "There are five explanations for this event and they are. . . ."

Write key points on an overhead transparency or chalkboard while presenting.

- Adjust the pace of the presentation to accommodate students who are taking notes.
- Present schematic diagrams that explain complex concepts or use concrete manipulatives whenever possible to accompany verbal information.
- Stop frequently and encourage students to ask questions about the presented information and have them summarize the content to peers.
- Ask students to predict what a test on the material might include.
- Include "errors" in your talk and ask students to try to find the errors.

Finally, check with students with disabilities after class to see if they obtained the necessary content or if they have any questions. Schedule extra help sessions, office hours, or study sessions during which students can obtain extra assistance or clarification on information presented verbally in class.

Plan for Special Problems

Sometimes there are special problems encountered by students with disabilities during oral presentations (Deshler, Ellis, & Lenz, 1996). Some of these include the following:

- The pace of the presenter is too rapid.
- Amount of information given is too great.
- Students lack prior knowledge on the presentation topic.
- Language is too difficult.
- Students have difficulties processing and organizing information.

Some presenters speak too rapidly for students with disabilities or students learning English as a second language to comprehend. When this occurs, ask lecturers to slow down and write major points on an overhead projector or chalkboard while speaking. The act of writing while speaking may slow the rate of presentation sufficiently for students. It is appropriate to ask presenters to repeat information to provide an additional opportunity for students to hear the same information. Tape-record important presentations that are presented rapidly, place recorded tapes on reserve or at a listening center, and encourage students to listen again to tapes for review. If variable speed tape recorders are available, students can play tapes at a comfortable speed for themselves.

See chapter 15 for a sample vocabulary check sheet.

The following scenario describes what Mrs. Goodwin does to help her students with disabilities become more familiar with new vocabulary in their general education classes.

CLASSROOM SCENARIO

Mrs. Goodwin

Mrs. Goodwin, a special education teacher, provides all her elementary students with lists of vocabulary that will be covered in future units. She passes the lists out a couple of weeks before the unit is introduced. Every student reads the words to her and to individual parents daily. This familiarizes students with upcoming vocabulary so when they hear the words in general education classes they are familiar with them. This often puts students with special needs one jump ahead of general education students and thus builds self-esteem for students with disabilities in their general education setting. The general education teachers tell Mrs. Goodwin that because of this extra practice students with disabilities are better able to keep up with classwork on the new units. Students also seem to enjoy using the vocabulary lists.

Finally, some students have severe processing and organizing difficulties during listening activities. These students may require oral information to be repeated slowly before they are able to comprehend it. Assistance from special education teachers and speech and language specialists can provide students extra review and practice on the information covered. Also, enlist the help of peer assistants, siblings, and parents to provide additional review and practice at home. Don't forget to use

Good note-taking skills are essential for school success.

the PASS variables to determine whether all information presented is essential for all students. When these lessons are adapted, some of the information may be eliminated for these special students.

Note Taking

Define the Purpose

Note taking provides students with a greater depth of processing of information presented orally (Gall et al., 1990). Notes also can be used to review information presented orally (Devine, 1987). Note-taking skills become increasingly important as grade levels increase (Deshler, Ellis, & Lenz, 1996)—secondary teachers expect students to have good note-taking skills. However, many students are never taught how to take good notes and can benefit from instruction on effective note taking. Several important skills are critical for successful note taking and are listed in the teacher checklist in Figure 11.7. Determine which skills students need help with and teach them. After that, your students will be ready for some note-taking instruction.

Teach Note-Taking Skills and Strategies

Several strategies can be explicitly taught to students to help them become better note takers (Gall et al., 1990). Teach students that the purpose of notes is to facilitate recall and comprehension of information presented during lectures, so notes can and should be used to review. Going over notes regularly, and particularly just before an exam, can increase a student's chances for success.

Be Prepared. Helping students learn how they can be prepared to take notes will promote more self-sufficiency. Be sure they have the right type of paper and pencils or pens to take notes. Encourage students to select the type of paper or pen that is best for them. As long as the notes are legible and organized, the type of paper and color of pen is irrelevant. In fact, allowing students to select their own writing materials may help motivate them during note-taking activities.

Teach How to Write Short Summaries. Showing students how to write summary ideas rather than entire sentences assists them in becoming better note takers. Demonstrate with examples of good notes and poor notes. Good notes contain major ideas in students' own words and can be used for studying. Poor notes contain lots of unnecessary words such as *the, and,* or *but;* or entire verbatim sentences. These practices may make it much more difficult to take notes efficiently.

Ask Questions for Clarification. Encouraging students to ask you to repeat information or clarify the major purpose of lessons helps you monitor whether they know what to write in their notes. A good way to start is to have students ask what the purpose of the lecture is. You can facilitate this

Does the student have:

_____ Listening skills

_____ Handwriting skills

      _____ Is the student's handwriting legible?

      _____ Can the student write rapidly enough?

_____ Keyboarding skills?

      _____ Can the student type fast enough?

      _____ Are computers and power sources readily available?

Can the student:

      _____ Determine the purpose of lectures?

      _____ Determine a plan of organization for notes?

      _____ Summarize and relate main ideas?

      _____ Write down main points?

      _____ Use abbreviations?

Does the student:

      _____ Read and revise notes?

      _____ Study notes?

Figure 11.7
Checklist for Prerequisite Skills for Note Taking

For Websites devoted to study skills, go to the Web Links module in chapter 11 of the Companion Website.

process by explicitly stating the purpose of the lecture and describing an overall plan of organization before beginning a lecture.

Teach Abbreviations. Using abbreviations reduces the amount of writing and increases the speed of note taking. Some students may be unaware that it is acceptable to use lots of abbreviations as long as they remember what the abbreviations represent. Teach commonly used abbreviations and have students generate a listing of words and possible abbreviations. For example, "w/" for *with;* "MD" for *doctor;* "<" for *less than;* and "ave." for *average* can be taught and are fairly easy to decipher later. Design practice activities containing common abbreviations and have students practice using and interpreting the abbreviations.

Use Specific Formats for Note Taking. Different note-taking formats are conducive to making notes for certain kinds of topics. Horton, Lovitt, and Christensen (1991) reported that particular column formats helped students perform better in class. Depending on the subject areas in which you teach you may choose a particular format and encourage students to use it consistently. Distribute blank sheets containing the format, explain how it works, and why you consider it an effective note-taking format. Figure 11.8 displays a note-taking format that you might consider. Show students the importance of leaving spaces in their notes for additions or changes after the lecture. For example, after reviewing notes, it may be necessary to add corrections and provide more detailed information in the remaining space in the left margin. Some students prefer to write notes on every other line, which is, of course, another means of providing extra space for later additions or corrections.

Supplying guided notes to students helps decrease the amount of writing and increase the focus on major ideas. Guided notes are similar to partial outlines, but usually contain more spaces for students to fill in important details during the lectures (Carman & Adams, 1984). Some teachers have students complete guided notes or partial outlines together as a class activity to ensure that students are obtaining critical information from lectures. Guided notes are especially beneficial for topics that contain a great deal of new vocabulary and concepts. Figures 11.9 and 11.10 contain examples of partial outlines and guided notes.

Class	Date
New Information	Questions or Comments

Figure 11.8
Sample Note-Taking Format

Class: <u>Social Studies</u>   Topic: <u>Products of Indiana</u>   Date: 4/1

Major Ideas	Details	Questions
Agriculture	**Major Crops:** <u>Corn</u>	**Where within the state are the various crops grown?**
Industry	**Major Industries** <u>Steel</u>	**What are the products of the major industries?** **Where are the major industrial areas located and why?**

Figure 11.9
Guided Notes

Teach Speed and Accuracy Techniques. Start by demonstrating what good note takers do. Have students share the ways they take notes. For example, some students never erase mistakes in their notes, they simply draw a single line through errors. Erasing takes valuable time from listening and note-taking activities. Encouraging students to develop methods and strategies with which they feel comfortable will help them be more effective. Students are more likely to use note-taking strategies they like than ones imposed on them, especially if the student-developed techniques are just as effective as those provided by teachers.

Teach Students How to Study Using Notes. Don't forget to show students what to do with their notes. Many students take notes, close their notebooks after class, and never look at them again. Direct students to review notes after each class and make any corrections or clarifications.

Initially, provide many of the elements of the partial outline for your students.
As students learn the format you can leave more elements blank.

ARTHROPODS

I. What is an arthropod?
   A. *Largest phylum of animals*
   B. *More than ¾ of all animals*

II. Characteristics of arthropods.
   A. Jointed legs
   B. *Exoskeleton*
   C. *Special heart and blood*

III. Types of arthropods
   A. Crustaceans
      1. *Crabs*
      2. *Lobsters*
   B. Insects
      1. *Beetles*
      2.
      3.
   C. Centipedes
   D. Millipedes

Figure 11.10
Partial Outline

They should also jot down questions they may have to clarify later. Show students how they can use "sticky notes" to attach to various pages in their notes to remind them of places for questions. Sometimes use of gimmicks such as brightly colored sticky notes enhances motivation for reviewing notes. Distribute fancy sticky notes as rewards for note takers who try hard.

Finally, teach students how to study using their notes by helping them identify the most important information to study. Then show them how to generate study strategies to facilitate recall and understanding of that important information (Meltzer et al., 1996). Demonstrate strategies to help them remember information in their notes. Explain how they can use their notes to supplement their textbooks when studying for exams.

> Teach students test-taking strategies to enhance their performance on exams as described in chapter 12 and memory strategies as described in chapter 10.

The LINKS Strategy. Four note-taking strategies were developed by researchers to teach students to use cues from teachers to record only the most relevant information from lectures. The LINKS strategy stands for **L**isten, **I**dentify verbal cues, **N**ote **K**ey words, and **S**tack information into outline format (Deshler, Schumaker, Alley, Clark, & Warner, 1981). The first two steps encourage students to listen for teacher cues during the lecture. These teacher cues include *organizational cues* (e.g., "Now we will talk about. . . "), *emphasis cues—verbal* (e.g., "Now listen carefully to this. . . "), and *emphasis cues—nonverbal* (e.g., stress, volume, or pace of speaking). When students identify a cue, they are taught to make a circle (a *"link for listening"*) on the left margin of their paper. Then they are taught to note *key words* following each cue, writing notes in telegraphic style, including the following:

1. Write words, not complete sentences.
2. Abbreviate words.
3. Do not use any punctuation.
4. Draw a line through an error rather than erase.
5. Allow extra space to add more information.
6. Use synonyms. (Suritsky & Hughes, 1996, pp. 305–306)

The LINKS strategy teaches students to use a two-column format for taking notes. The main ideas go on the left side column (e.g., names of important people, places, or things) and supporting details (important attributes or characteristics) go on the right side column.

The AWARE Strategy. The AWARE strategy was developed for college students with learning disabilities, but can be adapted for students in secondary settings (Suritsky & Hughes, 1993). The five steps in AWARE are the following:

1. *A*rrange to take notes

   Arrive early
   Take seat near front/center
   Obtain pen/notebook
   Make note of date

2. *W*rite quickly

   Indent minor points
   Record some words without vowels
   Use common abbreviations
   Note personal examples

3. *A*pply cues

   Attend to accent and organization verbal cues
   Record cued lecture ideas
   Make a checkmark before cued ideas

4. *R*eview notes as soon as possible

5. *E*dit notes

   Add information you forgot to include
   Add personal details (Suritsky & Hughes, 1996, p. 308).

The AWARE strategy can easily be adapted for students in secondary schools. You might try this strategy in your college courses so you can teach it to students. Provide opportunities to review and offer feedback during the initial phases of instruction.

The Three and Five R's Strategies. Two additional note-taking strategies include three or five steps that all begin with the letter "R" (Alley & Deshler, 1979; Pauk, 1987). Both of these strategies combine ideas for taking and studying notes. The steps in the three-R strategy involve *reviewing, reading,* and *relating:* (a) *review* previous lecture notes and materials before class, (b) *read* the materials for class before class, and (c) *relate* the lecture topics to other known information. Teachers can practice with students how to choose and select appropriate materials to review before class, using class materials as examples (e.g., "What would be important to review before the next class?"). Strategies for reading class assignments can also be practiced (e.g., skim the entire reading assignment; read the assignment carefully, highlighting or taking notes; summarize what you have read and ask yourself questions about the material). When the lecture is presented, teachers can practice how students can relate the current material with other known information (e.g., "How does the voyage of Vasco da Gama remind you of Columbus' voyages?").

The five-R strategy is similar but includes more after-lecture studying hints. The first step is *record* important facts and details. The second step is *reduce* the notes to short phrases. The third step is *recite* the important information in your own words. The fourth step is *reflect* on the notes and add any information to them. The final step is *review* all notes and information. One helpful way for students to practice this strategy is in pairs or cooperative groups where students compare notes, and recite, reflect on, and review their notes with each other.

Any of these note-taking strategies can help students. Select a strategy, teach it, and monitor its effectiveness. Some students may develop a preference for one strategy over another. Encourage students to use the strategy that maximizes their performance.

Address Special Problems

Some students may experience great difficulties with note taking, in spite of attempts to teach all skills to make students successful. Table 11.1 lists some special problems that may be encountered by students when trying to take notes. The following ideas may help students overcome some of those problems.

- Encourage students to develop a format for taking notes with which they feel comfortable.
- Writing on every other line of the paper or only on one side or leaving a column blank seems to help many students.

Table 11.1

Special Problems with Note-Taking and Possible Adaptations

Note-Taking Problem	Possible Solutions
Note-taker is too slow	• Provide basic outline as handout • Model outlining on blackboard • Use overhead transparencies during lectures • Copy overhead transparencies for students
Legibility	• Show how illegibility can affect value of notes • Model "shorthand" and abbreviations • Provide a variety of paper and pens
Deciding what to write	• Organize lecture logically • Write key points on board or overhead as you lecture • Provide guided notes as handouts for students
Deciding how to organize	• Provide a note-taking format • Teach a particular note-taking strategy that suits your class
Learning how to use notes	• Show how to review, correct, and elaborate on notes • Model how to use notes for studying • Schedule time for reviewing notes during class

- Make sure students date each new lecture and page of notes so they can go back and request specific assistance with particular lectures.
- Tell students to write blank lines in their notes when they know they have missed something important. They can later request assistance from the teacher or a peer to fill in the missing information.
- Encourage the use of tape recorders during lectures so students can listen to the lectures again later.
- Assign peer assistants who can duplicate their notes for students experiencing great difficulties taking notes independently.

Finally, provide sufficient practice and feedback during note-taking activities so students with special needs gain sufficient confidence to take notes and to use their notes to help them study.

Research and Reference Skills

Although many general education students possess adequate knowledge of library and researching skills, students with special needs benefit from explicit instruction, practice, and feedback on the process (Hoover, 1993). Students need to know how to use reference materials including reference books, indexes (e.g., periodical guides), computerized catalogs, computerized literature searches, computerized searches of encyclopedias, and use of **search engines** on the **World Wide Web**. You can increase your students' motivation for these activities by always encouraging students to ask questions and to search for the answers. Statements like "That's an excellent question!" "What is a question we'd like to find the answer for?" and "How can we find the answer?" will show your students you value lifelong learning, library, and research skills.

Teach Library Skills

To get students started, provide maps of the interior of libraries that indicate where various sources are located, including the reference librarians. Arrange meetings with reference librarians so students become familiar with them and feel comfortable asking for assistance. Librarians can schedule special instructional sessions for classes and often will meet with smaller groups of students with special needs to provide extra guidance and practice searching the library. Arrange to have special educators work with librarians to devise specialized training sessions for students with disabilities.

Reference Books

Familiarizing your students with the reference materials available in the school and public libraries can be made into a motivating activity by challenging teams of students to locate topics within all available sources. Typical materials include dictionaries, encyclopedias, biographical sources, almanacs, and various specific guidebooks, such as medical guides or natural history guides. Most reference materials are located together in libraries and usually cannot be checked out. Because materials are shelved in alphabetical order, practice or reference sheets containing the alphabet may be necessary for younger students who have difficulty recalling alphabetical order. Summary guides listing reference books, types of information, and locations can serve as library guides for students. Setting up practice activities during which students are required to locate different pieces of information benefits all students. These activities can be exciting by arranging practice as part of a scavenger hunt game. Grouping students into scavenger hunt teams will help inspire them, perhaps demonstrating how much fun it is to "find" new information.

Databases

Many students will benefit from instruction on reference databases. Available databases may vary depending on whether the library is housed at an elementary, middle, or secondary school. High schools may have many more databases available than elementary schools. One very useful resource is ProQuest®, which contains Periodical Abstracts in periodical, scientific (peer-reviewed), and newspaper databases. By clicking on the appropriate source (e.g., children's, humanities, general interest), students can search for relevant articles in a variety of areas. ProQuest will provide the reference information (e.g., magazine title, issue number, date), and an abstract (brief summary) of all articles relevant to the topic entered in by the student. Such databases are not difficult to use, although basic familiarity with computer screens and use of the mouse is necessary to use them unassisted. The school librarian can provide specific information on the availability of various databases and how they can be used. Provide explicit practice with students with special needs, when necessary. Students should be able to locate relevant articles, copy down (or print out) identifying information, and know how to use this information to locate the articles. You can create library search activities, where you assign students in pairs or small groups to locate specific articles and identify where they can be found. If students learn to function independently with these skills, they will be able to write more thorough and informative research papers.

Library Catalogs

Library searches are quick and easy with today's computerized catalogs, but familiarity with particular computer systems is necessary. Searches can be completed by authors, titles, and subject areas, and searches can be completed on books, multimedia materials, and various databases of journals by topical area. Resulting search information is displayed and can be printed out or copied by hand.

Search results contain several important pieces of information. First, Library of Congress or Dewey Decimal System call numbers of books are identified, along with author and publication information of publishers, year, and city of publication. Longer formats are usually available and display abstracts of the materials. Model how reading abstracts and other displayed information helps students decide whether those materials should be included in their search. If materials appear relevant, students can either print the screen information, copy it, or save it to a disk, and then locate the book in the library using the call number. Give your students self-monitoring sheets containing reminders about what information they should keep for looking up materials and for their reference lists.

Searching by author or title can be simpler than searching by topic. A title or author's name will yield all sources containing that title or name. Searching by subject topic is a little more complex and guidance may be necessary to help narrow the descriptors. For example, if students select a broad descriptor like "pollution," several thousand entries might appear. Guide students in narrowing descriptors to focus their search efforts to a more restricted topic that yields a more realistic number of books or articles for them to scan. Divide the topic into smaller subtopics, such as air pollution, groundwater pollution, waste disposal, and agricultural pollution. The resulting search will then be narrower and more focused on the student's interest area.

Making informed decisions about which entries should be examined more closely can be difficult. The selection process requires critical thinking and students may need assistance focusing their thinking. Teach students to group potential sources into three categories: "Yes, definitely keep," "Maybe, look further and decide," and "No, do not keep." Model using relevant examples and ask students to assist you in making decisions about relevancy for various topics. Sample abstracts and topics can be distributed to pairs of students who can be asked to justify where the abstracts go. Finally, let students independently sort abstracts into three categories. Be sure to review what they do to verify that they understand the process.

The next step is to obtain the "yes" and "maybe" materials and determine if they should be included. If students do not do this component of the task well, they may experience great difficulties completing the remaining steps of the project. Some of your students with disabilities may have difficulty with this component because it relies on reading and thinking skills. Model some samples for the class by speaking aloud the "thinking" you use for inclusion and exclusion of sources. Say, for example, "I will keep this abstract on the hazards of using too much fertilizer because it sounds as if it fits with my topic of agricultural pollution. But I will discard this article on toxic dumps because it doesn't seem to be closely enough related to agricultural pollution." You can divide students into small groups for practicing this task and require students to defend verbally their reasons for including or excluding abstracts.

Computerized Literature Searches

Students need to become proficient at completing literature searches using computers. Similar procedures are used as in searching libraries for materials, but more specialized knowledge of each database is beneficial. Practice selecting descriptors by asking students to write the number of entries appearing for various descriptors. Practicing with narrowing descriptors is a good way to engage students in gaining the confidence they will need to do successful searches. Require students to practice reading the search results and pinpointing relevant sources. Don't forget to show students how to print, download, and save search results.

Computerized Searches of Encyclopedias. Many schools, in addition to many home computers, have encyclopedias on CD or online encyclopedia access. Model and demonstrate how students can search these encyclopedias using computers. Some entries have oral output accompanying them and are excellent resources for students with reading difficulties. Most CD or online encyclopedias are multimedia; contain video, audio, and printed entries; and are ideally suited for students with reading difficulties.

Use of Search Engines on the World Wide Web. So much information can be accessed via the **Internet** that students should become practiced in these search procedures as well. Most libraries have online access with numerous search engines to help students locate information on the Web. Become comfortable using computers and searching the Web, so you will feel confident showing your students how to access the wealth of knowledge on the Internet.

Plan for Special Problems

Because most information in libraries is accessed using alphabetical order, some students, especially those with more severe reading difficulties, may first require instruction in alphabetizing. Students with more severe disabilities may require assistance when having to rely on reading to find information (Scheid, 1993). However, school libraries also hold "higher interest, but low vocabulary" materials that may prove appropriate for students with lower reading levels. Audiovisual materials may be especially helpful for students with low reading levels. Assist these students in locating those materials and teach them how to use the video players, film projectors, computers, and other equipment necessary to access multimedia materials. Many computerized programs now have verbal presentations that accompany the visual displays on screens. These may be more ideally suited as reference materials for students with reading difficulties. It may also be necessary to establish a buddy system in which students with more severe disabilities are paired with peers who can accompany them to the library and assist with locating materials and even reading materials to them if necessary. These activities are also golden opportunities for increasing peer interactions by pairing students with and without disabilities on projects.

Help Students Prepare Reports and Projects

Assignments that involve writing papers are usually very challenging for students with disabilities as well as for other students in your classroom (Gall et al., 1990). This writing process can be taught directly by practicing some of the subskills involved in writing a report. Gall et al. (1990) list skills

For Websites for search engines, go to the Web Links module in chapter 11 of the Companion Website.

of planning, reading, thinking, organizing, and writing as all required for successful report writing. A checklist for collecting reference information, and a checklist for study skills for writing a school paper are provided in the *In the Classroom . . . for sharing with students* feature in the Companion Website.

Define the Writing Task

In defining the writing task, Gall et al. (1990) emphasize that it is important to explain the following:

- Purpose of the writing assignment
- Audience for the assignment
- Format for the paper both in terms of substance (book report, poem, short story, newspaper article, research report, other) and style (typewritten, handwritten, paper)
- Required length in pages and in scope and detail
- Date the assignment is due

This is also the time for students to estimate how long each step in the process will take and begin to plan a schedule for completing each step. Some of the steps may require additional subdividing. Have students record steps and due dates in their calendars. Finally, students can begin to work on the project according to their time schedule.

Select Topic.

Many students have difficulties selecting topics for their papers. Provide examples of topics that appear motivating and interesting to students, but that are manageable in scope. This allows students to either select their own idea, select one from the list, or adapt an idea from the provided list of acceptable alternatives. Students will be more likely to enjoy the paper if it covers a topic of interest to them. Help students focus their paper by providing sample topic sentences like, "This paper is intended to. . . ."

1. Make comparisons between _____ and _____.
2. Show the development of _____.
3. Evaluate and criticize _____.
4. Analyze why _____ happened.
5. Explore the consequences of _____. (Gall et al., 1990, p. 151)

You can give younger students interesting pictures from which paper topics can be selected and developed. For example, photographs of animals, space travel, nature scenes, and race cars might seem particularly appealing to some students. Similar directions can then be provided such that students are asked to compare sea lions with lions. You can also give self-monitoring sheets that contain similarities and differences such as "Did I include how my animals are similar or different in. . . .

- size
- color
- fur
- habitat
- intelligence
- feeding habits?"

Provide sample papers that address each purpose as models for students to see how the papers are constructed to answer the intended purpose. Maintain model papers from previous classes and put on reserve in the library. Seeing completed models helps students visualize the final product.

Develop a Writing Plan

The development of a writing plan is crucial for students. This component requires additional subdividing: Will books be needed from the library? Will reading and taking notes from those books be required? Will students need to interview experts on the topic? Will visits to museums be necessary? This plan will vary depending on the topic and purpose of the assignment.

Show students sample writing plans from different types of written projects. Again, model the development of plans during instruction. Have students complete partially developed plans before

The writing process might begin with the student creating a writing plan. Corrective guidance and feedback for this plan can build the student's confidence and motivation.

attempting to complete plans independently. Taking time to do this is almost more valuable than the writing project itself. These study skills exercises help most students learn how to become more proficient at writing tasks.

During the actual writing of assignments, have students bring in their plans for guidance and corrective feedback from you. This will ensure that the end products are in line with your expectations. This is also when to estimate the amount of time it may take to complete each step in the writing process and to revise the schedule for the entire project as necessary. Be sure to show students how it is best to allow some lead time near the end of their projected completion date in case some components consume more time than anticipated to finish.

Brainstorm Ideas

Once the writing topic has been selected, students need to brainstorm ideas of details that can be written about for that topic. Model how during the brainstorming process all ideas are written down and allow students opportunities to practice the brainstorming component. Then demonstrate how those ideas are evaluated later for relevancy and determinations are made as to whether to include them within the paper. After that, the relevant ideas are listed in order of importance for the project.

Find and Collect Information

Lead students to collect and find the necessary information for writing their papers. Students may use the library, World Wide Web, other reference materials, or interviews, depending on the paper topic and format required. Demonstrate how to find and collect information. The process of collecting information can be mysterious to students who have never completed projects independently before.

Organize Ideas and Information

At this stage students may write a more detailed outline for their paper. Notes from the obtained information can be included in the outline. Traditional outlines may or may not be used, but be sure to model how some organizational framework facilitates the organization of the paper and assists students in completing the written product. Some formats may consist of titles, main ideas, with supporting details under each main idea, and summary and conclusion sections. One key factor is to show students how to use the major purpose of the paper to guide the major subheadings for the paper.

In addition, show students how to take notes on index cards. Each card can be labeled with the name of the reference and contains major ideas from the material. Note cards can be kept in small boxes or held together with a rubber band. Later, those cards containing written summaries of major ideas from each of the references can be reorganized into any outline format and used to help students generate the first draft. The note cards are beneficial in helping students follow the sequence of information to organize the paper.

Write Draft of Paper

After completing the organizational outline or format, have students write the first draft of their paper. It should be relatively easy to write a first draft if note cards containing major points and outlines are used. Each organizational heading becomes a major section of the draft and students put that information into sentences in their own words. Then elaborations are added to those main ideas and details to complete the rough draft. At this point or earlier, you may need to explain why copying articles is illegal and called plagiarism, and explain how you want your students to cite the information they are using for their papers. This may be especially important if students are downloading complete documents from the Internet.

Obtain Feedback on Draft

Encourage students to obtain feedback from someone on their first drafts. The feedback provides them with information about what needs to be revised before completing their final versions. Teachers, parents, siblings, and peers can all be asked for feedback on draft versions.

Revise and Rewrite

Students should then incorporate the feedback into the revision of their draft. Explain to students how a revision process may involve several changes to their draft. This also helps students see where they are missing some information and thus require further research. One revision might involve augmenting content ideas with more information. Another revision might include altering the organizational framework based on feedback. Another revision may involve altering the overall format. Most revisions require grammatical, syntactical, semantic, and punctuation changes to improve the paper.

Proof and Edit Final Version

Even though you will probably hear your students groan, explain to them how important it is to edit the paper one more time. It is during this final editing and proofing stage, however, that additional errors are often detected. This may also be the time at which many students might give the paper to someone else to type for them. The Research Highlight describes one proofreading strategy using computers. An example checklist for writing a paper is provided in the *In the Classroom. . . for sharing with students* feature in the Companion Website.

If students have access to word processors, the entire writing process can be modified. See chapter 13 for information on using word processors to complete writing assignments.

Teach the Entire Process

Writing papers or completing independent projects is difficult for many students, but critical for success in secondary schools and higher education. Without instruction in the entire process of writing papers and completing independent projects, many students may fail to achieve in this important area. However, by providing extra instruction in the process of writing, students may be better prepared to write papers, and will be more likely to be successful in school.

The INSPECT Proofreading Strategy with Computers

McNaughton, Hughes, and Ofiesh (1997) taught high school students with learning disabilities a five-step proofreading strategy, called INSPECT:

The INSPECT Strategy

In your document,

1. **S**tart the speller checker,
   a. Place the cursor at the start of the text
   b. Under the "Tools" heading, select "Spelling"

2. **P**ick the correct alternatives
   a. Read the adjacent text to determine target vocabulary items
   b. Wait for all alternatives to appear
   c. Review all alternatives
   d. Look at the beginning and end of the alternatives
   e. Double-click on target

3. **E**liminate unrecognizable words
   a. Correct typos
   b. Write out parts of the word that are known
   c. Spell word phonetically
   d. Use * for unknown sections of the word
   e. Use a synonym

4. **C**orrect additional errors
   a. Print a copy of text
   b. Read from end, look for "wrong words,"—look at beginning and end of word
   c. Read from beginning, look for subject-verb agreement—slow down and focus on each sentence

5. **T**ype in your corrections
   a. Type in your corrections
   b. Run spelling checker
   c. Print final copy

Initially, the strategy was described, modeled, and practiced using investigator- and student-developed materials. During instruction the steps of the strategy were placed on charts in front of the students. Later students were asked to apply the strategy to their writing. Results indicated that all students increased their strategy usage, had few spelling errors on their written papers, and saw the value of using the strategy. Moreover, the number of spelling errors was similar to the number of spelling errors made by students without disabilities at the end of the intervention.

Note: From "Proofreading for Students with Learning Disabilities: Integrating Computer and Strategy Use," by D. McNaughton, C. Hughes, & N. Ofiesh, 1997, *Learning Disabilities Research & Practice, 12,* p. 20. Copyright 1997 by Lawrence Erlbaum Associates. Reprinted with permission. For more information, see Deshler, Ellis, and Lenz (1996).

Questions for Reflection

1. How could this strategy be adapted for different word processing programs?
2. How could this strategy be adapted for use without computers?
3. How could you evaluate the effectiveness of this strategy with your own students?
4. Could you create a similar strategy for use of grammar checkers?

Companion Website

To answer these questions online, go to the Research Highlights feature in chapter 11 of the Companion Website.

Technology Highlight

Inspiration and Kidspiration Software

Spatial organizers help make content more concrete and more familiar to students when studying various content areas. Graphic organizers can be used in almost any content area. Organizers can be used to teach sequence of events, cause-and-effect relationships, to compare and contrast ideas or concepts, or to illustrate hierarchies. Organizers can be used as story webs during the brainstorming phase of writing papers. Graphic organizers can be developed as story maps that include specific details to facilitate comprehension and learning about characters, plots, major events, and story themes. Organizers can be used to develop hierarchies of important-to-least-important content in science and social studies. Graphic organizers can also be used to design study guides to accompany content area textbooks.

Organizers can take many forms. Inspiration and Kidspiration software provide assistance in developing graphic organizers, webs, brainstorming, diagramming, outlining, and prewriting strategies. Both programs contain numerous templates that can be adapted to suit needs, but also offer the flexibility to allow users to create custom-made templates and designs. Directions for developing organizers appear fairly clear, and students who have some facility with computer use and various software programs typically experience little difficulty in developing organizers independently.

Both Inspiration and Kidspiration have extensive graphics' libraries that can be integrated within diagrams to help make the information even more concrete and meaningful to students. Libraries of content areas, such as animals, foods, shapes, or plants, organize colored graphics. Users can also import graphics of their own from personal photos or from the Internet into Inspiration documents. The technology also offers a wide range of fonts and colors that can be changed during production of an organizer. Various fonts and colors can be used to highlight specific organized details within a single graphic organizer. Both programs have features that enable users to switch from diagrams to outlines and vice versa very easily and are printable in either format. Kidspiration has the unique feature of adding sound to the program such that words entered into the organizers can be "read aloud" for students. Both also have features that allow the versions to be saved into word documents or, as mentioned earlier in the chapter 3 Integrating technology feature, have applets that can be used with AlphaSmarts and then combined with the full-scale programs on computers.

Inspiration is listed as being appropriate from grades 6 through 12, while Kidspiration is appropriate for K–5. However, both may be adaptable up or down in grade levels depending on the individual ability levels of your students. Sample organizers from each are provided. Contact *http://www.inspiration.com* for additional information. A 30-day free trial version is available to be downloaded from the Website. Refer to the chapter 11 Companion Website for links to Web casts describing how to use Inspiration software (*http://www.techmentor.org/webcasts.html*) and to other graphic organizer sites. See chapter 13 for an example of Inspiration software.

Summary

- Students with disabilities and those at risk for failure in school benefit from explicit instruction and practice in study skills.
- Personal organization skills, such as knowing about class times and schedules, using assignment notebooks and monthly planners, and organizing homework are important for success in school and can be effectively taught to students with special needs.
- Direct teaching of listening skills helps students with special needs be prepared to learn information presented orally in school.
- Teaching students ways to take notes, including writing short summaries, abbreviations, using specific note-taking formats, and specific note-taking strategies, facilitates learning from lectures and presentations.

- Practice and instruction using the library, including use of reference materials, indices, computerized literature searches, use of the World Wide Web, and use of Internet search engines, assists students with special needs in learning how to search for and locate resources for schoolwork.
- Direct instruction on how to write a research paper, including selecting topics, searching for information, organizing information, writing and editing first drafts, and preparing final versions is essential for most students with special needs. The technology feature provides one way to help students with these writing tasks.

Council for
Exceptional
Children

Teaching Study Skills

Information in this chapter links most directly to:

Standard 4—Instructional Strategies, particularly:

Skills:
- Use strategies to facilitate integration into various settings.
- Teach individuals to use self-assessment, problem solving, and other cognitive strategies to meet their needs.
- Select, adapt, and use instructional strategies and materials according to characteristics of the individual with exceptional learning needs.
- Use strategies to facilitate maintenance and generalization of skills across learning environments.

Standard 7—Instructional Planning

Knowledge:
- Theories and research that form the basis of curriculum development and instructional practice.
- Scope and sequences for general and special curricula.

- National, state or provincial, and local curricula standards.
- Technology for planning and managing the teaching and learning environment.

Skills:
- Identify and prioritize areas of the general curriculum and accommodations for individuals with exceptional learning needs.
- Develop and implement comprehensive, longitudinal individualized programs in collaboration with team members.
- Use task analysis.
- Sequence, implement, and evaluate individualized learning objectives.
- Incorporate and implement instructional and assistive technology into the educational program.
- Prepare and organize materials to implement daily lesson plans.
- Use instructional time effectively.
- Make responsive adjustments to instruction based on continual observations.

✓ Inclusion Checklist
Teaching Study Skills

If the student is having difficulty in study skills and test-taking skills, have you tried specific strategies for teaching:

- ❏ Personal organizational skills, such as:
  - ❏ Class and time schedules
  - ❏ Daily, weekly, monthly planners, and planning
  - ❏ Task analysis
  - ❏ Homework
  - ❏ Special problems
- ❏ Listening skills, such as:
  - ❏ Prerequisite skills, including:
    - ❏ Hearing the speaker
    - ❏ Attending to the speaker
    - ❏ Understanding the speaker
    - ❏ Understanding the vocabulary
    - ❏ Recognizing and selecting important points
    - ❏ Following the sequence of ideas
    - ❏ Understanding organizational cues (*first, then*)
    - ❏ Attending to transitional statements
    - ❏ Understanding verbal emphasis cues ("This is important.")
    - ❏ Understanding nonverbal cues (extra loud speech)
  - ❏ Teach listening skills, including:
    - ❏ Provide listening activities
    - ❏ Adjust lectures
  - ❏ Special problems, such as:
    - ❏ Lack of attention to speaker (coming, maintaining, vigilance)
    - ❏ Unable to hear the speaker
    - ❏ Pace of presenter is too rapid
    - ❏ Amount of information is too great
    - ❏ Lack of prior knowledge on topic
    - ❏ Language is too difficult
    - ❏ Processing and organizing difficulties
- ❏ Note-taking skills, such as:
  - ❏ Prerequisite skills, including the following:
    - ❏ Listening skills
    - ❏ Handwriting (legibility and speed)
    - ❏ Spelling skills
  - ❏ Note-taking adaptations, including the following:
    - ❏ Provide outlines
    - ❏ Provide copies of notes
    - ❏ Keyboarding (laptop) skills
    - ❏ Provide guided notes
  - ❏ Note-taking skills and strategies, including the following:
    - ❏ Be prepared
    - ❏ How to write short summaries
    - ❏ Ask questions for clarification
    - ❏ Using abbreviations
    - ❏ Choose the right format for note-taking
    - ❏ Speed and accuracy techniques
    - ❏ How to study using notes
    - ❏ The LINKS strategy
    - ❏ The AWARE strategy
    - ❏ The three-R and five-R strategies
  - ❏ Special problems, including the following:
    - ❏ Speed of writing
    - ❏ Legibility of writing
    - ❏ Deciding what to write
    - ❏ Organizing paper and notes
    - ❏ Making sense of notes later
    - ❏ Incomplete notes
    - ❏ Knowing what to do with notes
    - ❏ Modifying notes later
    - ❏ Studying notes
- ❏ Library skills, such as the following:
  - ❏ Reference books
  - ❏ Indices
  - ❏ Card catalogs via computers
  - ❏ Computerized literature searches
  - ❏ Computerized searches of encyclopedias
  - ❏ Use of search engines on the World Wide Web
  - ❏ Special problems
- ❏ Writing a report and independent projects, such as the following:
  - ❏ Define the writing task
  - ❏ Select topic
  - ❏ Develop writing plan
  - ❏ Brainstorm ideas
  - ❏ Find and collect information
  - ❏ Organize ideas and information
  - ❏ Write draft of paper
  - ❏ Obtain feedback on draft
  - ❏ Revise and rewrite
  - ❏ Proof and edit final version

Chapter 12

Chauncey Jones, 9
Columbus, OH
"Indian Bird"

Assessment

Objectives

After studying this chapter, you should be able to:

- Describe the use of norm-referenced tests, competency-based assessments, and teacher-made and criterion-referenced tests in inclusive settings.
- Identify and implement strategies to modify test formats to meet the needs of students with disabilities.
- Compare and contrast curriculum-based measurement, performance assessment, and portfolio assessments and their applications for students with special needs.
- Describe specific test-taking strategies for taking standardized tests, and how these strategies can be taught.
- Design and implement strategies for taking teacher-made tests such as multiple-choice, true-false, matching, and essay tests.
- Identify procedures and rationales for modifying grading and scoring of tests for students with special needs.

Tests are a significant component of education because they provide information relevant to placement, instruction, and future career decisions. Tests are also being used increasingly to evaluate the performance of schools. Tests, however, must be administered appropriately and interpreted correctly, or they can do more harm than good. Teachers should be aware of different types of tests, the purposes they serve, how they can be used, and how they can be interpreted. Skills for maximizing test performance and modifications to accommodate students with special needs are also necessary.

Types of Tests

In education, many different tests address many different, specific needs. One type of test is no "better" than another, because different tests serve different purposes. As a teacher, it is critical to understand what information specific tests provide, and what information they do not provide.

All educational testing serves to compare performance with some type of standard (Howell & Morehead, 1987). One major distinction made in testing is between **norm-referenced** and **criterion-referenced** testing. In norm-referenced testing, student performance is compared with the performance of other students. Students receive scores such as "85th percentile," which means that the student scored higher than 85% of other students on that particular test. In criterion-referenced testing, student performance is compared to specified criteria, usually considered as meeting minimal competency. A written test for a driver's license, in which individuals either pass or fail to meet a certain criterion, is a good example of a criterion-referenced test.

CLASSROOM SCENARIO

Nate

Mr. Montoya saw Nate in his middle-school resource room for 45 minutes per day. Although much of the time was devoted to basic skills development, Mr. Montoya also allocated time to helping Nate prepare for upcoming tests. Nate had particular difficulty taking tests in U.S. Constitution and government, and Mr. Montoya also was having difficulty helping him. For two days before the test he would work with Nate by reviewing the content and creating practice questions for Nate to answer. However, it seemed that no matter how well prepared Nate appeared to be, he did poorly on the test. When Mr. Montoya asked Nate why this was, he just shrugged his shoulders and said the test did not make any sense to him.

Assessment is a topic on the Praxis *Special Education: Core Knowledge* Tests.

Both norm-referenced and criterion-referenced testing can be **standardized,** which means that all students take the test under the same, or standard, conditions. The information that comes from the test results, then, assumes standardized testing conditions were applied (McLoughlin & Lewis, 2000). Standardized administration procedures are published in test manuals, and are expected to be closely followed for the test scores to be meaningful.

Another important distinction is whether a test is **summative** or **formative** in nature. Summative testing usually refers to tests given at the end of a particular educational period. Achievement tests given at the end of a school year are good examples of summative evaluation. The results tell how much has been accomplished throughout the educational period, and may provide implications for placement in the next educational period. Many norm-referenced tests are summative in nature, but criterion-referenced tests can also be summative if they are administered at the end of a particular educational experience.

Formative evaluation refers to testing that takes place at frequent intervals, so that learner progress can be evaluated. For example, students who are attempting to learn and remember 100 multiplication facts may take a weekly test on these facts, so that the rate of growth can be evaluated, and instructional modifications made (e.g., more time on task) when growth is unsatisfactory. Formative evaluation is most frequently used in basic skills areas.

Table 12.1
Examples of Reading Tests

Types of Test	Example Reading Test
Standardized, Norm-Referenced	Published reading achievement test administered under standardized conditions. Students may answer test questions on computerized answer sheets or give answers to an examiner in an individual administration. Student's score is compared with scores of a normative sample of students.
Criterion-Referenced	Students' test scores are compared with a certain pre-determined criterion level to be considered competent at reading at their grade level.
Curriculum-Based Assessment	Test is based on the reading curriculum materials being used in class.
Curriculum-Based Measurement	Students take brief tests of reading speed, accuracy, and comprehension. These scores are monitored over time to determine whether progress is adequate.
Performance Assessment	Student could be asked to "perform" on a variety of reading-related tasks, such as summarizing a passage, looking up a reference, or identifying a certain printed label in a store.
Portfolio Assessment	A variety of a student's products relevant to reading are collected, for example, list of books read, book reports written, or tape recordings of reading selections.

Evaluation can also be curriculum-based. This means that the tests are derived directly from the curriculum being taught (Fuchs, Fuchs, Allinder, & Hamlett, 1992). Most teacher-made tests are intended to evaluate student learning of the curriculum, and therefore are types of curriculum-based tests. Distinctions have been made between **curriculum-based assessment**—which could include any procedure that evaluates student performance in relation to the school curriculum, such as weekly spelling tests—and **curriculum-based measurement**—characterized by frequent, direct measurements of critical school behaviors, which could include timed (1–5 minute) tests of performance on reading, math, and writing skills (McLoughlin & Lewis, 2000). Curriculum-based measurement is formative in nature, and allows teachers to make instructional decisions about teaching and curriculum while learning is taking place.

Other types of tests include **performance assessments** and **portfolio assessments.** Performance assessments are usually curriculum-based, and require students to construct responses on real-world tasks, usually in ways that allow teachers to evaluate the student's thinking (Fuchs, 1994). Portfolio assessment is also usually curriculum-based, and consists of student products and other relevant information collected over time and displayed in a portfolio. All these types of tests have relevance to students with special needs. Table 12.1 provides examples of these types of tests applied in the context of reading.

Regardless of the type of test, it must be demonstrated to have **reliability** and **validity** to be of value. All measures of reliability seek to determine that the test is consistent in what it measures. No less important, validity refers to the extent to which a particular test measures what it is intended to measure. Validity is often evaluated by comparing different tests of the same skills or abilities (McLoughlin & Lewis, 2000). For example, students should receive similar scores on different standardized tests of reading achievement, if both tests are valid.

Tests commonly used in special education are listed in Figure 12.1.

Companion Website

Many tests useful for special education are distributed by Pro-Ed, Psychological Corporation, and American Guidance Service. For Websites devoted to these publishers, go to the Web Links module in chapter 12 of the Companion Website.

For more information on tests and their characteristics, see McLoughlin and Lewis (2000); Overton (1999); Salvia and Ysseldyke (2001).

Intelligence Tests
Kaufman Assessment Battery for Children (Kaufman & Kaufman, 1983) (American Guidance Service)
Stanford–Binet Intelligence Scale (4th ed.). (Thorndike, Hagen, & Sattler, 1986) (Riverside)
Wechsler Intelligence Scale for Children (3rd ed.). (Wechsler, 1991) (Psychological Corporation)

Achievement Tests
Kaufman Test of Educational Achievement (KTEA) (Kaufman & Kaufman, 1997) (American Guidance Service)
KeyMath—Revised (Connolly, 1988) (American Guidance Service)
Peabody Individual Achievement Test—Revised (PIAT—R) (Markwardt, 1989) (American Guidance Service)
Test of Written Language—3 (TOWL) (Hammill & Larsen, 1996) (PRO-ED)
Wide Range Achievement Test—3 (Wilkenson, 1993) (Jastak Associates)
Woodcock-Johnson III, Tests of Achievement (Woodcock, Johnson, & Mather, 2001) (Riverside)
Woodcock Reading Mastery Test—Revised (Woodcock, 1987) (American Guidance Service)

Figure 12.1
Types of Tests

Adapting Tests for Students with Special Needs

Norm-Referenced Tests

Some students with special needs exhibit difficulties with norm-referenced tests that may limit the reliability and validity of their test scores. Problems may include language or communication styles (e.g., the need for a sign language interpreter or communication board), the length of the testing, attentional difficulties, or reading difficulties when reading competence is not being tested. Another threat to the validity of individual scores of students with disabilities is that in some cases, individuals with disabilities are not included in the test's standardization sample (Fuchs, Fuchs, Benowitz, & Barringer, 1987). Further, some tests may not be fair for students from some culturally diverse backgrounds (Anderson & Webb-Johnson, 1995; Artiles & Zamora-Durán, 1997; Baca & Almanza, 1991; Cummins, 1984). Special considerations including modifications in the testing procedure may be helpful and necessary.

Unfortunately, substantive deviations from standardized administration procedures typically limit the usefulness of the test. If, for example, an individual student is provided with a calculator as a modification to assist with math computation on a problem-solving subtest, the resulting score cannot be fairly compared with students who did not have access to calculators. Even though it can be argued that problem solving, and not computation, is being evaluated, and the student in question has difficulty remembering math facts, it is unknown how the students in the standardization sample would have performed if they also had access to calculators. Therefore, the student's score cannot be easily interpreted with respect to the performance of the norm group (McLoughlin & Lewis, 2000). Nevertheless, there are some instances when modifications in administration of standardized tests may be appropriate, including use of calculators, and some states have published state-approved test accommodations (Johnson, Kimball, Brown, & Anderson, 2001; Massachusetts Department of Education, 1998).

Use Test Modifications

While performance on modified tests may not always be fairly compared with performance under standardized administration conditions, results still provide relevant information about the skills and abilities of individual students. Test modifications include the following:

For further discussion of multicultural issues in assessment, see chapter 5; see also Baca and Almanza (1991); Bennett (1999); Ford, Obiakor, and Patton (1995); Winzer and Mazurek (1998).

When testing modifications violate standardization procedures, it may be useful to provide separate administrations of the test—first, under standardized conditions; then, after a break, under modified conditions.

- Altering the timing or scheduling of the test
- Extending time limits
- Spreading the test over several shorter time sessions
- Administering the test over several days (Erickson, Ysseldyke, Thurlow, & Elliott, 1998)
- Changing the setting
- Changing to a smaller room
- Moving to a distraction-free room (Elliott, Kratochwill, & Schulte, 1998b)
- Testing individually (Massachusetts Department of Education, 1998)
- Altering the presentation of the test
- Simplifying the language
- Providing prompts and feedback (including reinforcement)
- Allowing teachers to read the test and turn the test pages
- Allowing audiotaped, large-print, or Braille versions
- Changing the response formats
- Allowing verbal versus written responses
- Allowing circling versus filling in the bubbles (McLoughlin & Lewis, 2000).

If students perform very differently under one or more reasonable modifications, the standardized test may not have provided an accurate depiction of the student's ability.

See also Elliott, Kratochwill, and Schulte (1998a) and the Massachusetts Department of Education (1998) for additional suggestions for modifying testing and testing procedures. For relevant Websites, go to the Web Links module in chapter 12 of the Companion Website.

Use Individually Administered Tests

Some tests themselves are expected to serve in part as modifications from the group-administered tests given to all students. That is, many of the tests used in special education are individually administered. In addition to providing more detailed information about student performance in a particular area, individually administered tests avoid some potential problems associated with group administration, such as reading directions, working independently, and using machine-scored answer sheets. For example, in group-administered tests of reading, students may respond to more complicated formats to assess reading skills, while on an individually administered test, a student's individual reading can be directly assessed through interaction with the examiner. Therefore, it may be appropriate to rely more on individually administered tests for students who have difficulty undertaking group tests independently.

Teach Test-Taking Skills

Some students do more poorly than others on norm-referenced tests because they lack test-taking skills. In other words, they may know much of the content, but do not understand how to apply that knowledge on the test (Scruggs, Bennion, & Lifson, 1985b; Scruggs & Mastropieri, 1988). In these cases, students can be given specific training in **test-taking skills** appropriate to relevant tests, or administered published practice tests and given feedback on their understanding of test formats (Scruggs & Mastropieri, 1992). Test-taking skills training, appropriate for many different types of tests, is discussed later in this chapter.

Increase Motivation

In other cases, students may have relevant skills, but not be sufficiently motivated to work their hardest during the test. This may be true for all other types of tests, as well as norm-referenced tests. While direct rewarding of test performance may violate standardization in some instances, other motivational strategies, such as those suggested in chapter 9, may be helpful in increasing the validity of the test performance of unmotivated students.

Improve Examiner Familiarity

Finally, some students perform more poorly on tests when they are unfamiliar with the test administrator. It has been seen that some students score better on standardized tests if they are familiar with the examiner than if they are responding to an examiner they have not met before. This appears to be particularly true of African American and Latino students (Fuchs & Fuchs, 1989), as well as students with learning disabilities (Fuchs, Fuchs, & Power, 1987). Try to arrange for an administrator who is well known by the student, such as a classroom teacher (McLoughlin & Lewis, 2000). If possible, try to arrange for the examiner to meet and interact with the student, even for a brief

If a test administrator is someone familiar to a student with special needs, the student might perform better on the test.

Companion Website

For information about accommodations for the SAT, contact SAT Services for Students with Disabilities, P.O. Box 6226, Princeton, NJ 08541-6226. For information about accommodations for the ACT, contact Special Testing—61, ACT Universal Testing, P.O. Box 4028, Iowa City, IA 52243-4028. For relevant Websites, go to the Web Links module in chapter 12 of the Companion Website.

period of time, outside the testing situation. Such established familiarity may improve the validity of test responses.

Request Modifications for College Entrance Exams

Among the most frequently administered tests for college entrance are the Scholastic Assessment Test (SAT) and the American College Testing (ACT). These are usually administered in a student's junior or senior year of high school. Both of these tests allow special accommodations to be made for students with disabilities (Learning Disabilities Association, 1994).

Students with disabilities may be offered accommodations if they meet eligibility requirements. Accommodations that can be requested include extended time, large type, alternative test form with accommodations required on the student's IEP, a reader or recorder, audiocassette with written form, a magnifying glass, or a four-function calculator.

Adapt Competency-Based and Statewide Assessment

Statewide competency testing has been developed to help develop common standards for educational attainment and to help establish educational accountability. In some states, performance on competency tests has become a requirement for graduation and other issues of school operation, and has been referred to as "high-stakes" testing. Maryland, for example, has been working toward linking statewide minimum competency testing to hiring practices and college admissions, and perhaps even to scholarship money (Chenoweth, 1996). Maryland has also created a separate version of the statewide test to assess the progress of schools and programs for students with severe cognitive developmental disabilities in achieving performance standards (Haigh, 1996). Most states today have statewide competency tests (Frase-Blunt, 2000).

Check with your state department of education for information about statewide competency tests and accommodations for students with disabilities.

Minimum competency tests share many characteristics with norm-referenced achievement tests. Although competency tests are oriented toward competencies students are expected to attain for promotion or graduation, they are also developed for comparative purposes. Minimum competency tests are also involved with Title I and No Child Left Behind legislation, which requires states to hold all students to the same expectations (CEC, 2002; Phillips, 1995). Therefore, allowing adaptations for special needs while still maintaining standardization is a concern of competency tests, and can be determined through consultation with test developers or appropriate educational agencies (e.g., school district or state department of education).

Use Test Modifications or Accommodations

In many cases, testing modifications or accommodations are considered appropriate because they better allow some students to demonstrate what they know. Beattie, Grise, and Algozzine (1983) studied minimum competency tests in Florida, and made the following suggestions for modifications for students with learning disabilities:

- Administering fewer subsections (30–40 items) of the test per testing session.
- Adding at least one example for each different set of items within any section of the test.
- Grouping items that measure similar skills in progressive order of difficulty.
- Placing answer options in vertical format with answer bubbles (horizontal ovals) to the right.
- Using left-justified formats for reading comprehension passages and placing them in separate boxes set off from the sentences testing comprehension.
- Using continuation arrows and stop signs to organize the flow of items within the tests. (Beattie, Grise, & Algozzine, 1983, pp. 76–77)

Beattie et al. (1983) compared a large print version of the test with a regular print version and reported only a small and statistically insignificant effect favoring larger print.

Most states provide standard accommodations that are permissible on statewide competency tests. For example, Washington state allows accommodations on the Washington Assessment for Student Learning (WASL) for students who are served in special education, English as a second language (ESL)/bilingual, migrant, or Section 504 programs:

- Aids—Provide English, visual, or native language dictionaries, except on the reading test; use appropriate physical supports or assists; isolate portions of the test; clarify directions.
- Scribe—Answer orally, point, use voice recognition technology, sign an answer, or use a word processor to indicate responses. A scribe records a student's response *verbatim* in the test booklet, without using punctuation or capital letters. The student then indicates how to edit the text.
- Large-print/Braille format—Students with visual impairments may request large-print or Braille versions of the test.
- Oral Presentation—If the student has a documented disability that affects reading, read the math items verbatim in English. (Johnson, Kimball, Brown, & Anderson, 2001, p. 255)

Check with your state department of education for information on permissible accommodations for statewide competency tests, including alternate assessments.

Use Alternate Assessments

Standard statewide assessments may not be appropriate for some students with disabilities. This may be because of the characteristics of the student, the instructional needs of the student, or the type of instruction that is considered most appropriate. In these cases, it may be possible to arrange for alternate assessment procedures. In the state of Virginia, for example, students for whom the state (Standards of Learning) competency tests are not considered appropriate may participate in the Virginia Alternate Assessment Program. These assessments are administered at age 8, 10, 13, and one year prior to the student's exit year. These assessments consist of a Collection of Evidence that measures student performance relevant to IEP objectives that access the state Standards of Learning. The assessment incorporates multiple forms of data collected over time, and could include, for example, work samples; student observations; interviews with teachers, parents, or employers; videotapes of social skills or life skills; and journal entries (Training and Technical Assistance Center at the College of William and Mary, 2002). It is understood that students participating in alternate assessment are working on educational goals other than those prescribed for the traditional diplomas (modified standard, standard, or advanced studies), and therefore would not be eligible for those diplomas (Virginia Department of Education, 2001).

See chapter 16 for information on differentiated or tiered diplomas.

Request Modifications on GED Tests

Competency tests also include the Tests of General Educational Development (GED). GED tests are intended to evaluate the knowledge and skills that were intended to have been acquired from a four-year high school program, or those that may have been acquired in a different manner, such as independent study or tutoring. Students with special needs who have not graduated from high school, but believe they have met high school graduation criteria, can take the GED tests. Individuals wishing to take the GED must be a resident of the state in which the test is administered, and

Technology Highlight

Software to Assist with Recordkeeping, Grading, and Monitoring Progress

The need to maintain clear, accurate records of student performance and progress is important in education, especially when monitoring progress of students with disabilities who are included in general education classes. Organized systems for creating and maintaining recordkeeping systems for students' assignments, homework, grades, attendance, maintaining portfolio assessment products, and monitoring progress will greatly reduce the amount of noninstructional time for teachers. Fortunately, recent advances in technology have greatly reduced the amount of teacher time for many of these tasks. Software is now available that facilitates all recordkeeping and progress-monitoring activities.

Curriculum-based measurement (CBM) is one way to monitor student progress in academic areas. In the future, curriculum-based measurement may be recommended as a way to help identify students with learning disabilities. As described in the text, teachers can develop their own CBM measures; however, some software is available to facilitate the process of using curriculum-based measurement in basic skills such as reading, math, and spelling (Fuchs, Hamlett, & Fuchs, 1990, 1997, 1998, 1999). Lynn and Doug Fuchs and colleagues have developed software—*Monitoring Basic Skills Progress*—that contains curriculum-based measurement tests in reading, spelling, and math. Students take the tests on the computer, which automatically scores and graphs student performance. Students are provided with immediate feedback on their progress, and teachers are provided with individual and class reports documenting performance and progress to date.

Software is also available to assist with managing students' assignments, homework, attendance, grades, and reports to both students and parents. *Grade Machine* (Misty City Software) contains features that allow teachers to upload student information from existing school database systems. In addition to tailoring systems to include a variety of recordkeeping formats, Grade Machine has features such as multilingual report writing (currently in Spanish, French, Russian, German, and English), electronic dissemination of reports to facilitate better home-school communication, and templates or customizing features for maintaining attendance, homework, assignments, behavior, seating plans, and grading terms and scales.

Newer software enabling the use of multimedia is available that can assist with the maintenance of portfolio assessment materials. Teachers can manage their own as well as their students' portfolios using available software. Teachers can show their students how to compile their own portfolios using the available technology. With the use of scanners, digital cameras, digital videos, and available software, student products can be collected on a single CD rather than in a huge box. For relevant Websites pertaining to these topics, go to the Web Links module in chapter 12 of the Companion Website.

usually are older than 18. Also, students must not be enrolled in a public school, so, as a teacher, you may have little direct interaction with students taking the GED. However, you may be able to provide information about the GED to students who are about to leave school without graduating, or to former students who may ask you for assistance in taking the GED.

Students with disabilities may fill out an "Application for Special Testing" and sign a release of information to have specific medical or psychological records sent to GED to be evaluated. Possible modifications that may be obtained include an audiocassette edition of the test (with printed reference copy), large-print version of the test, extended time for taking the test, use of a calculator, frequent breaks, and use of a private testing room (Learning Disabilities Association, 1993).

Contact the GED Testing Service for further information. Publications such as *GED Test Accommodations for Candidates with Specific Learning Disabilities* can be requested from this organization.

Adapt Teacher-Made and Criterion-Referenced Tests

Putnam (1992) surveyed a number of secondary teachers in Kansas, Indiana, and Florida to determine how testing was used in their classrooms. Teachers reported that an average of nearly half of a student's report card grades depended on test performance, the most important single factor in determining grades. They reported using tests they made themselves, tests published by a curriculum publisher, and combinations of the two. Notably, teachers reported that they gave an average of 11 tests over each 9-week grading period. Clearly, students' success in school is tied very closely with their performance on academic classroom tests.

Putnam (1992) concluded that an adolescent with mild disabilities who is enrolled in four content area classes may be required to take as many as 44 tests during a 45-day grading period! Clearly, helping students be successful in dealing with the challenges of testing is critical to promoting school success.

Modify Tests

In the earlier scenario, Nate performed well on answering questions on the chapter posed by the resource teacher, but performed poorly on the actual test covering the U.S. Constitution and government. Because he apparently knew much of the required information, it is possible that Nate did not fully understand the format of the teacher-made test. Although training in test-taking skills may be important for Nate in this case, it is also possible that the social studies teacher could be encouraged to make some modifications on the format of the test so that students will better understand what is required of them, as shown in the continuation of the scenario.

CLASSROOM SCENARIO

Nate

Mr. Montoya made an appointment to speak to Nate's social studies teacher, Ms. Leet. She acknowledged that Nate was not doing well on the tests, and expressed a willingness to help solve the problem. Mr. Montoya and Ms. Leet examined the tests together, and Mr. Montoya noted that he believed Nate did know the answer to several of the questions that he had answered incorrectly. It appeared that Nate was more likely to answer questions incorrectly when the items contained double negatives, contained potentially confusing options such as "(e) all of the above except (b)", or when the test called for matching two columns of information. While Mr. Montoya agreed to provide Nate with practice on test-taking skills, and to provide practice tests that more closely resembled Ms. Leet's tests, Ms. Leet agreed to make modifications in her test to make the individual items more understandable. She also asked her class to provide her with some sample items that they thought should be on the test.

With training in test-taking skills and test modifications, Nate's scores increased from an average of D– to an average of C–. In addition, Ms. Leet found that the average score of her entire class seemed to improve.

Unfortunately many teachers do not often make effective test modifications for students with special needs (Putnam, 1992). However, most teachers view reasonable testing modifications favorably (Gajria, Salend, & Hemrick, 1994; Jayanthi, Epstein, Polloway, & Bursuck, 1996). Salend (1995) reviewed the literature on testing modifications, and concluded that "lengthy, poorly designed, messy, or distracting tests can adversely affect student performance" (p. 85). Well-designed tests, however, can be useful for all students.

For more information, contact GED Testing Service, American Council on Education, One Dupont Circle, NW, Suite 250, Washington, DC 20036-1163. Telephone: (202) 939–9490. For relevant Websites, go to the Web Links module in chapter 12 of the Companion Website.

Modify Test Formats. Format modifications that can be generally employed on teacher-made tests—and that are acceptable to teachers (Gajria, Salend, & Hemrick, 1994)—include the following:

- Prepare typewritten, rather than handwritten, tests.
- Space items sufficiently to reduce interference.
- Provide space for students to respond on the test itself.
- Provide items in a predictable hierarchy.
- Administer more tests with fewer items, rather than fewer, longer tests.
- When not testing reading—adjust the reading level of the items, or provide assistance with reading when needed.
- Define unfamiliar or abstract words, if their meanings are not directly being tested.
- Provide models of correctly answered items.
- Change the test setting for students with special needs (e.g., a quiet space where the student can work privately).
- Allow more time for test completion for students who are slower with reading, writing, or processing test requirements.
- Allow students to dictate responses or to use communication boards to indicate their responses. (p. 238)

The scoring of test items is often most manageable when teachers create and use objective tests, containing true–false, multiple-choice, matching, and sentence completions. However, these types of tests do not always provide students with opportunities to demonstrate all their knowledge, and they may be confused by formats. The key is to write test items as clearly as possible. Good test construction takes a bit more effort but is an essential part of good teaching, especially if student success depends on their performance on tests.

True–False Items. True–false items can be modified to be more easily understandable to diverse learners, without altering the nature of the content being tested. First, an example of what is called for in the directions could be helpful. Circle the word *circle* to make it clear what is to be done, and write out the words *true* or *false* for clarity.

Finally, avoid double negatives. In the following example, students are expected to answer "false" to a statement that a phrase is *not* found in the U.S. Constitution:

T   F   The phrase "secure the blessings of liberty to ourselves and our posterity" is not found in the Constitution.

Many students with special needs may be familiar with phrases in the Constitution, but become confused about the meaning of the test question. If negative statements must be used, emphasize them with bold or underlining so that they will not be overlooked, and the test-taker is prompted to think more carefully.

Multiple-Choice Items. Multiple-choice tests are composed of a beginning statement (stem), and a choice of responses (options) that complete the statement, such as:

Circle one:

The order Hymenoptera includes the following:

   a. Japanese beetle
   b. honey bee
   c. paper wasp
   d. (b) and (c) but not (a)
   e. (a) and (b) but not (c)
   f. (a), (b), and (c)

This item as written could be confusing for many students. It could be made less confusing, and still test the same content, if some modifications were made. First, the word *circle* in the directions could be circled for emphasis. Second, the stem could be elaborated on. Third, the items (d), (e), and (f) could be modified or eliminated:

Circle the correct letter:

The order Hymenoptera includes the following types of insects:

a. Japanese beetle, Junebug
b. honey bee, paper wasp
c. Monarch butterfly, tiger moth
d. praying mantis, walkingstick
e. dragonfly, damselfly

It is also possible to reduce the number of item choices to simplify the test, for example, to include only choices (a), (b), and (c). This could be particularly helpful for students who read slowly, or students who have difficulty sustaining attention. However, it should also be taken into consideration that by reducing the number of answer choices, the probability of answering correctly by guessing is improved.

Additionally, requiring answers to multiple-choice items on separate answer sheets may also result in more incorrect answers, as students with special needs may answer less efficiently on separate answer sheets (Veit & Scruggs, 1986).

Matching Items. Many teachers use matching items on their tests, which require students to pair items in one column with items from another column, as in the following example:

Match the items in Column 2 and Column 1.

Column 1
1. Sojourner Truth
2. Jackie Robinson
3. Crispus Attucks
4. Thurgood Marshall
5. Booker T. Washington
6. Rosa Parks
7. Harriet Tubman
8. Langston Hughes
9. George Washington Carver
10. W. E. B. Dubois
11. Martin Luther King

Column 2
a. Sociologist and early leader of the NAACP.
b. First African American to play modern major league baseball.
c. U.S. Supreme Court Justice.
d. Helped slaves escape to the North.
e. First African American governor.
f. Killed in Boston Massacre.
g. Famous writer from the Harlem Renaissance period.
h. Principal of Tuskegee Institute; influential African American leader of the early 20th century.
i. Leader of the Civil Rights Movement.
j. Famous for agricultural research.
k. Former slave and abolitionist leader.
l. Pianist and famous jazz musician.
m. Helped start the modern Civil Rights movement with refusal to give up bus seat.

This particular matching format can create problems for some students with special learning needs, and may be confusing to students of more average abilities. The directions are unclear and lack specificity. The longer part of the pairs is presented on the right side of the test. There are many items to match, requiring much scanning and remembering for each item. Finally, there are more items in Column 2 than there are in Column 1, which may create further confusion.

According to Salend (1995), this test could be modified in several ways to make it "friend-lier" to all students. First, the number of items could be reduced. This can be done without detracting from the overall test length by simply creating another, shorter matching section in another part of the test in which all the deleted items are included. Second, the number of items in each column could be made to match, so that there is only one choice for each pair. Third, the directions could be more explicit and an example could be provided. Fourth, the lengthier items in the pairs could be placed first, with a blank to indicate the response choice from Column 2. Finally, the entire section of the test should be placed on one page. A modified version of the same test could look like the following:

Directions: Write the letter from Column 2 that best fits with each number in Column 1. The first item has been done for you.

Column 1	Column2
_F_ 1. Sociologist and early leader of the NAACP	A. Jackie Robinson
____ 2. First African American to play modern major league baseball	B. Crispus Attucks
____ 3. U.S. Supreme Court Justice	C. Thurgood Marshall
____ 4. Helped slaves escape to the North	D. Douglas Wilder
____ 5. First African American governor	E. Harriet Tubman
____ 6. Killed in Boston Massacre	F. W. E. B. Dubois

Many of the items that were included in the matching format could be rewritten into a multiple-choice format, for example:

6. Rosa Parks:
    a. Helped slaves escape to the North.
    b. Was a famous writer from the Harlem Renaissance period.
    c. Helped start the modern Civil Rights movement when she refused to give up her bus seat.

Multiple-choice items can test the same content, in a similar way, and appear much more understandable for many students.

Sentence Completion Items. In sentence completion items, a word or brief phrase is left blank at the end of a sentence, and the test-taker is required to produce the correct word to complete the sentence:

Thick deposits of windblown dust are known as _____.

The test-taker is expected to insert the correct word (*loess*) in the blank. Salend (1995) suggested several modifications for this type of test item, including adding answer choices that can be circled rather than rewritten, making the directions clear, and highlighting key words, such as the following:

Circle **the word below the blank space that correctly completes the sentence:**

Thick deposits of **windblown dust** are known as _____.
sediment
loess
abrasions

Such modifications can be helpful for students who may have difficulty with copying words from memory, word-retrieval, focusing attention, and spelling. If such modifications of this type are made, however, it may be important to consider that the item is now easier to answer, in that the student now must only recognize (rather than produce) the correct answer.

Essay Questions. On essay questions, a direct question about a subject is posed and students are expected to compose a response that answers the question in some detail:

- Essay question: Define and describe mollusks.

According to Salend (1995), essay questions could be modified to include a listing of relevant concepts that should be included in the essay, and a recommendation of how the essay might be organized:

- Essay question: **Define and describe mollusks.** In writing your answer, you may wish to mention *mantle* and *radula,* and provide several different examples of mollusks. You should also address the following questions:

  What type of animals are mollusks?
  What are the major classes of mollusks?
  What are body parts of mollusks?
  What are organ systems of mollusks?
  What are special structures of mollusks?

Without providing too much information, modifications can help focus students' thinking, and organize their responses.

Modify Scoring Procedures

In addition to format modifications of tests, you can also modify the way you score the tests. Modifications may be particularly relevant when spelling, grammar, and neatness are usually considered part of the grade on a test. Because spelling, grammar, and even neatness are not always directly taught in some classes, consider grading answers solely for content presented. If some students have particular difficulty in areas such as spelling and grammar, it probably is unnecessary to penalize these students in every class they take, particularly if they are doing all they can to improve in these areas. If it seems important to grade on spelling, grammar, and neatness, consider grading them separately from actual mastery of the content, and perhaps ascribing these areas less weight. It may also be helpful to reconsider giving partial credit for answers that are incorrect, but nonetheless demonstrate some knowledge of the content covered. It seems reasonable that answers that demonstrate even a little knowledge may be given more credit than answers that reflect no knowledge.

Using Curriculum-Based Measurement

Curriculum-based measurement (CBM) was developed to document student progress through the class curriculum and to assist teachers in creating more effective instructional environments for students (Fuchs et al., 1992). Fuchs, Fuchs, Hamlett, Phillips, and Bentz (1994) described two major distinguishing features of CBM.

First, CBM entails a standardized (but probably not norm-referenced) set of procedures for administration. These standardized procedures include sampling test items from classroom curricula, administering the test under the same or similar conditions, summarizing the test information, and using the test information in instructional decision making (Fuchs et al., 1992). These procedures have established reliability and validity in CBM, as well as its utility in the classroom (e.g., Fuchs, Fuchs, Hamlett, & Stecker, 1991).

The second distinguishing feature of CBM is its focus on a long-term curricular goal—that is, the goal that you wish students will achieve by the end of the year. To this extent, CBM differs from other types of continuous measurement (or formative evaluation), in which student progress is assessed directly through changing objectives and standards throughout the year. With CBM, the test domain remains constant from the beginning of the school year until the end.

For an example of CBM, consider the curriculum area of spelling (Fuchs et al., 1992). The teacher examines the level of the curriculum for an entire domain of words that students are expected to be able to spell by the end of the year. Then the teacher samples from this list, creating, say, 50 versions of a 20-item spelling test that include words that students will study throughout

Some students—for example, those with traumatic brain injury—may benefit from recording their responses on audiotape, and using this tape to prompt their written responses. Teachers could also accept audiotaped answers when appropriate.

Figure 12.2
Curriculum-based Measurement in Spelling Chart

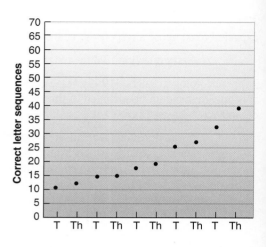

the year. The teacher administers one of these lists about twice a week under standardized administration procedures (e.g., words are read once every seven seconds and students write the words on lined, numbered paper). Student performance can be scored by means of measures that may be more sensitive than number of words spelled correctly, such as number of correct letter sequences (Fuchs & Fuchs, 1994).

Letter sequence scores can then be plotted over time, either for individual students or for the class as a whole (see Figure 12.2). Student progress can be plotted and the teacher can estimate whether students will attain end-of-year goals if they continue to progress at the current rate. If progress seems inadequate, teachers can increase time-on-task or individual work with specific difficult letter patterns (Fuchs et al., 1992).

Curriculum-based measurement is an excellent way to monitor the progress of all students, including those with special needs, toward end-of-year goals. In this way, instructional decisions can be made throughout the year to help ensure that students do meet their goals.

CBM has been used in all basic skill areas, including reading, spelling, writing, and mathematics. The following Research Highlight demonstrates how CBM was used to increase achievement in elementary math.

Research Highlight

Classwide Curriculum-Based Measurement

Fuchs, Fuchs, Hamlett, Phillips, and Bentz (1994) examined the influence of CBM on the mathematics achievement of students with learning disabilities, low-achieving students, and normally achieving students, in general education classes. They studied these three types of students in 40 classrooms in 11 schools, representing grades 2–5. Of the 40 classrooms, 20 served as comparison classrooms and 20 used CBM to monitor students' progress.

Every week in CBM classrooms, students took criterion-referenced tests based on the state curriculum standards for the grade level of that particular class. Students answered 25 questions on one of multiple forms of the test, and were given from 1.5 to 5 minutes to complete the test, depending on the grade level. Students scored their tests and entered their scores into a CBM computer program in pairs, and checked each other's data entry for accuracy. In some cases, data-entry clerks entered student scores. Students were asked to examine their graphed performance scores and ask themselves questions about their graphs (e.g., "Are my scores going up?" p. 522) and about their specific skills profiles (e.g., "Are my boxes getting darker?" p. 522) (see Figure 12.3). Every two weeks, teachers were provided computer-generated copies of each student's graph and skills profile, and a report summarizing the progress of the entire class. Teachers also received a graph of the progress of students at the 25th, 50th, and 75th percentile of the class, and a listing of students below the 25th percentile.

In 10 CBM classrooms (CBM-NoIN classrooms), no specific instructional recommendations were made. In the other 10 CBM classrooms (CBM-IN), specific recommendations were made on the reports, based on students' performance on the CBM measures. These recommendations included the following:

- Skills to teach during whole-class instruction
- How to create small groups for instruction in areas of common difficulty
- Recommendations for computer-assisted programs, including specific software recommendations for specific students
- Recommendations for classwide peer tutoring (see chapter 9), including which students should be paired to work on specific skills. Materials for implementing classwide peer tutoring were also provided.

After six months of instruction, results indicated that students demonstrated the highest gains and the highest rates of growth in the CBM-IN condition, in which weekly measurement was taken, and teachers were provided with specific suggestions for instruction. Observations indicated that CBM-IN teachers:

- addressed more skills.
- taught more operations skills.
- provided more one-to-one instruction.
- employed more peer-mediated instruction.
- used specific motivation systems more frequently.

Surveys indicated that teacher satisfaction with the CBM programs was very high; however, the greatest academic gains were achieved when the teachers actively considered the CBM data, and made instructional decisions based on these data, as recommended in the areas of specific whole-class instruction, small-group instruction, computer-assisted instruction, and classwide peer tutoring. Results suggested that computer-assisted curriculum-based measurement in mathematics, with specific instructional recommendations, can be effective in addressing the diverse learning needs of inclusive classrooms.

Questions for Reflection

1. How could CBM be adapted for other academic skills, such as reading or spelling?
2. What adaptations would be useful for students with special needs? Consider physical, sensory, cognitive, and behavioral domains.
3. How could you evaluate the effectiveness of CBM?
4. How could the principles of CBM be employed to monitor performance in areas such as creative writing or physics?

Companion Website

To answer these questions online, go to the Research Highlights feature in chapter 12 of the Companion Website.

Figure 12.3
CBM Student Feedback

Note: From "Classwide Curriculum-Based Measurement: Helping General Educators Meet the Challenge of Student Diversity," by L. S. Fuchs, D. Fuchs, C. L. Hamlett, N. B. Phillips, & J. Bentz, 1994, *Exceptional Children, 60,* p. 523. Copyright 1994 by CEC. Reprinted by permission.

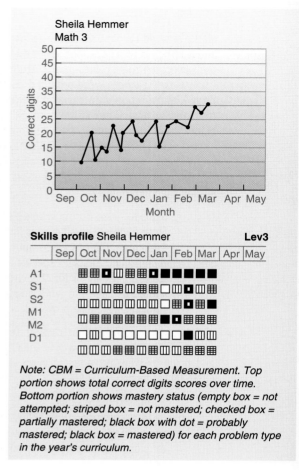

Note: CBM = Curriculum-Based Measurement. Top portion shows total correct digits scores over time. Bottom portion shows mastery status (empty box = not attempted; striped box = not mastered; checked box = partially mastered; black box with dot = probably mastered; black box = mastered) for each problem type in the year's curriculum.

Using Performance Assessment

Performance assessment addresses students' ability to interact (perform) appropriately with relevant instructional materials, and the content of instruction. As such, this type of assessment relies much less on direct recall of verbal information than do more typical classroom tests, and more on students' demonstration of understanding (Coutinho & Malouf, 1993). Performance assessment is helpful when testing students who may have word-finding (retrieval) problems, communication disorders, or other skills that limit verbal communication. For example, in an investigation by Scruggs, Mastropieri, Bakken, and Brigham (1993), students with learning disabilities performed relatively poorly on a more traditional test of their recall of vocabulary words after hands-on science instruction. However, they were much more able to demonstrate their knowledge in performance-based tests that required them to determine, for example, which of two minerals is harder, or whether a mineral contains calcite. Performance assessment is an effective way of measuring all students' comprehension of academic content in at least part of virtually all school subjects, including science, math, social studies, music, art, vocational education, and physical education.

Although performance assessments may vary widely, they often have three key elements in common:

1. Students construct their own responses, rather than selecting or identifying correct responses.
2. Teachers can observe student performance on tasks reflecting real-world or authentic requirements.
3. Student responses can reveal patterns in students' thinking and learning, as well as whether the question was correctly answered. (Fuchs, 1994)

To set up performance assessment measures, determine first exactly what you want students to be able to do after the instructional unit, and state it as a behavioral objective. For example, after an electricity unit you may think students should be able to demonstrate their knowledge of the properties of electricity by identifying which items in a set are conductors and which are insulators, using a battery, wires, and a small electric motor. You may also think they should be able to create series and parallel circuits, and increase the strength of an electromagnet. These objectives may be stated as follows:

- Given a small electric motor, a battery, wires, and connectors, and a set of 10 small objects, the student will demonstrate which are conductors and which are insulators with 100% accuracy.
- Given wires, light bulbs, batteries, and connectors, the student will construct a series circuit and a parallel circuit within 10 minutes with 100% accuracy.

The next step is to set up the materials and provide the opportunity for the student to perform on the test. Specific tasks can be placed at several stations around the classroom, and students can move from station to station individually, without observing another student's performance on the test.

It is important to specify to students ahead of time what criteria will be used in scoring their responses. Scoring is done by using a scoring rubric that lists test items and scoring criteria. For example, in a recent investigation of hands-on science education in an inclusive setting, students created ecosystems with stacked 2-liter soda containers, with an aquatic environment in the bottom container and a terrestrial environment in the top container (Mastropieri, Scruggs, Mantzicopoulos, et al., 1998). In the performance assessment for this unit, the following test item was used:

- Draw a picture of an ecosystem. Label all parts.

To score this item objectively, a scoring rubric was constructed by which responses could be evaluated. For this item, the scoring criteria included the following:

Scoring Rubric
3—picture with living and nonliving things appearing to interact in some general way. Living and nonliving things labeled.
2—picture of living and nonliving things not labeled, or labeled living, or labeled nonliving.
1—one of above or general relevant comment.
0—nothing of relevance.

Using this key, then, a picture drawn by a student that included both living and nonliving things, but with the items in the picture not labeled, would earn a score of 2 points. An example of a response to this particular item on a performance assessment is given in Figure 12.4. See if you can score #2 in Figure 12.4.

In some cases, the same rubric can be constructed to apply to a number of individual items. For instance, Fuchs (1994) provided a scoring rubric for a performance test in mathematics, taken from the Wisconsin School System, and shown in the *In the Classroom* feature on page 353.

Fuchs (1994) described the application of this scoring rubric with assessments that can be used four to six times each year, and that can be completed individually or in small groups. The test is intended to evaluate students' responses to real-life, age-appropriate situations representing practical applications of mathematics (see also Sammons, Kobett, Heiss, & Fennell, 1992). The problem is given as follows:

A group of five families on your block is going to have a garage sale in which clothes, toys, and books will be sold. Your family has 12 items to sell and will need 18 square feet to display these items; the Hamletts have 13 items and need 20 square feet; the Phillips, 7 items and 10 square feet; the Thompsons, 15 items and 15 square feet; and the Nelsons, 10 items and 30 square feet. Each family would like to have its own table or cluster of tables to oversee. The rental store tells you that you can rent tables measuring 6 feet by 2.5 feet for $6.00 per day. The garage where the sale will occur is 20 feet by 30 feet. Newspaper advertising costs $11.00 for the first 10 words and $1.50 for each additional word.

1. How many tables will you need? Explain how you got this number.
2. Draw a diagram showing how the tables can be arranged in the garage to allow the customers to move about with at least 4 feet between tables.
3. Write an ad for your sale that includes enough information.
4. How much money do you have to earn from your sale for the families to break even? (Fuchs, 1994, p. 23)

Ecosystems 1

NAME: _____   DATE: _____

SHORT ANSWER:

1. Tell me everything you can about an ecosystem.

an ecosystem is a place were living an nonliving things effect and depend on each other the living parts of an ecosystem is the plants animal. the non liv parts are to soil, water, air, light also and ecosystems

2. Draw a picture of an ecosystem. Label all parts.

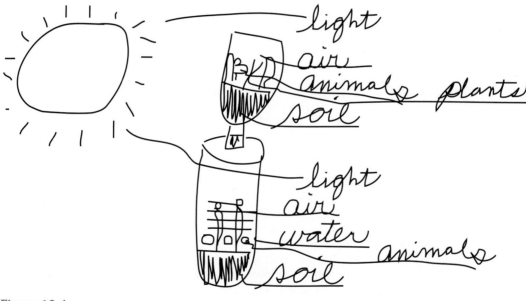

Figure 12.4
Student Response on Ecosystem Item on Performance-Based Assessment

Dalton, Tivnan, Riley, Rawson, and Dias (1995) described the uses of paper-and-pencil and hands-on performance assessments in fourth-grade science classes, and provided an example involving parallel circuits with scoring criteria and how one student with learning disabilities performed before and after instruction.

When you present a problem like this to the class, you also should present the scoring rubric, so that students are well aware of how their responses will be scored. An example of a score of 4 (exemplary response) is given in Figure 12.5.

Schirmer and Bailey (2000) described the development of a rubric for a writing assessment that was employed successfully for middle-school students who were deaf. They emphasized that the rubric should be a dynamic tool, capable of accommodating individual differences in student needs, content, assignments, and curriculum. That is, some students may benefit from a rubric that emphasizes word choice as a means for expanding vocabulary, while other students may benefit from a rubric that emphasizes organization of ideas.

In creating a writing assessment rubric, teachers should:

- Identify the qualities of writing.
- Create a scale.
- Define each quality by listing the characteristics that describe performance at each point on the scale. (Schirmer & Bailey, 2000, p. 55)

In the Classroom ...a feature for teachers

Sample Mathematics Scoring Rubric

4 Exemplary Response
  4.1 Complete, with clear, coherent, unambiguous, and insightful explanation
  4.2 Shows understanding of underlying mathematical concepts, procedures, and structures
  4.3 Examines and satisfies all essential conditions of the problem
  4.4 Presents strong supporting arguments with examples and counterexamples as appropriate
  4.5 Solution and work is efficient and shows evidence of reflection and checking of work
  4.6 Appropriately applies mathematics to the situation

3 Competent Response
  3.1 Gives a fairly complete response with reasonably clear explanations
  3.2 Shows understanding of underlying mathematical concepts, procedures, and structures
  3.3 Examines and satisfies most essential conditions of the problem
  3.4 Presents adequate supporting arguments with examples and counterexamples as appropriate
  3.5 Solution and work show some evidence of reflection and checking of work
  3.6 Appropriately applies mathematics to the situation

2 Minimal Response
  2.1 Gives response, but explanations may be unclear or lack detail
  2.2 Exhibits minor flaws in underlying mathematical concepts, procedures, and structures
  2.3 Examines and satisfies some essential conditions of the problem
  2.4 Draws some accurate conclusions, but reasoning may be faulty or incomplete
  2.5 Shows little evidence of reflection and checking of work
  2.6 Some attempt to apply mathematics to the situation

1 Inadequate Response
  1.1 Response is incomplete and explanation is insufficient or not understandable
  1.2 Exhibits major flaws in underlying mathematical concepts, procedures, and structures
  1.3 Fails to address essential conditions of the problem
  1.4 Uses faulty reasoning and draws incorrect conclusions
  1.5 Shows no evidence of reflection and checking of work
  1.6 Fails to apply mathematics to the situation

0 No attempt
  0.1 Provides irrelevant or no response
  0.2 Copies part of the problem but does not attempt a solution
  0.3 Illegible response

Note: To receive a particular score, a significant number of the associated criteria must be met.

Note: From *Connecting Performance Assessment to Instruction* (p. 24), by L. S. Fuchs, 1994, Reston, VA: Council for Exceptional Children. Copyright 1994 by CEC. Reprinted with permission.

Name: Marlena

1.   1 table: 6' × 2.5' = 15 sq.'

	sq. ft needed	# tables needed
Thompsons	15	15/15 = ①
Ours	18	18/15 = 1.2 → ②
Phillips	10	10/15 = .67 → ①
Hamletts	20	20/15 = 1.3 → ②
Nelsons	30	30/15 = ②

Total tables needed: 1 + 2 + 1 + 2 + 2 = ⑧

We'll need 8 tables because each table gives 15 sq.'.
2 families need 15 sq.' or less + therefore each need
1 table. 3 families need more than 15 sq.' but no more
than 30 sq.', so they each need 2 tables.
(2 families × 1 table) + (3 families × 2 tables) =

     2   +   6   = 8 tables

2.

20'

5'   30'

3.   Garage Sale. Toys, clothes, books. 325 Farm St.
Sat. June 20. 8 a.m. - 2 p.m.

    13 words   10 words @ $10.00
         + 3 words @
         3 × $1.50 $4.50
             ($14.50)

4.   ad costs $14.50
    tables cost 8 × $6.00 = $42.00 ⟩ ($56.50)
                 need to earn
                 to break even

Figure 12.5

Exemplary Response to the Performance Assessment Math Problem

Note: From *Connecting Performance Assessment to Instruction* (p. 24), by L. S. Fuchs, 1994, Reston, VA: Council for Exceptional Children. Copyright 1994 by CEC. Reprinted with permission.

Modified rubics could include traits and their definitions, and a scale for rating these traits. For example, Schirmer and Bailey (2000) created a rubric for a writing assessment, adapted from a published English series, that listed *traits*—including topic, content, story development, organization, text structure, voice/audience, word choice, sentence structure, and mechanics. Specific definitions were provided for each trait. For example, the definition of content was:

Good balance between central ideas and details; anecdotes and details enrich the central theme or story line; details and examples fit in well; ideas are clear, complete, and well-developed. (p. 55)

A performance test allows students to demonstrate their knowledge.

Since the definition provided clear criteria of the trait, a 5-point scale was used for each of these traits, with 1 = Many weaknesses, few or no strengths, to 5 = Many strengths, few or no weaknesses.

A rubric such as this can be modified to meet the needs of individual students, assignments, or grade level. For example, the writing rubric could be modified to include traits such as ideas, sentence fluency, purpose, complexity, or form. Rubrics can also be developed for writing process (including planning, drafting, revising), for specific types of writing, such as mystery stories, and for research reports (Schirmer & Bailey, 2000). As can be seen, a wide variety of rubrics can be developed to monitor performance and inform instruction in a number of different academic areas.

Using Portfolio Assessment

A *portfolio* has been defined as a "systematic and organized collection of evidence used by the teacher and student to monitor growth of the student's knowledge, skills, and attitudes" (Vavrus, 1990, p. 48). Using portfolios for assessment, teachers and students collect and organize relevant products to document performance and progress in different areas of academic and behavioral functioning (Wesson & King, 1996). These products can be collected in accordion folders, or in three-ring notebooks with pocketed dividers. You can refer to portfolios to document current functioning, to determine progress, to share information with parents and other teachers, and to plan appropriate interventions or modifications in the student's educational environment (Salend, 1998). Portfolios can be created in any area of student performance, including literacy (Hansen, 1992), math (Knight, 1992), and science (Hamm & Adams, 1991).

Student portfolios can be tailored to the specific needs of the classroom, the student, or the curriculum, and can therefore be considered quite versatile (Wesson & King, 1996). However, for these same reasons, portfolios may lack standardization and objectivity, and therefore teachers must ensure that judgments based on portfolio products are both reliable and valid (Scruggs & Mastropieri, 1994–1995). Helpful strategies include using multiple measures of the same skills or products, calculating interrater reliability (where different "experts" independently assess portfolio products), and making comparisons with more traditional measures (e.g., standardized tests, criterion-referenced measurement; see Wesson & King, 1992). Nevertheless, portfolios can provide authentic evidence of actual classroom performance that may be difficult to document by other methods. You can also use the portfolios to reflect on your own teaching.

Figure 12.6 provides a list of items that could be included in a literacy portfolio, while Figure 12.7 provides a list of items that could be included in a science portfolio.

As you select items for a portfolio, begin to determine the usefulness of each item. For example, consider the items, the organization of the portfolio, the involvement of the students in

- A tape of the student reading from a self-selected piece of literature. The student may reread the same piece periodically, thereby allowing the viewer of the portfolio to clearly see improvement.
- A checklist of skills the student has mastered, such as phonics rules or writing conventions like capitalization and punctuation.
- A log of books read during the year, including dates completed, authors, and student's appreciation ratings of the books.
- Copies of stories the student has written, including in some cases copies of all the draft stages the student has worked through.
- Pictures of a student's project, which shows understanding of a topic. For example, after studying volcanoes, the student may build a volcano and prepare a poster to illustrate how eruptions occur.
- Videotapes of students working cooperatively on language arts projects, such as putting on a skit to show understanding of a story.
- Notes the teacher makes while observing the student at work or conferencing with the student. These notes help the teacher document instructional decisions.
- A chart of progress using curriculum-based measures in reading and written expression.
- Charts the student has developed to track bits of information collected in relation to a nonfiction theme being composed.
- Excerpts from a student's journal and learning log.

Figure 12.6
Potential Items to Include in a Literacy Portfolio
Note: From "Portfolio Assessment and Special Education Students," by C. L. Wesson and R. P. King, 1996, *Teaching Exceptional Children, 28*(2), p. 44. Copyright 1996 by CEC. Reprinted with permission.

- Audiotape of oral reading from science materials collected and added to periodically throughout the year.
- Samples of written work completed throughout the year.
- Samples of laboratory booklets and notes kept throughout the year.
- Samples of formative evaluation measures completed.
- Summaries of performance-based assessments throughout the year.
- Copies of summative evaluation measures (end-of-term exams).
- Teacher observations and anecdotal records regarding performance during general education science class, updated periodically.
- Videotapes taken at various times throughout the year of the student during general education science classes.

Figure 12.7
Sample Portfolio Items for Science
Note: From *A Practical Guide for Teaching Science to Students with Special Needs in Inclusive Settings* (p. 115), by M. A. Mastropieri and T. E. Scruggs, 1993, Austin, TX: Pro-Ed. Copyright 1993 by CEC. Reprinted with permission.

designing the portfolio, any captions that could accompany photos or figures, and the summary statements describing the student goals (Salend, 1998). Salend provides a useful scoring rubric containing excellent, good, and fair performance indicators that can be applied to evaluating portfolios.

Applications for Students with Special Needs

In addition to the "traditional" uses of portfolio assessment in education, portfolio assessment can also be used to document the performance of students who have been referred to special education. Swicegood (1994) described how portfolios could be linked with individual student IEPs, by including work products that show growth on IEP objectives and by periodically completing summary sheets that link IEP objectives to documentation in the portfolio.

Wesson and King (1996) provided two case studies of the use of portfolios with students with disabilities. In the first study, a sixth-grade, general education teacher used a portfolio to chronicle the progress of a student, Tom, classified as seriously emotionally and behaviorally disturbed. Tom was described as having difficulties getting along with peers and frequently fighting with them, being argumentative and noncompliant with teachers, being socially isolated, and making limited academic progress.

Tom's portfolio was created very much along the lines of the literacy portfolio described previously; however, in Tom's case, his behavior was the subject of the portfolio. Contents included a videotape (updated regularly) of Tom's performance during cooperative group lessons, a description of Tom's outside-school social activities, and a list of narrative observations the teacher (or teacher's aide) had made as she watched Tom in social situations, including behavioral observations of Tom's problem behaviors.

In the second case study, a portfolio was created for Chris, a 16-year-old student with severe disabilities. Chris's teacher used a portfolio to document Chris's vocational experiences, which was intended to promote the student's vocational training. This portfolio included a videotape showing Chris working in academic and vocational settings, a transcript of an interview the teacher conducted with Chris, a vocational skill checklist, and a list of Chris's circle of friends [see chapter 8] and their roles in her life. Chris's teacher hoped the portfolio would be useful when Chris applies for jobs and works in the community (Wesson & King, 1996).

Teaching Test-Taking Skills

Tests are given frequently in school to determine how well students have learned various content areas and to determine their overall achievement levels. Many students with disabilities and at risk for failure in school perform poorly on tests, because of poor test-taking skills (Scruggs & Mastropieri, 1988).

Test-taking skills strategies help students with disabilities improve their performance on both standardized and teacher-made tests (Lee & Alley, 1981; Scruggs & Mastropieri, 1988, 1992). Several researchers have described a number of test-taking strategies that have been helpful for all types of learners (Hughes, 1996; Hughes, Schumaker, Deshler, & Mercer, 1988; Millman, Bishop, & Ebel, 1965; Millman & Pauk, 1969; Sarason, 1980; Scruggs & Marsing, 1988; Scruggs & Mastropieri, 1986; Scruggs & Mastropieri, 1992; Scruggs, Mastropieri, & Veit, 1986; Tolfa, Scruggs, & Bennion, 1985; Wine, 1971). This section describes test-taking strategies that are successful at increasing test performance of students with special needs.

General Preparation Strategies

General preparation strategies refer to things students can do to help generally when preparing for any exam (Scruggs & Mastropieri, 1992). Many students, but especially those with disabilities, will benefit from explicit instruction in each of these areas (Wood & Willoughby, 1995).

The first and most important general test strategy is academic preparation. See chapters 10 and 11 for more information in this area. The next general strategy is physical preparation, and includes getting enough rest and nourishment, particularly before studying and before taking the test. A positive attitude toward tests is also important, particularly as some research has indicated that students with special needs tend to have negative attitudes toward tests (Scruggs, Mastropieri, Tolfa, & Jenkins, 1985; Tolfa, Scruggs,

& Mastropieri, 1985). Improve test attitudes by helping students set realistic goals, providing practice tests, explaining the purpose of the particular test, rewarding effort, and training in test-taking skills.

Anxiety-reduction also can help, because too much anxiety can inhibit performance on tests (Lucangeli & Scruggs, 2003; Sarason, 1980). You can help students reduce anxieties during testing situations by encouraging their use of positive attributions—that is, by helping them focus on effort and strategies, rather than thinking about what their score will be or how others will do (see chapter 9). Teach students to recognize signs of tension in themselves—such as grinding teeth, biting fingernails, and by picking at hair or face—and to respond by consciously relaxing their muscles and controlling their breathing (see also Erwin & Dunwiddie, 1983).

Strategies for Standardized Tests

Teach General Strategies

You can teach students general strategies that they can apply across a number of standardized tests and testing situations (Pauk, 1987). These strategies include using separate answer sheets and elimination strategies, guessing effectively, and using time wisely.

Separate Answer Sheets. Most standardized tests require students to record their responses by filling a circle or "bubble" on separate answer sheets. Many younger students and students with disabilities have difficulties manipulating the separate answer sheet (Scruggs & Veit, 1986). Provide students with practice filling in the appropriate answer bubble "quick, dark, and inside the line." If practice tests are provided by the test publisher, provide instruction on the use of separate answer sheets (if not, make simulated answer sheets and test booklets when appropriate). Practice arranging test booklets and answer sheets so the numbers of the appropriate items match. Mark answers on the booklet and have students practice transferring marked responses to the correct locations on answer sheets (Scruggs & Mastropieri, 1992).

Use Elimination Strategies. If test-takers have some prior knowledge on the topic of the question, but are unsure of the exact answer, a good strategy is to eliminate response options they know are incorrect. For example, if there are four answer options and a test-taker can eliminate three of them, then the remaining option must be the correct response. If two out of four options can be eliminated (e.g., "I know that Carson City is not the capital of Florida or California"), then the test-taker has only two options left (e.g., Nevada or Montana). Many students with disabilities are unaware of elimination strategies, as they often do not even read all options (Scruggs, Bennion, & Lifson, 1985b). Provide students with practice items about which you know they have some prior knowledge, so they can practice using the elimination strategy. This strategy is an effective way of using partial knowledge to select a correct response from a listing of options.

Guess When Appropriate. Encourage guessing where appropriate, as many students with disabilities and at risk for school failure do not realize that guessing is better than leaving an item blank on most standardized tests. In fact, when students reported guessing, their scores on those items were higher than what would be expected by chance (Scruggs, Bennion, & Lifson, 1985a). Many normally achieving students know how to improve their scores by guessing, so it is appropriate to teach all students this strategy.

Use Time Wisely. Teach students to use time efficiently on familiar items, and not to waste time on items they are unlikely to answer correctly. Teach students to monitor their time as they take the test. That is, when the testing period is half over, they should be finished with about half the test.

Teach Specific Strategies for Standardized Tests

Strategies can be employed for specific subtests of standardized tests. These can be divided generally by the skills being tested.

Reading Comprehension Subtests

Most standardized reading comprehension subtests require students to read a specific passage, then answer questions about the passage. Teach students to read as much of the passage as possible, as they can still answer many of the questions even if they have skipped some unfamiliar words. Encourage students to read the entire question and every stem option before selecting responses. Teach students to check back in the passage when possible to verify that their answer choice was correct. When reading selections contain information such as train schedules, weather maps, or basketball schedules, teach students to quickly skim the information, then look to the questions and refer back to the table to identify answers.

Decoding Subtest Strategies

Decoding subtests, such as syllabication and vocabulary, may appear as unusual formats on standardized tests. Because most standardized tests are administered in groups, students do not respond orally and decode words, but are provided with formats that have them read silently to test those skills. Practice with these format demands can help students demonstrate all their knowledge. For example, the following item is representative of many decoding subtests:

- play
  a. plan
  b. yard
  c. afraid
  d. drag

Students are required to pick the word that contains the same sound as the underlined part of the word in the stem ("play"). Common errors with this type of subtest are identifying (a) as the answer because it contains the same beginning letters, or identifying (b) as the correct answer because it contains the same letter as one underlined in the stem. Provide students with practice with this format. Teach them to say the underlined sound of the word to themselves, and be certain they have found an answer that matches this sound, and not the appearance of the stem word.

Mathematics Computation Subtests

Mathematics computation subtests require students to look at test items, compute answers on scratch paper, and select the correct answer from the options provided. Provide students with practice using scratch paper and identifying the correct answer from an array of choices. One strategy for handling scratch paper is to divide the paper into quarters, and compute each item within one of the quarters. Teach students to rewrite the problem into the format that they are most comfortable with. For example, when problems are presented horizontally like: $368 + 499 =$, teach them that they can transfer those numbers to the vertical format:

$$368 \\ + 499$$

Practice checking answers that are selected on the answer sheet with the answers that were computed on the scratch paper. Be sure students have sufficient practice with mathematics vocabulary that will be used in word problems. Review words like *sum, product, difference, quotient,* and other words that may appear on the test.

Mathematics Concepts Subtests. Mathematics concepts subtests cover a range of skills in math and are presented in a variety of formats on standardized tests. Model examples in which you read the question, rephrase it, and then think aloud through to the solution. Some math problems may contain boxes to indicate missing values, as in the following example:

    1. What number should be in the ☐ ?

      $524 - ☐ = 425 + 75$
      a. 500
      b. 75
      c. 24
      d. 425

Practice solving problems before the test using those types of boxes or other symbols that may be used on standardized tests. If specific formats that will be used are not known (and this is likely),

Encouraging the use of scratch paper, demonstrating how they can align test problems with the space for answers and allowing students to ask questions during a math exam are all accommodations important for students with special needs.

practice solving problems throughout the year using different answering formats. Be sure students are aware of any specialized vocabulary that may be included on the test.

Math Problem-Solving Subtests

Math problem solving can be complex for students with disabilities. Math problem solving requires reading the problem, determining what is known, figuring out what operation is called for, generating a plan for a solution, computing the solution, selecting the correct answer from the options, and marking the selected response appropriately on the answer sheet. Provide students with practice using their scratch paper, carefully matching the number of the problem on their scratch paper with the test booklet, along with being able to execute all the other necessary steps in the procedure for solving word problems.

If the math subtests contain written problems, students are often allowed to request assistance with reading. Tell students to practice requesting help with the reading if they need it. If test administrators are not allowed to provide assistance in an area, they will simply say "I cannot help you with that."

Some math problems do not contain all the necessary information to answer the question and students are asked to furnish the missing, but necessary information. For example:

3. Tyler is 66 inches tall. What else do you need to know to know how much he grew this year?
   a. How old he is this year.
   b. How tall he was last year.
   c. How tall his father is.
   d. How much his brother grew last year.

Practice with this type of format is necessary for students with disabilities to ensure successful performance. Model and demonstrate by thinking through the solution aloud. Have students practice using similar procedures.

Science and Social Studies Subtests

The formats for science and social studies exams parallel the formats employed in reading comprehension and mathematics subtests. Many items require students to read expository passages and then answer questions about the passages. Other items require students to examine charts, diagrams, reference materials, or maps and interpret them before selecting correct answers. Provide practice using these various formats with students when teaching throughout the year.

Teacher-Made Tests

Teachers sometimes use tests developed by textbook publishers to accompany adopted text materials. Other times they develop their own tests. Some items on both teacher-made and publisher-developed tests include objective tests that contain multiple-choice, matching, and true–false items, and written formats that contain short-answer, fill-in-the-blank, essay, and performance-based items (Putnam, 1992). Millman and Pauk (1969) and Carman and Adams (1972) describe many of these test-taking strategies. The general preparation strategies, and many of the general strategies described for standardized tests are also applicable to teacher-made tests. In addition, some specific strategies for teacher-made tests should be learned.

Objective Tests

Objective tests consist of items similar in format to the items on standardized tests. These types of tests contain multiple-choice, true–false, and matching items. All strategies described so far may be applicable for helping students prepare for objective tests. However, students should be familiar with the content on teacher-made tests, and they can use this knowledge, or partial knowledge, to improve their test scores. A list of strategies for taking objective tests is provided in the *In the Classroom . . . for sharing with students* feature in the Companion Website.

Written Tests

Students with special needs may have difficulty with written tests because of language and literacy problems. Some strategies can help these students become better test-takers on a variety of such tests.

Sentence Completion Items. These items are usually short sentences containing several blanks that need to be filled in with the correct answers, such as the following:

- The largest river in South America is the _____.

Encourage students to put something in the blank, even if the answer is only partially correct. Explain that many teachers give partial credit for some answers, but cannot provide any credit if the items are left blank. Have students guess if they are not completely sure, encourage them to use partial knowledge, and teach them to make the sentence sound logical.

Short-Answer Items. Short-answer tests and items usually require a phrase or several phrases or one to several sentences for responses, for example:

- What were the causes of the War of 1812?

Sometimes, lists of items are considered acceptable responses for short-answer items. Determine whether sentence fragments or lists will result in the same credit as complete sentences. Encourage the use of scratch paper to facilitate students' brainstorming or thinking, especially if complete sentences are required as responses.

Essay Questions. Essay tests may be difficult for students with disabilities, but several strategies exist to facilitate essay test performance. One strategy, referred to as SNOW, stands for:

Study the question
Note important points
Organize the information
Write directly to the point of the question (Scruggs & Mastropieri, 1992, p. 89)

Teach students how to implement each step of this strategy and provide corrective feedback on their performance. Have them study the questions by underlining the specific words that tell them what to do, such as *describe, define, explain, compare, contrast, list, justify,* or *critique.* Each of these words provides information on how the item should be answered, as shown in Figure 12.8.

Next, students should *note* important points that come to mind. Then they should *organize* their notes by numbering the main and supporting points in logical order for discussion. Finally, they should *write* concisely and directly to the point of the question.

	Command Words on Test Items and Their Implications
Word	*Possible Implications*
Discuss	Provide reasoning behind; give different points of view.
Describe	Give an overall impression; give examples.
Compare	Show how two or more things are similar; provide examples of common characteristics.
Contrast	Show how two or more things are different; provide examples of differing characteristics.
Explain	Clarify or simplify; describe the rationale behind.
Justify	Argue in favor of; defend.
Critique	Argue in opposition of; find fault with.
List	Give a simple list of elements.
Outline	Give a list of elements organized into a system.

Figure 12.8

Command Words and Their Explanations

Note: From *Teaching Test-Taking Skills: Helping Students Show What They Know* (p. 90), by T. E. Scruggs and M. A. Mastropieri, 1992, Cambridge, MA: Brookline. Copyright 1992 by Brookline. Reprinted with permission.

Performance Tests

Performance tests are designed to parallel the exact format of what has been taught and practiced, and are designed to provide better information about instruction (Baron, 1990). A practice test may be helpful for some students in preparing for the test. Teach students to read directions carefully, and not to answer too quickly if something looks familiar. Show them how to talk through the steps of answers before responding.

Other Test-Taking Strategies

Other test-taking strategies may be helpful in preparing students to take tests. One strategy is called **SCORER** (Carman & Adams, 1972). Each letter in SCORER represents clue words to help students perform better during testing situations: **S**chedule time; **C**lue words (or command words, see Figure 12.8); **O**mit hard items; **R**ead carefully; **E**stimate answers; and **R**eview work. This strategy has been successfully used with students of middle school age (Ritter & Idol-Maestas, 1986).

Another strategy, **PIRATES,** was developed by Hughes, Rule, Deshler, and Schumaker (1993) and Hughes and Schumaker (1991). PIRATES is a seven-step strategy designed to help students perform better on teacher-made tests. Each letter in PIRATES represents a step of the strategy. The steps of PIRATES are provided in the *In the Classroom . . . for sharing with students* feature in the Companion Website.

Another strategy is called ANSWER (Hughes, 1996). While PIRATES was originally designed for improving performance on objective tests, ANSWER is designed to assist students with essay-type exams. The steps in **ANSWER** can be summarized as:

- **A**nalyze the situation, by reading the item carefully, underlining important words, and estimating time needed;
- **N**otice requirements, by marking different parts of the question, and committing to a quality answer;
- **S**et up an outline, including main ideas, and checking outline ideas with the question;
- **W**ork in details, remembering previous learning and applying it in appropriate order, using abbreviations;
- **E**ngineer answer, writing an introductory paragraph, referring back to your outline, using topic sentences and additional details, and providing examples; and
- **R**eview work, checking the entire answer with all components of the question. (Hughes, 1996)

Grading and Scoring

Report Card Grades

Report card grading is an essential component of the U.S. educational system (Polloway, et al., 1994). This becomes obvious when you consider all the functions that grades serve for parents, teachers, students, guidance counselors, and administrators. As an example, Munk and Bursuck (2001) described a case of a student with learning disabilities who had received a grade of C in math:

> The special educator and general educator were pleased with the grade because it appeared to suggest average performance on the general education curriculum. However, the student's parents were displeased with the grade because of the significant time the student was spending on homework and preparing for quizzes. Similarly, the student interpreted positive feedback from his teachers to suggest that he was mastering the material and would be getting an A in the class; he was crestfallen on report card day to find the lower grade of C (p. 281).

In this case, there were three different sets of perceptions regarding the purpose of the grade: actual performance, time spent on assignments, or mastery of material. The grade may also have led to three different outcomes: satisfaction on the part of the teachers that the student was "succeeding" in the general education curriculum; determination on the part of parents to increase expectations; and demoralization on the part of the student (Munk & Bursuck, 2001).

As such, grading policies and procedures have been subjected to critical evaluation. Although the importance of grades in our society cannot be denied, several criticisms have been raised of current grading practices. It has been argued that grading is an ineffective motivator and it promotes competition over cooperation, subjects all students to universally applied standards, overlooks less-tangible learning outcomes, and emphasizes quality ratings over objective performance or mastery standards (Polloway et al., 1994). Selby and Murphy (1992) reported that students with learning disabilities, as well as their parents and teachers, may feel confusion and ambiguity about letter grades. Students with disabilities may feel helpless to achieve high grades and blame themselves for lower grades. Nevertheless, report card grading, in its current or a similar form, is likely to continue at least into the near future.

Recently, attention has been focused on grading practices involving students with disabilities. When the grades of students with learning disabilities—the largest disability category found in regular classrooms—have been examined, the results have not been very positive. Donahoe and Zigmond (1990) reported that students with learning disabilities consistently receive below average grades, with an overall grade average of about a "D." Zigmond, Levin, and Laurie (1985) reported that students with learning disabilities passed only about 75% of their classes during one academic year.

Across the country, standards for grading appear to be somewhat variable. Polloway et al. (1994) reported that about 39% of the districts surveyed had a specific policy for modifications in grading for students with disabilities (see also Rojewski, Pollard, & Meers, 1992). The most common responses involved modifications reflected in the students' IEPs, decisions made by a committee, and notations of accommodations noted on the report card.

Modify Grading Procedures

There appears to be no one "right" way to proceed when issuing report card grades to students with disabilities. However, following are some considerations that could be helpful in planning grading procedures (Bradley & Calvin, 1998; Christiansen & Vogel, 1998; Munk & Bursuck, 2001; Putnam, 1992; Rojewski, Pollard, & Meers, 1992; Salend, 1995):

1. *Consult school and district policy.* Many schools (although perhaps not the majority) have established official policies on issuing report card grades to students with disabilities. Find out whether your school has such a policy, and, if so, follow its guidelines. If revisions appear to be necessary in the policy, or if your district does not have a grading policy for students with disabilities, make recommendations to appropriate school personnel.

2. *Follow recommendations on the IEP.* IEPs typically state explicit goals and objectives for the academic year. These objectives can be made the basis for grading. For example, an objective on an IEP may state that the student will score 70% correct on tests given in a general education science class. This goal can be taken into consideration when determining the student's grade in the class.

3. *Make no grading modifications at all.* This approach is adopted by many regular classroom teachers, and there are some advantages to this approach. First, the grade the students earn reflects directly their success at performing in the inclusive environment of the regular classroom. Therefore, achieving an acceptable grade under these circumstances can be a source of pride. However, many students are simply not able to successfully compete in such an environment without any supports, and such a system may doom some students to failure. Carefully consider the effect of adopting such a policy.

4. *Use a pass–fail system.* Consider carefully what the minimum standard for a passing grade would be, considering attendance, effort, and performance. Using the PASS variables, prioritize class objectives so that students with disabilities or other special needs receive as much instruction on critical objectives as possible. At the end of the grading period, record with "pass" or "fail" (or "no pass") whether the student met these minimum criteria.

5. *Use a double-standard approach.* With this approach, students with disabilities can be graded using different standards for letter grades, such as "A," "B," "C," and so on. It may not be necessary simply to lower the standards, such that, for example, an "A" on the special education standard is equivalent to a "C" on the general education standard. It is also possible to consider the grade itself differently. For example, a grade on a special education standard could weight more heavily considerations such as effort, persistence, attitude, and progress (see Bursuck et al., 1996). Placing more importance on these areas also demonstrates to students that the grade they receive is more in their control than one that sets unrealistic academic standards and that may lead to resignation or quitting. A special education grading standard could also consider more carefully goals and objectives for the student documented on the student's IEP.

Often when different grading standards are applied, some notation is included that acknowledges that the standard is different. This could be done by a discreet note on the report card (e.g., "Special grading standard"), or could be done by recording the grade in some different way, for instance, by circling the letter awarded. Use of different grading standards can make goals more realistic and achievable for students. However, it is important to first determine that "normal" grading standards are not appropriate for particular students. If it seems that students may be able, with sufficient effort, to meet the same standards as the rest of the class, it may be best not to use a different standard.

For more information on report card grading modifications, see Munk and Bursuck (1998, 2001).

6. *Contracting.* In some cases it may be helpful to establish a formal contract with a student regarding report card grades (see chapter 7). The contract can specify what the student will do to earn a particular grade in the class. For example, to receive a "B," the contract may state that the student:

- will maintain an attendance rate of 90%.
- will be late no more than twice in a grading period.
- will turn in completed homework assignments 90% of the time.
- will participate satisfactorily in all class activities.
- will score 70% or higher on all class tests. Criteria can also be specified for other grades. The contract is then signed by the teacher, the student, and perhaps a parent. Grades are allocated according to the terms of the contract.

7. *Independent study.* Another possibility is to offer the class to a particular student without the normal course title (e.g., "World History"), but with the title "Independent Study in World History." The course is then set up to address the student's needs. The student may attend the "World History" class along with the other students, but the assignment requirements may be different, and the tests may be somewhat different or scored differently. Grades are assigned according to criteria established for the "Independent Study."

8. *Apply a decision-making model.* Use a systematic approach to grading students with disabilities. Bradley and Calvin (1998) recommend that you meet the following four criteria for developing effective grading practices:

- Frequent assessment
- Incorporation of critical learning elements (product, progress, and process)
- Accurate reporting of achievement to parent and student
- Provision of useful feedback indicating directions toward improvement (Bradley & Calvin, 1998, p. 27.)

Christiansen and Vogel (1998) suggest using a decision-making model to guide grading students with disabilities. Steps for the model include the following:

1. Determine the existing grading policies.
2. Know your theoretical grading approach.
3. Identify your co-teachers' grading approaches.
4. Develop grading procedures for individual students collaboratively with your co-teachers.

Munk and Bursuck (2001) surveyed parents of secondary students with and without disabilities on their perceptions of the purposes of report card grading. Although considerable agreement was noted, parents of students with disabilities were less likely to agree that report card grades effectively communicated general achievement and quality of work on the high school curriculum, or that they effectively conveyed the student's abilities to postsecondary schools or employers. However, none of the parents' comments suggested students should be given higher grades simply for trying hard, or that grades should serve a motivating purpose. Above all, parents supported adaptations tailored to their children's abilities that can be sensitive to changes in individual performance. Munk and Bursuck (2001) suggested that grading criteria be established ahead of time, so that students and parents can monitor progress more carefully, and misunderstandings can be avoided. In addition, teachers could consider changing the relative weights of assignments, and giving grades for both production and effort. With thoughtful modifications and effective communication, grading can be a useful and productive experience for everyone.

Many of the adaptations described for report card grading and test scoring in this chapter can also be applied to grading homework and seatwork assignments.

Summary

- Many types of tests are used in education; however, all tests must be reliable and valid to be useful.
- Norm-referenced testing compares the score of an individual with the scores of other students in a standardization sample.
- Modifications in standardized tests or administration procedures may detract from the validity of the test. However, such modifications as teaching test-taking skills, enhancing motivation, and enhancing examiner familiarity may improve test validity without compromising standardization.
- Competency-based and statewide testing assesses the skill levels of students and is being used more often in schools. Some modifications in these tests, or alternate assessments, may be appropriate for students with special needs.
- Teacher-made tests can be modified to obtain a clearer picture of student performance, without detracting from the test itself. Modifications can be applied to a variety of test formats.
- Curriculum-based measurement is an excellent means of documenting progress of all students, including students with disabilities or other special needs. Curriculum-based measurement allows the teacher to make instructional decisions as instruction is going on.
- Performance assessment evaluates student competence in particular instructional units. Because it focuses more on doing than writing or speaking, it may be particularly suited for diverse classrooms.
- Portfolio assessment is an ongoing means of obtaining information from student products and other sources. It is a particularly useful form of assessment that also has direct applications to some students with disabilities.
- Explicit instruction on general strategies to improve test performance, such as academic preparation, physical preparation, reducing anxieties, and increasing motivation, can improve the test performance of students with special needs.
- General strategies for improving standardized test performance include using separate answer sheets, using time wisely, elimination, and guessing strategies. Test-taking strategies for specific types of subtests can also improve standardized test performance.
- Test-taking strategies for teacher-made tests include strategies for taking objective tests; written tests, including fill-in-the-blank; short-answer; and essay tests.
- Some other test-taking strategies, such as SNOW, SCORER, PIRATES, and ANSWER, have been successfully taught to students with special needs and have improved their performance.
- Modifications can be made in grading and scoring the work of students with special needs. These modifications can be applied on report card grades, homework, and seatwork.

Assessment

Information in this chapter links most directly to:

Standard 8—Assessment, particularly:

Knowledge:
- Basic terminology used in assessment
- Legal provisions and ethical principles regarding assessment of individuals
- Use and limitations of assessment instruments
- National, state or provincial, and local accommodations and modifications

Skills:
- Gather relevant background information.
- Administer nonbiased formal and informal assessments.
- Use technology to conduct assessments.
- Develop or modify individualized assessment strategies.
- Interpret information from formal and informal assessments.
- Use assessment information in making eligibility, program, and placement decisions for individuals with exceptional learning needs, including those from culturally and/or linguistically diverse backgrounds.
- Report assessment results to all stakeholders using effective communication skills.
- Evaluate instruction and monitor progress of individuals with exceptional learning needs.
- Develop or modify individualized assessment strategies.
- Create and maintain records.

Inclusion Checklist
Assessment

When using and interpreting tests with students with disabilities and other special needs, have you considered:

- ❏ Different types of tests and their uses
- ❏ The reliability and validity of tests
- ❏ The use and possible adaptations of norm-referenced testing
- ❏ The use and possible adaptations of competency-based assessment
- ❏ Modifications of teacher-made and criterion-referenced tests, including:
  - ❏ General format modifications
  - ❏ True-false tests
  - ❏ Multiple-choice tests
  - ❏ Matching tests
  - ❏ Sentence completion items
  - ❏ Essay questions
  - ❏ Modify scoring procedures
- ❏ The uses of curriculum-based measurement
- ❏ The uses of performance assessment
- ❏ The uses of portfolio assessment and its special applications with students with disabilities
- ❏ Teaching test-taking skills, such as:
  - ❏ General test-taking strategies, including:
    - ❏ Academic preparation
    - ❏ Physical preparation
    - ❏ Improve attitudes
    - ❏ Reduce anxieties
- ❏ Strategies for standardized tests, such as:
  - ❏ General strategies, including:
    - ❏ Separate answer sheets
    - ❏ Elimination strategies
    - ❏ Guessing strategies
    - ❏ Using time wisely
  - ❏ Specific strategies for content area standardized tests, including:
    - ❏ Reading comprehension subtest strategies
    - ❏ Decoding subtest strategies
    - ❏ Mathematics computation subtests
    - ❏ Mathematics concepts subtests
    - ❏ Math problem-solving subtests
    - ❏ Science and social studies subtests
  - ❏ Teacher-made tests, such as:
    - ❏ Objective tests
    - ❏ Written tests
      - ❏ Sentence-completion tests
      - ❏ Short-answer tests
      - ❏ Essay tests
    - ❏ Performance-based tests
  - ❏ Other test-taking strategies, including:
    - ❏ SCORER
    - ❏ PIRATES
    - ❏ ANSWER
- ❏ Modifications in grading and scoring

Chapter 13

David Dow, 12
Perrysburg, Ohio
"Sunflowers"

Literacy

Objectives

After studying this chapter, you should be able to:

- Understand considerations and adaptive approaches relevant to basal textbooks, whole language, reading recovery, direct instruction, and code emphasis approaches.
- Describe adaptations for promoting word identification, including phonemic awareness, phonics, structural analysis, and basic sight words.
- Understand adaptations and technological advances to promote reading fluency, including repeated readings, curriculum-based measurement, classwide peer tutoring, and various computer programs.
- Design and implement strategies for teaching reading comprehension in inclusive settings.
- Describe and implement instructional and technological adaptations for written expression.
- Implement instructional strategies to enhance and improve spelling for students in inclusive settings.
- Describe and implement effective composition strategies such as self-regulation and self-instruction.

Over the years, much has been learned about the ways children learn to read and write (Brady & Shankweiler, 1991; Chall, 1983; Harris & Graham, 1992; Pressley, 1998; Snow, Burns, & Griffin, 1998; Stanovich, 1988). While many children begin to develop pre-literacy skills at early ages and proceed easily through developmental stages of reading, other students are much slower to develop reading skills, and may have difficulty with reading throughout their school years, and beyond. However, some approaches to reading have been found to be very helpful for improving literacy skills of students with disabilities and those at risk for school failure (Adams, 1990; Graham & Harris, 1994; Snow, Burns, & Griffin, 1998). This news is encouraging for students who will most likely need some specialized instruction in reading. Many of these strategies can be implemented by regular education teachers and supported by special education teachers. Today, there are several approaches to beginning reading instruction. It is important to understand these different approaches, because they carry different implications for students who are having difficulty learning to read.

Stages of Reading Development

Skills and understandings important for learning to read begin to develop almost at birth (Snow, Burns, & Griffin, 1998). Between the ages of birth to three, many children demonstrate understandings that will lead to later literacy. These include recognizing books by their cover, pretending to read, listening to stories, commenting on characters in books, attending to specific print, such as letters in names, and using purposive scribbling including letter-like forms and some features of standard writing. Between the ages of three and four, pre-literacy accomplishments can include understanding that it is print that is read in stories, understanding that letters can be individually named and can name some alphabet letters, attending to repeating (e.g., rhyming) sounds in language, and connecting information from a story to life experiences. Clearly, families can play a key role in promoting this skill development (Snow, Burns, & Griffin, 1998).

As children begin learning to read in school, they begin to go through a sequence of stages of reading development, beginning with pre-reading skills and continuing through expert reading (Chall, 1983; Cunningham & Stanovich, 1997; Lerner, 2000). After the early literacy or pre-reading stage (including phonemic awareness, discussed later), learners develop decoding skills (typically, grades 1–2), fluency and automaticity (grades 2–3), uses of reading for learning (grades 4–8), appreciation of multiple viewoints and levels of comprehension (including literal, inferential, critical, grades 9–12), and construction and reconstruction of reading for one's own purposes (including personal, professional, and civic purposes, college and beyond) (Chall, 1987; Lerner, 2000). Students with disabilities or other special needs may exhibit difficulties at any, or all, of these stages of learning to read.

For discussions of reading development, see Chall (1983, 1987); Cunningham and Stanovich (1997); Lerner (2000); Moats (1998b); Snow, Burns, and Griffin (1998).

Reading

CLASSROOM SCENARIO

Michelle

Michelle is a sincere, likeable seventh-grader. However, she has struggled with reading since first grade. She marvels at how easily some of her peers are able to read. She can't figure out why it seems so easy for them and yet is so difficult for her. Sometimes when she looks at the printed page, the words make no sense at all. They don't look a bit familiar to her, even when her teacher has her repeat the words over and over. She does her best to get by in school, by listening to other students read, by attending to what her teachers say about the text, and by studying the illustrations in her book. She never raises her hand in class, and sits quietly hoping she will not be noticed. Michelle really wants to learn to read better, but no one seems to be able to help her do so.

Using Basal Textbooks

The most traditional approach to reading instruction involves the use of **basal textbooks,** with a different text assigned for each grade level from kindergarten through middle school (Durkin, 1987). These textbooks contain short stories and comprehension questions designed to meet certain grade-level criteria. Some basal textbooks emphasize phonics; others highlight literature-based stories.

Most basal reading series include workbooks and work sheets that provide supplemental practice on comprehension and specific skills. In addition, the development of literacy is supported by language arts classes, typically distinct from reading classes, whereby students are provided separate spelling and grammar textbooks.

Developing Reading Skills Using Basals

Basal reading instruction is often conducted with small groups of students who are reading at a similar level. Teachers spend time working with each group, and groups spend independent time completing reading and associated workbook activities. Basals typically use vocabulary appropriate to the grade level, although new vocabulary words are frequently introduced before the selected readings. The controlled introduction of new words does not necessarily follow a sequence of phonics rules, and students with reading disabilities may experience difficulty with the vast number of sight words and word patterns encountered in the typical reading selection.

Some controversy has existed concerning the use of basal readers. It has been argued that because basal texts often become the single source of reading materials for students, the content and format of the textbooks need to be examined more critically (Dole, Rogers, & Osborn, 1987). Since then, many basal textbook approaches have been analyzed and researchers have published guidelines for selecting the most effective basal materials (Adoption Guidelines Project, 1990). Published criteria provide teachers with guidelines to help them be more objective in evaluating and selecting basal textbook series. Guidelines include information on beginning reading and decoding skills, comprehension instruction, skill instruction, and useful workbook activities (Adoption Guidelines Project, 1990).

Adapting Basal Approaches

If you have a student with serious reading difficulties and you are using a basal textbook approach, determine whether your basal offers a clear sequence of skills and sufficient review of newly learned skills generally considered beneficial to students with reading disabilities (Mather, 1992). Consult with the special education teacher to determine whether a different, more structured phonetic approach to reading instruction might be more helpful for that student, as a supplement or an alternative to the classroom materials. Because basal textbooks may contain a wide range of new vocabulary words, students with reading difficulties may benefit from alternative reading materials that include systematic phonics instruction, more practice with newly introduced word patterns, and reading with more familiar words. Information on these approaches is described later in this section.

Some basal series have attempted to provide a more balanced approach to literature and phonics instruction (Carnine, Silbert, & Kameeniu, 1997). Pinnell and Fountas (1999, 2001) provide listings of thousands of trade books by graded reading level that can be used to support whole language approaches to reading instruction.

The Whole Language Approach

The **whole language** approach to reading emphasizes meaning and integrates all literacy tasks within reading instruction. Whole language instruction is often theme based, and all traditional reading, writing, and language arts activities revolve around a central theme. A basic tenet of the approach is that the immersion of children in a literature-enriched environment promotes literacy. Many traditional skills such as phonics, sounding out words, spelling, grammar, and comprehension strategies are not directly taught, and there is an increased emphasis on meaning construction and use of context clues to figure out unknown words (Routman, 1991).

During whole language instruction, students engage in reading authentic literature independently and maintain journals documenting their progress and comprehension of reading materials. **Authentic literature** refers to trade books, real literature books (rather than the shortened versions of stories in basal textbooks), magazines, newspapers, and similar materials. The emphasis is placed on engaging students in literacy acts and promoting meaning. Many teachers have reported that when whole language was implemented in their schools, they no longer had reading group instruction and even their reading tables were removed from their classrooms. Stahl and Miller (1989) reported that whole language approaches might work best with very young children, as in the kindergarten years. Although many general educators advocate this approach to reading instruction, no efficacy studies documenting its specific effectiveness with students with serious reading disabilities are available to date (Pressley, 1998; Pressley & Rankin, 1994; Mastropieri & Scruggs, 1997). Nevertheless, some aspects of whole language instruction—for example, reading for meaning and integration of literacy activities—may be beneficial for all students.

Publishers of basal textbooks have distributed literature basals in an attempt to accommodate the whole language market (Snider, 1997). Although these texts do contain more authentic literature, they often fail to teach systematic phonics skills or to control vocabulary. Moreover, it has been noted that some literature basals have increased the variability in difficulty levels within a single text. As a teacher you may be expected to examine literature programs to determine their appropriateness for all students—including those with reading disabilities—before recommending their adoption.

Adapting Whole Language Approaches

Some estimate that as many as "25% of the students do not discover sound–symbol relationships on their own" (that is, without explicit instruction) (Snider, 1997, p. 54). Students with serious reading difficulties frequently have phonemic awareness deficits, and need special training to learn how words are composed of smaller, individual speech sounds (phonemes) (Liberman, Shankweiler, & Liberman, 1989; Pressley, 1998; Torgesen, 1994). Most students with reading problems benefit from instruction that includes explicit training in phonological awareness, letter recognition and formation, sound–symbol relationships, decoding practice using controlled texts, comprehension strategies, and motivational techniques (Moats, 1998a). Because whole language approaches typically do not include such components, they may be less beneficial for students with serious reading difficulties, without additional instructional support (Gersten & Dimino, 1993; Pressley & Rankin, 1994). Some commercially available literature programs have been designed for students with reading problems and may be useful in some cases. These programs include *Victory!* (Brigance, 1991) and *Learning Through Literature* (Dodds & Goodfellow, 1990–1991). It may be difficult, however, to find appropriate authentic literature for students who are reading at very low levels.

If you are using a whole language approach to reading, monitor the performance of struggling readers. Collect reading performance data, including reading rates, error rates, and comprehension levels over time to determine whether they are making sufficient progress (see chapter 12). Tape-record students' oral reading and review the tapes periodically to see if students are improving in overall reading competence. Make instructional decisions based on these performance data. Some research suggests that students with severe reading deficits may benefit from placement in inclusive classes using whole language if they are also receiving specialized reading instruction from special educators (Rudenga, 1992). It also may be possible for you to directly teach some of the skills necessary for reading texts used in whole language.

Consult special education teachers to determine the optimal instructional approach for any student with serious reading difficulties. Finally, if you have the opportunity as a teacher to examine literature programs to make recommendations for adoption, review what considerations have been made to meet the reading needs of all students.

Reading Recovery

Reading Recovery is a program that has been widely adopted in some states and school districts to help promote the early reading success of students at risk for reading failure. The program was developed by Marie Clay in New Zealand (Clay, 1985) and has extended to training programs in the United States. Reading Recovery identifies primary-age students who are not learning to read and provides them with one-to-one tutorial instruction for 30 minutes daily. Sessions emphasize reading from familiar books, instruction in letter-identification strategies, writing stories, assembling cut-up stories, and introducing the process of reading a new book. Additionally, teachers maintain daily records of students' reading progress. Keys to effective Reading Recovery instruction appear to be in the teacher's ability to analyze children's problems and devise appropriate instruction and feedback. Pinnell, DeFord, and Lyons (1988) and Clay and Watson (1987) provide lists of books suitable for students in Reading Recovery programs. One such book is Eric Carle's *The Very Hungry Caterpillar* (1994), which contains few words but has excellent pictures and a predictable story sequence. Nonreaders can use the pictures and predictable story lines to learn to use context clues when reading.

Some findings indicate that Reading Recovery is successful at improving reading for students at risk for reading failure. Unfortunately, few efficacy data are available to support all the claims made by those endorsing Reading Recovery (Hiebert, 1994). Some findings suggest that the program may be less successful with students who have moderate to severe reading difficulties (DeFord, Pinnell, Lyons, & Young, 1988) and that researchers have excluded data from these students when conducting program evaluations (Herman & Stringfield, 1995). Nevertheless, Reading Recovery has been considered effective for many young, struggling readers. If Reading Recovery is used in your school with students with severe reading problems, be certain that their progress is

For additional storybooks containing wonderful pictures suitable for younger students with reading difficulties, see Eric Carle's Website in the Web Links module in chapter 13 of the Companion Website.

For more information of the costs and benefits of Reading Recovery compiled by Bonnie Grossen, Gail Coulter, and Barbara Ruggles, go to the Web Links module in chapter 13 of the Companion Website.

Using literature is one methodology for teaching literacy.

carefully documented, and determine the steps that will be taken if acceptable progress is not being made.

Direct Instruction and Code Emphasis

Direct instruction is an instructional method that has proved successful with students with disabilities and those at risk for school failure. Direct instruction involves a systematic, teacher-led approach using materials that contain a controlled vocabulary and emphasize a **code approach** to reading instruction. For example, students are taught the sound–symbol relationships among letters and are provided sufficient practice decoding specific word patterns in reading passages before being presented with reading selections containing unfamiliar words (Carnine, Silbert, & Kameenui, 1997). Individual sounds and words are introduced systematically and practiced in isolation, in word lists, sentences, paragraphs, short stories, and accompanying workbook activities.

This approach employs what is referred to as the "code-emphasis" approach because the code system for the relationship between letters and sounds is explicitly taught. This approach may be particularly effective for students who lack phonemic awareness, who have not acquired the ability to sound out words, and who struggle with learning sight words (Kennedy & Backman, 1993; Polloway, Epstein, Polloway, Patton, & Ball, 1986; Wagner & Torgesen, 1987).

Curriculum materials are available that contain a code-emphasis approach to reading instruction. These materials include, for example, *Reading Mastery* (a basal series, Engelmann & Bruner, 1995), and *Corrective Reading: Decoding Series* (Engelmann, Becker, Hanner, & Johnson, 1988). Both of these reading series use an effective instruction model of delivery, including teacher modeling and demonstration, frequent student responding and feedback, and practice using the controlled vocabulary materials to teach reading. Students learn and practice specific word attack skills and apply these skills to reading passages. Because students with reading disabilities frequently rely too much on context cues (Johnson, 1992; Pressley, 1998; Stanovich, 1994), the materials encourage use of word attack skills, by, for example, not providing pictures or pictures that can be seen only after turning the page. Figure 13.1 contains a sample page from the *Corrective Reading Series.* The accompanying passage tells the story of "Chee, the Dog," who often speaks nonsense phrases. These phrases are included to compel students to focus on their word attack skills to read the words.

Other commercially available controlled vocabulary reading programs include the *Merrill Linguistic Reading Program* (published by SRA) and *Palo Alto Reading Program* (published by Harcourt,

Implementation of curriculum and instruction, including direct instruction, are topics on the Praxis *Special Education: Core Knowledge* Tests.

LESSON 18

1   cold   store   that   read   back
    soon   job   beans   helped
    ham   better   things   much

2   name   like   came
    note   bone   home

3   Gretta   Chee   let's   day
    pay   played   stay   someone
    saying   door   bigger   said
    I've   cook   other   some
    don't   can't   folks   didn't
    another   their   became   one

4

CHEE, THE DOG

Gretta got a little dog. She named the dog Chee. Chee got bigger and bigger each day.

On a very cold day, Gretta said, "Chee, I must go to the store. You stay home. I will be back."

Chee said, "Store, lots, of, for, no."

Then Gretta said, "Did I hear that dog say things?"

Chee said, "Say things can I do."

Gretta said, "Dogs don't say things. So I must not hear things well."

But Chee did say things. Gretta left the dog at home. When Gretta came back, Chee was sitting near the door.   [1]

Gretta said, "That dog is bigger than she was."

Then the dog said, "Read, read for me of left."

Gretta said, "Is that dog saying that she can read?" Gretta got a pad and made a note for the dog. The note said, "Dear Chee, if you can read this note I will hand you a bag of bones."

Gretta said, "Let's see if you can read." Chee said, "Dear Chee, if you can read this note, I will ham you a bag for beans."   [1]

Gretta said, "She can read, but she can't read well. Ho, ho."

Chee became very mad. She said "For note don't read ho ho."

Gretta said, "Chee gets mad when I say ho, ho."

Chee said, "Yes, no go ho ho."

Then Gretta felt sad. She said, "I didn't mean to make you mad. I don't like you to be sad. I will help you say things well."

Then Chee said, "Yes, well, of say for things."

So every day, Gretta helped Chee say things. She helped Chee read, too.   [1]

Chee got better and better at saying things. And she got better at reading. And she got bigger and bigger. When she was one year old, she was bigger than Gretta.

On a hot day Gretta left Chee at home, but when she got back, Chee met her at the door. "Did you have fun at the your job?" Chee asked.

"Yes, I did," Gretta said.

"I don't have much fun at home," Chee said. "I think I will get a job. I don't like to stay home."

"Dogs can't have jobs," Gretta said.

Chee said, "You have a job. So I will get a job, too."   [1]

Figure 13.1

Part of a Corrective Reading Lesson

Note: From *Corrective Reading: Decoding Strategies* (p. 26), by S. Engelmann, G. Johnson, D. Carnine, L. Meyer, W. Becker, J. Eisele, 1988, Chicago, Science Research Associates. Copyright 1988 by SRA/McGraw Hill. Reprinted by permission.

Brace, Jovanovich). A linguistic series teaches word *families (cat, fat, pat, mat, sat)* rather than individual letter sounds.

The *Edmark Reading Program* (published by Pro-Ed) is another example of a systematic reading program. *Edmark* is a sight-word program designed for students with few or no reading skills, and who have not benefited from an explicit phonics approach. Level I introduces the direct teaching of 150 sight words and word endings including *-ing, -ed,* and *-s,* and Level II introduces 200 more words and provides review on the first 150 words. Lessons are sequenced into small steps and include prereading, word identification, following directions, matching pictures and phrases, and reading storybooks.

Considerations and Adaptations

A commonly asked question of direct instruction approaches is whether students who are taught using a code-emphasis approach can transfer these reading skills to other, less-structured reading materials. Snider (1997) provided evidence that students with learning disabilities who were taught using the code-emphasis approach in special education settings successfully transferred their read-

Skill instruction is supported by a number of curricula including SRA's Reading Mastery *program.* (From *Reading Mastery 1, Presentations Book A* (rainbow edition, p. 73) by S. Englemann and E.C. Bruner, 1995, Columbus, OH: SRA Macmillan/McGraw Hill. Copyright 1995 by SRA Division of Macmillan/McGraw Hill School Publishing Co. Reprinted by permission.)

ing skills to literature-based books. However, she emphasized that such transfers to other, more "authentic" reading materials should be monitored, and not taken for granted.

Another frequently asked question is whether the redundancy and structure of a direct instruction approach decreases motivation in students. Students who have serious reading difficulties can respond well to this instructional approach, especially if the teacher is enthusiastic, builds praise and rewards into the instruction, makes students aware of the progress they are making, and monitors student fatigue. Further, students are more likely to respond positively if they can see that they are making progress in reading (see also chapter 9).

A third question concerns whether providing students with exclusively phonetic training can result in too little focus on comprehension of text. Most researchers today agree that reading instruction should be balanced, with time also allocated toward reading for pleasure, self-selecting reading materials, and focus on meaning and comprehension skills (Adams, 1990; Pressley, 1998; Pressley & Rankin, 1994). Ensure that your reading program provides all the elements necessary for students to become skilled and motivated readers.

Adaptations for Promoting Word Identification

Reading is often a slow and laborious process for individuals with serious reading difficulties; that is why most students with reading difficulties require additional instruction and practice at identifying words. Readers need to become fluent at word reading so they will be able to devote sufficient cognitive energy to comprehending what they read. Some have referred to this as "automaticity" (LaBerge & Samuels, 1974). However, before readers can acquire automaticity, they must be able to read individual words. **Phonemic awareness** deficits may be at the core of the reading difficulty (Blachman, 1991; Kennedy & Backman, 1993; Lyon, 1995; Wagner, Torgesen, & Rashotte, 1994). However, specific training in **phonemic awareness** and phonics promotes better reading (Fuchs, Fuchs, Thompson, et al., 2001; Vadasy, Jenkins, Antil, Wayne, & O'Conner, 1997).

Pocket charts help students practice sorting letters, words, and sounds. Pocket charts can be made for individual or whole-class use.

Phonemic Awareness

Phonemes are the smallest sound units that have meaning, such /t/ and /l/. Phonemic awareness training includes activities to provide instruction and practice at listening and using sounds in isolation initially, followed by the use of words in context and in a reading passage. The purpose of phonemic awareness training is for students to learn that words are composed of individual sounds that can be combined and separated to create new words. Later, they learn that these individual phonemes can be represented by letters. Sample phonemic awareness activities include the following:

- Discriminating sounds, for example: "Tell me if these two words have the same, or different, first sound: *cap—cat.*"
- Sound blending or making individual sounds into words, for example: "What word am I saying?: /c/—/a/—/t/?"
- Segmenting words into individual phonemes, for example: "How many sounds are in the word *fan?* What are the sounds?"
- Rhyming sounds, for example: "Tell me some words that rhyme with *fall.* Now, tell me some 'make-believe' words that rhyme with *fall.*"

Training programs are implemented daily for a short period of time. For example, Vadasy et al. (1997) taught children:

- Letter names and sounds
- Categorizing sounds
- Creating rhymes
- Onset-rime tasks, that is, segmenting words into beginning (initial sounds including the first consonant) and later sounds, such as "h-" "-op" for "hop"
- Phonogram exercises with magnetic letter boards
- Spelling words on magnetic letter boards
- Writing
- Storybook reading

Lovett, Lacerenza, et al. (2000) trained elementary-level students with reading disabilities in reading skills, and observed the greatest gains in a program that combined direct instruction in phonemic awareness and sound blending with word identification strategy training.

Research has documented the positive effects of phonemic awareness training on young children's reading performance (Fuchs, Fuchs, Thompson, et al., 2001; Lovett, Lacerenza, & Borden, 2000; O'Conner, Jenkins, & Slocum, 1995; Vadasy et al., 1997).

Gamelike activities are available that emphasize phonological awareness training. For example, Torgesen and Bryant (1994) developed *Phonological Awareness Training for Reading*, which is in a board game format. In one game, Rocky the Robot "speaks" only in phonemes or onset-rime constructions, and students must create the words Rocky is trying to say. For example, a teacher could say, "Rocky says, 'p-an.' What is he trying to say?" These materials provide instruction and practice with phonemic awareness skills over a 12- to 14-week period.

Several excellent activities for developing phonemic awareness are described in detail by Fischer (1993). One activity is playing "I Spy," with a letter sound. For example, a teacher might say: "I spy something that begins with the letter sound /m/ . . . or ends with the sound /t/ . . . " (Fischer, 1993, p. 91), and every student is required to generate an appropriate word. Another is to begin sentences such as "I went to my uncle's house and found a _____"; or, "On my way to school I saw a _____," and ask students to supply words with designated phonemes. Many activities can be designed as games, which can increase students' motivation.

Another program combines the use of mnemonic strategies using pictures to promote learning of sound–letter associations and sound segmentation skills (Telian, 1993, 1995). Mnemonic letter cards are used to introduce new sounds, and activities are provided for practicing learning letter sounds, blending and segmenting sounds in isolation and words for reading and spelling. The goal is to have the mnemonic strategies facilitate initial acquisition of the letters and associated sounds.

Computerized training programs are also available commercially. Pro-Ed distributes *Daisy Quest* and *Daisy Cow* (Adventure Learning Software), which provide practice on rhyming; beginning, middle, and ending sounds; sound blending; and segmenting. Curriculum Associates distributes a computerized program, *SuperSonic Phonics* that provides instruction in phonics skills such as beginning sound–symbol relationships and decoding.

Consult with special education teachers and speech and language specialists in your school if you suspect your students have phonemic awareness difficulties. These specialists can recommend specific practice activities to promote better phonemic awareness.

Phonics

Phonics has been defined as "the study of sound; the method of using sounds of a language when teaching people to read; or . . . the letter–sound correspondences" (Fischer, 1993, p. 1). Training in phonics refers to providing instruction in the sound–symbol associations among letters and symbols. Children who learn to read without any difficulties—and many do—may figure out this system independently. However, students without good phonics skills have to rely on visual memory, context clues, or picture clues to guess what the unfamiliar word is. Unfortunately, reliance on such clues is not always effective, especially when the many letter–sound relationships are unknown (Pressley, 1998). These students can benefit from explicit phonics instruction. It has been suggested that phonics instruction works best when it is integrated within a reading program and builds on a student's prior phonemic awareness knowledge. According to Stahl (1992), an exemplary phonics program:

- builds on students' knowledge about how print works.
- builds on a phonemic awareness foundation.
- is explicit, clear, and direct.
- is integrated within a reading and language arts program.
- emphasizes reading words rather than memorizing rules.
- includes learning onsets and rimes.
- emphasizes development of independent word recognition strategies.
- emphasizes development of fluency-building word recognition skills.

Instruction in phonics proceeds systematically; practice is provided using familiar words before new words are introduced. Usually, regular words are introduced before irregular words, and sufficient practice in reading and spelling is provided before introducing new vocabulary. In phonics-based programs, instruction follows a specific sequence of skills. Although variation exists, a possible sequence could include the following (see, for example, Polloway, Smith, & Miller, 2003):

1. Individual consonant and short vowel sounds
2. Simple patterns such as *vc* (vowel–consonant, e.g., "at," "it") and *cvc* (consonant–vowel–consonant, e.g., "bat," "hit").

For more information on phonemic awareness, see Adams, Foorman, Lundberg, and Beeler (1998).

Help beginning readers make alphabet books and individual letter books that contain all learned letters and illustrations of words containing those sounds. Children can add new letters and words as they learn them. Books can be illustrated and read to partners or parents.

Magnetic letter boards are useful for practicing new letter and word sounds and symbols. Children can make words using the magnetic letters and practice forming new words from a set of letters or letter sounds (e.g., /at/ words).

The Wilson Reading System, also designed for students with severe reading difficulties, uses a structured systematic approach including phonemic awareness training. To view materials, go to the Web Links module in chapter 13 of the Companion Website.

3. Consonant digraphs (e.g., *ch, sh, th*) and consonant blends (e.g., *bl, st, br*).
4. Long vowels, including final *e,* (such as "hope," "tape") and double vowels or vowel digraphs (such as "keep," "tail").
5. *r-* and *l-*controlled vowels, such as "car" and "call."
6. Diphthongs, such as *ow, oi, aw.*

Once these skills are mastered, students can learn higher level word analysis skills, such as compound words, prefixes and suffixes, contractions, and syllabication. It is important that these skills are taught to students who have demonstrated a need to learn these skills, that they are taught in the context of a reading program that also emphasizes meaning, and that the overall emphasis is on reading words, rather than memorizing rules. A variety of curriculum materials are available, in addition to *Corrective Reading* and *Reading Mastery,* that emphasize phonics skill instruction.

The *Saxon Phonics K, 1, and 2* materials (Simmons, 1996a, 1996b) provide systematic instruction beginning with auditory discrimination and sound-blending activities for reading and spelling, and reading and reading comprehension activities. Materials include alphabet strips, letter tiles, worksheets, readers, and letter, picture, and sight word cards.

The *Lindamood Phoneme Sequencing Program for Reading, Spelling, and Speech* (LIPs) materials were also designed to teach explicit phonological awareness and phonics skills to students who experienced difficulties learning to read by other methods (Lindamood & Lindamood, 1998). Kennedy and Backman (1993) demonstrated that the Lindamood and Lindamood method raised the reading achievement of students with learning disabilities after 50-minute daily sessions during a 6-week period. Specific training procedures included the following:

- Practicing auditory discrimination using letter sounds
- Associating speech sounds with the letters (symbols)
- Identifying speech sounds or words with their orthographic (spelled) symbols
- Using those sounds and symbols in reading and writing activities

Recipe for Reading (Traub, 1975) provides suggestions and activities for teaching sound–symbol associations in reading to students who have experienced difficulties learning to read the traditional ways. Traub (1975) sequences the order of skill development from beginning sounds, consonant–vowel–consonant sounds, two-syllable words, up to more complex rules including spelling with affixes. Exercises are designed to include auditory, visual, and kinesthetic (motor) practice by incorporating, seeing, saying, and writing activities. Figure 13.2 includes a sequence chart for introducing letter sounds from *Recipe for Reading.*

Students with severe to profound hearing loss are typically far less proficient than other students in phonological skills. During the elementary years, they appear to rely more on visual than acoustic cues of letters and words. In secondary school, and later in college, they may rely more on phonological information. Strategies recommended for teaching reading to students with severe hearing impairments include early access to language by means of signing, and simultaneous exposure to written texts. Reading skills of students with hearing impairments appears to be associated with language and vocabulary development (Marschark & Harris, 1996).

Structural Analysis

Structural analysis refers to the ability to examine structures of words and break them into pronounceable syllables. As students acquire some reading and phonics skills, they encounter more complex words during reading. When they encounter unknown words, they can be taught to use structural analysis to decode them. Structural analysis involves examining a word by familiar word parts, such as the prefix, suffix, syllables, or smaller word parts. Teach basic syllabication rules to help students.

Another strategy that uses structural analysis as well as some other steps is the **DISSECT strategy.** The DISSECT strategy teaches a multiple-step procedure for figuring out unfamiliar words (Ellis, 1996; Lenz, Schumaker, Deshler, & Beals, 1984). Each letter in DISSECT stands for one of the steps in the procedure. Each step of the strategy is:

STUDENT'S NAME _____

First Group	**Two-Syllable Words Using Consonant Blends**	ge—dge
(c-o-a-d-g-m-l-h-t)		Review: Hard-Soft c and g
i (as in Igloo)	Endings: ing-ang-ong-ung-ink-ank- onk-unk	"y" as a Vowel
k		Long Vowel in Syllable Division
p	"Magic e"	aw (as in straw)
ch (as in chin)	Review Tests Using "Magic e" Words	au (as in August)
u (as in up)	Detached Syllable "Magic e"	a (as in ball)
b	Two-Syllable Words Containing "Magic e"	oi (as in oil)
r		oy (as in boy)
f	ph (as in phone)	"ing" as an Ending
n	ea (as in eat)	VCV Spelling Rule
e (as in egg)	oa (as in soap)	Suffix: "ed"
s (as in sit)	ai (as in mail)	ew (as in grew)
sh	ee (as in tree)	tch (as in catch)
th (hard—as in that)	ay (as in play)	eigh (as in eight)
w	oe (as in toe)	ie (as in chief)
wh	Syllable Division	eu (as in Europe)
y (as in yes)	Review Tests: Two-Syllable Words	ei (as in ceiling)
v	er (as in her)	tion (as in action)
x	ir (as in bird)	ue (as in rescue)
z	ur (as in burn)	sion (as in division)
th (soft—as in thin)	ow (as in clown)	ow (as in snow)
qu (as in queen)	ou (as in ouch)	ch (as in school)
Review Tests: CVC Words	igh (as in light)	ea (as in head)
Two-Syllable Compound Words	Endings: ble-fle-tle-dle-gle- kle-ple-zle	oo (as in good)
Spelling Rule: ff-ll-ss		ew (as in few)
Detached Syllables	ild-old-ind-ost-olt	ei (as in vein)
Review Tests: CVC Detached Syllables	are (as in star)	ue (as in true)
Two-Syllable Words	or (as in horn)	ou (as in group)
Consonant Blends	oo (as in zoo)	sion (as in mansion)
Review Tests: Consonant Blends	Endings: ly-vy-by-dy-ty-fy-ny- py-sy	ea (as in great)
Detached Syllables—Consonant Blends		ch (as in machine)
	ck (as in black)	s (as in is)
Review Tests: Detached Syllable- Consonant Blends	Hard-Soft c	Affixes and Root Words
	Hard-Soft g	Spelling with Affixes

Figure 13.2
Sequence Chart
Note: From *Recipe for Reading* (2nd ed.), by N. Traub, 1975, Cambridge, MA: Educators Publishing Service. Copyright 1975 by Educators Publishing Service. Reprinted with permission.

- **D**iscover the context of the word.
- **I**solate the word's prefix.
- **S**eparate the word's suffix.
- **S**ay the word's stem.
- **E**xamine the word's stem using rules of 3s and 2s and segment into pronounceable parts.

    3s rule: underline 3 letters if stem begins with a consonant (example: re<u>new</u>al).
    2s rule: underline 2 letters if stem begins with a vowel (example: un<u>op</u>ened).
    repeat for all letters in stem.

- **C**heck with another person to see if you are correct.
- **T**ry finding the word in the dictionary.

Teaching students this strategy provides them with tools they can use independently when they encounter unfamiliar words.

Teach students other problem-solving strategies so they will become more independent readers. For example, show them how to use context clues to guess what the word might be, based on the rest of the sentence or paragraph, the title, subheadings, charts, graphs, and accompanying illustrations (Deshler, Ellis, & Lenz, 1996).

Software phonics programs are also available commercially. For example, *Phonics Based Learning to Read Programs* are available from *Special Times,* Special Education Software for grades K through 12. The programs are designed for grades 1 through 6 and include activities with words, sentences, and paragraphs and record student progress. Consult your special education teacher to determine whether additional work in phonics instruction may be appropriate for students experiencing reading difficulties. *Lexia Software* and *FastForWord* (Scientific Learning Corporation) are other approaches that emphasize phonics, phonemic awareness, and auditory discrimination. For more information on software for promoting reading, see the Technology Highlight. For Websites of these software publishers, go to the Web Links module in chapter 13 of the Companion Website.

Technology Highlight

Technology for Enhancing Literacy Instruction

Technological advances have provided numerous opportunities to assist with teaching literacy for students with disabilities. Many of the devices are referred to as assistive technologies in that students' access to the curriculum is enhanced either by enhancing the input or the output procedures, while others are referred to as software, as they are materials designed to enhance literacy. Both hardware and software devices are available that can be used to enhance literacy for students with disabilities.

Intellikeys, an alternative to the traditional keyboard, is a device used to assist with keyboarding skills. *Intellikeys* contains overlays consisting of large letters and numbers that are more accessible for some students with disabilities. *Intellikeys* keyboards come in standard forms but are also programmable, using the *Overlay Maker* software program, to meet individual needs. Keyboards plug into Usb ports. (Available from IntelliTools, Inc. 1720 Corporate Circle, Petaluma, CA 94954; 800-899-6687 (USA and Canada); Phone: 707-773-2000; Fax: 707-773-2001 or the Website.)

Software is available that provides speech-to-computerized text. For example, *Ereader* developed by *www.CAST.org* is a tool that when used with any computerized text adds the speech component. Text from word processing programs, other computerized programs, the Internet, scanned-in materials from classrooms, or any electronic text can be read orally to students once *Ereader* is installed onto a computer. Users can select the volume, speed, and pitch of the program and can alter the fonts and color of the text once text is imported into the *Ereader* program.

IntelliTalk (IntelliTools) provides speech components to word processing in male or female voices. *IntelliTalk's* read-aloud feature can read each letter as it is typed into the program and can read back what has been written. It is also available in a Spanish version. These "talking" word processor programs that provide speech output for highlighted words on word processing programs are assistive technologies that enable struggling readers and writers to have more access to literacy tasks.

Write: Outloud (Don Johnston Incorporated) is another word processing program that contains text-to-speech functions along with the typical word processing functions like spell checkers and search functions. This program was developed for children and is easy to learn to use. *Co: Writer* (Don Johnston Incorporated) contains word prediction components that predict words based on the initial few letters that are typed. Students select the desired word from the word choices that are supplied.

Numerous software programs are available to provide assistance with literacy instruction. Examine the software to determine whether it meets the needs of your students. Many of the Websites for these programs can be accessed from the Web Links module in chapter 13 of the Companion Website.

Basic Sight Vocabulary

Many words are used frequently at various grade levels and are often referred to as basic **sight words.** These irregular words cannot be easily decoded using phonics skills, and include words such as: *the, a, is, to,* and *one.* Many word lists are available that contain graded sight word lists (e.g., Dolch word lists). Students with reading difficulties may require additional practice at identifying and saying these words automatically. Figure 13.3 provides a list of commonly seen words referred to as sight words.

One suggestion for providing practice developing basic sight vocabulary is to have students make and use flashcards containing their sight words. Some time each day can be devoted to saying the sight words with a partner. Cards containing words pronounced correctly and quickly can be stacked together, cards containing words said correctly but slowly in another stack, and cards containing words unknown in a third stack. Maintain records of the number of words in each stack. Gradually add new words as sight words are mastered.

Some teachers prepare checklists that contain new words or difficult words for students to learn. The checklists are practiced daily at school and at home, and teachers and parents simply put a checkmark next to words read correctly under the appropriate date.

Finally, some teachers prepare large wall charts and prominently display listings of words they want students to master. Figure 13.4 has an example of a word wall chart. Charts can be changed as students master words. Word ladders can be constructed displaying words learned by students. Arrange ladders by placing words with similar sounds or patterns together. As new words are introduced, they can be added to the appropriate ladder. Time can be scheduled daily to have students go to the chart and practice saying the words as quickly as possible.

One program uses a combination of mnemonics with pictures and stories to promote learning irregular sight words. *Sight Words You Can See* (Castagnozzi, 1996) contains 7 sets of 12 sight words and accompanying mnemonic pictures and stories. The picture cues are used to trigger the memory for the sound of parts of the words. For example, a story about Wally the Walrus is used to help link the memory of the sound for the letter "w" and the "waw" sound, which is also linked with a symbolic wavy line to represent water underneath sight words containing that sound.

Students with moderate and severe disabilities may benefit from teaching specific sight words to enhance their classroom experience, daily living, and job skills (Browder & Xin, 1998). These could include words for shopping, cooking, reading warning labels, and reading signs for community recreation. Fletcher and Abood (1988) found that students with mild mental retardation who could read at nearly the fourth-grade level could not read the words on many warning labels, such as "inhale," "flammable,"

Chapter 15 contains a sample checklist for new vocabulary words.

a	came	her	look	people	too
after	can	here	looked	play	two
all	come	him	long	put	up
an	could	his	make	ran	us
and	day	house	man	run	very
are	did	how	mother	said	was
am	do	I	me	saw	we
as	don't	I'm	my	see	went
asked	down	if	no	she	were
at	for	in	not	so	what
away	from	into	now	some	when
back	get	is	of	that	where
be	go	it	old	the	will
because	going	just	on	then	with
before	good	keep	one	there	would
big	had	kind	or	they	you
boy	has	know	our	this	your
but	have	like	out	three	
by	he	little	over	to	

Figure 13.3

Sample Sight Words

Note: From *Guided Reading: Good First Teaching for All Children* by Irene Fountas and Gay Su Pinnell. Copyright © 1996 by Irene Fountas and Gay Su Pinnell. Published by Heinemann, a division of Reed Elsevier Inc., Portsmouth, NH. Reprinted with permission.

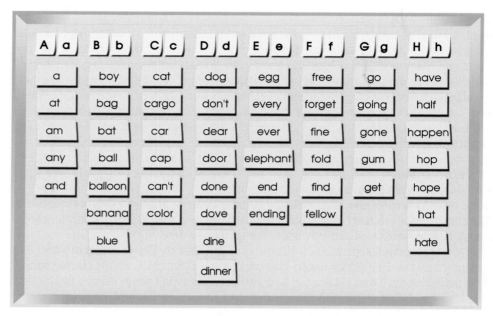

Figure 13.4
Wall Chart Containing Sight Words

and "inaccessible." Sight words have been taught using a variety of methods, including modeling, prompting, error correction, and feedback (Browder & Xin, 1998). Students' comprehension can be promoted by having them find the words in pictures or real settings, or by having them give definitions. Try using classroom peers and sight word cards to help promote sight word recognition.

Adaptations for Promoting Reading Fluency

Most students with reading difficulties require additional practice activities designed to help them read more fluently. Several procedures are available to promote fluency (Mastropieri, Leinhart, & Scruggs, 1999).

Repeated Readings

It has been suggested that, in learning to play the piano, no one would expect students to continuously sight-read new passages. Rather, students are expected to practice new pieces until they have become skilled and automatic, before they move on to new and more difficult pieces (Anderson, Hiebert, Scott, & Wilkinson, 1985; Samuels, 1981). Similarly, students who have struggled to learn to read a new passage should have the opportunity to re-read the passage until fluent, effortless reading is achieved. Having students read the same passage more than once is one way to increase fluency (O'Shea, Sindelar, & O'Shea, 1987). Students often enjoy the opportunity to repeat the same passage. As their familiarity of the passage increases, their fluency and comprehension should also increase. Record reading rates on a graph, and indicate which passages are "repeated readings" and which are first-time readings. You could set target rates (e.g., 140 words per minute) for reading selected passages, and provide rewards and encouregment for reaching these targets. To help develop fluency on these passages, provide extra practice on difficult words or phrases that slow students' rate.

Reading a single passage more fluently, through repeated readings, may not always bring about general improvements in reading fluency. However, continued practice on specific reading passages, and additional experience in fluent reading with repeated readings, may lead over time to more fluent reading overall (Mastropieri, Leinhart, & Scruggs, 1999).

Curriculum-Based Measurement

Curriculum-based measurement (CBM) can help monitor students' fluency progress. Time students' oral reading several days a week and chart their performance. Graphed reading rates will demonstrate to students the rate at which they are improving in reading fluency. The *Corrective Reading* materials contain passages that are identified in 100-word segments that can be used to complete regular timings using a standardized number of words. Some teachers prefer to time students for a designated amount of time. For example, 1- or 2-minute time segments can be used to measure the number of words read correctly. When either the number of words or the amount of time is held constant, the opposite is recorded on the graph.

Software is available that administers grade-level appropriate reading passages and maze comprehension tests, scores, and graphs individual student and class performance (Fuchs, Hamlett, & Fuchs, 1997). Research findings indicate that use of this CBM in general education classrooms helps improve reading fluency of students with disabilities (Fuchs, Fuchs, Hamlett, Phillips, & Bentz, 1994). In addition, combining the use of CBM with classwide peer tutoring in general education classes also helps promote reading improvement in students at risk for school failure (Phillips, Hamlett, Fuchs, & Fuchs, 1993).

Classwide Peer Tutoring

More time spent in oral reading can help develop fluency over time. Classwide peer tutoring, in which pairs of students take turns reading to each other, is one good way to dramatically increase the amount of time students spend reading in class. In classwide peer tutoring configurations, students can develop fluency using such other components as repeated readings, 1- or 2-minute timings, extra practice with difficult parts, and curriculum-based measurement.

Computer Programs

Software designed for computers can provide an alternative means of practicing reading decoding and fluency building activities. Students are usually highly motivated to use computers, and many programs contain gamelike formats to entice students to put forth extra effort. Computer software is available to help promote reading fluency, increase vocabulary, and promote reading comprehension. For example, *DLM Reading Fluency* (distributed by SRA) consists of four programs designed to promote reading decoding fluency: *Hint and Hunt I and II, Construct A Word I and II, Syllasearch I, II, III, and IV,* and *Word Wise I, II, and III.* Many of the activities are in gamelike format, contain speech and animated graphics, and hold students' attention while increasing decoding fluency. *Academic Skill Builders in Language Arts* (distributed by SRA) consist of gamelike programs that provide practice in making words.

Technological Adaptations to Promote Reading

New technological advances may be used to help promote reading for students with reading difficulties. Some technological advances include modification of printed materials with Braille, large-print, magnifying devices, use of Opticon and reading machines such as the Kurzweil Reader, and use of adaptive devices to facilitate page turning. Other adaptations involve the use of audiotape formats, including tape-recorded text, variable speed cassettes and speech compressors, listening centers, and enhancement of audiotape presentations.

New software programs are continually being developed that provide additional practice activities for students with reading difficulties. Many programs can be used independently by students while maintaining their attention due to the motivational nature of many programs. Above all, a classroom environment that encourages reading, no matter what the reading ability of the student, is important for reading success.

Reading Comprehension

CLASSROOM SCENARIO

Carmen

Carmen can read the words in the stories, but when someone asks him what the story is about, he can't remember. In fact, he isn't sure he ever understood what the words mean. For example, Ms. Simpson, his third-grade teacher, always has him read orally during class and consistently gives him praise for his reading efforts. However, whenever Ms. Simpson says, "Now tell me what the story is about in your own words," Carmen is lost. He is beginning to dislike reading class because more and more time is being devoted to questioning about the stories rather than just reading out loud.

In a maze task, students read a passage in which words have been omitted. For each omitted word, students select the word that fits best from several (generally three) options.

Refer to chapter 4 for additional information on technological adaptations.

Reading comprehension is the ultimate goal of reading. More than 20 years ago, Durkin (1978–1979) reported that teachers spent little time teaching children how to comprehend during reading. Reading comprehension research has accumulated greatly since that time, and has provided some effective strategies for improving reading comprehension for students with disabilities and other special needs (Mastropieri & Scruggs, 1997; Mastropieri, Scruggs, Bakken, & Whedon, 1996; Swanson, 2000; Talbott, Lloyd, & Tankersley, 1994). Students with reading comprehension difficulties often benefit from explicit instruction and practice using strategies that promote reading comprehension.

Strategies for Teaching Reading Comprehension in Inclusive Settings

Specific reading comprehension strategies can be taught for use before, during, and after reading passages. The strategies presented here are sequenced from those requiring the least to the most teacher instruction and from those having the least to the greatest effect on students' performance. In other words, although the strategies discussed first positively affect students' comprehension and take less time to teach, the strategies discussed later have a much greater impact on students' comprehension. They also require more instructional time and practice for students to master. As a teacher, you will have to decide which strategies you will use based on a number of factors, including the amount of instructional time available to you.

Use Basic Skills and Reinforcement Strategies

You may recall from chapter 9 that **reinforcement** refers to providing rewards or positive comments to students to encourage and motivate them as they work and answer comprehension questions successfully. Although reinforcement is effective, it may be best when combined with some of the strategies discussed in this section.

Vocabulary instruction refers to providing students with practice learning specific vocabulary words that will be encountered in the readings. Although teaching the vocabulary is beneficial, the effects on comprehension may be more pronounced when this strategy is combined with some of the self-questioning strategies described later.

Corrective feedback refers to providing students with immediate feedback when oral reading errors are committed. The idea is that students' comprehension will improve when they are given immediate feedback on decoding errors. Although this approach has some support for improving comprehension, the method may be more effective when combined with specific self-questioning reading comprehension strategies.

Repeated reading, as discussed previously, refers to having students re-read passages or stories to increase reading fluency and comprehension. Research has indicated that two or three repeated readings may help increase comprehension of the material (O'Shea, Sindelar, & O'Shea, 1987). Repeated readings can also help students read more fluently. However, use caution when assigning more than several repeated readings of the same passage because as the number of readings increase, students' motivation may decrease.

Direct instruction refers to the use of published curriculum materials such as *Corrective Reading* (Engelmann, Becker, Hanner, & Johnson, 1988) and *Reading Mastery* (Engelmann & Bruner, 1995). These materials contain scripted teacher presentations, introduce controlled vocabulary, and include specific comprehension questions throughout the stories. Research has indicated that this type of structured approach combined with the controlled introduction of new vocabulary using a systematic phonetic approach is effective at increasing both fluency and comprehension in students with disabilities and those at risk for school failure (Polloway, Epstein, Polloway, Patton, & Ball, 1986).

Create Text Enhancements

Text enhancements refer to additions designed to accompany text to promote comprehension and learning. Text enhancements can include illustrations, maps, diagrams, concept maps, visual spatial displays, semantic feature analysis charts, mnemonic pictures, and other adjunct aids developed to accompany text materials. Although publishers of curriculum materials frequently use text enhancements, they also may be developed by teachers, or students, or by teachers and students together during class activities.

Illustrations drawn to represent characters, events, places, and action in texts reinforce the sequence of events in the stories. Information can be organized into concept maps or spatially organized maps that show relationships among all events, people, and places. Mnemonic text enhancements can also be designed to promote memory of important concepts and features from

Examples of mnemonic and visual spatial illustrations are given in chapter 10. Text enhancement strategies are also described in chapter 15.

reading materials. If text enhancements are created before reading, provide students with explicit instruction on all features contained in the enhancements to activate students' prior knowledge on the topics. However, these enhancements may be developed during the reading process with students. Provide guidance by modeling and demonstrating during the development process. Finally, such enhancements can be used as review after finishing reading assignments.

Imagery, the process of visualizing content from readings, can also be taught to students as a reading comprehension strategy. Imagery may be a useful substitute when illustrations are unavailable. To assist students in using this strategy, model and demonstrate the imagery process. Break the strategy into three steps. First, tell students to read a passage. Second, have them think of a picture in their mind that represents important content in the story. Third, have students describe their "mental pictures" to you or a peer. Provide feedback on the quality of the image by adding any important features that may have been missing from their images. Although imagery has not yielded as powerful comprehension effects as some self-questioning strategies, it may be beneficial for some of your students.

Adjunct aids including study guides, outlines, guided notes, partial outlines, and highlighting and underlining are also examples of useful text enhancements. Adjunct aids are discussed in more detail in chapter 15.

Teach Specific Reading Comprehension Strategies

Asking students questions and teaching them to ask themselves questions about readings helps to promote reading comprehension. Overall guidelines for teaching reading comprehension strategies are given in Figure 13.5. Several questioning and self-questioning strategies that are particularly effective are listed in Figure 13.6. Most of these strategies were validated on students with learning disabilities. However, they may also be effective for other students with reading comprehension difficulties.

Activate Prior Knowledge. Several strategies help students activate their prior knowledge on topics before they begin reading. These strategies work best at the beginning of lessons when combined with other questioning strategies. One strategy for **activating prior knowledge** is the TELLS fact or fiction strategy (Idol-Maestas, 1985). TELLS fact or fiction is an acronym for:

- studying story **T**itles
- **E**xamining pages for clue words
- **L**ooking for important words
- **L**ooking for hard words
- describing the **S**etting of the story
- answering whether the story was **fact** or **fiction**

- Set clear objectives that are logically related to the use of each strategy for reading comprehension.
- Follow a specific instructional sequence:
  1. State the purpose of instruction.
  2. Provide instruction.
  3. Model use of the strategy.
  4. Prompt students to use the strategy following your model.
  5. Give corrective feedback.
  6. Provide guided practice of the strategy.
  7. Provide independent practice of the strategy.
- Inform students about the importance of the strategy.
- Monitor student performance.
- Encourage questioning that requires students to think about the strategies in relationship to the text.
- Encourage positive attributions.
- Teach for generalized use of the strategy.

Figure 13.5
Guidelines for Teaching Reading Comprehension

Activating Prior Knowledge Features:
- Teacher asks questions relevant to forthcoming readings
- Teacher teaches relevant vocabulary
- Teacher teaches using graphic organizers containing main ideas of forthcoming topic
- Students are taught to ask questions related to forthcoming topics
- Students complete activities containing relevant questions before reading

Summarization, Main Idea, Self-Monitoring, and Attribution Features:
- Students taught to ask questions about the reading material, such as "Who or what is the passage about?" "What is happening?"
- Students answer the questions they asked and summarize or paraphrase readings in their own words
- Students state what the whole passage is about in their own words
- Students initially use self-monitoring cards while learning strategy steps
- Teacher encourages independent monitoring of strategy use
- Teacher encourages appropriate strategy attributions
- Teacher encourages independent use of strategy

Text-Structure-Based:
- Teaches passage-specific strategies for different types of text structures, including main idea, list, order, compare–contrast, problem-solving passages, as well as narrative story grammar passages

Multicomponent Packages:*
- Incorporate all or many of the above features, students are taught to ask and answer questions about the reading materials
- Questioning typically includes summarizing, predicting, and clarifying
- Teacher has direct role in instruction first and students assume more independence gradually in most models

*In some models, students assume a more active role during initial phases of instruction

Figure 13.6

Features of Self-Questioning Research

Before starting to read, students attempt to answer the steps in TELLS and then check their answers after reading the passage.

Brainstorming with students is another strategy for activating prior knowledge. Before a lesson, present students with the major topic that will be introduced, and ask them to generate as many ideas as possible that are related or similar to that topic. Encourage participation from all students. Brainstorming can be a component of most questioning strategies, including those intended to activate prior knowledge.

K-W-L is another strategy used to access prior knowledge before reading (Ogle, 1986). During implementation of this strategy, students ask and answer three questions:

- "What do I **K**now about this topic?"
- "What do I **W**ant to know?"
- "What did I **L**earn?"

For the first question, teachers and students brainstorm ideas of related topics of which they have prior knowledge and categorize their ideas. For the second question, teachers and students discuss what they want to know from reading the information. For the final step, students write down information they learned after reading the passage. You can create worksheets containing columns for answering each of the K-W-L steps.

Additional strategies for activating prior knowledge include modified directed reading activities (Sachs, 1983, 1984), preteaching vocabulary (Snider, 1989), preteaching using visual spatial displays (Billingsley & Wildman, 1988), semantic feature analysis (Bos & Anders, 1990; Bos, Anders, Filip, & Jaffe, 1989), and POSSE (Englert & Mariage, 1991; Englert, Tarrant, Mariage, & Oxer, 1994) (POSSE stands for *p*redict ideas, *o*rganize thoughts, *s*earch for the structure, *s*ummarize the main idea, and *e*valuate, see chapter 15). Each of these procedures involves listing or discussing new topics and vocabulary before reading to activate students' prior knowledge. Other steps in these procedures include predicting findings or relationships, encouraging students to clarify and confirm their earlier predictions during reading, and reviewing all information after reading with respect to the prior knowledge strategies used.

Promote Self-Generated Questions. Many reading comprehension strategies require students to self-question before, during, and after reading. As such, these strategies promote **metacognition,** the awareness of one's own cognitive processes and how they can be enhanced (Montague, 1998). While good readers may develop these skills independently, students with special needs (and many other students) can benefit from metacognitive training. Asking questions about reading material helps to promote thinking about the information, which in turn facilitates comprehension.

One example of self-questioning was used by Wong and Jones (1982). They taught students with learning disabilities to ask themselves the following questions:

- What are you studying the passage for?
- Find the main idea/ideas in the paragraph and underline it/them.
- Think of a question about the main idea you have underlined. Remember what a good question should look like. (Look at the prompt.)
- Learn the answer to your question.
- Always look back at the questions and answers to see how each successive question and answer provides you with more information (Wong & Jones, 1982, p. 231).

This self-questioning strategy can be used to promote recall and comprehension for students with learning disabilities and other special needs.

Summarize and Paraphrase. Several researchers have developed steps for teaching students to summarize and paraphrase reading materials (Bakken, Mastropieri, & Scruggs, 1997; Ellis, 1996; Gajria & Salvia, 1992; Jenkins, Heliotis, Stein, & Haynes, 1987; Malone & Mastropieri, 1992; Wong, Wong, Perry, & Sawatsky, 1986). Although each study varied somewhat, similar components included the following:

1. Read a passage or short segment from a book.
2. Ask yourself who or what the passage is about.
3. Ask yourself what was happening in the passage.
4. Make up a summary sentence in your own words using the answers to the questions asked.

For example, Ellis (1996) described the **RAP** strategy for paraphrasing reading passages. The letters of the acronym stand for:

- **R**ead a paragraph.
- **A**sk yourself what the paragraph was about.
- **P**ut the main idea and two details in your own words. (p. 73)

Similarly, reading comprehension strategies used in classwide peer-tutoring interventions (e.g., Mathes & Fuchs, 1994; see chapter 8) include the following questioning steps:

- What is the most important who or what in the text?
- What is the most important thing about the who or what?
- Write a summary sentence. (e.g., Mastropieri, Scruggs, Mohler, et al., 2001, p. 21)

Semantic feature analysis organizes concepts and vocabulary using "relationship charts." Examples of strategies such as POSSE and semantic feature analysis are described in chapter 15.

Implementation of curriculum and instruction, including learning strategy instruction, are topics on the Praxis *Special Education: Core Knowledge* Tests.

Teach students to delete irrelevant and redundant information from their summary sentences and to use their own words. Include self-monitoring instructions that list the above procedures on cards or charts, and display them prominently during reading to help students master the strategy steps. For a sample self-monitoring card designed to accompany a summarization strategy, see the *In the Classroom . . . for sharing with students* feature in the Companion Website. In the early phases of instruction, ask students to answer the questions either verbally or in writing to verify whether all strategy steps have been implemented correctly.

Extensions to the questions can include teaching students to identify main ideas in stories and passages. For example, Wong, Wong, Perry, and Sawatsky (1986) taught students to (1) identify the main ideas in paragraphs, (2) summarize the information in those paragraphs, and (3) apply those skills to social studies material. It is frequently necessary to provide instruction on identifying main ideas first. Teach students that the main idea tells what the whole story (or paragraph) is about in a short summary sentence. Graves (1986) successfully taught students with learning disabilities to find the main ideas while using self-monitoring procedures. If students experience difficulties identifying main ideas from reading passages, introduce the topic of main ideas using pictures. Model, demonstrate, and provide sufficient practice describing main ideas from pictures. Once that skill has been mastered using pictures, provide practice using text materials.

Bakken, Mastropieri, and Scruggs (1997) taught high school students with learning disabilities to read and process text structure. Students were taught to examine paragraphs and identify how the information was structured. For example, some paragraphs contain a main idea—such as wind erosion—with supporting statements or examples. Some paragraphs present a list of information, such as chief exports of Guatemala. Others contain information presented as an ordered series, such as steps in the digestive process. Students who were trained to identify the text structure and create appropriate outlines outperformed other students on tests of recall and comprehension.

Teach students appropriate attributional statements to use when learning the reading comprehension strategies. For example, Borkowski, Weyhing, and Carr (1988) taught students to make statements like, "I need to try and use the strategy," and "I tried hard, used the strategy, and did well" (p. 49). Place large charts and posters that contain the attributional and strategy questions in the classroom and consider providing students with smaller index card versions of the questions.

Story Maps. Story-mapping strategies demonstrate for students that most stories follow a particular pattern, or story grammar. Teaching students to use that pattern can promote remembering information from individual stories. For example, Idol (1987) and Idol and Croll (1987) taught students to complete story-mapping worksheets while reading to discover the following information about the story:

1. The setting, including the characters, times, and places
2. The problem in the story
3. The goals in the story
4. The action in the story
5. The outcomes of the story

Their findings suggest that completing story grammar sheets can improve reading recall and comprehension.

Story grammar training cards can be designed similar to those provided in Figure 13.7. Provide instruction and practice using the sheets during reading activities. Encourage students to complete similar worksheets during independent reading.

Reciprocal Teaching. **Reciprocal teaching** is a reading comprehension strategy that contains four comprehension-fostering strategies: (1) summarizing, (2) predicting, (3) questioning, and (4) clarifying (Palincsar & Brown, 1984). In addition, during reciprocal teaching, students assume the role of teacher during instruction and take the lead on asking questions. Reciprocal teaching incorporates the following elements:

- Teacher and students silently read the reading selection.
- The teacher explains and demonstrates the four strategies, using "talk-alouds," or talking aloud about thought processes used. For example, a teacher might say, "To *summarize,* I

The Specific Skill Series (Boning, 1990) provides booklets for students to practice specific comprehension skills such as identifying the main idea, detecting sequence, using context, and making inferences. Students may learn these skills better if they are accompanied by direct instruction in the use of appropriate strategies.

Remind students that strategy use is beneficial to them, and prompt them to attribute success and failure to use (or lack of use) of the appropriate strategy. Additional information on attributions is presented in chapter 9.

| The setting: |
| The characters: |
| The time: |
| The place: |
| The problem in the story: |
| The goals in the story: |
| The action in the story: |
| The outcomes of the story: |

Figure 13.7
Story Grammar Training Card

might think to myself, 'What is this entire passage about? What is the overall topic, and what is being said about it?' " The talk-aloud may then describe a summary of the passage being considered, and why it is a good summary.

- Students then read another passage, and demonstrate out loud their strategy use for other students, while the teacher provides guidance and support (also known as "scaffolding"). Students construct their own comprehension questions.
- After practice, each student is expected to exhibit competence in the four strategies: summarizing, questioning, clarifying, and predicting (Palinscar & Brown, 1984; see also Lerner, 2000).

Rosenshine and Meister (1994) concluded that reciprocal teaching is more effective when direct skills-based teaching (on, for example, summarizing or predicting) occurs before the model is

Strategy instruction can help promote comprehension.

Many publishers of specialized educational materials have Websites. For a listing of relevant publisher's Websites, go to the Web Links module in chapter 13 of the Companion Website.

implemented. Moreover, they concluded that the reciprocal teaching model is powerful because it contains the following five "excellent instructional ideas":

1. Focusing on helping students acquire comprehension-fostering strategies instead of simply asking them comprehension questions.
2. Providing four specific comprehension-fostering strategies instead of the tens of "reading skills" that have appeared in reading workbooks.
3. Making provision for practicing the strategies while reading actual text.
4. Popularizing procedures for "scaffolding" or supporting students as they develop their strategies.
5. Popularizing the idea of students providing support for each other within reading groups (Rosenshine & Meister, 1994, p. 520).

Speece, MacDonald, Kilsheimer, and Krist (1997) described the successes and challenges of trying to implement reciprocal teaching with elementary-age students with learning and behavioral disabilities. For example, one teacher found that students initially had difficulty asking questions about text. However, by the end of the lessons, the teacher reported, "I was impressed with the students' participation and with their choice of questions that summarized large portions of the text:

Teacher: What do you think, Nell?

Nell: How can a doctor know that a person is dreaming?

Teacher: Excellent question, Nell! That is perfect; that is an amazing, great question. What do you think, Andy?

Andy: Why did the doctors need to learn about dreaming?

Teacher: That is another excellent question!" (Speece et al., 1997, p. 183)

As with all reading comprehension instruction, provide students with sufficient modeling, support, and guidance during the early learning phases. Later, students can be more independent in their use of the strategies (Stone, 1998).

Instructional Adaptations that Foster Reading Comprehension

Teaching students how to use comprehension strategies will enhance recall and comprehension. You might need to adapt the format of instructional materials and some assignments before using those materials with students with special needs. These adaptations may be required because students cannot read the materials, have limited writing abilities, or need more time to complete assignments. Possible alternative text formats and alternative teacher presentation ideas are listed in Figure 13.8 and the following *In the Classroom* feature.

Secondary Applications

Many students with special needs advance to secondary grade levels without completely mastering important reading skills. This is a particular problem, because formal reading instruction ceases to be a part of the general education curriculum at secondary levels. Nevertheless, there are things that secondary-level teachers can do to promote reading skill development in their classes. First, they can support intensive reading instruction in resource rooms or study periods, by working with the special education teacher and emphasizing newly learned skills in the general education classroom context. Secondary teachers can also promote use of word recognition strategies, such as the DISSECT strategy described previously (Ellis, 1996), to assist with independent reading skills, and text structure, outlining, and other strategies described previously (e.g., Bakken, Scruggs, & Mastropieri, 1997) to assist with text comprehension. Additionally, secondary teachers can provide opportunities to practice reading skills in content area instruction through classwide peer-tutoring interventions.

For example, Mastropieri, Scruggs, Mohler, et al. (2001) implemented classwide peer tutoring in middle-school English classes, which contained students with learning and behavior problems. Students worked in pairs, with the stronger reader reading first, for five minutes, followed by the second reader reading the same passage for five minutes. At the end of each reading turn, the tutoring partner would ask the reader story restatements or summarization strategies. Story restatements included, "What is the first thing you learned?" followed by, "What was the next thing you learned?" as often as needed to restate the story. Summarization strategies included, "What is the most important who or what in the text?" followed by, "What is the most important thing about the who or what in the text?" and "What is the summary sentence?" (see Mathes, Fuchs, Fuchs, Henley, & Sanders, 1994; see also chapter 8). After five weeks of the program, students who had participated in tutoring scored 82% correct on a reading comprehension test of different text materials, while control students who had not participated in tutoring scored 63% correct. Similar tutoring programs have helped improve learning of reading skills as well as subject area content for secondary students with disabilities including history, civics, and chemistry (Mastropieri, Scruggs, & Graetz, in press; Spencer, Scruggs, & Mastropieri, 2003). These programs may be useful because they provide all students with additional practice on academic content, and provide additional supervised reading practice for students with special needs.

Lists of award-winning high-interest, low-vocabulary, and picture books by readability level can be found in *The Reading Teacher* (Chamberlain & Leal, 1999; Leal & Chamberlain-Solecki, 1998).

- Highlight text
- Alter font, spacing, and colors of text
- Magnify text
- Tape-record text
- Use language masters for practice with difficult words
- Use talking computerized programs (scan texts)
- Use Braille formats
- Rewrite text supplements using more familiar vocabulary
- Rewrite text supplements at a lower reading level
- Supplement with high-interest, low-vocabulary texts

Figure 13.8
Adapting Text Formats

In the Classroom ...a feature for teachers

Alternative Teaching Suggestions

- Supplement texts with
  advance organizers
  illustrations
  graphic organizers
  visual spatial displays
  concrete manipulatives
  summary charts
      audiovisual aids
      computer programs
      descriptive video
      study guides
      guided notes
- Preteach
  difficult vocabulary
  new concepts
  organizational structure of text
  reading comprehension strategies
- Provide sufficient practice activities
- Use teacher effectiveness variables
- Use peers and cooperative groups
- Modify assignments
  Reduce reading or writing requirements
  Permit oral formats (e.g., tape-recorded answers)
  Supply alternative materials such as audiovisual or computer formats

Written Expression

Written language refers to handwriting, spelling, and composition. One or all of these may be especially problematic for students at risk for school failure. However, adaptations can be made in each area to promote success in inclusive classrooms.

Handwriting

Competent handwriting is a functional necessity for students at all grade levels in school. However, the inability to write well can often be attributed to more than a lack of fine motor skills. For example, some students with learning disabilities may exhibit what has been referred to as **dysgraphia,** or extreme difficulty with writing. Other students experience difficulty copying from the chalkboard or overhead projector, or what is referred to as "far-point copying." Still others have difficulty copying from models on or near their desks, or "near-point copying." Finally, forming letters from memory can present handwriting problems for some students (Hallahan, Kauffman, & Lloyd, 1999).

No matter what the difficulty, students need to acquire fluency with the mechanical aspects of handwriting or they will experience difficulties composing written work. Illegible, dysfluent, and laborious handwriting interferes with students' abilities to complete written assignments in a timely fashion, take notes in classes, read and study materials they have written, and undertake writing tasks (Graham, 1992). Some have suggested that illegibly written assignments receive lower grades and less careful consideration by teachers. Graham and Weintraub (1996) provided a thorough analysis of research on handwriting. Their general findings are summarized here:

1. Handwriting problems are greatest among students who have academic difficulties.
2. Students develop their own style of writing regardless of script style taught.

3. Successful handwriting instruction for students with handwriting difficulties emphasizes the following:

- Use paper with more space between lines (Graham, 1992).
- Provide models of the order, number, and direction of strokes (Graham & Miller, 1980).
- Provide sufficient practice tracing, copying, and writing from memory (Furner, 1970).
- Use behavioral techniques such as cueing, shaping, and positive practice (Mabee, 1988).
- Teach self-regulation behaviors such as self-verbalizations during tracing, copying, and writing from memory activities (Robin, Armel, & O'Leary, 1975).
- Use self-assessment as part of the handwriting instruction (Kosiewicz, Hallahan, & Lloyd, 1981).
- Use self-instruction and self-correction as part of the handwriting instruction (Kosiewicz, Hallahan, Lloyd, & Graves 1982).

Incorporate Self-Regulation and Self-Instruction Strategies

It is important to model all the steps of the procedures and to provide practice opportunities for students in using self-regulation and self-instruction procedures. Some basic self-instructions include defining tasks to be undertaken, focusing attention on tasks, reviewing necessary strategic steps, self-evaluating and self-correcting, self-control, and self-reinforcement. Harris and Graham (1992) provided some descriptive statements illustrating self-instruction statements. Following is a sample handwriting lesson using self-regulation and self-instruction procedures.

Daily review:	Yesterday we practiced writing the letter "g" in cursive. Everybody, write that letter twice for me right now. [checks]. Very good! I can see you all know how to write a cursive "g!"
Statement of purpose:	Today, I am going to show you how I can help myself learn to write the new letter, "q," in cursive.
Teacher presentation:	First, I ask myself: What is the first step? Then, I have to concentrate, be careful, and think of all of the steps involved. I will say all of the steps for writing a cursive "q" as I write it [demonstrates to group]. I place my pen on line of the paper and move up to the top of the "q." Without taking my pen off the paper, I make a *circle* around to the top again. Then, I go *down* below the line, then *loop* back to the top again. Finally, I *finish* on an upswing. Remember, [repeats model] "Up, circle, down, loop, finish." Now I can look at my new cursive "q" and see how well it matches the model cursive "q." Let's see. . . . It looks as if I did a pretty good job! I stayed on the line and went above and below the lines at the right places. Now I'll practice writing another "q."
Guided practice:	Now let's all try doing a "q" together. What do we do first? What's the first step, Leon? [Leon: "You go up."] Good, I go up, like this. Everybody do it correctly? What is the next step, Lori?
Independent practice:	Ok, I think it looks as if we are all catching on to how to write our new cursive letters. I want you to write the letter "q" for the rest of this page. Remember to think about the steps you need to do each time. I'd like to hear you restate the steps. And remember to compare each letter with the models at the tops of the page and to reward yourself for writing good letters. Does anyone have any questions?
Formative evaluation:	OK, everybody stop. Now, circle all the letters that you wrote well with your purple pens. Then, turn in your papers to me. I think you all did a very good job with the letter "q" today!

Manuscript vs. Cursive Writing

Debate exists over whether manuscript (printing) or cursive (handwriting) both need to be taught, or which system for teaching each should be used (Frose, 1981; Graves, 1994). Some claim that manuscript resembles print more closely and therefore facilitates reading, especially for students who experience difficulties learning to read. Some also claim that students with learning difficulties need to learn only one system, and that learning both cursive and manuscript creates confusion. Others assert that children can write faster using the cursive system, and usually are more motivated to learn to write using a cursive system than a manuscript system. Unfortunately, little evidence is available to completely support or refute such claims. Therefore, you will need to decide what works best for your individual students.

Some handwriting programs have been developed to teach handwriting skills efficiently and systematically. The *D'Nealian Handwriting* system (Thurber & Jordan, 1981) teaches students a manuscript style that leads more naturally into cursive writing. The *Cursive Writing Program* (SRA) provides a systematic introduction of handwriting letters, words, and then sentences. *SRA Lunchbox Handwriting* (SRA) introduces writing using plastic overlays and tracing activities. *Handwriting Zaner-Bloser* (Zaner-Bloser, 2003) provides materials for handwriting instruction from kindergarten through eighth grade.

Although many script styles exist, the quality of handwriting can be evaluated according to legibility, shape, size, spacing, alignment, line quality; speed and ease of writing; slant; uppercase and lowercase letter formations; and manuscript and cursive script styles. Your goal then will be to set criteria for what your students should focus on first, and find an instructional system that will support students' efforts.

For materials and criteria for evaluating handwriting, see Gardner (1998).

Technological Adaptations

Computers and typewriters are effective alternatives for students who have great difficulties with handwriting. Keyboarding and typing skills need to be mastered and can be taught using one of several computerized programs, including *StickyBear Typing* (Optimum Resource), *Kids on Keys* (Spinnaker), *Type to Learn* (Sunburst), *Type* (Broderbund), and *Microtype: The Wonderful World of Paws* (South Western Publishing). Advantages of using word processors include neatness, ease, increased fluency, availability of spelling and grammar checks, and increased motivation. However, because students may not always have access to computers, supplement these programs with at least some basic handwriting skills for those with sufficient fine motor ability. For students who lack fine motor skills, voice input devices can be added to computers, enabling the students to enter information orally and receive typed output. If technological adaptations are unavailable, assign scribes for students who cannot write independently. Figure 13.9 provides additional suggestions for students experiencing handwriting difficulties.

- Regular pencil or pen
- Pencil or pen with special grip, or larger size
- Pencil or pen with special grip and special paper
- Typewriter/word processor/computer to keyboard instead of writing
- Word processor/computer with spell checker to improve spelling
- Computer with keyguard, support for arm, and so on, to improve accuracy
- Computer with word prediction software to decrease needed keystrokes
- Single switch or other way of accessing keyboards
- Voice recognition software to operate computer

Figure 13.9

Alternatives for Students Who Experience Handwriting Difficulties

Note: Information developed by Dr. Penny Reed. From *Has Technology Been Considered? A Guide for IEP Teams* (p. 30), by A. C. Chambers, 1997, Albuquerque, NM: CASE/TAM Assistive Technology Policy and Practice Group. Reprinted with permission.

Spelling

CLASSROOM SCENARIO ━━━━━

Mario

Mario, a fourth-grader with learning disabilities, is included in Ms. Wills' general education class for all subjects. Ms. Wills has weekly spelling tests every Friday. On Mondays new spelling lists containing 20 words are distributed and time is allocated throughout the week to study independently to prepare for Friday's test. But Mario is failing spelling. His recent weekly test scores are: 50%, 45%, 30%, 40%, and 35% correct. He tries hard to learn the words, but he can't pronounce some of the words on the list. Both he and Ms. Wills are becoming frustrated with spelling.

CLASSROOM SCENARIO ━━━━━

James

James is an eleventh-grader with a terrific personality who has severe writing disabilities. He is included in every general education class. His grades are satisfactory, but recently he is having more difficulties in his history class. Ms. Washburn, his U.S. history teacher has begun taking points off his tests and assignments for misspellings. In other words, even if James has the correct answer but has misspelled some words he loses credit. Consequently, this term his grade is barely passing. Once he went to Ms. Washburn for assistance and she cut him off abruptly, saying, "You can't expect me to spoon-feed you, James. You want to attend college, don't you? Then you better get going and improve the quality of all of your work, and that includes your spelling performance." James has become nervous about attending history class and has started having stomachaches before class. He has missed the last 4 days of history class.

For detailed reviews of spelling research with students with disabilities, see Graham (1999, 2000); Gordon, Vaughn, and Schumm (1993); Fulk and Stormont-Spurgin (1995); and Moats (1995).

Spelling can be a complex and difficult task for students with reading and writing difficulties. Efficient spellers rely on good memory, phonological awareness, phonemic awareness, orthographic skills, phonics skills, and self-checking skills, all of which are often deficit areas for many students with disabilities. Research has identified a number of effective spelling strategies that can be implemented in inclusive settings (Fulk & Stormont-Spurgin, 1995).

It has been suggested that competence in spelling can be acquired without explicit instruction, and that enough reading and writing activities can develop spelling competence (the natural learning approach). However, research evidence suggests that reading and writing alone contribute only modestly to spelling achievement, and that at least some spelling instruction is necessary for learners to acquire needed skills. This is particularly true for many students with disabilities and other special learning needs (Graham, 2000).

First, ensure that students can read the words on their spelling lists. Many times spelling lists are distributed without checking to see if all students can read the words. If students are unable to decode spelling words, they will surely encounter difficulties learning how to spell them.

One strategy is to shorten the list length for students with spelling problems. It has been demonstrated that providing students with shorter spelling lists can improve their spelling performance on weekly tests (Bryant, Drabin, & Gettinger, 1981). This means asking students with disabilities to learn 10 rather than 20 words, or 5 rather than 10, in a week. Introduce a small number of words daily, rather than providing a large list all at once. Introduce and practice three or four words on Monday, then on Tuesday review those words and introduce a few more words. This helps students master words daily before new words are introduced. However, shortening the list will not help if the words themselves are beyond the current abilities of the students.

Select Words from Reading and Writing Activities

Spelling words that are relevant to students' reading and writing activities can be easier to learn, and students may be more likely to see the importance of learning to spell these words. Additionally, students can apply their decoding skills in reading to the spelling lists.

Provide distributed practice sessions over time (Gettinger, Bryant, & Fayne, 1982). Distributed practice—providing shorter, more frequent periods for studying, rather than fewer, longer periods—may be beneficial for students with disabilities. For example, several 15-minute spelling activity sessions scheduled throughout the school day could reinforce learning better than one 45-minute block.

Peer-tutoring sessions also can help students with special needs. Provide students with extra opportunities to practice spelling their new words (Delquadri, Greenwood, Stretton, & Hall, 1983) after they have been trained in peer-tutoring procedures. Peer spelling sessions can be scheduled regularly. Flashcards can be used and students can record their daily performance by stacking cards spelled correctly together. Keeping the stack of misspelled words to review several times within a single tutoring session or in additional sessions can help students be more successful on tests. Alternatively, simple word lists can also be used as tutoring materials. Tutors can check off words spelled correctly. Students can be matched in almost any way for spelling tutoring sessions, because the tutors can view the correct spellings on the word lists. Using tutoring for spelling can increase time-on-task, including increasing opportunities for responding and increasing feedback on spelling performance.

Show students mnemonic strategies to remember the difficult or unpredictable parts of words, for example, the "s" in "island." Mnemonic spelling strategies consist of creating a sentence that contains the difficult word and another smaller word that includes the most difficult part of the word. Mnemonics can thus provide the students with a "reason" that a certain word should be spelled the way it is (Mastropieri & Scruggs, 1991). Focus on those parts and create strategies to promote learning the correct way to spell them. Shefter (1974) identified mnemonic strategies for some difficult words, for example:

- It is **VILE** to allow special pri**VILE**ge.
- Don't **MAR** your writing with bad gram**MAR**.
- You **GAIN** when you buy a bar**GAIN**.
- Draw **ALL** the lines par**ALL**el. (Shefter, 1974, p. 19)

Similarly, teach the distinction between homonyms by making up sentences using the same procedures. For example:

- A princi**PAL** is your **PAL**; a princip**LE** is a ru**LE**.
- A lett**ER** is written on station**ER**y; the j**AR** is station**AR**y.

Sometimes an interactive illustration can be shown to help students remember the correct spelling, as in the mnemonic, "She screamed E-E-E as she walked by the cemetery," to help remember the three e's in cemetery (Figure 13.10).

Self-Instructional and Self-Monitoring Strategies

Strategies are often taught so students can use them independently. Self-monitoring strategies, helpful during spelling instruction (Reid & Harris, 1993), teach students to self-monitor their attention to task, use of particular studying strategies, and spelling performance. Listed on a "self-monitoring" card, these strategies teach students to:

- say the spelling word.
- write and say the spelling word.
- check the spelling.
- trace and say the word.
- write the word without looking.
- check the spelling.

Repeat the above steps as necessary (adapted from Harris, Graham, & Freeman, 1988).

Find opportunities throughout the day for tutoring pairs to practice their spelling words. Even 10-minute sessions scheduled immediately after recess or lunch can be helpful. Information on designing and implementing peer tutoring is provided in chapter 8.

Dowling (1995) provides an entire book of mnemonic spellings for difficult words. Chapter 10 contains additional examples of mnemonic strategies to promote learning.

Figure 13.10
Mnemonic Spelling Strategy
Note: From *Teaching Students Ways to Remember: Strategies for Learning Mnemonically* (p. 84), by M. A. Mastropieri &
T. E. Scruggs, 1991, Cambridge, MA: Brookline. Reprinted with permission.

Self-Questioning

Wong (1986) used a similar set of self-questions for improving spelling performance. She directed
students to ask themselves the following questions:

- Do I know this word?
- How many syllables do I hear?
- I'll spell out the word.
- Do I have the right number of syllables down?
- If yes, is there any part of the word I am unsure of the spelling?
- Now, does it look right to me?
- When I finish spelling, I'll tell myself I've worked hard. (Wong, 1986)

Cover–Copy–Compare or Study–Test–Study

Teach students to say the word, look at the model, and study the spelling. Then *cover* the model
and try to *copy* the word from memory. Finally, look at the model and *compare* their spelling with
that model. Repeat the steps until the spelling of the word is mastered. Show students how paper
can be folded into several columns. The first column contains the "model" or correctly spelled
word. The remaining columns are used to write new spelling words and are compared with the first
column models. A similar procedure is referred to as the study–test–study technique. Finally, many
spelling strategies include attributional and motivational components to help promote better
spelling and overall studying habits (Fulk, 1997).

Curriculum and Software

Some research suggests that computers can help improve spelling performance (MacArthur,
Haynes, Malouf, Harris, & Owings, 1990). Some computer software contains drill-and-practice formats in which students practice spelling new words over and over. Other software resembles computer games, and students practice spelling words in more gamelike formats. The commercially
available *StickyBear Spellgrabber* (Optimum Resource) contains first- through fourth-grade high-
frequency words. Various interactive gamelike features provide practice spelling the words. *The
Spelling Rules* (Optimum Resource) teaches spelling using 21 rules across six levels using a variety of exercises. *Spell It 3* (Davidson) teaches more than 3,600 words using word lists, word
search puzzles, crossword puzzles, and other activities.

Many curriculum materials also are available commercially to teach spelling, including *Corrective Spelling Through Morphographs* and *Spelling Mastery* (Dixon & Engelmann, 1990). These programs emphasize systematic approaches using a direct instruction format and spelling patterns. Both programs recommend daily lessons of 15 to 20 minutes and have supplemental activities to provide practice with the new words.

The *Directed Spelling List* and the *Spelling for Writing List* (Graham, Harris, & Loynachan, 1994, 1996) are word lists based on analyses of commonly used words that are problematic for students. The *Spelling for Writing List* contains 335 words ordered from first through third grade, and the *Directed Spelling List* has additional word listings suitable for teaching students with disabilities. Instructions encourage students to think actively about word patterns while spelling.

Adapt Spelling Objectives

Spelling may not be as important during some written activities as it is during other activities, so you need to prioritize spelling objectives for your class. It may be helpful to consider spelling separately, or not at all, when students with spelling difficulties are completing assignments without access to spelling assistance. For example, during written essay exams, knowledge of the content, rather than spelling, is probably the major objective, so consider focusing the weight of the evaluation on content knowledge (see the case of James in the earlier scenario).

Teach students compensation skills. For example, model how to use dictionaries to look up unknown words and how to use spell checkers on word processing programs. Use electronic items, such as *Speak and Spell* (Texas Instruments), a handheld spell checker, and make them available in class. Encourage students to check their work, or proofread in peer partner groups.

Written Communication

Written expression is a high level of communication that involves integration of language, spelling, and reading skills. Students with special needs frequently experience problems with writing assignments due to their deficits in reading, spelling, or language. Research has demonstrated the effectiveness of strategies designed to promote better writing (Harris & Graham, 1992; Wong, 1998). Effective planning, revising, and rewriting strategies have improved students' written products. To improve writing, involve students more actively in the writing process by having them write daily, choose their own topics, and revise their papers—often in collaboration with peers (Graves, 1985). Englert and Mariage (1996) used a peer questioning activity ("Sharing Chair") to help primary-grade students expand their journal ideas. For example, students asked Frank questions about his journal entry on getting a new bicycle:

Frank:	[Reading his story] Me and my brother got a new Huffy.
Joe:	What color is it?
Frank:	Red and white.
Ned:	Who bought it for you?
Frank:	My dad.
Joe:	Do you guys have the same bikes?
Frank:	No. My brother's is a different color.
Joe:	Is yours better than his?
Frank:	No.
Joe:	What color is your brother's?
Frank:	Blue and white.
Sam:	Do you guys ever ride it?
Frank:	Yes.
Dan:	What store did you get it from?
Frank:	From the bike shop. (Englert & Mariage, 1996, p. 158)

Such activities can help enforce the idea that writing is communication to an audience, and that peers can be helpful in expanding and improving the communication. Peer groups can also be used in editing and revising activities (Englert & Mariage, 1996). Ask students to review and provide positive feedback and suggestions for each others' written work, and to collaborate in the revision process.

Problem Definition
Sizing up the nature and demands of the task:
"What is it I have to do here?"
"What am I up to?"
"What is my first step?"
"I want to write a convincing essay."

Focusing of Attention and Planning
Focusing on the task at hand and generating a plan:
"I have to concentrate, be careful . . . think of the steps."
"To do this right I have to make a plan."
"First I need to . . . then . . . "

Strategy
Engaging and implementing writing or self-regulating strategies:
"First I will write down my essay writing reminder."
"The first step in writing an essay is . . . "
"My goals for this essay are . . . ; I will self-record on . . . "

Self-Evaluating and Error Correcting
Evaluating performance, catching and correcting errors:
"Have I used all of my story parts—let me check."
"Oops, I missed one; that's okay, I can revise."
"Am I following my plan?"

Coping and Self-Control
Subsuming difficulties or failures and dealing with forms of arousal:
"Don't worry, worry doesn't help."
"It's okay to feel a little anxious, a little anxiety can help."
"I'm not going to get mad, mad makes me do bad."
"I can handle this."
"I need to go slow and take my time."

Self-Reinforcement
Providing reward:
"I'm getting better at this."
"I like this ending."
"Wait 'til my teacher reads this!"
"Hurray—I'm done!"

Figure 13.11
The Six Basic Types of Self-Instruction
Note: From *Helping Young Writers Master the Craft: Strategy Instruction and Self-Regulation in the Writing Process* (p. 85), by K. R. Harris and S. Graham, 1992, Cambridge, MA: Brookline. Reprinted with permission.

Beal (1996) described the importance of comprehension monitoring while making revisions and demonstrated that effective writers use self-monitoring during the revision process. She also described research that demonstrated effective strategy training for young writers. Combining these strategies with self-regulation and self-instructions has greatly improved the writing performance of students with special needs (Wong, 1998).

Self-Regulation and Self-Instructional Writing Strategies

The importance of teaching students effective strategies combined with self-regulation and self-instruction is emphasized generally in this text, and extends to teaching writing skills. Strategic instruction can promote effective writing strategies and positive attitudes toward writing. As with all strategic instruction, model the self-instruction and strategy before asking students to implement it.

Six basic types of self-instruction exist, which are presented with examples in Figure 13.11. Provide students with these types of self-instruction, and discuss how they can be helpful in completing writing tasks. With this background understanding, they may be more able to appreciate the value and purpose of more specific strategy instruction.

How to Identify Story Grammar: Story grammar strategies were described in the reading comprehension section of this chapter, but can also be applied effectively as composition strategies (Harris & Graham, 1992). Model all steps of the story grammar strategy, making smaller individual charts containing steps for students. Discuss when the strategy is useful and how to use all the steps involved, and provide examples of how the strategy will benefit students in a variety of situations. After reviewing previously learned relevant information, a sample dialogue for the presentation of this strategy follows:

Statement of purpose:	Today we are going to learn an exciting new strategy that will help us when we write stories! This strategy will be helpful when you write stories in this class, when you write stories in your other classes, and whenever you want to write any stories. [Note: This informs students when and under what circumstances the strategy will be useful for them.] The strategy is called a Story Mapping Strategy.
Presentation of information:	Whenever I want to write a story, I will first remember the steps of this story mapping strategy because those steps will help me write a better story. [Note: This informs students about the self-regulatory steps of thinking about all strategic steps and helps with positive attributions by attributing success to strategy usage.] This means that it will be important for me to try to learn and remember all these steps. Then I will think of neat ideas for my stories! I will try to think up ideas of fun things that I have done or that I would like to do. Those types of ideas would all make good stories. What other kinds of things could I think about? [Elicit responses, provide feedback]. Next, I will use the questions in our story mapping strategy. Can you see these questions on the overhead? The first one says . . . ; [read each question aloud]

- Who is in the story?
- When does the story take place?
- Where does the story take place?
- What happens in the story?
- What do the characters in the story do?
- Why did those things happen in the story?
- How do the characters feel?
- How does the story end?

Before I begin to write a story, I am going to think about these questions and write the answers on a small piece of paper like the one I have given you. [Note: This provides "think-aloud models" for students.] First, I am going to think about what I need to do. I need to write a story and use our story mapping strategy.

Second, I am going to think about each of the questions in the story mapping strategy. . . . [review questions]. Third, I am going to check myself to see how I am doing. I can say things like "I am working hard and using the strategy. I will try to think of more characters that can be in the story. I have lots of time, so I can keep working." Fourth, I can give myself positive feedback for trying hard and using the strategy. Now I am going to use all these steps to write a story. I want you to watch and listen as I go through all of the steps. First, I am going to. . . . [Continue to use the steps as the story is written]

Storybook Weaver Deluxe, a multimedia program, contains story-starting images to help improve students' writing skills. For the Website of MECC, the publisher, go to the Web Links module in chapter 13 of the Companion Website.

After modeling all the steps for self-regulation, have students practice the steps in the strategy with partners. Furnish practice sessions during which students complete the self-talk of the regulation and self-instruction phases while completing the story grammar. Such practice sessions enable students to master both the strategy and the self-regulatory components.

Modeling the writing process with students, in a variety of contexts, can help them see how the process works before they begin to put it into practice.

Some research has been conducted in which a story grammar strategy has been presented by computers (Bahr, Nelson, & Van Meter, 1996). The FrEdWriter (Starshine, 1990) public domain software was used to program specific questions as text-based prompts. During the computerized instruction, story grammar questions appeared on the screen to prompt students' thinking and preplanning stories.

Choose Effective Composition Strategies. Many students with disabilities benefit from explicit instruction and practice with specific strategies designed to promote better written compositions. As you review the strategies that follow, think about different grade and ability levels of students and choose which applications you think will be effective for individual students.

Thinking About Writing

Students can be taught to use action words, action helper words, and describing words as they write (Harris & Graham, 1992). You can use pictures and have students describe the action they see taking place in the pictures. For example, brainstorm lists relevant to students' age and backgrounds and post them in the room:

Action words tell what is happening and what people are doing:

ran
drove
slept
climbed
skied
swam
jogged
played

Action helper words tell more about the action:

ran *fast*
drove *slowly*
slept *soundly*
climbed *carefully*
skied *rapidly*
swam *quickly*
jogged *silently*
played *joyfully*

Describing words provide more information about something:

pretty puppy
happy child
tall man
broken pencil
colorful flowers
beautiful scene
delicious meal
enthusiastic teacher

Harris and Graham (1992) also describe a three-step strategy to use when students become more proficient at writing. Model for students how to:

1. THINK—Who will read this? Why am I writing this?
2. PLAN what to say.
3. WRITE and say more. (Harris & Graham, 1992, p. 48)

The TREE strategy is designed to help students plan and take notes about what to say in their essays.

- Note **T**OPIC sentence
- Note **R**EASONS
- **EX**AMINE reasons—Will my reader buy this?
- Note **E**NDING (Harris & Graham, 1992, p. 49)

Finally, the SPACE strategy is designed to help students think about more details that need to be included in their stories.

- Note **S**ETTING
- Note **P**URPOSE
- Note **A**CTION
- Note **C**ONCLUSION
- Note **E**MOTIONS (Harris & Graham, 1992, p. 49)

When teaching students these strategies, use the model of effective instruction and include models, demonstrations, and guided practice to promote independent and fluent strategy usage.

Essays Using Computers

Some researchers have developed strategy-based models for writing "compare-and-contrast" essays using computers. In the following Research Highlight, a project designed by Bernice Wong and colleagues is described. This investigation provides further information on the benefits of strategic approaches to writing for students with learning disabilities.

Support for Research Reports

Teachers frequently assign research reports as longer-term homework assignments. Such projects are often overwhelming to students with special needs, but teaching students specific strategies helps students successfully complete the assignments. Several important skills are required for writing a research report, including the following:

- Brainstorming topics
- Selecting a topic
- Finding relevant sources
- Reading and note taking
- Organizing the paper's outline
- Filling in details in the outline
- Writing a rough draft
- Proofing and correcting the draft version
- Completing a final version

Research Highlight

Strategies for Writing "Compare-and-Contrast" Essays

Wong, Butler, Ficzere, and Kuperis (1997) taught students with learning disabilities to plan, write, and revise "compare-and-contrast" essays. Teachers taught students to use the strategy using models, demonstrations, and "think-aloud" procedures similar to those described for teaching the story grammar strategy. Students worked with partners during the writing process. During the planning stage students were taught to generate topics and brainstorm interesting ways to compare and contrast those topics. For example, students brainstormed ways of comparing and contrasting rock concerts with school concerts. Planning sheets were used to record and organize ideas. For a sample planning sheet, see the *In the Classroom . . . for sharing with students* feature in the Companion Website.

Planning sheets guide thinking about the major themes to be compared and contrasted in the essay. Ideas for each theme are identified and analyzed as to whether they represent similarities or differences between the two major categories. Students drew conclusions based on their thinking, and the final section of the planning sheet was completed as well as the writers' helper sheet, which can be found in the *In the Classroom . . . for sharing with students* feature in the Companion Website.

During the writing stage, students worked on word processors to compose their essays individually and were encouraged to refer to completed planning and writers' helper sheets. The helpers on the writing sheets encouraged students to think about the thesis and concluding statements of their essays and begin to compose their introductory and concluding statements. During the revision stage, students met with a teacher and their partner. Students served as critics for their partner's first draft. They were taught to look for and highlight ambiguities in each other's papers. Teachers also provided feedback on the appropriateness of the ideas and details used to support the major themes. For example, in an earlier study, the interactive feedback sessions sounded like this:

> I am going to read your essay now. When I come across any sentence that I don't understand, I am going to hum and hah, and ask you a question, okay? . . . So you see now, when you write, you've got to make sure you make yourself clear so people know what you mean, okay? So how can we fix this part so readers would understand what you wanted to say? (Wong, Butler, Ficzere, Kuperis, Corden, & Zelmer, 1994, p. 81)

All feedback was then used to complete revised versions of the compare-and-contrast essays. Wong et al. (1997) reported a substantial increase in the quality of students' final products after the intervention.

For more information, see Wong (1998).

Questions for Reflection

1. How could a similar strategy be adapted for other writing assignments, such as persuasive or opinion papers?
2. What adaptions would be useful for students with special needs? Consider physical, sensory, cognitive, and behavioral domains.
3. How could this strategy be adapted if computers were not available? Were there any particular benefits to the use of word processors?
4. How could you evaluate the effectiveness of this strategy?
5. With such structured strategy presentations, is there any danger of student creativity being inhibited? What are the dangers in *not* using a strategy such as this?

Companion Website

To answer these questions online, go to the Research Highlights feature in chapter 13 of the Companion Website.

Determine which of the above skills needs to be taught to your students. For example, you may have covered brainstorming in previous classes and can simply review the procedures with students. Once you determine which skill areas need instruction, prepare explicit instruction and provide plenty of opportunities for practice. For example, many students with disabilities require extensive instruction on "Finding relevant sources." Determine the types of search procedures students need to learn, and design appropriate instructional strategies to promote the acquisition of the procedures and provide ample practice opportunities.

Proofreading that Integrates Computers with Strategy Use

Although many students without disabilities know how to proofread their writing, students with disabilities may need explicit training in checking a paper for spelling and grammatical errors. Provide students instruction containing modeling and demonstrations along with guided practice in using this strategy. Large charts or cue cards are helpful for students to use when learning the new strategy steps. Provide students with opportunities to generalize this strategy to many different types of written products.

Adapt Instruction to Overcome Mechanical Obstacles

Many students become frustrated with writing assignments because they are overwhelmed with the mechanical obstacles of handwriting, spelling, and punctuation (Isaacson & Gleason, 1997). Isaacson and Gleason proposed eight methods for helping students overcome those obstacles:

> **Method 1:** *Allow dictation instead of writing.* Provide students the flexibility of thinking without any writing impediments; however, someone must be available to act as the scribe.
> **Method 2:** *Precue spelling of difficult words.* Write difficult words on the board or prominently displayed chart cards.
> **Method 3:** *Teach a word book strategy.* Have students maintain word books containing their own dictionaries of hard words, which they can refer to anytime to check their spelling.
> **Method 4:** *Ask for help.* Encourage students to ask others (teachers, aides, other students) for assistance, and ensure that someone is available to help them.

Chapter 11 provides more detailed information on teaching report writing.

See the Research Highlight in chapter 11 for an example of proofreading combined with computer use. See also Hunt-Berg, Rankin, and Beukelman (1994) for a review of computer-supported writing and Wetzel (1996) for a discussion on speech recognition and computers.

Story webs can help the writing process.

Method 5: *Encourage invented spelling.* Encourage students to write their "best guess" of a word's spelling, to encourage creativity and writing fluency. However, at some point students must learn to identify and correct any misspellings. Invented spelling can facilitate writing by helping students focus on their ideas, but it is unlikely to improve spelling.

Method 6: *Encourage peer collaboration.* This approach establishes a cooperative approach to writing and may be beneficial during brainstorming, preplanning, and revising stages.

Method 7: *Encourage self-checking.* Teach students specific self-checking strategies. Some strategies include re-reading to make sure that sentences make logical sense, that capital letters are used appropriately, and that punctuation and spelling are accurate.

Method 8: *Use technology.* Computers have become more available and more versatile for classroom use. Computer-assisted writing may prove to be a positive alternative for students with writing difficulties.

Curriculum Materials

Some materials are commercially available to promote writing competencies for students with disabilities. *Reasoning and Writing* (published by SRA) uses a direct instruction format to provide practice learning how to think and write from beginning levels—using pictures—to more advanced levels. *Expressive Writing* (Engelmann & Silbert, 1983) is another material using a direct instruction approach that contains approximately 50 lessons for students who can read at the third grade level or above and teaches writing and editing skills. *Writers at Work* (Morocco & Nelson, 1990) is designed for upper elementary-age students, emphasizes a process approach to writing, and includes prewriting, drafting, revising, editing, and proofreading practice. *Written Expression* (Warden, Allen, Hipp, Schmitz, & Collett, 1988) targets learners of all ages from elementary to advanced and emphasizes the three stages of writing: prewriting, composing, and editing. *Moving Up in Grammar* (SRA) is designed for upper elementary students and provides activities to improve grammar, such as use of nouns and verbs, capitalization, adjectives and adverbs, and pronouns.

Many computerized programs also are commercially available, such as *Bank Street Writer Plus* (published by Broderbund), *Write This Way* (produced by Hartley), *Print Shop* (Broderbund), *Kidwriter* (Spinnaker), and *The Children's Writing and Publishing Center* (The Learning Company). Carefully examine the features of programs to determine whether your students have the necessary skills to benefit from the software. Some programs also teach keyboarding skills so that students can make optimal use of computerized programs designed to improve written composition.

Summary

- Many approaches exist for teaching students to read. Many students with reading disabilities lack phonemic awareness and phonics skills, and overuse context cues when trying to read. Teachers should select reading programs that consider these areas of need.
- Phonemic awareness is the understanding that words are composed of smaller speech sounds (phonemes). Systematic instruction in phonemic awareness can be beneficial for students who lack this understanding.
- Sequenced phonics instruction is also usually helpful for students with reading problems. Phonics instruction is most helpful when it is used in conjunction with other reading and language arts activities, when it focuses on reading words rather than learning rules, and when it includes learning onsets and rimes.
- Reading comprehension strategies can be employed before, during, or after reading. These strategies include basic skills instruction and text enhancements. Self-monitoring and self-questioning strategies are among the most effective reading comprehension strategies.
- Handwriting problems can be addressed by providing models and sufficient practice, using behavioral techniques, and teaching self-regulation and self-instruction strategies.
- A variety of strategies has been described for improving problem spelling performance. These

include using the appropriate difficulty level and providing additional practice, mnemonic strategies, and self-instructional and self-monitoring strategies.

- Written communication problems can be addressed by using collaborative peer groups, teaching self-

regulation and self-instruction strategies, and using story grammar and effective specific composition strategies. Adapting instruction for students' special needs can promote more inclusive classroom environments.

Teaching Study Skills

Information in this chapter links most directly to:

Standard 4—Instructional Strategies, particularly:

Skills:

- Use strategies to facilitate integration into various settings.
- Teach individuals to use self-assessment, problem solving, and other cognitive strategies to meet their needs.
- Select, adapt, and use instructional strategies and materials according to characteristics of the individual with exceptional learning needs.
- Use strategies to facilitate maintenance and generalization of skills across learning environments.

Standard 7—Instructional Planning

Knowledge:

- Theories and research that form the basis of curriculum development and instructional practice.
- Scope and sequences of general and special curricula.
- National, state or provincial, and local curricula standards.
- Technology for planning and managing the teaching and learning environment.

Skills:

- Identify and prioritize areas of the general curriculum and accommodations for individuals with exceptional learning needs.
- Develop and implement comprehensive, longitudinal individualized programs in collaboration with team members.
- Use task analysis.
- Sequence, implement, and evaluate individualized learning objectives.
- Incorporate and implement instructional and assistive technology into the educational program.
- Prepare and organize materials to implement daily lesson plans.
- Use instructional time effectively.
- Make responsive adjustments to instruction based on continual observations.

Inclusion Checklist
Literacy

If the student is having difficulty in literacy, have you done the following:

Reading

- ❑ Carefully examined approaches to reading and adaptations to these approaches, including the following:
  - ❑ Basal textbook approaches
  - ❑ Whole language approaches
  - ❑ Reading Recovery approaches
  - ❑ Direct instruction approaches
- ❑ Considered adaptations for promoting word identification, such as:
  - ❑ Phonological or phonemic awareness
  - ❑ Phonics
  - ❑ Structural analysis
  - ❑ Sight words
- ❑ Considered adaptations to promote reading fluency, including the following:
  - ❑ Repeated readings
  - ❑ Curriculum-based measurement
  - ❑ Peer tutoring
  - ❑ Computer programs
- ❑ Considered technological adaptations to promote reading

Reading Comprehension

- ❑ Considered strategies for teaching reading comprehension in inclusive settings, such as:
  - ❑ Basic skills and reinforcement strategies
  - ❑ Text enhancement strategies
  - ❑ Specific reading comprehension strategies, including the following:
    - ❑ Activating prior knowledge
    - ❑ Self-generated questions
    - ❑ Summarizing and paraphrasing
    - ❑ Using story maps
    - ❑ Reciprocal teaching
- ❑ Considered instructional adaptations that facilitate reading comprehension, including the following:
  - ❑ Alternative text formats
  - ❑ Alternative presentation strategies
  - ❑ Alternative assignments

Written Expression: Handwriting

- ❑ Considered various adaptations, including the following:
  - ❑ Cursive versus manuscript
  - ❑ Provide models
  - ❑ Provide wider lined paper
  - ❑ Provide self-instructions and self-corrections
  - ❑ Provide practice tracing and copying
  - ❑ Considered technological adaptations

Spelling

- ❑ Considered strategies such as:
  - ❑ Reduce list length
  - ❑ Ensure that students can read the words
  - ❑ Provide distributed practice
  - ❑ Use peer tutoring
  - ❑ Use mnemonic strategies
  - ❑ Use self-instructional strategies
  - ❑ Teach self-monitoring strategies
  - ❑ Employ computer-assisted instruction
  - ❑ Use specialized curriculum materials
  - ❑ Employ special classroom adaptations

Written Communication

- ❑ Considered self-regulation, self-instruction, and writing strategies, such as:
  - ❑ Story grammar
  - ❑ Action words and modifiers, TREE, SPACE, and PLANS strategies
  - ❑ Compare-and-contrast essays using computers
  - ❑ Strategies for writing research reports
  - ❑ Proofreading by integrating computer and strategy use
- ❑ Specific teaching adaptations to overcome the mechanical obstacles to writing

Chapter 14

Justin Carrico, 10
Portland, OR
"Color Block"

Mathematics

Objectives

After studying this chapter, you should be able to:

- Describe, evaluate, and implement various strategies for teaching mathematics from early number concepts to more advanced computations such as quadratic equations.

- Provide instructional strategies for such concepts as counting, one-to-one correspondence, numeration, geometry, number lines, writing numbers, and understanding symbols.

- Describe and implement strategies for remembering addition and subtraction facts.

- List early addition and subtraction problem-solving strategies and multiplication and division concepts such as count-bys and count-ons, and describe how they can be implemented with students with special needs.

- Identify teaching strategies for incorporating calculators and introducing new vocabulary for multiplication and division facts, and describe when these strategies are appropriate.

- Understand and implement multiplication and division algorithm strategies such as priority of operations, Demonstration Plus Permanent Model, and modeling of long division.

- Describe and implement strategies in mathematics for operations on money, time, and fractions.

- Explain the use of manipulative materials and strategies for computation, solving quadratic equations, and problem solving in algebra.

- Describe and evaluate strategies for mathematical reasoning such as graduated coaching, providing support for inventing concepts and procedures, and teaching functional math.

Mathematics is the academic discipline concerned with the solution of problems that involve quantity or number. Mathematics includes such branches as arithmetic, algebra, geometry, trigonometry, and calculus. Always an important field of study in education, mathematics has taken on increasing importance in modern society. According to the National Research Council (1989):

> Mathematics is the key to opportunity. No longer just the language of science, mathematics now contributes in direct and fundamental ways to business, finance, health, and defense. For students, it opens doors to careers. For citizens, it enables informed decisions. For nations, it provides knowledge to compete in a technological economy. To participate fully in the world of the future, America must tap the power of mathematics. (p. 1)

Mathematics has been described as the key to opportunity.

Students with disabilities will also need to gain proficiency in mathematics to fully participate in society. For this to occur, teachers must be fluent in a variety of teaching techniques that will allow students with disabilities—as well as students with other, diverse learning needs—to meet their greatest potential in math.

Mathematics Education

CLASSROOM SCENARIO

Matthew

Mr. Martin tells his fourth-grade class, "Open your readers to page 80." After this has been done, and the class has begun reading, Mr. Martin notices that Matthew is still flipping pages in his book.

"We're on page 80, Matthew," Mr. Martin says. However, after another two minutes, Matthew is still flipping through pages. Mr. Martin approaches Matthew's desk and finds the place for him. After class, Mr. Martin discovers that Matthew could not find his place because he does not know what the number "80" looks like, and was ashamed to admit this in front of the class.

"This is a real problem," Mr. Martin tells the special education teacher, "but this is reading class, not math class. What should I do?"

Through much of U.S. history, mathematics was taught as a set of facts, rules, and procedures for dealing with numbers and quantitative concepts. More recently, reform in mathematics education initiated by the National Council of Teachers of Mathematics (NCTM) (1989) resulted in the *Curriculum and Evaluation Standards for School Mathematics* (NCTM, 1989; see also NCTM, 1991, 1995; Rivera, 1997). In 2000, these standards were revised to become the *Principles and Standards for School Mathematics* (NCTM, 2000). In it, six overarching principles are provided to describe features of high-quality mathematics education. These principles include equity, curriculum, teaching, learning, assessment, and technology. Standards are proposed for all students K–12 in the following areas:

- Number and Operations
- Algebra
- Geometry
- Measurement
- Data Analysis and Probability
- Problem Solving
- Reasoning and Proof
- Communication
- Connections
- Representations

For example, the Number and Operations Standard specifies that all students *understand numbers, understand meanings,* and *compute fluently.* Expectations for these standards vary by grade level. In grades 3–5, expectations for understanding meanings include "understand various meanings of multiplication and division"; "understanding the effects of multiplying and dividing whole numbers"; and "understand and use properties of operations, such as the distributivity of multiplication over addition" (NCTM, 2000, p. 148).

It has become clear that in recent years the NCTM standards have had a significant effect on school mathematics programs (Pressley & McCormick, 1995). Unfortunately, the 1989 NCTM standards made no overt reference to students with disabilities, and therefore provided no specific information on how to address the individual needs of students with disabilities (Rivera, 1998). In the 2000 version, NCTM did address the area of disabilities, in their Equity Principle:

> All students, regardless of their personal characteristics, backgrounds, or physical challenges, must have opportunities to study—and support to learn—mathematics. Equity does not mean that every student should receive identical instruction; instead, it demands that reasonable and appropriate accommodations be made as needed to promote access and attainment for all students. (NCTM, 2000, p. 11)

NCTM suggested that students with disabilities and other special needs may need accommodations in the form of language support, increased time, oral rather than written assignments, peer mentoring, and cross-age tutoring (NCTM, 2000). Unfortunately, many special education and general education teachers are not aware of the NCTM standards (Maccini & Gagnon, 2002). This chapter presents a number of strategies that may be useful in teaching mathematics to students with special needs in inclusive settings.

Mathematics and Students with Disabilities

Some students with disabilities exhibit little difficulty in learning mathematics. For most others, however, math is an extremely challenging subject area. For example, Mrs. Consuela has been using classroom peers to tutor Marcy in her multiplication tables for the past 3 weeks. Although Marcy seems to learn some facts, she forgets them as soon as new ones are introduced. Overall, her progress can be described as minimal. Not only has Marcy not learned her multiplication facts, she also is beginning to fall further behind in other, perhaps more important, areas of math.

Like Marcy, most students with disabilities or other special needs do experience some difficulties with math. McLeskey and Waldron (1990) reported that 64% of students with learning disabilities were achieving below grade level in mathematics. Montague (1996) summarized the types of difficulties many students with learning disabilities may exhibit in the area of mathematics (see also Miller & Mercer, 1997):

- Memory and strategic deficits can differentially affect mathematics performance, causing some students to experience difficulty conceptualizing mathematical operations,

The NCTM *Principles and Standards for School Mathematics* is available from the National Council for Teachers of Mathematics, 1902 Association Drive, Reston, VA 20191, or online through the Council's Website. Go to the Web Links module in chapter 14 of the Companion Website.

representing and automatically recalling math facts, conceptualizing and learning algorithms [e.g., computational procedures] and mathematical formulae, or solving mathematical word problems.

- Language and communication disorders may interfere with students' functioning when they are expected to read, write, and discuss ideas about mathematics.
- Deficiencies in processes and strategies specifically associated with solving mathematical word problems also can interfere with students' conceptual understanding of problem situations and how to address those situations mathematically.
- Low motivation, poor self-esteem, and a history of academic failure can arrest a student's desire to value mathematics and to become confident in his or her ability to become mathematically literate. (Montague, 1996, p. 85)

Students with mental retardation may exhibit many or all of the above difficulties, as well as problems with acquiring math concepts, remembering and executing math facts and procedures, and mathematical reasoning (Mastropieri, Bakken, & Scruggs, 1991). Students with emotional or behavioral disorders often score similarly to students with learning disabilities on tests of mathematics achievement (Scruggs & Mastropieri, 1986), and also may exhibit difficulties with motivation, attention, and concentration (Hallahan & Cottone, 1997).

For students with hearing impairments and communication disorders (as well as those for whom English is a second language) math may be an area of relative strength. Nevertheless, many of these students may have difficulty with the English language and communication aspects of mathematics (Schroeder & Strosnider, 1997). Students with visual impairments may also generally perform well on mathematics tasks, if appropriate adaptations are made (see chapter 4). Finally, some students with physical disabilities may need specific assistance if concrete manipulative materials are used (see chapter 4).

Strategies for Teaching Math in Inclusive Settings

Carnine (1998) recommends five major components that can be useful in designing effective mathematics instruction. These include the following:

- Focus on "big ideas"; that is, generalizable concepts rather than individual details.
- Teach "conspicuous" strategies (neither too broad or too specific) for conducting math operations and solving problems (see also Montague, 1998).
- Make efficient use of time on prioritized objectives.
- Communicate strategies in a clear, explicit manner.
- Provide practice and review to promote retention.

For all students, and particularly for those with cognitive or intellectual disabilities, development of mathematical understandings can be facilitated by progressing from concrete representations of quantity, to semiconcrete representations, and finally to abstractions (Miller & Mercer, 1993a). Mathematics functioning also has been improved by direct instruction, reinforcement, mnemonics, and cognitive strategy training (Kroesbergen & Van Luit, 2003; Mastropieri, Scruggs, Davidson, & Rana, in press; Stein, Silbert, & Carnine, 1997). Effective strategies for teaching students with learning difficulties in math in inclusive environments are discussed in the following sections.

Early Number Concepts

Most children begin school already familiar with many elementary number concepts. These concepts are represented by words like *more, less, any, none, none left, together, how many,* and *each.* These concepts are necessary for the development of more complex understandings. It may become clear, however, from student responses to teacher questions (e.g., "Do you want more?" "Which container holds fewer pencils?") or by a student's statements that such concepts have not been mastered. Understanding of these concepts can be promoted be applying the strategies for teaching language concepts (see chapter 13). For example, during snack period, after a student eats one cracker the teacher could say, "Do you want more?" When the student begins to reply correctly, the teacher could ask,

"What do you want?" prompting the student to reply, "More crackers." Later, the teacher could hold two crackers in one hand and three in the other, and ask, "Which hand has more crackers?"

Teaching Students to Count

Learning to count is a type of factual (serial list) learning, and is best acquired with practice. Counting seems to be a very simple skill, but can appear very complicated to those who have not mastered it. Be sure to address all the components of counting in early numeracy. *Acoustic counting* refers to saying numbers in sequence (see below). *Point counting* refers to pointing to objects as each number name is said. Done correctly, pointing and counting are *synchronized*. *Resultative counting* refers to the understanding that the order in which items are counted is irrelevant to obtaining the correct total. *Counting on* is the ability to begin counting with a number other than 1 (and is a good way to introduce adding). *Skip counting* or "count-bys" is counting by groups of numbers, such as 2s and 5s. Finally, *subitizing* means totaling small numbers of objects (e.g., 4 pennies) without directly counting (Van Luit & Schopman, 2000).

Begin with just a few numbers, such as "One, two, three," and have students clap their hands each time they count. Students who are having more difficulty may benefit from practicing with a larger group of students. As number sequences are mastered, add a few numbers at a time. For additional time-on-task, ask peers to count with students who are still learning. Use of rhythms or regular emphasis may also help develop counting skills. Following is an example:

Teacher: Everybody, we've been learning to count to three. Let's all do it together! Ready? Count with me: One, two, three.

Students: [Counting with teacher] One, two, three.

Teacher: One, two, three, good! Now I'm going to show you how to count more numbers. Listen: *One,* two, three, *four,* five, six! Listen again: *One,* two, three, *four,* five, six! Now, let's all try it together! Ready? Count with me: *One,* two, three, *four,* five, six!

Students: [Counting with teacher] *One,* two, three, *four,* five, six.

Teacher: That was very good! Now, let's try it again.

Although group practice is helpful, it is also important to determine that individual students have mastered counting skills by asking them to count independently.

Lots of practice counting objects can help young students with special needs learn early number concepts.

Figure 14.1
Before later concepts can be mastered effectively, it is important that students understand the concept of numerical equivalence.

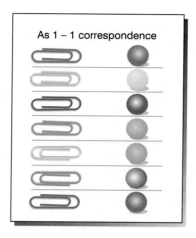

One-to-One Correspondence

One-to-one correspondence is the concept that sets of different objects (beads, blocks, and so on) can be matched according to quantity. That is, even though blocks are not the same as beads, a set of three blocks is equivalent to a set of three beads with respect to quantity. You can enforce this correspondence by exhibiting two sets of objects, and asking students to match them item for item, as shown in Figure 14.1.

Helping Students Master Numeration

As the series of names of numbers is mastered, students should be introduced to the concept of counting *things*. Counting the students in the class, or the pencils in a jar, are early means of demonstrating how similar objects can be counted. Again, practice, additional time-on-task, and use of peer assistance can help enforce the concept of numeration. Such activities can include both group counting and individual counting. Following is an example:

Teacher: Class, we're going to count the number of students who are present today. Everyone count together, and follow along with me as I point to each student in order. Ready? Go: [teacher points] One, two, three, four . . . .

Group performances can help individual students receive additional practice. Individual counting activities [e.g., "Now you try it by yourself, Marie"] can help ensure all students have learned appropriately.

Introducing Geometry in Early Years

It may be helpful to introduce the concept of shapes during the acquisition of early math concepts. Although precise rules that define particular geometric shapes can be provided later, you can teach students to identify simple shapes such as circle, square, and triangle by the presentation of many examples and through teacher questioning.

Teacher: What shape is this? [exhibits a circle]
Students: Circle.
Teacher: That's correct! It's a circle.

Use different types of circles to enforce the relevant attributes of a circle—that shape is what matters, and not other attributes such as color and size:

Teacher: What shape is this? [exhibits a big circle]
Students: Circle.

Companion Website

Many of the materials described in this chapter are available through Delta Education and Steck-Vaughn. For relevant Websites, go to the Web Links module in chapter 14 of the Companion Website.

Teacher: That's correct! It's a circle.

Teacher: Now, what shape is this? [exhibits a little circle]

Students: [less certain] Circle?

Teacher: That's correct! It's a little circle, but it's still a circle. You see, it can still be a circle, even if it's little.

Presenting noninstances also enforces the concept of circle:

Teacher: Is this a circle? [exhibits a square]

Students: No.

Teacher: That's right! It is *not* a circle.

Also, provide students with different shapes, and ask that they hold up the shape that matches the teacher's label:

Teacher: This is my triangle [demonstrates]. Now you show me your triangle.
             [Students hold up triangles]

Teacher: That's correct! Those are all triangles.

Addition and Subtraction Concepts

Using such materials as beads, buttons, dried beans, or commercially available base 10 blocks (distributed by companies such as Delta Education or Steck-Vaughn), you can help students learn concepts of addition and subtraction by counting. For example, show students 5 beans, and ask them to add 4 more. Demonstrate how to select 4 beans to add, and employ a "counting on" strategy, where they start at 5 and add the 4 beans, counting up to 9. You can also teach students to "take away," by starting with 9 beans and taking away 4, to leave the difference, 5.

Counting with Number Lines

A helpful intermediate step between counting actual objects and operating with numbers is the use of a **number line.** Number lines are lines with marks to represent quantity. Here is an example:

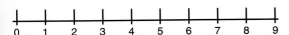

Teach students to place their pencil on the "0," and count forward (i.e., to the right), touching each number as they count. To add, have students place their pencils on the first addend, and count forward using the second addend. For example, to add $2 + 3$, students place their pencil on the 2, and then count forward: 1(3), 2(4), 3(5). Their pencils are now on the 5, the correct sum. To subtract, train students to place their pencil on the minuend, count to the left by the value of the subtrahend, and note the number of the difference. For example, the subtraction problem $5 - 2$ is solved by placing the pencil on the 5, counting two steps to the left: 1(4), 2(3), and noting the difference, 3. The relationship between operations with number lines and adding and subtracting beans and buttons should be made explicit. Also, number lines are useful when practicing "count-ons" and "count-backs," as precursors of learning addition and subtraction facts.

Some students with physical disabilities may benefit from physical assistance by teachers, aides, or peers when using number lines. For example, a helper can guide students' hands if they are having difficulty controlling the pencil on the number line. Additionally, enlarge or darken the number line to accommodate students with fine motor control difficulties or visual impairments. Students with visual impairments also may benefit from tactual, three-dimensional, or raised number lines (see chapter 4).

At a later time, number lines that include negative numbers can be substituted to help students understand concepts of negative numbers:

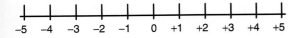

In the above example, addition and subtraction operate the same as in the number line of positive integers. For example, to compute the problem $(-3) +4$, have students place their pencils on the −3 and count four positive steps (to the right): 1(−2), 2(−1), 3(0), 4(+1) to arrive at the sum, +1.

Writing Numbers

Some students have difficulty learning to write numbers and may benefit from the use of models, stencils, or copying over dashed-line numbers. Additional practice may be required. Some students may reverse numbers when they write. Although many reversals may be obvious (e.g., 3), other reversals may not. A reversed 2, for example, may look like a 6, and suggest a problem with number facts, when the true problem is writing, as shown in the following illustration:

$$
\begin{array}{r}
3 \\
+\ 6 \\
\hline
5
\end{array}
$$

Bley and Thornton (2001) suggested a strategy for remembering the spatial orientation of 3, 5, 7, and 9. That is, the curved part of 3 and 5 can be represented with the right hand; the 7 and 9 can be represented with the right hand and right forearm. That is, if 3, 5, 7, and 9 are written correctly, they can be imitated with the right hand.

Some number writing reversals involve two digits. For example, 18 can be written as 81. Again, practice, feedback, and self-correction can be helpful in eliminating these reversals.

Understanding Symbols

Ginsburg (1998a, 1998b) described the case of a first grader who could answer problems such as 3 + 4 = ?, but could not explain what was meant by the "plus" and "equal" symbols. She could not describe the meaning of "plus" and when asked about "equals" in the problem, she said:

Toby:	. . . it tells you three plus four, three plus four, so it's telling you, that, um, I think, the, um, the end is coming up—the end.
Interviewer:	The end is coming up—what do you mean, the end is coming up?
Toby:	Like, if you have equals, and so you have seven, then. [She is gesturing to the problem on the table.] So if you do three plus four equals seven, that would be right. (p. 42)

Other children may state that = means "makes," as in "6 + 3 *makes* 9" (Ginsburg, 1998a). As students acquire skill in mathematics, question them to determine that they also understand concepts represented by mathematical symbols. If not, reemphasize previous concept-building activities, such as equivalence.

Addition and Subtraction Computation

Touch Math

Even when students have mastered the concepts of addition and subtraction, they may not necessarily be able to calculate addition and subtraction problems quickly and accurately. One method for assisting in calculation, the number line, has already been described. Number lines may become more difficult when numbers become larger, however. Another strategy for assisting with calculating arithmetic problems quickly is ***Touch Math*** materials (Innovative Learning Concepts). These materials represent quantity by dots on each of the numbers 1–9, as shown in Figure 14.2.

1 2 3 4 5 6 7 8 9

Figure 14.2

Touch Math Numbers

Note: Reprinted with permission of Innovative Learning Concepts.

Many two-digit reversals occur when writing numbers in the teens. Remind students that the teens are "backward" numbers for writing, because the number 1 is written first (e.g., 16), even though the second number is said first (e.g., *six*-teen).

Students learn that each number is associated with a certain number of dots ("touch points"), which can be counted forward or backward to compute sums and differences. Note that the numbers 1–5 have solid dots, the total representing the quantity of the number. After 5, *Touch Math* uses circled dots, or "double touch points," each of which represents the quantity 2. Students learn to touch each of the touch points once, and to touch each double touch point twice, with their pencil when counting. For example, to compute the quantity

students are taught to start with the larger number, 7, and count forward, touching each of the double touch points in the 6 twice. So students start with 7 and count "8, 9, 10, 11, 12, 13," to arrive at the answer. To subtract, students are taught to start with the minuend and count backward on the subtrahend, using the touch points. A complete set of *Touch Math* materials has been developed, along with worksheets and teacher materials, and is available from Innovative Learning Concepts.

Individual students can be taught to use *Touch Math* methods if they are having particular difficulty remembering addition and subtraction facts, and you want them to engage in computation problems with the rest of the class. In some cases, particularly in the primary grades, teachers use *Touch Math* with the whole class. However, if remembering math facts is a classroom standard, it may be important to continue to teach these facts.

Remembering Addition and Subtraction Facts

Many students, including those without disabilities, have difficulty remembering addition and subtraction facts, particularly if the teacher does not devote enough time to learning them. Nevertheless, many schools still require that these facts be mastered. In addition, mastery of these facts can be a significant source of accomplishment for many students, and provide a basis for success in other aspects of math (Garnett, 1992).

One way to ensure that math facts are learned is to spend enough time teaching them. This can be done with whole-class activities, in which the entire class responds to teacher questioning. Students can respond orally as a class to teacher questions ("Class, what is 4 plus 7?"), or hold up numbers at their desks ("Class, hold up the answer to 6 plus 3."). Additionally, pairs of students can drill each other using flashcards. Assigning facts to be mastered at home can also provide additional time-on-task.

Students who appear to be learning at a slower rate may be able to practice difficult facts with a partner. You can provide opportunities for students to practice using flashcards independently. Additionally, students can also use calculator-type machines and computer software, such as *Math Blaster* (Davidson), to practice math facts.

When teaching facts, it is important to stress commutativity, that is, for example, $2 + 3 = 3 + 2$. Students who understand commutativity must master only half as many facts. Bley and Thornton (2001) suggested that reversible cards be used to demonstrate the equivalence of, for example, $2 + 3$ and $3 + 2$. Use a card similar to the following, embedded with tags or paper clips:

2 + 3

Teachers can reverse the card ($3 + 2$) to show that both sides represent the same fact.

Bley and Thornton's Addition Strategies

Bley and Thornton (2001) described several strategies to assist students with addition facts. Looking at the matrix of 100 addition facts, they were able to demonstrate that most can be mastered with the following specific strategies:

1. Nineteen facts involve addition with zero (e.g., $3 + 0 = 3$). For students who understand that addition with zero does not change the number, these facts are easy.

2. Forty-five facts involve "count-ons," that is, addition with 1, 2, or 3 that can be "counted on" to the other addend. For example, when students encounter 8 + 2, they can start with the 8 and count on by two: "9, **10**" (holding up fingers as they count if needed), with 10 the sum. For 8 + 3, students can start with the 8 and count on by three: "9, 10, **11**", with 11 the sum. Altogether, 64 of the 100 addition facts involve "zero facts" or "count-ons."

3. Of the remaining 36 facts (not covered by zero or count-ons), six facts involve "doubles," and can be represented by images or pictures of doubles (Figure 14.3). That is, 4 + 4 is the "spider" fact: the spider has four legs on each side. The fact 5 + 5 is the "finger fact," with 5 fingers on each hand. The fact 6 + 6 is the "egg carton" fact, with 6 eggs in each half of the

Double	Visual cue	Auditory cue
2+2		The car fact (2 front tires, 2 back tires)
3+3		The grasshopper fact (3 legs on each side)
4+4		The spider fact (4 legs on each side)
5+5		The fingers fact (10 fingers)
6+6		The egg carton fact (6 in each half)
7+7		The 2 week fact (14 days)
8+8		The crayon fact (8 in each row)
9+9		The double 9 domino fact

Figure 14.3

Doubles Facts

Note: Reprinted with permission from Bley, N. S. & Thornton, C. A. (1989). *Teaching mathematics to the learning disabled* (2nd ed.). Austin, TX: Pro-Ed, p. 185.

carton; 7 + 7 is known as the "two-week" fact, with 7 days in each week; 8 + 8 is the "crayon" fact, because each row holds eight crayons. Finally, 9 + 9 is the "double-9 domino" fact, where each side of a domino contains nine dots. Double facts also exist for 2 + 2 and 3 + 3 (see Figure 14.3), but these are also covered by "count-ons."

4. In addition to the zero, count-on, and doubles facts, eight additional facts represent "doubles plus one," which means their sum is one more than the double. For example, 4 + 5 is the same as the doubles fact (spider) 4 + 4 = 8 plus one, or 9. The fact 6 + 7 is the same as the doubles fact (egg carton) 6 + 6 = 12 plus one, or 13. The doubles and doubles-plus-one facts, together with the previously described facts, account for 78 facts in all.

5. Of the remaining 22 facts, 10 are referred to as "pattern 9" facts, and can be learned by the following rule: the sum of a + 9 fact can be obtained by subtracting one from the other addend and adding ten. For example, to add 9 + 5, subtract 1 from the 5 (= 4) and add 10 to make 14. To add 9 + 7, subtract 1 from the 7 (= 6) and add 10 to make 16.

6. Two additional facts (6 + 4 and 4 + 6) are "other 10 sums," or other sums to 10, and two others (7 + 4 and 4 + 7) are "10 plus 1" sums. Altogether, zero, count-ons, doubles, doubles plus one, pattern 9, other 10 sums, and other 10 plus one sums account for 92 facts of the 100 addition facts, leaving only eight.

7. There is no specific rule for learning the remaining eight facts; however, commutativity reveals that these are actually only four facts, each of which can be expressed two ways: 5 + 7 (7 + 5); 8 + 4 (4 + 8); 8 + 5 (5 + 8); and 8 + 6 (6 + 8). Use of the Bley and Thornton strategies are likely to prove helpful in assisting students who have difficulty recalling math facts.

Subtraction Facts

Most students find it more difficult to learn subtraction facts than addition facts. One advantage, however, is that all subtraction facts are the inverse of particular addition facts and can be easily checked. That is, 9 − 5 = 4 is the inverse fact of 4 + 5 = 9. Use of base 10 blocks or other manipulatives can help enforce this concept. Some instructional materials (e.g., *Connecting Math Concepts,* published by SRA) teach these facts together, as number families. In this case, the number family would include 4 + 5 = 9; 5 + 4 = 9; 9 − 5 = 4; and 9 − 4 = 5.

Bley and Thornton (2001) provided several strategies to assist with subtraction facts. Of the 100 total subtraction facts, these include 27 "count-backs" when subtracting 1, 2, or 3 (e.g., for 11 − 2, "10, **9**"). You can teach this technique by modeling and prompting:

Teacher:	We're going to solve the problem 8 − 3 using count-backs. Listen to me show you how to do it: "I must solve the problem 8 − 3. I'm going to say the first number, then count back on my fingers by three. Here I go: Eight [holds up fist]—seven, six, **five**" [holds up one finger for each number as it is counted, for a total of three fingers]. Now, let's all do it together, everybody hold up your fist [counts with students]: Eight—seven, six, **five.** [students respond] Five, correct.
Students:	[with teacher] Eight—seven, six, **five.**
Teacher:	Good! So, 8 − 3 equals?
Students:	Five.
Teacher:	Five, good.

There are also 19 "zero" facts, which involve subtracting zero from a number (e.g., 9 − 0) or subtracting two identical numbers whose difference equals zero (e.g., 4 − 4). An additional 15 facts are referred to as "count-ups," when the difference can be counted up by 1, 2, or 3. For example, for 12 − 9, start at the subtrahend, 9, and count up to the minuend, 12, holding up fingers as you count, if needed: "9 − 10, 11, **12**," counting 3).

Bley and Thornton (2001) also list 7 "10-frame" facts, where the student imagines a "frame" of two rows of five, and calculates from these.

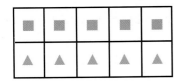

For example, for the fact $10 - 7$, subtracting 7 from the 10-frame removes all the top row and two of the bottom row, leaving 3. Bley and Thornton (2001) also include $9 - 5$ and $9 - 4$ in this series, beginning with a frame of 9 (5 on top, 4 on the bottom).

Finally, Bley and Thornton list six facts as "new doubles," which means when subtracted, doubles are revealed in the difference and subtrahend (e.g., $8 - 4 = 4$). Altogether, these strategies account for 74 subtraction facts, leaving 26 "harder facts" that must be learned through drill and practice, and application of addition rules. These harder facts include the following:

- $(17, 16, 15, 14, 13) - 9;$
- $(17, 15, 14, 13, 12) - 8;$
- $(16, 15, 13, 12, 11) - 7;$
- $(15, 14, 13, 11) - 6;$
- $(14, 13, 12, 11) - 5;$ and
- $(13, 12, 11) - 4.$ (Bley & Thornton, 2001)

Use of tutoring pairs, computer software, and homework can help promote mastery of these facts. Charts, such as the following, that demonstrate students' progress toward completion can help promote motivation and persistence of effort:

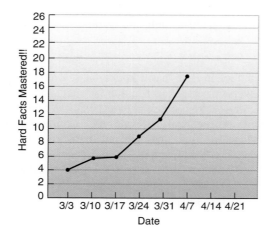

> Bley and Thornton (2001) provide a wide variety of strategies appropriate for helping students with learning disabilities learn math. These strategies could be helpful for many students who are having difficulty with math.

Place Value and Regrouping

Place value is a concept that is linked to our base 10 system, and students must learn this concept as they use numbers of more than one digit. An early problem in understanding place value is documented in an interview by Ginsburg (1997) with Chris, a second grader:

Interviewer: Now I'm going to ask you something about 14. How come you wrote 14 with a 1 and then a 4?

Chris: 'Cause that's how I write 14.

Interviewer: I notice that when you write 14 you have a 1, and on the right of that is a 4. What does that 4 stand for?

Chris: 'Cause it's 14.

Interviewer: All right. What does the 1 stand for?

Chris: That's how you write 14. . . .

Interviewer: Can you write the number one hundred twenty-three? That's right. What does that 1 mean?

Chris: 1.

Interviewer: Just 1. And what does that 2 mean? What does it stand for? What is it telling us?

Chris: 2.

Interviewer: Just 2. And the 3? What does that tell us?

Chris: Just 3. (p. 26)

Another student, Dan, identified the following problem as correct:

```
 38
+ 4
———
 78
```

Dan argued that the 4 was "where it's supposed to be. . . . Because that's where you mostly put the first number for numbers" (Behrend, 1994, p. 75, cited in Thornton, Langrall, & Jones, 1998, p. 150).

Students like Chris and Dan need to learn that numbers represent different values, depending on what place they hold. Use of **base 10 blocks** can be helpful in establishing this concept. First, students learn to count individual base 10 units. They next learn that units are combined as groups of 10, and that groups of 10 are combined as groups of 100. Therefore, the quantity 111 can be represented as follows:

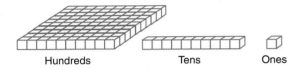

Hundreds   Tens   Ones

When students like Chris understand the concept of place value, they will be able to explain that the 1 in the quantity 123 represents 1 hundred, the 2 represents 2 tens, or twenty, and the 3 represents three units. You can practice place value by having students build, count, and record numbers from different values of 1s, 10s, and 100s.

Students can also learn to add and subtract with base 10 blocks. Making certain the appropriate values are lined up, they add or subtract within each column, as shown in Figure 14.4.

Understanding of regrouping in addition occurs when the values of any column exceed 10. These units must then be combined and placed in the next higher value, as shown in Figure 14.5. It is also important for students to see how numbers are used to represent these concepts, by recording number values when the building and counting have been completed.

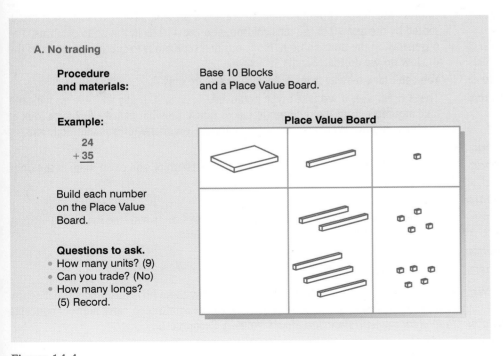

Figure 14.4

Base 10 Representation of 24 + 35

Note: From *Building Understanding with Base Ten Blocks* (p. 21), by P. Mclean, M. Laycock, and M. A. Smart, 1990, Hayward, CA: Activity Resources. Copyright 1990 by Activity Resources. Reprinted with permission.

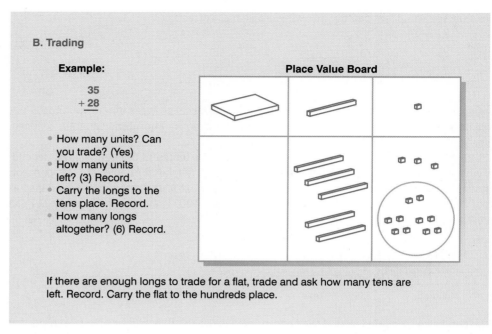

Figure 14.5

Representation of 35 + 28

Note: From *Building Understanding with Base Ten Blocks* (p. 21), by P. McLean, M. Laycock, and M. A. Smart, 1990, Hayward, CA: Activity Resources. Copyright 1990 by Activity Resources. Reprinted with permission.

For regrouping in subtraction, students must learn to "trade up" for 10 of a particular value in the higher column. For example, for the problem 14 − 6, students learn that the one 10 must be traded for 10 units and added to the 4 units in the units column. Subtracting 6 from the 14 units, then, leaves 8, the difference:

Teacher: [shows base 10 block representation] Here is a problem, 14 − 6. The 14 is represented by the one 10 in the tens column, and the 4 units in the units columns. The 6 is below, in the units column. Now, our first problem is to subtract the 6 from the 4. How do we do that, Sandi?

Sandi: You can't take 6 away from 4, because there are only 4.

Teacher: That's right. See, if we take away [removes], 1, 2, 3, 4, that's all there is, we can't take any more from that column [replaces units]. So what can we do? Let's look at the tens column. We have one 10 piece here. How many units is that, Ramon?

Ramon: 10.

Teacher: 10, good! It's 10 units. So, let's trade the 10 for 10 units, and place them in the units column. Now, can we subtract 6?

Students: Yes.

Teacher: Yes! So we have 14 units, and let's take away 6. Count with me [with students]: 1, 2, 3, 4, 5, 6. We took away 6. How many are left?

Students: 8.

Teacher: Good! There are 8 left.

When students have acquired the concept, you can show them how this procedure is represented using written numbers. A useful book of activities for learning such early number concepts is *Building Understanding with Base Ten Blocks* (Activity Resources).

Teaching Early Problem Solving with Addition and Subtraction

You can help promote the idea that mathematical operations have meaning by using manipulatives at the early stages of learning number concepts. As students move into the area of problem solving, these concepts can be enforced. Miller and Mercer (1993b) demonstrated the effectiveness of

Manipulative materials can help teach and reinforce important math concepts.

a graduated word problem sequence strategy for teaching math problem solving. The training consisted of three levels of instruction: (a) concrete, (b) semiconcrete, and (c) abstract. Each level contained four instructional steps: (a) providing an advance organizer, (b) demonstrating and having students model skills, (c) guided, and (d) independent practice with feedback.

The word used in the word problems matched the manipulative objects in the concrete and semiconcrete levels. For example, if students were learning to subtract using cubes (concrete level), the word *cubes* was used in the problem (semiconcrete level):

$$
\begin{array}{r}
4 \text{ cubes} \\
- \underline{2 \text{ cubes}} \\
\text{cubes}
\end{array}
$$

During the abstract level of instruction, the difficulty of word problems is increased gradually from simple words, phrases, and sentences, such as:

$$
\begin{array}{r}
8 \text{ pieces of candy} \\
- \underline{8 \text{ pieces of candy sold}} \\
\text{are left}
\end{array}
$$

to more elaborate sentences:

$$
\begin{array}{l}
\text{Jennie had 4 pens.} \\
\underline{\text{She lost 2 of them.}} \\
\text{She has \_\_\_\_\_ pens left}
\end{array}
$$

Finally, students created their own word problems. This investigation demonstrated how students with learning problems in mathematics could learn to solve word problems by introducing increasing levels of complexity (see Maccini & Hughes, 2000, for an extension to algebra problem solving).

Students who have difficulty determining the operation for solving problems (e.g., addition, subtraction) can construct problems like this on their own. Bley and Thornton (2001) suggested several steps, summarized as follows:

1. Eliminate what's not needed (e.g., color and size when not relevant).
2. Present a short problem, such as those given previously, that gives only the relevant data. Eliminate any unnecessary information (e.g., 3 apples, bought 2 more apples).

3. Tell what is missing. What is missing should be the solution of the problem (together there are _____ apples).

4. Write in numerals for number words. Some students can understand problems better if they see numbers (e.g., 9) rather than words (e.g., nine).

5. Compute two-step problems separately. Color code each step.

6. Use picture choices, for example, show two picture representations of the problem—such as 3 apples being added to 3 more or 2 apples being removed from a group of 3—and ask the student to choose the correct one.

Multiplication and Division Concepts

Multiplication and division concepts can be enforced through the use of manipulatives, such as base 10 blocks. Show students, for example, a set of 3 units, and ask them to put together 4 such sets. After this has been done, inform students that they have a set of 3, four *times*. By counting total units, it can be seen that 3 taken four times, or 4 times 3, is 12.

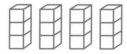

To enforce division concepts, students can be shown a set of 12 units, and asked how many separate groups of 3 they can make. It can then be shown that they can *divide* 12 units into 4 sets of 3. Therefore, 12 divided by 4 is 3. These concepts may not be acquired rapidly by all students, but repeated practice activities, such as those found in *Building Understanding with Base Ten Blocks* (Activity Resources), can be helpful. It may also be important to extend the activities beyond base 10 blocks to enhance generalization of the concept to, for example, beans, beads, or buttons.

Count-Bys

A useful bridge between learning multiplication concepts and learning multiplication facts is the use of count-bys. Students who have learned to count by 2 (2, 4, 6, 8, and so on) can use their fingers or pencil tallies to count up to 2×6 (2, 4, 6, 8, 10, *12*). Students also easily learn to count by 5s, because all numbers end in 5 or 0:

Teacher: The problem is 5×4, so I'm going to *count by* 5, four times. Watch me [hold up fist and count with fingers]: 5, 10, 15, *20*. So 4 times 5 is 20! Let's all do it together. Count by 5, four times, and keep track on your fingers:

Students: [counting with teacher] 5, 10, 15, *20*.

Teacher: Good! 5 times 4 is 20!

It may be helpful to learn to count by other numbers as an introduction to fact learning with those numbers. In fact, *Touch Math* uses strategies involving count-bys to compute multiplication and division facts.

Multiplication and Division Facts

Many students who have found a way to remember or otherwise deal with addition and subtraction facts can nonetheless have difficulty remembering multiplication and division facts. It is harder for them to apply simple strategies such as finger counting to multiplication and division facts, and after learning addition and subtraction facts, the sheer number of total facts to be learned can be overwhelming.

Remember that the learning of multiplication and division facts is more of a verbal learning task than a mathematical reasoning task. That is, while understanding concepts relevant to multiplication and division (e.g., 6 groups of 4) involves mathematical reasoning, immediate recall of the fact ("What is 6 times 4?") requires verbal memory. Because that is the case, strategies for increasing verbal memory are appropriate, given that students understand the concepts. Use drill and practice with flashcards; computer activities, such as *Math Blaster* (Davidson); peer tutoring; and homework assignments.

Identify exactly how many multiplication facts students actually need to learn, so that students will not feel overwhelmed—they may already know more than they think they do. That is, students who understand relevant concepts already know the ×0 and ×1 facts (that is, any number multiplied by zero is zero, and any number multiplied by one is the same number). Students who know addition facts and understand relevant concepts already know the remaining ×2 facts ($3 \times 2 = 3 + 3$). Students who know how to count by 5s know or can easily determine the ×5 facts. Finally, students can use the **bent finger strategy** for calculating the ×9 facts (see Mastropieri & Scruggs, 2002). Using this strategy, students hold their two hands, palms down, in front of them. They then count from left to right on their fingers by the number of the fact, and bend down the relevant finger. That is, for 9 ×5, students count to 5 starting with their left little finger to their left thumb, and bend down that thumb. Then, the fingers to the left of the bent finger represent the 10s and the fingers to the right of the bent finger represent the 1s of the product. In the case of 9 ×5, there are 4 fingers to the left and 5 fingers to the right of the bent finger, so the answer is 45.

So, if students already know, or can cope with, the ×0, ×1, ×2, ×5, and ×9 facts, and if they understand the principle of commutativity ($6 \times 4 = 4 \times 6$), you can show them that they only have 15 facts left to learn! Use charts and game formats to monitor their progress toward remembering all 100 facts.

These 15 facts still may not be easy for all students to learn, and many students may not automatically recognize the reverse (commutativity) of each fact. However, there is a mnemonic strategy that might be helpful in some cases (see chapter 10). Using the pegword strategy, rhyming words are developed for all numbers (*1* is *bun, 2* is *shoe,* and so on). Pegwords for relevant numbers higher than 10 are *12* is *elf; 16* is *sitting,* and *18* is *aiding. Twenty* is represented as *twin-ty,* so *21* is *twin buns. Thirty* is *dirty* or *thirsty; 40* is *party; 50* is *gifty* (i.e., *gift-wrapped*); and *60* is *witchy.* Using these pegwords, sentences can be developed for each of the 15 remaining facts (see Mastropieri & Scruggs, 1991):

Fact	Pegword strategy
Three times three is nine.	**Tree** to **tree** is **line.**
Three times four is twelve.	**Tree** in **door** is **elf.**
Three times six is eighteen.	**Tree** losing **sticks** needs **aiding.**
Three times seven is twenty-one.	**Tree** in **heaven** has **twin buns.**
Three times eight is twenty-four.	**Tree** at a **gate** has **twin doors.**
Four times four is sixteen.	**Door**-by-**door sitting.**
Four times six is twenty-four.	**Door** with **sticks,** has **twin doors.**
Four times seven is twenty-eight.	**Door** in **heaven** has **twin gates.**
Four times eight is thirty-two.	**Door** in **gate** has **dirty shoe.**
Six times six is thirty-six.	**Sticks, sticks,** and **dirty sticks.**
Six times seven is forty-two.	**Sticks** in **heaven** for **party shoe.**
Six times eight is forty-eight.	**Sticks** in **gate** is a **party gate.**
Seven times seven is forty-nine.	**Heaven** to **heaven** has **party line.**
Seven times eight is fifty-six.	**Heaven's gate** has **gifty sticks.**
Eight times eight is sixty-four.	**Gate** to **gate** is **witchy door.**

Sticks,		Sticks, and		Dirty Sticks
6	×	6	=	36

Figure 14.6
***Mnemonic Pictures of 4 × 4 = 16 and
6 × 6 = 36***
Note: From *Mnemonic Math Facts* by M. A. Mastropieri
and T. E. Scruggs, 1990, Fairfax, VA: Graduate School of
Education, George Mason University.

Door	by	Door,		Sitting
4	×	4	=	16

Some of these facts are easy to imagine; for example, tree to tree line is simply a line between two (not twin) trees. Others, however, may be more difficult for students to imagine automatically. In these cases, a picture of the mnemonic may be helpful, such as the pictures for 4 × 4 = 16 and 6 × 6 = 36, shown in Figure 14.6.

A couple of hints should help you make the most out of this pegword strategy: Hint 1—Guide students to learn to say the paired mnemonics together, such as "Heaven's gate has gifty sticks; seven times eight is fifty-six." Hint 2—Reserve these strategies for the facts students appear to be having the most difficulty with, rather than teaching all 15.

Calculators

It is sometimes recommended that computers and calculators be used to replace memorization of math facts and computation exercises. Nevertheless, most schools remain committed to mastery of facts and computation procedures as important mathematics objectives. Of course, if students are not required to memorize math facts, then it is not necessary that time be spent on these objectives. However, in some cases, it may become evident that students are simply not succeeding at memorizing facts and are beginning to lose valuable instructional time in other areas of math because of this problem (remember Marcy, who forgets facts from one tutoring session to another). In such cases, it may be prudent to allow individual students to use calculators for help with computation, while proceeding to other math objectives. If such a decision is made, however, make sure the following have been accounted for:

1. Have all possible strategies for increasing fact learning been attempted?
2. Has the student exhibited *documented failure* over time in memorizing math facts, to the extent that affect and motivation are affected negatively?
3. Are other areas of math functioning being affected negatively, because time allocations have begun to favor fact learning?

If these conditions have been met, it may be prudent to allow students to use calculators. For example, Horton, Lovitt, and White (1992) found that junior high school students with mild mental retardation performed similarly to nondisabled students in computation problems when they used calculators. Without calculators, however, their performance was lower.

Students may need training to operate calculators in their math classes. Provide lessons that include modeling, practice, and feedback on the use of calculators to solve specific types of problems. One set of materials that may be helpful is the *Calc-U-Vue* and *Student Calc-U-Vue* calculators (Learning Resources). The *Calc-U-Vue* calculator is made to be displayed on the overhead projector, so you can demonstrate the math functions it can perform. Student activities to promote calculator use can be found in the activity guide *Calculator Companions* (Learning Resources) (Duffie, Rutherford, & Schectman, 1990). Consider training students in the use of a calculator even if math facts and operations are being taught.

Finally, simply because a decision is made to use calculators does not mean that students may *never* learn math facts. Students should be retested periodically for their capacity to learn facts. It could be that with increasing age and cognitive development, or more familiarity with other aspects of math, fact learning can be attained at a future date.

Arithmetic Vocabulary

In addition to number concepts, algorithms, and procedures, students in math classes are generally required to learn and apply many vocabulary words. These words include *addend, sum, minuend, subtrahend, difference, product,* and *divisor.* For some students with disabilities or other special learning needs, this vocabulary can be confusing and difficult to learn. Prioritize your objectives so that you spend time teaching the most important vocabulary words.

One strategy for teaching math vocabulary is to provide additional time-on-task, use flashcards and peer tutors, and monitor progress toward mastery. Also consider using verbal elaboration strategies that will help tie the vocabulary words to the numbers they are intended to represent. For example, demonstrate to students how 3 is really the *difference* between 8 and 5; therefore, the term *difference* has some meaning. To help students remember that the *multiplier* is the number on the bottom of the multiplication problem, next to the multiplication sign (when presented vertically), draw the multiplication sign to represent a pair of *pliers* (see Mastropieri & Scruggs, 1991). The *pliers* show which number is the multi*plier.* For another example, on a division problem, place *quotation marks* on the *quot*ient.

$$8 \overline{) \ 24 } \ \ ^{``3"}$$

Overall, you can best promote mathematics vocabulary learning with a combination of methods for conceptual enhancement, additional drill and practice, and verbal elaboration.

Multiplication and Division Algorithms

Priority of Operations

Students must learn the order of arithmetic operations in more complex problems. That is, the sequence that must be followed to accurately solve any problem.

$$5 + 4 \times 3 - 2 =$$

To successfully solve this problem, students must know that the multiplication of the terms 4 and 3 must be done first, followed by the addition of 5 and subtraction of 2. The use of the following mnemonic might help some of your students remember the order in which math operations must be done: "*My Dear Aunt Sally*, who says, '*M*ultiply and *d*ivide before you *a*dd and *s*ubtract.'" In this case,

$$5 + (4 \times 3) - 2 =$$

where (4×3) is calculated first, followed by the addition and subtraction. An alternative strategy is "*Please excuse my dear Aunt Sally,*" where *p* and *e* stand for *p*arenthetical expression and *e*xponents, respectively.

Another math procedure students need to learn is the sequence to follow when multiplying numbers of two or more digits. Learning how to do this kind of problem is often complicated because handwritten figures are not often placed in proper relationship to one another. Try having students use graph paper, as shown here.

```
        1   3   1
    x   1   2
    ─────────────
        2   6   2
    1   3   1
    ─────────────
    1   5   7   2
```

Demonstration Plus Permanent Model

Another appropriate strategy for addressing problems in computational arithmetic skills is the **Demonstration Plus Permanent Model** (Rivera & Smith, 1987). In the first part of this approach, the teacher demonstrates how to complete a particular type of problem, for example, subtraction with regrouping or long division. The problem is written on the student's page or somewhere easily accessible and left for the student to refer to in completing similar problems. The model can be written on a 3-×-5-inch index card, so the students can carry it in a pocket, or math folder, and use it when needed. Over time, the permanent model can be faded out.

Modified Long Division

Some students exhibit extreme difficulty with long division. Even for students who can complete other computational procedures, the numerous procedures and skills required for long division may appear overwhelming. If such strategies as reteaching preskills, drill and practice, use of peer assistants, and displaying permanent models are not ultimately successful, it may be helpful to employ a simpler procedure for long division. This procedure lacks some of the precision of traditional long division, but it employs a simpler format that some students may find beneficial (see also Reisman, 1977).

To use modified long division, construct the problem as usual, but draw a line straight down vertically from the end of the problem:

```
23) 4859 |
         |
         |
```

Now, ask students to guess the solution to the entire problem, "How many 23s are there in 4,859?" Even if students have difficulty estimating the answer closely, a good first guess might be 100. So, tell students to write the 100 to the right of the vertical line and multiply 23 by 100 and subtract from the dividend, like this:

```
23) 4859 | 100
    2300 |
    2559 |
```

Then, ask students the same question again, with respect to the difference, "How many 23s are there in 2559?" Since 100 times 23 is 2300, it makes sense to try 100 again. So, you write 100 again below the first 100, multiply 23 again by 100, and subtract from 2559:

```
23)  4859 | 100
    -2300 | 100
     2559 |
    -2300 |
      259
```

The remainder is now 259, so a good next guess would be 10:

```
    ⎞ 4859 │ 100
23  ⎠ -2300 │ 100
       2559 │  10
      -2300
        259
       -230
         29
```

Subtracting 230 from 259 leaves 29, so we subtract one more 23, and compute a remainder of 6. This number is smaller than the divisor, 23, so we cannot go any farther. Adding all estimates yields a sum of 211 with a remainder of 6 (or 6/23), the correct solution.

```
    ⎞ 4859 │ 100
23  ⎠ -2300 │ 100
       2559 │  10
      -2300 │ + 1
        259 │ 211 , r. 6
       -230
         29
         23
          6
```

One advantage of modified long division is that it allows students to view the entire problem at once. Because of this, they may be less likely to become entangled in a maze of algorithmic procedures. Nevertheless, students may still need much practice learning and applying the steps of the modified long division procedure.

Error Analysis for Diagnosis

When correcting student products, it is not enough simply to know whether the problem has been answered correctly or incorrectly. Rather, it is important to determine the *type* of error students make, whether such error types are consistently found in the work of some students, and what type of remedial instruction is indicated by these error patterns. Figure 14.7 lists common error types in arithmetic computation, and possible explanations for them. Remember, before a firm conclusion

> "Lots" of additional practice is still a valid way to make students more confident, and teachers more aware that a student understands the procedure (Jones, Wilson, & Bhojwani, 1998).

> When introducing new concepts, program gradual changes in difficulty level and provide additional practice when needed so that students are mostly successful in learning new procedures, such as long division (Jones, Wilson, & Bhojwani, 1998).

Error Examples	Possible Explanations	Suggested Interventions
$2 + 2 = 8$	1. Inadequate fact mastery. 2. Failure to apply learned strategies (e.g., "count-ons"). 3. Reversal (2 = 6).	1. Reteach facts. 2. Reteach strategies. 3. Teach strategies for writing orientation.
$22 - 9 = 27$	1. Inadequate fact mastery. 2. Regrouping error. 3. Reversed subtraction ($9 - 2 = 7$).	1. Reteach facts. 2. Reteach regrouping. 3. Reteach procedures.
$22 \times 12 = 66$	1. Place value error: $22 (1 \times 22) + 44 (2 \times 22) = 66$ 2. Algorithmic error (incorrect alignment of addends in problem solution): $\begin{array}{r} 22 \\ \times 12 \\ \hline 44 \\ 22 \\ \hline 66 \end{array}$	1. Reteach place value concepts. 2. Reteach algorithms, using Demonstration and Permanent Model, graph paper.

Figure 14.7
Sample Error Analysis Procedures

can be drawn about a particular error type, it is best to obtain evidence that such errors occur repeatedly in a given student's work.

Problem Solving

Use of Word Meanings

Implied mathematical operations (e.g., add, multiply) are represented by the language of word problems. One problem that students with cognitive, language, or intellectual disabilities wrestle with is understanding how words are used in word problems, and what specific operations are implied by these words. Many mathematics educators have criticized a strategy known as the *clue word* or *key word* approach (not the same as the mnemonic keyword method) to solving word problems. In this approach, students are provided with key operation words and relevant operations, such as the following:

> in all, together, total = add or multiply
> left, remaining = subtract
> each = divide

Students are encouraged to look in the problem for one of these words, and then employ the associated operation with the numbers presented. The reason this method is criticized is that students may learn to use the method mindlessly, without carefully reasoning through problems (Kilpatrick, 1985).

However, the real issue may not be quite as simple as this. Words convey meanings, and to the extent that these meanings aid in problem solution, a careful analysis of the meaning of words is appropriate. "In all" does in fact convey the idea of combining quantities (and thus, perhaps, addition or multiplication); "remaining" does suggest diminishing quantity (and thus, perhaps, subtraction). For students who have language learning disabilities or language delays, it is important to enforce the understanding of word meanings to solve word problems.

It is true that the mindless substitution of "each" for "divide," for example, may not be an appropriate strategy in most cases (it may be appropriate for a last-ditch effort during a timed math test). However, it is also important that students learn to attend to the language of mathematics, and attempt to derive meaning from that language. A problem that states a particular overall quantity and requests unstated information regarding "each," or "for one," certainly seems to be implying some type of division operation, and students should learn to use such cues in determining how to solve the problem.

In fact, the **"ask for one, tell for one"** strategy may be useful in helping students determine implied operations. That is, if a larger quantity and another quantity are given (10 cookies, 5 children), and the problem "asks for one (or each)" (e.g., "How many cookies does 1 child get?"), the operation is probably division. If a quantity associated with an individual unit ("tells for one") is given (2 cookies for one child), and a larger number is requested ("How many cookies do 5 children get?"), the operation is probably multiplication. Encourage students to review their decisions, and use different sources of information before making a decision, such as visualizing, using manipulatives, or drawing pictures of the problem.

Cognitive Strategies

Montague (1992) successfully trained students to use a seven-step strategy to solve word problems: (a) read, (b) paraphrase, (c) visualize, (d) hypothesize, (e) estimate, (f) compute, and (g) check. Students were also given metacognitive training in implementing these cognitive processes.

Similarly, Shiah, Mastropieri, Scruggs, and Fulk (1994–1995) trained students with mathematics learning disabilities to use a computer program that included the following steps:

1. *Read* about the problem
2. *Think* about the problem
3. *Decide* the operation
4. *Write* the math sentence
5. *Do* the problem
6. *Label* the answer
7. *Check* every step

Use of steps like these can help your students solve word problems of the following type:

There are 8 bookshelves in a library. Each bookshelf holds 26 books. How many books are in the library altogether?

Begin by providing students with the list from Shiah et al. (1994–1995), so that they can check off the steps as they are completed. Be sure to train students on how to undertake each of the steps. For example, for Step 2, "Think about the problem," students should be told to use visualization (Montague, 1992), and draw pictures and identify and circle cue words or phrases (Case, Harris, & Graham, 1992). For the current example, students could visualize or draw a library with 8 bookshelves. Each one of the bookshelves holds 26 books. Alternately, to guide thinking, cue words such as *each* ("tells for one"), *bookshelf, books,* and *altogether* could be circled. Thinking about the problem should lead to the operation decision, and writing the math sentence (i.e., $8 \times 26 = \_\_\_\_\_$). After this step, students compute the answer, label the answer, and check every step. To enforce use of the systematic procedures, you could supply students with a self-monitoring sheet, in which they can check off each step as they complete it. The *In the Classroom . . . for sharing with students* feature in the Companion Website presents an example of a problem-solving self-monitoring sheet.

Metacognition and Mathematics

Lucangeli, Coi, and Bosco (1998) have provided evidence that students who have difficulty in math problem solving also exhibit low levels of metacognitive awareness in math. For example, elementary students classified as "poor problem solvers" were more likely to believe that the size of the numbers, and not the number of steps or the complexity of the problem, was the most important factor in determining difficulty of word problems. Training in metacognitive awareness has resulted in increased performance in mathematics, as illustrated in the Research Highlight.

Money

One of the primary uses of mathematics in adult life involves calculations involving money, and it is important to involve students in this area as soon as possible after basic counting skills have been mastered. An early concept students could learn is to identify coins of different values. This can be done through providing drill and practice and demonstrating instances and noninstances of coin

Thornton, Langrall, and Jones (1998) described a student with special needs in mathematics who was able to draw pictures to help solve even nonroutine math problems.

Some students need more emphasis on functional math including learning how to write a check, how to balance a checkbook, or how to plan for household expenses.

Research Highlight

Metacognitive Training in Mathematics

Lucangeli, Cornoldi, and Tellarini (1998) implemented an extended program in metacognitive awareness training to improve mathematics functioning of Italian students. In Part I of the training, students were trained to be aware of general and specific metacognitive goals. For example, students were taught the following:

1. To differentiate among cognitive processes (e.g., attention, language, memory) and to recognize cognitive interconnections.
2. To recognize specific mental abilities for problem solving, such as understanding the sequential nature of a problem solution.
3. To recognize one's own cognitive style (e.g., analytic, impulsive, independent) and to develop implications for mathematics.
4. To have a positive attitude toward mathematics learning through, for example, positive attributions.
5. To recognize anxiety when executing mathematical tasks, and to apply appropriate strategies for relieving anxiety.

In Part II of the training program, students were taught specific metacognitive control processes in solving word problems. These processes included prediction ("Will you solve this problem correctly?"), planning ("Correctly sequence the steps for solving this problem"), monitoring ("Describe the strategies necessary for solving the problem"), and evaluation ("Have you correctly solved the problem?").

Experimental condition fourth-grade students received metacognitive training for two to three hours a week for about six months. At the end of this period, trained students significantly outperformed untrained control condition students both on tests of metacognitive awareness in mathematics as well as tests of mathematics achievement. Further, students who had been characterized as having special learning problems in math exceeded the performance of untrained, normally achieving students on several measures of metacognition and achievement.

Questions for Reflection

1. How could you determine that your students are in need of metacognitive training in mathematics?
2. What strategies would be appropriate for reducing anxiety? (See also chapters 7 and 12.)
3. How could these procedures be adapted for secondary-level students studying higher level mathematics?
4. Would metacognitive training such as this be useful in other academic areas, such as biology or chemistry? How could it be used?
5. How could you evaluate whether your training had been successful?

Companion Website

To answer these questions online, go to the Research Highlights feature in chapter 14 of the Companion Website.

values (simulated coins and bills, including coins and bills that can be displayed on an overhead projector, are available from Delta Education and Steck-Vaughn):

Teacher: [demonstrates] Class, this is a nickel. What is it?

Students: A nickel.

Teacher: Good! It is a nickel! Now, look at your coins and hold up a nickel.

Students: [hold up nickels].

Teacher: Good! Those are all nickels! [correct when appropriate] Now look carefully [holds up a dime]. Is this a nickel?

Students: No.

Teacher: No, this is *not* a nickel, that's correct! Now, look again [holds up a penny]. Is this a nickel?

Students: No.

Teacher: No, this is not a nickel either. Everybody, show me a nickel again.

Students: [hold up nickels].

Teacher: Good, those are all nickels.

Once students have learned to name coins, they need to learn the value of each coin. Again, direct teaching, drill and practice—perhaps using flashcards with the coin on one side and the value on the other—will help enforce these values. When values are mastered, students will be ready to learn to count change. This task can be very difficult for some learners with special needs, because of the overall complexity of the task. However, a simple sequence of instruction, with extensive practice activities, may prove helpful, as shown in the following *In the Classroom* feature.

A good material for practice activities is *Coin Stamp Mathematics* (Activity Resources). Students use stamps of coin values to display the answers to computation problems involving money. The advantage of these materials is that students (who have already been taught relevant concepts and procedures, and who need additional practice) can work independently, and

In the Classroom ...a feature for teachers

Sequence of Coin Counting Skills

1. *Count numbers of the same coins.* Start with different numbers of pennies, and have students count by 1s (e.g., 7 pennies = 7 cents). Then move to higher values, and count by the relevant numbers. For example, count by 5s to calculate the value of 4 nickels = 20 cents; count by 10s to calculate the value of 6 dimes = 60 cents; and 25s to calculate the value of 3 quarters = 75 cents.

2. *Teach count-on strategies with same coin values plus pennies.* That is, for 3 dimes and 3 pennies, count: "10, 20, 30 cents, 31, 32, 33 cents." For two quarters and four pennies, count: "25, 50 cents, 51, 52, 53, 54 cents."

3. *For more complex combinations of coins, teach students to first sort coins into groups containing multiples of ten.* That is, two dimes is one group, one quarter and one nickel is one group. So, for these groups, count: "10, 20 cents; (on fingers) 30, 40, 50 cents."

4. *For making change, teach students to count up from the given value, counting first to a 10s or 25s value, and then counting up to the dollar value.* For example, for making change for one dollar for a 27 cent purchase, count up: "[in pennies] 28, 29, 30; [in dimes] 40, 50; [in quarters] 75, 1 dollar."

More advanced calculations with money involve decimal values, which should be taught in conjunction with decimal concepts and procedures. These are described in a following section.

produce a "permanent product" that can be checked by the teacher, aide, or a peer at a later time. However, remember, as with all practice activities, the sooner feedback is delivered on errors, the more helpful it will be, and the opportunity of "practicing errors" will be minimized. If you as a teacher are unable to provide immediate feedback, ask a peer to score the practice activities, or provide students with an answer key so that they can score their own work after they have finished. Alternatively, the software programs *Let's Learn About Money* (Troll Software, Cambridge Development Laboratory) or *Money Works* (MECC) can provide useful practice.

A more advanced material that may help develop skill with money values is *Using Dollars and Sense* (Fearon/Janus/Quercus). Another money curriculum that may be useful is *Remarkable Math Money* (SRA/McGraw-Hill).

Time

An important skill for all students is telling time. Materials, such as student clocks that can be set to specific times, are available from suppliers such as Delta Education and Steck-Vaughn. Generally, students are best taught by employing a specific set of subskills, as shown in the following *In the Classroom* feature.

Teachers can model times or specific features of a clock on their own model, and ask students to repeat the time on their own clock models. For example, for subskill No. 2, "Recognize the hour hand," teachers can demonstrate 4 o'clock on their own clock, and say,

Teacher: Class, on my clock the hour hand is pointing to the 4. What is the hour hand pointing to?

Students: 4.

Teacher: Good! It's pointing to the 4. That 4 stands for 4 o'clock. What does it stand for?

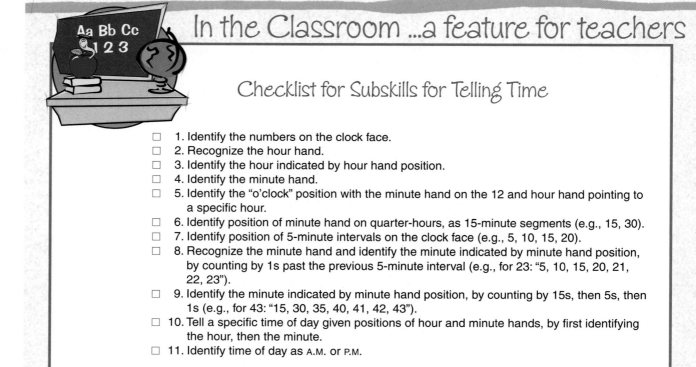

In the Classroom ...a feature for teachers

Checklist for Subskills for Telling Time

- ☐ 1. Identify the numbers on the clock face.
- ☐ 2. Recognize the hour hand.
- ☐ 3. Identify the hour indicated by hour hand position.
- ☐ 4. Identify the minute hand.
- ☐ 5. Identify the "o'clock" position with the minute hand on the 12 and hour hand pointing to a specific hour.
- ☐ 6. Identify position of minute hand on quarter-hours, as 15-minute segments (e.g., 15, 30).
- ☐ 7. Identify position of 5-minute intervals on the clock face (e.g., 5, 10, 15, 20).
- ☐ 8. Recognize the minute hand and identify the minute indicated by minute hand position, by counting by 1s past the previous 5-minute interval (e.g., for 23: "5, 10, 15, 20, 21, 22, 23").
- ☐ 9. Identify the minute indicated by minute hand position, by counting by 15s, then 5s, then 1s (e.g., for 43: "15, 30, 35, 40, 41, 42, 43").
- ☐ 10. Tell a specific time of day given positions of hour and minute hands, by first identifying the hour, then the minute.
- ☐ 11. Identify time of day as A.M. or P.M.

Students: 4 o'clock.

Teacher: Good, 4 o'clock. Now, everyone set your own hour hand to 4 o'clock [teacher observes students and provides feedback].

Peer partners, who are fluent in telling time, can be assigned to students who need more practice. Use of the time telling checklist may be helpful in targeting the exact skills students need to practice. Peers can also be helpful in promoting other students' knowledge of time throughout the day. The software program *Clock Works* (MECC) may also provide helpful practice.

Finally, students who can recognize numbers but have difficulty learning to tell time may benefit from digital clocks and watches that display time in numerical formats that may be more easily recognizable. Steck-Vaughn distributes a clock that displays the time with both digital and clock-face display. Use of digital timepieces can help students' knowledge of time while they are learning to tell time.

Fractions

Initial teaching of fractions should involve as much as possible the students' own experiences. Most children know about sharing things, such as cookies, by breaking them into halves or other parts. Children are also usually aware that pizzas and pies are sliced into pieces. Use this knowledge to develop more advanced concepts of fractions. One helpful material to use is the "Fraction Burger" (Delta Education), in which the equally proportioned layers of a hamburger (e.g., meat, tomato, bun) are each made of different fractions (e.g., 3/3, 5/5) that total the same size circle. There is also a version for demonstration on the overhead projector. Demonstrate the different ways of creating a circle with different fraction pieces, and have students demonstrate their conceptual knowledge by posing simple problems, such as the following:

- "Show the whole burger in two halves."
- "Show me the whole slice of onion in three thirds."
- "Show me the whole lettuce leaf made of eight eighths."
- "Show me a whole circle made of one half (burger) and two fourths (cheese)."
- "Show me two burgers made of eight fourths."

Another educational material, *Fraction Flip Charts* (Delta Education), employs laminated fraction overlays to demonstrate the equivalence of different fractions (e.g., 2/8 = 1/4).

When students have learned relevant concepts, they must also learn how to represent fraction concepts in writing, and to perform computations on fractions. One problem many students may have with fractions is in reducing them to their lowest values. For students who have less of a mathematical "sense," fractions that need to be reduced may not appear as obvious as they may for other students. To help students determine whether a fraction may be reduced, a self-monitoring sheet may be helpful. For an example self-monitoring sheet for reducing fractions, go to the *In the Classroom . . . for sharing with students* feature in the Companion Website.

Decimals

If students have exhibited proficiency on aspects of arithmetic, procedures for using decimals should not be an overwhelming challenge. Procedures for adding and subtracting numbers with decimals involve keeping the decimal points aligned; again, graph paper may be useful for this purpose. For multiplication and division of decimals, additional practice and permanent models may be helpful.

Even if students learn to calculate with decimals, they may be less certain what decimal numbers mean. To enforce decimal concepts, *Decimal Squares* (Scott Resources) may be helpful. Decimal squares represent decimal values on cards that have been divided into 100 or 1,000 smaller components. Transparency versions are also available for demonstrating on the overhead projector. For example, to demonstrate a decimal value of .32, a card can be shown that represents a square divided into 100 equal parts, for which 32 squares are shaded. Students can also be shown that this proportion is equivalent to a square divided into 1,000 parts, for which 320 squares are shaded; therefore, .320 = .32. When 32 of 1,000 squares are shaded, this represents not .32, but .032 (see also Figure 14.8).

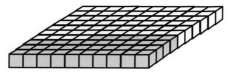

Figure 14.8
Base 10 blocks can be used to demonstrate decimal values such as .36 and .360.

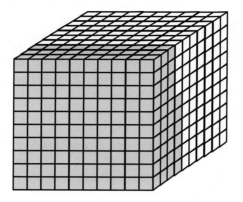

Davidson has produced motivational *Math Blaster* software for pre-algebra, algebra, and geometry.

Area and Volume Concepts

Provide Visual Representations

Concepts of area and volume can be enhanced with visual depictions. A book of overhead transparencies, *A Clear View of Area and Volume Formulas* (Delta Education), may be helpful in promoting understanding of area and volume. In this material, moveable transparency representations help clarify the formulas in computing the area of trapezoids or triangles, and in estimating the area of a circle. Some transparencies demonstrate how a triangle represents half of a trapezoid or rectangle, and why the equation 1/2bh (where b = base and h = height), for determining area, is logical. Other transparencies promote the concepts of volume of three-dimensional figures. Three-dimensional representations of solids are also available from Delta Education. These figures are matched for height so that comparisons can be more easily made. Additionally, they can be filled with water, to demonstrate relative volume measures.

Teach "Big Ideas."

Kameenui, Chard, and Carnine (1996) emphasized the importance of teaching "big ideas" in mathematics, so that students would have a more general idea of themes, rather than a large number of unrelated formulas and problem solutions. For example, they demonstrated that volume formulas should all proceed from the "big idea" that all represent the product of the area of the base and a multiple of the height. Then, rather than teaching separate formulas for rectangular prism, rectangular wedge, rectangular cylinder, triangular pyramid, rectangular pyramid, conic pyramid, and sphere, they can all be demonstrated to be functions of the products of base area and height. For example, for figures in which the sides go straight up, such as rectangular prism (box) or cylinder, the volume is the area of the base times the height (B × h). For figures that come to a point, such as pyramids and cones, the formula is the area of the base times 1/3 of the height (B × 1/3h) (see also Carnine, 1998). Teaching students that different procedures can stem from a common principle can help enforce understanding of the relevant concept as well as memory for specific formulae.

Algebra

Algebra is an important branch of mathematics, required for more advanced problem solving in a variety of fields in business and industry. Algebra involves the use of letters, such as x and y, to represent unknown quantities in the solution of problems. Because of the complex and abstract nature of algebra, many students may feel anxious and insecure about studying it.

CLASSROOM SCENARIO

Brenda

Ever since Brenda started in algebra, she has exhibited problems with her attitude. Previously a hardworking, sincere student, she becomes angry and frustrated whenever she is confronted with an algebra problem. "This is stupid!" Brenda exclaims. "Why should I have to learn this? What difference does it make? I hate algebra!" She doesn't seem to want to make the attempt to learn. Her ninthgrade teacher, Ms. Moon, is considering placing her in a remedial math class.

Many students with disabilities and other special needs have problems with algebra (Maccini, McNaughton, & Ruhl, 1999). These problems stem, in part, from students' prior achievement in more basic skill areas, students' perception of self-efficacy, and the content of instruction. General strategies for addressing achievement problems in secondary-level mathematics include organized, explicit teaching of important concepts, providing many examples of new concepts that address the overall range of the concept, and teaching to prioritized, general objectives (Jones, Wilson, & Bhojwani, 1998).

Use Manipulatives to Teach Negative Numbers

Many students with disabilities or other special needs have difficulty acquiring the concept of negative numbers, as in $-3 + 4 = 1$. One way of enhancing this concept is by the use of number lines, as described earlier. The student can be shown to identify -3 on the number line, three places to the left of zero. Then, by counting four places to the right, obtaining the answer of $+1$. If this use follows other addition and subtraction problems using number lines, the concept may be strengthened. Another way of promoting the concept of negative numbers is by using the example of financial debt. One who owes $5, for example, must earn $5 before having 0 dollars (no surplus but no debt).

A third way of teaching about negative numbers is through the use of **algebra tiles** (Delta Education). These manipulatives use dark-colored pieces to represent positive integers and lighter-colored pieces to represent negative numbers. The positive and negative tiles can be placed together to represent an equation, such as the following:

The three lighter-colored pieces "cancel out" three of the darker pieces, leaving only one positive integer, or 1. Workbook activities for using algebra tiles to solve problems involving negative numbers are given in *Manipulative Interludes in Algebra* (Delta Education).

Teach Algebraic Representations Early

You can begin to teach algebraic representations at an early level of problem solving. For example, students can learn to solve a problem represented as $2 + 3 =$ __; or, $2 + 3 = ?$; or, $2 + 3 = x$. When students learn that x stands for an unknown quantity, they can also begin to solve equations such as $2 + x = 5$. Again, the concept of equivalence should be helpful in targeting the concept that both sides of the equation must represent the same quantity (Ginsburg, 1997). Using algebra tiles, a rectangular-shaped piece is used for the x value, so $2 + 3 = x$ is represented as follows:

The sets of two and three pieces can easily be combined to reveal the answer, $5 = x$ or $x = 5$.

Teach Computation Strategies

Some algebraic notation and conventions must be learned in order to compute algebraic equations. These generally represent examples of rule learning, and must be understood, practiced, and applied. For example, the rule that like quantities, such as $2x + 3x$, can be summed to equal $5x$ can be practiced and conceptualized using algebra tiles. Manipulatives can also be employed to demonstrate that unlike quantities, such as $2a + 3b$, cannot be added.

Mnemonic strategies may be helpful for learning and remembering some of these algorithms. For example, consider the problem:

$$(x + 4)(x + 2) = x^2 + 6x + 8$$

Students should recognize that the parentheses mean that each "symbol and digit" in parentheses must be multiplied by one another as in any other two-or-more-digit multiplication problem. To expand the left side of the equation into the values of the right side, it is necessary to multiply in a specific order. The first step is to multiply the *first* terms, $(x)(x) = x^2$. The second steps are to sum the products of the *outer* (x) (2) and the *inner* (x) (4) terms, $2x + 4x = 6x$. The final step is to multiply the *last* terms, $(2)(4) = 8$. Added together, they provide the answer, $x^2 + 6x + 8$. To remember the sequence of this operation, it may be helpful to remember the mnemonic acronym FOIL, which stands for **F**irst terms, **O**uter terms + **I**nner terms, and **L**ast terms (Kilpatrick, 1985).

Teach Strategies for Solving Quadratic Equations

In a quadratic equation, the unknown variable is squared, and the equation can be written in the form

$$ax^2 + bx + c = 0.$$

There are three ways to solve quadratic equations, two of which are factoring the equation and completing the square. Algebra tiles again can be helpful in developing understanding of these concepts, by using the square version of the x variable to represent x^2. A third method involves the use of an equation developed by mathematicians:

$$x = \frac{-b \pm \sqrt{b^2 - 4ac}}{2a}$$

If the numbers in the quadratic equation are used to replace a, b, and c, the equation is relatively simple to solve. For example, if the quadratic equation is $x^2 + 8x + 15 = 0$, then a = 1, b = 8, and c = 15. Replacing these values in the formula results in the value

$$\frac{-8 \pm \sqrt{8^2 - 4(1 \bullet 15)}}{2 \bullet 1}$$

One problem with this method is remembering the equation. One possible method is the use of a mnemonic strategy, using a bee with a minus sign for a stinger for $-b$, a "square" bee for b^2, four aces for 4ac, and a TWA airplane for 2a (TWoA):

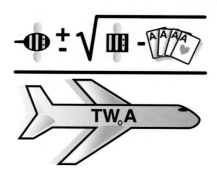

Such a strategy, of course, should be practiced many times, and particular attention must be paid to the elements that are *not* represented mnemonically (+ / −, and square root). Finally, students should have many opportunities practicing the application of this equation in the solution of problems. Remember, as with any academic strategy, students must be taught to *identify* the situation in which a particular strategy is called for, *remember* the steps of the strategy, and correctly *apply* the strategy in the appropriate context.

Teach Problem-Solving Strategies

Students can benefit from self-questioning strategies for solving algebra word problems. Hutchinson (1993) developed a strategy-based model for solving algebra word problems to accommodate students with learning disabilities. Hutchinson used a model that considered two separate phases: problem representation and problem solution (Janvier, 1987). Problem representation refers to an internal representation of the words of the problem. Problem solution refers to the solution planning and solution execution of the problem to obtain the answer. Hutchinson employed different problem types: relational problems, proportion problems, problems that employed two variables, and problems that employed two equations. For example, for relational problems, students were required to identify the relational statement that provided information about one unknown quantity in terms of its relationship to another unknown quantity. Then, the solution focused on procedures and order of operations. One relational problem was,

> *A man walks 6 km farther than his son. If the total distance walked by both is 32 km, how far did each walk? (p. 38)*

Students were then directed to use self-questioning for solving algebra problems, as shown in the worksheet in Figure 14.9. For an example of self-questioning for representing algebra word problems, see the *In the Classroom . . . for sharing with students* feature in the Companion Website.

In this instance, you would prompt students to think through the fact that the man's son walked x km, and the man, who walked 6 km farther, walked $x + 6$ km. Using the worksheet questions, then, students could identify the goal, the unknowns, the knowns, the type of problem, and the equation. These two distances, x km and $x + 6$ km, totaled 32 km, can be represented by the equation:

$$x + (x + 6) = 32$$

Goal: _____

What I don't know: _____

What I know: _____

Kind of problem: _____

Equation: _____

Solving the equation: _____

Solution: _____

Compare with goal.

Check.

Figure 14.9

Structured Worksheet

Note: From "Effects of Cognitive Strategy Instruction on Algebra Problem Solving of Adolescents with Learning Disabilities," by H. L. Hutchinson, 1993, *Learning Disability Quarterly, 16,* p. 40. Copyright 1993 by Council for Learning Disabilities. Reprinted with permission.

Using the problem solution strategy, students were able to obtain the correct answer, 13 km.

$$x + (x + 6) = 32$$

or,

$$2x + 6 = 32$$
$$(2x + 6) - 6 = 32 - 6$$
$$2x = 26$$
$$x = 13$$

so,

$$\text{man walked } x + 6 = 19 \text{ km}$$
$$\text{son walked } x = 13 \text{ km}$$

Students then compare their solution to the stated goal, and check by replacing obtained values in the original problem. Self-monitoring sheets such as the ones used by Hutchinson can be made available to all students, but particularly emphasized for students who exhibit difficulties executing all steps of problem solution correctly.

Similarly, Lang (2001) taught an algebra problem-solving strategy employed with students with learning disabilities, students who spoke English as a second language, and students considered at risk for math failure. The following strategy steps were used in each example problem:

1. If I use this strategy, I will be successful.
2. What do we know?
3. What don't we know?
4. How can we represent the unknowns?
5. How can we represent the knowns?
6. Do we need more than one equation?
7. What is the equation(s)?
8. Substitute the knowns into the equation(s).
9. Solve the equation(s).
10. Have I checked my answer?

Students went through each step of the strategy as they solved algebra problems. Lang (2001) reported that students who were taught the strategy significantly outperformed comparison students in strategy use, and that strategy use was significantly correlated with achievement on both immediate and delayed posttests of algebra problem-solving skills (for another application, see Maccini & Hughes, 2000).

Mathematical Reasoning Problems

Use Graduated Coaching

The NCTM *Standards* stress the promotion of reasoning to solve novel problems involving quantities, and many mathematics educators have long promoted the value of reasoning tasks over calculation and simple word problems (Schoenfeld, 1989). Taken in this sense, problem solving refers to problem solution when the means are not immediately apparent. Such tasks are thought to promote reasoning skills, rather than the simple application of a procedure. For example, consider the "Magic Square" problem (Schoenfeld, 1989). In this problem, a square is drawn with nine cells, as shown:

The problem is to fill in the cells using each of the numbers 1–9, in such a way that all rows, columns, and diagonals sum to the same number. Because the procedures for solving this problem are not immediately obvious, use of reasoning skills is required.

However, some students with cognitive or intellectual disabilities, or students with difficulties maintaining sustained attention to academic tasks, may exhibit difficulties with problems such as this. In these cases, students may not exhibit the degree of insight required to solve the problem without assistance. If the goal of such activities is to promote student thinking, then segmenting the task into achievable components might meet the requirement of promoting thinking, and still lead to a satisfactory solution.

When students studying a problem such as this do not appear to be able to proceed with the problem, teachers, aides, or peers could provide sequenced prompts that help the student proceed in an appropriate direction without directly providing answers. Try solving the problem yourself, and compile a list of coaching questions you could ask to help direct a student's reasoning process when needed (example: "What is the total sum of all nine cells?"). For a possible sequence of coaching steps for this Magic Square problem, go to the *In the Classroom . . . for sharing with students* feature in the Companion Website.

Although some students may have difficulty solving the Magic Square problem completely independently, many students will be able to answer the smaller questions stated, and use reasoning skills to help them arrive at a solution. By using **graduated coaching** steps such as those previously described, students can be successful with the task and also use some of their own higher-level thinking skills. When constructing such coaching steps, it is important that the steps provide no more information than is necessary. Ideally, students will arrive at problem solutions by answering questions posed to them by teachers, aides, or other students.

Provide Support for Inventing Concepts and Procedures

Some mathematics educators have suggested that students should spend considerable time inventing their own ways of doing mathematics. For example, Davis and Maher (1996) describe as a positive example a videotape of a math classroom, in which second-grade students, after playing simple games, are asked to invent ways of solving addition problems:

> In the videotaped classroom, the teacher poses the problem $87 + 24 = ?$, and asks the children to invent some ways to find the answer. One girl says, "Eighty and twenty are a hundred. Six and four is ten, so seven and four are eleven, so the answer is one hundred and eleven." [There is not even a six in the problem! This is really an instance of taking the initiative!] (1996, p. 75)

The girl in the example may indeed have benefited from having "invented" her own way to solve a problem (here she is using an example of "10 + 1" sums, described previously). Certainly, at least, she has demonstrated her understanding of relevant concepts. However, if this type of activity characterizes mathematics instruction in your classroom, it is important that you ensure that all students are benefiting. As stated previously, students with cognitive or intellectual disabilities do not always function well on tasks that place heavy requirements on learner insight, such as "inventing" mathematical procedures. In this case, it is very possible that second-grade students with cognitive or intellectual disabilities could exhibit difficulty even following the reasoning of the girl in the example. When having the class "invent" math concepts or procedures, be certain that all students have ample opportunity to think problems through for themselves, and that their understanding of these invented concepts is carefully monitored.

Teach Functional Math

Many students do not go into advanced math classes, but instead place more emphasis on basic skills and what is called **functional math.** Functional math includes aspects of mathematics that serve individuals in their daily living. These topics include using the calendar, writing checks and keeping checking and savings bank accounts, calculating household expenses, filling out income tax forms, and paying bills. These skills are important for students to acquire, regardless of the program they are in (Patton, Cronin, Bassett, & Koppel, 1998). A useful textbook reference on this subject is *Practical Mathematics for Consumers* (Staudacher & Turner, 1994). A list of topics from the table of contents is provided in Figure 14.10. Some materials from *Essential Mathematics for Life* (Glencoe/McGraw-Hill) also provide activities for functional math. Because many of these topics may not necessarily be on the curriculum for other students—who may be assumed (correctly or not) to already have these skills—some time for small-group teaching of these topics may need to be arranged.

Technology Highlight

Multimedia Mathematics

Many computer-assisted math software programs are commercially available. Software can be used to provide drill and practice, to provide instruction, and to provide tutorial assistance. Some programs, for example, provide drill and practice on learning basic math facts. Other software programs provide more instructional components to assist in learning how to solve word problems.

One promising problem-solving program uses multimedia. Math problem solving has been enhanced with the use of multimedia using contextualized problems (e.g., Goldman & Hasselbring, 1997; Hasselbring & Moore, 1996). Contextualized problems are math problems designed to simulate real-life experiences that require applications of math problem solving. Researchers hypothesized that if students were given more realistic scenarios as math problems that were presented in an interesting multimedia format, they would see the value of learning math and their motivation to solve problems would increase.

Video-based projects on CDs called *Ben's Pet Project* and *The Adventures of Jasper Woodbury* were developed that involve algebra, geometry, statistics, and other math problem-solving skills. Since the episodes are video-based on CDs, students can replay them as frequently as necessary. Stories are interesting and consist of real-life scenarios; for example, Ben heard about a lumber sale, then he and a friend visited a pet store. At the pet store they have to decide whether they can financially afford to purchase both a pet and a cage for the pet. Throughout the story Ben and his friend are confronted with both relevant and irrelevant information that must be sorted through to solve the problem. Students are required to figure out what information is necessary to solve all the problems along the way in order to answer the final question. Researchers have demonstrated the success of these contextualized multimedia programs.

Refer to the chapter 14 Companion Website for additional links related to math.

---

1. Covering Expenses	10. Healthful Eating
2. Making and Changing Budgets	11. Buying Personal Items
3. Salary	12. Getting the Best Value
4. Take-Home Pay	13. Buying a Vehicle
5. Banking	14. Maintaining a Vehicle
6. Using a Checking Account	15. Credit Card Math
7. Finding a Place to Live	16. Loans and Interest
8. Furnishing an Apartment	17. Budgeting for Recreation
9. Choosing and Buying Groceries	18. Planning a Trip

Figure 14.10
Functional Math Topics
Note: From *Practical Mathematics for Consumers,* by C. Staudacher and S. Turner, 1994, Paramus, NJ: Globe Fearon. Adapted with permission.

Instead of advanced math classes, some students need more emphasis on functional math, including learning how to write a check, balance a checkbook, or budget household expenses.

Summary

- Mathematics has been considered the "key to opportunity" in society. However, many students with disabilities and other special needs exhibit problems learning mathematics. Appropriate curriculum, effective teaching, and specific strategy instruction can help alleviate many of these problems.
- Basic number and operation concepts (e.g., addition, subtraction) can be enforced by direct teaching, number lines, and manipulatives such as base 10 blocks. Learning of vocabulary concepts can be promoted by direct teaching, manipulatives, and verbal elaboration including mnemonic strategies.
- Learning of basic math facts can become a significant obstacle to many students with disabilities and other special needs. When possible, promote memory of basic facts through direct teaching, increased learning time, peer tutoring, specialized software, and independent study strategies. Additionally, use specific strategies for promoting recall of specific facts. If basic fact learning seems unproductive and frustrating, consider using calculators to continue progressing on other areas of mathematics functioning. Return to fact learning when it appears it may be profitable.
- Math word problem solving can be facilitated by using a concrete to semiconcrete to abstract sequence of instruction. In addition, use specific problem-solving strategies including a seven-step self-monitoring strategy, judicious use of clue words, highlighting, imagery, pictures, and other problem-solving strategies.
- Important money and time concepts can be enforced by direct teaching, increased practice, manipulatives, models, and providing a careful sequence of skills.
- Specific manipulative materials (commercially available or teacher-made) can be helpful in promoting learning of fractions and decimals. Specific self-monitoring and other strategies can also be useful in promoting these concepts.
- Promote concepts in algebra by providing early concept development, computation strategies, manipulatives such as algebra tiles, mnemonics, and self-monitoring strategies.
- Provide sufficient guidance and support when employing "invention" or "discovery" strategies. If students exhibit difficulty, break conceptual tasks into smaller units, and allow students to use their reasoning skills on these subskills.
- Ensure that students are acquiring sufficient "practical" mathematics skills for use in transition to community life and future employment. Curriculum materials are available that provide for instruction in these practical areas.

Mathematics

Information in this chapter links most directly to:

Standard 4—Instructional Strategies, particularly:

Skills:
- Use strategies to facilitate integration into various settings.
- Teach individuals to use self-assessment, problem solving, and other cognitive strategies to meet their needs.
- Select, adapt, and use instructional strategies and materials according to characteristics of the individual with exceptional learning needs.
- Use strategies to facilitate maintenance and generalization of skills across learning environments.

Standard 7—Instructional Planning

Knowledge:
- Theories and research that form the basis of curriculum development and instructional practice.
- Scope and sequences for general and special curricula.
- National, state or provincial, and local curricula standards.
- Technology for planning and managing the teaching and learning environment.

Skills:
- Identify and prioritize areas of the general curriculum and accommodations for individuals with exceptional learning needs.
- Develop and implement comprehensive, longitudinal individualized programs in collaboration with team members.
- Use task analysis.
- Sequence, implement, and evaluate individualized learning objectives.
- Incorporate and implement instructional and assistive technology into the educational program.
- Prepare and organize materials to implement daily lesson plans.
- Use instructional time effectively.
- Make responsive adjustments to instruction based on continual observations.

Inclusion Checklist
Mathematics

If the student is having difficulty in mathematics, have you tried specific strategies for teaching:

- ❑ Beginning number concepts, including the following:
  - ❑ Direct teaching
  - ❑ Teach as language concepts
  - ❑ Manipulatives for one-to-one correspondence
- ❑ Addition, subtraction, multiplication, and division concepts
  - ❑ Direct teaching
  - ❑ Number lines
  - ❑ Base 10 blocks
  - ❑ Other manipulatives
  - ❑ Count-by strategies
- ❑ Arithmetic vocabulary concepts
  - ❑ Direct teaching
  - ❑ Manipulatives
  - ❑ Verbal elaboration
  - ❑ Mnemonics
- ❑ Writing numbers
  - ❑ Drill and practice
  - ❑ Hand-and-arm strategy for spatial orientation
- ❑ Math facts
  - ❑ Drill and practice
  - ❑ Concrete to abstract teaching
  - ❑ Touch Math
  - ❑ Increase learning time
  - ❑ Peer tutoring
  - ❑ Software
  - ❑ Independent study strategies
  - ❑ Reversible cards for addition commutativity
  - ❑ Bley and Thornton strategies (count-ons, doubles, etc.)
  - ❑ Strategies for ×0, ×1, ×2, ×5 facts
  - ❑ Bent finger strategy for ×9 facts
  - ❑ Teach commutativity
  - ❑ Formative evaluation, progress charts
  - ❑ Mnemonic pegword strategies
- ❑ Calculators
  - ❑ Determine when calculators are needed
  - ❑ Use teaching materials for calculators
- ❑ Math procedures
  - ❑ Direct teaching
  - ❑ Graph paper
  - ❑ Base 10 blocks
  - ❑ Mnemonics for priority of operations
  - ❑ Demonstration Plus Permanent Model

- ❑ Self-monitoring
- ❑ Modified long division
- ❑ Problem solving
  - ❑ Concrete to semiconcrete to abstract sequences
  - ❑ Bley and Thornton problem-solving strategies
  - ❑ Seven-step self-monitoring strategy
  - ❑ Use of clue words
  - ❑ "Ask for one, tell for one" strategy
  - ❑ Highlighting
  - ❑ Imagery
  - ❑ Pictures
- ❑ Money
  - ❑ Direct teaching
  - ❑ Manipulatives
  - ❑ Coin Stamp Math
  - ❑ Counting strategies
  - ❑ Sequence of coin-counting skills
  - ❑ Strategies for making change
  - ❑ Time
  - ❑ Clock models
  - ❑ Peer assistance
  - ❑ Digital clocks
- ❑ Fractions and decimals
  - ❑ Direct teaching
  - ❑ Fraction Burger
  - ❑ Other manipulatives
  - ❑ Self-monitoring for reducing fractions
  - ❑ Decimal Squares
- ❑ Geometry
  - ❑ Manipulatives
  - ❑ Visual representations
  - ❑ Teach "big ideas"
- ❑ Algebra
  - ❑ Early concept development
  - ❑ Computation strategies
  - ❑ Algebra tiles
  - ❑ Direct teaching
  - ❑ Mnemonics for solving quadratic equations
  - ❑ Self-monitoring strategies for problem solving
- ❑ Mathematical reasoning
  - ❑ Coaching strategies
  - ❑ Provide support for inventing concepts and procedures
- ❑ Practical math
  - ❑ Appropriate curriculum materials
  - ❑ Individual or small-group teaching when needed

Chapter 15

Alita Vaughn, 10
Chicago, IL
"Fish"

Science and Social Studies

Objectives

After studying this chapter, you should be able to:

- Describe and apply strategies for adapting textbook- or content-oriented approaches in science and social studies such as content enhancements, semantic feature analysis, and mnemonic strategies.
- Identify criteria for selecting and adopting textbooks for your class or school district.
- Evaluate and implement strategy instruction for using content area textbooks such as text organization, text structure, and essential information in content textbooks.
- Describe and evaluate methods for adapting textbook materials to accommodate diverse learners in the classroom.
- Discuss considerations and adaptations to science activities and ways to make appropriate adaptations for teaching process skills.
- Provide methods and strategies for adapting activities in specific science content areas, including life science, earth science, and physical science activities for diverse learners.
- Describe and apply methods for adapting social studies with students with special needs.
- Discuss ways for adapting inquiry-oriented approaches in science and social studies.

Science and social studies are academic disciplines concerned with concepts and knowledge of the physical and social world around us (Brophy, 1990; Rutherford & Ahlgren, 1990), and as such are important subject areas for all students. Both subjects, however, present unique challenges to teachers who must adapt their instruction, materials, and procedures to accommodate students with special needs.

Adaptations for students with special needs must reflect the approach to instruction being used in the class (Scruggs & Mastropieri, 1993). That is, many schools employ a **textbook-oriented** (or content-oriented) approach in which students are taught and learn content information about science and social studies. With this approach, adaptations may focus on teacher presentations and student independent learning from textbooks. Other schools may embrace an **activities-oriented** approach to learning, in which students undertake specific projects, experiments, or other activities to enhance their understanding of the subject. With this approach, adaptations may focus on physical activities as well as reading and writing requirements. Using either approach, teachers may emphasize an **inquiry-based** model of learning, in which students use their knowledge or experiences to invent, discover, or construct new knowledge. Adaptations for inquiry-based learning may focus on supports or enhancements to promote the thinking and reasoning process in students with special needs.

Adapting Textbook/Content-Oriented Approaches

CLASSROOM SCENARIO

Jeffrey

As Mr. Sterner's sixth-grade science class enters the room on Monday of the second week of school, Mr. Sterner booms, "Pick up your science lab materials on your way to your seat. Open up your textbooks to Activity 2–1 in Chapter 2 on page 26 and follow the instructions. If you have any problems with the steps see me." After most of the class appears to have begun working, Mr. Sterner notices that Jeffrey hasn't even started the activity. Mr. Sterner speaks with Jeffrey and realizes Jeffrey can't follow through with the activity because he can't read what to do. Although embarrassed, Jeffrey agrees to work through the activity with one of his peers. At the end of the day, Mr. Sterner approaches Jeffrey's special education teacher. "I know Jeffrey has a learning disability, but doing well in science this year is somewhat dependent on Jeffrey being able to read. We will do most of the activities in cooperative groups, but how will Jeffrey get the content background he needs unless he can read the text?"

Curriculum and instruction and their implementation across different educational placements are topics on the Praxis *Special Education: Core Knowledge* Tests.

Adapting Science and Social Studies Instruction

Most instruction in social studies and science involves teaching and learning of content based on relevant textbook materials (Brophy, 1990). Carefully planned and executed presentations can address a variety of special learning needs, and enhance learning for all students. Learning can also be improved by specific strategies for promoting independent textbook study.

Effective Teacher Presentations

You can enhance learning of science and social studies in inclusive classrooms by using the teacher effectiveness variables (Larrivee, 1985), described in detail in chapter 6. Students learn more content when you plan for content coverage (by considering scope and sequence, objectives, curriculum, and pacing), and deliver instruction systematically (by using academic engaged time, teacher presentation, practice activities, review, and formative evaluation).

Use of the SCREAM variables (see chapter 6) can make your presentations easy to understand. Organizing your science or social studies content around "big ideas" will make subordinate concepts easier to understand (Carnine & Kameenui, 1992). For example, the model of convection can be developed to describe the behavior of water in a boiling pot, the Earth's mantle, and air masses, as well as atmospheric convection (Woodward, 1994). Emphasize the organization of your presentations with outlines and important information highlighted on the chalkboard or overhead projector, and refer frequently to this outline. Speak in a clear, direct manner, and avoid ambiguous language. Actively model excitement and enthusiasm about the content being covered. Repeat new or unfamiliar vocabulary or concepts, and provide multiple instances of new concepts (e.g., *saprophytic, nullification, hegemony*) to strengthen comprehension. Use mnemonics or other elaborations to promote recall of new vocabulary (see chapter 10). Maximize engagement by frequent questioning and appropriate feedback. Use student responses to determine whether you are moving too quickly or too slowly through the content, and adjust your instruction accordingly.

Overall, in making teacher presentations, be certain to highlight the most important information, then model and demonstrate strategies for remembering and comprehending that information. Students in inclusive classrooms can benefit from the demonstrated strategies, and may begin to develop their own strategies independently (Bulgren, Deshler, & Schumaker, 1997).

Content Enhancements

The general teacher effectiveness variables can help promote science and social studies learning for all students. However, researchers also have developed a number of **content enhancement** strategies (Bulgren, Deshler, & Schumaker, 1993; Bulgren, Schumaker, & Deshler, 1988, 1994a, 1994b) that teachers can use to further increase science and social studies learning. Content enhancement strategies follow clear planning, explanation, and evaluation phases during instruction (Bulgren & Lenz, 1996). Content enhancements are designed to meet both group and individual student needs while maintaining the integrity of the content. The design identifies difficult aspects of the content and provides instructional procedures that facilitate learning while involving the students in active learning procedures (Lenz, Bulgren, & Hudson, 1990).

Content enhancements make use of devices such as graphic organizers, study guides, charts, diagrams, outlines, visual spatial displays, mnemonics, and imagery to promote learning and comprehension. Content enhancements are provided in the context of effective instructional procedures, as described previously. These include informing students of the purpose of instruction, increasing motivation, and using effective instructional principles. Research has indicated that students with disabilities in inclusive classrooms have improved their performance when science and social studies teachers apply content enhancement strategies in their teaching (Bulgren et al., 1994b). These include the "lesson organizer" routine and the "concept mastery" routine.

The *lesson organizer routine* is a visual advanced organizer to introduce and accompany lessons (Lenz, Marrs, Schumaker, & Deshler, 1993). The organizer does the following:

- Introduces the topic
- Changes difficult vocabulary to familiar vocabulary
- Teaches students relationships among concepts
- Identifies appropriate strategies for learning
- Graphically demonstrates relationships of lessons to an entire unit
- Graphically displays organization of the content
- Provides self-testing questions

As teachers present the visual displays and share information with students, they help show how the information is related to previously learned content. The organizer also functions as a teacher-planning device in that the sequences of content, concepts, and vocabulary are identified before instruction to ensure a developmentally appropriate lesson. In addition, the lesson plan identifies how previously covered concepts link with new content.

The *concept mastery routine* addresses the teaching of difficult concepts (Bulgren et al., 1993). This content enhancement is designed around a concept diagram, a visual device that includes the following components:

- Concept name
- Class or category of concept
- Important information associated with concept
- Instances and noninstances of the concept
- Blank space for additions to the diagram
- Concept definition (Bulgren et al., 1993)

Specific instructional steps are provided for teachers to use when implementing the concept mastery routine. Figure 15.1 contains a sample concept diagram.

Several other strategy packages or strategies involving multiple steps are available to promote content area learning. The packages described next have been shown to be helpful for students with disabilities.

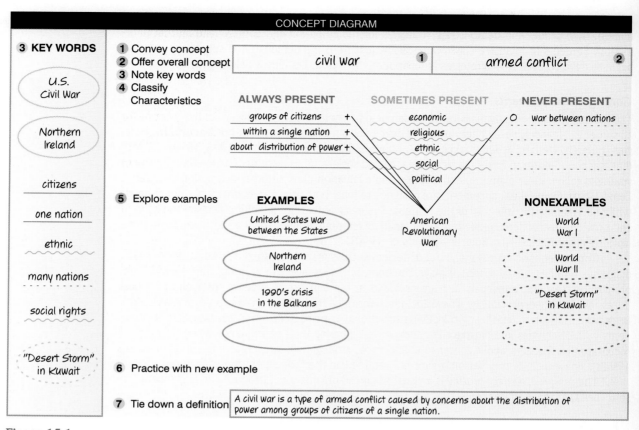

Figure 15.1

Sample Concept Diagram

Note: From *Teaching Adolescents with Learning Disabilities: Strategies and Methods* (2nd ed., p. 453), by D. D. Deshler, E. S. Ellis, and B. K. Lenz (Eds.), 1996, Denver, CO: Love Publishing. Reprinted with permission.

Companion Website

Software for producing concept maps, concept diagrams, relationship charts, diagrams, and other visual displays has been developed by Inspiration Software, Portland, Oregon. For relevant Websites, go to the Web Links module in chapter 15 of the Companion Website.

Semantic Feature Analysis

Semantic feature analysis is an activity intended to help students learn the vocabulary and major concepts from a science or social studies chapter (Bos & Anders, 1990; Bos, Anders, Filip, & Jaffe, 1989). Bos and her colleagues demonstrated that semantic feature analysis facilitated learning more vocabulary than dictionary methods (Bos & Anders, 1990). To use semantic feature analysis, first, analyze the content within a chapter and develop a relationship chart (see Figure 15.2). The chart contains all the vocabulary in a hierarchy of main ideas to lesser ideas. The main ideas are placed along separate columns on the top of the chart, and the related vocabulary are listed in separate rows along the left side of the chart. Several blank spaces can remain to add new ideas that result from class discussions. During instruction, present the information on the chart and have students participate in the discussion of the vocabulary and related concepts. After the discussion, students complete the relationship chart by marking whether or not words in the rows and columns are positively or negatively related or unrelated (Bos & Anders, 1987).

Posse

Englert and Mariage (1991) developed and validated the effectiveness of a strategy called **POSSE** (Englert, Tarrant, Mariage, & Oxer, 1994), an acronym for:

Predicting ideas from prior knowledge
Organizing predictions based upon the forthcoming text structure
Searching/**S**ummarizing for main ideas within the text structure
Evaluating comprehension

	Important Ideas						
	Type of Life		Location			Extinct?	
Important Words	Plant	Animal	Sea	Land	Lakes	Not Extinct	Extinct
Trilobites							
Crinoids							
Giant cats							
Coral							
Bryozoans							
Guide fossils							
Dinosaurs							
Fresh water fish							
Brachiopods							
Small horses							
Ferns							
Enormous winged bugs							
Trees							

Key: + = positive relationship; – = negative relationship; 0 = no relationship; ? = uncertain.

Figure 15.2
Sample Semantic Feature Relationship Chart
Note: From "Semantic Feature Analysis: An Interactive Teaching Strategy for Facilitating Learning from Text," by C. S. Bos and P. L. Anders, 1987, *Learning Disabilities Focus, 3*(1), p. 57. Copyright 1987 Erlbaum. Reprinted with permission.

Analyze the chapters and design strategy think sheets and cue cards as displayed in Figure 15.3. During instruction, POSSE begins with prediction activities. Guide students to predict the content that will be covered and activate student prior knowledge including related information they know. Attempt to involve all students in the discussion as they record their predictions on the think sheets. During the organizing component, ask students to organize their ideas into semantically related groups. For example, for a unit on whales, students could organize their ideas into types of whales, things whales eat, physical characteristics, and behavior of whales. Guide students in their thinking to facilitate the organization process. In the search/summarize component, students read the text, identify main ideas, and generate questions. The final component, evaluation, involves comparing, clarifying, and predicting information learned from reading. Students use this information to generate questions and record answers on their think sheets.

Use Mnemonic Strategies

Keyword, pegword, and letter strategies can be extremely useful for helping students remember vocabulary, terminology, and factual information involving science and social studies. These mnemonic strategies are described in detail in chapter 10, and should be used whenever students exhibit difficulty remembering important content. Create strategies for class presentations and ask students to create their own strategies in group activities. For example, after information has been organized in a graphic organizer or relationship chart, ask students which information seems most

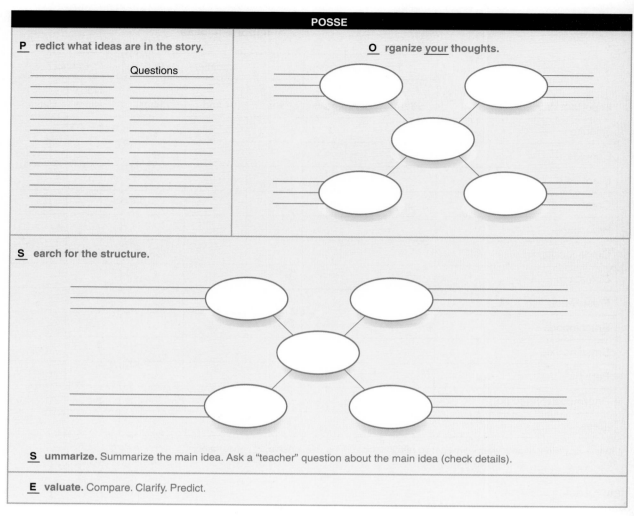

Figure 15.3
POSSE Sheets

Note: From "Lesson Talk as the Work of Reading Groups: The Effectiveness of Two Interventions," by C. S. Englert, K. L. Tarrant, T. V. Mariage, and T. Oxer, 1994, *Journal of Learning Disabilities, 27,* pp. 171, 175. Reprinted with permission.

important, and have them create effective mnemonic strategies to remember this information, using techniques described in chapter 10.

Modify Worksheet Activities

Some students with special needs are able to address the content required in worksheet activities, but may have difficulty with the mechanical aspects of writing necessary to complete the activity in the allotted time. Figure 15.4 includes a regular education class assignment in science and a modified version of the same assignment for students with special needs. The modified assignment reduces the amount of reading and writing, but covers the same major concepts. Amy Sturgeon, a fourth-grade teacher, has developed these modified worksheets to accompany many of her science and social studies assignments. She reports that students with disabilities are better able to keep up with the pace of instruction using the modified sheets and are obtaining the same type of practice using the key concepts from the lessons.

In addition to effective instruction and use of content enhancements to promote comprehension, another important area to consider is teaching students to learn independently from content area textbooks.

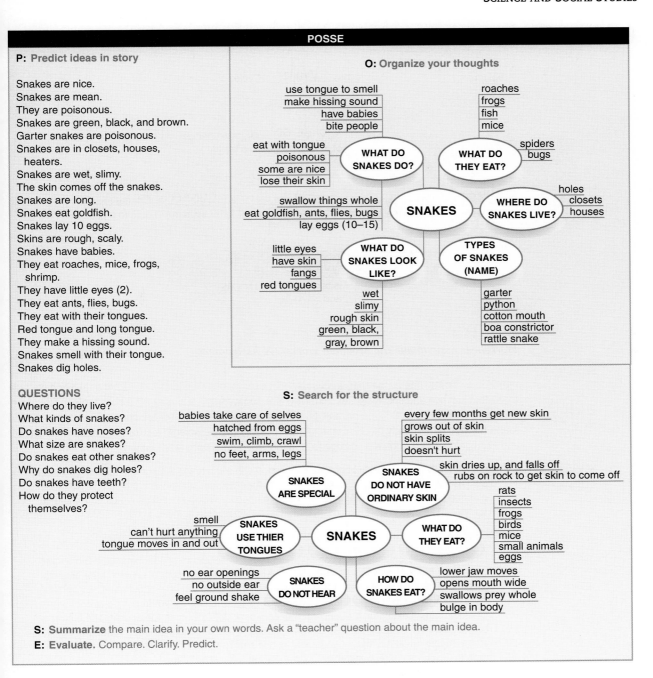

Figure 15.3
Continued

Promoting Independent Learning from Textbooks

A large proportion of learning that takes place in science and social studies comes from independent studying of textbooks (Brophy, 1990). Moreover, the amount of independent studying from textbooks increases substantially with each successive grade level (Deshler, Ellis, & Lenz, 1996). For assignments, students are required to read chapters or sections of chapters and answer questions. Teachers often move rapidly from chapter to chapter because enormous pressures exist to cover content in science and social studies in school (Bulgren & Lenz, 1996). Science and social studies textbooks are often complex, contain high readability levels and many formats, and introduce a significant number of new vocabulary words and concepts (Bulgren & Lenz, 1996; Chiang-Soong & Yager, 1993; Mastropieri & Scruggs, 1994). Some textbook analyses have indicated that science textbooks introduce more new vocabulary

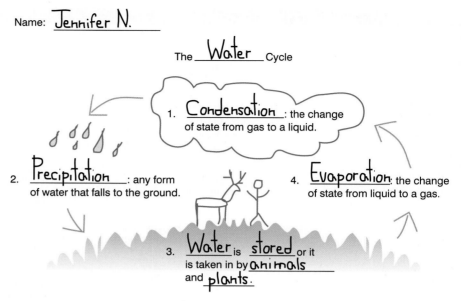

Name: Jennifer N.

The ___Water___ Cycle

1. ___Condensation___ : the change of state from gas to a liquid.

2. ___Precipitation___ : any form of water that falls to the ground.

4. ___Evaporation___: the change of state from liquid to a gas.

3. ___Water___ is ___stored___ or it is taken in by ___animals___ and ___plants___.

Figure 15.4
Worksheet Assignment and Modified Worksheet Assignment

words in a similar time frame than foreign language textbooks (Yager, 1983). Other analyses have indicated that science and social studies textbooks are "unfriendly" and difficult for students to use (Armbruster & Anderson, 1988). Jitendra et al. (2001) evaluated middle-school geography textbooks, and found them to be generally inconsiderate of poor readers and dense with factual information. Gelzheiser and D'Angelo (2000) quoted a passage from a fourth-grade history textbook:

> On April 19, 1775, fighting broke out between British soldiers and Americans in Massachusetts. Two battles were fought. One was at Lexington, the other at Concord. These battles were the beginning of the American Revolution, or the Revolutionary War. A revolution is a complete and often violent change in government. (Larkin, Cunningham, & Dearstyne, 1985, p. 133)

Glezheiser and D'Angelo (2000, p. 26) evaluated the text as follows:

> First, the passage is difficult because extensive background knowledge is assumed, as is the case with many history textbooks (Paxton, 1999). Many fourth grade poor readers will not be familiar with terms such as "British," "revolution," and "government;" the concepts of "battle" and "war," also pose challenges. Similarly, most fourth grade students would not be able to locate Massachusetts, Lexington, or Concord. Students have difficulty with these terms and concepts because they are abstract, because history textbooks overload students with information instead of developing understanding (Paxton, 1999), and because many elementary teachers have little time to devote to content area instruction (Johnson & Janisch, 1998).

Given these analyses, it is not surprising that studying from textbooks can be frustrating for many students with disabilities and those at risk for school failure. Unfortunately, the needs of diverse students are not always considered when adoption decisions are made (Fiore & Cook, 1994). The first thing to do is determine whether textbooks effectively promote understanding. This important feature of textbooks is referred to as text "considerateness."

Criteria for Selecting Considerate Textbooks

In our analysis of science textbooks (Mastropieri & Scruggs, 1994), we noted that readability levels were often higher than the assigned grade levels, a large number of new vocabulary words were introduced in every chapter, and more than 95% of the text copy and subsequent test questions were exercises in factual recall (see also Chiang-Soong & Yager, 1993). Taken together, such findings suggest that students with special needs will encounter great difficulties with most textbooks in science and social studies, a concern shared by many teachers (Bean, Zigmond, & Hartman, 1994). The following recommendations can guide your evaluation of textbook choices if you are asked to make an adoption decision (Armbruster & Anderson, 1988; Chambliss, 1994; Mastropieri & Scruggs, 1993).

Average number of syllables per 100 words

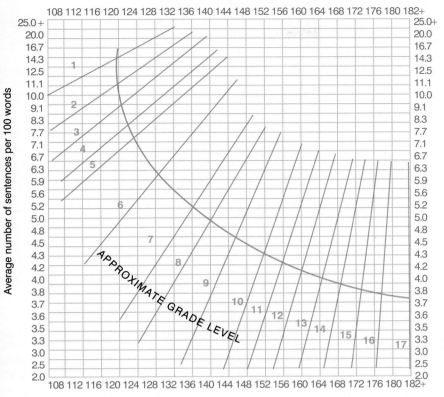

1. Randomly select three text samples of exactly 100 words, beginning with the beginning of a sentence. Count proper nouns, numerals, and initializations as words.

2. Count the number of sentences in each 100-word sample, estimating the length of the last sentence to the nearest one-tenth.

3. Count the total number of syllables in each 100-word sample. Count one syllable for each numeral or initial or symbol; for example, 1990 is one word and four syllables, LD is one word and two syllables, and "&" is one word and one syllable.

4. Average the number of sentences and number of syllables across the three samples.

5. Enter the average sentence length and average number of syllables on the graph. Put a dot where the two lines intersect. The area in which the dot is plotted will give you an approximate estimated readability.

6. If there is a great deal of variability in the syllable or sentence count across the three samples, more samples can be added.

Figure 15.5
Fry's Readability Graph and Formula
Note: From "Fry's Readability Graph: Clarifications, Validity, and Extension to Level 17," by E. Fry, 1977, *Journal of Reading, 21,* pp. 242–252.

1. Evaluate readability.
   a. Is the reading level appropriate for learners?
   b. Complete readability levels for chapters throughout the text and check for consistency (see Figure 15.5).
   c. Is the language understandable?
   d. Are new concepts thoroughly explained, with multiple examples, before proceeding to additional concepts?

2. Consider the adequacy of content coverage for the age group.
   a. Compared with other textbooks, is the coverage too cursory? Too detailed?
   b. Does the content covered reflect scope and sequence in local, state, or national guidelines?
   c. Are objectives addressed toward factual recall or higher order thinking?
3. Evaluate the text structure.
   a. Use the headings and subheadings, develop an outline, and evaluate the organization that is revealed.
   b. Do concepts follow a logical, sequential hierarchy?
   c. Are subheadings informative?
   d. Is the page layout well organized with respect to margin notes, paragraphs, charts, diagrams, and illustrations?
   e. Are order and transitional words like *first, second, next,* and *in contrast* used to promote comprehension?
4. Evaluate text coherence.
   a. Are text enhancements such as illustrations, charts, maps, and diagrams related to the narrative text?
   b. Are the text enhancements clear and understandable?
   c. Is the sequence of the text easy to follow?
   d. Is the language clear and explicit?
5. Evaluate instructional strategies and assessment procedures.
   a. Are assessment activities aligned with instructional objectives?
   b. Are study strategies embedded within the text?
   c. Are there a variety of activities that are relevant to instructional objectives, and are the directions clear and easy to follow?
   d. Are different types of assessment procedures, including curriculum-based, performance-based, and portfolio assessments, included?
6. Evaluate attractiveness.
   a. Does the text have a pleasing appearance?
   b. Will students like the appearance of the text?
   c. Will you enjoy teaching with the text?
7. Evaluate supplemental teacher materials.
   a. What materials accompany the text?
   b. Will they help modify instruction for students with special needs?

One readability measure is provided in Figure 15.5. Other readability measures exist, including those available on some word processing programs such as Microsoft Word™. However, in some cases there may be some problems with standard readability measures. For example, if a long, difficult word is appropriately presented several times to promote redundancy and familiarity, the text readability level will increase. This is also true for textual elaborations that promote comprehension but may increase sentence length. In addition to readability formulas, consider simply having your students read the text aloud and asking them comprehension questions.

Consider using these or similar guidelines when evaluating textbooks. Volunteer to be a member of your school district's textbook adoption committees. Your input on the selection of appropriate textbooks will benefit all students, but especially those with special learning needs.

Many general education students may also benefit from explicit instruction in expository text study strategies.

Strategy Instruction for Using Content Area Textbooks

Successful students develop many effective study skills and strategies that they use when studying textbooks independently. However, students with special needs may require explicit instruction in the use of these strategies. Learning how to predict text structures, how to highlight or outline essential information, and how to use content enhancements such as lesson organizers, spatial organizers, illustrations, charts, graphs, and diagrams are strategies for effectively using textbooks.

Many related strategies for studying from textbook materials (such as organizational and study skills, and reading comprehension strategies) are described in chapters 11 and 13. Additionally, many of the suggestions in chapter 6 will prove beneficial for presenting science and social studies content. Many of these strategies are appropriate for all expository text materials and therefore would be helpful for many other secondary-level classes, such as business education, foreign languages, home economics, and physical education as discussed in chapter 16.

Familiarize Students with Text Organization.   Textbooks contain organizational features intended to help students learn academic content. Unfortunately, however, many students with special needs may not figure out text organization independently. Taking time to teach students how the features of their textbooks are organized can help students learn more easily and make the use of textbooks more valuable. Begin by pointing out to students how to use design features such as:

The overall parts of the text

table of contents
glossary
index
references
appendices

The organizational system of text

units
chapters within units
sections within chapters

Specific features within chapters or units

chapter objectives
chapter openers (motivating stories)
chapter outlines
types and levels of headings and subheadings
use of boldface type, underlining, or colors
vocabulary
illustrations
maps, charts, diagrams, graphs
chapter, section, or lesson summaries
follow-up activities or extensions
end-of-section, chapter, and unit questions
check for understanding
different question-and-answer formats
skill builders
application problems
critical or creative thinking extensions

Features associated with supplemental materials

workbooks
lab books
activity sheets
student directions
amount and types of practice activities
formats of materials

Understanding the organization of a textbook can enhance students' comprehension of the content area information presented. Use the effective instruction principles (as described in chapter 6) when designing lessons to teach students about text features.

The Use of Text Structures.   Science and social studies textbooks are written differently than narratives. Narrative prose tells stories, while expository prose explains theories and presents and explains facts, dates, people, predictions, generalizations, and conclusions (Slater, 1988). Researchers who have analyzed science and social studies textbooks report that expository textbooks use several distinct types of structures (Cook, 1983; Cook & Mayer, 1988; Grimes, 1975; Meyer, 1975; Niles, 1965). Text structures include, for example:

- *Time–order*—information is provided in a chronological sequence; clue words include *next, later, after this.*
- *Cause–effect*—events or actions are related as causes with consequences; clue words include *because, caused, resulted in.*
- *Compare–contrast*—similarities or differences are highlighted among concepts, events, or other phenomena; clue words include *in contrast, similar, differ, difference between.*
- *Enumeration*—items are listed by number; clue words include *one, another, the next, finally.*
- *Sequence*—items are placed in a specific order; clue words include *first, second, third.*
- *Classification*—types of items are placed into groups; clue words include *type of, labeled, classified, member of, group.*
- *Main idea*—an overriding thought or concept is presented (often in the first sentence), followed by supporting or elaborating statements (Bakken, 1995; Bakken, Mastropieri, & Scruggs, 1997; Cook, 1983; Cook & Mayer, 1988; Mayer, 1985; Smith & Friend, 1986).

All types of text structures may appear throughout a single science or social studies textbook. Therefore, students are likely to encounter many structures not only within a single textbook, but also within a single chapter. Students must understand these structures to be able to realize what information is important for them to learn and remember (Mayer, 1984, 1985).

Once passage structures are identified, structure-specific reading comprehension strategies can be used to improve understanding and recall. Bakken, Mastropieri, and Scruggs (1997) successfully taught students with learning disabilities to recognize main idea, list (enumeration), and order passage types and to apply structure-specific reading comprehension strategies. For example, when studying main idea passages, students were taught to write down the main idea, and then write supporting statements. For order passages, they were taught to write down the items in the appropriate sequence presented. These students outperformed students who were given more general training, either to paraphrase information or to answer questions about the passages.

Show How to Identify Essential Information in Content Texts. Highlighting and outlining are used to increase learning and memory of text. Both of these techniques have been adapted to increase learning of students with special needs (Chan & Cole, 1986; Horton, Boone, & Lovitt, 1990; Horton & Lovitt, 1989; Horton, Lovitt, Givens, & Nelson, 1989). Highlighting or underlining identifies the critical information in text or notes (Armbruster & Anderson, 1988; Chan & Cole, 1986). Information highlighted with bright colors, such as fluorescent yellow, stands out dramatically from the text, and can be used to quickly find important information. Underlining is usually done in pencil or pen, but brightly colored highlighting pens can also be used. Brightly colored sticky notes can be used when students are not allowed to write in their textbooks.

The most difficult aspect of highlighting or underlining for students is choosing which information is most important. Without training, many students with disabilities or at risk for school failure may be unable to discern what is important to highlight or underline and may highlight or underline everything on a page. Obviously, this defeats the purpose of highlighting.

When using actual science or social studies text materials, proceed through a highlighting activity in which you describe verbally why you are selecting certain sections to highlight and not others. Say, for example:

- "This looks like a new science concept, therefore I will highlight it. This next section just provides more information on the new concept, so I won't highlight it."
- "This looks like an important person in this history chapter so I will highlight her, but this next section just presents more information on what she did, so I won't highlight that."
- "This looks like an important vocabulary word so I'll highlight it, but I already know what the next word means, so I won't highlight that."

Specific text structures such as list, order, or compare–contrast may not always be easy to identify in textbook passages. Teach students to use paragraph summary or restatement strategies when they cannot identify a specific text structure.

Show students how to examine the features associated with their textbook. For example, boldface text often accompanies only important information and therefore should be highlighted. Point out how the organizational subheadings sometimes provide clues as to whether something is essential, and how some valuable information is presented in maps, figures, charts, and diagrams within the text. Teach students that answering the questions from the *In the Classroom . . . for sharing with students* feature in the Companion Website can help them determine what to highlight.

Finally, provide guided practice in which students work with partners or in small groups and practice identifying important information for highlighting. Stop occasionally and ask students whether they think some of the points meet the criteria for highlighting. Have students share with each other their rationale for the selections they made to highlight. Independent practice and corrective feedback on whether students highlighted appropriate information can reinforce student learning. Positive attribution statements for using the strategy appropriately can also reinforce mastery.

Teach Outlining. Outlining is another study strategy that students can use while studying science and social studies textbooks independently. Before expecting students to outline, be sure they can identify different text structures. If the texts they are using contain a variety of structures, familiarize students with their formats. Point out how textbooks are organized under various levels of subheads, which often can be used as levels in outlines. Then be sure to teach or review how to develop outlines. Start off by teaching that determining the main idea is a first step. Follow up by selecting supporting ideas and details for each major idea. Before requiring students to create outlines independently, provide them with partially completed outlines in which they complete missing information as they study independently. Outlines set up like this are called **framed outlines,** and have been used to promote textbook learning of students with and without disabilities (Lovitt, Rudsit, Jenkins, Pious, & Benedetti, 1986). Figure 15.6 displays an example of a framed outline that can be used for your teaching.

Outlining is also a useful strategy when students are unable to highlight directly in their textbooks.

Social Studies Resources is a Website that helps students find links for research projects. Other Websites can help students find historical documents. To find these Websites, go to the Web Links module in chapter 15 of the Companion Website.

Title: Types of Mountains

I. Folded Mountains
  A. Formed by the "folding" of rock layers
    1. Most occurred when _____.
    2. When this (1) happened, the rocks _____.
  B. Many important mountain ranges are folded mountains.
    1. The world's highest mountains, including _____
       and _____, are folded mountains.
    2. In the United States, _____ are folded mountains.
II. _____ Mountains
  A. Formed when molten rock rises through the Earth's crust.
    1. Molten rock is known as _____.
    2. Pools of _____ get bigger, and _____.
  B. _____ mountains are found in the United States.
    1. The Black Hills of South Dakota.
    2. The _____ Mountains.
III. Fault-Block Mountains
  A. Formed when _____.
  B. Found in the Western United States.
    1. The Sierra Nevadas are fault-block mountains.
    2. The _____ are fault-block mountains.

Figure 15.6
Sample Framed Outline

Introduce Study Guides. Study guides take on a variety of forms and can be developed by teachers, students, or by both teachers and students using "partially completed" study guides similar to partially completed outlines. Lovitt and Horton and their colleagues studied the effects of various study guides on textbook comprehension of students with and without disabilities (Horton et al., 1990; Horton & Lovitt, 1989; Horton et al., 1989). Students used information in the science and social studies textbooks to complete short-answer questions on the study guide form. In some studies students used computerized versions of the study guides. Students who used the study guides consistently outperformed students who did not have instruction using study guides. To create a study guide for your students, include critical features such as the formulation of questions, the use of vocabulary, the amount of content coverage, and a predictable format for the guide. Before developing study guides to accompany the science or social studies textbooks, consider the following:

1. The amount of content you will cover on a single study guide (chapter, unit)
2. The amount of information on a single page (delete unnecessary information)
3. The type of study guide you will use (question–answer, framed outline, schematic graph, graphic organizer)
4. The size of the font used (not too small, but not too large)
5. The sophistication of language used
6. The format of the questions (fill-in-the-blank, open-ended, or multiple-choice)
7. Whether the order of questions parallels the order within the text
8. The amount of time and assistance available for completion
9. The type of instruction used to show students how to study using the completed and corrected study guide
10. The use of motivational pictures or other features

Similar to the development of mnemonic strategies (see chapter 10) and other teacher-developed materials, try developing a few study guides annually to accompany your text. Save them or share them with another teacher who may also develop a few to share with you. Do not pressure yourself to complete the entire text at one time or you may become overwhelmed. Over time, you will have accompanying study guides developed for entire textbooks in science and social studies.

Teach Learning Strategies

Deshler and Schumaker and their colleagues at the University of Kansas Institute for Research in Learning Disabilities developed some excellent learning strategies including an instructional model for optimal delivery of these strategies (Deshler, Ellis, & Lenz, 1996; Deshler & Schumaker, 1988; see also Deshler & Schumaker, 1986). Learning strategies should be implemented slowly over time to ensure that all students master all steps involved in learning and generalizing strategies. Key elements in the learning strategies model are listed in the following *In the Classroom* feature. The intent of instruction in the learning strategies is for students to become independent at implementing the strategies in their own studying.

MultiPass. A useful learning strategy for reading science and social studies textbooks is **MultiPass** (Schumaker, Deshler, Alley, Warner, & Denton, 1982). The steps in MultiPass are similar to the SQ3R strategy—survey, question, read, recite, and review (McCormick & Cooper, 1991). With MultiPass, students are taught to review textbook reading materials three times, first to "survey," second to "size up," and third to "sort out."

During the "survey" pass, students familiarize themselves with the organization of the text chapter, including the title, beginning paragraphs, subheadings, summary paragraphs, and the major ideas. Teach students to make associations with the information in this chapter and previously read chapters. Finally, teach students to summarize the information in the chapter in their own words.

For the "size up" pass, teach students more study techniques to use when reviewing the chapter:

- Identify highlighted information.
- Read the questions at the end of the chapter.
- Make up questions from statements.
- Skim text to find answers to questions.
- Paraphrase answers without looking back at the chapter.

Other strategies that emphasize repeated readings are PQRST (preview, question, read, state, test), triple-S (scan, search, summarize), and OARWET (overview, achieve, read, write, evaluate, test)(see Mastropieri & Scruggs, 2002).

In the Classroom ...a feature for teachers

Steps in Learning Strategy Model

Step 1: Pretest learners and have students make a commitment to learning.
Step 2: Present and describe the learning strategy.
Step 3: Model strategy usage using think alouds and provide initial student practice with the strategy.
Step 4: Provide additional rehearsal and verbal elaboration practice with the strategy.
Step 5: Provide controlled practice and feedback with the strategy (guided practice).
Step 6: Provide advanced practice and feedback with the strategy (independent practice).
Step 7: Provide positive feedback for learning strategy and enlist support for generalization of self-use of strategy.
Step 8: Provide generalization and maintenance training, support, and feedback.

Note: From "An Instructional Model for Teaching Students How to Learn," by D. D. Deshler and J. B. Schumaker, 1988, in J. L. Graden, J. E. Zins, & M. J. Curtis (Eds.), *Alternative Instructional Delivery Systems: Enhancing Instructional Options for All Students,* Washington, DC: National Association of School Psychologists.

Finally, for the "sort out" phase, teach students to test themselves on the information in the chapter. In addition, throughout all three phases of instruction, students can use self-monitoring procedures to ensure they have completed all necessary steps, including appropriate attribution. An example attribution statement to teach students is: "Using MultiPass should help me do better on the next test."

IT FITS. **IT FITS** was developed to help students with learning difficulties remember important information from science textbooks (King–Sears, Mercer, & Sindelar, 1992). IT FITS is an acronym for steps in creating mnemonic keyword strategies. King-Sears et al. taught students with learning disabilities to use the IT FITS strategy:

Identify the term.
Tell the definition of the term.
Find a keyword.
Imagine the definition doing something with the keyword.
Think about the definition doing something with the keyword.
Study what you imagined until you know the definition. (King-Sears et al., 1992, p. 27)

One student in this investigation reported using the strategy to learn the meaning of *acoustic*. After *identifying* the term, he *told* the definition of the term ("having to do with hearing"), then *found* a keyword ("stick"). Next, he *imagined* the definition doing something with the keyword, by considering the stick that his bandleader used, which made a noise when it was tapped. He then *thought* about this definition, and *studied* what he imagined until he remembered the keyword. Results indicated that students learned more science vocabulary when they used and implemented the IT FITS strategy.

TRAVEL. Boyle and Weishaar (1997) taught students with learning disabilities to use the TRAVEL strategy for developing their own cognitive organizers to improve their comprehension and recall of text content. This strategy is described in the following Research Highlight.

The IT FITS strategy was originally used with science textbooks, but the same procedures can be applied to social studies textbook learning (see also Fulk, 1994).

See chapter 10 for additional information on developing and applying keyword mnemonic strategies.

Research Highlight

Creating Cognitive Organizers to Enhance Text Learning

Boyle and Weishaar (1997) employed a strategy to train high school students (grades 10, 11, and 12) with learning disabilities how to create their own cognitive organizers, that is, a spatial representation of information in the text being studied. Following are the steps in the **TRAVEL** strategy:

Topic: Write down the topic and circle it.

Read: Read a paragraph.

Ask: Ask what the main idea and three details are and write them down.

Verify: Verify the main idea by circling it and linking its details.

Examine: Examine the next paragraph and Ask and Verify again.

Link: When finished with the story, link all circles. (Boyle & Weishaar, 1997, p. 230)

Students in the TRAVEL condition were taught to apply this strategy to text on a variety of topics (e.g., flash floods). In another experimental condition, students were provided with a cognitive organizer previously generated by experts, and given training in its use. Students were trained to review the "map," read a paragraph, stop reading and find the main idea and details on the map, and then to start again on the next paragraph. A third control condition received no training or cognitive organizers.

Results revealed that students who used the TRAVEL strategy outperformed control condition students on tests of literal and inferential recall, on both below-grade level passages and grade-level passages. In addition, students who used this strategy in some cases outperformed students who had been provided with expert-generated cognitive organizers and training in their use. For example, students who generated their own cognitive organizers (TRAVEL) had an average comprehension score of 79.9% on grade-level passages. Students who were provided with expert-generated cognitive organizers scored 64.5%, and control students scored 46.0% correct on these same measures. Boyle and Weishaar (1997) concluded that "cognitive organizers offer a promising set of effective tools for teachers to use to increase learning among students with LD" (p. 234).

Questions for Reflection

1. Why do you think students with learning disabilities who generated their own cognitive organizers outperformed students who had been provided with cognitive organizers generated by experts?
2. How could this strategy be adapted for use by an entire class, as a whole-class activity?
3. How could students be included if their reading ability was far below the level of the textbook?
4. How could you evaluate whether the TRAVEL strategy had been successful? How could you determine whether students considered it useful?

Companion Website

To answer these questions online, go to the Research Highlights feature in chapter 15 of the Companion Website.

Adapting Textbook Materials to Accommodate Diverse Learners

Because textbooks are adopted for entire school districts, it is inevitable that the reading level of some books may be too difficult, and thus inaccessible for some students. A number of suggestions to help promote learning in these cases are presented in Figure 15.7.

Steps to Take Before Students Start to Read

Before assigning independent textbook reading, explain the purpose of the assignment. For example, you could say, "When you finish reading the section of your U.S. history text tonight, you will all be able to tell me the causes of the Civil War tomorrow at the beginning of class."

Provide organizers as overviews of the text structures and the content they will be studying. Organizers can be in many different formats, including visual spatial displays, relationship charts, timelines, or concept maps (see Figures 15.1, 15.2 and 15.3). Figure 15.8 provides an example spatially organized template from Inspiration Software that allows you or your students to create visual displays of historical events. Information from the visual display can be converted and printed in an outline format. Visual displays may or may not contain pictures, but they do graphically demonstrate relationships among concepts introduced in chapters or highlight important attributes of the forthcoming

---

Provide alternative text formats.
- Use published audiotapes of texts or develop your own.
- Use computerized text with audio components.
- Acquire enlarged-type versions of materials.
- As appropriate, use Braille versions of materials.
- Assign peers to read text.

Develop or plan for use of alternative curricular materials.
- Revise, rewrite text, deleting higher-level concepts and vocabulary; insert guided questions to use with simplified text.
- Prepare and distribute study guides, outlines, or guided notes.
- Prepare and distribute mnemonic illustrations.
- Supplement with software focused on simpler presentation of concepts.
- Use high-interest low-vocabulary materials.
- Use activities-based materials (see next section).
- Shorten reading and writing assignments.
- Develop pictorial versions of text materials.

Modify teaching presentations.
- Preteach difficult concepts and vocabulary.
- Provide concrete examples.
- Activate prior knowledge.
- Reduce amount of new information.
- Provide illustrative aids and spatial organizers.
- Use study guides.
- Encourage active participation.
- Schedule regular meetings with special needs students.
- Require frequent verbal responses to check for understanding.
- Provide additional review sessions.
- Use trade books as supplements.
- Use audiovisual supplements.
- Use flashcards for studying.
- Have students maintain journals containing new concepts and vocabulary.

Use peers (or parent volunteers) as assistants.
- To read or listen to reading.
- As study partners.
- To assist with writing tasks.

Figure 15.7

Suggestions for Adapting and Using Textbooks

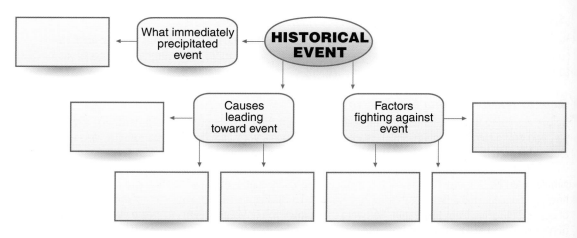

Figure 15.8
Template for Creating Visual Display for Historical Event
Note: Reprinted with permission from Inspiration Software, Portland, Ore.

content. Show a visual display of the upcoming content in science or social studies that depicts the relationships among the new concepts.

Timelines can be constructed to demonstrate graphically the sequence of important events, for example, the events leading up to the Civil War. Timelines may or may not include pictures or symbols, but do contain a chronological sequence in a graphic format. Design, develop, and show timelines that present detailed events covered in the next social studies chapter. The provision of advance organizers assists students in activating their prior knowledge on the topics, but also highlights for them critical information.

Present difficult concepts or vocabulary words to students with disabilities in class before having them read about the information independently. Use some of the suggestions described in the POSSE, MultiPass, Semantic Feature Analysis, or mnemonic strategies to introduce and teach these concepts first. Demonstrate how students can use context clues, glossaries, and dictionaries to figure out new words they will encounter in the text.

One special education teacher, Laura Goodwin, gives her students checklists of upcoming vocabulary and concepts her students will encounter in their general education classes. She has the students practice these words at home and at school to become familiar with the new words before hearing them for the first time in class. Although the vocabulary learning cannot be considered complete until students can use the words in the context of relevant classroom activities, familiarizing students with important terms can make later classroom learning much easier. Figure 15.9 contains a partial vocabulary checklist.

Steps to Take After Textbook Reading Activities

When textbook reading assignments have been completed, use several of the following suggestions to aid students who are at risk for school failure:

- Review major points in class.
- Pair students and have them verbally summarize key points to partners. Partners can give each other feedback and help reinforce major concepts and vocabulary.
- Provide extra help sessions for students who appear confused. Distribute study guide questions and assist students in finding and comprehending the answers to the questions.
- Instruct students to write summaries in visual spatial or graphical formats to indicate to you what they have learned.
- Provide practice tests indicating the precise format of questions and types of important information with which students should be familiar before the "test."
- Assign peer tutors to assist students who appear to have difficulties with new concepts.
- Encourage students to ask you for extra help if they are unsure of the information or they think they require extra assistance.

Companion
Website

Many related ideas and listings of technological advances for converting textbook materials into Braille and computerized formats are described in chapter 4. To locate state agencies for help, contact the National Library Service for the Blind and Physically Handicapped of the Library of Congress. For relevant Websites, go to the Web Links module in chapter 15 of the Companion Website.

For text adaptations for sighted students with severe reading disabilities, see chapter 13.

Vocabulary and Phrases

Direction: Place a check mark in the box if the student reads and defines the word correctly.

Chapter 4: Ecosystems   S = At School   H = At Home

	S	H	S	H	S	H	S	H	S	H
Vocabulary Words & Phrases	Mon	Mon	Tues	Tues	Wed	Wed	Thur	Thur	Fri	Fri
Ecosystem										
Producer										
Consumer										
Decomposer										
Community										
Predator										
Prey										
Parasite										
Host										

Figure 15.9
Sample Vocabulary Checklist
Note: From unpublished materials by M. A. Mastropieri and T. E. Scruggs, 1996, Fairfax, VA: Graduate School of Education, George Mason University. Reprinted with permission.

Adaptations for Students with Visual Impairments or Severe Reading Problems

As Mr. Sterner discovered of Jeffrey in the scenario at the beginning of this chapter, reading problems can significantly inhibit science learning. Students with visual impairments or severe reading problems will need to have written text available to them in alternative formats. Alternative formats include taped versions, computerized versions containing audio components, and larger print versions, or Braille formats for students with very limited vision. Services are available to assist with completing Braille versions of materials. Some special educators are trained to work with Braille and use Braillers and raised materials to make copies of class materials accessible in Braille and raised formats that can be used by students who are blind.

Use Classwide Peer Tutoring

Classwide peer tutoring can be an excellent way for all students to gain extra practice on the most important content of science and social studies units. For example, Maheady, Sacca, and Harper (1988) employed classwide peer tutoring in inclusive tenth-grade social studies classrooms to promote the learning of basic content of all students. Maheady et al. developed 30-item weekly study guides for the most important content of each chapter. The content areas included (a) Egyptians, beginnings of civilization, (b) Greek and Roman civilizations, (c) Middle Ages, (d) American and French Revolutions, and (e) World War I (Maheady et al., 1988, p. 54). Students tutored each other in pairs for about 30 minutes per day, two days per week, using items from the study guides (e.g., "What does imperialism mean?" "What is the governmental structure of the Communist party?"). When participating in the peer-tutoring condition, students scored over 21 percentage points higher than they scored before the intervention began. More recently, Mastropieri, Scruggs, Spencer, and Fontana (2003) implemented classwide peer tutoring using reading comprehension strategies and summary sheets in tenth-grade world history classes, in units on the World Wars. Students who had participated in tutoring outperformed students who had studied with guided notes, on chapter tests, unit tests, and end-of-year tests.

See chapter 8 for more discussion of classwide peer tutoring. Guided notes are discussed in chapter 11.

Students who are not reading at grade level can benefit from listening to textbooks on tapes, which are often available from the textbook publisher.

Classwide peer tutoring has also been used in inclusive high school chemistry classes (Mastropieri, Scruggs, & Graetz, in press). The tutoring materials contained basic information about chemistry concepts, as well as elaborations on that information. Elaborative questions were included in the materials to help link additional information to target concepts. Materials were designed so that if the target information was not known, a keyword or similar mnemonic strategy was provided. When the information was answered correctly by the tutoring partner, further elaborations on the content was prompted. A sample from these materials is shown in Figure 15.10 (see also Figure 10.10 in chapter 10). For example, to learn that a *molarity* is the concentration of a solute in a solution expressed in moles per liter, the first thing tutors would say is: "What is molarity?" If partners answered correctly, tutors skipped down the page and asked: "What else is important about molarity?"

If students were incorrect on the initial response, tutors presented the mnemonic strategy. In this case, tutors said:

> Think of the word 'moles' for mole, and remember the picture of a number of moles in solution, to remember molarity is the concentration of a solute in a solution, in moles per liter.

This information was then practiced. Following practice, tutors proceeded next to questions that elaborated on the target concept, such as "What else is important about molarity?" These questions were intended to promote recall and comprehension of the concept. Correct answers were also included on the tutoring materials and tutors provided corrective feedback continuously. Once students had completed practicing a set of about four to five concepts, students reversed roles, so that each student acted as both a tutor and a tutee. Results of this investigation revealed that students who had participated in tutoring scored much higher on unit tests than students in classes that did not participate in tutoring. This was true of normally-achieving students as well as students with learning disabilities (Mastropieri, Scruggs, & Graetz, in press).

What is molarity?

Concentration of a solute in a solution; moles per liter.

If your partner is correct, go to ⇒
If your partner doesn't know the answer, review the strategy.

Strategy: Think of the word "moles" for mole, and remember the picture of a number of moles in solution, to remember molarity is the concentration of a solute in a solution, in moles per liter.

Then ask: *What is the strategy to remember molarity?*

Then ask again: *What does molarity mean?*

⇒ Then ask:
What else is important about molarity?

[Answers include: molarity is a ratio, moles of solute divided by liters of solution]

Figure 15.10
What is molarity?
Note: From "Teaching Tutorial: Mnemonic Instruction," by T. Scruggs and M. A. Mastropieri, 2002, *TeachingLD.org*, p. 19. Copyright 2002 by the division for Learning Disabilities. Reprinted with permission.

Adapting Activities–Oriented Approaches in Science and Social Studies

An activities-oriented approach to teaching science and social studies can be used, rather than relying primarily on textbooks. Activities-oriented approaches rely on the execution of various activities and projects to develop conceptual understanding. Research has indicated that activities-oriented approaches frequently produce superior learning in general education science and social studies classes (Crabtree, 1983; Ochoa & Shuster, 1980; Shymansky, Kyle, & Alport, 1990). Some research indicates that activities-oriented approaches may be beneficial for students with disabilities when sufficient support is provided (Bay, Staver, Bryan, & Hale, 1992; Mastropieri et al., 1998; Scruggs, Mastropieri, Bakken, & Brigham, 1993). Some of the advantages of activities-oriented approaches to science and social studies education are that they de-emphasize vocabulary

Many manipulative materials for science learning are available from Delta Education and Carolina Biological Supply Company. For relevant Websites, go to the Web Links module in chapter 15 of the Companion Website.

Inductive thinking refers to construction of general rules or principles on the basis of specific observations. Constructing general principles of buoyancy on the basis of the properties of "clay boats" of different construction when placed in water is an example.

Check school policies before using new or unusual materials in the classroom.

learning and learning dependent on the reading of textbooks (areas of relative difficulty for many students with special needs). In addition, activities provide direct interaction with concrete, meaningful materials (areas of relative strength for many students with special needs). Two potential disadvantages to an activities approach are difficulty adjusting to the less-structured atmosphere of activities-oriented instruction, and the fact that some students may exhibit difficulty with inductive thinking often associated with such instruction (Mastropieri & Scruggs, 1994; Mastropieri, Scruggs, Boon, & Carter, 2001; Scruggs & Mastropieri, 1995a, 1995b).

A key to successful inclusive teaching when using activities-oriented approaches is to provide sufficient support and adaptations. However, many types of activities can be undertaken, and different activities may require different adaptations. For example, specific adaptations can help students succeed in specific aspects of science learning, including activities involving plants and animals, microscopes, mixtures and solutions, weather, rocks and minerals, astronomy, magnetism, force and motion, physics of sound, and optics. Adaptations can also be made to social studies activities, including mapping, investigating different cultures or historic time periods, role-playing citizen or government functions, and creating reenactments of historical events. The following sections describe adaptations that may help you more effectively include your students with disabilities in science and social studies activities.

Adapting Science Activities

Many science activities can be adapted for the special learning needs of students with disabilities. Both general and specific adaptations may be helpful when planning activities-oriented instruction in science. Many of these suggestions are described in more detail in *Barrier Free In Brief: Laboratories and Classrooms in Science and Engineering* (1991); "Science Education for Deaf Students," (Lang, 1994); *A Practical Guide for Teaching Science to Students with Special Needs in Inclusive Settings* (Mastropieri & Scruggs, 1993); "Guidelines for Adapting Science Activities for Including Students with Disabilities" (Mastropieri, 1997); *Teaching Chemistry to Students with Disabilities* (1993); *What Others Are Doing: Proceedings of a Working Conference on Science for Persons with Disabilities* (Stefanich, Bergan, & Paulsen, 1997); *Science Success for Students with Disabilities* (Weisgerber, 1993); and "Science Education for Students with Disabilities: The Visually Impaired Student in Chemistry" (Wohlers, 1994).

Science instruction is more meaningful when students can explore science concepts using hands-on materials.

Develop General Laboratory Procedures

Many adaptations can be implemented when using activities-oriented approaches that enable students with all types of disabilities to be more active participants in science. As you think through the activity process, review the PASS variables (see chapter 6): *P*rioritize all objectives and determine whether all objectives are necessary and critical for students with disabilities. Then, *a*dapt materials, the environment, or instructional procedures as needed to ensure success for all students. Use the *S*CREAM variables (e.g., structure, clarity, redundancy) to maximize the effectiveness of your teaching. Finally, *s*ystematically evaluate whether your instruction has been successful through performance activities (see chapter 12). After considering these PASS variables, consider a number of general procedures to address diverse learning needs.

List Rules. Explain, post, and strictly enforce laboratory rules. Speak privately with students who have behavioral difficulties and explain the necessity of adhering strictly to the posted rules during science. Often, students enjoy the activities so much they will try extra hard to control their behavior just to get to participate in them. Have a "cooling-off" place in the room designated for any students who lose control of their behavior. Generously use praise to reinforce following of the science lab rules.

Ensure Safety. Because safety is a major concern when using scientific equipment and materials, stabilize all scientific equipment and materials to avoid unnecessary spills. Velcro can be used to attach lighter objects to tables or trays, while string and trays can be used to hold larger and heavier objects. Use large, clear labels on all equipment and materials, including Braille labels when needed for students with visual impairments. Be sure there is sufficient space for easy mobility and access to materials around the room and lab tables for all students, including those with physical and visual disabilities.

Give Clear Directions. Be sure directions are clearly communicated, are parallel in construction, and follow a step-by-step process. List directions on the board or overhead projector so students can refer to them easily. Color code tasks by order of importance. For instance, tasks written in red must be completed by all students; while tasks written in other colors may be less important. Provide adapted lab booklets that contain extra lines or spaces for writing or drawing examples of specimens. Make Braille and textured versions of lab booklets when necessary. Furnish checklists of what needs to be accomplished in lab to assist students who have difficulties completing longer tasks. Frequently check on student progress during lab activities. If students are working in cooperative groups, verify that students with disabilities are active participants rather than observers while their peers complete all activities.

Enhance Stimulus Value. Implement closed circuit television (CCTV) to ensure that students with vision problems can see all phenomena being observed in labs. CCTV can show enlarged versions of anything being studied. Acquire extra lighting and magnifying lenses to help visibility when needed during lab activities. For example, a "Big Eye Lamp" (Big Eye Lamp, Inc.) is available that consists of a high-intensity light with a large magnifying lens attached. Use of such a device can enhance viewing of small objects for all students, but may be especially beneficial for students with low vision. It may also be helpful for students with less well-developed fine motor skills, for example, when they remove small animal bones from "owl pellets." Use videotapes and videodisks to enforce relevant concepts and provide redundancy; use descriptive video presentations for students who cannot see a television monitor clearly. Acquire extra microphones, stethoscopes, or tuning forks that can help students with hearing impairments hear or feel vibrations of various activities. For example, tuning forks can be placed in water and students with hearing impairments can observe the sound waves in the water.

Prepare for Spills. Prepare areas for spills by having plenty of clean-up materials handy. Place tarps on the floor before engaging in activities that may result in spills. This will save the floor or carpets and help keep custodians on your side. Have students bring in extra large shirts that can be worn as "lab coats" that will protect their clothing in case of spills. Put felt on desk surfaces that are particularly slippery to help stabilize materials. Use trays, slatted trays, or small tubs to hold smaller items on students' desks. Anchor these trays or receptacles with bags of

Publishers of specialized materials include the American Printing House for the Blind and the Lawrence Hall of Science. For relevant Websites, go to the Web Links module in chapter 15 of the Companion Website.

sand or marbles to reinforce and stabilize their positions. Then trays and tubs will reduce the area of any potential spills.

Make Adaptations for Teaching Process Skills. *Measuring and pouring:* Obtain adaptive equipment for measuring and pouring activities. The Lawrence Hall of Science at the University of California at Berkeley has many materials available to help students with visual and physical disabilities. Some of these materials were developed for the curriculum materials Science Activities for the Visually Impaired/Science Enrichment for the Physically Handicapped (SAVI/SELPH) and Full Option Science System (FOSS; Britannica). All of their adapted materials include enlarged labels in print and Braille formats. Some specific adapted materials include enlarged type and Braille on enlarged rulers and number lines, enlarged syringelike devices for measuring, enlarged graduated cylinders for measuring and pouring activities, and larger balance-scales containing a plastic guide that students with visual or cognitive impairments can touch to determine whether the sides of the scale are equivalent. Have students use "scooper" devices, for example, a plastic quart bottle with the bottom removed, for obtaining water from larger receptacles, rather than obtaining it directly from the tap.

Balancing and weighing: Obtain simpler and larger scales and balances for weighing materials. A spring scale that is suitable for students with visual impairments is made available by the American Printing House for the Blind. Other measuring devices such as measuring wheels that click at each rotation to assist with measuring larger areas are available from the American Foundation for the Blind. Devise your own measuring adaptations to suit the activities in your class. For example, when repeatedly using a specific measure on rulers, place a piece of tape or rubber band on the exact measure required to help students with motor or cognitive difficulties be more precise with measuring. Substitute three-dimensional articles made of different textures so students with visual impairments can feel objects that others are able to see to explore weight, texture, and simple measurements.

Charting/graphing and recording data: Most activities in science and many in social studies require students to record their observations on some type of chart, graph, pictorial, or narrative format. Students with disabilities may require some preinstruction with the specific charting or recording procedures for your class. Prefamiliarize students with various types of charts and graphs, such as graph paper, bar charts, frequency charts, and histograms using very concrete examples. Some of the STC (Science and Technology for Children) curriculum materials (available from Carolina Biological Supply Company) contain some excellent lessons for teachers to use to teach preskills in graphing, charting, and recording data. Try using some very familiar topics and construct class graphs. For example, create a class bar chart graph based upon students' favorite foods, colors, television shows, or sports, and demonstrate how the chart or graphic display arranges each student's favorite in a way that all can see if there is a "class favorite" more easily. Use pictures of the objects being graphed to help reinforce what the graph represents. For example, when graphing favorite colors, use shapes containing actual colors, place them on the graph, and write each student's name on his or her color selection. This helps comprehension of the concepts underlying graphing. The AIMS curriculum materials (Activities for Integrating Math and Science) have some excellent lessons that teach beginning graphing and recording data using very concrete, familiar objects.

Use larger graph paper for students with motor or visual difficulties. Label charts and graphs or use paper that has guidelines for students with reading and writing difficulties. Replace pencil or pen markings on charts or graphs with felt circles or squares, or some other textured materials, like Velcro, stickers, guide strips from computer paper, Braille dots, or tactile dots, so students with visual and cognitive disabilities can feel the differences in the types of items charted and the quantities associated with each item. Make three-dimensional graphs using clay, tiles, golf tees, pushpins, yarn, chicken wire, and other materials to help students' comprehension. Three-dimensional graphs in larger formats can be more easily made by students with fine motor difficulties. Students with visual impairments may record observations by drawing on a screen board (crayon on paper over a screen), using clay models, or using Braille numbers and raised lines.

Some computer programs make charts and graphs and may be especially helpful for students with disabilities. In addition, many newer computer programs collect, record, and graph data. These programs when used with other adaptations for accessing computers for students with disabilities will enable students with severe physical disabilities to participate more fully in recording data activities.

Finally, consider grouping students with and without disabilities to record and graph data co-operatively. Peers may be able to assist with some of the more difficult components of the task. However, monitor closely to verify whether students with disabilities are completing their share of the recording activities and to verify whether students with disabilities are comprehending the concepts from the experiences.

Monitor Progress. Increase the amount of time to complete lab activities and provide time guidelines for each component of the lab activities. Many students with disabilities work at a much slower pace than general education students. Check frequently to verify whether the students understand the purpose of the lab activities. Provide additional lab times during which students have access to the same materials but at a slower, more appropriate rate. Finally, provide sufficient redundancy with the activities to reinforce the learning and ensure students have generalized the learning.

Life Science Activities

Life science strands include living things, ecology, cells, genetics, and evolution. Many activities involving life sciences can be concrete and meaningful for students with disabilities. Further, in some cases, successful care of plants or animals can help students feel more a part of classroom activities. By considering the following adaptations, students with special needs may become more actively involved during science.

Activities involving plants

- Because most household plants die from overwatering, and small fish are frequently overfed, set up a strict schedule for watering and feeding, using specific amounts of water or fish food. Water syringes may help students deliver the precise amount of water needed by the plant, and food portions can be prepared ahead of time.
- After planting seeds, plan other science activities to do while plants are growing. Since some students may have difficulty sustaining interest or attention over longer time periods, consider using plants that grow and develop faster. For example, beans normally grow faster and flower sooner than peas. Further, consider acquiring Wisconsin Fast Plants, which develop much faster than most plants, from Carolina Biological Supply Company.
- To help students plant seeds at a standard depth, wrap a rubber band around a dowel or pencil, for a depth gauge.
- To help students directly observe root structure, grow plants in clear plastic "baggies," or in hydroponic (all water) containers. Students with visual impairments can also be encouraged to feel the sunlight in relation to a plant, and feel the effect of the sunlight on the development of the plant.

Activities involving animals

- Carefully consider the purpose of acquiring classroom animals. Many schools have specific restrictions regarding animals, so it is important to first check out these policies before acquiring any animals.
- Any animals' characteristics or peculiarities need to be noted. For example, hamsters are largely nocturnal, and you may wish to consider this fact when deciding on what animals to acquire. Reptiles must be kept warm (e.g., with special heaters), or they will not eat, and may catch "colds" and die. Newts' water must be kept clean, or they may not be able to detect the presence of food placed in their tank. Crayfish are prone to diseases that may spread rapidly to other crayfish. Isolate crayfish for five days, check for any sign of red tinge to the underside, and quarantine affected crawfish.
- When ordering animals from supply houses, make sure the outdoor climate is appropriate for the animal being shipped, and be certain it will arrive at a time when it can be immediately attended to by an adult. For example, ordering a butterfly kit in the winter may mean releasing them when the weather is too cold for survival.
- Some animals (e.g., reptiles) require live food, so consider the effect this may have on students in your class. Some students with emotional handicaps may react strongly to some animals, or to the behaviors of some animals. Finally, some students may be disposed to abuse animals in captivity, so be certain to promote an attitude of respect toward living things, and ensure that captive animals will be kept safe.

Some animals (e.g., guppies, snails, mealworms, crayfish, caterpillar/butterflies) are part of curriculum materials in science (e.g., FOSS, STC), and have specific roles to play in the activities. In other cases, the teacher must determine the purpose of animals in the classroom.

Activities for teaching anatomy

- A variety of three-dimensional models is available from supply companies, such as the Carolina Biological Supply Company. A large-scale model of a boy ("Dudley"), with simulated working organs, is available from Hubbard, and may be helpful for younger students or students with intellectual impairments. The *Visible Man/Visible Woman* also provides concrete information on anatomy. However, be careful that too much valuable instructional time is not lost on assembling models versus learning anatomy concepts.
- Students with hearing impairments who cannot use a stethoscope may be able to feel a pulse at the carotid or brachial arteries. Students with physical disabilities who cannot run in place can substitute another activity (such as raising or lowering the body from the arms of a wheelchair) to increase heartbeat.
- For students who do not have a good sense of their own bodies (e.g., younger students, students with cognitive or intellectual disabilities, or some students with emotional disturbance), use photographs, videotapes, and mirrors to reinforce body image.

Using Microscopes. When acquiring microscopes, consider the Brock "Magiscope" (Brock Optical). This sturdy microscope is simple to use and maintains sufficient light even when it is moved around. Projecting microscopes can project an image of a specimen on a screen or wall. Projected downward on a piece of paper, it can be copied over with special markers to produce a raised surface that can be experienced by students with visual impairments. Microscope images can also be displayed on large monitors for students with visual impairments, or printed from the screen and made into a three-dimensional image. When microscopes are not available, or their use is not practical, acquire large color pictures, or three-dimensional models of the microscopic objects being studied (see Scruggs & Mastropieri, 1994b). For example, Carolina Biological Supply Company supplies a "pull-apart" cell that presents cross-sectional layers of cell structure that can be observed by students.

Health Considerations. Students who have asthma or serious allergies may react negatively to dander in animal fur, or to molds or pollens in plants. Consider the health needs of all students before including specific animals or plants in the classroom.

NASA/Goddard Space Flight Center maintains a motivating Web page that includes links to student activities and curricula for teachers. For the Website, go to the Web Links module in chapter 15 of the Companion Website.

Showing video presentations of microscopic specimens can help students learn.

Earth Science Activities

Earth science covers meteorology, astronomy, geology, and oceanography. Many relevant activities can be conducted in the classroom to enhance comprehension in these areas. Unlike life sciences, students may be unfamiliar with many of the concepts and terms used, so be sure that relevant vocabulary is being learned.

Activities related to weather

- Some concepts, such as humidity or air pressure, may be more difficult for younger students or students with intellectual impairments. Use students' prior knowledge of, for example, hot showers versus dry oven heat, and traveling in an airplane or a fast elevator, to make the concepts more meaningful.
- Place a barometer in a glass container with a rubber top to demonstrate changes as a function of pressure generated by pushing or pulling on the rubber top.
- Available from the Lawrence Hall of Science are adapted thermometers, adapted graduated cylinders and beakers, and tactile floating scales (for measuring rainfall) to assist students with visual impairments.

Activities using rocks and minerals

- The FOSS materials feature an activity titled "Mock Rocks." The teacher creates "rocks" composed of such ingredients as water, flour, aquarium gravel, crushed oyster shells, and food coloring. Students disassemble these rocks into component parts, enforcing the concept that rocks are composed of many other components. Activities such as this may be helpful for students with cognitive or intellectual impairments.
- Models of "sedimentary rock" can be created from differently colored layers of sand or gravel, in white glue and water, or plaster of Paris. Use of alternate layers can represent the layers of rock built up over time.
- Many specimens and models of rocks and minerals are available from supply companies. Generally, larger, loose specimens are preferable to smaller examples glued on a card. Students with visual impairments should be able to feel many properties of minerals, including heft, cleavage (see especially, mica), fracture, and crystal faces. If students feel a specific place on a mineral before a scratch test, it may be possible to feel the scratch. It may be more difficult for students with visual impairments to detect color, luster, and streak, but students with some vision may detect these properties with illumination or magnification.

Physical Science Activities

Physical science activities can include sound, magnetism and electricity, force and motion, light, and powders, mixtures, and solutions. See also *Teaching Chemistry to Students with Disabilities* (1993).

Activities involving sound

- Students can observe and compare sounds made by different objects, and conduct experiments on variations in tension, thickness, and length of strings, cords, and rubber bands. Students may also examine the effect of sound-producing devices in vacuum chambers.
- Students with hearing impairments may have specific difficulties with this content area. For students with some hearing, amplification may be helpful. It may also be helpful to ensure that no other sound is detectable in the classroom other than the one being observed.
- Students with severe hearing loss may in many cases be able to feel the vibrations in different sound-producing objects. Carefully place tuning forks in water after being struck to demonstrate the vibrations in water. When using "waterphone bottle" (bottles filled with different levels of water) activities, indicate the level of the water with rubber bands placed around the bottles for students with visual impairments.

Activities involving magnetism and electricity

- Students can make simple connections from batteries to small motors and lightbulbs, identify conductors and insulators, and create series and parallel circuits, electromagnets, and telegraphs. Some science activities encourage students to find insulators and conductors by connecting circuits. Monitor these activities carefully and be certain that classroom wiring and outlets are inaccessible.

- The SAVI/SELPH science materials include electricity boards that are made to be easy to work with, including alligator clips and battery holders. These boards may be beneficial for students with visual and physical disabilities, as well as any students who lack well-developed fine motor skills. For students with more severe physical disabilities, wires can be permanently attached to most connections.
- For students who cannot see whether lightbulbs are lighted, substitute small electric motors, which can be heard when they are connected to a battery. When using electric motors with students with hearing impairments, attach a small paper flag to the rotor, so the movement can be observed when the power is connected.
- When constructing telegraphs, connect a lightbulb to flash, so that the message can be observed by students with hearing impairments.
- Students with mental retardation and younger students may have less well-developed preconceptions about electricity; for example, the battery as a power source, the current that travels through a conductor, and the concept of a "circuit" (Scruggs, Mastropieri, & Wolfe, 1995). Pretraining on some of these concepts may be helpful.

Activities related to force and motion

- Force and motion activities include investigations with simple machines (such as levers and pulleys), pendulum motion, and rubber-band-propelled airplanes. The concepts presented in force and motion activities are more abstract than they are in some other subjects; therefore, some concept-enhancement activities may be helpful for students with lower cognitive or intellectual functioning (Mastropieri, Scruggs, & Butcher, 1997; Scruggs & Mastropieri, 1995b). Provide and practice many examples from students' experiences of new concepts as they are investigated.
- See-saws, hammers, rakes, and crowbars are good examples of levers; ramps found around the schoolyard are good examples of inclined planes; playground swings and pendulum clocks are good examples of pendulums. Demonstrate how the principles learned in class generally apply to these more familiar objects.
- Software programs such as "Miner's Cave" (MECC) provide additional guided practice on concepts of simple machines.
- Acquire light sensors that detect variations in light by emitting a sound to help students with visual disabilities during activities using pendulums or other activities involving motion (available from American Printing House for the Blind). If used appropriately, the light sensor will provide auditory feedback each time the pendulum swings past the sensor.

Activities related to light and color

- Some activities involving light and color include making color wheels, using prisms, separating pigments with chromatographic paper, investigating printed colors with magnifying lenses, and mixing food coloring and differently colored light beams. The greatest concern for adaptations for light and color activities, of course, is for students with visual impairments.
- For students with residual vision, use large examples of intense colors, magnifying lenses, closed circuit television, and high illumination.
- For students with no vision, some color changes are detectable with a light sensor. Determine which colors can be detected before initiating the activity. Students can also feel the relative warmth of light from some lightbulbs (but remember, lightbulbs can get too hot to touch).
- A spray bottle filled with water can be used in some cases to demonstrate light rays.
- Some investigations involving light and color involve darkening the room. Check with your school's policy on lighting, and determine whether some students may have specific fears of the dark. Since some students who fear the dark are reluctant to admit it, carefully monitor students' responses to darkened rooms.

Activities to explore powders, mixtures, and solutions

- An important first consideration for creating mixtures and solutions, examining chemical properties and observing chemical changes, saturation, concentration, and separation is safety. Make certain that all students, including students with disabilities or other special needs, are familiar with specific rules about handling relevant materials. Such rules may include the following: never taste anything, clean up spilled substances immediately, avoid direct contact with the substances unless supervised, avoid blowing (or sneezing) into the powders, and use heat sources only with teacher supervision.

- Because spills are likely during these activities, consult the recommendations listed previously for spills (see p. 469–470).
- Mixing substances together often produces some sound, such as fizzing. Encourage students to employ their hearing when making observations. Stethoscopes or microphones can be used to amplify the sound. In some cases, light sensors can detect mixtures undergoing color changes.
- Students with visual impairments can be encouraged to feel powders and substances that are not harmful to touch. Additionally, students can feel paper or other filters before and after mixtures and solutions have passed through them.
- For students with physical disabilities and fine or gross motor difficulties, determine whether measuring and pouring is an essential part of that particular activity. If not, perhaps these students can concentrate more on the more central aspects of the activity and rely on peers for measuring and pouring liquids.

Social Studies Adaptations

Social studies activities can address motivational problems and negative reactions to independent textbook-based assignments for students who have problems with reading or writing. These activities might include producing plays, reenacting historical events, creating maps, preparing foods from other cultures and historical periods, making historical or cultural dioramas, and interacting with experts on cultural events or historical periods. Students can also engage in discussion or debate about current issues or historical events. Finally, students can participate in field trips to museums or historical sites. Overall, social studies activities ordinarily may not involve such a wide range of different materials and equipment as activities in science, and therefore fewer overall specific adaptations may be considered. General recommendations are noted in the following section, and are also found in Brophy (1990), Crabtree (1983), and Ochoa and Shuster (1980).

General Recommendations

As suggested throughout this book, Crabtree (1983) suggested that whole-class teaching devoted solely to textbooks and worksheets is not an optimal way of addressing the diverse needs of students. Instead, Crabtree recommended the following (see also Brophy, 1990):

- Design projects and activities relevant to the students' specific interests and needs.
- When texts are used, supplement them with equivalent materials that are easier to read, audiotaped textbooks, and relevant illustrations.
- Use a variety of resources for viewing and other interactions in a viewing center in the classroom.
- Use multimedia for presentations and project-based activities. The *Technology Highlight* feature describes the uses of technology to create multimedia social studies projects.
- Use a variety of structured role-play activities, simulations, and manipulative materials to enforce important concepts.

Because disability awareness is very much a social issue, determine whether you can plan disability awareness issues as a component of the curriculum. Even in history classes, many significant historical characters either had disabilities themselves or were very concerned with promoting rights of individuals with disabilities, for example, Alexander Graham Bell, Franklin Roosevelt, Dorothy Dix, or Julia Ward Howe.

Recommendations for specific activities

- When planning meals from other cultures or historical periods, consider whether any of your students have specific food allergies.
- Role-play and reenactment activities can be supplemented with videotape presentations of the events being role-played to enhance understanding of the activity. Keep in mind students' special needs when assigning roles; for example, in reenactments plan or adapt appropriate roles for students with mobility impairments.

The National Geographic Society has features for children on its Web page, including information and activities. Go to the Web Links module in chapter 15 of the Companion Website.

The Voyage of the Mimi I and II are excellent multimedia programs that integrate science and social studies while learning about whales or the Mayan culture, and are available from Wings for Learning by Sunburst. For the Website, go to the Web Links module in chapter 15 of the Companion Website.

Intercultural E-mail Classroom Connections helps students find keypals anywhere in the world, to promote multicultural studies. For the Website, go to the Web Links module in chapter 15 of the Companion Website.

The World Wide Web Virtual Library of Museums provides links to museums and zoos around the world. For the Website, go to the Web Links module in chapter 15 of the Companion Website.

Technology Highlight

Multimedia Social Studies Projects

Project-based learning and social studies is enhanced with the use of multimedia. Multimedia can take many forms—including use of text, pictures, sounds, graphics, and video, all combined within a single project. Many of the software described throughout this text and on the Companion Website offer alternatives to the traditional paper-pencil report. Combining various multimedia formats into a project often appeals to students with disabilities who may have stronger skills with multimedia than with literacy skills. Researchers have demonstrated that students with disabilities have been successful at completing multimedia projects in inclusive social studies classes (e.g., Ferretti & Okolo, 1996; Okolo, Cavalier, Ferretti, & MacArthur, 2000).

Various types of software and hardware can be used to develop projects. PowerPoint, for example, is a fairly simple-to-use software program that can assist students in developing basic multimedia projects. Since text, pictures, sounds, and animation are easy to insert into PowerPoint documents, students can design professional looking slide shows that contain multimedia with relatively little expertise. Students can practice presenting using some of the features of the program and develop professional looking handouts to accompany their presentations.

Digital cameras are less expensive now than ever before, and many schools help teachers purchase or have access to digital cameras in classrooms. Once students learn how to use digital cameras, they can learn how to upload and edit photos to use in their projects. Photos can be taken of projects that were completed during class, of peers dressed in era-specific clothing for social studies lessons, or of historical artifacts observed on field trips—all inserted within their multimedia-based projects.

Digital video is more widely available and can be used by students to enhance their projects. Students can shoot their own video or may need to access available videos that can be inserted with links into their multimedia projects. Since scanners are more widely available, students can learn to use them to insert graphics or photos to help enhance projects.

Web page development also offers students the opportunity to combine various multimedia features. Several programs are widely available for Web page development including Front Page and Dream Weaver. There are, however, software programs available that offer "templates" of Web pages that students can use to design, develop, and publish their own Websites (Web Workshop by Sunburst).

By using combinations of software programs and hardware aspects of multimedia, students' project-based learning can be enhanced considerably. Personalizing projects in this way increases individual ownership and motivation toward the entire process of completing projects.

Refer to the chapter 15 Companion Website for additional links for multimedia projects.

- In geography, relief maps may be helpful, not only for students with low vision, but for other students who may need assistance understanding the representative function of maps. Braille maps, raised globes, and illuminated globes are also available to assist students with visual impairments.
- Prepare students for visitors who come into the classroom to demonstrate, for example, instruments, clothing, lifestyles, and habits from different countries. Some students may need additional preparation in appropriate attending skills, and appropriate questions to ask.

Field Trips

Field trips can often allow students to obtain first-hand exposure to people and things that they may not be able to experience in the classroom. In addition to museums and zoos, field trips can include visits to historical sites, living farms, archeological sites, weather stations, observatories, and public parks, to name only a few possibilities. Many students with special needs may benefit at least as much as other students, particularly if they have had fewer relevant background experiences, or when they can benefit particularly from the enhanced stimulus value and added concreteness of the experience. However, field trips can become unpleasant experiences if not well planned and supervised. If you have not previously been to the field-trip site, visit it personally in advance of the trip. This visit will provide you with a great deal of information that will be helpful in planning the experience.

- Call the facility in advance and inform the staff that you will be attending, and inform them of any special needs your students may have. When students with physical disabilities are involved, for example, special needs may arise involving accessibility, viewing levels, seating, rest periods, overall length of the tour, and use of adaptive devices. Advance visitation and planning will help you provide the needed supports for students' needs.
- Students with visual impairments may require modifications or adaptations in lighting, printed materials, videotape presentations, seating arrangements, and in any visually presented information. Mobility considerations, use of magnifying lenses, and method of participation in demonstrations may also need to be considered.
- Considerations for students with hearing impairments may include the amount of background noise, seating, distance from speaker, interpreters, rate of speaker presentation, effective visual aids, and multisensory experiences, depending on the level of the hearing disability (Mastropieri & Scruggs, 1993; see also chapter 4).
- Students with cognitive or intellectual impairments may need preparation or on-site support of teachers, aides, or peers, to promote understanding of the information being presented.
- Students with attentional disorders may need assistance focusing attention on relevant exhibits, and efficiently sequencing their visit (Mastropieri & Scruggs, 1993; see also chapter 5).

Prepare your students before their visit. Prefamiliarize them with the purpose of the visit and the behaviors that will be expected of them. Practice any specific social skills that may need to be exhibited on the trip. If behavior management is likely to be a problem, set up a point system such as those described in chapter 8. Providing students with notebooks and giving them specific information to acquire may help focus their attention on the objectives of the field trip. Additional guidelines for teachers to consider on field trips are given in Figure 15.11 (see also Mastropieri & Scruggs, 1993).

Inquiry Learning in Science and Social Studies

Many advocates of science and social studies instruction strongly endorse inquiry and problem-solving approaches to teaching (Rutherford & Ahlgren, 1990). Inquiry approaches involve the presentation of questions and problems to students with less direct guidance during the problem solution stages. Although often associated with activities-oriented approaches, inquiry-based learning can also be a significant component of textbook-oriented learning. Inquiry approaches rely heavily upon students' ability to think, use insight, employ prior knowledge, make connections between previously covered content, and generate novel solutions. Unfortunately, however, students with disabilities and at risk for school failure may experience great difficulty with tasks that emphasize inquiry and problem-solving approaches (Mastropieri, Scruggs, & Butcher, 1997). This does not mean that attempting to teach problem-solving and thinking skills to students with special needs is unimportant. On the contrary, these skills are especially important for such students to learn. It has been seen that with appropriate adaptations students with disabilities and those at risk for school failure can benefit from inquiry-oriented and problem-solving instructional approaches. Many special educators advocate strongly for teaching students with disabilities active thinking skills. Adaptations for inquiry-oriented approaches in science and social studies will help your students with disabilities be more successful.

- Set learning objectives before the trip and discuss them with your students.
- Preview the field trip with students, including the procedures that will be involved and the behaviors they will be expected to exhibit. Obtain handouts of the facility, and preview them with the class.
- Practice any difficult or unusual vocabulary that students will encounter on the field trip, to maximize comprehension.
- Discuss the behavioral objectives for the trip, and describe your behavior management plan.
- Assign peer partners, buddies, or helpers when appropriate.
- During the trip, encourage active participation of all students.
- Use familiar and descriptive language whenever possible. Summarize information from the field trip to the students as they participate, and ask them to summarize what they have done.
- When it is not possible to touch or manipulate exhibits, describe sounds, odors, shapes, colors, and textures as much as possible.
- Emphasize multisensory presentations or examples whenever possible.
- Record the field trip, using photographs, videotape, or audiotape. Edit the recordings, and review them with the students after the field trip, emphasizing important objectives.
- Make a book of the field trip for the class, or create a book as a class activity, and review it with students.

Figure 15.11
Teacher Guidelines for Field Trips

Use a Problem-Solving Model for Social Studies Instruction

O'Brien (2000) proposed a problem-solving model for social studies instruction for students with learning disabilities:

> As indicated by the research, students with LD tend to rely too much on their own personal experiences to help make sense of new ideas, in part because they often lack necessary prior knowledge. One means to further these students' ability to engage in higher level thinking is to present them with problems that are based in their own communities. (p. 199)

O'Brien (2000) proposed a seven-step model for promoting problem solving in social studies:

Step 1: Provide context and introduce background. In O'Brien's example, he provided the problem of determining how some of the streets of Lawrence, Kansas (the students' hometown) were named.

Step 2: Generate the problem and demonstrate the use of maps.

Step 3: Generate possible solutions and question how to solve the "mystery."

Step 4: Research possible solutions.

Step 5: Reconsider possible solutions.

Step 6: Explain a solution.

Step 7: Reestablish the context. In the present instance, the effects of Quantrill's raid on the city of Lawrence and the introduction of the railroad can be included in the discussion.

In inclusive classes, students can work in pairs or cooperative learning groups to find and refine answers to problems. Once students have learned to apply the problem-solving strategy to hometown issues, they can investigate broad and complex issues, such as violence in society. Students can study a problem, propose solutions, and evaluate the possible consequences of their proposed solution.

Promote Active Thinking with Guided Questioning

Several studies have documented the positive effects of coaching students with disabilities through an active reasoning process to facilitate their performance. In fact, some recent research has suggested that students with mild cognitive and intellectual disabilities comprehend more and understand better when they actively reason through new information (e.g., Scruggs, Mastropieri, & Sullivan, 1994; Sullivan, Mastropieri, & Scruggs, 1995). For example, in a lesson on life science, dialogue similar to the following was provided:

Teacher: Some penguins carry their eggs on top of their feet. Why does this make sense?

Student: I don't know.

Teacher: Well, let's think. What do we know about penguins? For example, where do they live?

Student: In Antarctica.

Teacher: Good. And what is life like in Antarctica?

Student: Cold, icy,. . . . frozen.

Teacher: So, if it is cold and icy in Antarctica, why does it make sense that penguins carry their eggs on their feet?

Student: To keep them from getting frozen?

Teacher: Good. To keep them warm, to keep them from getting frozen. (see Mastropieri, Scruggs, & Sullivan, 1994, p. 453)

In this research, students with learning disabilities and mental retardation remembered and comprehended more information when they were prompted to actively reason through the information, as described in the example, than when they were directly provided with the same information. The following questioning procedures seemed particularly helpful:

- Select information that is logically related, and for which students have at least some prior knowledge to help them. Students are not likely to be able to reason through, for example, why there are seven days in a week, or why stars appear to twinkle, without provision of specific information relevant to the question.
- Students with cognitive and intellectual disabilities have been characterized as "inactive learners," and may not know how to go about reasoning through new information. If students do not immediately respond to questioning (e.g., "Why does it make sense that some bats fly near light?"), ask follow-up questions that help students activate relevant prior knowledge (e.g., "What do bats eat?").
- If they still do not draw relevant conclusions, provide relevant information in the context of the question (e.g., "If bats eat insects, and insects fly toward light, why does it make sense that bats fly near light?").

Such guided questioning has also been seen to promote thinking in science classes containing students with cognitive or intellectual disabilities, as seen in this example of a discussion of the effects of capillary action when flowers were placed in colored water:

Teacher: What do you think happened? I have a flower in blue water and a flower in green water, a white flower, right? Ken, what is the color of this flower?

Ken: Blue.

Sam: White.

Teacher: White and blue. Julie, what color is this flower?

Julie: Green.

Teacher: White and green. How did I get the colors there? How did I get the colors there, Shawn?

Shawn: That's from a stain in there like . . .

Teacher: A stain? What do you think? Ken, how did this blue get here?

Ken: . . . Oh, you watered it with food coloring.

Teacher: But I didn't put any up here, did I?

Ken: You put it in the dirt.

Teacher: But there's no dirt.

Ken: Oh.

Teacher: How did it get from there to here?

Student: I know. I know. It raised.

Teacher:	OK, Jimmy, what do you think?
Jimmy:	It went all the way up to here.
Teacher:	Went all the way through water? The what, Mary?
Mary:	A stem.
Teacher:	The stem. It went all the way through the stem, you're right. (Scruggs & Mastropieri, 1995b, p. 264)

This type of questioning may also be appropriate for promoting critical thinking in social studies subjects. For example, teachers can describe the nature and characteristics of harbors, and ask students why it makes sense that many cities are located on or near natural harbors.

Developmental Considerations

Recent research has demonstrated that students with learning disabilities and mild mental retardation can be coached to draw relevant inferences themselves—with appropriate support—and that they understand and remember better when they do. However, some additional research has demonstrated that some students, especially those with mental retardation, may lag far behind their age peers in reasoning skills. For example, following is a segment of an interview with an upper-elementary student with mild mental retardation when questioned about his conceptions about the nature of air. When asked where air is found, Martin replied:

Martin:	Outside.
Interviewer:	We find it outside. Does it do anything for you?
Martin:	It gives you goosebumps.
Interviewer:	Do you think there is air in this cup?
Martin:	No.
Interviewer:	What do we breathe?
Martin:	No [Put his ear to the cup on the scale.]
Interviewer:	You tried to listen to it? There wasn't any air in there?
Martin:	This was the cold. (Scruggs, Mastropieri, & Wolfe, 1995, p. 228)

The preconception that air is found "outside," and exists only as cold, wind, or a draft, is commonly held by preschool children (Driver, Asoko, Leach, Mortimer, & Scott, 1994). However, the individual in the previous interview was in the upper-elementary grades, and his reported preconceptions may be several years behind those of many of his more typical age peers. Teachers should consider these possible differences when planning inquiry-oriented instruction.

Further, in a more recent investigation, Mastropieri, Scruggs, and Butcher (1997b) reported that students with cognitive and intellectual disabilities were slower than their normally achieving peers to draw the correct inference in an activity investigating pendulum movement (i.e., the length of the string affects the rate of swing). Further, after completing the activity, they were less able to apply the concept to new problems. Similar findings were reported by Mastropieri, Scruggs, Boon, and Carter (2001) in a study of principles of buoyancy. These findings suggest that while normally achieving students can answer higher-level questions with only subtle coaching, students with disabilities may require extensive levels of coaching to draw the same inference. However, in many cases, more structured coaching did lead students to draw relevant inferences.

Scruggs and Mastropieri (1995b) observed students with mental retardation in inquiry-oriented science classes over an extended time period and concluded that these instructional practices could be effective in promoting understanding of science concepts. However, it was also reported that special problems may arise with respect to:

- attention (particularly, attention to the most important aspects of new concepts);
- memory for new vocabulary;
- logical reasoning in drawing inferences or solving problems; and
- outerdirectedness, or the tendency to be overly reliant upon the practices or conclusions of others.

These problems may be addressed, respectively, by redirecting attention; by enhancing memory with repetition and elaboration; by carefully guided questioning; and by acceptance and reinforcement of divergent, individualized responses.

Develop Students' Abilities to Use Deductive Reasoning

Woodward and Noell (1992) have recommended the use of deductive reasoning strategies, in addition to inductive reasoning strategies, to promote thinking and generalization of concept knowledge in students with special needs. For example, rather than providing several examples of pendulums to students and asking them to draw inductive conclusions about pendulum motion, teachers can directly provide the "rule" about pendulum motion, by saying something like the following:

> *Remember, the longer the string, the slower the swing. Let's say it together: "The longer the string, the slower the swing." That means, the longer the string is, the fewer swings the pendulum will make in 10 seconds. Watch me: You see this pendulum with a short string is swinging very fast, while this other pendulum with a long string is swinging very slowly.*

Next, teachers can apply different instances of pendulum motion, and ask students to make predictions:

> *Now, here are two new pendulums. This one has a short string, and the other one has a long string. Which one do you think will swing faster? Which one do you think will swing more times in 10 seconds? OK, now try it and see if you were right.*

Finally, teachers can provide more divergent examples to further promote generalized knowledge of the concept:

> *Now, look at this pendulum clock. This clock is running slow, because the pendulum is swinging too slowly. What can I do to the bob of the pendulum [indicate] to make it run faster? Should I make the pendulum longer or shorter? OK, let's try it.*

Although inductive thinking activities have been widely promoted in education for many years (e.g., Bruner, 1966), deductive thinking activities also are important, and in some cases, may provide more realistic thinking activities for some students with special learning needs.

Summary

- Much learning in science and social studies takes place in the context of textbook learning. To address the needs of diverse classrooms, teachers should evaluate their texts for "considerateness."
- Content enhancement devices are means for increasing recall and comprehension of content information, and include use of graphic organizers, study guides, diagrams, visual spatial displays, and mnemonics.
- Familiarization with text organization and structure can help students understand text content. Students can be taught to incorporate analysis of text structure into their study strategies. Highlighting, outlining, and study guides are also helpful.
- Textbooks can be adapted for students with reading problems with such methods as audiotaped texts, Braille or enlarged print versions, simplified texts, or modified presentations.
- Before assigned readings, students can be familiarized with new vocabulary, and provided with advance organizers such as visual spatial displays, timelines, or concept maps.
- After assigned readings, students can be provided with reviews and summaries of the readings, practice with peers, and extra help sessions.
- Activities-oriented instruction can be helpful for students who have reading problems, or who benefit from the enhanced concreteness and meaningfulness afforded by such instruction.

- A variety of adaptations are available for accommodating special needs in such science activity areas as balancing and weighing, activities with plants and animals, anatomy, microscope activities, weather, rocks and minerals, and activities involving sound and light. These adaptations address specific needs areas, and also can enhance comprehension of the associated concepts.
- Adaptations can also be incorporated into social studies areas, including role-play, simulation activities, and field trips.

- Inquiry-oriented approaches to science and social studies, found in both textbook and activities approaches, can also be adapted for students with special needs. These adaptations include use of hands-on materials, carefully structured questioning, redirecting attention, and reinforcing divergent, independent thinking.

Council for Exceptional Children

Teaching Study Skills

Information in this chapter links most directly to:

Standard 4—Instructional Strategies, particularly:

Skills:
- Use strategies to facilitate integration into various settings.
- Teach individuals to use self-assessment, problem solving, and other cognitive strategies to meet their needs.
- Select, adapt, and use instructional strategies and materials according to characteristics of the individual with exceptional learning needs.
- Use strategies to facilitate maintenance and generalization of skills across learning environments.

Standard 7—Instructional Planning

Knowledge:
- Theories and research that form the basis of curriculum development and instructional practice.
- Scope and sequences for general and special curricula.
- National, state or provincial, and local curricula standards.
- Technology for planning and managing the teaching and learning environment.

Skills:
- Identify and prioritize areas of the general curriculum and accommodations for individuals with exceptional learning needs.
- Develop and implement comprehensive, longitudinal individualized programs in collaboration with team members.
- Use task analysis.
- Sequence, implement, and evaluate individualized learning objectives.
- Incorporate and implement instructional and assistive technology into the educational program.
- Prepare and organize materials to implement daily lesson plans.
- Use instructional time effectively.
- Make responsive adjustments to instruction based on continual observations.

Inclusion Checklist
Science and Social Studies

If students are having difficulty learning from textbooks, have you tried the following:

- ❑ Strategies for adapting textbook approaches, including:
  - ❑ Effective instruction using the PASS variables
  - ❑ Content enhancement and related strategies, such as:
    - ❑ Lesson organizer routine
    - ❑ Content mastery routine
    - ❑ Semantic feature analysis
    - ❑ POSSE strategy
    - ❑ Modifying worksheet activities
  - ❑ Promoting independent learning from textbooks, by:
    - ❑ Familiarizing students with text organization
    - ❑ Text structure analysis strategies
    - ❑ Highlighting and underlining strategies
    - ❑ Outlines or study guides
  - ❑ Learning strategies, such as:
    - ❑ MultiPass
    - ❑ IT FITS strategy
  - ❑ Strategies for adapting textbook materials
  - ❑ Before reading textbook activities
  - ❑ After reading textbook activities
  - ❑ Adaptations for students with severe reading problems

If students are having difficulty learning from science activities, have you tried the following:

- ❑ General laboratory adaptations, including:
  - ❑ Effective use of rules
  - ❑ Safety considerations
  - ❑ Clarifying directions
  - ❑ Stimulus enhancement
  - ❑ Preparing for spills
  - ❑ Adaptations for process skills, including:
    - ❑ Adaptations for measuring and pouring
    - ❑ Adaptations for balancing and weighing
    - ❑ Adaptations for recording data

- ❑ Adaptations for life science activities, including:
  - ❑ Activities involving plants
  - ❑ Activities involving animals
  - ❑ Activities for teaching anatomy
  - ❑ Microscope activities
  - ❑ Health considerations
- ❑ Adaptations for earth science activities, including:
  - ❑ Activities related to weather
  - ❑ Activities using rocks and minerals
- ❑ Adaptations for physical science activities, including:
  - ❑ Activities involving sound
  - ❑ Activities related to force and motion
  - ❑ Activities related to light and color
  - ❑ Activities to explore powders, mixtures, and solutions

If students are having difficulty learning from social studies activities, have you tried the following:

- ❑ General adaptation strategies, such as addressing interest areas, supplementing texts, and using a variety of resources and role-play activities
- ❑ Recommendations for specific activities, such as planning meals from other cultures or time periods, role-play and reenactment activities
- ❑ Adaptations for mapping activities
- ❑ Adaptations for field trips

If students are having difficulty learning from inquiry approaches, have you tried the following:

- ❑ Promoting active thinking with guided questioning
- ❑ Considering students' preconceptions
- ❑ Addressing problems in attention, memory, reasoning, and outerdirectedness
- ❑ Using deductive, rather than inductive, models of thinking

Chapter 16

Lamont Marble, 16
Washington, D.C.
"Guitar"

Art, Music, Physical Education, Foreign Languages, Vocational Education, and Transitions

Objectives

After studying this chapter, you should be able to:

- Describe and implement adaptations for students with special needs in art, music, physical education, foreign languages, and vocational and career education.
- Understand the importance of setting realistic vocational and career goals and objectives as well as environmental, curriculum, and instructional strategies and modifications.
- Identify the meaning of transition and the purpose of planning and designing transition programs for students with disabilities.
- Gain understanding of the significance of teaching self-advocacy and self-determination skills toward promoting assertiveness and advocacy.
- Understand the importance of planning and transitioning for graduation, future education, job opportunities, and independent living.

Art, music, physical education, and foreign languages may at first appear to be quite different content area classes; however, these general education classes share some common features. The first three frequently include many students with disabilities because they are often the first classes selected for including students with disabilities. Students with disabilities who experience difficulties with language and literacy tasks may be more successful in art, music, or physical education. These classes, therefore, can be very important, particularly when appropriate accommodations are made to help all students achieve their potential.

Transition, career, and vocational education issues are critical as well, if students with disabilities are to become successful in later life. Planning, designing, and adapting career and vocational educational programs for students with disabilities will allow many individuals to have successful careers and become self-sufficient.

Transition programs help prepare students for changes—changes from one grade level to another, from preschool to elementary school, elementary to middle school, middle school to high school, and high school to life after high school. Preparing students for transitions after high school include vocational or career education, and directions to manage employment, supported living, or independent living arrangements.

Art, Music, and Physical Education

Art, music, and physical education are taught throughout elementary and secondary schools and usually include students with disabilities. In elementary schools, specialists or the general classroom teacher may teach these content areas. In either scenario, these subjects are important for students with special needs. Even if art, music, or the skills associated with physical education do not become part of individuals' lifetime career goals, they may become a focus for leisure-time activities.

Some students with disabilities have special talents in art, music, or physical education. For example, it has been noted that some individuals with Williams Syndrome, who have mild mental retardation, also may have special musical abilities and may be able to sing and/or play musical instruments very well. Some individuals with Asperger's syndrome (individuals with autism who are also intellectually high functioning) have been seen to be especially talented at composing music. One woman with Asperger's syndrome composes symphonies. The Association of Mouth and Foot Painting Artists is a group of individuals with physical disabilities who demonstrate talents at artwork. The Perkins School for the Blind in Massachusetts also distributes Christmas cards made by its students.

Some very talented musicians have disabilities, such as singer-songwriters Stevie Wonder and Jose Feliciano, who both are blind. Tom Cruise, Henry Winkler, and Cher have all said they have learning disabilities but have not allowed their disability to interfere with their opportunity for success. Figure 16.1 shows a letter written by Henry Winkler, the television and movie star who played the Fonz in the situation comedy *Happy Days,* to students with learning disabilities. In the letter, Winkler wishes the youngsters good luck and emphasizes that hard work pays off.

Many successful athletes have special needs as well. For example, Steve Sheffler, a professional basketball player, has a learning disability. When Steve was enrolled at Purdue University, he was an extremely successful basketball player, who openly talked about his learning disability to students on campus and in the local schools. Steve's success is attributable to his perseverance, hard work, and positive attitude. His learning disability did not limit Steve's reaching his goals, but allowed him through extra organizational skills and effort to reach his academic and athletic aspirations.

For information on the Mouth and Foot Artists, write to the Association of Handicapped Artists, Inc., 5150 Broadway, Depew, NY 14043–4085 or call 716–683–4624. For information on the Perkins School for the Blind, write to 175 North Beacon Street, Watertown, MA 02172 or call 617–924–3434.

Students with special needs often exhibit unique talents in music and art classes.

Henry Winkler

January 6, 1999

Dear Students,

Yes, I'm learning challenged and now that I'm older my memory seems to have fallen down a dark hole, so I'm really, really, really challenged.

On the other hand my life is good. I'm acting, directing, producing. I have a wonderful wife, three great kids and 2 dogs - a Labrador retriever named "Tootsie" and a King Charles Cavalier named "Monty".

When I was in school, a lot of subjects were very hard for me. I couldn't get math, I still can't spell and when I read, the words started doing the monster mash on the page. It was very hard to focus.

It is very important to know what it is you want to do and it is also very important to know that there is greatness in everyone of you - all the members of your class.

Just because we are learning challenged does not mean we are stupid. A learning challenge is not a disease, you can't catch it, and it is certainly not caused by lack of intelligence. As a matter of fact, we just have to figure out how to solve problems in other very creative ways.

I wish you all luck. I want you to be very proud of ourselves and remember that hard work, and knowing what you want, will always put you in good stead.

Self respect is cool so are all of you!

Warmly!

Henry Winkler

Figure 16.1

Copy of Letter Written By Henry Winkler to Students with Learning Disabilities

Note: Henry Winkler is best known for playing Arthur Fonzarelli (the "Fonz") on *Happy Days.* Winkler has also produced and directed several movies (*Cop and a Half, Memories of Me*) and starred in *Scream* and *The Waterboy.* Reprinted with permission of Fairdinkum Productions.

Figure 16.2
Mike Augspurger and Leni Fried with a prototype of their invention, a handcycle for wheelchair athletes, at their shop in Florence, MA.
Note: Photo by Kevin Gutting, *Daily Hampshire Gazette.* Copyright 1997 by *Daily Hampshire Gazette.* Reprinted with permission of the *Daily Hampshire Gazette.* All rights reserved.

For more information on Dance Umbrella, go to the Web Links module in chapter 16 of the Companion Website.

Part 2 of this book contains strategies that promote effective inclusion of students with disabilities in art, music, and physical education classes.

Opportunities for individuals with disabilities in physical and recreational activities have increased in recent years. Individuals are taking advantage of these opportunities, as evidenced by the growing number of participants in the Special Olympics and the increasing number of wheelchair basketball leagues. Organizations supporting wheelchair dancing and workshops designed to teach individuals who use wheelchairs to dance exist. For example, Dance Umbrella was organized in 1997 as the first International Festival of Wheelchair Dance. Moreover, technological advances are continually enhancing the development of adapted equipment that enables more individuals to participate in physical activities. Better designed wheelchairs for "road racing," and adapted skis for downhill skiing, and wheelchairs that can travel across sandy terrain, such as beaches, are just a few examples of advances that increase participation of all individuals in physical activities. Figure 16.2 shows a photo of a handcycle that can be used in competitive racing. However, all students with special needs will benefit greatly from participating in art, music, and physical education classes, even if they do not have special talents in those areas.

Teaching Strategies

Overall strategies discussed earlier in this text—including teacher effectiveness, behavior management, attention, memory, and motivation—can be helpful in including students with special needs in art, music, and physical education classes. The consistent use of the PASS variables will help ensure that objectives for these content areas are carefully prioritized and adapted for appropriate instruction. It may take some students longer than others to learn, but that will not diminish the benefits from participating in art, music, or physical education classes. By prioritizing objectives for students with disabilities and by working closely with special educators, the goals for art, music, and physical education for students with disabilities may be realized more effectively. In addition several specific strategies are described here for including students with disabilities in art, music, and physical education classes.

For Art

- Stock adapted materials and equipment when necessary, such as special grips, larger paper, brushes, and crayons, to promote better accessibility by students with motor difficulties. For example, bake regular size crayons in muffin tins to make extra large crayons for easier gripping; make paint brushes out of empty deodorant bottles by filling empty bottles with paint; or substitute large pieces of different textured sponges for paint brushes (Platt & Janeczko, 1991).
- Model and demonstrate fine and gross motor skills involved in using art materials, then provide students with ample opportunities to practice developing those skills (Kelchner, 1991).
- Enforce guidelines and rules to ensure safe use of materials. Some students may need reminders on using scissors, knives, fragile objects, paints, glue, and other equipment safely and appropriately.
- Prepare work areas ahead of time by covering floors with tarps and desks with garbage bags.
- Ask students to bring old, baggy shirts to wear as smocks to protect their school clothing.
- Place all art materials on tables and shelves that are accessible for all students (Rodriguez, 1984).
- Establish "clean-up" procedures and assign roles and responsibilities to students ahead of time.
- Provide ample opportunities for students to practice using new art materials and techniques. Use participation in art as a reward, as most students with special needs will work hard in other classes to gain the privilege of participating in art.
- Pair students with disabilities with general education students who can assist them with tasks as necessary. For example, some students may need help carrying materials from place to place within the room, while others may require reminders about the steps to complete a particular activity.
- Increase the level of art project complexity as students progress through the grade levels, while using task analysis to assist with teaching art activities (Spencer, 1992).
- Break longer-term art assignments into segments, provide self-monitoring charts containing subdivided tasks, and frequently check on students' progress toward the end goal of project completion.
- Monitor the pace of instruction when introducing new tasks and concepts. For example, if students appear to experience difficulty learning fundamental art concepts and skills, determine whether a special educator can give students additional practice.
- Provide experiences with many mediums, including computer art drawing using a light pen (Lancioni & Boelens, 1996).
- Showcase work from all types of artists, including those from culturally and linguistically diverse backgrounds and those with disabilities as models for students.
- Encourage creativity and a positive attitude toward art activities.
- Provide extra encouragement for students who appear to have special talents, including helping them access extra art classes at local universities or community centers.
- Integrate art activities with other content areas to help reinforce learning. Making and illustrating books is motivating and promotes learning. See, for example, Carle's (1988) *You Can Make a Collage: A Very Simple How-To Book* for step-by-step instructions for making collages that can be combined with other content areas or used just for art classes.

For Music

- Music may not require many adaptations if the class is singing songs or clapping along with a beat, but monitor the pace of introducing the new songs and rhythms to ensure students with disabilities have ample opportunities to learn new material. Meet with special education teachers to learn about music goals for students with disabilities (Atterbury, 1984).
- Adapt instruments as necessary so students with physical disabilities can play and handle them more easily. For example, insert handles or mallets through foam balls or use Velcro

Music is often a fun class for students with special needs in which they enjoy participating (Hock, Hasazi, & Patten, 1990).

to attach handles to gloves for an easier grip. Stabilize small instruments by clamping them to music stands or desks. Use rubber door stops to strum guitars (Campbell & Scott-Kassner, 1995).

- Modify response formats so students who are unable to vocalize responses may be able to tap out the beats to the music or, if unable to use their hands, students can tap with their feet, nod their heads, or blink their eyes (Atterbury, 1990).
- Allow students with hearing impairments to feel the vibrations from the musical instruments and vocal cords to help them participate and understand rhythm.
- Provide Braille or large-print music to students with visual impairments (Mark, 1996). The Library of Congress distributes tapes of music recorded at slower speeds to help individuals who are learning music by ear. It also has musical books and scores in Braille and large print, and recorded lessons for piano, guitar, voice, recorder, and other instruments.
- Provide extra opportunities for learning and practicing new words and music, and allow more time for practicing and reading the applications of music.
- Teach students memory strategies for how to read music to promote the rapid learning of the notes. For example, teach the mnemonic "**E**very **G**ood **B**oy **D**eserves **F**udge" for the notes on the lines in the treble clef (EGBDF) and "**A**ll **C**ows **E**at **G**rass" for the spaces in the bass clef (ACEG). Teach memory strategies such as the keyword method to promote learning of music history (Brigham & Brigham, 1998).
- Minimize reading activities for students with reading difficulties by presenting information orally or color-coding musical notes (Atterbury, 1983).
- Refer to the memory and study skills chapters to design accommodations for learning new content.
- Allow students with special talents to perform with upper grade-level bands, choirs, or other musical organizations.

For Physical Education

- Develop motor and sports skills. For example, discuss recommendations with physical therapists on the types and amounts of adaptations and physical exercise students with severe physical disabilities need.
- Maintain regular contact with specialists and the school nurse, concerning any students with special physical and/or health needs.
- Make minor adaptations to increase participation in physical education classes (Pangrazi & Dauer, 1997).
- Modify the way students are placed on competitive teams within physical education classes. For example, avoid having students selected for teams by team captains, as students with poor physical abilities may always be selected last. Consider alternative approaches such as random assignment or selecting teams beforehand to ensure the equality of the group.
- Modify activities to promote coordination by using stationary objects such as batting tees when practicing batting, or making it easier to retrieve practice balls by using backstops or goals (Pangrazi & Dauer, 1995).
- Modify activities when students tire more easily or have limited physical abilities. For example, shorten the running distances or size of playing areas, decrease the playing time or number of points necessary to win, allow balls to be caught or bounced in games like volleyball, or decrease the heights of baskets in basketball (Stillwell & Willgoose, 1997).
- Prioritize objectives and the modifications of game rules or response formats. For example, students in wheelchairs can participate in many of the same activities with modified rules. Allow students additional time to hold the ball before they throw it, when needed.
- Substitute standard-size equipment with more easily handled equipment, such as larger-than-regulation-size balls for students who have difficulties handling smaller balls. You also can attach Velcro to ends of balls and gloves, to make it easier for students to grasp and hold onto them. Provide practice developing skills to handle regulation-size mate-

Library of Congress resources include Websites for services for the blind and physically handicapped, and local libraries for distribution of talking tapes. For relevant Websites, go to the Web Links module in chapter 16 of the Companion Website.

More information can be found on the Websites of the National Wheelchair Basketball Association, Special Olympics, and United States Association for Blind Athletes. For relevant Websites, go to the Web Links module in chapter 16 of the Companion Website.

rials but provide that practice individually and build up to standard-size equipment when possible.

- Assign buddies, who can provide verbal descriptions and feedback of what is happening, to students with visual impairments. Add sounds to activities to help students orient appropriately, add the use of guide rails, use of sound-emitting devices such as light sensors on bases in baseball, and provide clear verbal descriptions of activities (Winnick & Short, 1985).
- Many students with disabilities have difficulties hearing or understanding directions in outdoor classes. Stand close to those who may have difficulties when giving directions in areas where acoustics are poor and many distractions exist. Use statements like: "When I say go, I want you to [provide explanation] . . . . Ready, GO!" This will help students listen first and prepare to begin the activity.
- Break directions into small steps and provide sufficient practice and review of previously learned skills before introducing new skills. Most students with disabilities require additional practice and review time before mastering new physical skills.
- When administering tests on the rules or history of sports, refer to the suggestions provided earlier in this text for adapting assignments, modifying tests and test formats, and decreasing language and literacy demands.
- Provide information on relevant sporting associations for after-school recreational participation such as the National Wheelchair Basketball Association, Special Olympics, or United States Association for Blind Athletes.
- Be enthusiastic and encourage all students to perform at their maximal potential. When students like physical activities, they will be more likely to continue them as part of their leisure-time activities later in life.

Foreign Languages

Although some students with disabilities have difficulty learning foreign languages, the classes are required for many students to meet high school and college graduation requirements (Sparks, Ganschow, & Javorsky, 1992). Issues surrounding the instructional methods used in foreign language classes have been discussed by Padilla, Fairchild, and Valadez (1990), but a variety of methods are currently used. Most methods share features similar to those used in whole language instruction—that is, that children learn their native languages by listening first, then speaking, and finally reading and writing (Javorsky, Sparks, & Ganschow, 1992). Such methods, which rely on good listening, phonemic awareness, and auditory discrimination skills, may prove especially problematic for students with learning disabilities who have difficulties with English. Those particular instructional procedures emphasize the very areas identified as problematic for students with disabilities.

Specialized procedures emphasize learning phonemic patterns of the foreign language and their relationship to the **orthography** or spelling patterns. Focusing on this aspect of the language may be much more successful with students with learning disabilities (Myer, Ganschow, Sparks, & Kenneweg, 1989). Other instructional recommendations, which have been described earlier in this text, include preferential seating, taping lectures, providing copies of lecture notes and overhead materials, and allowing ample practice and feedback opportunities.

Given the large amounts of new vocabulary that must be acquired within relatively short periods of time to learn any foreign language, it is recommended that specialized mnemonic strategies be used to facilitate learning of vocabulary. The keyword method, described in chapter 10, has been used successfully to increase foreign language vocabulary learning (Atkinson, 1975).

Encourage students to keep note cards containing new vocabulary and specific memory strategies for learning the new words. Allow time for students to share their memory strategies with one another. Arrange time for peer tutoring during which students can practice new vocabulary. Finally, encourage students to review the cards continually while learning new vocabulary and then periodically for reviewing previously learned words.

Audiocassettes are available in various languages that can be used as supplements to classroom instruction. Recently developed multimedia programs can also be used to supplement classroom instruction. Most second-language learning multimedia programs now enable students to

General procedures for teaching physical education are provided by Clements (1995) and Pangrazi and Dauer (1995), applications of adapting physical education classes for students with disabilities are provided by Block (1994) and Kaser, Collier, and Solava (1997), and modifications of various sports activities are described by Winnick and Short (1985).

Language Now! Learn Italian Now (Transparent Language) and Living Language Multimedia: Triple Play Plus: Italia Multimedia Games and Conversations (Random House/Syracuse Language Systems Program) are examples of computerized multimedia programs.

look, listen, speak, record and listen to their voice, and compare it with the one on the program. In addition, many programs contain realistic dialogues that can be played at various speeds depending upon the level of the learner.

Modifications in testing procedures are recommended and are similar to those suggested in chapter 12. Adaptations include providing longer testing periods, oral versus written exams, testing in distraction-free environments, and opportunities to demonstrate mastery of content in a variety of individually negotiated ways. Special accommodations can be designed and implemented for students based on their specific learning needs. Finally, it may be important to emphasize that students should be informed that if foreign language learning is difficult for them and they are required to complete the classes, then they should be prepared to spend more time than usual in preparing and studying for foreign language classes.

Vocational and Career Education

Vocational education is an extensive and varied field, which includes both secondary and postsecondary education. Vocational education is a most important content area, and may be particularly important in the education of individuals with special needs, many of whom may go directly to paid employment after leaving high school (Sarkees-Wircenski & Scott, 1995) and many of whom drop out of high school (Blackorby & Wagner, 1996; Love & Malian, 1997; Malian & Love, 1998; Wagner et al., 1991).

Overview of Vocational and Career Education

Vocational education and career education include a variety of educational programs intended to prepare students for employment and for life after high school (Grubb, 1996; Sarkees-Wircenski & Scott, 1995). Vocational education is generally considered to comprise seven areas associated with different labor markets: (a) agriculture, (b) business, (c) family and consumer sciences, (d) marketing, (e) health, (f) trade and industry, and (g) technical/communications. An overview of these is provided in Table 16.1. Familiarity with these areas can help you understand why the Carl D. Perkins Vocational Act of 1984 can make a difference in the lives of students with disabilities and students at risk for school failure.

The Carl D. Perkins Vocational Education Act of 1984

Vocational education has a long and varied history in the United States, and has been growing in importance in recent years. One of the most significant events in the history of vocational education was the passage of PL 98-524 or the Carl D. Perkins Vocational Education Act of 1984 (Asselin, Todd-Allen, & DeFur, 1998). Since passage of the Vocational Education Act of 1963, federal and state legislation has continued to encourage educational programs to provide services for students at risk because of disability or economic disadvantage. Under the Perkins Act, each state was obliged to provide educational programs and other activities designed to increase the participation of, and meet any special needs of, previously underserved groups of individuals, including the following:

1. Individuals with disabilities
2. Individuals from positions of economic disadvantage
3. Adults who need training and/or retraining
4. Single parents or homemakers
5. Individuals who would participate in programs designed to eliminate sex-bias or stereotyping in vocational education
6. Criminal offenders who are serving in a correctional institution

The Perkins Act also provides the Criteria for Services and Activities for the Handicapped and for the Disadvantaged (Title II, Part A). These require state boards providing vocational services and activities for individuals with disabilities or disadvantages to provide specific assurances;

Table 16.1
Vocational Education Areas

Vocational Area	Area of Study
Agricultural education promotes an understanding of the field of agriculture and identifies the role it plays in society ("agricultural literacy").	Caring for and production of agricultural plants and animals, forestry, agribusiness, agricultural economics, agronomy, crop science, dairy science, plant pathology, and veterinary technology.
Business education not only prepares students for occupations in business but also teaches students how to conduct their own business.	Skill development in the use of high-speed copiers, laser printers, fax machines, and computers including word processing; office management, accounting, economics, keyboarding, spreadsheets, computer graphics, networking, computer programming, paralegal secretarial, information and office technology.
Family and consumer science helps prepare students for family life, work life, and careers in family and consumer sciences.	Knowledge in nutrition, physical wellness, balancing family, home, personal, and work activities, travel services, textile and clothing, food science, interior decorating, and child and elder care.
Marketing education prepares students for marketing and management careers.	Learning about recruiting, training, financing, researching, communicating, and selling goods, ideas, and services.
Health occupations education provides information on careers in health services.	Introduces knowledge on dental hygienists and assistants, medical secretaries and receptionists, registered and licensed practical nurses, physicians, and dentists.
Trade and industrial education prepares students for multiple level careers from operatives to semi-skilled to skilled craftspersons such as carpentry, masonry, plumbing, and electricity.	Knowledge in a wide range of careers including electronics, auto and marine mechanics, culinary arts, collision repair, welding, heavy equipment mechanics, and barbering.
Technology education helps prepare students in technological literacy and for careers in technology–related areas.	Learning about technology and its effects on daily life including communications, broadcasting, robotics, photography, and use of recent technological advances.

for example, that equal access will be provided to individuals with disabilities or disadvantages in recruitment, enrollment, and placement, and that equal access will be provided for the full range of vocational programs. It also requires that individuals with disabilities or disadvantages will receive instruction in the least-restrictive environment, and will receive vocational services when appropriate as a component of the IEP, developed jointly by special educators and vocational educators (Asselin, Todd-Allen, & DeFur, 1998; Sarkees-Wircenski & Scott, 1995). Recent amendments to the Perkins Act (Carl D. Perkins Vocational and Applied Technology Education Act of 1990, PL 101-392) have authorized the largest amount of funds ever for vocational education (Sarkees-Wircenski & Scott, 1995).

As a result of federal and state legislation, states have established support programs intended to assist students with special needs in vocational programs. Students with disabilities and students considered at risk for dropping out of school have been provided with counseling, special coursework, and collaborative assistance from teacher teams to help them acquire entry-level job skills.

Modifications for Students with Special Needs

To make any modification to the curriculum to initiate vocational or career education, start by prioritizing objectives. For each instructional area of vocational content, ask whether each particular objective is absolutely necessary. Establish the most important objectives, and address these most intensively. Next, adapt environments, curriculum, and instruction to meet the needs of individual

Companion Website

For Websites for the Handbook on Section 504 of the Rehabilitation Act, Americans with Disabilities Act, and IDEA, go to the Web Links module in chapter 16 of the Companion Website.

As with all other areas of inclusive education of special needs, refer to the "PASS" variables (see chapter 1).

Some students with disabilities need to transition from more formal educational opportunities to learning vocational skills.

learners. Use effective teaching strategies, as presented in the teacher presentation variables: structure, clarity, redundancy, enthusiasm, appropriate pace, maximized engagement, questioning, and feedback. Finally, systematically evaluate whether acceptable progress toward prespecified objectives is being made.

Goals and Objectives

Goals and objectives specified for students with special needs in vocational programs should be, above all, realistic. Reviewing and prioritizing goals and objectives can be achieved by having vocational educators communicate with special educators about the entry-level expectations of the program, the objectives addressed in the program, and the exit expectations for students in the program. Such information can be useful in developing specific IEPs, and can help identify necessary teaching strategies and support services. Of course, it is necessary to prioritize all course or program objectives, to determine which are absolutely necessary, and which are most important. It can also be helpful to identify the many "exit points" for specific job descriptions for which students are training. Figure 16.3 provides examples of multiple exit points and entry-level competencies in masonry.

Environmental Modifications

Chapter 4 describes strategies for modifying the physical environment to accommodate special needs.

As with all school environments, vocational training areas can contain physical barriers to accessibility for all students. Barriers such as curbs, stairs, and doors can hinder access to the training area. Other barriers can be found in the training area itself (ramps, aisles, restrooms, and work stations). Examine all potential barriers to accessibility for vocational training areas, and modify environments as needed, using considerations discussed in chapter 4.

MULTIPLE EXIT POINTS AND ENTRY LEVEL COMPETENCIES IN MASONRY

TASK NO.	TASK NAME	POSSIBLE EXIT POINTS / DOT DESCRIPTIONS / DOT NO.	Cement Mason Helper 869.687-026	Bricklayer Helper 861.687-010	Stone Mason Helper 869.687-026	Cement Mason 844.364-010	Stone Mason 861.381-038	Bricklayer Construction 001.301-010
01	Spreading mortar		X	X	X	X	X	X
02	Laying brick to a line			X				X
03	Building a brick corner							X
04	Cutting brick and block			X	X		X	X
05	Determining spacing for standard-size brick							X
06	Laying out courses to sill and cornice height							X
07	Interpreting and using a line modular rule			X	X		X	X
08	Dimensioning and scaling a working drawing							X
09	Identifying names and uses of lines and symbols on a working drawing							X
10	Identifying different views and their uses on a working drawing							X
11	Setting batter boards		X	X		X		X
12	Inspecting grading at building site					X	X	X
13	Finishing grading at building site		X	X	X	X	X	X

Figure 16.3

Multiple Exit Points and Entry Level Competencies in Masonry

Note: From *Vocational Special Needs* (p. 338), by M. Sarkees-Wircenski and J. L. Scott, 1995, Homewood, IL: American Technical Publishers. Reprinted with permission.

Curriculum Modifications

Curriculum modifications for vocational education parallel those for other content areas previously discussed. Some particularly important areas to address are student affect, motivation, and positive peer relations. Figure 16.4 presents some sample problems that can be encountered in vocational training areas and suggested curriculum modifications. Following are some specific considerations for vocational education programs.

Plan for Safety Considerations. The most important consideration in any vocational program is safety. All students must be provided with basic safety instruction before undertaking activities in

Student affect, motivation, and peer relations are discussed in detail in chapters 7 and 9.

POSSIBLE PROBLEMS AND POSSIBLE MODIFICATIONS FOR VOCATIONAL EDUCATION

Problem	Possible Modifications
Safety	Use peer assistance; teach safety skills; reduce danger (e.g., holders for hot materials); use student safety profile.
Measuring	Preset measures, using tactual (e.g., rubber bands), or visual (e.g., color) guides.
Reading	Provide modified reading passages; use audiotapes; use peer assistance (see chapter 13).
Physical manipulation	Enhance grips with rubber bands, provide larger materials, use holders or hoists (see chapter 4).
Comprehension	Use multiple examples; use more concrete examples; provide additional practice; use summarization/restatement strategies (see chapter 13).
Memory	Provide repetition, enhance stimulus value, increase questioning, provide enactments, use organizational or mnemonic strategies (see chapter 10).
Feeling	Use sandpaper or other material to enhance tactual stimulus value.
Motivation	Increase student decision making; use goal-setting; use peer mediation; teach enthusiastically; use praise and rewards; create task-oriented classrooms (see chapter 9).
Fatigue	Provide frequent breaks; use supports to reduce effort requirements; use peer assistance.
Mobility	Provide sufficient aisle space; replace doorknobs with levers; use ramps where needed; plan ahead for emergencies; prepare work surfaces at appropriate height (see chapter 4).
Vision	Provide safety precautions; use closed-circuit television; enhance lighting; provide physical models; use peer assistance (see chapter 4).
Hearing	Plan for emergencies; use peer assistance; reduce reading requirements; provide visual cues and models (see chapter 4).
Attention	Use teacher proximity; direct appeal; peer assistance; self-monitoring; change activities frequently (see chapters 5 and 10).

Figure 16.4

Possible Problems and Possible Modifications for Vocational Education

that area. Even if some students require more time and practice acquiring safety techniques, additional time allocations can pay dividends, because a primary cause of accidents in laboratory settings is lack of understanding of safety rules and procedures.

One helpful way to address safety considerations is by developing a "safety profile" for individual students. An example of a safety profile is provided in the following *In the Classroom* feature. This profile, designed for a machine shop, provides specific competencies for safety in this setting, and the dates these competencies have been demonstrated. Although safety considerations are of great importance for all students, it is also important to consider carefully the characteristics of individual students with special needs, and how these specific characteristics may interact with safety concerns of particular instructional areas.

Modify Instructional Materials. Many students with special needs enrolled in vocational programs have limited reading skills. Teachers must ensure that appropriate adaptations are made for students with reading difficulties.

In the Classroom ...a feature for teachers

Student Safety Profile

General Laboratory

Student: _____ Date: _____

Trade and Industrial
Program: _____ Date of Entry: _____

Instructor: _____

Date of Safety
Orientation: _____

Date Student Completes Specific Objectives of Safety Orientation: _____

Specific Objectives	**Date Accomplished**
Develops awareness of hazard and becomes more safety conscious	_____
Develops a serious attitude toward safety	_____
Prepares for safety before entering work area	_____
Prepare for safety at work stations	_____
Understands color coding	_____
Practices safety procedures	_____
Prepares for safety on leaving shop	_____

Develops awareness of hazards and becomes more safety conscious.
Successfully responds to the following:

Date Competence Demonstrated

1. Why provide safety for yourself and others? _____
2. How does shop safety help production? _____
3. What laws and agencies regulate shop safety? _____
4. What are the causes of shop accidents? _____

Develops a serious attitude toward safety
1. Gives serious thought to work safety _____
2. Remains alert in the shop area _____
3. Works carefully _____
4. Remains calm and holds temper _____
5. Focuses attention on what is being done _____
6. Assumes responsibility for own safety and safety of others _____

Prepares for safety before entering shop
1. What are the characteristics of a training program? _____
  a. Determines what tools, machines, and materials are required _____
  b. Determines what hazards are involved _____
  c. Determines what skills are needed _____

2. What clothing and safety equipment to wear?
  a. Recognizes types of clothing suitable for the shop area _____
  b. Recognizes types of foot and leg covering _____
  c. Recognizes types of head covering _____
  d. Recognizes types of eye and face protection _____
  e. Recognizes types of hearing protection _____
  f. Recognizes types of hand and arm protection _____
  g. Recognizes types of lung and breathing protection _____

(continued)

	Date Competence Demonstrated

Prepares for safety on entering the shop
1. What safety provision to locate?
   a. Locates exit _____
   b. Locates emergency fire equipment _____
   c. Locates emergency aids _____
   d. Locates main power disconnect area _____
   e. Locates safety zones and lanes _____

2. What potential hazards to keep in mind?
   a. Identifies flammable materials _____
   b. Identifies mobile equipment _____
   c. Identifies activities of others _____

Prepares for safety at work station
1. Obtaining tools and materials
   a. Remembers where tool was obtained _____
   b. Follows established procedures for obtaining tools _____
   c. Checks condition of tool upon receipt _____
   d. Uses care in handling tools _____

2. What safety precautions to observe?
   a. Checks for the condition of floor openings and storage areas _____
   b. Checks for proper lighting _____
   c. Checks for proper ventilation _____
   d. Checks for caution areas and protective signs _____
   e. Checks for guardrails _____

3. What power is available?
   a. Uses electrical power safely _____
   b. Uses air power safely _____
   c. Uses hydraulic power safely _____

4. What solvents and chemicals are present?
   a. Checks the parts cleaning area _____
   b. Checks the dispensing containers _____

Practicing shop safety skills
1. Recognizes how to prevent bodily injuries
   a. Understands how to prevent slipping or falling _____
   b. Understands how to avoid injuries from lifting _____
   c. Understands how to avoid crushing injuries _____
   d. Understands how to avoid hand and arm injuries _____

2. Develops tool and machine safety skills
   a. Demonstrates hand tool safety skills _____
   b. Demonstrates power tool safety skills on the following machines:
      (1) Milling machines _____
      (2) Lathes _____
      (3) Shapers _____
      (4) Drill Presses _____
      (5) Power hacksaws _____
      (6) Band saws _____
      (7) Electrical discharge machines _____

	Date Competence Demonstrated
Understands color coding	
1. Recognizes safety color codes for shop machines and equipment	_____
Prepares to leave the school shop	
1. Stores tools, machines, and materials	
a. Stores hand and portable power tools	_____
b. Secures stationary power tools	_____
c. Stores usable materials and supplies	_____
2. Disposes of waste materials	
a. Disposes of scrap metal, filings, and chips	_____
b. Disposes of hot metal	_____
c. Disposes of waste liquids	_____
d. Disposes of sawdust and absorbent compounds	_____
3. Cleans the workbench and floor	
4. Stores safety equipment	_____
5. Cleans hands and other parts of body	_____
6. Performs final check of shop area	_____

Note: From *Vocational Special Needs* (pp. 344–345), by M. Sarkees-Wircenski and J. L. Scott, 1995, Homewood, IL: American Technical Publishers. Copyright 1995 by American Technical Publishers. Reprinted with permission.

In many cases, students learn vocational procedures from printed material such as lab manuals and textbooks. These materials can be modified for students with reading difficulties by using some of the following strategies:

- Rewrite the most important parts of the text in simpler language, highlighting the most important points. This modified text then can be used for other students with similar reading difficulties.
- Tape-record readings of the text, so students can listen independently, or use the tape recordings to assist their own reading. Be certain to include in the recording's references to figures, tables, and illustrations, and page numbers. Also include summaries of the information read.
- Create videotape presentations of vocational procedures, such as masonry, carpentry, or electrical wiring. Present the same information as in the text versions, but also include demonstrations of the procedures. All students may benefit from this type of modification.
- Teach unfamiliar vocabulary separately, using direct instruction, demonstrations and examples, and verbal elaborations such as the keyword method (see chapter 10). Some students can read adequately once they have become fluent with specialized vocabulary.

Since technical terms are of such importance in many vocational areas, it may be helpful to use a technical terms tabulation sheet, such as the one shown in Figure 16.5. This tabulation allows the instructor to identify each significant term to be encountered in a vocational unit, how each is applied in the text materials, and appropriate teaching strategies to be considered.

See chapter 13 for an extended discussion of text modifications for students with reading difficulties.

TECHNICAL TERMS TABULATION SHEET

Name _____ Text/Reference _____

Date _____ Chapter/Section _____ Pages _____

| Vocabulary Terms | Application in Text | | | | | Teaching Strategies | | | | | | Comments |
	Defined in text content	Illustrated	Included in index	Included in glossary	Included in review questions	Teacher lecture	Teacher demonstration	Word lists	Puzzle or game	Written assignment	Computer exercise	
Wheel alignment						X	X					Demonstrate
Stability	X					X		X				Illustrate with transparencies
Ball joint	X	X				X	X	X				Show actual ball joints
Spindle						X	X	X				Show actual spindle
Toe-in	X	X	X		X	X	X	X				Show with transparencies
Toe-out	X	X	X		X	X	X	X				Show with transparencies
Caster	X	X	X		X	X	X	X				Show with transparencies
Camber	X	X	X		X	X	X	X				Show with transparencies
Steering axis inclination angle	X	X	X		X	X	X	X				Chalkboard drawing
Steering knuckle	X		X			X	X	X				Show actual knuckle
Elongated holes	X					X	X					Chalkboard illustration
Control arms	X	X	X			X	X	X				Show actual control arms
Shims	X	X	X			X	X	X				Show shims
Visualiner	X	X	X			X	X					Audiovisual presentation
Lite-a-line	X	X	X			X	X					Audiovisual presentation
Tie-rods	X		X			X	X	X				

Figure 16.5

Technical Terms Tabulation Sheet

Note: From *Vocational Special Needs* (2nd ed., p. 237), by D. Kingsbury, 1985, Homewood, IL: American Technical Publishers. Reprinted with permission.

Select Computer Software. Vocational programs in recent years have seen the increased use of computer-assisted learning techniques, which can be helpful in promoting learning. When selecting software for vocational training programs that include students with special needs, several important questions should be answered:

1. Is the content presented in the software directly relevant to the objectives of the vocational unit?
2. Can the software be operated independently by students, or are adaptations or supervision required?
3. Is the information presented current and technically correct?
4. Is the pace of presentation of information compatible with special learning needs?

5. Do students consider the software more interesting and motivating than alternative approaches to learning the same information?
6. Will students have enough opportunities to practice using the software to make the activities worthwhile?
7. Is the particular software application an improvement over the instruction that is currently provided?

As with other instructional strategies, formative evaluation can help determine whether particular software applications are effective. Some possible adaptations for students with special needs using computer software include increased time-on-task, direct supervision, or using peers as tutors or "buddies," working on computer assignments in pairs.

Instructional Strategies

Appropriate instructional strategies for teaching students with special needs in vocational education are similar to instructional strategies appropriate for other classes. Overall, the "effective instruction" strategies described in chapter 6 are useful for vocational areas. Important variables to consider in effectively teaching all students include maximizing engaged time-on-task, appropriate content coverage, and pace of instruction. Further, teachers should maximize the effectiveness of instructional variables such as providing information, direct questioning, and feedback in response to teacher questions.

Refer to chapter 6 for a complete discussion on effective instruction, teacher presentation, and SCREAM variables.

Teach Procedures. Much learning in vocational classes is procedural. That is, students learn the procedures for undertaking specific vocational tasks, such as displaying or stocking merchandise, using a word-processing program, or installing a light-dimming system. As such, careful demonstrations and modeling, with a substantial amount of practice and feedback, can be particularly helpful. Simulations and role-playing can also be helpful when direct access to real situations is not available. Formative evaluation including task analysis can determine the rate of progress for individual students, and whether instruction should be modified or intensified. Task analysis can be particularly useful in determining the particular subtasks or subroutines that need additional practice or in developing a more refined sequence of skills and competencies that need to be mastered to execute any subtasks.

Increase Time on Task. As with many other areas of learning, increased time-on-task can be helpful in developing vocational skills. This can be accomplished by additional supervised time with the teacher or aide (when time is available), additional work with peers, or work with tutors. Choosing students who have recently mastered a particular vocational skill to act as tutors can be particularly helpful, because the tutee can gain important skill development, and the tutor can consolidate and reinforce previous learning.

Individualize Instruction. One teaching method that can be helpful in many vocational areas is individualizing instruction (Sarkees–Wircenski & Scott, 1995). Figure 16.6 provides an example of an individualized instruction assignment sheet for the task "Cleaning or replacing spark plugs" in the major block "Basic Engine Tune-Up." Using this procedure, the objectives for the task are clearly specified, and the activities to accomplish this task are identified. Three activities are specified: written assignments, audiovisual presentations, and laboratory assignments. In addition, instructor checkpoints are identified. On the assignment sheet, the sequence of activities and check points are clearly provided. Individualized instruction can be helpful in providing relevant activities that meet the needs of individual learners. However, many individualized instruction practices lean heavily on independent learning from provided practice activities. When implementing individualized procedures such as these, determine the level of independent learning that can reasonably be expected of individual students, and provide guided practice and supervision when needed.

Generalizable Skills

One critically important area of vocational education is the area of generalizable skills. These are skills that are necessary across many different areas of vocational training, and appear to be

INDIVIDUALIZED INSTRUCTION ASSIGNMENT SHEET

MAJOR BLOCK   Basic Engine Tune-up   NAME _____

TASK   Cleaning or replacing spark plugs

UNIT   223-9   TIME (est.)   2 hrs.   (act) _____

OBJECTIVE(S)

To remove and diagnose condition of spark plugs, analyze spark plug deposits, clean plugs, file electrodes, and set plug gap to specifications; plug gap to be within .001 of recommended setting. Ground electrode must be at right angle to center electrode. Install and torque to specifications. Correctly answer 16 of 20 test questions on spark plug types, application, and service procedures.

START ➡ W-1 ▷ W-2 ▷ A-1 ▷ L-1 ▷ C-1 ▷ L-2 ▷ L-3 ▷

C-2 ▷ L-4 ▷ C-3 ▷ ▷ ▷ ▷ ▷ ▷

▷ ▷ ▷ ▷ ▷ ▷ ▷ ▷

WRITTEN
W-1 Assignment Sheet 223-9
W-2 Assignment 223-9-1
W-3 _____
W-4 _____
W-5 _____
W-6 _____
W-7 _____

AUDIO VISUALS
A-1 Slide set 223-9
A-2 _____
A-3 _____
A-4 _____
A-5 _____
A-6 _____
A-7 _____

LABORATORY
L-1 Assignment 223-9-2
L-2 Install spark plugs
L-3 Performance test plugs
L-4 Secure work station
L-5 _____
L-6 _____
L-7 _____
L-7 _____
L-7 _____

CHECK POINT
C-1 Instructor check
C-2 Instructor check
C-3 Give test, evaluate, and
C-4   make next assigment
C-5 _____
C-6 _____
C-7 _____
C-7 _____
C-7 _____

Figure 16.6
Individualized Instruction Assignment Sheet

Note: From *Vocational Special Needs* (p. 406), by M. Sarkees-Wircenski and J. L. Scott, 1995, Homewood, IL: American Technical Publishers. Copyright 1995 by American Technical Publishers. Reprinted with permission.

closely related to success in a number of different fields. Greenan (1983) identified four areas of generalizable skills:

1. Mathematics
2. Communications
3. Interpersonal relations
4. Reasoning skills

Generalizable skills can be found generally in the cognitive and affective areas. In mathematics, generalizable skills are found in such areas as whole numbers, percentages, measurement and calculation, and estimation. In communications, generalizable skills include words and their meanings, reading, writing, speaking, and listening. In interpersonal relations, generalizable skills include work-related behaviors, instructional and supervisory conversations, and social conversations. Finally, generalizable skills in reasoning include listening and problem solving, verbal reasoning, and planning (see also Sarkees-Wircenski & Scott, 1995).

Students with disabilities and other special learning needs may lack the important generalizable skills necessary to succeed in a variety of vocational training areas. In planning curriculum it is important for vocational education teachers to work closely with academic teachers to identify important generalizable skill areas and ensure that these skills are taught and reinforced in all relevant classes (Greenan, 1986).

Specific strategies for teaching generalizable skills in academic, affective, and social skills areas are discussed in detail in chapters 7, 8, 13, and 14.

Transitions

Transitions are natural passages in life that happen continually as we move to new schools, new jobs, and join new recreational organizations. Students with special needs typically have more difficulties than do students without disabilities adjusting to new transitions. Planning for those transitions by making instructional accommodations can promote smoother and more successful transitions for students with disabilities.

What Does Transition Mean?

Transition is the process of planning for changes throughout a student's life. Most frequently, transition is referred to as the planning for a student's life after high school; however, planning for changes throughout life is a more accurate definition.

CLASSROOM SCENARIO

Quinetra

Quinetra is a 5-year-old with cerebral palsy who has gross and fine motor difficulties in addition to speech and language challenges. She has been enrolled in a half-day preschool program near her home. During preschool she receives physical therapy, occupational therapy, and speech and language therapy daily. Quinetra also participates in the activities that take place as part of the regular preschool program. Quinetra feels comfortable in this program, as she has been enrolled there for four years, and she has had the same teachers for the entire time. Beginning next fall, Quinetra will begin a regular education kindergarten program. This transition will involve moving to another building, the neighborhood public school, which is farther from her home, and is quite large in comparison to her preschool. This transition also means having a new general education kindergarten teacher, being included with many more students without disabilities, changing to new special education teachers and therapists, riding a bus to school, and having a much longer day away from home. How can you help prepare Quinetra, her family, her teachers, her new school, and all of her support personnel for this important transition?

Transitions, while exciting and challenging, can be traumatic events. Planning for transitions and preparing students with disabilities for those transitions can eliminate some of the difficult aspects of adjustment. Examples of transitions include the following:

- Attending preschool for the first time and separating from Mom and Dad and home-life
- Changing from half-day to full-day school programs
- Moving to first grade from kindergarten
- Moving to any new grade level

- Changing from elementary school to middle school
- Changing from middle school to high school
- Moving to new school buildings
- Attending college for the first time
- Returning to school after a summer vacation
- Changing school placements from special education settings to general education settings
- Changing to post-secondary school training and education
- Obtaining a job
- Joining recreational activities
- Moving to independent living arrangements
- Moving to a new community

IDEA defines transition services as coordinating services for students that promote the change from school to post-school. This means IDEA emphasizes only planning for transitions from high school to vocational education, post-secondary education, adult services, independent living, and community participation (Taymans & DeFur, 1994). The coordination of transition services is based on student preferences, interests, and abilities, and includes instruction, experiences in the community, development of employment, post-secondary, daily living, and vocational objectives (Asselin, Todd-Allen, & DeFur, 1998). However, it has been seen that planning for transitions at all ages promotes social and emotional well-being of students with disabilities (Wehman, 1996).

CLASSROOM SCENARIO

Jamal

Jamal is a 16-year-old with severe disabilities, who has recently begun a part-time job in a supported work environment. At age 22 he will graduate from his high school and, it is hoped, will engage in some meaningful adult activity. What needs to be done to prepare Jamal for the transition from public school to adult life? What services need to be coordinated? How can you help Jamal with self-advocacy skills and explain the differences between IDEA and ADA to him? How can you help him with the new community services and vocational rehabilitation services? How can you help Jamal prepare to be more independent in his life?

Planning for transitions helps prepare students for the expected changes that take place in their lives. The amount of planning for transitions and adaptations necessary varies depending upon the type of transition and the severity level of disability. Planning includes involving all individuals who will be affected by the transition, including the following:

the student
the parents
teachers
special education teachers
transition coordinators
specialists (e.g., speech and language, physical therapists, occupations therapists)
counselors
community representatives
advocates
support personnel (e.g., bus drivers, cafeteria workers, custodians, school secretary)
employers

Effective transition planning begins early, includes everyone who may be involved, provides an initial timeline, and involves continuous evaluation.

Make Preparations with Students to Plan for Transitions

Many students have a difficult time going to school from home for the first time. Many young children with disabilities may not have been exposed to many different situations and people. It can also be frightening to move to a new school, teachers, and peers. The new school may be farther from home, which means leaving home earlier in the morning, riding a new school bus, and having a longer school day. Students may become more tired, frightened, and anxious until they feel accepted in the new environment. Preparatory actions can be undertaken to ease transitions where everything is so different, otherwise students with disabilities may experience difficulties transitioning to the new site. Such actions include the following:

- Deciding on a time for optimal placement
- Establishing a transition timeline
- Preparing all individuals involved
- Establishing communication procedures
- Sharing information with all individuals
- Collecting data on student performance
- Visiting the new school with the student
- Arranging a meeting with new teachers and support personnel
- Allowing time to explore the new setting
- Planning activities to simulate the new environment to prepare the student
- Reviewing new procedures and explaining what the student can expect in the new environment
- Showing the student that you are supportive and will still be supportive even when the student is attending the new school
- Structuring the new environment for success
- Preparing new teachers and students for the new student with disabilities
- Attending the first day of the new school with the student
- Arranging a communication plan
- Scheduling follow-up evaluation times

Refer to chapters 1 and 2 for additional information on the legal aspects of Individual Transition Plans. For a sample Individual Transition Plan, see the Appendix.

Plan Transitions to Adulthood

Planning transitions for adulthood are vitally important for students with disabilities. All students with disabilities who have IEPs are required to have Individual Transition Plans (ITPs) when they reach the age of 14. Planning and instruction includes teaching students self-advocacy and self-determination skills; planning for future education, such as college or other post-secondary training; planning for future employment opportunities; and preparing students for independent living situations (Asselin, Todd-Allen, & DeFur, 1998; Beakley & Yoder, 1998).

CLASSROOM SCENARIO

Ricardo

Ricardo, an 18-year-old with learning disabilities, is preparing to move to the local university beginning the next fall semester. Ricardo has had special education services for his learning disabilities since third grade. He has particular difficulties with basic literacy tasks, especially reading and writing activities which tend to require a great deal of time to complete. He has never lived away from home, and his parents have always been very supportive of anything he has tried to do. However, his parents have also had a tendency to help him with everything, including organizing his schoolwork and his homework schedule. How can you help prepare Ricardo for the transition to college? How can you help Ricardo develop self-advocacy and self-determination skills? How can you prepare him for the changes from IDEA to ADA and describe what those changes will mean in terms of responsibilities that he will have to assume? What are all of the anticipated changes? What is a reasonable timeline for meeting the transition needs? How can you help prepare Ricardo to be successful with his transition from high school to college?

Self-Advocacy and Self-Determination Preparation

Many students with special needs are overly dependent on others and are passive with respect to decision making. Although making decisions is difficult, students with disabilities will eventually be required to participate more actively in that process for themselves. Therefore, it is vital that opportunities, instruction, and practice at becoming more independent and at decision making are a part of a student's curriculum. Thus, training in **self-advocacy** and **self-determination** skills is a must. This means that students may need assistance, instruction, and practice at learning how to become knowledgeable about themselves with respect to learning strengths, needs, preferences, interests, and rights and responsibilities. This knowledge can be used to request accommodations that promote more success at jobs, independent living, and post-secondary education. Sample self-advocacy skills include the following:

- Awareness of legal rights and responsibilities
- Requesting adaptations and accommodations (e.g., ADA requires that college students with disabilities go to professors, self-identify themselves as having disabilities, and request that specific adaptations be made)
- Meeting with vocational rehabilitation personnel
- Requesting assistance from social security offices
- Meeting with medical personnel and asking relevant questions
- Possessing appropriate social skills, such as requesting assistance, seeking clarification
- Having job-related skills and job-related social skills
- Thinking about and planning for the future with realistic goals
- Making informed choices
- Seeking assistance when necessary

To be successful and independent in their lives after formal schooling, students need to learn about their learning strengths and needs, to articulate those abilities and needs, and to participate actively in the IEP process.

Teach Strategies

The I PLAN strategy includes several steps to assist students in acquiring these necessary skills (Van Reusen, Bos, Schumaker, & Deshler, 1994). Specific steps from I PLAN include completing a detailed self-inventory of individual strengths and needs. Students evaluate and plan for the following transition areas:

The ultimate goal of education for students with special needs is to enable them to live and work as independently as they can, like their peers.

- Independent living skills
- Consumer and financial skills
- Legal and citizenship skills
- Community involvement skills
- Career and employment skills
- Family-living and social skills
- Recreational and leisure skills (Van Reusen, Bos, Schumaker, & Deshler, 1994)

The analysis also includes identifying, for example, strengths such as math computation, and social skills and needs such as reading, reading comprehension, and written expression. Specific goals are identified, such as independent living and career employment goals. Choices for student learning preferences are also included on the inventory. For example, student preferences for certain activities and listings of helpful materials and testing procedures are identified. Finally, accommodations that are necessary to help students succeed are listed. After the inventory is completed, students are taught to use communication skills more effectively by using PLAN and SHARE strategy prompts:

Plan

Provide the inventory to teachers
Listen and respond to the comments
Ask relevant questions
Name your goals

Share

Sit up straight
Have a nice tone of voice
Activate your thinking
Relax and remain calm
Engage in eye contact (Van Reusen, Bos, Schumaker, & Deshler, 1994)

Learning Assertiveness

Many students require explicit social skills instruction in assertiveness, such as requesting assistance, asking for clarification, and negotiating changes.

Provide instruction and role-play situations during which students can practice developing and refining these skills in a safe environment. Finally, provide opportunities to practice generalizing the skills in a variety of situations with a number of different adults. During high school, teachers assume major responsibilities for ensuring that students with disabilities are given a free and appropriate education (FAPE) as required by IDEA. Remember that teachers are part of the IEP team and are legally bound to implement IEP objectives and classroom modifications. However, once students leave high schools and enroll in colleges, they are no longer covered by IDEA. They do have rights and responsibilities identified in the Americans with Disabilities Act (ADA) and Section 504 of the Rehabilitation Act. Students, however, must meet any new classification criteria established at their respective institutions. Once student services are identified, usually with the assistance of personnel at a dean of students office, extended testing times, test administrations in a distraction-free environment, and provision of notes or copies of overhead materials may be made available. However, according to ADA, students have to be more assertive and identify themselves as having disabilities to their professors before they are guaranteed modifications to their educational programs. Then they need to notify professors of their learning needs. One method devised by some college students with disabilities is to compose a brief statement containing learning strengths and needs. Figure 16.7 contains a sample letter written by a college student, Toni, who has learning disabilities. Toni distributes the letter to all of her professors each semester during the first week of classes and then meets individually with them during the next week to discuss any follow-up questions or concerns.

Refer to chapter 8 for additional information on teaching social skills to students with special needs.

Refer to chapter 1 for more detailed information on the legal rights and responsibilities under all legislative acts.

Dear Professor:

I am Toni, a student enrolled in your class this semester. I have a learning disability. I learn best by seeing and hearing information rather than by reading. I can sit through lectures and not take any notes and do fairly well on exams. When I sit in lectures and try to take notes at the same time I usually do poorly on exams. I do not seem to be able to take notes and listen at the same time very well at all. When I have had the opportunity to have my textbooks provided on cassette audiotapes I can perform even better.

I have also noticed that I have a very keen sense of hearing but have the inability to filter out unwanted noises. This causes a problem for me in some lectures. To cope with this I usually sit near the front of the room so I can see the lecturer's face and try to lip read. Lecture outlines are also very helpful for me to be able to keep up with the information being presented in class. I tape record all of my lectures so that I am able to listen more carefully later on when studying for exams. I use the tapes and the lecture outlines as review. At that time I usually insert additional important points into the outline to help with studying and remembering important information.

I also do better on exams if I can take them in a private, very quiet room. I know that the Dean of Students Office has testing facilities that can be used to take my exams, and I would prefer to be able to take all of my exams for this class there.

I work very hard in school and am willing to try to work as hard as possible in your class. I am looking forward to learning in your class this semester. I can be reached by phone or by e-mail, but e-mail seems to be a more reliable method of communicating since my roommates and I are usually unavailable during the days.

Sincerely,

Toni Sanchez

Phone: 993-7346
E-mail: *toni@gmu.edu*

Figure 16.7
Self-Advocacy Letter to College Professors from Toni, a Student with Learning Disabilities

Toni has received positive feedback on her letter from her professors. Most professors report that the letter provided them with helpful background information and insights into Toni's learning strengths and needs. They also kept the letter on file for later referral. This letter documents the type of self-advocacy skills that will be necessary for students with disabilities.

Consider assisting students with disabilities while they are enrolled in middle and high school in developing statements similar to the one used by Toni. This activity familiarizes students with their learning needs, helps them communicate these needs whenever necessary, and provides them with practice for doing this when they no longer have the protective services of IDEA and have to be independent.

Assessment

Assessment for transition consists of collecting information on students from all available sources. This includes the current IEPs, the school permanent records, school guidance counselors, formal and informal interviews with students and their families, and the answers to formal and informal transition planning and **occupational surveys.** The collected information is compiled and evaluated by members of the transition team, who then make recommendations for the ITP.

A recently developed transition survey addresses the four domains of instruction, community experiences, employment, and postschool goals, required by IDEA. The *Transition Planning Inventory* (Clark & Patton, 1997) contains 46 transition planning statements organized around

Technology Highlight

Career Information Using Technology

Students with reading difficulties need access to career information. However, the traditional formats that rely on reading independently may be inappropriate for many of these students. Several alternatives exist for adapting this information for students. One alternative format is to provide the text material in audio formats. Recordings for the Blind and Dyslexic will make audio recordings of text materials for individuals with visual disabilities, including those who are blind and those with low vision, and for individuals with learning disabilities and dyslexia.

Another alternative is to obtain one of the electronic text readers, such as *Ereader* by CAST that will provide speech output for any electronic text. This software will be particularly useful for materials that are available electronically. Since many career surveys are now widely available on CDs, they can be combined with a program such as *Ereader* to provide the speech output necessary for students. For example, the *Career IQ and Interest Survey* electronically assesses broad interest areas of students, including aptitudes of general ability, verbal ability, numbers, perception, and space.

College information is also widely available on the Internet. By using a text-to-speech program, students with reading difficulties can access the information. For example, every university has a Website that contains its admission procedures. Catalogs, and course descriptions are generally available on the Internet. In addition, The Advocacy Institute provides on its Website a wealth of information about the transition from high school to college for students with learning disabilities—information on selecting colleges that have services for students with disabilities, applying to colleges, and for making a successful transition to college, including suggestions on getting help once there for students with learning disabilities.

Refer to the chapter 16 Companion Website for additional links for relating to career and college education.

---

the four IDEA domains on four separate forms: the student form, the home form, the school form, and the profile and further assessment recommendations form, and a supplemental fifth parent preferences and interest form. Raters indicate their level of agreement on a 5-point scale from strongly disagree to strongly agree with statements such as "Recognizes and accepts own strengths and limitations." Particular areas addressed and a sample item include the following:

- Employment: knows how to get a job
- Further education/training: knows how to gain entry into a college or university
- Daily living: manages own money
- Leisure activities: uses settings that offer entertainment
- Community participation: knows basic legal rights
- Self-determination: sets personal goals
- Communication: has needed speaking skills
- Interpersonal relationships: displays appropriate social behavior in a variety of settings*

---

*Note: From *Transition Planning Inventory: Administration and Scoring Guide,* by G. M. Clark and J. R. Patton, 1997, Austin, TX: Pro-Ed. Reprinted with permission.

The profile and further recommendations form presents a summary of responses across the individual forms and can be used to make generalizations regarding the strengths and individual needs. This information assists in determining whether or not additional information should be collected prior to designing ITPs.

Occupational surveys are also commercially available. For example, the *Occupational Aptitude Survey and Interest Schedule* (OASIS-2) (Parker, 1991) assesses whether students like, dislike, or have neutral feelings toward occupations and job activities from a pool of 240 items ranging across 12 vocational domains. The domains to be assessed include: artistic, scientific, nature, protective, mechanical, industrial, business detail, selling, accommodating, humanitarian, leading influencing, and physical performing (Parker, 1991). Findings from this survey help develop a more comprehensive transition plan in the post-secondary vocational and educational areas. In addition, Figure 16.8 presents a listing of commercially available tests that may also prove beneficial in assessing for transition.

Curriculum

Commercially prepared curriculum materials are available that provide examples of life skills and **life-centered career objectives** and materials (Brolin, 1989; Cronin & Patton, 1993; Glascoe & Miller, 1986; Lloyd & Brolin, 1997; Miller & Glascoe, 1986). Most curriculums are designed around basic competencies that are subdivided according to the needs of targeted students. One curriculum, for example, contains the following major areas: Daily Living Skills, Personal-Social Skills, and Occupational Guidance Preparation (Lloyd & Brolin, 1997). Each area is then subdivided into more specific level competencies and objectives that also contain teaching suggestions to develop skills for successful living in maintaining a home and accepting responsibility for community living. Other suggestions for integrating a life skills curriculum within the general curriculum are provided by Cronin and Patton (1993). Finally, Wehman (1996) recommended that teachers identify as many community-based sites as possible and integrate those sites into their curriculum for students with disabilities, especially individuals with moderate to severe disabilities. Integrating community-based sites will increase awareness of what is available in the community for later access by students.

Planning for Graduation

In many states, more demanding coursework (in, for example, algebra, geometry, or foreign languages) and passing state competency exams are being required for graduation (see, for example, the *Standards of Learning for Virginia Public Schools* in English, math, science, history, and social studies, 1995). At the same time, some more basic and vocational courses are being phased out to free teachers for the more demanding courses. Some students with disabilities may find it extremely difficult, because of their disability, to pass one or more of these classes, even if modifications are made. If a student's apparent inability to pass one or more particularly demanding courses appears to stand in the way of graduation, determine whether a substitute course could be included on the student's IEP that would be accepted toward the diploma (see fact sheets by Learning Disabilities Association, 1995).

States have variable policies toward awarding diplomas. Some states award what is known as differentiated or tiered diplomas, which may include certificates of attendance, standard diplomas, or advanced diplomas. For individuals who have not been able to meet all the requirements for a standard diploma, an attendance certificate can be awarded for those who nonetheless have stayed in school and satisfactorily met attendance requirements throughout their school career. For students who have gone significantly beyond graduation requirements, advanced diplomas are awarded to acknowledge this level of achievement. Any differentiated or tiered diploma may be associated with specific course and competence requirements. In your own school, find out what factors determine the type of diploma individual students will receive, and how students' post-secondary futures (employment, vocational training, college entrance) will be affected by the type of diploma received (Learning Disabilities Association, 1995).

Other states, attempting to ensure uniformly high standards, have begun to eliminate differentiated diplomas in favor of one more advanced diploma. Consultation with career counselors, vocational schools, parents, and community resources can help provide relevant information on how to best meet the needs of students with disabilities under these circumstances. Because IDEA allows students with disabilities to continue to attend school until age 22, some students with disabilities may be able to meet the higher requirements with the additional years of schooling.

Companion Website

Search your own state Department of Education Website to read about state competency testing and graduation requirements. For an example, go to the Web Links module in chapter 16 of the Companion Website.

Lanford and Cary (2000) discuss the issue of graduation requirements for students with disabilities.

	Employment	Further Educational Training	Leisure Activities	Daily Living	Community Participation	Health	Self-Determination	Communication	Interpersonal Relationships
Achievement									
Adult Basic Learning Examination		X						X	
Brigance Inventory of Essential Skills		X						X	
Iowa Test of Basic Skills		X						X	
Peabody Individual Achievement Test		X						X	
Woodcock-Johnson Psycho-Educational Battery		X						X	
Adaptive Behavior									
AAMR Adaptive Behavior Scales	X			X	X			X	X
Adaptive Behavior Inventory	X	X		X	X			X	X
Normative Adaptive Behavior Checklist	X		X	X	X			X	X
Scales of Independent Behavior	X		X	X	X			X	X
Vineland Adaptive Behavior Scale	X			X	X			X	X
Street Survival Skills Questionnaire				X	X	X			
Aptitude									
APTICOM Program	X	X							
Armed Services Vocational Aptitude Battery	X	X							
Differential Aptitude Test	X	X							
General Aptitude Test Battery (GATB)	X	X							
JEVS Work Sample System	X								
McCarron-Dial Evaluation System	X								
MESA	X								
Micro-TOWER System	X								
Occupational Aptitude and Interest Scale-2	X	X							
Talent Assessment Program	X								
TOWER System	X								

Figure 16.8

Commercially Available Assessment Measures

Note: From "Transitional Planning Assessment for Secondary-Level Students with Learning Disabilities," by G. M. Clark, 1996, *Journal of Learning Disabilities, 29*(1), pp. 91–92. Reprinted with permission.

Planning for Future Education

Applying for colleges is an arduous task for all students, but may be particularly overwhelming to students with disabilities. Provide additional assistance to those students to encourage them to pursue further education. Many resources are available commercially to help students learn more about colleges' and universities' programs and their services for students with disabilities. The Learning Disabilities Association of America provides one such listing (4156 Library Road, Pittsburgh, PA 15234). Another helpful resource is *The Complete Directory for People with Learning Disabilities* (Grey House Publishing) that contains information on products, resources, books, and services that are available to help individuals with learning disabilities. For example, names, addresses, and phone

	Employment	Further Educational Training	Leisure Activities	Daily Living	Community Participation	Health	Self-Determination	Communication	Interpersonal Relationships
Communication									
Communicative Abilities in Daily Living								X	
Woodcock Reading Mastery Test								X	
Individual Reading Placement Inventory								X	
Test of Written Language								X	
Functional Capacity									
Functional Assessment Profile	X			X			X	X	X
General Health Questionnaire						X			
Life Functioning Index	X	X		X				X	
Personal Capacities Questionnaire	X			X			X	X	X
Independent Living Behavior Checklist				X	X				
Learning Styles									
Learning Style Inventory	X							X	
Learning Styles and Strategies	X							X	
Manual Dexterity									
Crawford Small Part Dexterity Test	X								
Minnesota Rate of Manipulation Test	X								
Pennsylvania Bi-Manual Worksample	X								
Purdue Pegboard	X								

Figure 16.8
Continued

numbers are provided for government agencies, professional organizations, books for parents and individuals with disabilities, major catalogs, pamphlets, and instructional materials including videos, computer software, and study guides. Interested students and parents should contact their local state chapter of the Council for Exceptional Children for additional information on services provided within their region at the higher education level. Much of this information may also be available on the World Wide Web. Many of these resource guides are also available at your local library or local bookstore.

Provide information on the standards necessary for admission to the college that students wish to attend. For example, some colleges require courses in foreign languages, others require specific units (high school credits) in math and English, and most require submission of the Scholastic Assessment Test (SAT) or American College Testing (ACT) scores with the completed applications by prespecified dates. This information can help students select the courses for their last few years in high school. Additionally, they can prepare for taking the SAT or ACT by studying pamphlets, commercially available books, computer programs, or enrolling in classes designed to improve performance on the tests. Some students may qualify for adapted testing procedures on the SAT. For example, some may be allowed extended time to take the SAT; others may be given the SAT in a larger print format. Seek assistance from your local high school counselor to determine whether or not students qualify for testing adaptations and help them obtain and submit the appropriate application forms.

Most colleges now have Web pages and application forms that can be submitted via e-mail. Provide opportunities for students to access this information via the Internet so they will be able to peruse the information at later times independently. They can also practice writing their application forms on computers and decide whether or not they would like to submit their forms via e-mail or regular mail.

Planning for Future Job Opportunities

Provide opportunities to discuss future job options. Relate your class content to employment options and opportunities. Invite professionals from the community to discuss how their educational backgrounds assisted them in their vocations. Discuss what types of educational backgrounds are required for various professions. Plan field trips to community-based organizations so students can see first-hand the types of employment opportunities available. Use the expertise of your school guidance counselors to assist in disseminating job-related information. Integrate, whenever possible, relevant job-related information with your regular curriculum. Use published curriculum materials for assessing and teaching employment-related skills. The following Research Highlight describes successful employment placements for students with mental retardation (Heal, Gonzalez, Rusch, Copher, & DeStefano, 1990).

Research Highlight

Successful Placement for Competitive Employment for Students with Disabilities

Heal, Gonzalez, Rusch, Copher, and DeStefano (1990) compared the employment placements of 54 high school students and young adults with mental retardation who were in successful or unsuccessful employment placements in an attempt to uncover factors associated with the most successful employment situations. Staff and individuals from high school and community placement programs from across the United States were surveyed. Forty-six percent of both successful and unsuccessful employees were placed in food service jobs, followed by fewer placements in health-related, automotive, hotel/motel, office, and manufacturing positions. Support for the individuals with disabilities was identified as a major factor in successful employment placements. This support reportedly came from the home, follow-up support from transition agencies and placement specialists, and employment supervisors. Student ability, social skills, work attitude, quality of work, and absence of asocial behaviors were also reported as critical factors for maintaining a successful employment placement. The authors concluded, "the most important elements in success appear to be a persevering placement effort, including home support, employer support, skillful on-the-job supervision, and a sensitive match of the worker to the job" (p. 194).

Also see Doren and Benz (1998) for follow-up information on predictors of better employment for all students with disabilities.

Questions for Reflection

1. How could this information be used to improve transition for students with disabilities?
2. Why did vocational skills not rank as high as some factors in successful placements?
3. How can positive work attitudes be taught to students prior to transition?
4. What social skills would be of most importance in maintaining successful employment placements? (See chapter 7.)

Companion Website

To answer these questions online, go to the Research Highlights feature in chapter 16 of the Companion Website.

Planning for Independent Living Situations

Many students require information on preparing for future independent living situations. One important issue is selecting, managing, and maintaining a home. Questions to consider include the following:

- What are your residential options?
- Where would you like to live?
  - With family?
  - With friends?
  - In a residential group home?
  - In a supported living situation?
  - In a semi-independent living program?
  - In independent living arrangements?

Provide information on the types of resources that will be required to go with each type of living arrangement. For example, if students select an independent living arrangement as their first choice, then they need to realize what financial resources will be necessary to accomplish this goal. Many teachers have included units on planning for independent living within their regular curriculum and have reported that students have enjoyed the opportunities to gain familiarity with what is required to own a car and live in an apartment. Preparing budgets allows students to examine expenses they will incur and help them examine employment opportunities that will enable them to realize their goals. Efforts to increase awareness of future needs helps students to be more planful and successful later in life.

Other important living skills include caring for personal needs, getting around in the community, buying and preparing food, buying and maintaining clothing, engaging in community and civic activities, and selecting meaningful recreation and leisure activities (Kokaska & Brolin, 1985). Individuals preparing for independent living also need to know about credit and how it can be used effectively.

Finally, vocational, personal, and social skills are important in independent living, and are described in this chapter and in chapter 7. Information provided by Kokaska and Brolin (1985), Cronin and Patton (1993), and Lloyd and Brolin (1997) can be helpful in planning and implementing programs to facilitate independent living, in school settings and beyond. It is important that support for students with disabilities and other special needs not stop at the end of schooling, but that all individuals receive needed preparation and necessary support to ensure quality and fulfillment in all of their life's activities.

Summary

- Art, music, and physical education are important subject areas for students with disabilities. Prioritize objectives and adapt the environment, instructional materials, and procedures effectively in art, music, and physical education to ensure success for students with disabilities.
- Foreign languages may be particularly challenging for students with disabilities and extra care should be taken to ensure that sufficient modifications are in place to assist students with appropriate modifications.
- Vocational education and career education include a wide variety of educational programs that are intended to prepare students for employment and for living. Vocational education may be particularly important for students with disabilities or other special needs who become employed immediately after high school.
- Vocational education areas include agriculture, business, family and consumer sciences, marketing, health, trade and industry, and technical/communications.
- The Carl D. Perkins Vocational Act of 1984 was of significant importance in promoting access to vocational education for students with disabilities or other special needs.
- Special considerations for adapting instruction to students with special needs include modifying the

physical environment, choosing goals and objectives carefully, adapting curriculum materials, and adapting instructional procedures.

- Transitions in life are important and transition planning is critical for students with disabilities. All students with IEPs must have Individual Transition Plans by the age of 14 or the end of eighth grade.
- Prepare students of all ages for transitions, including transitions from home to preschool, to new schools, to new teachers, and most importantly for life after high school. Involve students, parents, teachers, counselors, transition coordinators, and community-based personnel as members of the transition team.
- Students with disabilities require instruction in self-advocacy and self-determination skills to provide them with skills to be more successful during and after high school. Provide ample practice in safe environments for the development of these skills.
- Prepare students for life after high school by using appropriate transition assessment measures, carefully evaluating the results, and designing and implementing life skills programs.
- Help prepare students for the appropriate high school graduate requirements necessary for their transition plans.
- Provide educational opportunities that prepare students with disabilities for future education, jobs, and independent or supported living arrangements.

Council for Exceptional Children

Art, Music, Physical Education, Foreign Languages, Vocational Education, and Transitions

Information in this chapter links most directly to:

Standard 4—Instructional Strategies, particularly:

Skills:
- Use strategies to facilitate integration into various settings.
- Teach individuals to use self-assessment, problem solving, and other cognitive strategies to meet their needs.
- Select, adapt, and use instructional strategies and materials according to characteristics of the individual with exceptional learning needs.
- Use strategies to facilitate maintenance and generalization of skills across learning environments.
- Use procedures to increase the individual's self-awareness, self-management, self-control, self-reliance, and self-esteem
- Use strategies that promote successful transitions for individuals with exceptional learning needs.

Standard 5—Learning Environments and Social Interactions

Skills:
- Teach self-advocacy.
- Create an environment that encourages self-advocacy and increased independence.

Standard 7—Instructional Planning

Knowledge:
- Theories and research that form the basis of curriculum develoment and instructional practice.
- Scope and sequences for general and special curricula.
- National, state or provincial, and local curricula standards.
- Technology for planning and managing the teaching and learning environment.

Skills:
- Identify and prioritize areas of the general curriculum and accommodations for individuals with exceptional learning needs.
- Develop and implement comprehensive, longitudinal individualized programs in collaboration with team members.
- Use task analysis.
- Sequence, implement, and evaluate individualized learning objectives.
- Incorporate and implement instructional and assistive technology into the educational program.
- Prepare and organize materials to implement daily lesson plans.
- Use instructional time effectively.
- Make responsive adjustments to instruction based on continual observations.

✓ Inclusion Checklist
Art, Music, Physical Education, Foreign Languages, Vocational Education, and Transitions

If you are teaching other content areas, have you considered modifications for students with special needs in:

- ❏ Art education, such as:
  - ❏ Prioritize objectives
  - ❏ Adapt environment
  - ❏ Adapt instructional materials
  - ❏ Adapt instructional procedures
- ❏ Music classes
  - ❏ Prioritize objectives
  - ❏ Adapt environment
  - ❏ Adapt instructional materials
  - ❏ Adapt instructional procedures
- ❏ Physical education
  - ❏ Prioritize objectives
  - ❏ Adapt environment
  - ❏ Adapt instructional materials
  - ❏ Adapt instructional procedures
- ❏ Foreign languages
  - ❏ Prioritize objectives
  - ❏ Adapt environment
  - ❏ Adapt instructional materials
  - ❏ Adapt instructional procedures

If you are planning career and vocational education, have you considered the following:

- ❏ Career and vocational education options:
  - ❏ Agricultural education
  - ❏ Business education
  - ❏ Family and consumer sciences
  - ❏ Marketing education
  - ❏ Health occupations education
  - ❏ Technical education
  - ❏ Technology education
  - ❏ Trade and industrial education

Have you considered modifications in career and vocational education, such as:

- ❏ The PASS variables:
  - ❏ Goals and objectives
  - ❏ Environmental modifications
  - ❏ Curriculum modifications
  - ❏ Safety considerations
  - ❏ Modifying instructional materials
  - ❏ Selecting computer software
  - ❏ Instructional strategies
  - ❏ Generalizable skills

Have you considered transition education, such as the following:

- ❏ What transition means:
  - ❏ Transitions from home to preschool
  - ❏ Transitions to a new school or teachers
  - ❏ Transitions to adulthood
- ❏ Self-advocacy and self-determination preparation:
  - ❏ Assessment for transition
  - ❏ Curriculum for transition
  - ❏ Planning for graduation
  - ❏ Planning for future education
  - ❏ Planning for future job opportunities
  - ❏ Planning for independent living situations

References

Chapter 1

Affleck, J. Q., Madge, S., Adams, A., & Lowenbraun, S. (1988). What's happening in self-contained special education classrooms? *Exceptional Children, 55,* 259–265.

Alaska Statutes, Title 14, Chapter 30, 1971.

Beattie v. Board of Education of City of Antigo, 172 N.W. 153, 154, 1919; Johnson, 1986, p. 2.

Bina, M. (1993). Mainstreaming, schools for the blind, and full inclusion: What shall the future of education for blind children be? *The Braille Monitor,* November, 1007–1010.

Blaska, J. (1993). The power of language: Speak and write using "person first." In M. Nagler (Ed), *Perspectives on disability* (2nd ed., pp. 25–32). Palo Alto, CA: Health Markets Research.

Boon, R., & Mastropieri, M. A. (1999). *Inclusion: What the teachers in the trenches really think.* Paper presented at the annual meeting of the Learning Disabilities Association, Atlanta.

Brown v. Board of Education, 347 U.S. 483 (1954).

Bryan, T. H., Bay, M., & Donahue, M. (1988). Implications of the learning disabilities definition for the regular education initiative. *Journal of Learning Disabilities, 21,* 21–28.

Bryan, J. H., & Bryan, T. H. (1988). Where's the beef? A review of published research on the Adaptive Learning Environment Model. *Learning Disabilities Focus, 4,* 9–14.

Carlberg, C., & Kavale, K. (1980). The efficacy of special versus regular class placement for exceptional children: A meta-analysis. *Journal of Special Education, 14,* 295–309.

Carr, M. N. (1993). A mother's thoughts on inclusion. *Journal of Learning Disabilities, 26,* 590–592.

Chung, S. (1998). *The compatibility of reform initiatives in inclusion and science education: Perceptions of science teachers.* Unpublished doctoral dissertation. West Lafayette, IN: Purdue University.

Code of Virginia, Section, 22.275.3, 1973.

Cook, B. G., Tankersley, M., Cook, L., & Landrum, T. J. (2000). Teachers' attitudes toward their included students with disabilities. *Exceptional Children, 67,* 115–135.

Council for Exceptional Children. (2002). No Child Left Behind has major implications for special education. *CEC Today, 9*(4), 4.

Deno, E. (1970). Special education as developmental capital. *Exceptional Children, 37,* 229–237.

Dev, P. C., & Scruggs, T. E. (1997). Mainstreaming and inclusion of students with learning disabilities: Perspectives of general educators in elementary and secondary schools. In T. E. Scruggs & M. A. Mastropieri (Eds.), *Advances in learning and behavioral disabilities* (Vol. 11, pp. 135–178). Greenwich, CT: JAI Press.

Diamond, S. C. (1993). Special education and the great god, inclusion. *Beyond Behavior, 4*(2), 3–6.

Diana vs. State Board of Education, Civ. No. C-70-37 RFP (N.D. Cal. 1970, 1973).

Educational Testing Service. (2002). *Special education: Core knowledge study guide.* Princeton, NJ: Author.

Elam, S. M., & Rose, L. C. (1995). Of the public's attitudes toward the public schools. *Phi Delta Kappan, 77,* 41–56.

Frymier, J. (1992). Children who hurt, children who fail. *Phi Delta Kappan, 74,* 257–259.

Fuchs, D., & Fuchs, L. S. (1988a). Evaluation of the Adaptive Learning Environments Model. *Exceptional Children, 55,* 115–127.

Fuchs, D., & Fuchs, L. S. (1988b). Response to Wang and Walberg. *Exceptional Children, 55,* 138–146.

Fuchs, D., & Fuchs, L. S. (1994). Inclusive schools movement and the radicalization of special education reform. *Exceptional Children, 60,* 294–309.

Fuchs, D., Fuchs, L. S., & Fernstrom, P. (1993). A conservative approach to special education reform: Mainstreaming through transenvironmental programming and curriculum-based measurement. *American Educational Research Journal, 30,* 149–177.

Fulk, B. J. M., & Hirth, M. A. (1994, April). *Perceptions of special education program effectiveness and attitudes toward inclusion.* Paper presented at the annual meeting of the American Educational Research Association, New Orleans. (ERIC Document Reproduction Service No. ED374595)

Gartner, A., & Lipsky, D. K. (1989). *The yoke of special education: How to break it.* New York: National Center on Education and the Economy.

Genshaft, J. L., Bireley, M., & Hollinger, C. L. (Eds.). (1995). *Serving gifted and talented students: A resource for school personnel.* Austin, TX: Pro-Ed.

Green, S. K., & Shinn, M. R. (1995). Parent attitudes about special education and reintegration: What is the role of student outcomes? *Exceptional Children, 61,* 269–281.

Grossman, H. (1995). *Teaching in a diverse society.* Boston: Allyn & Bacon.

Haring, N., Stern, G. G., & Cruickshank, W. M. (1958). *Attitudes of educators toward exceptional children.* Syracuse, NY: Syracuse University Press.

Honig v. Doe, 484 U.S. 305 S.Ct. 592, 98 L.Ed.2d 686, 43 Ed. Law Rep. 857 (1988).

Jenkins, J. R., & Heinen, A. (1989). Students' preferences for service delivery: Pull-out, in-class, or integrated models. *Exceptional Children, 55,* 516–523.

Johnson, T. P. (1986). *The principal's guide to the educational rights of handicapped students.* Reston, VA: National Association of Secondary School Principals.

Kauffman, J. M. (1989). The regular education initiative as a Reagan-Bush education policy: A trickle-down theory of education of the hard-to-teach. *Journal of Special Education, 23,* 256–278.

Kauffman, J. M. (1995). Why we must celebrate a diversity of restrictive environments. *Learning Disabilities Research & Practice, 10,* 225–232.

Kauffman, J. M., & Hallahan, D. P. (Eds.). (1995). *The illusion of full inclusion: A comprehensive critique of a current special education bandwagon.* Austin, TX: Pro-Ed.

Kavale, K. A., & Forness, S. R. (2000). History, rhetoric, and reality: Analysis of the inclusion debate. *Remedial and Special Education, 21,* 279–296.

Kliewer, C., & Biklen, D. (1996). Labeling: Who wants to be called retarded? In W. Stainback & S. Stainback (Eds.), *Controversial issues confronting special education: Divergent perspectives* (2nd ed., pp. 83–95). Boston: Allyn & Bacon.

Klingner, J. K., Vaughn, S., Schumm, J. S., Cohen, P., & Forgan, J. W. (1998). Inclusion or pull-out: Which do students prefer? *Journal of Learning Disabilities, 31,* 148–158.

Lane, H. (1995). The education of deaf children: Drowning in the mainstream and the sidestream. In J. M. Kauffman & D. P. Hallihan (Eds.), *The illusion of full inclusion* (pp. 275–287). Austin, TX: Pro-Ed.

Larrivee, B., & Cook, L. (1979). Mainstreaming: A study of the variables affecting teacher attitude. *Journal of Special Education, 13,* 315–324.

Larry P. v. Riles, 343 F. Supp. 1306 (N.D. Cal. 1972, *aff'd* 502 F.2d 963 (9th Cir. 1974), *further action* 495 F. Supp. 926 N.D. Cal. 1979), *aff'd* 793 F.2d 969 (9th Cir., 1984).

Lilly, M. S. (1992). Labeling: A tired, overworked, yet unresolved issue in special education. In W. Stainback & S. Stainback (Eds.), *Controversial issues confronting special education: Divergent perspectives* (pp. 85–95). Boston: Allyn & Bacon.

Lipsky, D. K., & Gartner, A. (1991). Restructuring for quality. In J. W. Lloyd, A. C. Repp, & N. N. Singh (Eds.), *The regular education initiative: Alternative perspectives on concepts, issues, and models* (pp. 43–56). Sycamore, IL: Sycamore.

Lloyd, J. W., Repp, A. C., & Singh, N. N. (Eds.). (1991). *The regular education initiative: Alternative perspectives on concepts, issues, and models.* Sycamore, IL: Sycamore.

Marston, D. (1987–1988). The effectiveness of special education: A time series analysis of reading performance in regular and special education settings. *Journal of Special Education, 21,* 13–26.

Martin, R. (1992). *Continuing challenges in special education law.* Urbana, IL: Carle Media.

Mastropieri, M. A., & Scruggs, T. E. (1997). What's special about special education? A cautious view toward full inclusion. *Educational Forum, 61,* 206–211.

Mills v. Board of Education, 348 F. Supp. 866 (D.D.C. 1972). Nevada Revised Statutes, Section 39.050 (1963).

Oberti v. Board of Education, 995 F.2d 1204 (3rd Cir. 1993).

Osborne, A. G., Jr. (1996). *Legal issues in special education.* Boston: Allyn & Bacon.

Padeliadu, S., & Zigmond, N. (1996). Perspectives of students with learning disabilities about special education placement. *Learning Disabilities Research & Practice, 11,* 15–23.

Palmer, D. S., Fuller, K., Arora, T., & Nelson, M. (2001). Taking sides: Parent views on inclusion for their children with severe disabilities. *Exceptional Children, 67,* 467–484.

Pennsylvania Association for Retarded Citizens v. Commonwealth of Pennsylvania (PARC), 334 F. Supp. 1257 (E.D. Pa. 1972).

Raynes, M., Snell, M., & Sailor, W. (1991). A fresh look at categorical programs for children with special needs. *Phi Delta Kappan, 73,* 326–331.

Rimland, B. (1993). Inclusive education: Right for some. *Autism Research Review International, 7,* 3.

Rothstein, L. F. (1999). *Special education law* (3rd ed.). New York: Longman.

Scruggs, T. E., & Mastropieri, M. A. (1996a). Teacher perceptions of mainstreaming/inclusion, 1958–1995: A research synthesis. *Exceptional Children, 63,* 59–74.

Scruggs, T. E., & Mastropieri, M. A. (1996b). Quantitative synthesis of survey research: Methodology and validation. In T. E. Scruggs & M. A. Mastropieri (Eds.), *Advances in learning and behavioral disabilities* (Vol. 10, pp. 209–223). Greenwich, CT: JAI Press.

Smith, T. E. C. (2001). Section 504, the ADA, and public schools: What educators need to know. *Remedial and Special Education, 22,* 335–343.

Smith, T. E. C., & Patton, J. R. (1999). *Section 504 and public schools: A practical guide.* Austin, TX: Pro-Ed.

Stainback, W., & Stainback, S. (1984). A rationale for the merger of regular and special education. *Exceptional Children, 51,* 102–111.

Stainback, W., & Stainback, S. (1990a). Inclusive schooling. In W. Stainback & S. Stainback (Eds.), *Support networks for inclusive schooling: Independent integrated education* (pp. 3–23). Baltimore: Brooks Publishing.

Stainback, W., & Stainback, S. (Eds.). (1990b). *Support networks for inclusive schooling: Independent integrated education.* Baltimore: Brooks Publishing.

Stainback, S., Stainback, W., & Forest, M. (Eds.). (1989). *Educating all students in the mainstream of regular education.* Baltimore: Brooks Publishing.

Stephens, V. P., & Price, M. (1992). Meeting the challenge of educating children at risk. *Phi Delta Kappan, 74,* 18–23.

Turnbull, A., Turnbull, R., Shank, M., & Leal, D. (1999). *Exceptional lives: Special education for today's schools.* Upper Saddle River, NJ: Merrill/Prentice-Hall.

U.S. Department of Education. (1999). *The Individuals with Disabilities Education Act Amendments of 1997. Final Regulations.* Washington, DC: Author.

U.S. Senate-House. (1994, March 21). *Goals 2000: Educate America Act* (Conference Report 103–446). Washington, D.C.: Author.

Vaughn, S., Elbaum, B. E., & Schumm, J. S. (1996). The effects of inclusion on the social functioning of students with learning disabilities. *Journal of Learning Disabilities, 29,* 598–608.

Vaughn, S., & Klingner, J. K. (1998). Students' perceptions of inclusion and resource room settings. *The Journal of Special Education, 32,* 79–88.

Wang, M. C., Reynolds, M. C., & Zollers, N. J. (1990). Adaptive instruction: An alternative service delivery approach. *Remedial and Special Education, 11*(1), 7–21.

Wang, M. C., & Walberg, H. J. (1988). Four fallacies of segregationism. *Exceptional Children, 55,* 122–128.

Watson v. City of Cambridge, 32 N.E. 864, 864 (1893); Johnson, 1986, pp. 1–2.

Wiederholt, J. L., Hammill, D. D., & Brown, V. L. (1993). *The resource program: Organization and implementation.* Austin, TX: Pro-Ed.

Will, M. (1986). Educating students with learning problems: A shared responsibility. *Exceptional Children, 52,* 411–415.

Yell, M. (1997). *The law and special education.* Columbus, OH: Prentice-Hall.

Zigmond, N., & Baker, J. (1994). Is the mainstream a more appropriate educational setting for Randy? A case study of one student with learning disabilities. *Learning Disabilities Research & Practice, 9,* 108–117.

Chapter 2

Adams, L., & Cesan, K. (1993). Metaphors of the co-taught classroom. *Preventing School Failure, 37*(4), 28–31.

Bauwens, J., Hourcade, J. J., & Friend, M. (1989). Cooperative teaching: A model for general and special

education integration. *Remedial and Special Education, 10*(2), 17–22.

Bradley, D. F., Bjorlykke, L., Mann, E., Homan, C., & Lindsay, J. (1993). *Empowerment of the general educator through effective teaching strategies.* Paper presented at the International Conference on Learning Disabilities, Baltimore, MD. (ERIC Document Reproduction Service No. ED368123)

Cook, L., & Friend, M. (1995). Co-teaching: Guidelines for effective practices. *Focus on Exceptional Children, 28*(3), 1–16.

Craig, S., Hull, K., Haggart, A. G., & Perez-Selles, M. (2000). Promoting cultural competence through teacher assistance teams. *Teaching Exceptional Children, 32*(3), 6–12.

Denton, M., & Foley, D. J. (1994). The marriage of special and regular education through inclusion. *Teaching and Change, 1,* 349–368.

Dougherty, J. W. (1994). Inclusion and teaming: It's a natural collaboration. *Schools in the Middle, 3*(4), 7–8.

Drasgow, E., Yell, M. L., & Robinson, T. R. (2001). Developing legally correct and educationally appropriate IEPs. *Remedial and Special Education, 22,* 359–373.

Ekstrand, R. E., & Edmister, P. (1984). Mediation: A process that works. *Exceptional Children, 51,* 163–167.

Ekstrand, R. E., Edmister, P., & Riggin, J. (1989). *Preparation for special education hearings.* Reston, VA: Council for Exceptional Children.

Forest, M., & Lusthaus, E. (1989). Promoting educational equity for all students. In S. Stainback, W. Stainback, & M. Forest (Eds.), *Educating all students in the mainstream of regular education* (pp. 47–49). Baltimore: Brookes Publishing.

French, N. (1998). Working together: Resource teachers and paraeducators. *Remedial and Special Education, 19,* 357–368.

Friend, M., & Cook, L. (1992). *Interactions: Collaboration skills for school professionals.* White Plains, NY: Longman.

Fuchs, D., Fuchs, L. S., Reeder, P., Gilman, S., Fernstrom, P., Bahr, M., & Moore, P. (1989). *Mainstream assistance teams: A handbook on prereferral intervention.* Nashville, TN: Peabody College of Vanderbilt University.

Gately, F. J., Jr., & Gately, S. E. (1993). *Developing positive co-teaching environments: Meeting the needs of an increasingly diverse student population.* Paper presented at the annual meeting of the Council for Exceptional Children, San Antonio, TX. (ERIC Document Reproduction Service No. ED358604)

Giangreco, M. F., Broer, S. M., & Edelman, S. W. (1999). The tip of the iceberg: Determining whether paraprofessional support is needed for students with disabilities in general education settings. *Journal of the Association for Persons with Severe Handicaps, 24,* 281–291.

Ginott, H. (1995). *Teacher and child.* New York: Collier.

Gordon, T. (1987). *T.E.T.: Teacher effectiveness training.* New York: David McKay.

Graden, J. L., Casey, A., & Bonstrom, O. (1985a). Implementing a prereferral intervention system: Part II: The data. *Exceptional Children, 51,* 487–496.

Graden, J. L., Casey, A., & Bonstrom, O. (1985b). Implementing a prereferral intervention system: Part I: The model. *Exceptional Children, 51,* 377–387.

Hardy, S. (2001). *A qualitative study of the instructional behaviors and practices of a dyad of educators in self-contained and inclusive co-taught secondary biology classrooms during a nine-week science instruction grading period.* Unpublished doctoral dissertation, George Mason University, Fairfax, VA.

Harris, K., Harvey, P., Garcia, L., Innes, D., Lynn, P., Munoz, D., Sexton, K., & Stocia, R. (1987). Meeting the needs of special high school students in regular classrooms. *Teacher Education and Special Education, 10,* 143–152.

Hines, R. A. (1994). The best of both worlds? Collaborative teaching for effective inclusion. *Schools in the Middle, 3*(4), 3–6.

Ianacone, R. N., & Stodden, R. A. (Eds.). (1987). *Transition issues and directions.* Reston, VA: The Council for Exceptional Children, Division on Mental Retardation and Developmental Disabilities.

IDEA 1997: Let's make it work. (1998). Reston, VA: Council for Exceptional Children.

Idol, L., Paolucci-Whitcomb, P., & Nevin, A. (1986). *Collaborative consultation.* Austin, TX: Pro-Ed.

Idol, L., & West, J. F. (1993a). *Effective instruction of difficult-to-teach students: An inservice and preservice professional development program for classroom, remedial, and special education teachers: Instructor's manual.* Austin, TX: Pro-Ed.

Idol, L., & West, J. F. (1993b). *Effective instruction of difficult-to-teach students: An inservice and preservice professional development program for classroom, remedial, and special education teachers: Participant's workbook.* Austin, TX: Pro-Ed.

The IEP Planner. (1996). Highland Park, IL: Rodan Associates. Indiana Department of Education. (2000). *Title 511 Indiana State Board of Education Article 7, Rules 3–16: Special Education Rules.* Indianapolis: Indiana Department of Education, Division of Special Education.

Katsiyannis, A., Hodge, J., & Lanford, A. (2000). Paraeducators: Legal and practice considerations. *Remedial and Special Education, 21,* 297–304.

Kluwin, T. N., Gonsher, W., Silver, K., & Samuels, J. (1996). The E.T. class: Education together! Team teaching students with hearing impairments and students with normal hearing together. *Teaching Exceptional Children, 29,* 92–100.

Kovaleski, J. F., Gickling, E. E., Morrow, H., & Swank, P. R. (1999). High versus low implementation of instructional support teams: A case for maintaining program fidelity. *Remedial and Special Education, 20,* 170–183.

Kozleski, E. B., & Jackson, L. (1993). Taylor's story: Full inclusion in her neighborhood elementary school. *Exceptionality, 4,* 153–175.

Latz, S., & Dogan, A. (1995). Co-teaching as an instructional strategy for effective inclusionary practices. *Teaching and Change, 2,* 330–351.

Lundeen, C., & Lundeen, D. J. (1993). *Effectiveness of mainstreaming with collaborative teaching.* Paper presented at the American Speech-Language-Hearing Annual Convention, Anaheim, CA. (ERIC Document Reproduction Services No. ED368127)

Mastropieri, M. A., & Scruggs, T. E. (2002). *Effective instruction for special education* (3rd ed.). Austin, TX: Pro-Ed.

Messersmith, J. L., & Piantek, G. A. (1988). Changing the "I" to "We": Effective mainstreaming through cooperative teaching. *NASSP Bulletin, 72*(510), 66–71.

Murawski, W. W., & Swanson, H. L. (2001). A meta-analysis of co-teaching research: Where are the data? *Remedial and Special Education, 22,* 258–267.

Nelson, M. C., & Stevens, K. B. (1981). An accountable consultation model for mainstreaming behaviorally disordered children. *Behavioral Disorders, 6*(2), 82–91.

Nowacek, E. J. (1992). Professionals talk about teaching together: Interviews with five collaborating teachers. *Intervention in School and Clinic, 27,* 262–276.

Phillips, L., Sapona, R. H., & Lubie, B. L. (1995). Developing partnerships in inclusive education: One school's approach. *Intervention in School and Clinic, 30,* 262–272.

Polloway, E. A., Patton, J. R., & Serna, L. (2001). *Strategies for teaching learners with special needs* (7th ed.). Upper Saddle River, NJ: Merrill/Prentice Hall.

Pugach, M. C., & Johnson, L. J. (1995). Unlocking expertise among classroom teachers through structured dialogue: Extending research on peer collaboration. *Exceptional Children, 62,* 101–110.

Reeve, P. T., & Hallahan, D. P. (1994). Practical questions about collaboration between general and special education. *Focus on Exceptional Children, 26*(7), 1–11.

Reinhiller, N. (1996). Coteaching: New variations on a not-so-new practice. *Teacher Education and Special Education, 19,* 34–48.

Ritter, D. R. (1978). Effects of a school consultation program upon referral patterns of teachers. *Psychology in the Schools, 15,* 239–243.

Trent, S. C. (1998). False starts and other dilemmas of a secondary general education collaborative teacher: A case study. *Journal of Learning Disabilities, 31,* 503–513.

Walther-Thomas, C., Korinek, L., McLaughlin, V. L., & Williams, B. T. (2000). *Collaboration for inclusive education.* Boston: Allyn & Bacon.

Weiss, M. P., & Brigham, F. J. (2000). Co-teaching and the model of shared responsibility: What does the research support? In T. E. Scruggs & M. A. Mastropieri (Eds.),

Advances in learning and behavioral disabilities (Vol. 14, pp. 217–245). Oxford, UK: JAI/Elsevier Science.

West, J. F., & Cannon, G. (1988). Essential collaborative consultation competencies for regular and special educators. *Journal of Learning Disabilities, 21*(1), 28, 56–63.

West, J. F., Idol, L., & Cannon, G. (1989a). *Collaboration in the schools: An inservice and preservice curriculum for teachers, support staff, and administrators: Instructor's manual.* Austin, TX: Pro-Ed.

West, J. F., Idol, L., & Cannon, G. (1989b). *Collaboration in the schools: An inservice and preservice curriculum for teachers, support staff, and administrators: Participant's workbook.* Austin, TX: Pro-Ed.

Zigmond, N. (1998, February). *Inclusion in secondary schools.* Paper presented at the Sixth Annual Pacific Coast Research Conference, LaJolla, CA.

Chapter 3

Algozzine, B. (1985). Low achiever differentiation: Where's the beef? *Exceptional Children, 52,* 72–75.

Algozzine, B., Ysseldyke, J. E., & McGue, M. (1995). Differentiating low-achieving students: Thoughts on setting the record straight. *Learning Disabilities Research & Practice, 10,* 140–144.

American Association on Mental Retardation Ad Hoc Committee on Terminology and Classification. (1992). *Mental retardation: Definition, classification, and systems of support.* Washington, DC: American Association on Mental Retardation.

American Psychiatric Association (APA). (1994). *Diagnostic and statistical manual of mental disorders: DSM-IV* (4th ed.). Washington, DC: American Psychiatric Association.

American Speech–Language Hearing Association (ASHA). (1993). Definitions: Communicative disorders and variations. *ASHA, 35* (Supple. 10), 40–41.

Apgar, V., & Beck, J. (Eds.). (1972). *Is my baby all right? A guide to birth defects.* New York: Simon & Schuster.

Bauermeister, J. J., & Jemail, J. A. (1975). Modification of "elective mutism" in the classroom setting: A case study. *Behavior Therapy, 6,* 246–250.

Beck, J. (1972). Spina bifida and hydrocephalus. In V. Apgar & J. Beck (Eds.), *Is my baby all right? A guide to birth defects* (pp. 288–298, 400–414). New York: Simon & Schuster.

Beirne-Smith, M., Ittenbach, R., & Patton, J. (2002). *Mental retardation* (6th ed.). Upper Saddle River, NJ: Merrill/Prentice Hall.

Benson, D. F., & Alfredo, A. (1996). *Aphasia: A clinical perspective.* New York: Oxford University Press.

Blackman, J. A. (Ed.). (1983). *Medical aspects of developmental disabilities in children birth to three.* Iowa City: University of Iowa Press.

Bos, C., & Tierney, R. J. (1984). Inferential reading abilities of mildly mentally retarded and nonretarded students. *American Journal of Mental Deficiency, 89,* 75–82.

Braswell, L., Bloomquist, M. L., & Barkley, R. A. (1991). *Cognitive behavioral therapy with ADHD children.* New York: Guilford Press.

Bricker, W. A., & Bricker, D. D. (1972). A program for language training for the severely handicapped child. *The Exceptional Child, 37,* 101–111.

Brigham, F. J., & Cole, J. E. (1999). Selective mutism: Developments in definition, etiology, assessment and treatment. In T. E. Scruggs & M. A. Mastropieri (Eds.), *Advances in learning and behavioral disabilities* (Vol. 13, pp. 183–216). Greenwich, CT: JAI Press.

Bryan, T. (1994). The social competence of students with learning disabilities over time: A response to Vaughn and Hogan. *Journal of Learning Disabilities, 27,* 304–308.

Bryan, T., Pearl, R., & Herzog, A. (1989). Learning disabled adolescents' vulnerability to crime: Attitudes, anxieties, experiences. *Learning Disability Quarterly, 5,* 51–60.

Bursuck, W. (1989). A comparison of students with learning disabilities to low achieving and higher achieving students on three dimensions of special competence. *Journal of Learning Disabilities, 22,* 188–194.

Bybee, J., & Zigler, E. (1992). Is outerdirectedness employed in a harmful or beneficial manner by students with and without mental retardation? *American Journal on Mental Retardation, 96,* 512–521.

Cannon, L., Crawford, D., Fleming, A., Gallagher, L., Gardsbane, H., Petersen, J., & Vinup, A. (2002). Report from the LDA past presidents think tank. *LDA Newsbriefs, 37*(1), 1–14, 21.

Case, L. P., Mamlin, N., Harris, K. R., & Graham, S. (1995). Self-regulated strategy development: A theoretical and practical perspective. In T. E. Scruggs & M. A. Mastropieri (Eds.), *Advances in learning and behavioral disabilities* (Vol. 9, pp. 21–46). Greenwich, CT: JAI Press.

Cawley, J. F., & Parmer, R. (1992). Arithmetic programming for students with disabilities: An alternative. *Remedial and Special Education, 13*(3), 6–18.

Ceci, S. J. (Ed.). (1986). *Handbook of cognitive, social, and neuropsychological aspects of learning disabilities* (Vol. 1). Hillsdale, NJ: Lawrence Erlbaum.

Centra, N. A. (1990). *A qualitative study of high school students in a resource program.* Unpublished doctoral dissertation, Syracuse University, Syracuse, NY.

Ciborowski, J. (1992). *Textbooks and the students who can't read them: A guide to teaching content.* Cambridge, MA: Brookline Books.

Cleaver, A., Bear, B., & Juvonen, J. (1992). Discrepancies between competence and importance in self-perceptions of children in integrated classes. *The Journal of Special Education, 26,* 125–138.

Clements, S. D. (1966). *Minimal brain dysfunction in children: Terminology and identification—Phase one of a three phase project.* Washington, DC: U.S. Department of Health, Education, and Welfare.

Conture, E. G. (1989). Why does my child stutter? In *Stuttering and your child: Questions and answers* (pp. 13–22). Memphis: Stuttering Foundation of America.

Cooney, J. B., & Swanson, H. L. (1987). Memory and learning disabilities: An overview. In H. L. Swanson (Ed.), *Advances in learning and behavioral disabilities: Memory and learning disabilities* (Supplement 2, pp. 1–40). Greenwich, CT: JAI Press.

Costello, M., & Holland, A. L. (Eds.). (1986). *Handbook of speech and language disorders.* San Diego: College Hill Press.

Cronin, M. E., & Patton, J. R. (1993). *Life skills instruction for students with special needs: A practical guide for integrating real life content into the curriculum.* Austin, TX: Pro-Ed.

Curlee, R. F. (1989). Does my child stutter? In *Stuttering and your child: Questions and answers* (pp. 7–12). Memphis: Stuttering Foundation of America.

DeFries, J. C., Gillis, J. J., & Wadsworth, S. J. (1993). Genes and genders: A twin study of reading disability. In A. M. Galaburda (Ed.), *Dyslexia and development: Neurological aspects of extraordinary brains* (pp. 187–294). Cambridge, MA: Harvard University Press.

Deshler, D. D., Ellis, E. S., & Lenz, B. K. (1996). *Teaching adolescents with learning disabilities: Strategies and methods* (2nd ed.). Denver: Love Publishing.

Donahoe, K., & Zigmond, N. (1990). Academic grades of ninth-grade urban learning-disabled students and low-achieving peers. *Exceptionality, 1,* 17–27.

Donahue, M. (1986). Phonological constraints on the emergence of two word utterances. *Journal of Child Language, 13,* 109–228.

Ellis, N. R. (1970). Memory processes in retardates and normals. In N. R. Ellis (Ed.), *Handbook of mental deficiency: Psychological theory and research* (Vol. 1, pp. 134–158). New York: McGraw-Hill.

Ellis, N. R. (Ed.). (1979). *Handbook of mental deficiency: Psychological theory and research* (2nd ed.). Hillsdale, NJ: Lawrence Erlbaum.

Englert, C. S., & Mariage, T. V. (1996). A sociocultural perspective: Teaching ways-of-thinking and ways-of-talking in a literacy community. *Learning Disabilities Research & Practice, 11,* 157–167.

Epstein, M. H., Kinder, D., & Bursuck, B. (1989). The academic status of adolescents with behavioral disorders. *Behavioral Disorders, 14,* 157–165.

Federal Register. (1977, December 29). *Procedures for evaluating specific learning disabilities.* Washington, DC: Department of Health, Education, and Welfare.

Forness, S. R., & Dvorak, R. (1982). Effects of test time-limits on achievement scores of behaviorally disordered adolescents. *Behavioral Disorders, 7,* 207–212.

Forness, S. R., Sinclair, E., & Guthrie, D. (1983). Learning disability discrepancy formulas: Their use in actual practice. *Learning Disability Quarterly, 6,* 107–114.

Franklin, K., & Beukelman, D. R. (1991). Augmentative communication: Directions for the future. In J. F. Miller (Ed.), *Research on child language disorders: A decade of progress* (pp. 321–337). Austin, TX: Pro-Ed.

Fuchs, D. (1998, April). *Is "LD" just a fancy term for "underachievement"?* Paper presented at the annual meeting of the Council for Exceptional Children, Minneapolis.

Fuchs, D., Fuchs, L., Mathes, P. G., & Lipsey, M. W. (2000). Reading differences between low-achieving students with and without learning disabilities: A meta-analysis. In R. Gersten, E. P. Schiller, & S. Vaughn (2000), *Contemporary special education research: Syntheses of the knowledge base on critical instructional issues* (pp. 81–104). Mahwah, NJ: Lawrence Erlbaum.

Fuchs, D., Fuchs, L., Mathes, P. G., Lipsey, M. W., & Roberts, P. H. (2000). Is "learning disabilities" just a fancy term for low achievement: A meta-analysis of reading differences between low achievers with and without the label. In R. Bradley, L. Danielson, & D. P. Hallahan (Eds.)(2002), *Identification of learning disabilities: Research to practice* (pp. 737–762). Mahwah, NJ: Lawrence Erlbaum.

Fulk, B. J. M., & Stormont-Spurgin, M. (1995). Spelling interventions for students with learning disabilities: A review. *Journal of Special Education, 28,* 488–513.

Gable, R. A., & Warren, S. F. (Eds.). (1993). *Advances in mental retardation and developmental disabilities* (Vol. 5). London: Jessica Kingsley Publishers.

Gallagher, J. J. (1998). The public policy legacy of Samuel A. Kirk. *Learning Disabilities Research & Practice, 13,* 11–14.

Gaskins, I., & Elliot, T. (1991). *Implementing cognitive strategy training across the school: The Benchmark manual for teachers.* Cambridge, MA: Brookline Books.

Graham, F. K., Ernhart, C. B., Thurston, D., & Craft, M. (1962). Development three years after perinatal anoxia and other potentially damaging experiences. *Topics in Early Childhood Special Education, 8,* 23–28.

Graham, S., & Harris, K. R. (1994). The effects of whole language on writing: A review. *Educational Psychologist, 29,* 187–192.

Graham, S., & Weintraub, N. (1996). A review of handwriting research: Progress and prospects from 1980 to 1994. *Educational Psychology Review, 8,* 7–87.

Gresham, F. M. (2002). Responsiveness to intervention: An alternative approach to the identification of learning disabilities. In R. Bradley, L. Danielson, & D. P. Hallahan (Eds.), *Identification of learning disabilities* (pp. 449–466). Mahwah, NJ: Lawrence Erlbaum.

Hallahan, D. P., & Cottone, E. A. (1997). Attention deficit hyperactivity disorder. In T. E. Scruggs & M. A. Mastropieri (Eds.), *Advances in learning and behavioral disorders* (Vol. 11, pp. 27–67). Greenwich, CT: JAI Press.

Hallahan, D. P., & Kauffman, J. M. (2003). *Exceptional learners: Introduction to special education* (9th ed.). Boston: Allyn & Bacon.

Hallahan, D. P., Kauffman, J. M., & Lloyd, J. W. (1999). *Introduction to learning disabilities* (2nd ed.). Needham Heights, MA: Allyn & Bacon.

Hammill, D. D., Leigh, J. E., McNutt, G., & Larsen, S. C. (1981). A new definition of learning disabilities. *Learning Disability Quarterly, 4,* 336–342.

Haring, N. G. (1969). *Minimal brain dysfunction in children: Educational, medical, and health related services—Phase two of a three phase project.* Washington, DC: U.S. Department of Health, Education, and Welfare.

Harris, K. R., & Graham, S. (1992). *Helping young writers master the craft: Strategy instruction and self-regulation in the writing process.* Cambridge, MA: Brookline Books.

Heath, N. (1996). The emotional domain: Self-concept and depression in children with learning disabilities. In T. E. Scruggs & M. A. Mastropieri (Eds.), *Advances in learning and behavioral disabilities* (Vol. 10, Part A, pp. 47–75). Greenwich, CT: JAI Press.

Hendrickson, J. M., & Frank, A. R. (1993). Engagement and performance feedback: Enhancing the classroom achievement of students with mild mental disabilities. In R. A. Gable & S. F. Warren (Eds.), *Advances in mental retardation and developmental disabilities* (Vol. 5, pp. 11–47). London: Jessica Kingsley Publishers.

Hetherington, E. M., & Parke, R. D. (1986). *Child psychology: A contemporary viewpoint* (3rd ed.). New York: McGraw-Hill.

Hollingsworth, M., & Woodward, J. (1993). Integrated learning: Explicit strategies and their role in problem-solving instruction for students with learning disabilities. *Exceptional Children, 59,* 444–455.

Hulit, L. M., & Howard, M. R. (1993). *Born to talk.* New York: MacMillian.

Hunt, N. (1967). *The world of Nigel Hunt.* New York: Garrett Publications.

Hynd, G. W., Marshall, R., & Gonzalez, J. (1991). Learning disabilities and presumed central nervous system dysfunction. *Learning Disability Quarterly, 14,* 283–296.

Jacobson, J. W., & Mulick, J. A. (1996). *Manual on diagnosis and professional practice in mental retardation.* Washington, DC: American Psychological Association.

Jensen, A. (1989). The relationship between learning and intelligence. *Learning and Individual Differences, 1,* 37–62.

Jones, K. L., Smith, D. W., Ulleland, C. N., & Streissguth, A. P. (1973). Patterns of malformation in offspring of chronic alcoholic mothers. *The Lancet, 1*(1267), 1271.

Kail, R., & Leonard, L. B. (1986). Sources of word-finding problems in language-impaired children. In S. J. Ceci (Ed.), *Handbook of cognitive, social, and neuropsychological aspects of learning disabilities* (Vol. 1, pp. 185–202). Hillsdale, NJ: Lawrence Erlbaum.

Kauffman, J. M. (2001). *Characteristics of emotional and behavioral disorders of children and youth* (7th ed.). Upper Saddle River, NJ: Merrill/Prentice Hall.

Kavale, K. A. (1981). The relationship between auditory perceptual skills and reading ability: A meta-analysis. *Journal of Learning Disabilities, 14,* 539–546.

Kavale, K. A. (1987). Theoretical issues surrounding severe discrepancy. *Learning Disabilities Research, 3,* 12–20.

Kavale, K. A. (1995). Setting the record straight on learning disability and low achievement: The tortuous path of ideology. *Learning Disabilities Research & Practice, 10,* 145–152.

Kavale, K. A., & Forness, S. R. (1992). Learning difficulties and memory problems in mental retardation: A meta-analysis of theoretical perspectives. In T. E. Scruggs & M. A. Mastropieri (Eds.), *Advances in learning and behavioral disabilities* (Vol. 7, pp. 177–219). Greenwich, CT: JAI Press.

Kavale, K. A., & Forness, S. R. (1995). *The nature of learning disabilities.* Hillsdale, NJ: Lawrence Erlbaum.

Kavale, K. A., Forness, S. R., & Duncan, B. (1996). Defining emotional disturbance or behavioral disorders: Divergence or convergence. In T. E. Scruggs & M. A. Mastropieri (Eds.), *Advances in learning and behavioral disabilities* (Vol. 10, Part A, pp. 1–45). Greenwich, CT: JAI Press.

Kavale, K. A., Fuchs, D., & Scruggs, T. E. (1994). Setting the record straight on learning disability and low achievement: Implications for policymaking. *Learning Disabilities Research & Practice, 9,* 70–77.

Kavale, K. A., Mathur, S. R., Forness, S. R., Rutherford, R. B., Jr., & Quinn, M. M. (1997). Effectiveness of social skills training for students with behavior disorders: A meta-analysis. In T. E. Scruggs & M. A. Mastropieri (Eds.), *Advances in learning and behavioral disabilities* (Vol. 11, pp. 1–26). Greenwich, CT: JAI Press.

Keogh, B. K. (1994). A matrix of decision points in the measurement of learning disabilities. In G. R. Lyon (Ed.), *Frames of reference for the assessment of learning disabilities: New views on measurement issues* (pp. 15–26). Baltimore: Brookes Publishing.

Kirk, S. A. (1962). *Educating exceptional children.* Boston: Houghton Mifflin.

Korinek, L., & Polloway, E. A. (1993). Social skills: Review and implications for instruction for students with mild mental retardation. In R. A. Gable & S. F. Warren (Eds.), *Advances in mental retardation and developmental disabilities* (Vol. 5, pp. 71–97). London: Jessica Kingsley Publishers.

Lerner, J. (2000). *Learning disabilities: Theories, diagnosis, and teaching strategies* (8th ed.). Boston: Houghton-Mifflin.

Lewis, R. B. (1993). *Special education technology: Classroom applications.* Pacific Groves, CA: Brookes Publishing.

Liberman, I. Y., & Shankweiler, D. (1991). Phonology and beginning reading: A tutorial. In L. Reiben & C. A.

Perfetti (Eds.), *Learning to read: Basic research and its implications* (pp. 3017). Hillsdale, NJ: Lawrence Erlbaum.

Lloyd, J. W., Talbott, E., Tankersley, M., & Trent, S. C. (1993). Using cognitive-behavioral techniques to improve classroom performance of students with mild mental retardation. In R. A. Gable & S. F. Warren (Eds.), *Advances in mental retardation and developmental disabilities* (Vol. 5, pp. 99–116). London: Jessica Kingsley Publishers.

Lloyd, L. L., Fuller, D. R., & Arvidson, H. H. (1997). *Augmentative and alternative communication: A handbook of principles and practices.* Boston: Allyn & Bacon.

Lucangeli, D., Galderisi, D., & Cornoldi, C. (1995). Specific and general transfer effects following metamemory training. *Learning Disabilities Research & Practice, 10,* 11–21.

Lyon, G. R., Fletcher, J. M., Shaywitz, S. E., Shaywitz, B. A., Torgesen, J. K., Wood, F. B., Schulte, A., & Olson, R. (2001). Rethinking learning disabilities. In C. E. Finn, Jr., A. J. Rotherham, & C. R. Hokanson, Jr. (Eds.), *Rethinking special education for a new century* (pp. 259–287). Washington, DC: Thomas B. Fordham Foundation.

MacMillan, D. L. (1982). *Mental retardation in school and society* (2nd ed.). Boston: Little Brown.

MacMillan, D. L., Gresham, F. M., & Bocian, K. M. (1998). Discrepancy between definitions of learning disabilities and school practices: An empirical investigation. *Journal of Learning Disabilities, 31,* 314–326.

Marder, C., & D'Amico, R. (1992). *How well are youth with disabilities really doing? A comparison of youth with disabilities and youth in general* (SRI International, Contract 300-87-0054). Washington, DC: U.S. Department of Education, Office of Special Education Programs. (ERIC Document Reproduction Service No. 369233)

Margalit, M. (1993). Social skills and classroom behavior among adolescents with mild mental retardation. *American Journal on Mental Retardation, 97,* 685–691.

Martin, C. J., Boersma, F. J., & Bulgarella, R. (1968). Verbalization of associative strategies by normal and retarded children. *The Journal of General Psychology, 78,* 209–218.

Mastropieri, M. A. (1987). Statistical and psychometric issues surrounding severe discrepancy: A discussion. *Learning Disabilities Research, 30,* 29–31.

Mastropieri, M. A., & Scruggs, T. E. (1997). Best practices in promoting reading comprehension in students with learning disabilities. *Remedial and Special Education, 18,* 197–213.

Mastropieri, M. A., & Scruggs, T. E. (2002). Discrepancy models in the identification of learning disabilities: A response to Kavale. In R. Bradley, L. Danielson, & D. P. Hallahan (Eds.), *Identification of learning disabilities* (pp. 449–466). Mahwah, NJ: Lawrence Erlbaum.

Mastropieri, M. A., Scruggs, T. E., Bakken, J. P., & Whedon, C. (1996). Reading comprehension: A synthesis of research in learning disabilities. In T. E. Scruggs & M. A. Mastropieri (Eds.), *Advances in learning and behavioral disabilities* (Vol. 10, Part B, pp. 201–223). Greenwich, CT: JAI Press.

Mastropieri, M. A., Scruggs, T. E., & Butcher, K. (1997). How effective is inquiry learning for students with mild disabilities? *Journal of Special Education, 31,* 199–211.

Mather, N., & Roberts, R. (1994). Learning disabilities: A field in danger of extinction? *Learning Disabilities Research & Practice, 9,* 49–58.

McLeskey, J., & Waldron, N. (1990). The identification and characteristics of students with learning disabilities in Indiana. *Learning Disabilities Research, 5,* 72–78.

McPhail, J. C., & Stone, C. A. (1995). The self-concept of adolescents with learning disabilities: A review of literature and a call for theoretical elaboration. In T. E. Scruggs & M. A. Mastropieri (Eds.), *Advances in learning and behavioral disabilities* (Vol. 9, pp. 193–226). Greenwich, CT: JAI Press.

Meltzer, L. (1996). Strategic learning in students with learning disabilities: The role of self-awareness and self-perception. In T. E. Scruggs & M. A. Mastropieri (Eds.), *Advances in learning and behavioral disabilities* (Vol. 10, Part B, pp. 181–200). Greenwich, CT: JAI Press.

Mercer, C. D., & Snell, M. E. (1977). *Learning theory research in mental retardation: Implications for teaching.* Upper Saddle River, NJ: Merrill/Prentice Hall.

Merrill, K. W. (1990). Differentiating low achieving students and students with learning disabilities: An examination of performances on the Woodcock-Johnson psycho-educational battery. *The Journal of Special Education, 24,* 296–305.

Montague, M. (1995). Cognitive instruction and mathematics: Implications for students with learning disorders. *Focus on Learning Problems in Mathematics, 17,* 39–49.

Montague, M., & Applegate, B. (1993). Middle school students' mathematical problem solving: An analysis of think-aloud protocols. *Learning Disability Quarterly, 16,* 19–32.

Montague, M., Fiore, T., Hocutt, A., McKinney, J. D., & Harris, J. (1996). Interventions for students with attention deficit hyperactivity disorder: A review of the literature. In T. E. Scruggs & M. A. Mastropieri (Eds.), *Advances in learning and behavioral disabilities* (Vol. 10, Part B, pp. 23–50). Greenwich, CT: JAI Press.

Moore, G. P., & Hicks, D. M. (1994). Voice disorders. In G. H. Shames, E. H. Wiig, & W. A. Secord (Eds.), *Human communication disorders: An introduction* (4th ed., pp. 292–335). New York: Merrill/Macmillan.

National Joint Committee on Learning Disabilities. (1989, September 18). *Letter from NJCLD to member organizations: Topic: Modifications to the NJCLD definition of learning disabilities.* Washington, DC: Author.

O'Grady, W., Dobrovolsky, M., & Aronoff, M. (1997). *Contemporary linguistics: An introduction* (3rd ed.). New York: St. Martin's Press.

Olsen, R., Wise, B., Conners, F., Rack, J., & Fulker, D. (1989). Specific deficits in component reading and language skills: Genetic and environmental influences. *Journal of Learning Disabilities, 22,* 339–348.

Palson, K. (1986). *Essence of Kirstin.* Medfield, MA: Author.

Powers, T. V., & Neel, R. S. (1997). Aggressive behavior in children with behavioral disorders: A critical review of identification and intervention strategies. In T. E. Scruggs & M. A. Mastropieri (Eds.), *Advances in learning and behavioral disabilities* (Vol. 11, pp. 69–86). Greenwich, CT: JAI Press.

Riccio, C. A., Gonzalez, J. J., & Hynd, G. W. (1994). Attention deficit-hyperactivity disorder (ADHD) and learning disabilities. *Learning Disability Quarterly, 17,* 311–322.

Schalock, R. L., Stark, J. A., Snell, M. E., Coulter, D. L., Polloway, E. A., Luckasson, R., Reiss, S., & Spitalnik, D. M. (1994). The changing conception of mental retardation: Implications for the field. *Mental Retardation, 32,* 181–193.

Schargel, F. P., & Smink, J. (2001). *Strategies to help solve our school dropout problem.* Eye on Education.

Schiefelbusch, R. L., & Lloyd, L. L. (Eds.). (1974). *Language perspectives: Acquisition, retardation, and intervention.* Baltimore: University Park Press.

Schoenwald, S. K., Thomas, C. R., & Henggeler, S. W. (1996). Treatment of serious antisocial behavior. In T. E. Scruggs & M. A. Mastropieri (Eds.), *Advances in learning and behavioral disabilities* (Vol. 10, Part B, pp. 1–22). Greenwich, CT: JAI Press.

Schwartz, R. G. (1994). Phonological disorders. In G. H. Shames, E. H. Wiig, & W. A. Secord (Eds.), *Human communication disorders: An introduction* (4th ed., pp. 251–290). New York: Merrill/Macmillan.

Scott, M. S., & Greenfield, D. B. (1992). A comparison of normally achieving, learning disabled and mildly retarded students on a taxonomic information task. *Learning Disabilities Research & Practice, 7,* 59–67.

Scott, M. S., & Perou, R. (1994). Some observations on the impact of learning disabilities and mild mental retardation on the cognitive abilities of young school children. In T. E. Scruggs & M. A. Mastropieri (Eds.), *Advances in learning and behavioral disabilities* (Vol. 8, pp. 215–234). Greenwich, CT: JAI Press.

Scruggs, T. E., & Marsing, L. (1988). Teaching test-taking skills to behaviorally disordered students. *Behavioral Disorders, 13,* 240–244.

Scruggs, T. E., & Mastropieri, M. A. (1984). Issues in generalization: Implications for special education. *Psychology in the Schools, 21,* 397–403.

Scruggs, T. E., & Mastropieri, M. A. (1986). Academic characteristics of behaviorally disordered and learning disabled children. *Behavioral Disorders, 11,* 184–190.

Scruggs, T. E., & Mastropieri, M. A. (1992). Effective mainstreaming strategies for mildly handicapped students. *Elementary School Journal, 92,* 389–409.

Scruggs, T. E., & Mastropieri, M. A. (1993). Teaching students with mild mental retardation. In R. A. Gable & S. F. Warren (Eds.), *Advances in mental retardation and developmental disabilities* (Vol. 5, pp. 117–125). London: Jessica Kingsley Publishers.

Scruggs, T. E., & Mastropieri, M. A. (1994). The construction of scientific knowledge by students with mild disabilities. *Journal of Special Education, 28,* 307–321.

Scruggs, T. E., & Mastropieri, M. A. (1994–1995). Assessing students with learning disabilities: Current issues and future directions. *Diagnostique, 20,* 17–31.

Scruggs, T. E., & Mastropieri, M. A. (1995a). Reflections on "Scientific reasoning of students with mental retardation: Investigating preconceptions and conceptual change." *Exceptionality, 5,* 249–257.

Scruggs, T. E., & Mastropieri, M. A. (1995b). Science and mental retardation: An analysis of curriculum features and learner characteristics. *Science Education, 79,* 251–271.

Scruggs, T. E., & Mastropieri, M. A. (2002). On babies and bathwater: Addressing the problems of assessment and identification of learning disabilities. *Learning Disability Quarterly, 25,* 155–168.

Scruggs, T. E., Mastropieri, M. A., & Wolfe, S. (1995). Scientific reasoning of students with mental retardation: Investigating preconceptions and conceptual change. *Exceptionality, 5,* 223–244.

Shinn, M. R., Ysseldyke, J. E., Deno, S. L., & Tindal, G. A. (1986). A comparison of differences between students labelled learning disabled and low achieving on measures of classroom performance. *Journal of Learning Disabilities, 19,* 545–552.

Sinclair, M. F., Christenson, S. L., Evelo, D. L., & Hurley, C. M. (1998). Dropout prevention for youth with disabilities: Efficacy of a sustained school engagement procedure. *Exceptional Children, 65,* 7–21.

Spitz, H. H. (1973). The channel capacity of educable mental retardates. In D. K. Routh (Ed.), *The experimental psychology of mental retardation* (pp. 133–156). Chicago: Aldine.

Spitz, H. H. (1979). Beyond field theory in the study of mental deficiency. In N. R. Ellis (Ed.), *Handbook of mental deficiency, psychological theory, and research* (pp. 121–142). Hillsdale, NJ: Lawrence Erlbaum.

Steele, R. G., Forehand, R., Armistead, L., & Brody, G. (1995). Predicting alcohol and drug use in early adulthood: The role of internalizing and externalizing behavior problems in early adolescence. *American Journal of Orthopsychiatry, 65,* 380, 388.

Stuttering Foundation of America. (1997). *The child who stutters at school: Notes to the teacher.* Memphis: Author.

Sullivan, G. S., & Mastropieri, M. A. (1994). Social competence of individuals with learning disabilities. In T. E. Scruggs & M. A. Mastropieri (Eds.), *Advances in learning and behavioral disabilities* (Vol. 8, pp. 171–213). Greenwich, CT: JAI Press.

Swanson, H. L. (Ed.). (1987). *Advances in learning and behavioral disabilities: Memory and learning disabilities* (Supplement 2). Greenwich, CT: JAI Press.

Swanson, H. L., Cooney, J. B., & O'Shaughnessy, T. E. (1998). Learning disabilities and memory. In B. Y. L. Wong (Ed.), *Learning about learning disabilities* (2nd ed., pp. 107–162). San Diego, CA: Academic Press.

Talbott, E., & Coe, M. C. (1997). A developmental view of aggression and achievement. In T. E. Scruggs & M. A. Mastropieri (Eds.), *Advances in learning and behavioral disabilities* (Vol. 11, pp. 87–100). Greenwich, CT: JAI Press.

Thousand, J. S., & Villa, R. A. (1990). Strategies for educating students with severe disabilities within their local home schools and communities. *Focus on Exceptional Children, 23*(3), 1–24.

Tur-Kaspa, H., & Bryan, T. (1994). Social information-processing skills of students with learning disabilities. *Learning Disabilities Research & Practice, 9,* 12–23.

U.S. Department of Education. (2001). *To assure the free appropriate public education of all children with disabilities: Twenty-third annual report to Congress on the implementation of the Individuals with Disabilities Education Act.* Washington, DC: Author.

U.S. Department of Education, Office of Special Education Programs. (2002). *Specific learning disabilities: Finding common ground.* Washington, DC: Author.

Vaughn, S., & Hogan, A. (1994). The social competence of students with learning disabilities over time: A within-individual examination. *Journal of Learning Disabilities, 27,* 292–303.

Walker, H. M., Colvin, G., & Ramsey, E. (1995). *Antisocial behavior in school: Strategies and best practices.* Pacific Grove, CA: Brooks/Cole.

Whitman, T. L. (1990). Self-regulation and mental retardation. *American Journal on Mental Retardation, 94,* 347–362.

Wilson, L. R. (1985). Large-scale learning disability identification: The reprieve of a concept. *Exceptional Children, 52,* 44–51.

Wilson, V. L. (1987). Statistical and psychometric issues surrounding severe discrepancy. *Learning Disabilities Research, 3,* 24–28.

Wolraich, M. L. (1983). Hydrocephalus. In J. A. Blackman (Ed.), *Medical aspects of developmental disabilities in children birth to three* (pp. 137–141). Iowa City: University of Iowa Press.

Woodward, J. (1994). Effects of curriculum discourse style on eighth graders' recall and problem solving in earth science. *Elementary School Journal, 94,* 299–314.

Woodward, J., Baxter, J., & Scheel, C. (1997). It's what you take for granted when you take nothing for granted: The problems with general principles of instructional design. In T. E. Scruggs & M. A. Mastropieri (Eds.), *Advances in*

learning and behavioral disabilities (Vol. 11, pp. 199–234). Greenwich, CT: JAI Press.

Ysseldyke, J. E., Algozzine, B., & Epps, S. (1983). A logical and empirical analysis of current practice in classifying students as handicapped. *Exceptional Children, 50,* 160–166.

Ysseldyke, J. E., Algozzine, B., Shinn, M. R., & McGue, M. (1982). Similarities and differences between low achievers and students classified as learning disabled. *Journal of Special Education, 16,* 73–85.

Zeaman, D., & House, B. J. (1963). The role of attention in retardate discrimination learning. In N. R. Ellis (Ed.), *Handbook of mental deficiency: Psychological theory and research* (pp. 159–263). Hillsdale, NJ: Lawrence Erlbaum.

Zeaman, D., & House, B. J. (1979). A review of attention theory. In N. R. Ellis (Ed.), *Handbook of mental deficiency, psychological theory, and research* (pp. 63–120). Hillsdale, NJ: Lawrence Erlbaum.

Chapter 4

AAMR Ad Hoc Committee on Terminology and Classification. (1992). *Mental retardation: Definition, classification, and systems of support.* Washington, DC: American Association on Mental Retardation.

American Academy of Child and Adolescent Psychiatry. (2000). *No. 29. Psychiatric medication for children and adolescents Part II: Types of medications.* Retrieved March 2, 2003, from http://www.aacap.org/publications/factsfam/29.htm.

American Printing House for the Blind. (1989). *Instructional aids, tools, and supplies for people who are visually handicapped.* Louisville, KY: Author.

American Psychiatric Association (APA). (1994). *Diagnostic and statistical manual of mental disorders: DSM-IV* (4th ed.). Washington, DC: American Psychiatric Association.

Beirne–Smith, M., Ittenbach, R., & Patton, J. (1998). *Mental retardation* (5th ed.). Upper Saddle River, NJ: Merrill/Prentice Hall.

Beirne-Smith, M., Ittenbach R., & Patton, J. (2001). *Mental retardation* (6th ed.). Upper Saddle River, NJ: Merrill/Prentice Hall.

Berla, E. P. (1981). Tactile scanning and memory for a spatial display by blind students. *Journal of Special Education, 15,* 341–350.

Bigelow, A. (1991). Spatial mapping of familiar locations in blind children. *Journal of Visual Impairments and Blindness, 85*(3), 113–117.

Bigge, J. L. (1991) *Teaching individuals with physical and multiple disabilities* (3rd ed.). Upper Saddle River, NJ: Merrill/Prentice Hall.

Biklen, D. (1990). Communication unbound: Autism and praxis. *Harvard Educational Review, 60,* 291–314.

Bleck, E. E. (1975a). Cerebral palsy. In E. E. Bleck & D. A. Nagel (Eds.), *Physically handicapped children—A medical atlas for teachers* (pp. 37–99). New York: Grune & Stratton.

Bleck, E. E. (1975b). Myelomeningocele, meningocele, spina bifida. In E. E. Bleck & D. A. Nagel (Eds.), *Physically handicapped children—A medical atlas for teachers* (pp. 181–192). New York: Grune & Stratton.

Bleck, E. E., & Nagel, D. A. (1975). *Physically handicapped children—A medical atlas for teachers.* New York: Grune & Stratton.

Bondy, A. (1996). What parents can expect from public school programs. In C. Maurice, G. Green, & S. C. Luce (Eds.), *Behavioral interventions for young children with autism* (pp. 323–330). Austin, TX: Pro-Ed.

Braman, B. J., Brady, M. P., Linehan, S. L., & Williams, R. E. (1995). Facilitated communication for children with autism: An examination of face validity. *Behavioral Disorders, 21*(1), 110–116.

Briggs, G. (2001). *Drugs in pregnancy and lactation* (6th ed.). Baltimore: Williams and Wilkins.

Brown, L. W. (1997). Seizure disorders. In M. L. Batshaw (Ed.), *Children with disabilities* (4th ed., pp. 553–593). Baltimore: Paul Brookes.

Burgess, D. M., & Streissguth, A. P. (1992). Fetal alcohol syndrome and fetal alcohol effects: Principles for educators. *Phi Delta Kappan, 74,* 24–29.

Byrom, E., & Katz, G. (Eds.). (1991). *HIV prevention and AIDS education: Resources for special educators.* Reston, VA: Council for Exceptional Children.

Caldwell, T. H., Sirvis, B., Todaro, A. W., & Accouloumre, D. S. (1991). *Special health care in the school.* Reston, VA: The Council for Exceptional Children.

Caldwell, T. H., Todaro, A. W., & Gates, A. J. (1991). Special health care needs. In J. L. Bigge (Ed.), *Teaching individuals with physical and multiple disabilities* (3rd ed., pp. 50–74.). Upper Saddle River, NJ: Merrill/Prentice Hall.

Christiansen, R. O. (1975). Diabetes. In E. E. Bleck & D. A. Nagel (Eds.), *Physically handicapped children: A medical atlas for teachers* (pp. 123–131). New York: Grune & Stratton.

Clayman, C. B. (1994). *The American Medical Association family medical guide.* New York: Random House.

Cohen, L. H. (1994). *Train go sorry: Inside a deaf world.* Boston: Houghton Mifflin.

Cohen, S. D., Joyce, C. M., Rhoades, K. W., & Welks, D. M. (1987). Educational programming for head injured students. In M. Ylvisaker (Ed.), *Head injury rehabilitation: Children and adolescents* (pp. 383–409). San Diego: College Hill.

Cronin, B. J., & King, S. R. (1990). The development of the Descriptive Video Service. *Journal of Visual Impairment and Blindness, 86*(12), 503–506.

Daneman, D., & Frank, M. (1996). The student with diabetes mellitus. In R. H. A. Haslam & P. J. Valletutti (Eds.), *Medical problems in the classroom: The teacher's role in diagnosis and management* (3rd ed., pp. 97–113). Austin, TX: Pro-Ed.

Downing, J. E., Ryndak, D. L., & Clark, D. (2000). Paraeducators in inclusive classrooms: Their own

perceptions. *Remedial and Special Education, 21,* 171–181.

Engel, J. (1995). Concepts of epilepsy. *Epilepsia, 36,* 23–29.

Federal Interagency Head Injury Task Force. (1990). *The National Head Injury Foundation.* [Pamphlet]. Washington, DC: Author.

Feldman, W. (1996). Chronic illness in children. In R. H. A. Haslam & P. J. Valletutti (Eds.), *Medical problems in the classroom: The teacher's role in diagnosis and management* (3rd ed., pp. 115–124). Austin, TX: Pro-Ed.

Forest, M., & Lusthaus, E. (1989a). Circles and maps. In S. Stainback, W. Stainback, & M. Forest (Eds.), *Educating all students in the mainstream of regular education* (pp. 43–57). Baltimore: Paul Brookes.

Forest, M., & Lusthaus, E. (1989b). Promoting educational equity for all students. In S. Stainback, W. Stainback, & M. Forest (Eds.), *Educating all students in the mainstream of regular education* (pp. 47–49). Baltimore: Paul Brookes.

Frith, G. H. (1982). *The role of the special education paraprofessional: An introductory text.* Springfield, IL: Charles C. Thomas.

Giangreco, M. F., Broer, S. M., & Edelman, S. W. (1999). The tip of the iceberg: Determining whether paraprofessional support is needed for students with disabilities in general education settings. *The Journal of the Association for Persons with Severe Handicaps, 24,* 281–291.

Giangreco, M. F., Cloninger, C., & Iverson, V. (1990). *Cayuga-Onondaga assessment for children with handicaps—Version 6.0.* Stillwater: National Clearinghouse of Rehabilitation Training Materials at Oklahoma State University.

Giangreco, M. F., Edelman, S., & Dennis, R. (1991). Common professional practices that interfere with integrated delivery of services. *Remedial and Special Education, 12*(2), 16–24.

Graetz, J. (2003). *Promoting social behaviors for adolescents with autism with social stories.* Unpublished doctoral dissertation, George Mason University, Fairfax, VA.

Grandin, T. (1995). *Thinking in pictures: And other reports of my life with autism.* New York: Doubleday.

Grandin, T., & Scariano, M. (1986). *Emergence: Labelled autistic.* California: Arena Navato.

Gray, C., & Garand, J. (1993). Social stories: Improving responses of students with autism with accurate social information. *Focus on Autistic Behavior, 8,* 1–10.

Griffin, H. C., & Gerber, P. J. (1982). Tactile development and its implication for the development of blind children. *Education of the Visually Handicapped, 13,* 116–123.

Griffith, H. W., & Moore, S. (2002). *Complete guide to prescription and nonprescription drugs.* New York: Penguin Putnam.

Hack, S., & Klee, B. (2001). *Guide to psychiatric medications for children and adolescents.* New York University Child Study Center. Retrieved March 2,

2003, from http://www.aboutourkids.org/articles/guidetopsychmeds.html.

Hallahan, D. P., & Kauffman, J. M. (2003). *Exceptional children: Introduction to special education* (9th ed.). Boston: Allyn & Bacon.

Hallenbeck, M. J., & McMaster, D. (1991). Disability simulation. *Teaching Exceptional Children, 23*(3), 12–15.

Harder, J. (1996). Orthopedic problems and sports injuries in children. In R. H. A. Haslam & P. J. Valletutti (Eds.), *Medical problems in the classroom: The teacher's role in diagnosis and management* (3rd ed., pp. 261–300). Austin, TX: Pro-Ed.

Haslam, R. H. A. (1996). Common neurologic disorders in children. In R. H. A. Haslam & P. J. Valletutti (1996), *Medical problems in the classroom: The teacher's role in diagnosis and management* (3rd ed.). Austin, TX: Pro-Ed.

Haslam, R. H. A., & Valletutti, P. J. (1996). *Medical problems in the classroom: The teacher's role in diagnosis and management* (3rd ed.). Austin, TX: Pro-Ed.

Heward, W. L. (1999). *Exceptional children: An introduction to special education* (6th ed.). Upper Saddle River, NJ: Merrill/Prentice Hall.

Hull, J. M. (1990). *Touching the rock.* New York: Pantheon Books.

Jones, C., & Lopez, R. (1988). *Direct and indirect effects on infant of maternal drug use.* Rockville, MD: NIDA.

Jones, K. L., Smith, D. W., Ulleland, C. N., & Streissguth, A. P. (1973). Patterns of malformation in offspring of chronic alcoholic mothers. *The Lancet, 1*(1267), 1271.

Kamps, D. M., Leonard, B., Potucek, J., & Garrison-Harrell, L. (1995). Cooperative learning groups in reading: An integration strategy for students with autism and general classroom peers. *Behavioral Disorders, 21*(1), 89–109.

Kanner, L. (1943). Autistic disturbances of affective contact. *Nervous Child, 2,* 217–250.

Kelly, T. E. (1996). The role of genetic mechanisms in childhood disabilities. In R. H. A. Haslam & P. J. Valletutti (Eds.), *Medical problems in the classroom: The teacher's role in diagnosis and management* (3rd ed., pp. 125–160). Austin, TX: Pro-Ed.

Kerr, M. M., & Nelson, C. M. (2002). *Strategies for addressing behavior problems in the classroom* (4th ed.). Upper Saddle River, NJ: Merrill/Prentice Hall.

Leppert, M. O., & Capute, A. J. (1996). Cerebral palsy and associated dysfunctions. In R. H. A. Haslam & P. J. Valletutti (Eds.), *Medical problems in the classroom: The teacher's role in diagnosis and management* (3rd ed., pp. 341–360). Austin, TX: Pro-Ed.

Lindley, L. (1990, August). Defining TASH: A mission statement. *TASH Newsletter, 16*(8), 1.

Lovaas, O. I., & Newsom, C. D. (1976). Behavior modification with psychotic children. In H. Leitenberg (Ed.), *Handbook of behavior modification and therapy* (pp. 303–360). Upper Saddle River, NJ: Merrill/Prentice Hall.

Luterman, D. M. (1986). *Deafness in perspective.* San Diego: College Hill Press.

Luterman, D. M. (1996). *Counseling the communicatively disordered and their families* (3rd ed.). Austin, TX: Pro-Ed.

McDougle, C. J. (1998). NIH grant awarded for research in autism. *Reporter: Indiana Resource Center for Autism, 3*(2), 9.

Meadow-Orlans, K. P. (1990). Research on developmental aspects of deafness. In D. F. Moores & K. P. Meadow-Orlans (Eds.), *Educational and developmental aspects of deafness* (pp. 283–298). Washington, DC: Gallaudet University Press.

Michael, R. J. (1992). Seizures: Teacher observations and record keeping. *Intervention in School and Clinic, 27,* 212.

Michaud, L., Duhaime, A., & Lazar, M. F. (1997). Traumatic brain injury. In M. L. Batshaw (Ed.), *Children with disabilities* (4th ed., pp. 595–617). Baltimore: Paul Brookes.

Mitchell, D. C. (1983). Spina bifida. In J. Umbreit (Ed.), *Physical disabilities and other health impairments: An introduction.* Upper Saddle River, NJ: Merrill/Prentice Hall.

Myles, B. S., Simpson, R. L., & Smith, S. M. (1996). Impact of facilitated communication combined with direct instruction on academic performance of individuals with autism. *Focus on Autism and Other Developmental Disabilities, 11*(1), 37–44.

National Head Injury Foundation. (1985). *Questions about traumatic head injury.* [Brochure]. Southboro, MA: Author.

Obiakor, F. E., Mehring, T. A., & Schwenn, J. O. (1997). *Disruption, disaster, and death: Helping students deal with crises.* Reston, VA: Council for Exceptional Children.

Ogletree, B. T. (1998). The communicative context of autism. In R. L. Simpson & B. S. Myles (Eds.), *Educating children and youth with autism: Strategies for effective practice* (pp. 141–172). Austin, TX: Pro-Ed.

Padden, C., & Humphries, T. (1988). *Deaf in America: Voices from a culture.* Cambridge, MA: Harvard University Press.

Paul, P. V., & Quigley, S. P. (1990). *Education and deafness.* New York: Longman.

Paul, P. V., & Quigley, S. P. (1994). *Language and deafness* (2nd ed.). San Diego: Singular Publishing Group.

Petersen, S., & Straub, R. L. (1992). *School crisis survival guide.* West Nyack, NY: Center for Applied Research in Education.

Pipitone, P. (1992). Acquired pediatric brain damage: Diverse causes. *Headlines, 3*(5), 5.

Plumb, I. J., & Brown, D. C. (1990). SPAN: Special peer action network. *Teaching Exceptional Children, 56,* 291–304.

Reagan, T. (1990). Cultural considerations in the education of deaf children. In D. F. Moores & K. P. Meadows-Orlans (Eds.), *Educational and developmental aspects of deafness* (pp. 73–84). Washington, DC: Gallaudet University Press.

Rimland, B. (1992a). A facilitated communication "horror story." *Autism Research Review, 6*(1), 1, 7.

Rimland, B. (1992b). Facilitated communication: Problems, puzzles and paradoxes: Six challenges for researchers. *Autism Research Review, 5*(4), 3.

Rimland, B. (1993). Facilitated communication under siege. *Autism Research Review International, 7*(1), 2, 7.

Ritvo, E. R., & Freeman, B. J. (1978). National Society of Autistic Children definition of the syndrome autism. *Journal of Autism and Developmental Disorders, 8,* 162–170.

Ross, D. B., & Koening, A. J. (1991). A cognitive approach to reducing stereotypic head rocking. *Journal of Visual Impairment & Blindness, 85*(1), 17–19.

Ruble, L. A., & Dalrymple, N. J. (1996). An alternative view of outcome in autism. *Focus on Autism and Other Developmental Disabilities, 11*(1), 3–14.

Rudigier, A. F., Crocker, A. C., & Cohen, H. J. (1990). The dilemma of childhood: HIV infection. *Children Today, 19,* 26–29.

Ryan, L., Ehrlich, S., & Finnegan, L. (1987). Cocaine abuse in pregnancy: Effects in the fetus and newborn. *Neurotoxicology and Tetralogy, 9,* 295–299.

Sacks, O. (1993–1994) (December 27, 1993/January 3, 1994). A neurologist's notebook: An anthropologist on Mars. *The New Yorker, LXIX*(44), 106–125.

Sacks, S. Z., Rosen, S., & Gaylord-Ross, R. (1990). Visual impairment. In N. Haring & L. McCormick (Eds.), *Exceptional children and youth* (5th ed., pp. 403–446). Upper Saddle River, NJ: Merrill/Prentice Hall.

Sailor, W., Gee, K., & Karasoff, P. (1993). Full inclusion and school restructuring. In M. E. Snell (Ed.), *Instruction of students with severe disabilities* (pp. 1–30). Upper Saddle River, NJ: Merrill/Prentice Hall.

Salend, S. J., & Longo, M. (1994). The roles of the education interpreter in mainstream settings. *Teaching Exceptional Children, 26*(4), 22–28.

Sapon-Shevin, M. (1992). Celebrating diversity, creating community: Curriculum that honors and builds on differences. In S. Stainback & W. Stainback (Eds.), *Curriculum considerations in inclusive classrooms: Facilitating learning for all students.* Baltimore: Paul Brookes.

Scadden, L. (1987). Implications of the research and development of modern technology on the education of the blind and visually handicapped students. In M. C. Wang, M. C. Reynolds, & H. J. Walberg (Eds.), *Handbook of special education: Research and practice, learner characteristics and adaptive education* (Vol. 1, pp. 203–222). Oxford, England: Pergamon Press.

Schwartz, I. S., Billingsley, F. F., & McBride, B. M. (1998). Including children with autism in preschools: Strategies that work. *Young Exceptional Children, 1*(2), 19–26.

Simpson, R. L., & Myles, B. S. (1995). Facilitated communication and children with disabilities: An enigma in search of a perspective. *Focus on Exceptional Children, 27*(9), 1–16.

Simpson, R. L., & Myles, B. S. (1998). Controversial therapies and interventions with children and youth with autism. In R. L. Simpson & B. S. Myles (Eds.), *Educating children and youth with autism: Strategies for effective practice* (pp. 315–331). Austin, TX: Pro-Ed.

Simpson, R.L., & Zionts, P. (2000). *Autism: Information and resources for professionals and parents* (2nd ed.). Austin, TX: Pro-Ed.

Snell, M. E. (Ed.). (1993). *Instruction of students with severe disabilities.* Upper Saddle River, NJ: Merrill/Prentice Hall.

Snell, M. E., & Brown, F. (1993). Instructional planning and implementation. In M. E. Snell (Ed.), *Instruction of students with severe disabilities* (pp. 99–151). Upper Saddle River, NJ: Merrill/Prentice Hall.

Spiegel, G. L., Cutler, S. K., & Yetter, C. E. (1996). What every teacher should know about epilepsy. *Intervention in School and Clinic, 32*(1), 34–38.

Stainback, S., & Stainback, W. (1992). *Curriculum consideration in inclusive classrooms: Facilitating learning of all students.* Baltimore: Paul Brookes.

Stewart, D. A., & Kluwin, T. N. (2001). *Teaching deaf and hard of hearing students: Content, strategies, and curriculum.* Needham Heights, MA: Allyn & Bacon.

Thomas, J. (1991). Not disabled—just deaf. *Let's Talk, 33*(20), 30.

Turnbull, A. P., & Morningstar, M. E. (1993). Family and professional interaction. In M. E. Snell (Ed.), *Instruction of students with severe disabilities* (pp. 31–60). Upper Saddle River, NJ: Merrill/Prentice Hall.

Umbreit, J., & Blair, K. (1996). The effects of preference, choice, and attention on problem behavior at school. *Education and Training in Mental Retardation and Developmental Disabilities, 31,* 151–161.

U.S. Department of Education. (1999). *The Individuals with Disabilities Act Amendments of 1997. Final Regulations.* Washington, DC: Author.

U.S. Department of Education. (2001). *Twenty-third annual report to Congress on the implementation of the Individuals with Disabilities Education Act.* Washington, DC: Author.

Valletutti, P. J. (1996). The crucial role of the teacher. In R. H. A. Haslam & P. J. Valletutti (Eds.), *Medical problems in the classroom: The teacher's role in diagnosis and management* (3rd ed., pp. 1–26). Austin, TX: Pro-Ed.

Vincent, L. J., Poulsen, M. K., Cole, C. K., Woodruff, G., & Griffith, D. R. (1991). *Born substance exposed, educationally vulnerable.* Reston, VA: Council for Exceptional Children.

Warren, D. H. (1984). *Blindness and early childhood development* (2nd ed.). New York: American Foundation for the Blind.

Ylvisaker, M., & Feeney, T. J. (1998). School reentry after traumatic brain injury. In M. Ylvisaker (Ed.), *Traumatic brain injury rehabilitation: Children and adolescents*

(2nd ed., pp. 369–387). Boston: Butterworth-Heinemann.

Chapter 5

American Psychiatric Association (APA). (1994). *Diagnostic and statistical manual of mental disorders: DSM–IV* (4th ed.). Washington, DC: American Psychiatric Association.

Anderson, M. G., & Webb-Johnson, G. (1995). Cultural contexts, the seriously emotionally disturbed classification, and African American learners. In B. A. Ford, F. E. Obiakor, & J. M. Patton (Eds.), *Effective education of African American exceptional learners: New perspectives* (pp. 151–188). Austin, TX: Pro-Ed.

Artiles, A. J., & Trent, S. C. (1994). Overrepresentation of minority students in special education: A continuing debate. *The Journal of Special Education, 27,* 410–437.

Artiles, A. J., & Zamora-Durán, G. (1997). *Reducing disproportionate representation of culturally diverse students in special and gifted education.* Reston, VA: Council for Exceptional Children.

Baca, L. M., & Almanza, E. (1991). *Language minority students with disabilities.* Reston, VA: Council for Exceptional Children.

Baca, L. M., & Cervantes, H. T. (1998). *The bilingual special education interface* (3rd ed.). Upper Saddle River, NJ: Merrill/Prentice Hall.

Barkley, R. A. (1990). *Attention deficit hyperactivity disorder: A handbook for diagnosis and treatment.* New York: Guilford Press.

Barkley, R. A. (1998). *Attention deficit hyperactivity disorder: A handbook for diagnosis and treatment* (2nd ed.). New York: Guilford Press.

Barkley, R. A. (2000). *Taking charge of ADHD: The complete, authoritative guide for parents.* New York: Guilford Press.

Bassuk, F., & Rubin, L. (1987). Homeless children: A neglected population. *American Journal of Orthopsychiatry, 57,* 279–286.

Bender, W. N. (1997). *Understanding ADHD: A practical guide for teachers and parents.* Upper Saddle River, NJ: Merrill/Prentice Hall.

Bennett, C. I. (1999). *Multicultural education: Theory and practice* (4th ed.). Boston: Allyn & Bacon.

Biederman, J., Faranone, S. V., Keenan, K., Benjamin, J., Krifcher, B., Moore, C., Sprich-Buckminster, S., Ugaglia, K., Jellinek, M. S., Steingard, R., Spencer, T., Norman, D., Kolodny, R., Kraus, I., Perrin, J., Keller, M. B., & Tsuang, M. T. (1992). Further evidence for family-genetic risk factors in attention deficit hyperactivity disorder. *Archives of General Psychiatry, 48,* 633–642.

Bireley, M. (1995). Identifying high ability/high achievement giftedness. In J. L. Genshaft, M. Bireley, & C. L. Hollinger (Eds.), *Serving gifted and talented students: A resource for school personnel* (pp. 49–65). Austin, TX: Pro-Ed.

Bryen, D. N. (1974). *Special education and the linguistically diverse child.* Reston, VA: Council for Exceptional Children.

Burns, S. (1991). Homelessness demographics, causes, and trends. *Homewords, 3*(4), 1–3.

Caplan, P., & Dinardo, L. (1986). Is there a relationship between child abuse and learning disability? *Canadian Journal of Behavioral Science, 18,* 367–380.

Cavazos, L. F. (1990, March). U.S. Department of Education report to Congress on the education for homeless children and youth program for the period October 1, 1988 through September 30, 1989.

Cherkes-Julkowski, M., Sharp. S., & Stolzenberg, J. (1997). *Rethinking attention deficit disorders.* Cambridge, MA: Brookline Books.

Chinn, P. C., & Hughes, S. (1987). Representation of minority students in special education classes. *Remedial and Special Education, 8*(4), 41–46.

Clark, B. (2001). *Growing up gifted* (6th ed.). Upper Saddle River, NJ: Merrill/Prentice Hall.

Connors, C. K. (1980). *Food additives and hyperactive children.* New York: Plenum Press.

Council for Exceptional Children (CEC). (1992). *Children with ADD: A shared responsibility.* Reston, VA: Council for Exceptional Children.

Crenshaw, T. M., Kavale, K. A., Forness, S. R., & Reeve, R. E. (1999). Attention deficit hyperactivity disorder and the efficacy of stimulant medication: A meta-analysis. In T. E. Scruggs & M. A. Mastropieri (Eds.), *Advances in learning and behavioral disabilities* (Vol. 13, pp. 135–165). Greenwich, CT: JAI.

Cummins, J. (1984). *Bilingualism and special education: Issues in assessment and pedagogy.* San Diego, CA: College Hill Press.

Davis, G. A. (1995). Identifying the creatively gifted. In J. L. Genshaft, M. Bireley, & C. L. Hollinger (Eds.), *Serving gifted and talented students: A resource for school personnel* (pp. 67–82). Austin, TX: Pro-Ed.

Davis, G. A., & Rimm, S. B. (1989). *Education of the gifted and talented* (2nd ed.). Englewood Cliffs, NJ: Prentice Hall.

de Melendez, W. R., & Ostertag, V. (1997). *Teaching young children in multicultural classrooms: Issues, concepts, and strategies.* New York: Delmar Publishers.

Diamond, L. J., & Jaudes, P. K. (1983). Child abuse in a cerebral-palsied population. *Developmental Medicine and Child Neurology, 25,* 169–174.

Diaz-Rico, L. T., & Weed, K. Z. (1995). *The crosscultural, language, and academic development handbook: A complete K–12 reference guide.* Boston: Allyn & Bacon.

Donovan, S., & Cross, C. (Eds.). (2002). *Minority students in special and gifted education.* Washington, DC: National Research Council.

Eighteenth annual report affirms CEC's policy on inclusive setting. (1997). *CEC Today, 3*(7), 1, 4–5.

Feingold, B. (1975). *Why your child is hyperactive.* New York: Random House.

Feldhusen, J. F. (1992). *Talent identification and development in education (TIDE)*. Sarasota, FL: Center for Creative Learning.

Feldhusen, J. F., & Moon, S. (1995). The educational continuum and delivery of services. In J. L. Genshaft, M. Bireley, & C. L. Hollinger (Eds.), *Serving gifted and talented students: A resource for school personnel* (pp. 103–121). Austin, TX: Pro-Ed.

Fuchs, D. (1987). Effects of examiner familiarity on LD and MR students' language performance. *Remedial and Special Education, 8*(4), 47–52.

Fuchs, D., & Fuchs, L. S. (1989). Effects of examiner familiarity on Black, Caucasian, and Hispanic children: A meta-analysis. *Exceptional Children, 55,* 303–308.

Fuchs, L. S., & Fuchs, D. (1984). Examiner accuracy during protocol completion. *Journal of Psychoeducational Assessment, 2,* 101–108.

Gallagher, J. J., & Gallagher, S. A. (1994). *Teaching the gifted child* (4th ed.). Boston: Allyn & Bacon.

Garbarino, J. (1987). What can the school do on behalf of the psychologically maltreated child and the community? *School Psychology Review, 16,* 181–187.

Garbarino, J., Brookhouser, P. E., & Authier, K. J. (Eds.). (1987). *Special children special risks: The maltreatment of children with disabilities*. Hawthorn, NY: Aldinede Gruyter.

Gardner, D. P. (1983). *A nation at risk: The imperative for education reform*. Washington, DC: U.S. Department of Education.

Gardner, H. (1983). *Frames of mind: The theory of multiple intelligences*. New York: Basic Books.

Gardner, H. (1999). *Intelligence reframed: Multiple intelligences for the 21st century*. New York: Basic Books.

Gardner, H., & Hatch, T. (1989). Multiple intelligences go to school: Educational implications of the theory of multiple intelligences. *Educational Researcher, 18*(8), 4–9.

Genshaft, J. L., Bireley, M., & Hollinger, C. L. (Eds.). (1995). *Serving gifted and talented students: A resource for school personnel*. Austin, TX: Pro-Ed.

Germinario, V., Cervalli, J., & Ogden, E. H. (1992). *All children successful: Real answers for helping at risk elementary students*. Lancaster, PA: Technomic.

Gregory, D. A., Starnes, W. T., & Blaylock, A. W. (1988). Finding and nurturing potential giftedness among Black and Hispanic students. In A. A. Ortiz & B. A. Ramirez (Eds.), *Schools and the culturally diverse exceptional student: Promising practices and future directions* (pp. 76–85). Reston, VA: Council for Exceptional Children.

Grossman, H. (1995). *Teaching in a diverse society*. Boston: Allyn & Bacon.

Grossman, R. (1997, July 6). What is an American. *Chicago Tribune Magazine*, pp. 11–16, 21. Sunday July 6, 1997, Chicago Tribune.

Guetzloe, E. C. (1991). *Depression and suicide: Special education students at risk*. Reston, VA: Council for Exceptional Children.

Hallahan, D. P., & Cottone, E. A. (1997). Attention deficit hyperactivity disorder. In T. E. Scruggs & M. A. Mastropieri (Eds.), *Advances in learning and behavioral disorders* (Vol. 11, pp. 27–67). Greenwich, CT: JAI Press.

Hallahan, D. P., & Kauffman, J. M. (2003). *Exceptional learners: Introduction to special education* (9th ed.). Boston: Allyn & Bacon.

Hardman, M. L., Drew, C. J., Egan, M. W., & Wolf, B. (1993). *Human exceptionality: Society, school, and family* (4th ed.). Boston: Allyn & Bacon.

Harry, B. (1992). *Cultural diversity, families, and the special education system*. New York: Teachers College Press.

Harry, B. (1994). *The disproportionate representation of minority students in special education*. Alexandria, VA: National Association of State Directors of Special Education.

Harry, B. (1995). African American families. In B. A. Ford, F. E. Obiakor, & J. M. Patton (Eds.), *Effective education of African American exceptional learners* (pp. 211–234). Austin, TX: Pro-Ed.

Heflin, L. J., & Rudy, K. (1991). *Homeless and in need of special education*. Reston, VA: Council for Exceptional Children.

Helge, D. (1991). *Rural, exceptional, at risk*. Reston, VA: Council for Exceptional Children.

Heward, W. L., & Orlansky, M. D. (1992). *Exceptional children* (4th ed.). New York: Merrill/MacMillan.

Hollinger, C. (1995). Stress as a function of gender: Special needs of gifted girls and women. In J. L. Genshaft, M. Bireley, & C. L. Hollinger (Eds.), *Serving gifted and talented students: A resource for school personnel* (pp. 269–283). Austin, TX: Pro-Ed.

Hynd, G. W., Marshall, R., & Gonzales, J. (1991). Learning disabilities and presumed central nervous system dysfunction. *Learning Disability Quarterly, 14,* 283–296.

Jones, C. B. (1991). *Sourcebook for children with attention deficit disorder: A management guide for early childhood professionals and parents*. Tucson, AZ: Communication Skill Builders, Inc.

Jones, E. D., & Southern, W. T. (1991). Conclusions about acceleration: Echoes of debate. In W. T. Southern & E. D. Jones (Eds.), *The academic acceleration of gifted children* (pp. 223–228). New York: Teachers College Press.

Kauffman, J. M. (2001). *Characteristics of emotional and behavioral disorders of children and youth* (7th ed.). Upper Saddle River, NJ: Merrill/Prentice Hall.

Kavale, K. A. (1982). The efficacy of stimulant drug treatment for hyperactivity: A meta-analysis. *Journal of Learning Disabilities, 15,* 280–289.

Kerr, M. M., & Nelson, C. M. (2002). *Strategies for managing behavior problems in the classroom* (4th ed.). Upper Saddle River, NJ: Merrill/Prentice Hall.

Kitano, M. K. (1991). A multicultural educational perspective on serving culturally diverse gifted. *Journal for the Education of the Gifted, 15*(1), 4–19.

Klein, M., & Stern, L. (1971). Low birth weight and the battered child syndrome. *American Journal of Disabled Children, 122,* 15–18.

Kline, D. F. (1977). *Child abuse and neglect: A primer for school personnel.* Reston, VA: Council for Exceptional Children.

Knapp, M. S., & Turnbull, B. J. (1991). Alternatives to conventional wisdom. In M. S. Knapp & P. M. Shields (Eds.), *Better schooling for children of poverty: Alternatives to conventional wisdom* (pp. 329–353). California: McCutchen Publishing Corporation.

Kollar, J. L. (1993). *Multicultural bibliography.* Huntington Beach, CA: Teacher Created Materials.

Leone, P. E. (1991). *Alcohol and other drugs: Use, abuse, and disabilities.* Reston, VA: Council for Exceptional Children.

Lombardi, T. P., Odell, K. S., & Novotny, D. E. (1990). Special education and students at risk: Findings from a national study. *Remedial and Special Education, 12,* 52–62.

Lynch, E. W. (1992). Developing cross-cultural competence. In E. W. Lynch & M. J. Hanson (Eds.), *Developing cross-cultural competence* (pp. 35–59). Baltimore: Brookes Publishing.

Maag, J. W., & Reid, R. (1994). Attention deficit hyperactivity disorder: A functional approach to assessment and treatment. *Behavioral Disorders, 20,* 5–23.

MacMillan, D. L. (1991). *Hidden youth: Dropouts from special education.* Reston, VA: Council for Exceptional Children.

MacMillan, D. L., & Reschly, D. J. (1998). Overrepresentation of minority students: The case for greater specificity or reconsideration of the variables examined. *Journal of Special Education, 32,* 15–24.

Maker, C. J. (Ed.). (1993). *Critical issues in gifted education: Programs for the gifted in the regular classroom.* Austin, TX: Pro-Ed.

Markel, G., & Greenbaum, J. (1996). *Performance breakthroughs for adolescents with learning disabilities or ADD: How to help students succeed in the regular education classroom.* Champaign, IL: Research Press.

Miksic, S. (1987). Drug abuse management in adolescent special education. In M. M. Kerr, C. M. Nelson, & D. L. Lambert, *Helping adolescents with learning and behavior problems* (pp. 226–253). Upper Saddle River, NJ: Merrill/Prentice Hall.

Montague, M., Fiore, T., Hocutt, A., McKinney, J. D., & Harris, J. (1996). Interventions for students with attention deficit hyperactivity disorder: A review of the literature. In T. E. Scruggs & M. A. Mastropieri (Eds.), *Advances in learning and behavioral disabilities* (Vol. 10, Part B, pp. 23–50). Greenwich, CT: JAI Press.

Muccigrosso, L., Scavarda, M., Simpson-Brown, R., & Thalacker, B. E. (1991). *Double jeopardy: Pregnant and parenting youth in special education.* Reston, VA: Council for Exceptional Children.

Ortiz, A. A., & Garcia, S. B. (1988). A prereferral process for preventing inappropriate referrals of Hispanic students to special education. In A. A. Ortiz & B. A. Ramirez (Eds.), *Schools and the culturally diverse exceptional student: Promising practices and future directions* (pp. 6–18). Reston, VA: Council for Exceptional Children.

Ortiz, A., & Yates, J. R. (1983). Incidence of exceptionality among Hispanics: Implications for manpower training. *NAEB Journal, 7,* 41–51.

Ovando, C. J., & Collier, V. P. (1998). *Bilingual and ESL classroom: Teaching in multicultural contexts* (2nd ed.). Boston: McGraw-Hill.

Patton, J. M. (1997). Disproportionate representation in gifted programs: Best practices for meeting this challenge. In A. J. Artiles & G. Zamora-Durán (Eds.), *Reducing disproportionate representation of culturally diverse students in special and gifted education* (pp. 59–86). Reston, VA: Council for Exceptional Children.

Patton, J. M. (1998). The disproportionate representation of African Americans in special education: Looking behind the curtain for understanding and solutions. *Journal of Special Education, 32,* 25–31.

P.L. 100–297, Sec. 4103. definitions (gifted).

Plummer, D. L. (1995). Serving the needs of gifted children from a multicultural perspective. In J. L. Genshaft, M. Bireley, & C. L. Hollinger (Eds.), *Serving gifted and talented students: A resource for school personnel* (pp. 285–300). Austin, TX: Pro-Ed.

Ramirez, G., Jr., & Ramirez, J. L. (1994). *Multiethnic children's literature.* Albany, NY: Delmar Publishers.

Renzulli, J. S. (1978). *The enrichment triad model: A guide for developing defensible programs for gifted and talented.* Weathersfield, CT: Creative Learning Press.

Renzulli, J. S. (1982). Dear Mr. and Mrs. Copernicus: We regret to inform you . . . . *Gifted Child Quarterly, 26,* 11–14.

Renzulli, J. S., & Reiss, S. M. (1991). The school wide enrichment model: A comprehensive plan for the development of creative productivity. In N. Colangelo & G. A. Davis (Eds.), *Handbook of gifted education* (pp. 111–141). Boston: Allyn & Bacon.

Riccio, C. A., Hynd, G. W., & Cohen, M. J. (1997). Etiology and neurobiology of ADHD. In W. N. Bender (Ed.), *Understanding ADHD: A practical guide for teachers and parents* (pp. 23–44). Upper Saddle River, NJ: Merrill/Prentice Hall.

Rossi, P. H. (1990). The old homeless and the new homeless in holistic perspective. *American Psychologist, 45,* 954–959.

Rueda, R. (1997). Changing the context of assessment: The move to portfolios and authentic assessment. In A. J. Artiles & G. Zamora-Durán (Eds.), *Reducing disproportionate representation of culturally diverse* students in special and gifted education. Reston, Va: Council for Exceptional Children.

Rueda, R., & Prieto, A. G. (1979). Cultural pluralism: Implications for teacher education. *Teacher Education and Special Education, 2*(4), 4–11.

Schwanz, K. A., & Kamphaus, R. W. (1997). Assessment and diagnosis of ADHD. In W. N. Bender (Ed.), *Understanding ADHD: A practical guide for teachers and parents* (pp. 81–106). Upper Saddle River, NJ: Merrill/Prentice Hall.

Separate and unequal. (1993). *U.S. News & World Report, 115*(23), 46–60.

Serna, L. A., Forness, S. R., & Nielsen, M. E. (1998). Intervention versus affirmation: Proposed solutions to the problem of disproportionate minority representation in special education. *Journal of Special Education, 32,* 48–51.

Silverman, L. K. (1995). Highly gifted children. In J. L. Genshaft, M. Bireley, & C. L. Hollingsworth (Eds.), *Serving gifted and talented students: A resource for school personnel.* Austin, TX: Pro-Ed.

Slavin, R. E., Karweit, N. L., & Madden, N. A. (1989). *Effective programs for students at risk.* Boston: Allyn & Bacon.

Smith, L. (1975). *Your child's behavior chemistry.* New York: Random House.

Spitzer, R. L., Gibbon, M., Skodol, A. E., Williams, J. B. W., & First, M. B. (Eds.). (1994). *DSM–IV Casebook: A learning companion to the diagnostic and statistical manual of mental disorders* (4th ed.). Washington, DC: American Psychiatric Press, Inc.

Stephens, V. P., & Price, M. (1992). Meeting the challenge of educating children at risk. *Phi Delta Kappan, 74,* 18–23.

Stephens, V. P., Varble, M. E., & Taitt, H. (1993). Instructional and organizational change to meet minority and at risk students' needs. *Journal of Staff Development, 14*(4), 40–43.

Sternberg, R. J. (1991). Giftedness according to the triarchic theory of human intelligence. In N. Colangelo & G. A. Davis (Eds.), *Handbook of gifted education* (pp. 45–54). Boston: Allyn & Bacon.

Stronge, J. H., & Tenhouse, C. (1990). *Educating homeless children: Issues and answers.* Bloomington, IN: Phi Delta Kappa Educational Foundation.

Terman, L. (1925). Mental and physical traits of a thousand gifted children. In L. Terman (Ed.), *Genetic studies of genius* (Vol. 1). Stanford, CA: Stanford University Press.

U.S. Department of Education. (1993). Office of Educational Research and Improvement. *National excellence: A case for developing America's talent.* Washington, DC: Author.

U.S. Department of Education. (1996). *Eighteenth annual report to Congress on the implementation of the Individuals with Disabilities Education Act.* Washington, DC: Author.

U.S. Department of Education. (1998). *Twentieth annual report to Congress on the implementation of the Individuals with Disabilities Education Act.* Washington, DC: Author.

U.S. Department of Education. (2001). *To assure the free appropriate public education of all children with disabilities: Twenty-third annual report to Congress on the implementation of the Individuals with Disabilities Education Act.* Washington, DC: Author.

Van Tassel-Baska, J. (Ed.). (1990). *A practical guide to counseling the gifted in a school setting.* Reston, VA: Council for Exceptional Children.

Vincent, L. J., Poulsen, M. K., Cole, C. K., Woodruff, G., & Griffith, D. R. (1991). *Born substance exposed, educationally vulnerable.* Reston, VA: Council for Exceptional Children.

Wagner, C. L., Tewey, S., & Megivern, M. (1991). *Abuse and neglect of exceptional children.* Reston, VA: Council for Exceptional Children.

Wagner, M. (1995). *The contributions of poverty and ethnic background to the participation of secondary students in special education.* Washington, DC: U.S. Department of Education.

Wagner, M., Blackorby, J., Cameto, R., & Newman, L. (1993). *What makes a difference? Influences on postschool outcomes of youth with disabilities.* Menlo Park, CA: SRI International.

Watson, D. L., & Rangel, L. (1989). Don't forget the slow learner. *Clearinghouse, 62,* 266–268.

Winzer, M. A., & Mazurek, K. (1998). *Special education in multicultural contexts.* Upper Saddle River, NJ: Merrill/Prentice Hall.

Wolraich, M., Milich, R., Stumbo, P., & Schultz, F. (1985). The effects of sucrose ingestion on the behavior of hyperactive boys. *Pediatrics, 106,* 742–747.

Chapter 6

Alberto, P. A., Troutman, A. C., & Feagin, J. R. (2002). *Applied behavior analysis for teachers* (6th ed.). Upper Saddle River, NJ: Merrill/Prentice Hall.

Bettencourt, E. M., Gillett, M. H., Gall, M. D., & Hull, R. E. (1983). Effects of teacher enthusiasm training on student on-task behavior and achievement. *American Educational Research Journal, 20,* 435–450.

Biddle, B. J., & Anderson, D. S. (1986). Theory, methods, knowledge, and research on teaching. In M. C. Wittrock (Ed.), *Handbook on research on teaching* (3rd ed., pp. 230–252). New York: MacMillan.

Brigham, F. J., Scruggs, T. E., & Mastropieri, M. A. (1992). The effect of teacher enthusiasm on the learning and behavior of learning disabled students. *Learning Disabilities Research & Practice, 7,* 68–73.

Brophy, J. (1981). Teacher praise: A functional analysis. *Review of Educational Research, 51,* 5–32.

Brophy, J. E., & Good, T. L. (1986). Teacher behavior and students achievement. In M. C. Wittrock (Ed.),

Handbook on research on teaching (3rd ed., pp. 328–375). New York: MacMillan.

Carnine, D. (1976). Effects of two teacher presentation rates on off-task behavior, answering correctly, and participation. *Journal of Applied Behavior Analysis, 9,* 199–206.

Danielson, C. (1996). *Enhancing professional practice: A framework for teaching.* Alexandria, VA: Association for Supervision and Curriculum Development.

Doyle, W. (1986). Classroom organization and management. In M. C. Wittrock (Ed.), *Handbook on research on teaching* (3rd ed., pp. 392–431). New York: MacMillan.

Englert, C. S. (1983). Measuring special education teacher effectiveness. *Exceptional Children, 50,* 247–254.

Englert, C. S. (1984). Effective direct instruction practices in special education settings. *Remedial and Special Education, 5,* 38–47.

Gleason, M., Carnine, D., & Vala, N. (1991). Cumulative versus rapid introduction of new information. *Exceptional Children, 57,* 353–358.

Haynes, M. C., & Jenkins, J. R. (1986). Reading instruction in special education resource rooms. *American Educational Research Journal, 23,* 161–190.

Larrivee, B. (1985). *Effective teaching for successful mainstreaming.* New York: Longman.

Leinhardt, G., Zigmond, N., & Cooley, W. W. (1981). Reading instruction and its effect. *American Educational Research Journal, 18,* 343–361.

Mastropieri, M. A. (1989). Using general education teacher effectiveness literature in the preparation of special education personnel. *Teacher Education and Special Education, 12,* 170–172.

Mastropieri, M. A. (1995). L'instruzione mnemonica e l'interrogazione elaborativa: Strategie per ricordarsi e per pensare. In C. Cornoldi & R. Vianello (Eds.), *Handicap e apprendimento: Ricerche e proposte di intervento* (pp. 117–124). Bergamo, Italy: Juvenilia.

Mastropieri, M. A., & Scruggs, T. E. (1984). Generalization: Five effective strategies. *Academic Therapy, 19,* 427–431.

Mastropieri, M. A., & Scruggs, T. E. (1987). *Effective instruction for special education.* Austin, TX: Pro-Ed.

Mastropieri, M. A., & Scruggs, T. E. (1997). What's special about special education? A cautious view toward full inclusion. *Educational Forum, 61,* 206–211.

Mastropieri, M. A., & Scruggs, T. E. (2002). *Effective instruction for special education* (3rd ed.). Austin, TX: Pro-Ed.

Mastropieri, M. A., Scruggs, T. E., & Bohs, K. (1994). Mainstreaming an emotionally handicapped student in science: A qualitative investigation. In T. E. Scruggs & M. A. Mastropieri (Eds.), *Advances in learning and behavioral disabilities* (Vol. 8, pp. 131–146). Greenwich, CT: JAI.

Mastropieri, M. A., Scruggs, T. E., Mantzicopoulos, P. Y., Sturgeon, A., Goodwin, L., & Chung, S. (1998). "A place where living things affect and depend upon each other": Qualitative and quantitative outcomes associated with

inclusive science teaching. *Science Education, 82,* 163–179.

Pressley, M., & McCormick, C. B. (1995). *Advanced educational psychology for educators, researchers, and policymakers.* New York: HarperCollins.

Rosenshine, B., & Stevens, R. (1986). Teaching functions. In M. C. Wittrock, *Handbook on research on teaching* (3rd ed., pp. 376–391). New York: MacMillan.

Scruggs, T. E., & Mastropieri, M. A. (1984). Issues in generalization: Implications for special education. *Psychology in the Schools, 21,* 397–403.

Scruggs, T. E., & Mastropieri, M. A. (1994a). The effectiveness of generalization training: A quantitative synthesis of single subject research. In T. E. Scruggs & M. A. Mastropieri (Eds.), *Advances in learning and behavioral disabilities* (Vol. 8, pp. 259–280). Greenwich, CT: JAI Press.

Scruggs, T. E., & Mastropieri, M. A. (1994b). Successful mainstreaming in elementary science classes: A qualitative investigation of three reputational cases. *American Educational Research Journal, 31,* 785–811.

Scruggs, T. E., & Mastropieri, M. A. (1995). What makes special education special? An analysis of the PASS variables in inclusion settings. *Journal of Special Education, 29,* 224–233.

Scruggs, T. E., Mastropieri, M. A., & Sullivan, G. S. (1994). Promoting relational thinking skills: Elaborative interrogation for mildly handicapped students. *Exceptional Children, 60,* 450–457.

Sindelar, P. T., Smith, M. A., Harriman, N. E., Hale, R. L., & Wilson, R. J. (1986). Teacher effectiveness in special education programs. *Journal of Special Education, 20,* 195–207.

Smith, L. (1977). Aspects of teacher discourse and student achievement in mathematics. *Journal for Research in Mathematics Education, 8,* 195–204.

Smith, L., & Land, M. (1981). Low-inference verbal behaviors related to teacher clarity. *Journal of Classroom Interaction, 17,* 37–42.

Stokes, T., & Baer, D. (1977). An implicit technology of generalization. *Journal of Applied Behavior Analysis, 10,* 349–367.

Sullivan, G. S., Mastropieri, M. A., & Scruggs, T. E. (1995). Reasoning and remembering: Coaching thinking with students with learning disabilities. *Journal of Special Education, 29,* 310–322.

Walberg, H. J. (1986). Syntheses on research on teaching. In M. C. Wittrock (Ed.), *Handbook on research on teaching* (3rd ed., pp. 214–229). New York: MacMillan.

Wittrock, M. C. (Ed.). (1986). *Handbook on research on teaching* (3rd ed.). New York: MacMillan.

Chapter 7

Alberto, P. A., Troutman, A. C., & Feagin, J. R. (2002). *Applied behavior analysis for teachers* (6th ed.). Upper Saddle River, NJ: Merrill/Prentice Hall.

Allison, T. S., & Allison, S. L. (1971). Time-out from reinforcement: Effect on sibling aggression. *Psychological Record, 21,* 81–86.

Barrish, H. H., Saunders, M., & Wolf, M. M. (1969). Good Behavior Game: Effects of individual contingencies for group consequences on disruptive behavior in the classroom. *Journal of Applied Behavior Analysis, 2,* 119–124.

Bauer, A. M., & Shea, T. M. (1988). Structuring classrooms through level systems. *Focus on Exceptional Children, 21,* 1–12.

Bauer, A. M., Shea, T. M., & Keppler, R. (1986). Level systems: A framework for the individualization of behavior management. *Behavioral Disorders, 12,* 28–35.

Becker, W. C., Madsen, C. H., & Arnold, C. R. (1967). The contingent use of teacher praise in reducing behavior problems. *The Journal of Special Education, 1,* 287–307.

Bijou, S. W., Peterson, R. F., & Ault, M. H. (1968). A method to integrate descriptive and experimental field studies at the level of data and empirical concepts. *Journal of Applied Behavior Analysis, 1,* 175–191.

Brigham, F. J., Bakken, J., Scruggs, T. E., & Mastropieri, M. A. (1992). Cooperative behavior management: A technique for improving classroom behavior. *Education and Training of the Mentally Retarded, 27,* 3–12.

Brigham, F. J., Scruggs, T. E., & Mastropieri, M. A. (1992). The effect of teacher enthusiasm on the learning and behavior of learning disabled students. *Learning Disabilities Research & Practice, 7,* 68–73.

Brown, A. L. (1987). Metacognition, executive control, self-regulation, and other more mysterious mechanisms. In F. E. Weinert & R. H. Klewe (Eds.), *Metacognition, motivation, and understanding* (pp. 117–140). Mahwah, NJ: Lawrence Erlbaum.

Buchard, J. D., & Barrera, F. (1972). An analysis of time out and response cost in a programmed environment. *Journal of Applied Behavior Analysis, 5,* 271–282.

Cambone, J. (1992). Tipping the balance. In T. Hehir & T. Latus (Eds.), *Special education at century's end: Evolution of theory and practice since 1970* (pp. 351–374). Reprint series No. 23, *Harvard Educational Review.* Cambridge, MA: President and Fellows of Harvard College.

Canter, L. (1979). *Assertive discipline workshop leader's manual.* Santa Monica, CA: Lee Canter & Associates.

Canter, L. (1990). *Back to school with Assertive Discipline.* Santa Monica, CA: Lee Canter & Associates.

Canter, L. (1992). *Lee Canter's Assertive Discipline middle school workbook: Grades 6–8.* Santa Monica, CA: Lee Canter & Associates

Canter, L., & Canter, M. (1993). *Succeeding with difficult students: New strategies for reaching your most challenging students.* Santa Monica, CA: Lee Canter & Associates

Carlson, C. S., Arnold, C. R., Becker, W. C., & Madsen, C. H. (1968). The elimination of tantrum behavior of a child in an elementary classroom. *Behavior Research and Therapy, 6,* 117–119.

Cartledge, G. (1996). *Cultural diversity and social skills instruction: Understanding gender and ethnic differences.* Champaign, IL: Research Press.

Cooper, J. O. (1974). *Measurement and analysis of behavioral techniques.* Upper Saddle River, NJ: Merrill/Prentice Hall.

Council for Children with Behavioral Disorders. (1990). Position paper on behavior reduction strategies with children with behavioral disorders. *Behavioral Disorders, 15,* 243–260.

DiGangi, S. O., & Maag, J. W. (1992). A component analysis of self-management training with behaviorally disordered youth. *Behavioral Disorders, 17,* 181–290.

Dreikurs, R., & Cassel, P. (1992). *Discipline without tears* (2nd ed.). New York: Hawthorn.

Elksnin, L. K. (1994). Promoting generalization of social skills. *LD Forum, 20* (1), 35–37.

Forness, S. R., & Kavale, K. A. (1996). Treating social skill deficits in children with learning disabilities: A meta-analysis of the research. *Learning Disability Quarterly, 19,* 2–13.

Foxx, R. M., & Shapiro, S. T. (1978). The timeout ribbon: A nonexclusionary timeout procedure. *Journal of Applied Behavior Analysis, 11,* 125–136.

Gagnon, J. C., & Leone, P. E. (2002). Alternative strategies for school violence prevention. In R. J. Skiba & G. G. Noam (Eds.), *Zero tolerance: Can suspension and expulsion keep schools safe?* (pp. 101–125). San Francisco: Jossey-Bass.

Goodman, H., Gottlieb, J., & Harrison, R. H. (1972). Social acceptance of EMR children integrated into a non-graded elementary school. *American Journal of Mental Deficiency, 76,* 412–417.

Gresham, F. (1998). Social skills training: Should we raze, remodel, or rebuild? *Behavioral Disorders, 24,* 19–25.

Harris, V. W., & Sherman, J. A. (1973). Use and analysis of the "Good Behavior Game" to reduce disruptive classroom behavior. *Journal of Applied Behavior Analysis, 6,* 405–417.

Hazel, J. S., Schumaker, J. B., Sherman, J. A., & Sheldon, J. (1995). *ASSET: A social skills program for adolescents* (2nd ed.). Champaign, IL: Research Press.

Horner, R. H., & Sugai, G. (1999). Developing positive behavioral support systems. In G. Sugai & T. Lewis (Eds.), *Developing positive behavioral support for students with challenging behaviors* (pp. 15–23). Arlington, VA: Council for Exceptional Children. (ERIC Document Reproduction Service No. 435155)

Hughes, C. A., Ruhl, K. L., & Misra, A. (1989). Self-management with behaviorally disordered students in school settings: A promise unfulfilled? *Behavioral Disorders, 14,* 250–262.

Jackson, N. F., Jackson, D. A., & Monroe, C. (1983). *Getting along with others.* Champaign, IL: Research Press.

Jenkins, J. R., & Gorrafa, S. (1974). Academic performance of mentally handicapped children as a function of token economies and contingency contracts. *Education and Training of the Mentally Retarded, 9,* 183–186.

Jones, D. B., & Van Houten, R. (1985). The use of daily quizzes and public posting to decrease the disruptive behavior of secondary school students. *Education and Treatment of Children, 8,* 91–106.

Kavale, K. A., & Forness, S. R. (1995). Social skill deficits and training: A meta-analysis of the research in learning disabilities. In T. E. Scruggs & M. A. Mastropieri (Eds.), *Advances in learning and behavioral disabilities* (Vol. 9, pp. 119–160). Greenwich, CT: JAI Press.

Kavale, K. A., Mathur, S., Forness, S. R., Rutherford, R. B., Jr., & Quinn, M. M. (1997). Effectiveness of social skills training for students with behavior disorders: A meta-analysis. In T. E. Scruggs & M. A. Mastropieri (Eds.), *Advances in learning and behavioral disabilities* (Vol. 11, pp. 1–26). Greenwich, CT: JAI Press.

Kerr, M. M., & Nelson, C. M. (2002). *Strategies for managing behavior problems in the classroom* (4th ed.). Upper Saddle River, NJ: Merrill/Prentice Hall.

Kuypers, D. S., Becker, W. C., & O'Leary, K. D. (1968). How to make a token system fail. *Exceptional Children, 35,* 101–109.

Long, N. J., & Morse, W. C. (Eds.). (1996). *Conflict in the classroom: The education of at-risk and troubled students* (2nd ed.). Austin, TX: Pro-Ed.

Long, N. J., Wood, M. M., & Fecser, F. A. (2001). *Life space crisis intervention: Talking with students in conflict.* Austin, TX: Pro-Ed.

Maag, J. (1999). *Behavior management: From theoretical implications to practical applications.* San Diego, CA: Singular Publishing Group.

Madsen, C. H., Becker, W. C., & Thomas, D. R. (1968). Rules, praise, and ignoring: Elements of elementary classroom control. *Journal of Applied Behavior Analysis, 1,* 139–150.

Martin, G., & Pear, J. (2002). *Behavior modification: What it is and how to do it* (7th ed.). Upper Saddle River, NJ: Merrill/Prentice Hall.

Mastropieri, M. A., Jenne, T., & Scruggs, T. E. (1988). A level system for managing problem behaviors in a high school resource program. *Behavioral Disorders, 13,* 202–208.

Mastropieri, M. A., & Scruggs, T. E. (2002). *Effective instruction for special education* (3rd ed.). Austin, TX: Pro-Ed.

Mayer, G. R., Nafpaktitis, M., Butterworth, T., & Hollingsworth, P. (1987). A search for the elusive setting events of school vandalism: A correlational study. *Education and Treatment of Children, 10,* 259–270.

McGinnis, E., & Goldstein, A. P. (1984). *Skillstreaming the elementary school child.* Champaign, IL: Research Press.

McGinnis, E., & Goldstein, A. P. (1990). *Skillstreaming in early childhood.* Champaign, IL: Research Press.

McIntosh, R., Vaughn, S., & Zaragosa, N. (1991). A review of social interventions for students with learning disabilities. *Journal of Learning Disabilities, 24,* 451–458.

McLaughlin, T. F., & Malaby, J. E. (1976). An analysis of assignment completion and accuracy across time under fixed, variable, and extended token exchange periods in a classroom token economy. *Contemporary Educational Psychology, 1,* 346–355.

Merritt-Petrashek, C. A. (1996). Emotional first aid: Bandaids for the bumps. In N. J. Long & W. C. Morse (Eds.), *Conflict in the classroom: The education of at-risk and troubled students* (2nd ed., pp. 429–442). Austin, TX: Pro-Ed.

Montague, M., & Lund, K. A. (1991). *Job-related social skills: A curriculum for adolescents with special needs.* Ann Arbor, MI: Exceptional Innovations.

Moore, R. J., Cartledge, G., & Heckaman, K. (1994). The effects of social skill instruction and self-monitoring on game-related behaviors of adolescents with emotional or behavioral disorders. *Behavioral Disorders, 20,* 253–266.

Nelson, C. M., & Rutherford, R. B., Jr. (1983). Timeout revisited: Guidelines for its use in special education. *Exceptional Education Quarterly, 3,* 3–13.

Nelson, J. R., & Sugai, G. (1999). Schoolwide application of positive behavioral supports. In G. Sugai & T. Lewis (Eds.), *Developing positive behavioral support for students with challenging behaviors* (pp. 25–34). Arlington, VA: Council for Exceptional Children. (ERIC Document Reproduction Service No. 435155)

Parker, J., & Asher, S. (1987). Peer acceptance and later personal adjustment: Are low-accepted children "at risk"? *Psychological Bulletin, 102,* 357–389.

Prater, M. (1992). Using self-monitoring to improve on-task behavior and academic skills of an adolescent with mild handicaps across special and regular education settings. *Education and Treatment of Children, 15,* 43–55.

Redl, F., & Wineman, D. (1965). *Controls from within: Techniques for the treatment of the aggressive child.* Glencoe, IL: Free Press.

Rosenberg, M. S., Wilson, R., Maheady, L., & Sindelar, P. T. (1997). *Educating students with behavioral disorders* (2nd ed.). Boston: Allyn & Bacon.

Rosenthal-Malek, A. L., & Yoshida, R. K. (1994). The effects of metacognitive strategy training on the acquisition and generalization of social skills. *Education and Training in Mental Retardation and Developmental Disabilities, 29,* 213–221.

Rutherford, R., Chipman, J., DiGangi, S., & Anderson, K. (1992). *Teaching social skills: A practical instructional approach.* Ann Arbor, MI: Exceptional Innovations.

Salend, S., & Gordon, B. D. (1987). A group-oriented timeout ribbon procedure. *Behavioral Disorders, 12,* 131–137.

Salzberg, C. L., Lignugaris/Kraft, B., & McCuller, G. L. (1988). Reasons for job loss: A review of employment termination studies of mentally retarded workers. *Research in Developmental Disabilities, 9,* 153–170.

Scruggs, T. E. (1992). Single subject methodology in the study of learning and behavioral disorders: Design, analysis, and synthesis. In T. E. Scruggs & M. A. Mastropieri (Eds.), *Advances in learning and behavioral disabilities* (Vol. 7, pp. 223–248). Greenwich, CT: JAI Press.

Scruggs, T. E., & Mastropieri, M. A. (1984). Issues in generalization: Implications for special education. *Psychology in the Schools, 21,* 397–403.

Scruggs, T. E., & Mastropieri, M. A. (1994a). The effectiveness of generalization training: A quantitative synthesis of single subject research. In T. E. Scruggs & M. A. Mastropieri (Eds.), *Advances in learning and behavioral disabilities* (Vol. 8, pp. 259–280). Greenwich, CT: JAI Press.

Scruggs, T. E., & Mastropieri, M. A. (1994b). Successful mainstreaming in elementary science classes: A qualitative investigation of three reputational cases. *American Educational Research Journal, 31,* 785–811.

Skiba, R., & Casey, A. (1985). Interventions for behavior disordered students: A quantitative synthesis and methodological critique. *Behavioral Disorders, 10,* 239–252.

Snapshots 2: Video for Special Education. Videotape to accompany Hallahan, D. P., & Kauffman, J. M. (1997). *Exceptional learners: Introduction to Special Education.* Boston: Allyn & Bacon.

Stokes, T. F., & Baer, D. M. (1977). An implicit technology of generalization. *Journal of Applied Behavior Analysis, 10,* 349–367.

Sugai, G., & Lewis, T. (Eds.). (1999). *Developing positive behavioral support for students with challenging behaviors.* Arlington, VA: Council for Exceptional Children. (ERIC Document Reproduction Service No. 435155)

Sullivan, G. S., & Mastropieri, M. A. (1994). Social competence of individuals with learning disabilities. In T. E. Scruggs & M. A. Mastropieri (Eds.), *Advances in learning and behavioral disabilities* (Vol. 8, pp. 171–213). Greenwich, CT: JAI Press.

Twyman, J. S., Johnson, H., Buie, J. D., & Nelson, C. M. (1994). The use of a warning procedure to signal a more intrusive timeout contingency. *Behavioral Disorders, 19,* 243–253.

Van Houten, R., Nau, P. A., MacKenzie-Keating, S. E., Sameoto, D., & Colavecchia, B. (1982). An analysis of some variables influencing the effectiveness of reprimands. *Journal of Applied Behavior Analysis, 15,* 65–83.

Vaughn, S., Levine, L., & Ridley, C. (1986). *PALS: Problem-solving and affective learning strategies.* Chicago: Science Research Associates.

Vaughn, S., McIntosh, R., & Hogan, A. (1990). Why social skills training doesn't work: An alternative model. In T. E. Scruggs & B. Y. L. Wong (Eds.), *Intervention research in learning disabilities* (pp. 279–303). New York: Springer Verlag.

Walker, H. M., McConnell, S., Holmes, D., Todis, B., Walker, J., & Golden, N. (1988). *The Walker social skills curriculum: The ACCEPTS program.* Austin, TX: Pro-Ed.

Walker, H. M., Todis, B., Holmes, D., & Horton, G. (1988). *The walker social skills curriculum: The ACCESS program.* Austin, TX: Pro-Ed.

Wertz, M. G., Zigmond, N., & Leeper, D. C. (2001). Paraprofessional proximity and academic engagement: Students with disabilities in primary aged classrooms. *Education and Training in Mental Retardation and Developmental Disabilities, 36,* 424–440.

Zabel, M. K. (1986). Timeout use with behaviorally disordered students. *Behavioral Disorders, 12,* 15–21.

Zaragosa, N., Vaughn, S., & McIntosh, R. (1991). Social skills interventions and children with behavior problems: A review. *Behavioral Disorders, 16,* 260–275.

Zirpoli, T. J., & Melloy, K. J. (1997). *Behavior management: Applications for teachers and parents* (2nd ed.). Upper Saddle River, NJ: Merrill/Prentice Hall.

Chapter 8

Britannica, Inc. (1991). *Full Option Science System.* Chicago: Author.

Cole, D. A., Vandercook, T., & Rynders, J. (1988). Comparison of two peer interaction programs: Children with and without severe disabilities. *American Educational Research Journal, 25,* 415–439.

Cook, S., Scruggs, T. E., Mastropieri, M. A., & Casto, G. C. (1985–1986). Handicapped students as tutors. *Journal of Special Education, 19,* 483–492.

Delquadri, J., Greenwood, C. R., Whorton, D., Carta, J. J., & Hall, R. V. (1986). Classwide peer tutoring. *Exceptional Children, 52,* 535–542.

Ferretti, R. P., MacArthur, C. D., & Okolo, C. M. (2001). Teaching for historical understanding in inclusive classrooms. *Learning Disability Quarterly, 24,* 59–71.

Forest, M., & Lusthaus, E. (1989). Promoting educational equity for all students. In S. Stainback, W. Stainback, & M. Forest (Eds.), *Educating all students in the mainstream of regular education* (pp. 47–49). Baltimore: Paul Brookes.

Fuchs, D., & Fuchs, L. S. (1992). *Classwide peer tutoring to accommodate student diversity in reading* [videotape]. Nashville, TN: Peabody College, Vanderbilt University.

Fuchs, D., Fuchs, L., Mathes, P. G., & Martinez, E. A. (2002). Preliminary evidence on the social standing of students with learning disabilities in PALS and No-PALS classrooms. *Learning Disabilities Research & Practice, 17,* 205–215.

Fuchs, D., Fuchs, L. S., Mathes, P. G., & Simmons, D. C. (in press). Peer-assisted learning strategies: Making classrooms more responsive to diversity. *American Educational Research Journal.*

Fuchs, D., Mathes, P. G., & Fuchs, L. S. (1995). *Peabody peer-assisted learning strategies (PALS): Reading methods.* Nashville, TN: Peabody College, Vanderbilt University.

Fuchs, L. S., Fuchs, D., Karns, K., & Phillips, N. (1995). *Peabody peer-assisted learning strategies (PALS): Math methods.* Nashville, TN: Peabody College, Vanderbilt University.

Fuchs, L. S., Fuchs, D., Phillips, N. B., Hamlett, C. L., & Karns, K. (1995). Acquisition and transfer effects of classwide peer-assisted learning strategies in mathematics for students with varying learning histories. *School Psychology Review, 24,* 604–620.

Gable, R. V., & Kerr, M. M. (1980). Behaviorally disordered adolescents as academic change agents. In R. B. Rutherford, Jr., A. G. Prieto, & J. E. McGlothlin (Eds.), *Severe behavior disorders of children and youth* (Vol. 4). Reston, VA: Council for Children with Behavioral Disorders.

Goodman, H., Gottlieb, J., & Harrison, R. H. (1972). Social acceptance of EMR children integrated into a non-graded elementary school. *American Journal of Mental Deficiency, 76,* 412–417.

Greenwood, C. R., Delquadri, J. C., & Hall, R. V. (1989). Longitudinal effects of classwide peer tutoring. *Journal of Educational Psychology, 81,* 371–383.

Hall, R. V., Delquadri, J., Greenwood, C. R., & Thurston, L. (1982). The importance of opportunity to respond to children's academic success. In E. Edgar, N. Haring, J. Jenkins, & C. Pious (Eds.), *Mentally handicapped children: Education and training* (pp. 107–140). Baltimore: University Park Press.

Higgins, T. S. (1982). *A comparison of two methods of practice on the spelling performance of learning disabled adolescents.* Unpublished doctoral dissertation, Georgia State University, Atlanta.

Iano, R. P., Ayers, D., Heller, H. B., McGettigan, J. F., & Walker, V. S. (1974). Sociometric status of retarded children in an integrative program. *Exceptional Children, 40,* 267–271.

Jenkins, J. R., & Jenkins, L. M. (1981). *Cross age and peer tutoring: Help for children with learning problems.* Reston, VA: Council for Exceptional Children.

Johnson, D. W., & Johnson, R. T. (1986). Mainstreaming and cooperative learning strategies. *Exceptional Children, 52,* 553–561.

Johnson, D. W., Johnson, R., Dudley, B., Ward, M., & Magnuson, D. (1995). The impact of peer mediation training on the management of school and home conflicts. *American Educational Research Journal, 32,* 829–844.

Johnson, D. W., Johnson, R. T., & Holubec, E. J. (1991). *Cooperation in the classroom.* Edina, MN: Interaction Book Company.

Johnson, D. W., Maruyama, G., Johnson, R., Nelson, D., & Skon, L. (1981). The effects of cooperative, competitive, and individualistic goal structures on achievement: A meta-analysis. *Psychological Bulletin, 89,* 47–62.

Kane, B. J., & Alley, G. R. (1980). A peer-tutored, instructional management program in computational mathematics for incarcerated, learning disabled juvenile delinquents. *Journal of Learning Disabilities, 13,* 39–42.

Kerr, M. M., & Nelson, C. M. (2002). *Strategies for addressing behavior problems in the classroom* (4th ed.). Upper Saddle River, NJ: Merrill/Prentice Hall.

Krouse, J., Gerber, M. M., & Kauffman, J. M. (1981). Peer tutoring: Procedures, promises, and unresolved issues. *Exceptional Education Quarterly, 1*(4), 107–115.

Maheady, L., & Harper, G. F. (1987). A class-wide peer tutoring program to improve the spelling test performance of low income, third- and fourth-grade students. *Education and Treatment of Children, 10,* 120–133.

Maheady, L., Harper, G. F., & Sacca, K. (1988). A classwide peer tutoring system in a secondary, resource room program for the mildly handicapped. *Journal of Research and Development in Education, 21*(3), 76–83.

Maheady, L., Sacca, M. K., & Harper, G. F. (1988). Classwide peer tutoring with mildly handicapped high school students. *Exceptional Children, 55*(1), 52–59.

Mastropieri, M. A., & Scruggs, T. E. (1985–1986). Early intervention for socially withdrawn children. *Journal of Special Education, 19,* 429–441.

Mastropieri, M. A., & Scruggs, T. E. (1993). *A practical guide for teaching science to students with special needs in inclusive settings.* Austin, TX: Pro-Ed.

Mastropieri, M. A., Scruggs, T. E., Graetz, J., Fontana, J., Cole, V., & Gersen, A. (2002, July). *Teacher-researcher partnerships to promote success in inclusive secondary science and social studies classes.* Paper presented at the OSEP Research Project Directors' Conference, Washington, DC.

Mastropieri, M. A., Scruggs, T. E., Mantzicopoulos, P. Y., Sturgeon, A., Goodwin, L., & Chung, S. (1998). "A place where living things affect and depend upon each other": Qualitative and quantitative outcomes associated with inclusive science teaching. *Science Education, 82,* 163–179.

Mastropieri, M. A., Scruggs, T. E., Mohler, L. J., Beranek, M. L., Spencer, V., Boon, R. T., & Talbott, E. (2001). Can middle school students with serious reading difficulties help each other and learn anything? *Learning Disabilities Research & Practice, 16,* 18–27.

Mastropieri, M. A., Scruggs, T. E., Spencer, V., & Fontana, J. (2003). Promoting success in high school world history: Peer tutoring versus guided notes. *Learning Disabilities Research & Practice.*

Mathes, P. G., Fuchs, D., Fuchs, L. S., Henley, A. M., & Sanders, A. (1994). Increasing strategic reading practice with Peabody Classwide Peer Tutoring. *Learning Disabilities Research & Practice, 9,* 44–48.

Mathes, P. G., & Fuchs, L. S. (1994). The efficacy of peer tutoring in reading for students with mild disabilities: A best-evidence synthesis. *School Psychology Review, 23,* 59–80.

McMaster, K. N., & Fuchs, D. (2002). Effects of cooperative learning on the academic achievement of students with learning disabilities: An update of Tateyama-Sniezek's review. *Learning Disabilities Research & Practice, 17,* 107–117.

O'Connor, R. E., & Jenkins, J. R. (1996). Cooperative learning as an inclusion strategy: A closer look. *Exceptionality, 6,* 29–51.

Osguthorpe, R. T., & Scruggs, T. E. (1986). Special education students as tutors: A review and analysis. *Remedial and Special Education, 7*(4), 15–26.

Ragland, E. U., Kerr, M. M., & Strain, P. S. (1978). Effects of social initiations on the behavior of withdrawn autistic children. *Topics in Early Childhood Special Education, 13,* 565–578.

Scruggs, T. E., & Mastropieri, M. A. (1994). Successful mainstreaming in elementary science classes: A qualitative investigation of three reputational cases. *American Educational Research Journal, 31,* 785–811.

Scruggs, T. E., & Mastropieri, M. A. (1998). Peer tutoring and students with special needs. In K. Topping & S. Ehly (Eds.), *Peer assisted learning* (pp. 165–182). Mahwah, NJ: Lawrence Erlbaum.

Scruggs, T. E., Mastropieri, M. A., & Richter, L. L. (1985). Peer tutoring with behaviorally disordered students: Social and academic benefits. *Behavioral Disorders, 10,* 283–294.

Scruggs, T. E., Mastropieri, M. A., Veit, D. T., & Osguthorpe, R. T. (1986). Behaviorally disordered students as tutors: Effects on social behaviors. *Behavioral Disorders, 12,* 36–44.

Scruggs, T. E., & Osguthorpe, R. T. (1986). Tutoring interventions within special education settings: A comparison of cross-age and peer tutoring. *Psychology in the Schools, 23,* 187–193.

Scruggs, T. E., & Richter, L. (1988). Tutoring learning disabled students: A critical review. *Learning Disability Quarterly, 11,* 274–286.

Sharpley, A. M., Irvine, J. W., & Sharpley, C. F. (1983). An examination of the effectiveness of cross-age tutoring program in mathematics for elementary school children. *American Educational Research Journal, 20,* 103–111.

Sindelar, P. T. (1982). The effects of cross-age tutoring on the comprehension skills of remedial reading students. *The Journal of Special Education, 16,* 199–206.

Singh, R. K. (1982). *Peer tutoring: Its effects on the math skills of students designated as learning disabled.* Unpublished doctoral dissertation, American University, Washington, D.C.

Slavin, R. E. (1991). Synthesis of research on cooperative learning. *Educational Leadership, 48*(5), 71–82.

Slavin, R. E., & Karweit, N. L. (1985). Effects of whole class, ability grouped, and individualized instruction on mathematics achievement. *American Educational Research Journal, 22,* 351–367.

Slavin, R. E., Madden, N. A., & Leavey, M. (1984). Effects of team assisted individualization on the mathematics achievement of academically handicapped and nonhandicapped students. *Journal of Educational Psychology, 76,* 813–819.

Spencer, V. G., Scruggs, T. E., & Mastropieri, M. A. (2003). Content area learning in middle school social studies classrooms and students with emotional or behavioral disorders: A comparison of strategies. *Behavioral Disorders, 28,* 77–93.

Stainback, W., & Stainback, S. (1990). Facilitating peer supports and friendships. In W. Stainback & S. Stainback (Eds.), *Support networks for inclusive schooling* (pp. 51–63). Baltimore: Paul Brookes.

Stevens, R. J., & Slavin, R. E. (1991). When cooperative learning improves the achievement of students with mild disabilities: A response to Tateyama-Sniezek. *Exceptional Children, 57,* 276–280.

Tateyama-Sniezek, K. M. (1990). Cooperative learning: Does it improve the academic achievement of students with handicaps? *Exceptional Children, 56,* 426–437.

Topping, K. (1988). *The peer tutoring handbook: Promoting cooperative learning.* Cambridge, MA: Brookline Books.

Topping, K., & Ehly, S. (Eds.). (1998). *Peer-assisted learning.* Mahwah, NJ: Lawrence Erlbaum.

Young, C. C., & Kerr, M. M. (1979). The effects of a retarded child's social initiations on the behavior of severely retarded school-aged peers. *Education and Training of the Mentally Retarded, 14,* 185–190.

Chapter 9

American Psychiatric Association. (1994). *Diagnostic and statistical manual of mental disorders* (4th ed.). Washington, DC: Author.

Amerikaner, M., & Summerlin, M. L. (1982). Group counseling with learning disabled children: Effects of social skill and relaxation training on self-concept and classroom behavior. *Journal of Learning Disabilities, 15,* 340–343.

Battle, J., & Blowers, T. (1982). A longitudinal comparitive study of the self-esteem of students in regular and special education classes. *Journal of Learning Disabilities, 12,* 596–607.

Bettencourt, E. M., Gillett, M. H., Gall, M. D., & Hull, R. E. (1983). Effects of teacher enthusiasm training on student on-task behavior and achievement. *American Educational Research Journal, 20,* 435–450.

Borkowski, J. G., Weyhing, R. S., & Carr, M. (1988). Effects of attributional retraining on strategy-based reading comprehension in learning disabled students. *Journal of Educational Psychology, 80,* 46–53.

Brigham, F. J., Scruggs, T. E., & Mastropieri, M. A. (1992). The effect of teacher enthusiasm on the learning and behavior of learning disabled students. *Learning Disabilities Research & Practice, 7,* 68–73.

Brophy, J. (1981). Teacher praise: A functional analysis. *Review of Educational Research, 51,* 5–32.

Brophy, J. (1987). Synthesis of research on strategies for motivating students to learn. *Educational Leadership,* 40–48.

Carlson, C. L., Booth, J. E., Shin, M., & Canu, W. H. (2002). Parent-, teacher-, and self-rated motivational styles in ADHD subtypes. *Journal of Learning Disabilities, 35,* 104–113.

Dev, P. (1997). Intrinsic motivation and academic achievement: What does their relationship imply for the classroom teacher? *Remedial and Special Education, 18*(1), 12–19.

Ford, M. E. (1995). Motivation and competence development in special and remedial education. *Intervention in School and Clinic, 31,* 70–83.

Fuchs, D., Fuchs, L. S., Reeder, P., Gilman, S., Fernstrom, P., Bahr, M., & Moore, P. (1989). *Mainstream assistance teams: A handbook on pre-referral intervention.* Nashville, TN: Peabody College of Vanderbilt University.

Fuchs, L. S., Fuchs, D., & Deno, S. (1985). Importance of goal ambitiousness and goal mastery to student achievement. *Exceptional Children, 52,* 63–71.

Fulk, B. J. M., & Mastropieri, M. A. (1990). Training positive attitudes: "I tried hard and did well!" *Intervention in School and Clinic, 26,* 79–83.

Fulk, B. M., & Montgomery-Grimes, D. J. (1994). Strategies to improve student motivation. *Intervention in School and Clinic, 30,* 28–33.

Harter, S., Whitesell, N. R., & Junkin, L. J. (1998). Similarities and differences in domain-specific and global self-evaluations of learning-disabled, behaviorally disordered, and normally achieving adolescents. *American Educational Research Journal, 35,* 653–680.

Heath, N. (1996). The emotional domain: Self-concept and depression in children with learning disabilities. In T. E. Scruggs & M. A. Mastropieri (Eds.), *Advances in learning and behavioral disabilities: Theoretical perspectives* (Vol. 10A, pp. 47–76). Greenwich, CT: JAI.

Katz, M. (1997). *On playing a poor hand well.* New York: W. W. Norton.

Knaus, W., & McKeever, C. (1977). Rational-emotive education with learning disabled children. *Journal of Learning Disabilities, 10,* 16–20.

Lavoie, R. (1996). *How difficult can this be? Understanding learning disabilities: Frustration, anxiety, tension, the FAT city workshop.* Alexandria, VA: PBS Video.

Lawrence, E. A., & Winschel, J. F. (1975). Locus of control: Implications for special education. *Exceptional Children, 41,* 483–490.

Lepper, M. R., & Hodell, M. (1989). Intrinsic motivation in the classroom. In C. Ames & R. Ames (Eds.), *Research on motivation in education: Goals and cognitions* (Vol. 3, pp. 73–105). San Diego: Academic Press.

Licht, B. (1992). Achievement-related beliefs in children with learning disabilities. In L. J. Meltzer (Ed.), *Strategy assessment and instruction for students with learning disabilities: From theory to practice* (pp. 195–220). Austin, TX: Pro-Ed.

Lo, F. G. (1985). The effects of a rational emotive education program on self-concept and locus of control among learning disabled adolescents. *Dissertation Abstracts International, 46,* 2973A.

Locke, E. A., & Latham, G. P. (1990). *A theory of goal setting and task performance.* Upper Saddle River, NJ: Merrill/Prentice Hall.

Lovitt, T. C. (1995). *Tactics for teaching.* Upper Saddle River, NJ: Merrill/Prentice Hall.

Mamlin, N., Harris, K. R., & Case, L. P. (2001). A methodological analysis of research on locus of control and learning disabilities: Rethinking a common assumption. *Journal of Special Education, 34,* 214–225.

Martin, G., & Pear, J. (1978). *Behavior modification: What it is and how to do it.* Upper Saddle River, NJ: Merrill/Prentice Hall.

Mastropieri, M. A., & Scruggs, T. E. (1994). *Effective instruction for special education* (2nd ed.). Austin, TX: Pro-Ed.

Mastropieri, M. A., & Scruggs, T. E. (2002, April). *Overcoming special education's greatest challenge: Motivating students to learn!* Paper presented at the annual meeting of the Council for Exceptional Children, New York.

Mastropieri, M. A., Scruggs, T. E., Bakken, J., & Brigham, F. J. (1992). A complex mnemonic strategy for teaching states and capitals. Comparing forward and backward associations. *Learning Disabilities Research & Practice, 7,* 96–103.

Mastropieri, M. A., Scruggs, T. E., & Bohs, K. (1994). Mainstreaming an emotionally handicapped student in science: A qualitative investigation. In T. E. Scruggs & M. A. Mastropieri (Eds.), *Advances in learning and behavioral disabilities* (Vol. 8, pp. 131–146). Oxford, UK: Elsevier Science/JAI.

Mastropieri, M. A., Scruggs, T. E., & Butcher, K. (1997). Counseling individuals with learning disabilities: Research, practice, and future issues. In T. E. Scruggs & M. A. Mastropieri (Eds.), *Advances in learning and behavioral disabilities* (Vol. 8, pp. 131–146). Oxford, UK: Elsevier Science/JAI.

McMaster, K. N., & Fuchs, D. (2002). Effects of cooperative learning on the academic achievement of students with learning disabilities: An update of Tateyama-Sniezek's review. *Learning Disabilities Research & Practice, 17,* 107–117.

Mishna, F. (1996). Finding their voice: Group therapy for adolescents with learning disabilities. *Learning Disabilities Research & Practice, 11,* 249–258.

Murray, C. (2002). Supportive teacher-student relationships: Promoting the social and emotional health of early adolescents with high-incidence disabilities. *Childhood Education, 78,* 285–290.

Murray, C. & Greenberg, M. T. (2001). Relationships with teachers and bonds with schools: Social emotional adjustments for children with and without disabilities. *Psychology in the Schools, 38,* 25–41.

Nicholls, J. G. (1989). *The competitive ethos and democratic education.* Cambridge, MA: Harvard University Press.

Omizo, M. M., & Omizo, S. A. (1987). The effects of group counseling on classroom behavior and self-concept among elementary school children. *The Exceptional Child, 34,* 57–61.

Paris, S. G., & Cross, D. R. (1983). Ordinary learning: Pragmatic connections among children's beliefs, motives, and actions. In J. Bisanz, G. Bisanz, & R. Kail (Eds.), *Learning in children* (pp. 137–169). New York: Springer-Verlag.

Pressley, M., & McCormick, C. B. (1995). *Advanced educational psychology for educators, researchers, and policymakers.* New York: HarperCollins.

Scruggs, T. E., & Mastropieri, M. A. (1983). Self-esteem differences by sex and ethnicity: Native American, handicapped Native American, and Anglo children. *Journal of Instructional Psychology, 10,* 177–179.

Scruggs, T. E., & Mastropieri, M. A. (1994a). The effectiveness of generalization training: A quantitative synthesis of single subject research. In T. E. Scruggs & M. A. Mastropieri (Eds.), *Advances in learning and behavioral disabilities* (Vol. 8, pp. 259–280).

Scruggs, T. E., & Mastropieri, M. A. (1994b). Successful mainstreaming in elementary science classes: A qualitative investigation of three reputational cases. *American Educational Research Journal, 31,* 785–811.

Wright, E. L., & Govindarajan, G. (1995). Discrepant event demonstrations. *Science Teacher, 62*(1), 25–28.

Zimmerman, B. J., Bandura, A., & Martinez-Pons, M. (1986). Development of a structured interview for assessing student use of self-regulated learning strategies. *American Educational Research Journal, 23,* 614–628.

Chapter 10

Abramowitz, A. J., O'Leary, S. G., & Futtersak, M. W. (1988). The relative impact of long and short reprimands on children's off-task behavior in the classroom. *Behavior Therapy, 19,* 243–247.

Abramowitz, A. J., O'Leary, S. G., & Rosen, L. S. (1987). Reducing off-task behavior in the classroom: A comparison of encouragement and reprimands. *Journal of Abnormal Child Psychology, 15,* 155–163.

American Psychiatric Association. (1994). *Diagnostic and statistical manual of mental disorders* (4th ed.). Washington, DC: Author.

Ashbaker, M. H., & Swanson, L. H. (1996). Short-term memory and working memory operations and their contribution to reading in adolescents with and without learning disabilities. *Learning Disabilities Research & Practice, 11,* 206–213.

Atkinson, R. C. (1975). Mnemotechnics in second-language learning. *American Psychologist, 30,* 821–828.

Atkinson, R. C., & Shiffrin, R. M. (1971). The control of short-term memory. *Scientific American, 225,* 82–90.

Baker, J. G., Ceci, S. J., & Herrmann, D. (1987). Semantic structure and processing: Implications for the learning disabled child. In H. L. Swanson (Ed.), *Advances in learning and behavioral disabilities: Memory and learning disabilities* (Supplement 2, pp. 83–109). Greenwich, CT: JAI.

Barkley, R. A. (1998). *Attention deficit hyperactivity disorder: A handbook for diagnosis and treatment* (2nd ed.). New York: Guilford Press.

Beirne-Smith, M., Ittenbach, R., & Patton, J. (2001). *Mental Retardation* (6th ed.). Upper Saddle River, NJ: Merrill/Prentice Hall.

Bos, C., & Anders, P. L. (1990). Interactive teaching and learning: Instructional practices for teaching content and strategic knowledge. In T. E. Scruggs & B. Y. L. Wong (Eds.), *Intervention research in learning disabilities* (pp. 166–185). New York: Springer-Verlag.

Bredderman, T. (1983). Effects of activity-based elementary science on student outcomes: A quantitative synthesis. *Review of Educational Research, 53,* 499–518.

Brigham, F. J., Scruggs, T. E., & Mastropieri, M. A. (1995). Elaborative maps for enhanced learning of historical information: Uniting spatial, verbal, and imaginal information. *Journal of Special Education, 28,* 440–460.

Brown, A. L. (1978). Knowing when, where, and how to remember: A problem of metacognition. In R. Glaser (Ed.), *Advances in instructional psychology* (pp. 77–157). Hillsdale, NJ: Lawrence Erlbaum.

Browning, W. G. (1983). *Memory power for exams.* Lincoln, NE: Cliff Notes.

Bulgren, J. A., Hock, M. F., Schumaker, J. B., & Deshler, D. D. (1995). The effects of instruction in a paired associates strategy on the information mastery performance of students with learning disabilities. *Learning Disabilities Research & Practice, 10,* 22–37.

Burchers, S., Burchers, M., & Burchers, B. (1997). *Vocabulary cartoons: Building an educated vocabulary with visual mnemonics.* Punta Gorda, FL: New Monic Books.

Burchers, S., Burchers, M., & Burchers, B. (2000). *Vocabulary cartoons II: Building an educated vocabulary with sight and sound memory aids.* Punta Gorda, FL: New Monic Books

Cade, T., & Gunter, P. L. (2002). Teaching students with severe emotional or behavioral disorders to use a musical mnemonic technique to solve basic division calculations. *Behavioral Disorders, 27,* 208–214.

Chen, K. (1973). Pronunciability in verbal learning of the deaf. *The Journal of Psychology, 84,* 89–95.

Cohen, R. L. (1989). Memory for action events: The power of enactment. *Educational Psychology Review, 1,* 57–80.

Cornoldi, C., & Caponi, B. (1993). *Memoria e metacognizione: Attivita didattiche per imparare a ricordare* [Memory and metacognition: Teaching activities for learning how to remember]. Trento, Italy: Erickson.

Cornoldi, C., & Vianello, R. (1992). Metacognitive knowledge, learning disorders, and mental retardation. In T. E. Scruggs & M. A. Mastropieri (Eds.), *Advances in learning and behavioral disabilities* (vol. 7, pp. 107–134). Greenwich, CT: JAI.

Craik, F. I. M., & Lockhart, R. S. (1972). Levels of processing: A framework for memory research. *Journal of Verbal Learning and Verbal Behavior, 11,* 671–684.

Crossairt, A., Hall, R. V., & Hopkins, B. L. (1973). The effects of experimenter's instructions, feedback, and praise on teacher praise and student attending behavior. *Journal of Applied Behavior Analysis, 6,* 89–100.

Dickens, V. J. (1977). *Paired-associate recognition learning and mediational strategy reporting as a function of hearing ability.* Unpublished doctoral dissertation, University of North Carolina, Chapel Hill.

Flavell, J. H., & Wellman, H. M. (1977). Metamemory. In R. V. Kail & W. Hagen (Eds.), *Perspectives on the development of memory and cognition* (pp. 3–33). Hillsdale, NJ: Lawrence Erlbaum.

Forness, S. R., & Kavale, K. A. (1996). Can 700 studies be wrong? Mega-analysis of special education meta-analyses. *Focus on Research: Newsletter of the Division for Research, Council for Exceptional Children, 9*(3), 4–15.

Forness, S. R., & Kavale, K. A. (1997). Mega-analysis of meta-analyses: What works in special education and related services. *Teaching Exceptional Children, 29*(6), 4–9.

Fulk, B. J. M. (1994). Mnemonic keyword strategy training for students with learning disabilities. *Learning Disabilities Research & Practice, 9,* 179–185.

Fulk, B. J. M., Mastropieri, M. A., & Scruggs, T. E. (1992). Mnemonic generalization training with learning disabled adolescents. *Learning Disabilities Research & Practice, 7,* 2–10.

Gelzheiser, L. M. (1984). Generalization from categorical memory tasks to prose by learning disabled adolescents. *Journal of Educational Psychology, 76,* 1128–1138.

Hallahan, D. P., & Cottone, E. A. (1997). Attention deficit hyperactivity disorder. In T. E. Scruggs & M. A. Mastropieri (Eds.), *Advances in learning and behavioral disabilities* (Vol. 11, pp. 27–68). Greenwich, CT: JAI.

Harris, K., Graham, S., Reid, R., McElroy, K., & Hamby, R. S. (1994). Self-monitoring of attention versus self-monitoring of performance: Replication and cross-task comparison studies. *Learning Disability Quarterly, 17,* 121–139.

Heward, W. L. (2000). *Exceptional children* (6th ed.). Upper Saddle River, NJ: Merrill/Prentice Hall.

James, W. (1890/1952). *Principles of psychology.* Chicago: Encyclopedia Britannica.

Jensen, A. R., & Rohwer, W. D. (1963). The effect of verbal mediation on the learning and retention of paired-associates by retarded adults. *American Journal of Mental Deficiency, 68,* 80–84.

Kavale, K. A., & Forness, S. R. (1992). Learning difficulties and memory problems in mental retardation: A meta-analysis of theoretical perspectives. In T. E. Scruggs & M. A. Mastropieri (Eds.), *Advances in learning and behavioral disabilities* (Vol. 7, pp. 177–219).

Kendall, P. C., & Braswell, L. (1985). *Cognitive behavior therapy for impulsive children.* New York: Guilford Press.

Kerr, M. M., & Nelson, C. M. (2001). *Strategies for managing behavior problems in the classroom* (4th ed.). Upper Saddle River, NJ: Merrill/Prentice Hall.

King-Sears, M. E., Mercer, C. D., & Sindelar, P. T. (1992). Toward independence with keyword mnemonic: A strategy for science vocabulary instruction. *Remedial and Special Education, 13,* 22–33.

Lerner, J. (1993). *Learning disabilities: Theories, diagnosis, and teaching strategies* (6th ed.). Boston: Houghton-Mifflin.

Lerner, J. W., Lowenthal, B., & Lerner, S. R. (1995). *Attention deficit disorders: Assessment and teaching.* Pacific Grove, CA: Brooks/Cole.

Lloyd, J. W., Hallahan, D. P., Kosiewicz, M. M., & Kneedler, R. D. (1982). Effects of self-assessment and self-recording on attention to task and academic productivity. *Learning Disability Quarterly, 5,* 216–227.

Lloyd, J. W., & Landrum, T. (1990). Self-recording of attending to task: Treatment components and generalization effects. In T. E. Scruggs & B. Y. L. Wong (Eds.), *Intervention research in learning disabilities.* New York: Springer-Verlag.

Lucangeli, D., Galderisi, D., & Cornoldi, C. (1995). Specific and general transfer effects following metamemory training. *Learning Disabilities Research & Practice, 10,* 11–21.

Mastropieri, M. A., Jenkins, V., & Scruggs, T. E. (1985). Academic and intellectual characteristics of behaviorally disordered children and youth. *Severe Behavior Disorders Monographs, 8,* 86–104.

Mastropieri, M. A., & Scruggs, T. E. (1989a). Constructing more meaningful relationships: Mnemonic instruction for special populations. *Educational Psychology Review, 1,* 83–111.

Mastropieri, M. A., & Scruggs, T. E. (1989b). Mnemonic social studies instruction: Classroom applications. *Remedial and Special Education, 10*(3), 40–46.

Mastropieri, M. A., & Scruggs, T. E. (1991). *Teaching students ways to remember: Strategies for learning mnemonically.* Cambridge, MA: Brookline Books.

Mastropieri, M. A., Scruggs, T. E., Bakken, J., & Brigham, F. J. (1992). A complex mnemonic strategy for teaching states and capitals: Comparing forward and backward associations. *Learning Disabilities Research & Practice, 7,* 96–103.

Mastropieri, M. A., Scruggs, T. E., & Butcher, K. (1997). How effective is inquiry learning for students with mild disabilities? *Journal of Special Education, 31,* 199–211.

Mastropieri, M. A., Scruggs, T. E., & Fulk, B. J. M. (1990). Teaching abstract vocabulary with the keyword method: Effects on recall and comprehension. *Journal of Learning Disabilities, 23,* 92–96.

Mastropieri, M. A., Scruggs, T. E., Graetz, J., Fontana, Coles, V., & Gerson, A. (in press). Mnemonic strategies: What are they? How can I use them? And how effective are they? In M. Riley (Ed.), *Best practices for all children in the inclusionary classroom.* Boston: Massachusetts Learning Disabilities Association.

Mastropieri, M. A., Scruggs, T. E., Mantzicopoulos, P., Sturgeon, A., Goodwin, L., & Chung, S. (1998). "A place where living things affect and depend on each other": Qualitative and quantitative outcomes associated with inclusive science teaching. *Science Education, 82,* 163–179.

Mastropieri, M. A., Scruggs, T. E., & Whedon, C. (1997). Using mnemonic strategies to teach information about U.S. presidents: A classroom-based investigation. *Learning Disability Quarterly, 20,* 13–21.

Mastropieri, M. A., Scruggs, T. E., Whittaker, M. E. S., & Bakken, J. P. (1994). Applications of mnemonic strategies with students with mental disabilities. *Remedial and Special Education, 15*(1), 34–43.

Montague, M., Fiore, T., Hocutt, A., McKinney, J. D., & Harris, J. (1996). Interventions for students with attention deficit hyperactivity disorder: A review of the literature. In T. E. Scruggs & M. A. Mastropieri (Eds.), *Advances in learning and behavioral disabilities: Intervention research* (Vol. 10, Part B, pp. 23–50). Greenwich, CT: JAI.

Paivio, A., & Okovita, H. W. (1971). Word imagery modalities and associative learning in blind and sighted subjects. *Journal of Verbal Learning and Verbal Behavior, 101,* 506–510.

Prater, M., Joy, R., Chilman, B., Temple, J., & Miller, S. R. (1991). Self-monitoring of on-task behavior by adolescents with learning disabilities. *Learning Disability Quarterly, 14,* 164–177.

Pressley, M., & McCormick, C. B. (1995). *Advanced educational psychology for educators, researchers, and policymakers.* New York: HarperCollins.

Putnam, M. L. (1992). Characteristics of questions on tests administered by mainstream secondary classroom teachers. *Learning Disabilities Research & Practice, 7,* 129–136.

Redl, F. (1952). *Controls from within: Techniques for the treatment of the aggressive child.* Glencoe, IL: Free Press.

Rey, H. A. (1962). *The stars: A new way to see them.* Boston: Houghton Mifflin.

Rooney, K. J., Hallahan, D. P., & Lloyd, J. W. (1984). Self-recording of attention by learning disabled students in the regular classroom. *Journal of Learning Disabilities, 17,* 360–364.

Russell, F. (1975). *The Pima Indians.* Tucson: University of Arizona Press.

Scott, M. S., & Perou, R. (1994). Some observations on the impact of learning disabilities and mild mental retardation on the cognitive abilities of young grade school children. In T. E. Scruggs & M. A. Mastropieri (Eds.), *Advances in learning and behavioral disabilities* (Vol. 8, pp. 215–234). Greenwich, CT: JAI.

Scruggs, T. E., & Brigham, F. J. (1991). Utility of musical mnemonics. *Perceptual and Motor Skills, 72,* 881–882.

Scruggs, T. E., & Cohn, S. J. (1983). Learning characteristics of verbally gifted students. *Gifted Child Quarterly, 27,* 169–172.

Scruggs, T. E., & Mastropieri, M. A. (1985). Spontaneous verbal elaboration in gifted and non-gifted youths. *Journal for the Education of the Gifted, 9,* 1–10.

Scruggs, T. E., & Mastropieri, M. A. (1989). Reconstructive elaborations: A model for content area learning. *American Educational Research Journal, 26,* 311–327.

Scruggs, T. E., & Mastropieri, M. A. (1990). Mnemonic instruction for learning disabled students: What it is and what it does. *Learning Disability Quarterly, 13,* 271–281.

Scruggs, T. E., & Mastropieri, M. A. (1992). Classroom applications of mnemonic instruction: Acquisition, maintenance, and generalization. *Exceptional Children, 58,* 219–229.

Scruggs, T. E., & Mastropieri, M. A. (1995). Science and mental retardation: An analysis of curriculum features and learner characteristics. *Science Education, 79,* 251–271.

Scruggs, T. E., & Mastropieri, M. A. (2000). The effectiveness of mnemonic instruction for students with learning and behavior problems: An update and research synthesis. *Journal of Behavioral Education, 10,* 163–173.

Scruggs, T. E., Mastropieri, M. A., Bakken, J. P., & Brigham, F. J. (1993). Reading vs. doing: The relative effectiveness of textbook-based and inquiry-oriented approaches to science education. *Journal of Special Education, 27,* 1–15.

Scruggs, T. E., Mastropieri, M. A., Jorgensen, C., & Monson, J. A. (1986). Effective mnemonic strategies for gifted learners. *Journal for the Education of the Gifted, 9,* 105–121.

Scruggs, T. E., Mastropieri, M. A., Levin, J. R., & Gaffney, J. S. (1985). Facilitating the acquisition of science facts in learning disabled students. *American Educational Research Journal, 22,* 575–586.

Scruggs, T. E., Mastropieri, M. A., & Sullivan, G. S. (1994). Promoting relational thinking skills: Elaborative interrogation for mildly handicapped students. *Exceptional Children, 60,* 450–457.

Scruggs, T. E., Prieto, A., & Zucker, S. (1981). Classroom hearing assessment: An operant training procedure for the non-verbal, autistic child. *Monographs in Behavioral Disorders, 4,* 89–95.

Shiffrin, R. M., & Schneider, W. (1980). Controlled and automatic human information processing: II. Perceptual learning, automatic attending, and a general theory. In J. G. Seamon (Ed.), *Human memory: Contemporary readings* (pp. 24–41). New York: Oxford University Press.

Sullivan, G. S., Mastropieri, M. A., & Scruggs, T. E. (1995). Reasoning and remembering: Coaching thinking with students with learning disabilities. *Journal of Special Education, 29,* 310–322.

Swanson, H. L. (1994). The role of working memory and dynamic assessment in the classification of children with learning disabilities. *Learning Disabilities Research & Practice, 4,* 190–202.

Terrill, M. C. (2002). *Mnemonic strategy vocabulary instruction with learning disabled high school students.* Unpublished master's project, George Mason University, Fairfax, VA.

Tulving, E. (1972). Episodic and semantic memory. In E. Tulving & W. Donaldson (Eds.), *Organization of memory* (pp. 381–403). New York: Academic Press.

Tulving, E. (1983). *Elements of episodic memory.* Oxford: Oxford University Press.

Uberti, H. Z., Scruggs, T. E., & Mastropieri, M. A. (2003). Key words make the difference! Mnemonic instruction in inclusive classrooms. A classroom application. *Teaching Exceptional Children, 35*(3), 56–61.

Underwood, B. J. (1983). *Attributes of memory.* Glenview, IL: Scott, Foresman.

Veit, D. T., Scruggs, T. E., & Mastropieri, M. A. (1986). Extended mnemonic instruction with learning disabled students. *Journal of Educational Psychology, 78,* 300–308.

Walker, J. M., & Buckley, N. K. (1968). The use of positive reinforcement in conditioning attending behavior. *Journal of Applied Behavior Analysis, 1,* 245–250.

Willott, P. C. (1982). *The use of imagery as a mnemonic to teach basic multiplication facts to students with learning disabilities.* Unpublished doctoral dissertation, West Virginia University, Morgantown.

Yates, F. (1966). *The art of memory.* Chicago: University of Chicago Press.

Zimler, J., & Keenan, J. M. (1983). Imagery in the congenitally blind: How visual are visual images? *Journal of experimental psychology: Learning, memory, and cognition, 9,* 269–282.

Zirpoli, T. J., & Melloy, K. J. (1997). *Behavior management: Appications for teachers and parents.* Upper Saddle River, NJ: Merrill/Prentice Hall.

Chapter 11

Alley, G., & Deshler, D. D. (1979). *Teaching the learning disabled adolescent: Strategies and methods.* Denver: Love Publishing.

Carman, R. A., & Adams, W. R. (1984). *Study skills: A student's guide for survival* (2nd ed.). New York: Wiley.

Carter, C., Bishop, J., Kravits, S. L., & Bucher, R. D. (2002). *Keys to effective learning* (3rd ed.). Upper Saddle River, NJ: Merrill/Prentice Hall.

Deshler, D. D., Ellis, E. S., & Lenz, B. K. (Eds.). (1996). *Teaching adolescents with learning disabilities: Strategies and methods* (2nd ed.). Denver: Love Publishing.

Deshler, D. D., Schumaker, J. B., Alley, G. R., Clark, F. L., & Warner, M. M. (1981). *LINKS: A listening/notetaking strategy.* Unpublished manuscript. Lawrence, KS: University of Kansas Institute for Research in Learning Disabilities.

Deshler, D. D., Schumaker, J. B., & Lenz, B. K. (1984). Academic and cognitive interventions for LD adolescents: Part I. *Journal of Learning Disabilities, 17,* 108–117.

Devine, T. G. (1987). *Teaching study skills* (2nd ed.). Boston: Allyn & Bacon.

Gall, M. D., Gall, J. P., Jacobsen, D. R., & Bullock, T. L. (1990). *Tools for learning: A guide for teaching study skills.* Alexandria, VA: Association for Supervision and Curriculum Development.

Gaskins, I., & Elliot, T. (1991). *Implementing cognitive strategy training across the school: The Benchmark manual for teachers.* Cambridge, MA: Brookline Books.

Hoover, J. J. (1993). *Teaching study skills to students with learning problems.* Boulder, CO: Hamilton.

Horton, S. V., Lovitt, T. C., & Christensen, C. C. (1991). Notetaking from textbooks: Effects of a columnar format on three categories of secondary students. *Exceptionality, 2*(1), 19–40.

Hughes, C. A., Ruhl, K. L., Schumaker, J. B., & Deshler, D. D. (2002). Effects of instruction in an assignment completion strategy on the homework performance of students with learning disabilities in general education classes. *Learning Disabilities Research & Practice, 17,* 1–18.

Hutchins, R. M. (1952). *Great books of the western world.* Chicago, IL: Britannica.

Kerr, M. M., & Nelson, C. M. (2002). *Strategies for addressing behavior problems in the classroom* (4th ed.). Upper Saddle River, NJ: Merrill/Prentice Hall.

Luckie, W. R., & Smethurst, W. (1997). *Study power: Study skills to improve your learning and your grades.* Cambridge, MA: Brookline Books.

Mastropieri, M. A., & Scruggs, T. E. (2002). *Effective instruction for special education* (3rd ed.). Austin, TX: Pro-Ed.

McNaughton, D., Hughes, C. A., & Ofiesh, N. (1997). Proofreading for students with learning disabilities: Integrating computer and strategy use. *Learning Disabilities Research & Practice, 12,* 16–28.

Meltzer, L. J., Roditi, B. N., Haynes, D. P., Biddle, K. R., Paster, M., & Taber, S. E. (1996). *Strategies for success: Classroom teaching techniques for students with learning problems.* Austin, TX: Pro-Ed.

Mercer, C. D., & Mercer, A. R. (1998). *Teaching students with learning problems* (5th ed.). Upper Saddle River, NJ: Merrill/Prentice Hall.

O'Melia, M. C., & Rosenberg, M. S. (1994). Effects of cooperative homework teams on the acquisition of mathematics skills by secondary students with mild disabilities. *Exceptional Children, 60,* 538–548.

Pauk, W. (1987). *Study skills for junior and community colleges.* Clearwater, FL: Reston–Stuart.

Polloway, E. A., Epstein, M. H., Bursuck, W. D., Jayanthi, M., & Cumblad, C. (1994). A national survey of homework practices of general education teachers. *Journal of Learning Disabilities, 27,* 500–509.

Polloway, E. A., Foley, R. M., & Epstein, M. H. (1992). Homework problems of students with learning disabilities and nonhandicapped students. *Learning Disabilities Research & Practice, 7,* 203–209.

Rafoth, M. A., Leal, L., & DeFabo, L. (1993). *Strategies for learning and remembering: Study skills across the curriculum.* Washington, DC: NEA Professional Library.

Scheid, K. (1993). *Helping students become strategic learners: Guidelines for teaching.* Cambridge, MA: Brookline Books.

Suritsky, S. K., & Hughes, C. A. (1993). *Notetaking strategy training for college students with learning disabilities.* Unpublished manuscript. College Park: Pennsylvania State University.

Suritsky, S. K., & Hughes, C. A. (1996). Notetaking strategy instruction. In D. D. Deshler, E. S. Ellis, & B. K. Lenz (Eds.), *Teaching adolescents with learning disabilities: Strategies and methods* (2nd ed., pp. 267–312). Denver: Love Publishing.

Wilson, H. W. (1987). *Reader's guide to periodical literature.* New York: H. W. Wilson.

Wood, E., Woloshyn, V. E., & Willoughby, T. (Eds.). (1995). *Cognitive strategy instruction for middle and high schools.* Cambridge, MA: Brookline Books.

Chapter 12

Anderson, M. G., & Webb-Johnson, G. (1995). Cultural contexts, the seriously emotionally disturbed classification, and African American learners. In B. A. Ford, F. E. Obiakor, & J. M. Patton (Eds.), *Effective education of African American exceptional learners: New perspectives* (pp. 151–188). Austin, TX: Pro-Ed.

Artiles, A. J., & Zamora-Durán, G. (1997). *Reducing disproportionate representation of culturally diverse students in special and gifted education.* Reston, VA: Council for Exceptional Children.

Baca, L. M., & Almanza, E. (1991). *Language minority students with disabilities.* Reston, VA: Council for Exceptional Children.

Baron, J. B. (1990). Performance assessment: Blurring the edges among assessment, curriculum, and instruction. In A. B. Champaign, B. E. Lovitts, & B. J. Callinger (Eds.), *Assessment in the service of instruction* (pp. 127–148). Washington, DC: American Association for the Advancement of Science.

Beattie, S., Grise, P., & Algozzine, B. (1983). Effects of test modification on minimum competency performance of learning disabled students. *Learning Disability Quarterly, 6,* 75–77.

Bennett, C. I. (1999). *Multicultural education: Theory and practice* (4th ed.). Boston: Allyn & Bacon.

Bradley, D. F., & Calvin, M. B. (1998). Grading modified assignments. *Teaching Exceptional Children, 31*(2), 24–29.

Bursuck, W. D., Polloway, E. A., Plante, L., Epstein, M. H., Jayanthi, M., & McConeghy, J. (1996). Report card grading and adaptations: A national survey of classroom practices. *Exceptional Children, 62,* 301–318.

Carman, R. A., & Adams, W. R. (1972). *Study skills: A student's guide for survival.* New York: Wiley.

Chenoweth, K. (1996). 2004: Maryland's reform odyssey. *Black Issues in Higher Education, 12*(26), 10–12.

Christiansen, J., & Vogel, J. R. (1998). A decision model for grading students with disabilities. *Teaching Exceptional Children, 31*(2), 30–35.

Connolly, A. J. (1988). *KeyMath revised: A diagnostic inventory of essential mathematics.* Circle Pines, MN: American Guidance Service.

Council for Exceptional Children (CEC) (2002). No child left behind has major implications for special education. *CEC Today, 9*(4), 4.

Coutinho, M., & Malouf, D. (1993). Performance assessment and children with disabilities: Issues and possibilities. *Teaching Exceptional Children, 25*(4), 63–67.

Cummins, V. (1984). *Bilingualism and special education: Issues in assessment and pedagogy.* San Diego, CA: College Hill Press.

Dalton, B., Tivnan, T., Riley, M. K., Rawson, P., & Dias, D. (1995). Revealing competence: Fourth-grade students with and without learning disabilities show what they know on paper-and-pencil and hands-on performance assessment. *Learning Disabilities Research & Practice, 10,* 198–214.

Donahoe, K., & Zigmond, N. (1990). Academic grades of ninth-grade urban learning-disabled students and low-achieving peers. *Exceptionality, 1,* 17–27.

Elliott, S. N., Kratochwill, T. R., & Schulte, A. A. G. (1998a). *The assessment accommodation checklist.* Monterey, CA: CTB/McGraw-Hill.

Elliott, S. N., Kratochwill, T. R., & Schulte, A. A. G. (1998b). The assessment accommodation checklist: Who, what, where, when, why, and how? *Teaching Exceptional Children, 31*(2), 10–14.

Erickson, R., Ysseldyke, J., Thurlow, M., & Elliott, J. (1998). Inclusive assessments and accountability systems: Tools of the trade in educational reform. *Teaching Exceptional Children, 31*(2), 4–9.

Erwin, B., & Dunwiddie, E. T. (1983). *Test without trauma.* New York: Grosset and Dunlap.

Ford, B. A., Obiakor, F. E., & Patton, J. M. (Eds.). (1995). *Effective education of African American exceptional learners: New perspectives.* Austin, TX: Pro-Ed.

Frase-Blunt, M. (2000). High stakes testing a mixed blessing for special students. *CEC Today, 7*(2), 1, 5, 7, 15.

Fuchs, D., & Fuchs, L. S. (1989). Effects of examiner familiarity on Black, Caucasian, and Hispanic children: A meta-analysis. *Exceptional Children, 55,* 303–308.

Fuchs, D., Fuchs, L. S., Benowitz, S., & Barringer, K. (1987). Norm-referenced tests: Are they valid for use with handicapped students? *Exceptional Children, 54,* 263–271.

Fuchs, D., Fuchs, L. S., & Power, M. H. (1987). Effects of examiner familiarity of LD and MR students' language performance. *Remedial and Special Education, 8*(4), 47–52.

Fuchs, L. S. (1994). *Connecting performance assessment to instruction.* Reston, VA: Council for Exceptional Children.

Fuchs, L. S., & Fuchs, D. (1994). Academic assessment and instrumentation. In S. Vaughn & C. Bos (Eds.), *Research issues in learning disabilities: Theory, methodology, assessment, and ethics* (pp. 233–245). New York: Springer-Verlag.

Fuchs, L. S., Fuchs, D., Allinder, R. M., & Hamlett, C. L. (1992). Diagnostic spelling analysis within curriculum-based measurement: Implications for students with learning disabilities. In T. E. Scruggs & M. A. Mastropieri (Eds.), *Advances in learning and behavioral disabilities* (Vol. 7, pp. 35–55). Greenwich, CT: JAI Press.

Fuchs, L. S., Fuchs, D., Hamlett, C. L., Phillips, N. B., & Bentz, J. (1994). Classwide curriculum-based measurement: Helping general educators meet the challenge of student diversity. *Exceptional Children, 60,* 518–537.

Fuchs, L. S., Fuchs, D., Hamlett, C. L., & Stecker, P. M. (1991). Effects of curriculum-based measurement and consultation on teacher planning and student achievement in mathematics operations. *American Educational Research Journal, 28,* 617–641.

Fuchs, L. S., Hamlett, C., & Fuchs, D. (1990). *Basic spelling.* Austin, TX: Pro-Ed.

Fuchs, L. S., Hamlett, C., & Fuchs, D. (1997). *Basic reading.* Austin, TX: Pro-Ed.

Fuchs, L. S., Hamlett, C., & Fuchs, D. (1998). *Basic math computation.* Austin, TX: Pro-Ed.

Fuchs, L. S., Hamlett, C., & Fuchs, D. (1999). *Basic math concepts and applications.* Austin, TX: Pro-Ed.

Gajria, M., Salend, S. J., & Hemrick, M. A. (1994). Teacher acceptability of testing modifications for mainstreamed students. *Learning Disabilities Research & Practice, 9,* 236–243.

Haigh, J. A. (1996, April). *Maryland School Performance Program. Outcomes, standards, & high-stakes accountability: Perspectives from Maryland and Kentucky.* Paper presented at the Annual Convention of the Council for Exceptional Children, Orlando. (ERIC Document Reproduction Service No. ED394256)

Hamm, M., & Adams, D. (1991). Portfolio assessment. *The Science Teacher, 58*(5), 18–21.

Hammill, D. D., & Larsen, S. C. (1996). *Test of written language.* Austin, TX: Pro-Ed.

Hansen, J. (1992). Literacy portfolios: Helping students know themselves. *Educational Leadership, 49*(8), 68–66.

Howell, K. W., & Morehead, M. K. (1987). *Curriculum-based evaluation for special and remedial education.* New York: Merrill/McMillan.

Hughes, C. (1996). Memory and test-taking strategies. In D. D. Deshler, E. S. Ellis, & B. K. Lenz (Eds.), *Teaching adolescents with learning disabilities: Strategies and methods* (2nd ed., pp. 209–266). Denver: Love Publishing.

Hughes, C. A., Rule, K. L., Deshler, D. & Schumaker, J. B. (1993). Test-taking strategy instruction for adolescents with emotional and behavioral disorders. *Journal of Emotional and Behavioral Disorders, 1,* 189–198.

Hughes, C. A., & Schumaker, J. B. (1991). Test taking strategy for adolescents with learning disabilities. *Exceptionality, 2,* 205–221.

Hughes, C. A., Schumaker, J. B., Deshler, D. D., & Mercer, C. D. (1988). *The test-taking strategy.* Lawrence, KS: Edge Enterprises.

Jayanthi, M., Epstein, M. H., Polloway, E. A., & Bursuck, W. D. (1996). A national survey of general education teachers' perceptions of testing adaptations. *Journal of Special Education, 30,* 99–115.

Johnson, E., Kimball, K., Brown, S. O., & Anderson, D. (2001). A statewide review of the use of accommodations in large-scale, high-stakes assessments. *Exceptional Children, 67,* 251–264.

Kaufman, A., & Kaufman, N. (1983). *The Kaufman assessment battery for children.* Circle Pines, MN: American Guidance Service.

Kaufman, A. S., & Kaufman, N. L. (1997). *Kaufman test of educational achievement.* Circle Pines, MN: American Guidance Service.

Knight, P. (1992). How I use portfolios in mathematics. *Educational Leadership, 49*(8), 71–72.

Learning Disabilities Association. (1993). *Fact sheet: Tests of General Educational Development (GED Tests).* Pittsburgh: Author.

Learning Disabilities Association. (1994). *Fact sheet: Entrance Tests for Postsecondary Programs.* Pittsburgh: Author.

Learning Disabilities Association. (1995). *Fact sheet: Learning disabilities and educational standards.* Pittsburgh: Author.

Lee, P., & Alley, G. R. (1981). *Training junior high school LD students to use a test-taking strategy.* Lawrence, KS: Kansas University. (ERIC Reproduction Service No. ED-217649)

Lucangeli, D., & Scruggs, T.E. (2003). Test anxiety, perceived competence, and academic achievement in secondary school students. In T.E. Scruggs & MA. Mastropieri (Eds.), *Identification and assessment: Advances in learning and behavioral disabilities* (pp. 223–230). Oxford, UK: Elsevier Science.

Markwardt, F. C. (1989). *Peabody individual achievement test—Revised.* Circle Pines, MN: American Guidance Service.

Massachusetts Department of Education. (1998). *The Massachusetts Comprehensive Assessment System: Requirements for the participation of students with disabilities (A guide for educators and parents).* Boston, MA: Massachusetts Department of Education.

Mastropieri, M. A., Scruggs, T. E., Mantzicopoulos, P. Y., Sturgeon, A., Goodwin, L., & Chung, S. (1998). "A place where living things affect and depend on each other": Qualitative and quantitative outcomes associated with inclusive science teaching. *Science Education, 82,* 163–179.

McLoughlin, J. A., & Lewis, R. B. (2000). *Assessing special students* (5th ed.). Upper Saddle River, NJ: Merrill/Prentice Hall.

Millman, J., Bishop, C. H., & Ebel, R. (1965). An analysis of test wiseness. *Educational and Psychological Measurement, 25,* 707–726.

Millman, J., & Pauk, W. (1969). *How to take tests.* New York: McGraw Hill.

Munk, D., & Bursuck, W. D. (1998). Report card adaptations for students with disabilities: Types and acceptability. *Intervention in School and Clinic, 33,* 306–308.

Munk, D., & Bursuck, W. D. (2001). What report card grades should and do communicate: Perceptions of parents of secondary students with and without disabilities. *Remedial and Special Education, 22,* 280–287.

Overton, T. (1999). *Assessment in special education* (3rd ed.). Upper Saddle River, NJ: Merrill/Prentice Hall.

Pauk, W. (1987). *Study skills for junior and community colleges.* Clearwater, FL: Reston–Stuart.

Phillips, S. E. (1995). *All students, same test, same standards: What the new Title I legislation will mean for the educational assessment of special education students.* Oak Brook, IL: North Central Regional Educational Lab. (ERIC Document Reproduction Service No. ED394269)

Polloway, E. A., Epstein, M. H., Bursuck, W. D., Roderique, T. W., McConeky, J. L., & Jayanthi, M. (1994). Classroom grading: A national survey of policies. *Remedial and Special Education, 15*(3), 162–170.

Putnam, M. L. (1992). The testing practices of mainstream secondary classroom teachers. *Remedial and Special Education, 13*(5), 11–21.

Ritter, S., & Idol-Maestas, L. (1986). Teaching middle school students to use a test-taking strategy. *Journal of Educational Research, 79,* 350–357.

Rojewski, J. W., Pollard, R. R., & Meers, G. D. (1992). Grading secondary vocational education students with disabilities: A national perspective. *Exceptional Children, 59,* 68–76.

Salend, S. (1995). Modifying tests for diverse learners. *Intervention in School and Clinic, 31,* 84–90.

Salend, S. (1998). Using portfolios to assess student performance. *Teaching Exceptional Children, 31*(2), 36–43.

Salvia, J., & Ysseldyke, J. E. (2001). *Assessment* (8th ed.). Boston: Houghton Mifflin.

Sammons, K. B., Kobett, B., Heiss, J., & Fennell, F. S. (1992, February). Linking instruction and assessment in the mathematics classroom. *Arithmetic Teacher,* 11–15.

Sarason, I. G. (Ed.). (1980). *Test anxiety: Theory, practice and applications* (pp. 3–14). Hillsdale, NJ: Lawrence Erlbaum.

Schirmer, B. R., & Bailey, J. (2000). Writing assessment rubric: An instructional approach with struggling writers. *Teaching Exceptional Children, 33,* 52–58.

Scruggs, T. E., Bennion, K., & Lifson, S. (1985a). An analysis of children's strategy use on reading achievement tests. *The Elementary School Journal, 85,* 479–484.

Scruggs, T. E., Bennion, K., & Lifson, S. (1985b). Learning disabled students' spontaneous use of test-taking skills on reading achievement tests. *Learning Disability Quarterly, 8,* 205–210.

Scruggs, T. E., & Marsing, L. (1988). Teaching test-taking skills to behaviorally disordered students. *Behavioral Disorders, 13,* 240–244.

Scruggs, T. E., & Mastropieri, M. A. (1986a). Academic characteristics of behaviorally disordered and learning disabled children. *Behavioral Disorders, 11,* 184–190.

Scruggs, T. E., & Mastropieri, M. A. (1986b). Improving the test-taking skills of behaviorally disordered and learning disabled students. *Exceptional Children, 53,* 63–68.

Scruggs, T. E., & Mastropieri, M. A. (1988). Are learning disabled students 'test-wise'?: A review of recent research. *Learning Disabilities Focus, 3,* 87–97.

Scruggs, T. E., & Mastropieri, M. A. (1992). *Teaching test-taking skills: Helping students show what they know.* Cambridge, MA: Brookline Books.

Scruggs, T. E., & Mastropieri, M. A. (1994–1995). Assessing students with learning disabilities: Current issues and future directions. *Diagnostique, 20,* 17–31.

Scruggs, T. E., Mastropieri, M. A., Bakken, J. P., & Brigham, F. J. (1993). Reading vs. doing: The relative effectiveness of textbook-based and inquiry-oriented approaches to science education. *Journal of Special Education, 27,* 1–15.

Scruggs, T. E., Mastropieri, M. A., Tolfa, D., & Jenkins, V. (1985). Attitudes of behaviorally disordered students toward tests. *Perceptual and Motor Skills, 60,* 467–470.

Scruggs, T. E., Mastropieri, M. A., & Veit, D. (1986). The effects of coaching on the standardized test performance of learning disabled and behaviorally disordered students. *Remedial and Special Education, 7*(5), 37–41.

Scruggs, T. E., & Veit, D. T. (1986). Can LD students effectively use separate answer sheets? *Perceptual and Motor Skills, 63,* 155–160.

Selby, D., & Murphy, S. (1992). Graded or degraded: Perceptions of letter-grading for mainstreamed learning-disabled students. *B.C. Journal of Special Education, 16,* 92–104.

Swicegood, P. (1994). Portfolio-based assessment practices. *Intervention in School and Clinic, 30*(1), 6–15.

Thorndike, R. L., Hagen, E., & Sattler, J. (1986). *Stanford-Binet intelligence scale* (4th ed.). Chicago: Riverside.

Tolfa, D., Scruggs, T. E., & Bennion, K. (1985). Format changes in reading achievement tests: Implications for students with learning disabilities. *Psychology in the Schools, 22,* 387–391.

Tolfa, D., Scruggs, T. E., & Mastropieri, M. A. (1985). Attitudes of behaviorally disordered students toward tests: A replication. *Perceptual and Motor Skills, 61,* 963–966.

Training and Technical Assistance Center at the College of William and Mary. (2002). *Virginia's alternate assessment program.* Williamsburg, VA: Author.

Vavrus, L. (1990). Put portfolios to the test. *Instructor, 100*(1), 48–53.

Veit, D. T., & Scruggs, T. E. (1986). Can learning disabled students effectively use separate answer sheets? *Perceptual and Motor Skills, 63,* 155–160.

Virginia Department of Education. (2001). *Virginia Alternate Assessment Program (VAAP): Guidelines for participation.* Richmond, VA: Author.

Wechsler, D. (1991). *Wechsler intelligence scale for children* (3rd ed.). San Antonio, TX: Psychological Corporation.

Wesson, C. L., & King, R. P. (1992). The role of curriculum-based measurement in portfolio assessment. *Diagnostique, 18*(1), 27–37.

Wesson, C. L., & King, R. P. (1996). Portfolio assessment and special education students. *Teaching Exceptional Children, 28*(2), 44–48.

Wilkenson, G. S. (1993). *Wide range achievement test—Revision 3.* Wilmington, DE: Jastak Associates.

Wine, J. (1971). Test anxiety and the direction of attention. *Psychological Bulletin, 76,* 92–104.

Winzer, M. A., & Mazurek, K. (1998). *Special education in multicultural contexts.* Upper Saddle River, NJ: Merrill/Prentice Hall.

Wood, W., & Willoughby, T. (1995). Cognitive strategies for test-taking. In E. Wood, V. E. Woloshyn, & T. Willoughby (Eds.), *Cognitive strategy instruction for middle and high schools* (pp. 245–258). Cambridge, MA: Brookline Books.

Woodcock, R. W. (1987). *Woodcock reading mastery tests* (Rev.). Circle Pines, MN: American Guidance Service.

Woodcock, R. W., Johnson, M. B. & Mather, N. (2001). *Woodcock-Johnson III, Tests of achievement.* Circle Pines, MN: American Guidance Service.

Zigmond, N., Levin, E., & Laurie, T. (1985). Managing the mainstream: An analysis of teacher attitudes and student performance in mainstreaming high school programs. *Journal of Learning Disabilities, 18,* 535–541.

Chapter 13

Adams, M. J. (1990). *Beginning to read.* Cambridge, MA: Massachusetts Institute of Technology Press.

Adams, M. J., Foorman, B. R., Lundberg, I., & Beeler, T. (1998). *Phonemic awareness in young children.* Baltimore: Brookes Publishing.

Adoption Guidelines Project. (1990). *A guide to selecting basal reading programs.* Champaign, IL: Center for the Study of Reading, University of Illinois at Urbana–Champaign.

Anderson, R. C., Hiebert, E. H., Scott, J. A., & Wilkinson, I. A. G. (1985). *Becoming a nation of readers: The report of the commission on reading.* Washington, DC: National Academy of Education, Commission on Education and Public Policy.

Bahr, C. M., Nelson, N. W., & Van Meter, A. M. (1996). The effects of text-based and graphics-based software tools on planning and organizing stories. *Journal of Learning Disabilities, 29,* 355–370.

Bakken, J. P., Mastropieri, M. A., & Scruggs, T. E. (1997). Reading comprehension of expository science material and students with learning disabilities: A comparison of strategies. *Journal of Special Education, 31,* 300–324.

Ball, E. W., & Blachman, B. A. (1988). Phoneme segmentation training: Effect on reading readiness. *Annals of Dyslexia, 38,* 208–225.

Beal, C. R. (1996). The role of comprehension monitoring in children's revision. *Educational Psychology Review, 8,* 219–238.

Billingsley, B. S., & Wildman, T. M. (1988). The effects of prereading activities on the comprehension monitoring of learning disabled adolescents. *Learning Disabilities Research, 4,* 36–44.

Blachman, B. A. (1991). Early intervention for children's reading problems: Clinical applications of the research in phonological awareness. *Topics in Language Disorders, 12*(1), 51–65.

Boning, R. A. (1990). *Specific skills series* (4th ed.). Blacklick, OH: SRA.

Borkowski, J. G., Weyhing, R. S., & Carr, M. (1988). Effects of attributional retraining on strategy-based reading comprehension in learning-disabled students. *Journal of Educational Psychology, 80*(1), 46–53.

Bos, C. S., & Anders, P. L. (1990). Effects of interactive vocabulary instruction on the vocabulary learning and reading comprehension of junior high learning disabled students. *Learning Disability Quarterly, 13,* 31–42.

Bos, C. S., Anders, P. L., Filip, D., & Jaffe, L. E. (1989). The effects of an interactive instructional strategy for enhancing reading comprehension and content area learning for students with learning disabilities. *Journal of Learning Disabilities, 22*(6), 384–390.

Brady, S. A., & Shankweiler, D. P. (Eds.). (1991). *Phonological processes in literacy: A tribute to Isabelle Y. Liberman.* Hillsdale, NJ: Lawrence Erlbaum.

Brigance, A. H. (1991). *Victory!* East Moline: Linguisystems.

Browder, D. M., & Xin, Y. P. (1998). A meta-analysis and review of sight word research and its implications for teaching functional reading to individuals with moderate and severe disabilities. *Journal of Special Education, 32,* 130–153.

Bryant, N. D., Drabin, I. R., & Gettinger, M. (1981). Effects of varying unit size on spelling achievement of learning disabled children. *Journal of Learning Disabilities, 14,* 200–203.

Carle, E. (1994). *The very hungry caterpillar.* New York: Philomel Books.

Carnine, D., Silbert, J., & Kameenui, E. J. (1997). *Direct instruction reading* (2nd ed.). Upper Saddle River, NJ: Merrill/Prentice Hall.

Castagnozzi, P. (1996). *Sight words you can see.* East Weymouth, MA: Castagnozzi Learning Materials.

Chall, J. S. (1983). *Stages of reading development.* New York: McGraw Hill Book Company.

Chall, J. S. (1987). Reading development in adults. *Annals of Dyslexia, 37,* 240–251.

Chamberlain, J., & Leal, D. J. (1999). Caldecott Medal books and readability levels: Not just picture books. *The Reading Teacher, 52,* 898–902.

Clay, M. (1985). *Early detection of reading difficulties.* Portsmouth, NH: Heinemann.

Clay, M., & Watson, B. (1987). *Reading recovery book list.* Auckland, New Zealand: University of Auckland.

Cunningham, A., & Stanovich, K. (1997). Early reading acquisition and its relation to reading experience and ability ten years later. *Developmental Psychology, 33,* 934–945.

DeBeni, R., & Pazzaglia, F. (1991). *Lettura e metacognizione.* Trento, Italy: Edizioni Centro Studi Erickson.

DeFord, D. E., Pinnell, G. S., Lyons, C. A., & Young, P. (1988). *Reading recovery: Volume IX, report of the follow-up studies.* Columbus, OH: Ohio State University.

Delquadri, J. C., Greenwood, C. R., Stretton, K., & Hall, R. V. (1983). The peer tutoring spelling game: A classroom procedure for increasing opportunity to respond and spelling performance. *Education and Treatment of Children, 6,* 225–239.

Deshler, D. D., Ellis, E. S., & Lenz, B. K. (1996). *Teaching adolescents with learning disabilities: Strategies and methods* (2nd ed.). Denver: Love Publishing.

Dixon, R., & Engelmann, S. (1980). *Corrective spelling through morphographs.* Blacklick, OH: Science Research Associates.

Dixon, R., & Engelmann, S. (1990). *Spelling mastery* [curriculum materials levels A–F]. Chicago: Science Research Associates.

Dodds, T., & Goodfellow, F. (1990–1991). *Learning through literature.* Desoto, TX: SRA McGraw-Hill.

Dole, J. A., Rogers, T., & Osborn, J. (1987). Improving the selection of basal reading programs: A report on the textbook adoption guidelines project. *Book Research Quarterly, 3,* 18–36.

Dowling, D. (1995). *303 dumb spelling mistakes.* Lincolnwood, IL: National Textbook Company.

Durkin, D. (1978–1979). What classroom observations reveal about reading comprehension instruction. *Reading Research Quarterly, 14,* 481–533.

Durkin, D. (1987). Influences on basal reader programs. *The Elementary School Journal, 87,* 331–341.

Ellis, E. (1996). Reading strategy instruction. In D. Deshler, E. S. Ellis, & B. Lenz (Eds.), *Teaching adolescents with learning disabilities: Strategies and methods* (2nd ed., pp. 61–125). Denver: Love Publishing.

Engelmann, S., Becker, W., Hanner, S., & Johnson, G. (1988). *Corrective reading: Decoding strategies.* Chicago: Science Research Associates.

Engelmann, S., & Bruner, E. (1995). *Reading mastery.* Blacklick, OH: Science Research Associates.

Engelmann, S., & Silbert, J. (1983). *Expressive writing 1 & 2.* Chicago: Science Research Associates.

Englert, C. S., & Mariage, T. V. (1991). Making students partners in the comprehension process: Organizing the reading "POSSE." *Learning Disability Quarterly, 14,* 123–138.

Englert, C. S., & Mariage, T. V. (1996). A sociocultural perspective: Teaching ways-of-thinking and ways-of-talking in a literacy community. *Learning Disabilities Research & Practice, 11,* 157–167.

Englert, C. S, Tarrant, K. L., Mariage, T. V., & Oxer, T. (1994). Lesson talk as the work of reading groups: The effectiveness of two interventions. *Journal of Learning Disabilities, 27,* 165–185.

Fischer, P. E. (1993). *The sounds and spelling patterns of English: Phonics for teachers and parents.* Morrill, ME: Oxton House, Publishers.

Fletcher, D., & Abood, D. (1988). An analysis of the readability of product warning labels: Implications for curriculum development for persons with moderate and severe mental retardation. *Education and Training in Mental Retardation, 23,* 224–227.

Frose, V. (1981). Handwriting: Practice, pragmatism, and progress. In V. Forse & S. B. Straw (Eds.), *Research in language arts: Language and schooling* (pp. 227–243). Baltimore, MD: University Park Press.

Fuchs, D., Fuchs, L. S., Thompson, A., Al Otaiba, S., Yen, L., Yang, N. J., Braun, M., & O'Connor, R. E. (2001). Is reading important in reading-readiness programs? A randomized field trial with teachers as program implementers. *Journal of Educational Psychology, 93,* 251–267.

Fuchs, L. S., Fuchs, D., Hamlett, C. L., Phillips, N. B., & Bentz, J. (1994). Classwide curriculum-based measurement: Helping general educators meet the challenge of student diversity. *Exceptional Children, 60,* 518–537.

Fuchs, L. S., Hamlett, C. L., & Fuchs, D. (1997). *Monitoring basic skills progress: Basic reading* (2nd ed., MacIntosh). Austin, TX: Pro-Ed.

Fulk, B. M. (1997). Think while you spell: A cognitive motivational approach to spelling instruction. *Teaching Exceptional Children, 29*(4), 70–71.

Fulk, B. M., & Stormont-Spurgin, M. (1995). Spelling interventions for students with disabilities: A review. *Journal of Special Education, 28,* 488–513.

Furner, B. (1970). An analysis of the effectiveness of a program of instruction emphasizes the perceptual-motor nature of learning in handwriting. *Elementary English, 47,* 61–69.

Gardner, M. (1998). *Test of handwriting skills.* Austin, TX: Pro-Ed.

Gajria, M., & Salvia, J. (1992). The effects of summarization instruction on text comprehension of students with learning disabilities. *Exceptional Children, 58,* 508–516.

Gersten, R., & Dimino, J. (1993). Visions and revisions: A special education perspective on the whole language controversy. *Remedial and Special Education, 14*(4), 5–13.

Gettinger, M., Bryant, N. D., & Fayne, H. R. (1982). Designing spelling instruction for learning disabled children: An emphasis on unit size, distributed practice, and training for transfer. *Journal of Special Education, 16,* 339–448.

Gordon, J., Vaughn, S., & Schumm, J. S. (1993). Spelling interventions: A review of literature and implications for instruction for students with learning disabilities. *Learning Disabilities Research & Practice, 8,* 175–181.

Graham, S. (1992). Issues in handwriting instruction. *Focus on Exceptional Children, 25,* 1–14.

Graham, S. (1999). Handwriting and spelling instruction for students with learning disabilities: A review. *Learning Disability Quarterly, 22,* 78–98.

Graham, S. (2000). Should the natural learning approach replace spelling instruction? *Journal of Educational Psychology, 92,* 325–348.

Graham, S., & Harris, K. R. (1994). The effects of whole language on writing: A review. *Educational Psychologist, 29,* 187–192.

Graham, S., Harris, K. R., & Loynachan, C. (1994). The spelling for writing list. *Journal of Learning Disabilities, 27,* 210–214.

Graham, S., Harris, K. R., & Loynachan, C. (1996). The directed spelling thinking activity: Application with high-frequency words. *Learning Disabilities Research & Practice, 11,* 34–40.

Graham, S., & Miller, L. (1980). Handwriting research and practice: A unified approach. *Focus on Exceptional Children, 13,* 1–16.

Graham, S., & Weintraub, N. (1996). A review of handwriting research: Progress and prospects from 1980 to 1994. *Educational Psychology Review, 8,* 7–87.

Graves, A. W. (1986). Effects of direct instruction and meta-comprehension training on finding main ideas. *Learning Disabilities Research, 1*(2), 90–100.

Graves, D. H. (1985). All children can write. *Learning Disability Focus, 1*(1), 36–43.

Graves, D. H. (1994). *A fresh look at writing.* Portsmouth, NH: Heinemann.

Hallahan, D. P., Kauffman, J. M., & Lloyd, J. W. (1999). *Introduction to learning disabilities* (2nd ed.). Boston: Allyn & Bacon.

Harris, K. K., Graham, S., & Freeman, S. (1988). Effects of strategy training on metamemory among learning disabled students. *Exceptional Children, 54,* 332–338.

Harris, K. R., & Graham, S. (1992). *Helping young writers master the craft: Strategy instruction and self-regulation in the writing process.* Cambridge, MA: Brookline Books.

Herman, R., & Stringfield, S. (1995, April). *Ten promising programs for educating disadvantaged students: Evidence of impact.* Paper presented at the annual meeting of the American Educational Research Association, San Francisco, CA.

Hiebert, E. H. (1994). Reading Recovery in the United States: What difference does it make to an age cohort? *Educational Researcher, 23*(9), 15–25.

Hunt-Berg, M., Rankin, J. L., & Beukelman, D. R. (1994). Ponder the possibilities: Computer-supported writing for struggling writers. *Learning Disabilities Research & Practice, 9,* 169–178.

Idol, L. (1987). Group story mapping: A comprehension strategy for both skilled and unskilled readers. *Journal of Learning Disabilities, 20*(4), 196–205.

Idol, L., & Croll, V. J. (1987). Story-mapping training as a means of improving reading comprehension. *Learning Disability Quarterly, 10,* 214–229.

Idol-Maestas, L. (1985). Getting ready to read: Guided probing for poor comprehenders. *Learning Disability Quarterly, 8,* 243–254.

Isaacson, S., & Gleason, M. M. (1997). Mechanical obstacles to writing: What can teachers do to help students with learning problems? *Learning Disabilities Research & Practice, 12,* 188–194.

Jenkins, J. R., Heliotis, J. D., Stein, M. L., & Haynes, M. C. (1987). Improving reading comprehension by using paragraph restatements. *Exceptional Children, 54,* 54–59.

Johnson, P. H. (1992). Understanding reading disability: A case study approach. In T. Heir & T. Latus (Eds.), *Special education at century's end: Evolution of theory and practice since 1970* (pp. 275–304). Reprint series No. 23, *Harvard Educational Review.* Cambridge, MA: President and Fellows of Harvard College.

Jordon, D. R. (1977). *Dyslexia in the classroom* (2nd ed.). Upper Saddle River, NJ: Merrill/Prentice Hall.

Kennedy, K. M., & Backman, J. (1993). Effectiveness of the Lindamood Auditory Discrimination in Depth Program with students with learning disabilities. *Learning Disabilities Research & Practice, 4,* 253–259.

Kosiewicz, M., Hallahan, D., & Lloyd, J. (1981). The effects of an LD student's treatment choice on handwriting performance. *Learning Disability Quarterly, 4,* 278–286.

Kosiewicz, M., Hallahan, D., Lloyd, J., & Graves, A. (1982). Effects of self-instruction and self-correction procedures on handwriting performance. *Learning Disability Quarterly, 5,* 71–81.

LaBerge, D., & Samuels, S. (1974). Toward a theory of automatic information processing in reading. *Cognitive Psychology, 6,* 293–323.

Leal, D. J., & Chamberlain-Solecki, J. (1998). A Newbery Medal winning combination: High student interest plus appropriate readability levels. *The Reading Teacher, 51,* 712–714.

Lenz, B. K., Schumaker, J. B., Deshler, D. D., & Beals, V. L. (1984). *The word identification strategy.* Lawrence: University of Kansas.

Lerner, J. (2000). *Learning disabilities: Theories, diagnosis, and teaching strategies.* Boston: Houghton Mifflin.

Liberman, I. Y., & Shankweiler, D. (1974). Reading and the awareness of linguistic segments. *Journal of Experimental Child Psychology, 87,* 576–586.

Liberman, I. Y., Shankweiler, D., & Liberman, A. M. (1989). The alphabetic principle and learning to read. In D. Shankweiler & I. Y. Liberman (Eds.), *Phonology and reading disability: Solving the reading puzzle* (pp. 1–33). Ann Arbor: University of Michigan.

Lindamood, P., & Lindamood, P. (1998). *The Lindamood Phoneme Sequencing Program for reading, spelling, and speech (LIPs).* Austin, TX: Pro-Ed.

Lovett, M. W., Lacerenza, L., & Borden, S. L. (2000). Putting struggling readers on the PHAST track: A program to integrate phonological and strategy-based remedial reading instruction and maximize outcomes. *Journal of Learning Disabilities, 33,* 458–476.

Lovett, M. W., Lacerenza, L., Borden, S. L., Frijters, J. C., Steinbach, K. A., & DePalma, M. (2000). Components of effective remediation for developmental reading disabilities: Combining phonological and strategy-based instruction to improve outcomes. *Journal of Educational Psychology, 92,* 263–283.

Lyon, G. R. (1995). Research initiatives in learning disabilities: Contributions from scientists supported by the National Institute of Child Health and Human Development. *Journal of Child Neurology, 10*(Suppl.1), 120–126.

Mabee, W. S. (1988). The effects of academic positive practice on cursive letter writing. *Education and Treatment of Children, 11,* 143–148.

MacArthur, C. A. (1996). Using technology to enhance the writing processes of students with learning disabilities. *Journal of Learning Disabilities, 29,* 344–354.

MacArthur, C. A., Haynes, J. A., Malouf, D. B., Harris, K., & Owings, M. (1990). Computer assisted instruction with learning disabled students: Achievement, engagement, and other factors that influence achievement. *Journal of Educational Computing Research, 6,* 311–328.

Malone, L. D., & Mastropieri, M. A. (1992). Reading comprehension instruction: Summarization and self-monitoring training for students with learning disabilities. *Exceptional Children, 58*(3), 270–279.

Marschark, M., & Harris, M. (1996). Success and failure in learning to read: The special case (?) of deaf children. In C. Cornoldi & J. Oakhill (Eds.), *Reading comprehension difficulties: Processess and intervention* (pp. 279–300). Mahwah, NJ: Lawrence Erlbaum.

Mastropieri, M. A., Leinhart, A., & Scruggs, T. E. (1999). Strategies to promote reading fluency. *Intervention in School and Clinic, 34,* 278–292.

Mastropieri, M. A., & Scruggs, T. E. (1991). *Teaching students ways to remember: Strategies for learning mnemonically.* Cambridge, MA: Brookline Books.

Mastropieri, M. A., & Scruggs, T. E. (1992). *Teaching students ways to remember: Strategies for learning mnemonically.* Cambridge, MA: Brookline Books.

Mastropieri, M. A., & Scruggs, T. E. (1997). Best practices in promoting reading comprehension in students with learning disabilities: 1976 to 1996. *Remedial and Special Education, 18,* 197–213.

Mastropieri, M. A., Scruggs, T. E., Bakken, J. P., & Whedon, C. (1996). Reading comprehension: A synthesis of research in learning disabilities. In T. E. Scruggs & M. A. Mastropieri (Eds.), *Advances in learning and behavioral disabilities* (Vol. 10, Part B, pp. 201–227). Greenwich, CT: JAI.

Mastropieri, M. A., Scruggs, T. E., & Graetz, J. (in press). Reading comprehension for secondary students. *Learning Disability Quarterly.*

Mastropieri, M. A., Scruggs, T. E., Mohler, L. J., Beranek, M. L., Spencer, V., Boon, R. T., & Talbott, E. (2001). Can middle school students with serious reading difficulties help each other and learn anything? *Learning Disabilities Research & Practice, 16,* 18–27.

Mather, N. (1992). Whole language reading instruction for students with learning disabilities: Caught in the crossfire. *Learning Disabilities Research & Practice, 7,* 87–95.

Mathes, P. G., Fuchs, D., Fuchs, L. S., Henley, A. M., & Sanders, A. (1994). Increasing strategic reading practice with Peabody Classwide Peer Tutoring. *Learning Disabilities Research & Practice, 9,* 44–48.

Mathes, P. G., & Fuchs, L. S. (1993). Peer-mediated reading instruction in special education resource rooms. *Learning Disabilities Research & Practice, 8,* 233–243.

McNaughton, D., Hughes, C., & Ofiesh, N. (1997). Proofreading for students with learning disabilities: Integrating computer and strategy use. *Learning Disabilities Research & Practice, 12,* 16–28.

Moats, L. C. (1995). *Spelling: Development, disability, and instruction.* Baltimore: York Press.

Moats, L. C. (1998a). Reading, spelling, and writing disabilities in the middle grades. In B. Y. L. Wong (Ed.), *Learning about learning disabilities* (2nd ed., pp. 367–389).

Moats, L. C. (1998b). Teaching decoding. *American Educator, 22,* 42–51.

Montague, M. (1998). Research on metacognition in special education. In T. E. Scruggs & M. A. Mastropieri (Eds.), *Advances in learning and behavioral disabilities* (Vol. 12, pp. 151–184). Greenwich, CT: JAI.

Morocco, C., & Nelson, A. (1990). *Writers at work.* Blalick, OH: SRA.

O'Conner, R. E., Jenkins, J. R., & Slocum, T. (1995). Transfer among phonological tasks in kindergarten: Essential instructional content. *Journal of Educational Psychology, 87,* 202–217.

Ogle, D. M. (1986). K-W-L: A teaching model that develops active reading of expository text. *The Reading Teacher, 39,* 564–570.

O'Shea, L. J., Sindelar, P. T., & O'Shea, D. (1987). The effects of repeated readings and attentional cues on the reading fluency and comprehension of learning disabled readers. *Learning Disabilities Research, 2,* 103–109.

Palincsar, A. S., & Brown, A. L. (1984). Reciprocal teaching of comprehension fostering and comprehension monitoring activities. *Cognition and Instruction, 1,* 117–175.

Phillips, N. B., Hamlett, C. L., Fuchs, L. S., & Fuchs, D. (1993). Combining classwide curriculum-based measurement and peer tutoring to help general educators provide adaptive education. *Learning Disabilities Research & Practice, 8,* 148–156.

Pinnell, G. S., DeFord, D. E., & Lyons, C. A. (1988). *Reading Recovery: Early interventions for at risk first graders.* Arlington, VA: Educational Research Service.

Pinnell, G. S., & Fountas, I. C. (1999). *Matching books to readers: Using leveled books in guided reading, K–3.* Portsmouth, NH: Heinemann.

Pinnell, G. S., & Fountas, I. C. (2001). *Leveled books for readers, grades 3–6: A companion volume to guiding readers and writers.* Portsmouth, NH: Heinemann.

Polloway, E. A., Epstein, M. H., Polloway, C. H., Patton, J. R., & Ball, D. W. (1986). Corrective reading program: An effectiveness with learning disabled and mentally retarded students. *Remedial and Special Education, 7*(4), 41–47.

Polloway, E. A., Smith, T. E. C., & Miller, L. (2003). *Language instruction for students with disabilities* (3rd ed.). Denver: Love Publishing.

Pressley, M. (1998). *Reading instruction that works: The case for balanced teaching.* New York: Guilford.

Pressley, M., & Rankin, J. (1994). More about whole language methods of reading instruction for students at-risk for early reading failure. *Learning Disabilities Research & Practice, 9,* 156–168.

Reid, R., & Harris, K. R. (1993). Self-monitoring of attention versus self-monitoring of performance: Effects on attention and academic performance. *Exceptional Children, 60,* 29–40.

Robin, A. L., Armel, S., & O'Leary, D. K. (1975). The effects of self-instruction on writing deficiencies. *Behaviour Therapy, 6,* 178–187.

Rosenshine, B., & Meister, C. (1994). Reciprocal teaching: A review of the research. *Review of Educational Research, 64,* 479–530.

Routman, R. (1991). *Invitations: Changing as teachers and learners K–12.* Portsmouth, NH: Heinemann.

Rudenga, E. A. V. (1992). *Incompatibility? Ethnographic case studies of learning disabled students in a whole language classroom.* Unpublished doctoral dissertation, Purdue University, West Lafayette, IN.

Sachs, A. (1983). The effects of three prereading activities on learning disabled students' reading comprehension. *Learning Disability Quarterly, 6,* 248–251.

Sachs, A. (1984). Accessing scripts before reading the story. *Learning Disability Quarterly, 7,* 226–228.

Samuels, J. (1981). Some essentials of decoding. *Exceptional Education Quarterly, 2*(1), 11–25.

Scott, M. S., Perou, R., Greenfield, D. B., & Swanson, L. (1993). Rhyming skills: Differentiating among mildly mentally retarded, learning disabled, and normally achieving students. *Learning Disabilities Research & Practice, 8,* 215–222.

Scruggs, T. E., Mastropieri, M. A., & Sullivan, G. S. (1994). Promoting relational thinking skills: Elaborative interrogation for mildly handicapped students. *Exceptional Children, 60,* 450–457.

Shefter, H. (1974). *6 minutes a day to perfect spelling.* New York: Pocket Books.

Simmons, D. C., Gunn, B., Smith, S. B., & Kameenui, E. J. (1994). Phonological awareness: Applications of instructional design. *LD Forum, 19*(2), 7–10.

Simmons, L. (1996a). *Saxon phonics 1: An incremental development: Student workbook.* Norman, OK: Saxon Publishers, Inc.

Simmons, L. (1996b). *Saxon phonics 1: An incremental development: Teacher's manual.* Norman, OK: Saxon Publishers, Inc.

Snider, V. E. (1989). Reading comprehension performance of adolescents with learning disabilities. *Learning Disability Quarterly, 12,* 87–96.

Snider, V. E. (1997). Transfer of decoding skills to a literature basal. *Learning Disabilities Research & Practice, 12,* 54–62.

Snow, C. E., Burns, M. S., & Griffin, P. (Eds.). (1998). *Preventing reading difficulties in young children.* Washington, DC: National Academy Press.

Speece, D. L., MacDonald, V., Kilsheimer, L., & Krist, J. (1997). Research to practice: Preservice teachers reflect on reciprocal teaching. *Learning Disabilities Research & Practice, 12,* 177–187.

Spencer, V. G., Scruggs, T. E., & Mastropieri, M. A. (2003). *Content area learning in middle school social studies classrooms and students with emotional or behavioral disorders: A comparison of strategies. Behavioral Disorders, 28,* 77–93.

Stahl, S. A. (1992). Saying the "p" word: Nine guidelines for exemplary phonics instruction. *The Reading Teacher, 45*(8), 618–625.

Stahl, S. A., & Miller, P. D. (1989). Whole language and language experience approaches for beginning reading: A quantitative research synthesis. *Review of Educational Research, 59,* 87–116.

Stanovich, K. E. (Ed.). (1988). *Children's reading and the development of phonological awareness.* Detroit: Wayne State University Press.

Stanovich, K. E. (1994). Romance and reality: *The Reading Teacher, 47,* 280–291.

Starshine, D. (1990). An inexpensive alternative to word processing—FrEd Writer. *Reading Teacher, 43,* 600–601.

Stone, C. A. (1998). The metaphor of scaffolding: Its utility for the field of learning disabilities. *Journal of Learning Disabilities, 31,* 344–364.

Suid, M. (1981). *Demonic mnemonics.* New York: Dell Publishing.

Sullivan, G. S., Mastropieri, M. A., & Scruggs, T. E. (1996). Reasoning and remembering: Coaching thinking with students with learning disabilities. *Journal of Special Education, 29,* 310–322.

Swanson, H. L. (2000). Intervention research for students with learning disabilities: A comprehensive meta-analysis of group design studies. In T. E. Scruggs & M. A. Mastropieri (Eds.), *Educational interventions: Advances in learning and behavioral disabilities* (Vol. 14, pp. 1–154). Oxford, UK: Elsevier Science.

Talbott, E., Lloyd, J. W., & Tankersley, M. (1994). Effects of reading comprehension interventions with students with learning disabilities. *Learning Disability Quarterly, 17,* 223–232.

Telian, N. A. (1993). *Telian multisensory mnemonic letter card program.* Stoughton, MA: Telian Learning Concepts.

Telian, N. A. (1995). *Instructor's manual for sound segmentation reading therapy.* Stoughton, MA: Telian Learning Concepts.

Thompson, K. L. (1993). *The cognitive reading strategies program: Teacher's program prospectus.* Alexandria, VA: K. L. Thompson.

Thompson, K. L., & Taymans, J. M. (1994). Development of a reading program: Bridging the gaps among decoding, literature, and thinking skills. *Intervention in School and Clinic, 30*(1), 17–27.

Thurber, D. N., & Jordan, D. (1981). *D'Nealian handwriting.* Glenview, IL: Scott, Foresman.

Torgesen, J. K. (1994). Learning disabilities theory: Issues and advances. In S. Vaughn & C. Bos (Eds.), *Research issues in learning disabilities* (pp. 3–21). New York: Springer-Verlag.

Torgesen, J. K., & Bryant, B. R. (1994). *Phonological awareness training for reading.* Austin, TX: Pro-Ed.

Traub, N. (1975). *Recipe for reading* (2nd ed.). Cambridge, MA: Educators Publishing Service.

Vadasy, P. F. (1997). *Phonological awareness training materials.* Seattle, WA: Washington Research Institute.

Vadasy, P. F., Jenkins, J. R., Antil, L. R., Wayne, S. K., & O'Conner, R. E. (1997). Community-based early reading intervention for at-risk first graders. *Learning Disabilities Research & Practice, 12,* 29–39.

Wagner, R. K., & Torgesen, J. K. (1987). The nature of phonological processing and its causal role in the acquisition of reading skills. *Psychological Bulletin, 101,* 192–212.

Wagner, R. K., Torgesen, J. K., & Rashotte, C. A. (1994). Development of reading-related phonological processing abilities: New evidence of bidirectional causality from a latent variable study. *Developmental Psychology, 30,* 73–87.

Warden, R., Allen, J., Hipp, K., Schmitz, J., & Collett, L. (1988). *Written expression.* San Antonio, TX: Psychological Corporation.

Wetzel, K. (1996). Speech recognizing computers: A written communication tool for students with learning disabilities. *Journal of Learning Disabilities, 29,* 371–380.

Wong, B. Y. L. (1986). A cognitive approach to teaching spelling. *Exceptional Children, 53,* 169–173.

Wong, B. Y. L. (1998). Reflections on current attainments and future directions in writing intervention research in learning disabilities. In T. E. Scruggs & M. A. Mastropieri (Eds.), *Advances in learning and behavioral disabilities* (Vol. 12, pp. 127–149). Greenwich, CT: JAI.

Wong, B. Y. L., Butler, D. L., Ficzere, S. A., & Kuperis, S. (1997). Teaching adolescents with learning disabilities and low achievers to plan, write, and revise compare and contrast essays. *Learning Disabilities Research & Practice, 12,* 2–15.

Wong, B. Y. L., Butler, D. L., Ficzere, S. A., Kuperis, S., Corden, M., & Zelmer, J. (1994). Teaching problem learners revision skills and sensitivity to audience through two instructional modes: Teacher versus student-student interactive dialogue. *Learning Disabilities Research & Practice, 9,* 78–90.

Wong, B. Y. L., & Jones, W. (1982). Increasing metacomprehension in learning disabled and normally achieving students through self-questioning training. *Learning Disability Quarterly, 5,* 228–240.

Wong, B. Y. L., Wong, R., Perry, N., & Sawatsky, D. (1986). The efficacy of a self-questioning summarization strategy for use by underachievers and learning disabled adolescents in social studies. *Learning Disabilities Focus, 2*(2), 20–35.

Zaner-Bloser handwriting. (2003). Columbus, OH: Zaner-Bloser.

Chapter 14

Bley, N. S., & Thornton, C. A. (2001). *Teaching mathematics to students with learning disabilities* (4th ed.). Austin, TX: Pro-Ed.

Carnine, D. (1998). Instructional design in mathematics for students with learning disabilities. In D. Rivera (Ed.), *Mathematics education for students with learning disabilities* (pp. 119–138). Austin, TX: Pro-Ed.

Case, L. P., Harris, K. R., & Graham, S. (1992). Improving the mathematical problem-solving skills of students with learning disabilities: Self-regulated strategy development. *Journal of Special Education, 26,* 1–19.

Davis, R. B., & Maher, C. A. (1996). A new view of the goals and means for school mathematics. In M. C. Pugach & C. L. Warger (Eds.), *Curriculum trends, special education, and reform: Refocusing the conversation.* New York: Teachers College Press.

Duffie, W. B., Rutherford, T. K., & Schectman, A. J. (1990). *Calculator companions: Classroom activity guide to overhead and student calculators.* Deerfield, IL: Learning Resources.

Garnett, K. (1992). Developing fluency with basic number facts: Interventions for students with learning disabilities. *Learning Disabilities Research & Practice, 7,* 210–216.

Ginsburg, H. P. (1997). Mathematics learning disabilities: A view from developmental psychology. *Journal of Learning Disabilities, 30,* 20–33.

Ginsburg, H. P. (1998a). Mathematics learning disabilities: A view from developmental psychology. In D. Rivera (Ed.), *Mathematics education for students with learning disabilities* (pp. 22–58). Austin, TX: Pro-Ed.

Ginsburg, H. P. (1998b). Toby's math. In R. J. Sternberg & T. Ben-Zeev (Eds.), *The nature of mathematical thinking* (pp. 175–202). Hillsdale, NJ: Lawrence Erlbaum.

Goldman, S. R., & Hasselbring, T. S. (1997). Achieving meaningful mathematics literacy for students with learning disabilities. *Journal of Learning Disabilities, 30,* 198–208.

Hallahan, D. P., & Cottone, E. A. (1997). Attention deficit hyperactivity disorder. In T. E. Scruggs & M. A. Mastropieri (Eds.), *Advances in learning and behavioral disabilities* (Vol. 11, pp. 27–67). Greenwich, CT: JAI Press.

Hasselbring, T. S., & Moore, P. R. (1996). Developing mathematical literacy through the use of contextualized learning environments. *Journal of Computing in Childhood Education, 7*(3–4), 199–222.

Horton, S. V., Lovitt, T. C., & White, O. R. (1992). Teaching mathematics to adolescents classified as educable mentally handicapped: Using calculators to remove the computational onus. *Remedial and Special Education, 13*(3), 36–60.

Hutchinson, N. L. (1993). Effects of cognitive strategy instruction on algebra problem solving of adolescents with learning disabilities. *Learning Disability Quarterly, 16,* 34–63.

Janvier, C. (1987). *Problems of representation in the teaching and learning of mathematics.* Mahwah, NJ: Lawrence Erlbaum.

Jones, E. D., Wilson, R., & Bhojwani, S. (1998). Mathematics instruction for secondary students with learning disabilities. In D. Rivera (Ed.), *Mathematics education for students with learning disabilities* (pp. 177–199). Austin, TX: Pro-Ed.

Kameenui, E. J., Chard, D. J., & Carnine, D. W. (1996). The new school mathematics and the age-old dilemma of diversity: Cutting or untying the Gordian knot. In M. C. Pugach & C. L. Warger (Eds.), *Curriculum trends, special education, and reform: Refocusing the conversation* (pp. 94–105). New York: Teachers College Press.

Kilpatrick, J. (1985). Doing mathematics without understanding it: A commentary on Higbee and Kunihira. *Educational Psychologist, 20*(2), 65–68.

Kroesbergen, E. H., & Van Luit, J. E. H. (2003). Mathematics interventions for children with special needs: A meta-analysis. *Remedial and Special Education, 24,* 97–114.

Lang, C. (2001). *The effects of self-instructional strategies on problem solving in algebra for students with special needs.* Unpublished doctoral dissertation, George Mason University, Fairfax, VA.

Lucangeli, D., Coi, G., & Bosco, P. (1998). Metacognitive awareness in good and poor math problem solvers. *Learning Disabilities Research & Practice, 12,* 219–244.

Lucangeli, D., Cornoldi, C., & Tellarini, M. (1998). Metacognition and learning disabilities in mathematics. In T. E. Scruggs & M. A. Mastropieri (Eds.), *Advances in learning and behavioral disabilities* (Vol. 12, pp. 219–244). Greenwich, CT: JAI Press.

Maccini, P., & Gagnon, J. (2002). Perceptions and application of NCTM standards by special and general education teachers. *Exceptional Children, 68,* 325–344.

Maccini, P., & Hughes, C. (2000). Effects of a problem-solving strategy on the introductory algebra performance of secondary students with learning disabilities. *Learning Disabilities Research and Practice, 15,* 10–21.

Maccini, P., McNaughton, D., & Ruhl, K. (1999). Algebra instruction for students with learning disabilities: Implications from a research review. *Learning Disability Quarterly, 22,* 113–126.

Mastropieri, M. A., Bakken, J. P., & Scruggs, T. E. (1991). Mathematics instruction for individuals with mental retardation: A perspective and research synthesis. *Education and Training in Mental Retardation, 26,* 115–129.

Mastropieri, M. A., & Scruggs, T. E. (1990). *Mnemonic math facts.* Unpublished materials. Fairfax, VA: George Mason University, Graduate School of Education.

Mastropieri, M. A., & Scruggs, T. E. (1991). *Teaching students ways to remember: Strategies for learning mnemonically.* Cambridge, MA: Brookline Books.

Mastropieri, M. A., & Scruggs, T. E. (2002). *Effective instruction for special education.* Austin, TX: Pro-Ed.

Mastropieri, M. A., Scruggs, T. E., Davidson, T., & Rana, R. (in press). Instructional interventions for students with mathematics learning disabilities. In B. Y. L. Wong (Ed.), *Learning about learning disabilities* (3rd ed.). New York: Elsevier Science.

McLeskey, J., & Waldron, N. L. (1990). The identification and characteristics of students with learning disabilities in Indiana. *Learning Disabilities Research, 5,* 72–78.

Miller, S. P., & Mercer, C. D. (1993a). Using data to learn about concrete-semiconcrete-abstract instruction for students with math disabilities. *Learning Disabilities Research & Practice, 8,* 89–96.

Miller, S. P., & Mercer, C. D. (1993b). Using a graduated word problem sequence to promote problem-solving skills. *Learning Disabilities Research & Practice, 8,* 169–174.

Miller, S. P., & Mercer, C. D. (1997). Educational aspects of mathematics disabilities. *Journal of Learning Disabilities, 30,* 47–56.

Montague, M. (1992). The effects of cognitive and metacognitive strategy instruction on the mathematical problem solving of middle school students with learning disabilities. *Journal of Learning Disabilities, 25,* 230–248.

Montague, M. (1996). What does the "New View" of school mathematics mean for students with mild disabilities? In M. C. Pugach & C. L. Warger (Eds), *Curriculum trends, special education, and reform: Refocusing the conversation* (pp. 84–93). New York: Teachers College Press.

Montague, M. (1998). Cognitive strategy instruction in mathematics for students with learning disabilities. In D. Rivera (Ed.), *Mathematics education for students with learning disabilities* (pp. 177–199). Austin, TX: Pro-Ed.

National Council of Teachers of Mathematics. (1989). *Curriculum and evaluation standards for school mathematics.* Reston, VA: Author. (ERIC Document Reproduction Service No. ED304336)

National Council of Teachers of Mathematics. (1991). *Professional standards for teaching mathematics.* Reston, VA: Author.

National Council of Teachers of Mathematics. (1995). *Assessment standards for school mathematics.* Reston, VA: Author.

National Council of Teachers of Mathematics. (2000). *Principles and standards for school mathematics.* Reston, VA: Author.

National Research Council. (1989). *Everybody counts: A report to the nation on the future of mathematics education.* Washington, DC: National Academy Press.

Patton, J. R., Cronin, M. E., Bassett, D. S., & Koppel, A. E. (1998). A life skills approach to mathematics instruction: Preparing students with learning disabilities for the real-life math demands of adulthood. In D. Rivera (Ed.), *Mathematics education for students with learning disabilities* (pp. 201–218). Austin, TX: Pro-Ed.

Pressley, M., & McCormick, C. (1995). *Advanced educational psychology for educators, researchers, and policymakers.* New York: HarperCollins.

Rappaport, D. (1975). The new math and its aftermath. *School Science and Mathematics,* 563–570.

Reisman, F. K. (1977). *Diagnostic teaching of elementary school mathematics: Methods and content.* Chicago: Rand McNally.

Rivera, D. P. (1997). Mathematics education and students with learning disabilities: Introduction to the special series. *Journal of Learning Disabilities, 30,* 2–19.

Rivera, D. P. (1998). Mathematics education and students with learning disabilities. In D. Rivera (Ed.), *Mathematics education for students with learning disabilities* (pp. 1–31). Austin, TX: Pro-Ed.

Rivera, D. P., & Smith, D. D. (1987). Influence of modeling on acquisition and generalization of computational skills: A summary of research findings from three sites. *Learning Disability Quarterly, 10,* 69–80.

Schoenfeld, A. H. (1989). Teaching mathematical thinking and problem solving. In L. B. Resnick & L. E. Klopger (Eds.), *Toward the thinking curriculum: Current cognitive research* (pp. 83–103). Washington, DC: Association for Supervision and Curriculum Development.

Schroeder, B., & Strosnider, R. (1997). Box-and-whisker what? Deaf students learn—and write about—descriptive statistics. *Teaching Exceptional Children, 29*(3), 12–17.

Scruggs, T. E., & Mastropieri, M. A. (1986). Academic characteristics of behaviorally disordered and learning disabled children. *Behavioral Disorders, 11,* 184–190.

Shiah, R. L., Mastropieri, M. A., Scruggs, T. E., & Fulk, B. J. M. (1994–1995). The effects of computer assisted instruction on the mathematical problem solving of students with learning disabilities. *Exceptionality, 5,* 131–161.

Staudacher, C., & Turner, S. (1994). *Practical mathematics for consumers* (2nd ed.). Paramus, NJ: Globe Fearon.

Stein, M., Silbert, J., & Carnine, D. (1997). *Designing effective mathematics instruction: A direct instruction approach* (3rd ed.). Upper Saddle River, NJ: Merrill/Prentice Hall.

Thornton, C. A., Langrall, C. W., & Jones, G. A. (1998). Mathematics instruction for elementary students with learning disabilities. In D. Rivera (Ed.), *Mathematics education for students with learning disabilities* (pp. 139–154). Austin, TX: Pro-Ed.

Van Luit, J. E. H., & Schopman, E. A. M. (2000). Improving early numeracy of young children with special educational needs. *Remedial and Special Education, 21,* 27–40.

Chapter 15

Armbruster, B. B., & Anderson, T. H. (1988). On selecting considerate content area textbooks. *Remedial and Special Education, 9*(1), 47–52.

Bakken, J. P. (1995). *Reading comprehension of expository science material and students with learning disabilities: A comparison of strategies.* Unpublished doctoral dissertation, West Lafayette, IN: Purdue University.

Bakken, J. P., Mastropieri, M. A., & Scruggs, T. E. (1997). Reading comprehension of expository science material and students with learning disabilities: A comparison of strategies. *Journal of Special Education, 31,* 300–324.

Barrier Free In Brief–Laboratories and Classrooms in Science and Engineering. (1991). Washington, DC: American Association for the Advancement of Science.

Bay, M., Staver, J. R., Bryan, T., & Hale, J. B. (1992). Science instruction for the mildly handicapped: Direct instruction versus discovery teaching. *Journal of Research in Science Teaching, 29,* 555–570.

Bean, R. M., Zigmond, N., & Hartman, D. K. (1994). Adapted use of social studies textbooks in elementary classrooms: Views of classroom teachers. *Remedial and Special Education, 15,* 216–226.

Bos, C. S., & Anders, P. L. (1987). Semantic feature analysis: An interactive teaching strategy for facilitating learning from text. *Learning Disabilities Focus, 3*(1), 55–59.

Bos, C. S., & Anders, P. L. (1990). Effects of interactive vocabulary instruction on the vocabulary learning and reading comprehension of junior high learning disabled students. *Learning Disability Quarterly, 13,* 31–42.

Bos, C. S., Anders, P. L., Filip, D., & Jaffe, L. E. (1989). The effects of an interactive instructional strategy for enhancing reading comprehension and content area learning for students with learning disabilities. *Journal of Learning Disabilities, 22*(6), 384–390.

Boyle, J. R., & Weishaar, M. (1997). The effects of expert-generated versus student-generated cognitive organizers on the reading comprehension of students with learning disabilities. *Learning Disabilities Research & Practice, 12,* 228–251.

Brophy, J. (1990). Teaching social studies for understanding and higher-order applications. *Elementary School Journal, 90,* 351–417.

Bruner, J. (1966). *Toward a theory of instruction.* Cambridge, MA: Harvard University Press.

Bulgren, J. A., Deshler, D. D., & Schumaker, J. B. (1993). *The content enhancement series: The concept mastery routine.* Lawrence, KS: Edge Enterprises.

Bulgren, J. A., Deshler, D. D., & Schumaker, J. B. (1997). Use of a recall enhancement routine and strategies in inclusive secondary classes. *Learning Disabilities Research & Practice, 12,* 198–208.

Bulgren, J. A., & Lenz, B. K. (1996). Strategic instruction in the content areas. In D. D. Deshler, E. S. Ellis, & B. K. Lenz (Eds.), *Teaching adolescents with learning disabilities: Strategies and methods* (2nd ed., pp. 409–473). Denver: Love Publishing.

Bulgren, J. A., Schumaker, J. B., & Deshler, D. D. (1988). Effectiveness of a concept teaching routine in enhancing the performance of LD students in secondary-level mainstream classes. *Learning Disability Quarterly, 11,* 3–17.

Bulgren, J. A., Schumaker, J. B., & Deshler, D. D. (1994a). *The content enhancement series: The concept anchoring routine.* Lawrence, KS: Edge Enterprises.

Bulgren, J. A., Schumaker, J. B., & Deshler, D. D. (1994b). The effects of a recall enhancement routine on the test performance of secondary students with and without learning disabilities. *Learning Disabilities Research & Practice, 9,* 2–11.

Carnine, D., & Kameenui, E. (1992). *Higher order thinking: Designing curriculum for mainstreamed students.* Austin, TX: Pro-Ed.

Chambliss, M. J. (1994). Evaluating the quality of textbooks for diverse learners. *Remedial and Special Education, 15,* 348–362.

Chan, L. K. S., & Cole, P. G. (1986). The effects of comprehension monitoring training on the reading competence of learning disabled and regular class students. *Remedial and Special Education, 7*(4), 33–40.

Chiang-Soong, B., & Yager, R. E. (1993). Readability levels of the science textbooks most used in secondary schools. *School Science & Mathematics, 93,* 24–27.

Cook, L. K. (1983). *Instructional effects of text-structure-based reading strategies on the comprehension of scientific prose.* Unpublished doctoral dissertation, University of California, Santa Barbara.

Cook, L. K., & Mayer, R. E. (1988). Teaching readers about the structure of scientific text. *Journal of Educational Psychology, 80,* 448–456.

Crabtree, C. (1983). A common curriculum in the social studies. In G. Fenstermacher & J. Goodlad (Eds.), *Individual differences and the common curriculum* (82nd yearbook of the National Society for the Study of Education, Part I, pp. 248–281). Chicago: University of Chicago Press.

Deshler, D. D., Ellis, E. S., & Lenz, B. K. (Eds.). (1996). *Teaching adolescents with learning disabilities: Strategies and methods* (2nd ed.). Denver: Love Publishing.

Deshler, D. D., & Schumaker, J. B. (1986). Learning strategies: An instructional alternative for low-achieving adolescents. *Exceptional Children, 52,* 583–590.

Deshler, D. D., & Schumaker, J. B. (1988). An instructional model for teaching students how to learn. In J. L. Graden, J. E. Zins, & M. J. Curtis (Eds.), *Alternative instructional delivery systems: Enhancing instructional options for all students.* Washington, DC: National Association of School Psychologists.

Driver, R., Asoko, H., Leach, J, Mortimer, E., & Scott, P. (1994). Constructing scientific knowledge in the classroom. *Educational Researcher, 23*(7), 5–12.

Englert, C. S., & Mariage, T. V. (1991). Making students partners in the comprehension process: Organizing the reading "POSSE." *Learning Disability Quarterly, 14,* 123–138.

Englert, C. S, Tarrant, K. L., Mariage, T. V., & Oxer, T. (1994). Lesson talk as the work of reading groups: The effectiveness of two interventions. *Journal of Learning Disabilities, 27,* 165–185.

Ferretti, R. P., & Okolo, C. M. (1996). Authenticity in learning: Multimedia design projects in the social studies for students with disabilities. *Journal of Learning Disabilities, 29,* 450–460.

Fiore, T. A., & Cook, R. A. (1994). Adopting textbooks and other instructional materials: Policies and practices that address diverse learners. *Remedial and Special Education, 15,* 333–347.

Fry, E. (1977). Fry's readability graph: Clarifications, validity, and extension to level 17. *Journal of Reading, 21,* 242–252.

Fulk, B. J. M. (1994). Mnemonic keyword strategy training for students with learning disabilities. *Learning Disabilities Research & Practice, 9,* 179–185.

Glezheiser, L. M., & D'Angelo, C. (2000). Historical fiction and informational texts that support social studies standards: An annotated bibliography. *The Language and Literacy Spectrum, 10,* 26–39.

Grimes, J. E. (1975). *The thread of discourse.* The Hague, Holland: Mouton & Co.

Horton, S. V., Boone, R. A., & Lovitt, T. C. (1990). Teaching social studies to learning disabled high school students: Effects of a hypertext study guide. *British Journal of Educational Technology, 21,* 118–131.

Horton, S. V., & Lovitt, T. C. (1989). Using study guides with three classifications of secondary students. *Journal of Special Education, 22*(4), 447–462.

Horton, S. V., Lovitt, T. C., Givens, A., & Nelson, R. (1989). Teaching social studies to high school students with academic handicaps in a mainstreamed setting: Effects of a computerized study guide. *Journal of Learning Disabilities, 22,* 102–107.

Jitendra, A., Nolet, V., Xin, Y. P., Gomez, O., Renouf, K., Iskold, L., & DaCosta, J. (2001). An analysis of middle school geography textbooks: Implications for students with learning problems. *Reading & Writing Quarterly: Overcoming Learning Difficulties, 17,* 151–173.

Johnson, M. J., & Janisch, C. (1998). Connecting literacy with social studies content. *Social Studies and the Young Learner,* 6–9.

King-Sears, M. E., Mercer, C. D., & Sindelar, P. T. (1992). Toward independence with keyword mnemonics: A strategy for science vocabulary instruction. *Remedial and Special Education, 13,* 22–33.

Lang, H. G. (1994). Science education for deaf students: Looking into the next millennium. In G. P. Stefanich & J. Egelston-Dodd (Eds.), *Proceedings of a working conference on science for persons with disabilities* (pp. 97–109). Cedar Falls, IA: University of Northern Iowa.

Larkin, D. F., Cunningham, J. T., & Dearstyne, B. W. (1985). *New York yesterday and today.* Morristown, NJ: Silver Burdett.

Larrivee, B. (1985). *Effective teaching for successful mainstreaming.* New York: Longman.

Lenz, B. K., Bulgren, J., & Hudson, P. (1990). Content enhancement: A model for promoting the acquisition of content by individuals with learning disabilities. In T. E. Scruggs & B. Y. L. Wong (Eds.), *Intervention research in learning disabilities* (pp. 122–165). Oxford, UK: Elsevier Science.

Lenz, B. K., Marrs, R. W., Schumaker, J. B., & Deshler, D. D. (1993). *The content enhancement series: The lesson organizer routine.* Lawrence, KS: Edge Enterprises.

Lovitt, T., Rudsit, J., Jenkins, J., Pious, C., & Benedetti, D. (1986). Adapting science materials for regular and learning disabled seventh graders. *Remedial and Special Education, 7*(10), 31–39.

Maheady, L., Sacca, M. K., & Harper, G. F. (1988). Classwide peer tutoring with mildly handicapped high school students. *Exceptional Children, 55,* 52–59.

Mastropieri, M. A. (1995). L'instruzione mnemonica e l'interrogazione elaborativa: Strategie per ricordarsi e per pensare. In C. Cornoldi & R. Vianello (Eds.), *Handicap e apprendimento: Ricerche e proposte di intervento* (pp. 117–124). Bergamo, Italy: Juvenilia.

Mastropieri, M. A., Scruggs, T. E., Mantzicopoulos, P. Y., Sturgeon, A., Goodwin, L., & Chung, S. (1998). "A place where living things affect and depend on each other": Qualitative and quantitative outcomes associated with inclusive science teaching. *Science Education, 82,* 163–179.

Mastropieri, M. A. (1997). Guidelines for adapting science activities for including students with disabilities. In G. P. Stefanich, E. C. Bergan, & J. C. Paulsen (Eds.), *What others are doing: Proceedings of a working conference on science for persons with disabilities* (pp. 5–23). Cedar Falls, IA: University of Northern Iowa.

Mastropieri, M. A., & Scruggs, T. E. (1993). *A practical guide for teaching science to students with special needs in inclusive settings.* Austin, TX: Pro-Ed.

Mastropieri, M. A., & Scruggs, T. E. (1994). Text-based vs. activities-oriented science curriculum: Implications for students with disabilities. *Remedial and Special Education, 15,* 72–85.

Mastropieri, M. A., & Scruggs, T. E. (1997). Best practices in promoting reading comprehension in students with learning disabilities: 1976 to 1996. *Remedial and Special Education, 18,* 197–213.

Mastropieri, M. A., & Scruggs, T. E. (2002). *Effective instruction for special education* (3rd ed.). Austin, TX: Pro-Ed.

Mastropieri, M. A., Scruggs, T. E., Boon, R., & Carter, K. B. (2001). Correlates of inquiry learning in science: Constructing concepts of density and buoyancy. *Remedial and Special Education, 22,* 130–137.

Mastropieri, M. A., Scruggs, T. E., & Butcher, K. (1997). How effective is inquiry learning for students with mild disabilities? *Journal of Special Education, 31,* 199–211.

Mastropieri, M. A., Scruggs, T. E., & Graetz, J. (in press). Reading comprehension for secondary students. *Learning Disability Quarterly.*

Mastropieri, M. A., Scruggs, T. E., Spencer, V., & Fontana, J. (2003). Promoting success in high school world history: Peer tutoring versus guided notes. *Learning Disabilities Research and Practice.*

Mayer, R. E. (1984). Aids to prose comprehension. *Educational Psychologist, 19,* 30–42.

Mayer, R. E. (1985). Structural analysis of science prose: Can we increase problem-solving performance? In B. K. Britton & J. B. Black (Eds.), *Understanding expository prose* (pp. 65–87). Hillsdale, NJ: Lawrence Erlbaum.

McCormick, S., & Cooper, J. O. (1991). Can SQ3R facilitate learning disabled students' literal comprehension of expository test? Three experiments. *Reading Psychology, 12,* 239–271.

Meyer, B. J. F. (1975). *The organization of prose and its effects on memory.* Amsterdam: North Holland Publishing.

Niles, O. S. (1965). Organization perceived. In H. Herber (Ed.), *Developing study skills in secondary schools.* Newark, DE: International Reading Association.

O'Brien, J. (2000). Enabling all students to learn in the laboratory of democracy. *Intervention in School and Clinic, 35,* 195–206.

Ochoa, A. S., & Shuster, S. K. (1980). *Social studies in the classroom, K–6.* Boston: Houghton Mifflin.

Okolo, C. M., Cavalier, A. R., Ferretti, R. P., & MacArthur, C. A. (2000) Technology, literacy, and disabilities: A review of the research. In R. M. Gersten & Schiller, E. P. (Eds)., *Contemporary special education research: Syntheses of the knowledge base on critical instructional issues* (pp. 179–250). Mahwah, NJ: Lawrence Erlbaum.

Paxton, R. J. (1999). A deafening silence: History textbooks and the students who read them. *Review of Educational Research, 69,* 315–339.

Rutherford, F. J., & Ahlgren, A. (1990). *Science for all Americans.* New York: Oxford University Press.

Schumaker, J. B., Deshler, D. D., Alley, G. R., Warner, M. M., & Denton, P. H. (1982). Multipass: A learning strategy for improving reading comprehension. *Learning Disability Quarterly, 5,* 295–304.

Scruggs, T. E., & Mastropieri, M. A. (1993). Current approaches to science education: Implications for mainstream instruction of students with disabilities. *Remedial and Special Education, 14*(1), 15–24.

Scruggs, T. E., & Mastropieri, M. A. (1994a). The construction of scientific knowledge by students with mild disabilities. *Journal of Special Education, 28,* 307–321.

Scruggs, T. E., & Mastropieri, M. A. (1994b). Refocusing microscope activities for special students. *Science Scope, 17,* 74–78.

Scruggs, T. E., & Mastropieri, M. A. (1995a). Science education for students with behavior disorders. *Education and Treatment of Children, 3,* 322–334.

Scruggs, T. E., & Mastropieri, M. A. (1995b). Science and mental retardation: An analysis of curriculum features and learner characteristics. *Science Education, 79,* 251–271.

Scruggs, T. E., Mastropieri, M. A., Bakken, J. P., & Brigham, F. J. (1993). Reading vs. doing: The relative effects of textbook-based and inquiry-oriented approaches to science learning in special education classrooms. *Journal of Special Education, 27,* 1–15.

Scruggs, T. E., Mastropieri, M. A., & Sullivan, G. S. (1994). Promoting relational thinking skills: Elaborative interrogation for mildly handicapped students. *Exceptional Children, 60,* 450–457.

Scruggs, T. E., Mastropieri, M. A., Sullivan, G. S., & Hesser, L. S. (1993). Improving reasoning and recall: The differential effects of elaborative interrogation and mnemonic elaboration. *Learning Disability Quarterly, 16,* 233–240.

Scruggs, T. E., Mastropieri, M. A., & Wolfe, S. (1995). Scientific reasoning of students with mental retardation: Investigating preconceptions and conceptual change. *Exceptionality, 5,* 223–244.

Shymansky, J. A., Kyle, W. C., & Alport, F. (1990). A reassessment of the effects of inquiry-based science curricula of the 60's on student performance. *Journal of Research in Science Teaching, 27,* 127–144.

Slater, W. H. (1988). Current theory and research on what constitutes readable expository text. *The Technical Writing Teacher, 15,* 196–206.

Smith, P. L., & Friend, M. (1986). Training learning disabled adolescents in a strategy for using text structure to aid recall of instructional prose. *Learning Disabilities Research, 2,* 38–44.

Stefanich, G. P., Bergan, E. C., & Paulsen, J. C. (Eds.). (1997). *What others are doing: Proceedings of a working conference on science for persons with disabilities.* Cedar Falls, IA: University of Northern Iowa.

Sullivan, G. S., Mastropieri, M. A., & Scruggs, T. E. (1995). Reasoning and remembering: Coaching thinking with students with learning disabilities. *Journal of Special Education, 29,* 310–322.

Teaching chemistry to students with disabilities. (1993). Washington, DC: American Chemical Society Committee on Chemists with Disabilities.

Weisgerber, R. A. (1993). *Science success for students with disabilities.* Reading, MA: Addison-Wesley.

Wohlers, H. D. (1994). Science education for students with disabilities: The visually impaired student in chemistry. In G. P. Stefanich & J. Egelston-Dodd (Eds.), *Proceedings of a working conference on science for persons with disabilities* (pp. 51–64). Cedar Falls, IA: University of Northern Iowa.

Woodward, J. (1994). The role of models in secondary science instruction. *Remedial and Special Education, 15,* 94–104.

Woodward, J., & Noell, J. (1992). Science instruction at the secondary level: Implications for students with learning disabilities. In D. Carnine & E. J. Kameenui (Eds.), *Higher order thinking: Designing curriculum for mainstreamed students* (pp. 39–58). Austin, TX: Pro-Ed.

Yager, R. E. (1983). The importance of terminology in teaching K–12 science. *Journal of Research in Science Teaching, 20,* 577–578.

Chapter 16

Asselin, S. B., Todd-Allen, M., & DeFur, S. (1998). Transition coordinators: Define yourselves. *Teaching Exceptional Children, 30*(3), 11–15.

Atkinson, R. C. (1975). Mnemotechnics in second-language learning. *American Psychologist, 30,* 821–828.

Atterbury, B. W. (1983). Success strategies for learning-disabled students. *Music Educators Journal, 69*(18), 29–31.

Atterbury, B. W. (1984). Music teachers need your help. *Journal of Learning Disabilities, 17*(2), 75–77.

Atterbury, B. W. (1990). *Mainstreaming exceptional learners in music.* Upper Saddle River, NJ: Merrill/Prentice Hall.

Beakley, B. A., & Yoder, S. L. (1998). Middle schoolers learn community skills. *Teaching Exceptional Children, 30*(3), 16–21.

Blackorby, M. R., & Wagner, M. (1996). Longitudinal postschool outcomes of youths with disabilities: Findings from the National Longitudinal Transition Study. *Exceptional Children, 62,* 399–413.

Block, M. E. (1994). *A teacher's guide to including students with disabilities in regular physical education.* Baltimore, MD: Brooks Publishing.

Brigham, F. J., & Brigham, M. M. (1998). Using mnemonic keywords in general music classes: Music history meets cognitive psychology. *Journal of Research and Development in Education, 31,* 205–213.

Brolin, D. (1989). *Life centered career education: A competency based approach.* Reston, VA: Council for Exceptional Children.

Campbell, P. S., & Scott-Kassner, C. (1995). *Music in childhood: From preschool through the elementary grades.* New York: Schirmer Books.

Carle, E. (1988). *You can make a collage: A very simple how-to book.* Palo Alto, CA: Klutz Press.

Clark, G. M. (1996). Transition planning assessment for secondary-level students with learning disabilities. *Journal of Learning Disabilities, 29,* 91–92.

Clark, G. M., & Patton, J. R. (1997). *Transition planning inventory: Administration and scoring guide.* Austin, TX: Pro-Ed.

Clements, R. L. (Ed.). (1995). *Games and great ideas: A guide for elementary school physical educators and classroom teachers.* Westport, CT: Greenwood Press.

Cronin, M. E., & Patton, J. R. (1993). *Life skills instruction for all students with special needs: A practical guide for integrating real-life content into the curriculum.* Austin, TX: Pro-Ed.

Day, M. (Ed.). (1997). *Preparing teachers of art.* Reston, VA: National Art Education Association.

Doren, B., & Benz, M. R. (1998). Employment inequality revisited: Predictors of better employment outcomes for young women with disabilities in transition. *Journal of Special Education, 31,* 425–442.

Elksnin, L. K., & Elksnin, N. (1996). Strategies for transition to employment settings. In D. D. Deshler, E. S. Ellis, & B. K. Lenz (Eds.), *Teaching adolescents with learning disabilities* (2nd ed., pp. 525–578). Denver: Love Publishing.

Future transition planning for life: A guide to a student's transition into employment, independent living, & recreation. (1996). Lafayette, IN: Greater Lafayette Area Special Services.

Galbraith, L. (Ed.). (1995). *Preservice art education: Issues and practice.* Reston, VA: National Art Education Association.

Glascoe, L. G., & Miller, L. S. (1986). *Life centered career education activity book two.* Reston, VA: Council for Exceptional Children.

Greenan, J. P. (1983). Identification and validation of generalizable skills in vocational programs. *Journal of Vocational Education Research, 8*(3), 46–71.

Greenan, J. P. (1986). The validation of generalizable mathematics skills assessment instruments for students with handicapping conditions. *Career Development of Exceptional Individuals, 9*(2), 77–88.

Grubb, W. N. (Ed.). (1996). *Education through occupations in American high schools.* New York: Teachers College Press.

Heal, L. W., Gonzalez, P., Rusch, F. R., Copher, J. I., & DeStefano, L. (1990). A comparison of successful and unsuccessful placements of youths with mental handicaps into competitive employment. *Exceptionality, 1,* 181–195.

Henrico County Public Schools, Glen Allen, VA. (1990). *Agriscience education for the middle school.* Glen Allen, VA: Vocational Curriculum and Resource Center. (ERIC Document Reproduction Service No. ED407500)

Hock, M., Hasazi, S. B., & Patten, A. (1990). Mainstreaming: Collaboration for learning: Strategies for program success. *Music Education Journal, 77,* 44–48.

Ianacone, R. N., & Stodden, R. A. (Eds.). (1987). *Transition issues and directions.* Reston, VA: The Council for Exceptional Children, Division on Mental Retardation and Developmental Disabilities.

Javorsky, J., Sparks, R. L., & Ganschow, L. (1992). Perceptions of college students with and without specific learning disabilities about foreign language courses. *Learning Disabilities Research & Practice, 7,* 31–44.

Kaser, S. L., Collier, D., & Solava, D. G. (1997). Sport skills for students with disabilities. *Journal of PE, Recreation, and Dance, 68*(1), 50–53.

Kelchner, T. A. (1991). *Art for the mentally retarded: Methodology and techniques for a broad based approach.* Williamsport, PA: Williamsport Area High School. (ERIC Document Reproduction Service No. ED335281)

Kokaska, C. J., & Brolin, D. E. (1985). *Career education for handicapped individuals.* Upper Saddle River, NJ: Merrill/Prentice Hall.

Lancioni, G. E., & Boelens, H. (1996). Teaching students with mental retardation and other disabilities to make simple drawings through a computer system and special cards. *Perceptual and Motor Skills, 83,* 401–402.

Lanford, A. G., & Cary, L. G. (2000). Graduation requirements for students with disabilities. *Remedial and Special Education, 21,* 152–160.

Learning Disabilities Association. (1993). *Fact sheet: Tests of General Educational Development (GED) Tests.* Pittsburgh: Author.

Learning Disabilities Association. (1994). *Fact sheet: Entrance tests for postsecondary programs.* Pittsburgh: Author.

Learning Disabilities Association. (1995). *Fact sheet: Learning disabilities and educational standards.* Pittsburgh: Author.

Lloyd, R. J., & Brolin, D. E. (1997). *Life centered career education: Modified curriculum for individuals with moderate special needs.* Reston, VA: Council for Exceptional Children.

Love, L., & Malian, I. M. (1997). What happens to students leaving secondary special education services in Arizona? Implications for educational program improvement and transition services. *Remedial and Special Education, 18,* 261–269.

Malian, I. M., & Love, L. (1998). Leaving high school: An ongoing transition study. *Teaching Exceptional Children, 30*(3), 4–10.

Mark, M. L. (1996). *Contemporary music education* (3rd ed). New York: Schirmer Books.

Miller, L. S., & Glascoe, L. G. (1986). *Life centered career education activity book one.* Reston, VA: Council for Exceptional Children.

Myer, B., Ganschow, L., Sparks, R., & Kenneweg, S. (1989). Cracking the code: Helping students with specific learning disabilities. In D. McAlpine (Ed.), *Defining the essentials for the foreign language classroom* (pp. 112–120). Lincolnwood, IL: National Textbook Company.

National FFA Center. (1996). *Bridging horizons: An advisor's guide to FFA involvement for members with disabilities.* Alexandria, VA: Nation FFA Center.

Padilla, A. M., Fairchild, H. H., & Valadez, C. M. (Eds.). (1990). *Foreign language education: Issues and strategies.* Newbury Park, CA: Sage Publications.

Pangrazi, R. P., & Dauer, V. P. (1995). *Dynamic physical education for elementary school children.* Boston: Allyn & Bacon.

Pangrazi, R. P., & Dauer, V. P. (1997). *Dynamic physical education for secondary school children* (3rd ed). Boston: Allyn & Bacon.

Parker, R. M. (1991). *OASIS-2: Occupational aptitude survey and interest schedule* (2nd ed.). Austin, TX: Pro-Ed.

Platt, J. M., & Janeczko, D. (1991). Adapting art instruction for students with disabilities. *Teaching Exceptional Children, 24*(1), 10–12.

Rodriguez, S. (1984). *The special artist's handbook: Art activities and adaptive aids for handicapped students.* Palo Alto, CA: Dale Seymour Publications.

Sarkees-Wircenski, M., & Scott, J. L. (1995). *Vocational special needs.* Homewood, IL: American Technical Publishers.

Sitlington, P., Newbert, D. A., Begun, W., Lombard, R. C., & Leconte, P. J. (1996). *Assess for success: Handbook on transition assessment.* Reston, VA: Council for Exceptional Children.

Smith, P. (1996). *The history of American art education: Learning about art in America's schools.* Westport, CT: Greenwood Press.

Sparks, R., Ganschow, L., & Javorsky, J. (1992). Diagnosing and accommodating the foreign language learning difficulties of college students with learning disabilities. *Learning Disabilities Research & Practice, 7,* 150–159.

Spencer, I. (1992). *Recent approaches to art instruction in special education: A review of the literature.* (ERIC Document Reproduction Service No. ED301469)

Standards of learning for Virginia public schools. (1995). Commonwealth of Virginia: Richmond, VA: Board of Education.

Stillwell, J. L., & Willgoose, C. E. (1997). *The physical education curriculum* (5th ed). Boston: Allyn & Bacon.

Taymans, J. M., & DeFur, S. (1994). Preservice and inservice development for school to adult life transition. *Career Development for Exceptional Children, 17,* 171–186.

Van Reusen, A. K., Bos, C. A., Schumaker, J. B., & Deshler, D. D. (1994). *The self-advocacy strategy for education and transition planning.* Lawrence, KS: Edge Enterprises.

Wagner, M., Newman, L., D'Amico, R., Jay, E. D., Butler-Nalin, P., Marder, C., & Cox, R. (1991). *Youth with disabilities: How are they doing? The first comprehensive report from the National Longitudinal Transition Study of Special Education Students.* Menlo, Park: CA: SRI International. (ERIC Document Reproduction Service No. ED341228)

Wehman, P. (1996). *Life beyond the classroom.* Baltimore: Brooks Cole.

West, L. L., Corbey, S., Boyer-Stephens, A., Jones, B., Miller, R. J., & Sarkees-Wiercenski, M. (1992). *Integrating transition planning into the IEP process.* Reston, VA: Council for Exceptional Children.

Winnick, J. P., & Short, F. X. (1985). *Physical fitness testing of the disabled: Project unique.* Champaign, IL: Human Kinetics Publishers, Inc.

Name Index

Abood, D., 381
Abramowitz, A. J., 279
Accouloumre, D. S., 103, 109, 115
Adams, A., 20
Adams, D., 355
Adams, L., 51
Adams, M. J., 369, 375, 377
Adams, W. R., 306, 320, 361
Affleck, J. Q., 20
Ahlgren, A., 447, 477
Alberto, P. A., 162, 188, 198, 214
Alfredo, A., 63
Algozzine, B., 69, 341
Allen, J., 405
Alley, G. R., 228, 322, 323, 357, 460
Allinder, R. M., 337
Allison, S. L., 198
Allison, T. S., 198
Almanza, E., 143, 144, 338
Alport, F., 467
Amerikaner, M., 258
Anders, P. L., 291, 387, 450, 451
Anderson, D., 338, 341
Anderson, K., 211
Anderson, M. G., 142, 338
Anderson, R. C., 382
Anderson, T. H., 454, 458
Antil, L. R., 375
Apgar, V., 76
Armbruster, B. B., 454, 458
Armel, S., 393
Armistead, L., 81
Arnold, C. R., 192
Aronoff, M., 63
Arora, T., 22
Artiles, A. J., 142, 338
Arvidson, H. H., 64
Ashbaker, M. H., 284
Asoko, H., 480
Asselin, S. B., 492, 493, 504, 505
Atkinson, R. C., 284, 292, 491
Atterbury, B. W., 489, 490
Augspurger, M., 488
Ault, M. H., 188
Authier, K. J., 146
Ayers, D., 220

Baca, L. M., 139, 143, 144, 338
Baer, D. M., 162, 204, 214

Bahr, C. M., 401
Bahr, M., 38, 255
Bailey, J., 352, 354, 355
Baker, J. G., 22, 285
Bakken, J. P., 70, 289, 292, 293, 350, 384, 387, 388, 391, 412, 458, 467
Ball, D. W., 373, 384
Bandura, A., 253
Barkley, R. A., 83, 126, 127, 129, 131, 282
Baron, J. B., 362
Barrera, F., 197
Barringer, K., 338
Bassett, D. S., 441
Bassuk, E., 146
Battle, J., 253
Bauer, A. M., 200, 201
Bauermeister, J. J., 82
Bauwens, J., 51
Baxter, J., 71
Bay, M., 19, 467
Beakley, B. A., 505
Beal, C. R., 399
Beals, V. L., 378
Bean, R. M., 454
Bear, B., 69
Beattie, S., 341
Beck, J., 76
Becker, W. C., 191, 192, 197, 373, 374, 384
Beeler, T., 377
Behrend, 421
Beikelman, D. R., 404
Beirne-Smith, M., 75, 76, 78, 111, 112, 276
Bender, W. N., 127, 129
Benedetti, D., 459
Bennett, C. I., 143, 338
Bennion, K., 339, 358
Benowitz, S., 338
Benson, D. F., 63
Bentz, J., 348–349, 350, 383
Benz, M. R., 513
Bergan, E. C., 468
Berla, E. P., 92
Bettencourt, E. M., 172, 264, 265
Beukelman, D. R., 63
Bhojwani, S., 429, 437
Biederman, J., 127
Bigelow, A., 92
Bigge, J. L., 93, 94, 101, 109, 110, 115
Bijou, S. W., 188

Biklen, D., 20, 118
Billingsley, B. S., 387
Billingsley, F. F., 118
Billingsley, P., 113–114
Bina, M., 22
Bireley, M., 10, 131, 133, 134, 136
Bishop, C. H., 357
Bishop, J., 306
Blachman, B. A., 375
Blackman, J. A., 76, 373, 375, 378
Blackorby, J., 147
Blackorby, M. R., 492
Blackstone, S. W., 119
Blair, K., 116
Blaska, J., 8
Blaylock, A. W., 134
Bleck, E. E., 100, 101, 103
Bley, N. S., 417–420, 423–424
Block, M. E., 491
Bloomquist, M. L., 83
Blowers, T., 253
Bocian, K. M., 69
Boelens, H., 489
Boersma, F. J., 78
Bohs, K., 156, 261
Bondy, A., 118
Bonstrom, O., 39
Boon, R., 21, 468, 480
Boone, R. A., 458
Booth, J. E., 247
Borden, S. L., 376
Borkowski, J. G., 257, 388
Bos, C. A., 506–507
Bos, C. S., 77, 291, 387, 450, 451
Bosco, P., 431
Boyle, J. R., 461, 462
Bradley, D. F., 363, 364
Brady, M. P., 118
Brady, S. A., 369
Braman, B. J., 118
Braswell, L., 83, 280
Bredderman, T., 289
Bricker, D. D., 78
Bricker, W. A., 78
Brigance, A. H., 372
Briggs, G., 105
Brigham, F. J., 51, 52, 53, 82, 172, 191, 202, 264, 289, 293, 298, 350, 467
Brody, G., 81

Broer, S. M., 54, 113
Brolin, D. E., 510, 514
Brookhouser, P. E., 146
Brophy, J., 156, 166, 172, 248, 265, 266, 447, 475
Browder, D. M., 381, 382
Brown, A. L., 212, 285, 388, 389
Brown, D. C., 113
Brown, F., 114
Brown, L. W., 104
Brown, S. O., 338, 341
Brown, V. L., 18
Browning, W. G., 296
Bruner, E. C., 373, 375
Bruner, J., 481
Bryan, J. H., 19
Bryan, T. H., 19, 69, 71, 467
Bryant, B. R., 377
Bryant, N. D., 395, 396
Bryen, D. N., 141
Buchard, J. D., 197
Bucher, R. D., 306
Buckley, N. K., 279
Buie, J. D., 193
Bulgarella, R., 78
Bulgren, J., 449, 453
Bullock, T. L., 306
Burchers, B., 295
Burchers, M., 295
Burchers, S., 295
Burgess, D. M., 105
Burns, M. S., 369, 370
Burns, S., 146
Bursuck, B., 82
Bursuck, W. D., 69, 310, 314, 343, 363, 364, 365
Butcher, K., 71, 258, 259, 290, 474, 477, 480
Butler, D. L., 403
Butterworth, T., 207
Bybee, J., 78
Byrom, E., 106

Cade, T., 298
Caldwell, T. H., 103, 109, 115
Calvin, M. B., 363, 364
Cambone, J., 186
Cameto, R., 147
Campbell, P. S., 490
Canter, L., 186, 191, 193, 195, 204, 205, 206, 207
Canter, M., 186, 191, 193, 195, 204, 205, 206
Canu, W. H., 247
Caplan, P., 145
Caponi, B., 285, 286
Capute, A. J., 100, 101
Carlberg, C., 22
Carle, E., 372, 489
Carlson, C. L., 247
Carlson, C. S., 192

Carman, R. A., 306, 320, 361
Carnine, D., 173, 371, 373, 374, 412, 436, 448
Carr, M. N., 22, 257, 388
Carta, J. J., 229
Carter, C., 306
Carter, K. B., 468, 480
Cartledge, G., 212, 213–214
Cary, L. G., 510
Case, L. P., 71, 257, 431
Casey, A., 39, 215
Cassel, P., 186
Castagnozzi, P., 381
Casto, G. C., 228
Cavalier, A. R., 476
Cavazos, L. F., 146
Cawley, J. F., 71
Ceci, S. J., 71, 285
Centra, N. A., 72
Cervalli, J., 147
Cervantes, H. T., 139
Cesan, K., 51
Chall, J. S., 369, 370
Chamberlain, J., 391
Chamberlain-Solecki, J., 391
Chambers, A. C., 394
Chambliss, M. J., 454
Chan, L. K. S., 458
Chard, D. J., 436
Chen, K., 292
Chenoweth, K., 340
Cher, 486
Cherkes-Julkowski, M., 127
Chiang-Soong, B., 453, 454
Chilman, B., 280
Chinn, P. C., 142
Chipman, J., 211
Christensen, C. C., 320
Christensen, S. L., 83
Christiansen, J., 363, 365
Christiansen, R. O., 105
Chung, S., 24, 289
Clark, B., 135, 136
Clark, D., 113
Clark, F. L., 322
Clark, G. M., 508, 509, 511
Clay, M., 372
Clayman, C. B., 100, 103, 105
Cleaver, A., 69
Clements, R. L., 491
Clements, S. D., 67, 68
Cloninger, C., 114
Coe, M. C., 82
Cohen, H. J., 106
Cohen, L. H., 96
Cohen, M. J., 127
Cohen, P., 21
Cohen, R. L., 288
Cohen, S. D., 104
Cohn, S. J., 291
Coi, G., 431

Colavecchia, B., 192
Cole, C. K., 105, 147, 149
Cole, D. A., 221
Cole, J. E., 82
Cole, P. G., 458
Collett, L., 405
Collier, D., 491
Collier, V. P., 141
Colvin, G., 81, 84
Conners, F., 69
Connolly, A. J., 338
Connors, C. K., 127
Conture, E. G., 63
Cook, B. G., 24
Cook, L., 24, 51, 52
Cook, L. K., 458
Cook, R. A., 454
Cook, S., 228, 229
Cooney, J. B., 71
Cooper, J. O., 460
Copher, J. I., 513
Corden, M., 403
Cornoldi, C., 71, 175, 285, 293, 286, 432
Costello, M., 62
Cottone, E. A., 71, 131, 279, 412
Coutinho, M., 350
Crabtree, C., 467, 475
Craft, M., 76
Craig, S., 38
Craik, F. I. M., 289
Crenshaw, T. M., 132
Crocker, A. C., 106
Croll, V. J., 388
Cronin, B. J., 94
Cronin, M. E., 80, 441, 510, 514
Cross, C., 139
Cross, D. R., 247
Crossairt, A., 279
Cruickshank, W. M., 24
Cruise, T., 486
Cumblad, C., 310, 314
Cummins, J., 141
Cummins, V., 338
Cunningham, A., 370
Cunningham, J. T., 454
Curlee, R. F., 62
Curtis, M. J., 461
Cutler, S. K., 108

Dalrymple, N. J., 118
Dalton, B., 352
D'Amico, R., 83
Daneman, D., 105
D'Angelo, C., 454
Dauer, V. P., 490, 491
Davidson, T., 412
Davis, G. A., 134, 136
Davis, R. B., 441
Dearstyne, B. W., 454
DeFabo, L., 309
DeFord, D. E., 372

DeFries, J. C., 69
DeFur, S., 492, 493, 504, 505
Delquardi, J., 229–230, 396
de Melendez, W. R., 137, 143, 144
Dennis, R., 114
Deno, E., 16
Deno, S. L., 69, 255
Denton, P. H., 460
Deshler, D. D., 71, 305, 306, 315, 318, 319, 322, 323, 330, 357, 362, 378, 380, 449, 450, 453, 460, 461, 506–507
DeStefano, L., 513
Dev, P. C., 21, 24, 247
Devine, T. G., 306, 315, 317–318, 319
Diamond, L. J., 43, 145
Diamond, S. C., 22
Dias, D., 352
Diaz-Rico, L. T., 142
Dickens, V. J., 292
DiGangi, S. Q., 202, 211
Dimino, J., 372
Dinardo, L., 145
Dixon, R., 398
Dobrovolsky, M., 63
Dodds, T., 372
Dole, J. A., 371
Donahoe, K., 69, 363
Donahue, M., 19
Donovan, S., 139
Doren, B., 513
Dougherty, J. W., 50
Dowling, D., 396
Down, J. L., 78
Downing, J. E., 113
Drabin, I. R., 395
Drasgow, E., 48
Dreikurs, R., 186
Driver, R., 480
Dudley, B., 240
Duffie, W. B., 427
Duhaime, A., 104
Duncan, B., 81
Dunwiddie, E. T., 358
Durkin, D., 370, 384
Dvorak, R., 86

Ebel, R., 357
Edelman, S. W., 54, 113, 114
Edmister, P., 47, 49
Ehly, S., 225
Ehrlich, S., 105
Eisele, J., 374
Ekstrand, R. E., 47, 49
Elam, S. M., 21
Elbaum, B. E., 21
Elksnin, L. K., 214
Elliot, T., 306
Elliott, J., 339
Elliott, S. N., 339
Ellis, E. S., 71, 305, 306, 315, 318, 319, 330, 378, 380, 387, 391, 450, 453, 460

Ellis, N. R., 77
Engel, J., 104
Engelmann, S., 373, 374, 375, 384, 398, 405
Englert, C. S., 70, 387, 398, 450, 452
Epps, S., 69
Epstein, M. H., 82, 310, 314, 343, 363, 373, 384
Erickson, R., 339
Ernhart, C. B., 76
Erwin, B., 358
Evelo, D. L., 83

Fairchild, H. H., 491
Fayne, H. R., 396
Feagin, J. R., 162, 188, 198, 214
Fecser, F. A., 207
Feeney, T. J., 104
Feingold, B., 127
Feldhusen, J. F., 133, 136
Feldman, W., 105
Feliciano, J., 486
Fennell, F. S., 351
Fernstrom, P., 22, 38, 255
Ferretti, R. P., 237, 476
Ficzere, S. A., 403
Filip, D., 387, 450
Finnegan, L., 105
Fiore, T., 84, 131, 279, 454
First, M. B., 126
Fischer, P. E., 377
Flavell, J. H., 285
Fletcher, D., 381
Foley, R. M., 310
Fontana, J., 233, 465
Foorman, B. R., 377
Ford, B. A., 338
Ford, M., 247, 255
Forehand, R., 81
Forest, M., 20, 50, 112, 220
Forgan, J. W., 21
Forness, S. R., 19, 22, 67, 69, 76, 81, 82, 86, 107, 132, 209, 211, 215, 285, 292
Fountas, I. C., 371, 381
Foxx, R. M., 199
Frank, A. R., 78
Frank, M., 105
Franklin, K., 63
Frase-Blunt, M., 340
Freeman, B. J., 117
Freeman, S., 396
French, N., 54
Fried, Leni, 488
Friend, M., 51, 52, 458
Frith, G. H., 113
Frose, V., 394
Fry, E., 455
Frymier, J., 10
Fuchs, D., 19, 22, 38, 39, 69, 143, 225, 229, 230, 231, 233, 234, 241, 255, 264, 337, 338, 339, 342, 347, 348–349, 350, 375, 376, 383, 391

Fuchs, L. S., 19, 22, 38, 69, 143, 225, 229, 230, 231, 233, 255, 337, 338, 339, 342, 347, 348–349, 350, 351, 353, 354, 375, 376, 383, 387, 391
Fulk, B. J. M., 24, 70, 257, 295, 395, 397, 430, 461
Fulker, D., 69
Fuller, D. R., 64
Fuller, K., 22
Furner, B., 393
Futtersak, M. W., 279

Gable, R. A., 77, 78
Gable, R. V., 228
Gaffney, J., 294, 296
Gagnon, J. C., 207, 208
Gajria, M., 343, 344, 387
Galderisi, D., 71, 285
Gall, J. P., 306
Gall, M. D., 172, 264, 265, 317, 319, 326, 327
Gallagher, J. J., 134, 136
Gallagher, S. A., 134, 136
Ganschow, L., 491
Garand, J., 119
Garbarino, J., 145, 146
Garcia, L., 52
Garcia, S. B., 142, 143
Gardner, H., 133, 145
Gardner, M., 394
Garnett, K., 417
Garrison-Harrell, L., 120
Gartner, A., 20
Gaskins, I., 71, 306
Gately, F. J., Jr., 51
Gately, S. E., 51
Gates, A. J., 109, 115
Gaylord-Ross, R., 92
Gee, K., 112
Gelzheiser, L. M., 298, 454
Genshaft, J. L., 10, 131, 133, 136
Gerber, M. M., 229
Gerber, P. J., 92
Germanario, V., 147
Gersten, R., 372
Gettinger, M., 395, 396
Giangreco, M. F., 54, 113, 114
Gibbon, M., 126
Gickling, E. E., 38
Gillett, M. H., 172, 264, 265
Gillis, J. J., 69
Gilman, S., 38, 255
Ginott, H., 31
Ginsburg, H. P., 416, 420, 437
Givens, A., 458
Glascoe, L. G., 510
Gleason, M., 173, 404
Golden, N., 211
Goldman, S. R., 442
Goldstein, A. P., 211
Gonzalez, J. J., 69, 71

Gonzalez, P., 513
Good, T., 156, 166, 172
Goodfellow, F., 372
Goodman, H., 209, 220
Goodwin, L., 289
Gordon, B. D., 199
Gordon, J., 395
Gordon, T., 31
Gorrafa, S., 196
Gottlieb, J., 209, 220
Govindarajan, G., 261
Graden, J. L., 39, 461
Graetz, J., 120, 233, 298, 391, 466
Graham, F. K., 76
Graham, S., 70, 71, 280, 369, 392, 393, 395, 396, 398, 399, 400, 401, 402, 431
Grandin, T., 117
Graves, A., 393
Graves, D. H., 388, 394, 398
Gray, C., 119
Green, S. K., 22
Greenan, J. P., 502, 503
Greenbaum, J., 129
Greenfield, D. B., 77
Greenwood, C. R., 229–230, 396
Gregory, D. A., 134
Gresham, F. M., 69, 70, 215
Griffin, H. C., 92
Griffin, P., 369, 370
Griffith, D. R., 105, 147, 149
Grimes, J. E., 458
Grise, P., 341
Grossman, H., 10
Grossman, R., 138, 140–141
Grubb, W. N., 492
Guetzloe, E. C., 147, 150
Gunter, P. L., 298
Guthrie, D., 69
Gutting, Kevin, 488

Hagen, E., 338
Haggart, A. G., 38
Haigh, J. A., 340
Hale, J. B., 467
Hall, R. V., 229–230, 279, 396
Hallahan, D. P., 19, 20, 21, 51, 69, 70, 71, 75, 81, 111, 131, 133, 279, 280, 392, 393, 412
Hallenbeck, M. J., 109
Hamby, R. S., 280
Hamlett, C. L., 230, 337, 342, 347, 348–349, 350, 383
Hamm, M., 355
Hammill, D. D., 18, 67, 338
Hanner, S., 373, 384
Hansen, J., 355
Harder, J., 100
Hardy, S., 53
Haring, N. G., 24, 67, 68
Harper, G. F., 232, 465
Harris, J., 84, 131, 279

Harris, K. R., 52, 70, 71, 257, 280, 282, 369, 393, 396, 397, 398, 399, 400, 401, 402, 431
Harris, M., 378
Harris, V. W., 201
Harrison, R. H., 209, 220
Harry, B., 139, 143
Harter, S., 248, 253
Hartman, D. K., 454
Harvey, P., 52
Hasazi, S. B., 489
Haslam, R. H. A., 100, 103, 104
Hasselbring, T. S., 442
Hatch, T., 133
Haynes, J. A., 397
Haynes, M. C., 165, 387
Hazel, J. S., 211
Heal, L. W., 513
Heath, N., 72, 248
Heckaman, K., 212, 213–214
Heflin, L. J., 146, 147, 151
Heinen, A., 21
Heiss, J., 351
Helge, D., 147
Heliotis, J. D., 387
Heller, H. B., 220
Hemrick, M. A., 343, 344
Hendrickson, J. M., 78
Henggeler, S. W., 81
Henley, A. M., 230, 391
Herman, R., 372
Herrmann, D., 285
Herzog, A., 72
Hetherington, E. M., 76
Heward, W., 95, 97, 276
Hicks, D. M., 62, 63
Hiebert, E. H., 372, 382
Higgins, T. S., 228
Hines, R. A., 51
Hipp, K., 405
Hirth, M. A., 24
Hock, M., 489
Hocutt, A., 84, 131, 279
Hodell, M., 268
Hodge, J., 54
Hogan, A., 71, 215
Holland, A. L., 62
Hollinger, C. L., 10, 131, 133, 134, 136
Hollingsworth, M., 71
Hollingsworth, P., 207
Holmes, D., 211
Holubec, E. J., 236, 239, 241
Hoover, J. J., 324
Hopkins, B. L., 279
Horner, R. H., 207, 208
Horton, G., 211
Horton, S. V., 320, 426, 458, 460
Hourcade, J. J., 51
House, B. J., 77
Howard, M. R., 62
Howell, K. W., 336

Hudson, P., 449
Hughes, C. A., 202, 212, 315, 322, 323, 330, 357, 362, 423, 440
Hughes, S., 142
Hulit, L. M., 62
Hull, J. M., 92
Hull, K., 38
Hull, R. E., 172, 264, 265
Humphries, T., 96
Hunt, N., 78–79
Hunt-Berg, M., 404
Hurley, C. M., 83
Hutchinson, H. L., 439, 440
Hynd, G. W., 69, 71, 127

Ianacone, R. N., 48
Iano, R. P., 220
Idol, L., 388
Idol-Maestas, L., 362, 385
Innes, D., 52
Irvine, J. W., 229
Isaacson, S., 404
Ittenbach, R., 75, 76, 78, 111, 112, 276
Iverson, V., 114

Jackson, D. A., 211
Jackson, L., 50
Jackson, N. F., 211
Jacobsen, D. R., 306
Jacobson, J. W., 75
Jaffe, L. E., 387, 450
Janeczko, D., 489
Janisch, C., 454
Janvier, C., 439
Jaudes, P. K., 145
Javorsky, J., 491
Jayanthi, M., 310, 314, 343
Jemail, J. A., 82
Jenkins, J. R., 21, 165, 196, 226, 230, 238–239, 375, 376, 387, 459
Jenkins, L. M., 226, 230
Jenkins, V., 357
Jenne, T., 200
Jensen, A. R., 77, 291
Jitendra, A., 454
Johnson, D. W., 233, 234, 235, 236, 239, 240, 241
Johnson, E., 338, 341
Johnson, G., 373, 374, 384
Johnson, H., 193
Johnson, L. J., 52
Johnson, M. B., 338
Johnson, M. J., 454
Johnson, P. H., 373
Johnson, R., 233
Johnson, R. T., 233, 234, 235, 236, 239, 240, 241
Johnson, T. P., 3, 5, 21
Jones, C., 105
Jones, C. B., 129
Jones, D. B., 198

Jones, E. D., 136, 429, 437
Jones, G. A., 421, 431
Jones, K. L., 76, 105
Jones, W., 387
Jordan, D., 394
Jorgensen, C., 292
Joy, R., 280
Joyce, C. M., 104
Junkin, L. J., 248, 253
Juvonen, J., 69

Kail, R., 70
Kameenui, E. J., 371, 373, 436, 448
Kamphaus, R. W., 128
Kamps, D. M., 120
Kane, B. J., 228
Kanner, L., 115
Karasoff, P., 112
Karns, K., 230
Karweit, N. L., 145, 233
Kaser, S. L., 491
Katsiyannis, A., 54
Katz, G., 106
Kauffman, E. A., 133
Kauffman, J. M., 19, 20, 21, 69, 70, 75, 80,
    81, 82, 111, 149, 229, 392
Kaufman, A. S., 338
Kaufman, N. L., 338
Kavale, K. A., 19, 22, 67, 76, 81, 82, 131,
    132, 209, 211, 215, 285, 292
Keenan, J. M., 292
Kelchner, T. A., 489
Kelly, T. E., 100, 103, 105
Kendall, P. C., 280
Kennedy, K. M., 373, 375, 378
Kenneweg, S., 491
Keogh, B. K., 70
Keppler, R., 200, 201
Kerr, M. M., 116, 149, 187, 192, 194, 198,
    224, 228, 278, 281, 314
Kilpatrick, J., 430, 438
Kilsheimer, L., 390
Kimball, K., 338, 341
Kinder, D., 82
King, R. P., 355, 356, 357
King, R. S., 94
King–Sears, M. E., 461
Kingsbury, D., 496
Kirk, S., 67
Kitano, M. K., 139
Klein, M., 145
Kliewer, C., 20
Kline, D. F., 148
Klingner, J. K., 21
Kluwin, T. N., 99
Knapp, M. S., 147
Knaus, W., 258
Kneedler, R. D., 280
Knight, P., 355
Kobett, B., 351
Koening, A. J., 93

Kokaska, C. J., 514
Kollar, J. L., 143
Koppel, A. E., 441
Korinek, L., 34, 78
Kosiewicz, M. M., 280, 393
Kovaleski, J. F., 38
Kozleski, E. B., 50
Kratochwill, T. R., 339
Kravits, S. L., 306
Krist, J., 390
Kroesbergen, E. H., 412
Krouse, J., 229
Kuperis, S., 403
Kuypers, D. S., 197
Kyle, W. C., 467

LaBerge, D., 375
Lacerenza, L., 376
Lancioni, G. E., 489
Land, M., 172
Landrum, T. J., 24, 280
Lane, H., 22
Lanford, A. G., 54, 510
Lang, H. G., 440, 468
Langrall, C. W., 412, 431
Larkin, D. F., 454
Larrivee, B., 24, 156, 166, 167
Larsen, S. C., 67, 338
Latham, G. P., 255
Laurie, T., 363
LaVole, R., 270
Lawrence, E. A., 257
Laycock, M., 421, 422
Lazar, M. F., 104
Leach, J., 480
Leal, D., 13, 391
Leal, L., 309
Leavey, M., 234
Lee, P., 357
Leeper, D. C., 192
Leigh, J. E., 67
Leinhart, A., 382
Lenz, B. K., 71, 305, 306, 315, 318, 319,
    330, 378, 380, 449, 450, 453, 460
Leonard, B., 120
Leonard, L. B., 70
Leone, P. E., 147, 148, 149, 207, 208
Lepper, M. R., 268
Leppert, M. O., 100, 101
Lerner, J., 68, 276, 281, 370, 389
Levin, E., 363
Levin, J. R., 294
Lewis, R. B., 63, 336, 337, 338, 339
Liberman, A. M., 372
Liberman, I. Y., 70, 372
Licht, B., 248
Lifson, S., 339, 358
Lignugaris/Kraft, B., 209
Lilly, M. S., 20
Lindamood, P., 378
Lindley, L., 112

Linehan, S. L., 118
Lipsey, M. W., 69
Lipsky, D. K., 20
Lloyd, J. W., 19, 69, 70, 78, 280, 384,
    392, 393
Lloyd, L. L., 64, 78, 119
Lloyd, R. J., 510, 514
Lo, F. G., 258, 259
Locke, E. A., 255
Lockhart, R. S., 289
Lombardi, T. P., 147
Long, N. J., 207
Longo, M., 99
Lopez, R., 105
Lovaas, O. I., 115, 117
Love, L., 492
Lovett, M. W., 376
Lovitt, T. C., 269, 320, 426, 458, 459, 460
Lowenbraun, S., 20
Loynachan, C., 398
Lubie, B. L., 53
Lucangeli, D., 71, 285, 358, 431, 432
Luckie, W. R., 306
Lund, K. A., 210
Lundberg, I., 377
Lundeen, C., 51
Lundeen, D. J., 51
Lusthaus, E., 50, 112, 220
Luterman, D. M., 95, 96
Lynch, E. W., 140
Lynn, P., 52
Lyon, G. R., 69, 70, 375
Lyons, C. A., 372

Maag, J. W., 126, 202, 204
Mabee, W. S., 393
MacArthur, C. A., 397, 476
MacArthur, C. D., 237
Maccini, P., 423, 440
MacDonald, V., 390
MacKenzie-Keating, S. E., 192
MacMillan, D. L., 69, 76, 139, 147
Madden, N. A., 145, 234
Madge, S., 20
Madsen, C. H., 191, 192
Magnuson, D., 240
Maheady, L., 206, 232, 465
Maher, C. A., 441
Maker, C. J., 133, 134
Malaby, J. E., 196
Malian, I. M., 492
Malone, L. D., 387
Malouf, D. B., 350, 397
Mamlin, N., 71, 257
Mantzicopoulos, P., 241, 289, 351
Marder, C., 83
Margalit, M., 78
Mariage, T. V., 70, 387, 398, 450, 452
Mark, M. L., 490
Markel, G., 129
Marrs, R. W., 449

Marschark, M., 378
Marshall, R., 69
Marsing, L., 86, 357
Marston, D., 22
Martin, C. J., 78
Martin, G., 188, 190, 199, 268
Martin, R., 12
Martinez, E. A., 229
Martinez-Pons, M., 253
Maruyama, G., 233
Mastropieri, M. A., 19, 21, 24, 47, 69, 70,
    71, 72, 77, 78, 82, 156, 158, 162,
    170–171, 172, 174, 180, 190, 199,
    200, 203, 204, 209, 222, 224, 228,
    229, 232–233, 236, 238, 241, 250,
    253, 257, 258, 259, 261, 264, 268,
    276, 289, 290, 291, 292, 293, 294,
    295, 296, 297, 298, 309, 339, 350,
    351, 355, 356, 357–358, 361, 362,
    371, 382, 384, 387, 388, 391, 396,
    397, 412, 425, 426, 427, 430, 447,
    453, 454, 458, 460, 465, 466, 467,
    468, 472, 474, 477, 479, 480
Mather, N., 69, 70, 338, 371
Mathes, P. G., 69, 229, 230, 231, 232,
    387, 391
Mathur, S. R., 82, 215
Mayer, G. R., 207
Mayer, R. E., 458
Mazurek, K., 139, 141, 142, 143, 338
McBride, B. M., 118
McConnell, S., 211
McCormick, C., 156, 248, 283, 411
McCormick, S., 460
McCuller, G. L., 209
McDougle, C. J., 117
McElroy, K., 280
McGettigan, J. F., 220
McGinnis, E., 211
McGue, M., 69
McIntosh, R., 211, 215
McKeever, C., 258
McKinney, J. D., 84, 131, 279
McLaughlin, T. F., 196
McLaughlin, V. L., 34
McLean, P., 421, 422
McLeskey, J., 69, 70, 411
McLoone, B., 294
McLoughlin, J. A., 336, 337, 338, 339
McMaster, D., 109
McMaster, K. N., 234, 241, 264
McNaughton, D., 330, 437
McNutt, G., 67
McPhail, J. C., 72
Meadow-Orlans, K. P., 95
Meers, G. D., 363
Megivern, M., 145, 147
Mehring, T. A., 109
Meister, C., 389, 390
Melloy, K. J., 189, 277
Meltzer, L. J., 72, 322

Mercer, C. D., 78, 357, 411, 412, 422, 461
Merrill, K. W., 69
Merritt-Petrashek, C. A., 206–207
Messersmith, J. L., 52
Meyer, L., 374
Michael, R. J., 108
Michaud, L., 104
Mihsna, F., 258
Miksic, S., 149
Milich, R., 127
Miller, L., 377, 393
Miller, L. S., 510
Miller, P. D., 371
Miller, S. P., 411, 412, 422
Miller, S. R., 280
Millman, J., 357, 361
Misra, A., 202, 212
Mitchell, D. C., 103
Moats, L. C., 370, 372, 395
Mohler, L. J., 232–233, 387, 391
Monroe, C., 211
Monson, J. A., 292
Montague, M., 71, 84, 131, 210, 279, 283,
    387, 411–412, 430, 431
Montgomery–Grimes, D. J., 257
Moon, S., 133
Moore, G. P., 62, 63
Moore, P., 38, 255
Moore, P. R., 442
Moore, R. J., 212, 213–214
Morehead, M. K., 336
Morningstar, M. E., 112
Morocco, C., 405
Morrow, H., 38
Morse, W. C., 207
Mortimer, E., 480
Muccigrosso, L., 147, 149
Mulick, J. A., 75
Munk, D., 363, 365
Munoz, D., 52
Murawski, W. W., 53
Murphy, S., 363
Myer, B., 491
Myles, B. S., 118

Nafpakitis, M., 207
Nagel, D. A., 100
Nau, P. A., 192
Neel, R. S., 81
Nelson, A., 405
Nelson, C. M., 116, 149, 187, 192, 193,
    194, 198, 199, 224, 278, 281, 314
Nelson, D., 233
Nelson, J. R., 208
Nelson, M., 22
Nelson, M. C., 50
Nelson, N. W., 401
Nelson, R., 458
Newman, L., 147
Newsom, C. D., 115, 117
Nicholls, J. G., 248, 251

Niles, O. S., 458
Noell, J., 481
Novotny, D. E., 147
Nowacek, E. J., 52

Obiakor, F. E., 109, 338
O'Brien, J., 478
Ochoa, A. S., 467, 475
O'Connor, R. E., 238–239, 375, 376
Odell, K. S., 147
Ofiesh, N., 330
Ogden, E. H., 147
Ogle, D. M., 386
Ogletree, B. T., 118
O'Grady, W., 63
Okolo, C. M., 237, 476
Okovita, J. W., 292
O'Leary, D. K., 393
O'Leary, K. D., 197
O'Leary, S. G., 279
Olsen, R., 69
O'Melia, M. C., 314
Omizo, M. M., 258
Omizo, S. A., 258
Ortiz, A. A., 142, 143
Osborn, J., 371
Osborne, A. G. Jr., 10, 11, 21
Osguthorpe, R. T., 228, 229
O'Shaughnessy, T. E., 71
O'Shea, D., 382, 384
O'Shea, L. J., 382, 384
Ostertag, V., 137, 143, 144
Ovando, C. J., 141
Overton, T., 337
Owings, M., 397
Oxer, T., 387, 450, 452

Padden, C., 96
Padeliadu, S., 21
Padilla, A. M., 491
Paivio, A., 292
Palincsar, A. S., 388, 389
Palmer, D. S., 22
Palmer, R., 71
Palson, K., 77
Pangrazi, R. P., 490, 491
Paris, S. G., 247
Parke, R. D., 76
Parker, R. M., 510
Patten, A., 489
Patton, J. M., 134, 139, 276, 338
Patton, J. R., 12, 47, 75, 76, 78, 80, 111, 112,
    373, 384, 441, 508, 509, 510, 514
Pauk, W., 323, 357, 358, 361
Paul, P. V., 95, 96
Paulsen, J. C., 468
Paxton, R. J., 454
Pear, J., 188, 190, 199, 268
Pearl, R., 72
Perez-Selles, M., 38
Perou, R., 77, 292

Perry, N., 387, 388
Petersen, S., 109
Peterson, R. F., 188
Phillips, L., 53
Phillips, N. B., 230, 348–349, 350, 383
Phillips, S. E., 340
Piantek, G. A., 52
Pinnell, G. S., 371, 372, 381
Pious, C., 459
Pipitone, P., 103
Platt, J. M., 489
Plumb, I. J., 113
Plummer, D. L., 134
Pollard, R. R., 363
Polloway, C. H., 373, 384
Polloway, E. A., 47, 78, 310, 314, 343, 363,
    373, 377, 384
Potucek, J., 120
Poulsen, M. K., 105, 147, 149
Power, M. H., 339
Powers, T. V., 81
Prater, M., 202, 280
Pressley, M., 156, 248, 283, 369, 371, 372,
    373, 375, 377, 411
Price, M., 10, 138, 145
Prieto, A. G., 139, 283
Pugach, M. C., 52
Putnam, M. L., 283, 343, 361, 363

Quigley, S. P., 95, 96
Quinn, M. M., 82, 215

Rack, J., 69
Rafoth, M. A., 309
Ragland, E. U., 224
Ramirez, G., Jr., 143
Ramirez, J. L., 143
Ramsey, E., 81, 84
Rana, R., 412
Rangel, L., 147
Rankin, J. L., 371, 372, 375, 404
Rashotte, C. A., 375
Rawson, P., 352
Raynes, M., 20
Reagan, T., 96
Redl, F., 192, 206, 277
Reed, P., 394
Reeder, P., 38, 255
Reeve, P. T., 51
Reeve, R. E., 132
Reid, R., 126, 280, 396
Reinhiller, N., 51, 52
Reisman, F. K., 428
Reiss, S. M., 135
Renzulli, J. S., 133, 135
Repp, A. C., 19
Reschly, D. J., 139
Reynolds, M. C., 19
Rhoades, K. W., 104
Riccio, C. A., 71, 127
Richter, L., 228, 229

Riggin, J., 47
Riley, M. K., 352
Rimland, B., 22, 118
Rimm, S. B., 134, 136
Ritter, D. R., 50
Ritter, S., 362
Ritvo, E. R., 117
Rivera, D. P., 411, 428
Roberts, P. H., 69
Roberts, R., 69, 70
Robin, A. L., 393
Robinson, T. R., 48
Roderique, T. W., 363
Rodriguez, S., 489
Rogers, T., 371
Rohwer, W. D., 291
Rojewski, J. W., 363
Rooney, K. J., 280
Rose, L. C., 21
Rosen, L. S., 279
Rosen, S., 92
Rosenberg, M. S., 206, 314
Rosenshine, B., 175, 177, 389, 390
Rosenthal-Malek, A. L., 212, 215
Ross, D. B., 93
Rossi, P. H., 146
Rothstein, L. F., 10, 11
Routman, R., 371
Rubin, L., 146
Ruble, L. A., 118
Rudenga, E. A. V., 372
Rudiger, A. F., 106
Rudsit, J., 459
Rudy, K., 146, 147, 151
Rueda, R., 139, 412
Ruhl, K. L., 202, 212, 315, 362, 437
Rusch, F. R., 513
Russell, F., 285
Rutherford, R. B., Jr., 82, 199, 211, 215,
    447, 477
Rutherford, T. K., 427
Ryan, L., 105
Ryndak, D. L., 113
Rynders, J., 221

Sacca, K., 232
Sacca, M. K., 465
Sachs, A., 387
Sacks, O., 117
Sacks, S. Z., 92
Sailor, W., 20, 112
Salend, S. J., 99, 199, 343, 344, 346, 347,
    355, 357, 363
Salvia, J., 337, 387
Salzberg, C. L., 209
Sameoto, D., 192
Sammons, K. B., 351
Samuels, J., 382
Samuels, S., 375
Sanchez, T., 508
Sanders, A., 230, 391

Sapon-Shevin, M., 113
Sapona, R. H., 53
Sarason, I. G., 357, 358
Sarkees-Wircenski, M., 492, 493, 495,
    497–499, 500, 501, 502, 503
Sattler, J., 338
Sawatsky, D., 387, 388
Scadden, L., 94
Scariano, M., 117
Scavarda, M., 147, 149
Schalock, R. L., 75
Schectman, A. J., 427
Scheel, C., 71
Scheid, K., 326
Schiefelbusch, R. L., 78
Schirmer, B. R., 352, 354, 355
Schmitz, J., 405
Schneider, W., 284
Schoenfeld, A. H., 440
Schoenwald, S. K., 81
Schopman, E. A. M., 413
Schroeder, B., 412
Schulte, A. A. G., 339
Schultz, F., 127
Schumaker, J. B., 211, 306, 315, 322, 357,
    362, 378, 449, 460, 461, 506–507
Schumm, J. S., 21
Schumm, S. J., 395
Schwanz, K. A., 128
Schwartz, I. S., 118
Schwartz, R. G., 62
Schwenn, J. O., 109
Scott, J. A., 382
Scott, J. L., 492, 495, 497–499, 500, 501,
    502, 503
Scott, M. S., 77, 292
Scott, P., 480
Scott-Kassner, C., 490
Scruggs, T. E., 19, 21, 24, 47, 69, 70, 71, 72,
    77, 78, 82, 86, 156, 158, 162, 170,
    172, 174, 180, 190, 199, 200, 203,
    204, 209, 222, 224, 228, 229,
    232–233, 236, 238, 241, 250, 253,
    258, 259, 261, 264, 268, 276, 283,
    289, 290, 291, 292, 293, 294, 295,
    296, 297, 298, 309, 339, 345, 350,
    351, 355, 356, 357–358, 361, 362,
    371, 382, 384, 387, 388, 391, 396,
    397, 412, 425, 426, 427, 430, 447,
    453, 454, 458, 460, 465, 466, 467,
    468, 472, 474, 477, 479, 480
Selby, D., 363
Serna, L., 47
Sexton, K., 52
Shank, M., 13
Shankweiler, D. P., 70, 369, 372
Shapiro, S. T., 199
Sharp, S., 127
Sharpley, A. M., 229
Sharpley, C. F., 229
Shea, T. M., 200, 201

Sheffler, S., 486
Shefter, H., 396
Sheldon, J., 211
Sherman, J. A., 201, 211
Shiah, R. L., 430, 431
Shiffrin, R. M., 284
Shin, M., 247
Shinn, M. R., 22, 69
Short, F. X., 491
Shuster, S. K., 467, 475
Shymansky, J. A., 467
Silbert, J., 371, 373, 405, 412
Silverman, L. K., 134
Simmons, D. C., 230
Simmons, L., 378
Simpson, R. L., 117, 118
Simpson-Brown, R., 147, 149
Sinclair, E., 69
Sinclair, M. F., 83
Sindelar, P. T., 206, 228, 382, 384, 461
Singh, N. N., 19
Singh, R. K., 228–229
Sirvis, B., 103, 109, 115
Skiba, R., 215
Skodol, A. E., 126
Skon, L., 233
Slater, W. H., 457
Slavin, R. E., 145, 233, 234, 236, 239, 241
Slocum, T., 376
Smart, M. A., 421, 422
Smethurst, W., 306
Smith, D. D., 428
Smith, D. W., 76, 105
Smith, L., 127, 172
Smith, P. L., 458
Smith, S. M., 118
Smith, T. E. C., 12, 377
Snell, M. E., 20, 78, 112, 114
Snider, V. E., 371, 372, 374, 387
Snow, C. E., 369, 370
Solava, D. G., 491
Southern, W. T., 136
Sparks, R., 491
Speece, D. L., 390
Spencer, I., 489
Spencer, V., 233, 391, 465
Spiegel, G. L., 108
Spitz, H. H., 77
Spitzer, R. L., 126
Stahl, S. A., 371, 377
Stainback, S., 8, 21, 22, 112, 220, 221
Stainback, W., 8, 21, 22, 112, 220, 221
Stanovich, K. E., 369, 370, 373
Starnes, W. T., 134
Starshine, D., 401
Staudacher, C., 441, 442
Staver, J. R., 467
Stecker, P. M., 347
Steele, R. G., 81
Stefanich, G. P., 468
Stein, M. L., 387, 412

Stephens, V. P., 10, 138, 145
Stern, G. G., 24
Stern, L., 145
Sternberg, R. J., 133
Stevens, K. B., 50
Stevens, R. J., 175, 177, 236, 241
Stewart, D. A., 99
Stillwell, J. L., 490
Stocia, R., 52
Stodden, R. A., 48
Stokes, T. F., 162, 204, 214
Stolzenberg, J., 127
Stone, C. A., 72, 390
Stormont-Spurgin, M., 70, 395
Strain, P. S., 224
Straub, R. L., 109
Streissguth, A. P., 76, 105
Stretton, K., 396
Stringfield, S., 372
Stronge, J. H., 146
Strosnider, R., 412
Stumbo, P., 127
Sturgeon, A., 289, 452
Sugai, G., 207, 208
Sullivan, G. S., 71, 174, 209, 290, 479
Summerlin, M. L., 258
Suritsky, S. K., 322, 323
Swank, P. R., 38
Swanson, H. L., 53, 71, 384
Swanson, L. H., 284, 285
Sweeney, D. P., 107
Swicegood, P., 357

Taitt, H., 138
Talbott, E., 78, 82, 384
Tankersley, M., 24, 78, 384
Tarrant, K. L., 387, 450, 452
Tateyama-Sniezek, K. M., 241
Taymans, J. M., 504
Telian, N. A., 377
Tellarini, M., 432
Temple, J., 280
Tenhouse, C., 146
Terrill, M. C., 295
Thalacker, B. E., 147, 149
Thomas, C. R., 81
Thomas, D. R., 191
Thompson, A., 375, 376
Thorndike, R. L., 338
Thornton, C. A., 417–420, 421,
    423–424, 431
Thousand, J. S., 80
Thurber, D. N., 394
Thurlow, M., 339
Thurston, D., 76
Thurston, L., 229–230
Tierney, R. J., 77
Tindal, G. A., 69
Tivnan, T., 352
Todaro, A. W., 103, 109, 115
Todd-Allen, M., 492, 493, 504, 505

Todis, B., 211
Tolfa, D., 357–358
Topping, K., 225, 228
Torgesen, J. K., 372, 373, 375, 377
Toy, K., 107
Traub, N., 378, 379
Trent, S. C., 53, 78, 142
Troutman, A. C., 162, 188, 198, 214
Tulving, E., 283
Tur-Kaspa, H., 69, 71
Turnbull, A. P., 13, 112
Turnbull, B. J., 147
Turnbull, R., 13
Turner, S., 441, 442
Twyman, J. S., 193

Uberti, H. Z., 295
Ulleland, C. N., 76, 105
Umbreit, J., 116
Underwood, B. J., 285

Vadasy, P. F., 375, 376
Vala, N., 173
Valadez, C. M., 491
Valletutti, P. J., 100, 105
Van Houten, R., 192, 197
Van Luit, J. E. H., 412, 413
Van Meter, A. M., 401
Van Reusen, A. K., 506–507
Van Tassel-Baska, J., 133
Vandercook, T., 221
Vanderheiden, G. C., 119
Varble, M. E., 138
Vaughn, S., 21, 71, 211, 215, 395
Veit, D. T., 229, 296, 345, 357, 358
Vernon, P., 141
Vianello, R., 175, 285, 293
Villa, R. A., 80
Vincent, L. J., 105, 147, 149
Vogel, J. R., 363, 365

Wadsworth, S. J., 69
Wagner, M., 147, 492
Wagner, R. K., 373, 375
Walberg, H. J., 19
Waldron, N., 69, 70, 411
Walker, H. M., 81, 84, 208, 210, 211
Walker, J. M., 211, 279
Walker, V. S., 220
Walther-Thomas, C., 34
Wang, M. C., 19
Ward, M., 240
Warden, R., 405
Warger, C. S., 145, 147
Warner, M. M., 322, 460
Warren, D. H., 92
Warren, S. F., 77, 78
Watson, B., 372
Watson, D. L., 147
Wayne, S. K., 375
Webb-Johnson, G., 142, 338

Wechsler, D., 338
Weed, K. Z., 142
Wehman, P., 504, 510
Weintraub, N., 70, 392
Weisberger, R. A., 468
Weishaar, M., 461, 462
Weiss, M. P., 51, 52, 53
Welks, D. M., 104
Wellman, H. M., 285
Werts, M. G., 192
Wesson, C. L., 355, 356, 357
Wetzel, K., 404
Weyhring, R. S., 257, 388
Whedon, C., 70, 296, 384
White, O. R., 426
Whitesell, N. R., 248, 253
Whitman, T. L., 78
Whittaker, M. E. S., 292
Whorton, D., 229
Wiederholt, J. L., 18
Wildman, T. M., 387
Wilkenson, G. S., 338
Wilkinson, I. A. G., 382
Will, M., 19
Willgoose, C. E., 490
Williams, B. T., 34
Williams, J. B. W., 126
Williams, R. E., 118
Willott, P. C., 296
Willoughby, T., 306, 357

Wilson, L. R., 69
Wilson, R., 206, 429, 437
Wilson, V. L., 69
Wine, J., 357
Wineman, D., 192, 206
Winkler, H., 486, 487
Winnick, J. P., 491
Winschel, J. F., 257
Winzer, M. A., 139, 141, 142, 143, 338
Wise, B., 69
Wohlers, H. D., 468
Wolfe, S., 78, 474, 480
Woloshyn, V. E., 306
Wolraich, M. L., 76, 127
Wonder, S., 486
Wong, B. Y. L., 387, 388, 397, 399, 403
Wong, R., 387, 388
Wood, E., 306
Wood, M. M., 207
Wood, W., 357
Woodcock, R. W., 338
Woodruff, G., 105, 147, 149
Woodward, J., 71, 448, 481
Wright, E. L., 261

Xin, Y. P., 381, 382

Yager, R. E., 453, 454
Yates, F., 292

Yates, J. R., 142
Yell, M., 10, 11, 48
Yetter, C. E., 108
Ylvisaker, M., 104
Yoder, S. L., 505
Yoshida, R. K., 212, 215
Young, C. C., 224
Young, P., 372
Ysseldyke, J. E., 69, 337, 339

Zabel, M. K., 198
Zamora-Durán, G., 142, 338
Zaragosa, N., 211
Zeaman, D., 77
Zelmer, J., 403
Zigler, E., 78
Zigmond, N., 22, 69, 192, 363, 454
Zimler, J., 292
Zimmerman, B. J., 253
Zins, J. E., 461
Zionts, P., 117, 118
Zirpoli, T. J., 189, 277
Zollers, N. J., 19
Zucker, S., 283

Subject Index

AAMR Ad Hoc Committee on Terminology and Classification, 112
ABC analysis, 188, 189
Abused children, 145–146, 147, 148
Academic engagement, 164–170, 173, 262
Academic on-task behavior, 165
Academic skills
    emotional disturbance and, 82–84
    mental retardation and, 78–79
    peer tutoring and, 228–229
Acceleration, 136
Acceptance
    social, 220–221
    statements promoting, 249–250
ACCEPTS, 210, 211
Accuracy techniques, for note taking, 321
Achievement tests, 338
Acoustic reconstructions, 295
Acquired immune deficiency syndrome (AIDS), 106
Acquisition, 160–161, 164
Acronym, 296
Acrostic, 297
ACT (American College Testing), 340, 512
Activating prior knowledge, 253, 385–387
Active listening, 31–32, 289–290
Active thinking, 478–480
Activities
    attention and, 278
    competitive and gamelike, 262–263
    cooperative learning, 236–237
    earth science, 473
    life science, 471–472
    mnemonic strategies and, 298
    physical science, 473–475
    practice, 176–178
    science, 468–471
    social studies and science, 452, 454, 475–476
    spelling, 396
Activities-oriented teaching approaches, for social studies and science, 447, 467–477
Adaptation, 50–51. *See also* Classroom adaptations
Adaptive behavior, 75, 78
Adaptive Learning Environments (ALEM), 19
Addition, problem solving with, 422–424

Addition computation, 416–417
Addition concepts, 415
Addition facts, 417–420
Adjunct aids, 385
Administrators, 43
Adoption Guidelines Project, 371
Adventitious disabilities, 91
Affect, 247
    improving, 252–270
    preconditions for, 248–252
Affective characteristics, 82
Affective disorders, 258
Age, tutoring and, 229
Agricultural education, 493
Alcohol abuse, 148–149
Algebra, 436–440
Algebra tiles, 437
Algorithms, multiplication and division, 427–429
Allergies, 105
Alphabet, manual, 97
AlphaSmart software, 73
Alternate assessments, 341
Alternative and augmentative communication (AAC), 62, 64–65, 101, 102, 117–118
Alternative teaching, 51
American Association on Mental Retardation (AAMR), 75, 112
American College Testing (ACT), 340, 512
American Federation of Teachers (AFT), 22
American Printing House for the Blind, 94
American Psychiatric Association (APA), 71, 117, 126–127, 128
American Sign Language (ASL), 96
American Speech–Language Hearing Association (ASHA), 62
Americans with Disabilities Act (ADA), 11, 12, 13, 507
Analytic touch, 92
Animals, activities teaching, 471
Annual reviews, 50
Anoxia, 76–77
ANSWER, 362
Answer sheets, 358
Antecedent, 129
Antidepressants, 107

Antipsychotic medications, 107
Aphasia, 63
Applet software, 73
Application, 72, 161–162, 164
Area concepts, 436
Arithmetic vocabulary, 427
Art education, 486–492
Arthritis, 104–105
Assertive discipline, 207
Assertiveness, 209, 507–508
Assessment
    ADHD, 128–129
    at-risk students, 150–151
    culturally and linguistically diverse students, 142–143, 144
    curriculum-based measurement, 347–350
    educational, 41–43
    emotional disturbance, 81
    gifted, creative, and talented students, 135–136
    grading and scoring, 363–365
    IDEA and, 14
    learning disabilities, 69–70
    mental retardation, 76
    motivation and affect, 253
    performance, 350–355
    portfolio, 355–357
    social skills, 210–211
    speech and language impairments, 64
    students with special needs, 338–347
    test types, 336–338
    test-taking skills, 357–362
    transitions, 508–510, 511–512
Assignment completion strategy, 315
Assistance, peer, 222–225
Association for Persons with Severe Handicaps (TASH), 20, 22, 112
Association for Retarded Citizens (ARC), 113
Association of Mouth and Foot Painting Artists, 486
Asthma, 105
At-risk students, 10, 145–151
Attention deficit disorder (ADD), 71, 126
Attention deficit hyperactivity disorder (ADHD), 71, 126–131, 132
Attention deficits, 71
    autism and, 283
    basic skills problems, 281

Attention deficits, *continued*
  extreme cases of, 281
  improving, 276–281
  intensive teacher-led instruction, 281
  self-monitoring, 282
  stimulant medications, 281, 283
  students with special needs, 276
Attitudes
  peer tutoring and, 228–229
  teacher, 22–25
Attorney fees, 14
Attribution training, 256
Attributions, 197–198, 256–258
Authentic literature, 371
Autism, 6, 8
  attention and, 283
  classroom adaptations, 117–120
  prevalence, definitions, and characteristics,
    115, 117
AWARE strategy, 323

Balancing, 470
Basal textbooks, 370–371
Base 10 blocks, 421–422
Basic skills problems, 281
*Beattie v. Board of Education of City of
    Antigo,* 6
Behavior
  abused and neglected children, 147
  defining, 187–188
  on-task, 165–167, 188, 190
  reinforcing, 193–194
  self-related, 209
  social, 169
  social skills and, 215
  task-related, 209
  See also Classroom behavior
Behavior problems, 116, 186–187, 198. *See
    also* Adaptive behavior; Classroom
    behavior; Social behavior
Behavioral interventions, 129–130, 131
Behavioral treatments, 215
Beliefs, irrational, 259
Bent finger strategy, 425
"Big ideas," 436
Bilingual special education, 141–142. *See
    also* Linguistically diverse students
Blindness, 9
Boardmaker, 102
Book reports, 311
Bound morpheme, 62
Braille, 92, 94
Brain factors, in mental retardation, 76
Brainstorming, 33, 328, 386
Bribes, 268
Brown v. Board of Education, 10, 20
Business education, 493

Calculators, 426–427
Calendars, 309
Cancer, 100

Career education, 492–503
Career information, 509
Career objectives, life-centered, 510
Carl D. Perkins Vocational Education Act,
    492–493
Case conference committee, 43, 45
Cataracts, 92
Cerebral palsy, 101–102
Charting, 470
Child abuse and neglect, 145–146, 147, 148
Child Abuse Prevention and Treatment Act, 145
Children's Defense Fund, 146
Chronic medical conditions, 109
Circle of Friends, 220–221
Clarification, questions for, 319–320
Clarity, 171–172
Class expectations, 313–314
Classroom activities. *See* Activities
Classroom adaptations
  ADHD, 129–131
  at-risk students, 151
  autism, 117–120
  culturally and linguistically diverse
    students, 143–145
  emotional disturbance, 84–86
  gifted, creative, and talented students,
    136–138
  hearing impairments, 97–99
  learning disabilities, 72–75
  mental retardation, 79–80
  multiple disabilities, 113–115, 116
  physical disabilities and other health-
    related impairments, 106–111
  severe disabilities, 113–115, 116
  speech and language impairments, 64–66
  visual impairments, 93–95
Classroom atmosphere, 190
Classroom behavior, 186
  behavior problems, 186–187
  confrontations, 204–206
  life space interviewing/life space crisis
    intervention, 206–207
  management strategies, 190–204
  observing and recording, 187–190
  schoolwide discipline systems, 207–208
Classroom diversity, 10
Classroom environment, 249–250
Classroom management, 167, 190–204
Classrooms
  collaboration and, 30–31
  personal investment in, 258–261
  task-oriented versus ego-oriented, 251–252
Classwide curriculum-based measurement,
    348–349
Classwide peer tutoring, 229–233, 383,
    465–466, 467
Cleft palate, 63
Clustering, 291
Code emphasis, 373–375
Cognitive-behavioral interventions, 130–131

Cognitive conflict, 261
Cognitive functioning, 77–78
Cognitive organizers, 462
Cognitive problem solving strategies, 430–431
Coin counting skills, 433
Collaboration, 29
  classroom scenario, 30–31
  communication and, 31–40
  intervention and, 34–40
  as partnerships, 50–56
  referrals and placements, 40–50
  school and parent responsibilities, 30
  student needs and, 31
College entrance exams, 340
Coloboma, 92
Color-related activities, 474
Command words, 362
Common goals, 32–33
Communication
  autism and, 117–118
  collaboration and, 31–40
  homework and, 56
  mental retardation and, 80
  paraprofessionals, 54
  parents and families, 54–57
  positive, 55–56
  total, 96
Communication board symbols, 119
Communication summary sheet, 34
Compare-and-contrast essays, 403
Compensatory education, 151
Competency-based assessment, 340–343
Competitive activities, 262–263
Competitive employment, 513
Complementary instruction, 51
Composition strategies, 401. *See also* Written
    expression
Computation strategies, 438
Computerized literature searches, 326
Computers
  AlphaSmart and Applet software, 73
  career information, 509
  collaborative learning and, 237
  IEP software, 47
  INSPECT proofreading strategy, 330
  Inspiration and Kidspiration software, 331
  mathematics, 442
  memory and, 299–300
  News-2-You and *Boardmaker* software, 102
  reading, 383
  recordkeeping, grading, and progress
    monitoring software, 342
  social studies, 476
  vocational education, 500–501
  written expression, 402, 404
Concept diagram, 450
Concept mastery routine, 449
Concepts, 160
  addition and subtraction, 415
  area and volume, 436
  inventing, 441

multiplication and division, 424
number, 412–413
Conceptual learning, 160, 163
Concrete examples, 286–288
Conductive, 95
Conflict resolution, 240
Confrontations, 204–206
Congenital disabilities, 91
Consequent, 129
Consultants, 17
Consultation, prereferral, 39
Consultation services, 17
Consumer Action Network (CAN), 22
Consumer science. See Family and consumer science
Content, social skills and, 209
Content coverage, planning for, 156–164
Content enhancement, 449, 450
Content-oriented teaching approaches, for social studies and science, 447, 448–467
Context, of behavior, 188, 189
Contingent observation, 199
Continuum of services, 16
Contracts/contracting, 202, 256
Conversation skills, 209
Cooperative homework teams, 314–315
Cooperative learning, 233–241, 263–264
Coping skills, 209
Corporal punishment, 196
Corrective feedback, 384
Corrective reading lesson, 374
Correspondence, one-to-one, 414
Co-teaching, 51–53
Council for Children with Behavioral Disorders (CCBD), 22, 196
Council for Exceptional Children (CEC), 15, 22, 106, 113, 126, 128, 129, 340
Council for Learning Disabilities (CLD), 22
Counseling interventions, 258
Counselors, 43
Count-bys, 424
Counterproductive statements, 255
Counting, 413, 415–416, 433
Cover–copy–compare, 397
Crawfordsville Community School Corporation, 42
Creative students, 134. See also Gifted, creative, and talented students
Criterion-referenced tests, 336, 337, 343–347
Critical thinking, 160
Cross-age tutoring, 229
Culturally diverse students, 10, 138–145, 463–466, 467
Curriculum
    content coverage and, 157, 158
    mental retardation and, 80
    social skills, 212
    spelling, 397–398
    transitions, 510
    vocational education, 495
    written expression, 405

Curriculum-based assessment, 337
Curriculum-based measurement (CBM), 337, 347–350, 382–383
Curriculum materials. See Materials
Cursive writing, 394
Cystic fibrosis, 100

Daily planners, 309–310
Daily routines and schedules, 73
Dance Umbrella, 488
Data, charting, and recording, 470
Data collection, 328
Databases, 325
Deaf-blindness, 6, 8
Deafness, 6, 8
Debriefing, 199–200
Decimals, 435
Decision making, 258, 260
Decoding, 44, 359
Deductive reasoning, 481
Delivery rate, 173
Demonstration Plus Permanent Model, 428
Depersonalization, 32
Descriptive Video Service, 94
Development, inquiry learning and, 480–481
Developmental delay, 9, 14
Developmental Disabilities Assistance and Bill of Rights Acts, 11
Developmental disability. See Mental retardation
Diabetes, 105
Diabetic retinopathy, 92
Diagnosis, error analysis for, 429–430
Diagnostic and Statistical Manual–IV (DSM–IV), 117, 126, 128
Diagnosticians, 43
Dialogue, coaching, 175
Diana v. Board of Education, 10
Diplegia, 100
Direct appeals, 192, 277, 278
Direct instruction, 373–375, 384
Directions, 74, 469
Disabilities, types of, 6, 8–9. See also specific disabilities
Disability awareness, 113–114
Disability issues, parents and, 56
Disability resources, 57
Disagreements, 57
Discipline, 14, 167, 207–208
Discrepancy, 68, 69–70
Discrimination learning, 159, 163
DISSECT strategy, 378–379
Distraction-free environments, 73
Diverse learners, 10. See also Culturally diverse students; Linguistically diverse students
Division algorithms, 427–429
Division concepts, 424
Division facts, 424–426
Division for Learning Disabilities (DLD), 22
Down syndrome, 75–76
Drafts, 329
Dropout prevention, 83–84

Drugs. See Medications
Due process, 13, 48–49
Duration recording, 189
Dyscalculia, 68
Dysgraphia, 68, 392
Dyslexia, 68

Early childhood education, 13–14
Early intervention services, 4
Earth science activities, 473
Editing, 329
Education
    compensatory, 151
    mathematics, 410–411
    multicultural, 140 (see also Culturally diverse students; Linguistically diverse students)
    planning for, 511–513
Educational evaluation/assessment, 41–43
Educational placement. See Placements
Educational programming, for hearing impairments, 96
Educational rights, 5–6
Education for All Handicapped Children Act, 3, 11, 13. See also Individuals with Disabilities Education Act
Education for All Handicapped Children Act Amendments, 11, 13
Education of the Handicapped Act Amendments, 11
Effective communication, 117–118
Effective instruction
    content coverage, 156–164
    overview of, 155–156
    PASS variables, 180–182
    strategies, 164–180
Effort, praise and rewards for, 265–270
Ego-oriented classrooms, 251–252
Elaboration, 291, 295
Electricity, activities involving, 473–474
Elementary and Secondary Education Act (ESEA), 14, 151
Elementary school report cards, 127
Elimination strategies, 358
Emergency procedures, for physical disabilities and other health-related impairments, 108
Emotional disturbance, 6, 8–9
    causes of, 81
    characteristics of, 81–84
    classroom adaptations, 84–86
    identification and assessment of, 81
    prevalence and definitions, 80–81
Emotional functioning, 71–72
Employment, competitive, 513
Enactments, 288–289
Enrichment, 136
Enthusiasm, 172–173, 191, 264, 265
Environment
    emotional disturbance and, 86
    hearing impairments and, 98

Environment, *continued*
  learning disabilities and, 73
  mental retardation and, 76
  motivation and affect, 249–250
  PASS variables, 181
  physical disabilities and other health-
    related impairments, 110
  speech and language impairments and,
    64, 65
  supportive, 167
  visual impairments and, 93
  vocational education, 494–495
Epilepsy, 104
Episodic memory, 283
Error analysis for diagnosis, 429–430
Essay questions, 347, 361
Essays, 402, 403
Ethnicity. *See* Culturally diverse students;
    Linguistically diverse students
Evaluation
  collaborative learning, 237–238
  educational, 41–43
  emotional disturbance and, 86
  formative, 179
  gifted, creative, and talented students,
    137–138
  hearing impairments and, 99
  learning disabilities and, 75
  mental retardation and, 80
  physical disabilities and other health-
    related impairments, 111
  speech and language impairments and, 66
  systematic, 181–182
Event recording, 189
Examiner familiarity, 339–340
Examples, concrete, 286–288
Exclusionary clause, 67
Expectations, 313–314
External locus of control, 257
External memory, 285
Extrinsic motivation, 247

Facilitated communication, 118
Facilities, special, 18
Factual learning, 159, 163
Fairness, 270
Families
  mental retardation and, 80
  motivation and affect, 256
  multiracial, 140–141
  as partners, 54–57
  poverty, 149
Family and consumer science, 493
Fatigue, 108
Federal government updates, 15
Federal Interagency Head Injury Task Force, 103
Federal Register, 67
Feedback, 167
  corrective, 384
  reports and projects, 329
  soliciting, 260–261
  teacher presentations, 175–176

Feelings
  projecting, 190–191
  validating, 193
Fetal alcohol syndrome (FAS), 105
Field trips, 477, 478
Fingerspelling, 96, 97
Five-R strategy, 323
Fluency, 160–161, 164, 382–383
Focus, 86
Force-related activities, 474
Foreign languages, 491–492
Formal management systems, 193
Formative evaluation, 179
Formative tests, 336
Fractions, 435
Framed outlines, 459
Free and appropriate education, 13
Free morpheme, 62
Fry's readability graph and formula, 455
Full inclusion, 8, 19–22
Functional mathematics, 441–442

Games
  good behavior, 201–202
  motivation and affect, 262–263
  social skills and, 213–214
GED tests, 341–343
General education assistance team, 38
General education classroom, 17, 21
General education prereferral request,
    34–36, 37
General education teachers, 43, 49–50
General laboratory procedures, 469
Generalizable skills, 501–503
Generalization, 72, 161–162, 164, 204,
    214–215
Genetics, mental retardation and, 75–76
Geometry, 414–415
Gifted and Talented Children's Education
    Act, 11, 131
Gifted, creative, and talented students, 10,
    131, 133–138
Glaucoma, 92
Goal setting, 255–256
Goals
  common, 32–33
  cooperative learning, 236
  learning disabilities and, 74
  shared, 31
  summarizing, 33
  vocational education, 494, 495
  writing, 47–48
Good Behavior Game, 201–202
Grading, 342, 363–365
Graduated coaching, 440–441
Graduation, planning for, 510
Graphic presentation, 190
Graphing, 470
Groups. *See* Collaborative learning
Guessing, 358
Guided notes, 321
Guided questioning, 478–480

Hand signals, 98
Handwriting, 392–394
Health, life science activities and, 472
Health-care needs, of students with severe
    and multiple disabilities, 115
Health occupations education, 493
Health-related impairments, 6, 9
  classroom adaptations, 106–111
  prevalence, definitions, and
    characteristics, 99–101
  types of, 101–106
Hearing impairments, 9
  classroom adaptations, 97–99
  educational programming, 96
  prevalence, definitions, and characteristics, 95
Hemiplegia, 100
Hidden gifted, creative, and talented
    students, 134
Higher-incidence disabilities, 61
  emotional disturbance, 80–86
  learning disabilities, 67–74
  mental retardation, 74–80
  speech or language impairments, 62–66
Highlighting, 458–459
High-risk students. *See* At-risk students
Homeless children, 146, 148
Homework, 56, 310–313, 314–315
Honig v. Doe, 11
Human immunodeficiency virus (HIV), 106
Hydrocephaly, 76

Ideas, 328, 329, 436
IDEA 7: Let's make it work, 43
Identification
  ADHD, 128–129
  at-risk students, 150–151
  culturally and linguistically diverse
    students, 142–143
  emotional disturbance, 81
  gifted, creative, and talented students,
    135–136
  learning disabilities, 69–70
  mental retardation, 76
  production versus, 162
  speech and language impairments, 64
  word, 375–382
IEP Planner, 46
Ignoring, 191–192
Illustrations, 287–288
Imagery, 288, 385
Inclusion, 7–8
Inclusion movements, 19–22
Inclusive teaching, 3
  historical scenarios, 4–6
  least-restrictive environment, 7–10
  legal foundations, 10–15
  mathematics, 412–442
  PASS variables, 180–182
  reading comprehension, 384–390
  service delivery models, 16–25
  severe and multiple disabilities and, 114
  teacher effectiveness in, 167

Independent learners, 306
    listening skills, 315–319
    note taking, 319–324
    organizational skills, 306–315
Independent learning, 453–462
Independent living situations, 514
Indiana Department of Education, 37
Individualized education plan (IEP), 13, 14,
    44, 46, 47, 48
Individualized instruction, 501, 502
Individualized Transition Plan (ITP), 48
Individually administered tests, 339
Individuals with Disabilities Education Act
    (IDEA), 3, 8–9, 11, 12–14, 15, 43, 44,
    46, 48, 61, 92, 100, 129, 508–509
Industrial education, 493
Information
    collecting, 328
    organizing, 329
Inquiry learning, for social studies and
    science, 448, 477–481
In-school suspension, 195
In-seat behavior, 188
INSPECT proofreading strategy, 330
Inspiration software, 331
Instruction
    complementary, 51
    direct, 373–375, 384
    emotional disturbance and, 86
    feedback during, 167
    gifted, creative, and talented students,
        137–138
    intensive teacher-led, 281
    learning and, 163
    learning disabilities and, 73–74
    mental retardation and, 80
    PASS variables, 181
    physical disabilities and other health-
        related impairments, 111
    reading comprehension, 391, 392
    social studies and science, 448
    speech and language impairments and, 65
    systematic, 181
    vocabulary, 384
    vocational education, 501–503
    See also Effective instruction; Inclusive
        teaching
Instructional appropriateness, 167
Instructional delivery systems, 114
Instructional materials. *See* Materials
Instructional strategies. *See* Teaching
    strategies
Intangible rewards, 269–270
Intellectual disability. *See* Mental retardation
Intellectual functioning, 77–78
Intellectually gifted students, 134
Intelligence tests, 338
Intensive teacher-led instruction, 281
Interfering information, 288
Internal locus of control, 257
International Festival of Wheelchair
    Dance, 488

Internet, 299–300, 326, 509
Interpersonal skills, 232
Interpreters, 99
Interval recording, 189
Interventions, 34–40
    behavioral, 129–130, 131
    cognitive-behavioral, 130–131
    counseling, 258
Intrinsic motivation, 247
Invention, of mathematical concepts and
    procedures, 441
Irrational beliefs, 259
IT FITS, 461

Job interview skills, 209
Job opportunities planning for, 513

Keyword method, 292–295
Kidspiration software, 331
Knowledge, prior, 253, 385–387

Laboratory procedures, 469
Language, 62
    literacy and, 70–71
    mental retardation and, 78
Language cards, 98
Language impairment, 6, 9
    causes of, 63
    classroom adaptations, 64–66
    identification and assessment of, 64
    prevalence, definitions, and
        characteristics, 62–63
Language therapists. *See* Speech/language
    therapists
Larry P. v. Riles, 10
Larynx, 63
Law, inclusive teaching and, 10–15
Learning, active, 289–290
Learning, cooperative, 233–241
Learning, fun and enjoyable, 261–265
Learning, independent, 453–462
Learning, inquiry, 477–481
Learning, learning disabilities and, 75
Learning, planning for, 158–162
Learning disabilities
    causes of, 68–69
    characteristics of, 70–72
    classroom adaptations, 72–75
    identification and assessment of, 69–70
    prevalence and definitions of, 66–68
    specific, 6, 9
Learning Disabilities Association, 340, 343, 510
Learning problems, 162–164
Learning strategies, 71, 460, 461
Least-restrictive environment, 3, 7–10,
    13, 14
Lectures, listening skills and, 317–318
Legal background, inclusive teaching,
    10–15
Legal proceedings, 10–11
Legislation, 10–11, 15
Lesson organizer routine, 449

Lessons
    concrete and meaningful, 261
    model, 179–180
    practice activities and, 178
Letter strategies, 292, 296–298
Level systems, 200–201
Library catalogs, 325–326
Library skills, 324–326
Life-centered career objectives, 510
Life science activities, 471–472
Life Space Crisis Intervention (LSCI),
    206–207
Life Space Interviewing (LSI), 206–207
Light-related activities, 474
Linguistically diverse students, 10, 138–145,
    463–466, 467
LINKS strategy, 322
Listening, active, 31–32
Listening skills, 315–319
"Listen, then look, then listen" instruction
    sequence, 98–99
Literacy portfolio, 356
Literacy, 70–71, 369
    reading, 370–383
    reading comprehension, 383–392
    written expression, 392–405
Literature, authentic, 371
Literature searches, computerized, 326
Locus of control, 257
Long division, modified, 428–429
Long-term memory, 284
Lower-incidence disabilities, 91
    autism, 115, 117–120
    hearing impairments, 95–99
    physical disabilities and other health-
        related impairments, 99–111
    severe and multiple disabilities,
        111–115, 116
    visual impairments, 92–95

Magnetism, activities involving, 473–474
Mainstreaming, 7–8
Mandated inclusion, 23–25
Manipulation, 288–289
Manipulatives, 437
Manual alphabet, 97
Manuscript writing, 394
Marketing education, 493
Masonry, 495
Massachusetts Department of Education,
    338, 339
Matching items, 345–346
Materials
    curriculum, 158
    emotional disturbance and, 86
    gifted, creative, and talented students,
        136–137
    hearing impairments and, 98
    learning disabilities and, 73
    mental retardation and, 80
    motivation and affect, 250
    PASS variables, 181

Materials, *continued*
  physical disabilities and other health-related impairments, 110
  social skills, 212
  social studies and science, 463–466, 467
  speech and language impairments and, 64
  tutoring, 232
  visual impairments and, 94
  vocational education, 496, 499, 500
  written expression, 405
Mathematical reasoning problems, 440–441
Mathematics, 71, 409–410
  addition and subtraction computation, 416–417
  addition and subtraction concepts, 415
  addition and subtraction facts, 417–420
  algebra, 436–440
  area and volume concepts, 436
  arithmetic vocabulary, 427
  calculators, 426–427
  cooperative learning in, 234
  counting, 413, 415–416
  decimals, 435
  education, 410–411
  error analysis for diagnosis, 429–430
  fractions, 435
  functional, 441–442
  geometry, 414–415
  metacognition and, 431, 432
  money, 431, 433–434
  multimedia, 442
  multiplication and division algorithms, 427–429
  multiplication and division concepts, 424
  multiplication and division facts, 424–426
  number concepts, 412–413
  number lines, 415–416
  number writing, 416
  numeration, 414
  one-to-one correspondence, 414
  performance assessment, 353, 354
  place value and regrouping, 420–422
  problem solving, 422–424, 430–431
  reasoning problems, 440–441
  scoring rubric, 353
  students with disabilities and, 411–412
  symbols, 416
  time, 434–435
Mathematics computation subtests, 359
Mathematics concept subtests, 359–360
Mathematics disability, 68
Mathematics problem-solving subtests, 360
Meaningfulness, 251, 261, 285–286
Measurements, 470
Mechanical obstacles, 404–405
Medical guidelines, for physical disabilities and other health-related impairments, 106–108

Medications
  attention deficits, 131, 132, 281, 283
  physical disabilities and other health-related impairments, 107
Memory, 71, 283
  aspects of, 283–284
  improving, 285–292
  mnemonic techniques and, 292–301
  students with special needs, 285
Mental retardation, 6, 9
  causes of, 75–76
  characteristics of, 77–79
  classroom adaptations, 79–80
  identification and assessment of, 76
  prevalence and definitions of, 75
Meta-analysis, 69
Metacognition, 71, 387, 431, 432
Metamemory, 284, 285
Microcephaly, 76
Microscopes, 472
Mills v. Board of Education, 10
Mimetic reconstructions, 295
Minerals, activities involving, 473
Mixtures, activities involving, 474–475
Mnemonic techniques, 292–301, 426, 451–452
Model lesson, 179–180
Models/modeling, 94, 254
Modified long division, 428–429
Money, 431, 433–434
Monthly planners, 309–310
Mood stabilizers, 107
Morphemes, 63
Morphology, 62
Motion-related activities, 474
Motivation, 247
  assessment and, 339
  improving, 252–270
  preconditions for, 248–252
Movement, 278
Moving, 108–109
Multicultural awareness, 145
Multicultural education, 140. *See also*
  Culturally diverse students;
  Linguistically diverse students
Multilingual pocket translators, 142
Multimedia mathematics, 442
Multimedia social studies projects, 476
MultiPass, 460–461
Multiple-choice tests, 344–345
Multiple disabilities, 6, 9
  classroom adaptations, 113–115, 116
  prevalence, definitions, and characteristics, 111–112
Multiplication algorithms, 427–429
Multiplication concepts, 424
Multiplication facts, 424–426
Multiracial families, 140–141
Muscular dystrophy, 103
Music education, 486–492

National Council of Teachers of Mathematics (NCTM), 410–411, 440
National Council on Disabilities, 96
National Education Association (NEA), 22
National Head Injury Foundation, 103
National Joint Committee on Learning Disabilities, 67
National Research Council, 139, 409
Needs, 31
Needs assessment, 144
Negative attributions, 197, 257
Negative numbers, 437
Neglected children, 145–146, 147, 148
Nephritis, 100
Nephrosis, 100
Neurological impairments, 100
News-2-You, 102
No Child Left Behind Act (NCLB), 14–15
Nondiscriminatory testing, 13
Norm-referenced tests, 336, 337, 338–340
Note taking, 319–324
Number concepts, 412–413
Number lines, 415–416
Numbers
  negative, 437
  writing, 416
Numeration, 414
Nurses, school, 43

OARWET, 460
Oberti v. Board of Education of the Borough of Clementon School District, 11
Objective tests, 361
Objectives
  content coverage, 156
  cooperative learning, 234–235
  mental retardation and, 80
  prioritizing, 180–181
  spelling, 398
  vocational education, 494, 495
  writing, 47–48
Observation, classroom behavior, 187–190
Occupational surveys, 508
Occupational therapists, 43
Office of Special Education and Rehabilitative Services, 15
Office of Special Education Programs, 15
One-to-one correspondence, 414
On-task behavior, 165–167, 188, 190
On-the-spot training, 212–214
Operational definitions, 188
Operations, priority of, 427–428
Oral presentations, 66, 94
Organization, 73
  memory and, 291
  reports and projects, 329
  text, 457
Organizational skills, 306–315
Organizational strategies, 71
Orthography, 491
Orthopedic impairment, 6, 9, 100
Outlines, 322

Outlining, 458–459
Overcorrection, 195
Overjustification, 268
Overlearning, 253, 290

Pacing, 158
Paired associates, 159
PALS level system, 201
Parallel teaching, 51
Paraphrasing, 387–388
Paraplegia, 100
Paraprofessionals, 43, 54, 113
Parent advisory groups, 56
Parental rights, 42
Parent participation, 13
Parent responsibilities, 30
Parents
    concerns of, 43–44
    motivation and affect, 256
    as partners, 54–57
    teenage, 149–150
Partnerships, collaborations as, 50–56
PASS variables, 180–182
Peabody classwide peer tutoring, 231–232
Peer assistance, 222–225
Peers
    attention and, 279
    mental retardation and, 80
    motivation and affect, 249
    social initiation, 224–225
    See also Collaborative learning
Peer training, 222–225
Peer tutoring, 75, 225–233, 383,
        465–466, 467
Pegword method, 292, 296
Pennsylvania Association for Retarded
        Children (PARC) v. Commonwealth
        of Pennsylvania, 10
Performance, self-monitoring of, 282
Performance assessment, 337, 350–355
Performance criteria, 268–269
Performance tests, 362
Periodic reviews, 75
Perkins Act, 11
Perkins School for the Blind, 486
Perkins Vocational Education Act,
        492–493
Persona, feeling and caring, 190–191
Personal Adjustment Level System. See PALS
        level system
Personal investment, 258–261
Personal organizational skills, 306–315
Personnel, school, 43
Phonemic awareness, 70, 375–377
Phonics, 375, 377–378
Phonology, 62
Physical abuse, 147
Physical disabilities
    classroom adaptations, 106–111
    prevalence, definitions, and
        characteristics, 99–101
    types of, 101–106

Physical education, 486–492
Physical environment
    emotional disturbance and, 86
    hearing impairments and, 98
    learning disabilities and, 73
    physical disabilities and other health-
        related impairments, 110
    speech and language impairments and, 64, 65
    visual impairments and, 93
Physical neglect, 147
Physical science activities, 473–475
Physical therapists, 43
Pictorial reconstructions, 295
Picture Exchange Communication System
        (PECS), 116
Pictures, 286–288, 298
PIRATES, 362
Place value, 420–422
Placements
    collaboration and, 40–50
    competitive employment, 513
    students with severe and multiple
        disabilities, 112
PLAN, 507
Planners, 309–310
Planning
    content coverage, 156–164
    daily, weekly, and monthly planners and,
        309–310
    education, 511–513
    graduation, 510
    independent living situations, 514
    job opportunities, 513
    learning, 158–162
    peer tutoring, 230
    transitions, 505
    writing, 327–328
Plants, activities involving, 471
Play interaction skills, 209
Pocket translators, 142
Portfolio assessment, 337, 355–357
Positioning, 108–109
Positive attributions, 197–198, 256–258
Positive behavioral supports (PBS),
        207–208
POSSE, 450–451, 452–453
Postlingual, 95
Pouring, 470
Poverty, family, 149
Powders, activities involving, 474–475
PQRST, 460
Practice, memory and, 290
Practice activities, 176–178
Pragmatics, 63
Praise, 176, 191–192, 265–270
Pregnancy, teenage, 149–150
Prelingual, 95
Prereferral consultation, 39
Prereferral intervention team, 34
Presentations
    formats for, 74
    graphic, 190

    video, 286
    See also Oral presentations; Teacher
        presentations
Prior knowledge, 253, 385–387
Problem behavior. See Behavior problems
Problem solving, 160, 163
    addition and subtraction, 422–424
    algebra, 439–440
    cognitive strategies, 430–431
    social studies, 478
    word meanings, 430
Problem-solving skills, 209
Procedural learning, 160, 163
Procedures, 236, 501
Process skills, 470–471
Production, identification versus, 162
Progress, monitoring, 33, 255–256, 342, 471
Projects, 326–331
Proofreading, 329, 404
Proximity, 192, 277
Psychologists, school, 43
Psychostimulants, 107
Punishment, 195–196

Quadratic equations, 438–439
Quadriplegia, 100
Questions/questioning, 74
    clarification, 319–320
    essay, 347, 361
    guided, 478–480
    self-generated, 387, 397
    teacher presentations, 173–175

Race. See Culturally diverse students;
        Linguistically diverse students
RAP strategy, 387
Reading
    basal textbooks, 370–371
    direct instruction and code emphasis,
        373–375
    Peabody classwide peer tutoring in,
        231–232
    reading fluency, 382–383
    reading recovery, 372–373
    spelling and, 396
    technological adaptations, 383
    textbooks, 463–464, 465
    whole language approach, 371–372
    word identification, 375–382
Reading comprehension, 383–384
    inclusive teaching, 384–390
    instructional adaptations, 391, 392
    secondary applications, 391
    subtests, 358–359
Reading development, stages of, 370
Reading disability, 68
Reading fluency, 382–383
Reading problems, 465
Reading recovery, 372–373
Reading skills, 371
Reasoning, 71, 481
Reasoning problems, 440–441

Reciprocal teaching, 388–390
Reconstructive elaborations, 295
Recording, 187–190, 470
Recordkeeping, 342
Redundancy, 172
Reference books, 325
Reference skills, 324–331
Referral form, sample, 40
Referral process, steps in, 36
Referrals, 40–50
Regrouping, 420–422
Regular Education Initiative, 19
Reinforcement, 193–194, 268, 279–280, 384
Relationship charts, 291
Reliability, 337
Repeated readings, 382, 384
Report cards, 127, 363–365
Reports, 326–331, 402, 404
Reprimands, 192–193, 194
Research, on reprimands, 194
Research reports, 402, 404
Research skills, 324–331
Research support, 52–53
Resources, disability, 57
Resource services, 17–18
Response cost, 197
Responsibilities
    paraprofessionals, 54
    school and parent, 30
Retinitis pigmentosa, 92
Retinopathy of prematurity, 92
Review, 178–179
Reviews
    annual, 50
    periodic, 75
Revisions, 329
Rewards, 196–197, 265–270
Rewriting, 329
Rheumatic fever, 100
Rights
    educational, 5–6
    parental, 42
Rocks, activities involving, 473
Routines, daily, 73
Rule learning, 160, 163
Rules, 191, 236, 469

Safety
    science activities and, 469
    vocational education, 495–496, 497–499
Same-age tutoring, 229
SAT (Scholastic Assessment Test), 340, 512
Schedules/scheduling
    daily, 73
    peer tutoring, 232
    post and review, 307–309
Schizophrenia, 81
Scholastic Assessment Test (SAT), 340, 512
School administrators, 43
School nurses, 43
School personnel, 43

School psychologists, 43
School responsibilities, 30
School specialists, 43
Schools, special, 18
Schoolwide discipline systems, 207–208
Science, 447–448
    activities-oriented approaches, 467–477
    cooperative learning in, 236
    inquiry learning in, 477–481
    portfolio assessment, 356
    textbook/content-oriented approaches,
        448–467
Science activities, 468–471
Science subtests, 360
Scope, 157
SCORER, 362
Scoring, 347, 363–365
Scoring rubrics, 351, 353
SCREAM, 73–74, 181
Search engines, 324, 326
Section 504, 11–12, 44, 46, 126–131, 507
Seizures, 108
Selective mutism, 81
Selective serotonin reuptake inhibitors
        (SSRI), 107
Self-advocacy, 506–508
Self-contained services, 17–18
Self-determination, 506–508
Self-efficacy, 252, 253–254
Self-esteem, 252, 253, 259
Self-generated questions, 387
Self-help skills, 209
Self-instruction, 130, 202–204, 393, 396,
        399–401
Self-monitoring, 71, 130, 202, 203, 282, 396
Self-questioning, 397
Self-recording, 280–281
Self-regulation, 71, 393, 399–401
Self-related behaviors, 209
Semantic feature analysis, 450
Semantic maps, 291
Semantic memory, 71, 283
Semantics, 62
Sensorineural, 95
Sentence completion items, 346, 361
Sequence, 157
Sequence chart, 379
Serial list, 159
Service delivery models, 16–25
Services
    continuum of, 16
    related, 18–19, 44
    resource and self-contained, 17–18
    transition, 48
Severe disabilities
    classroom adaptations, 113–115, 116
    prevalence, definitions, and
        characteristics, 111–112
Sexual abuse, 147
SHARE, 507
Shared goals, 31

Short-answer items, 361
Short-term memory, 284
Sickle-cell anemia, 100
Sight words, 381–382
Signaling systems, 98
Signing Exact English, 96
Sign language, 96, 97
Sincerity, 191
Snapshots 2, 197
Social acceptance, 220–221
Social behavior, 169
    emotional disturbance and, 81–82
    mental retardation and, 78
Social competence, 118–120
Social-emotional functioning, 71–72
Social initiation, 224–225
Social models, 254
Social skills, 208–210
    assessment, 210–211
    behavioral treatments, 215
    curriculum materials and, 212
    generalization, 214–215
    improving, 211–212
    on-the-spot training, 212–214
Social studies, 447–448
    activities-oriented approaches, 467–477
    inquiry learning in, 477–481
    subtests, 360
    textbook/content-oriented approaches,
        448–467
Social workers, 43
Sociometric measure, 210
Software
    AlphaSmart and Applet, 73
    career information, 509
    Individualized Education Plans, 47
    Inspiration and Kidspiration, 331
    mathematics, 442
    News-2-You and Boardmaker, 102
    reading, 383
    recordkeeping, grading, and progress
        monitoring, 342
    social studies, 476
    vocational education, 500–501
Solutions, activities involving, 474–475
Sound, activities involving, 473
Special education, bilingual, 141–142
Special education teachers, 43, 50
Special Friends, 221
Special needs students. See Students with
        special needs
Special Olympics, 488
Special schools and facilities, 18
Specificity, 69
Speech, 62
Speech impairment, 6, 9
    causes of, 63
    classroom adaptations, 64–66
    identification and assessment of, 64
    prevalence, definitions, and
        characteristics, 62–63

Speech/language therapists, 43
Speed techniques, for note taking, 321
Spelling, 395–398
Spills, 469–470
Spina bifida, 103
Standardized tests, 336, 337, 358–360
Statewide assessment, 340–343
Station teaching, 51
Stimulant medications, 107, 132, 281, 283
Stimulus value, 469
Story grammar, 400–401
Story grammar training card, 389
Story maps, 388
Strategy instruction, 456–457, 506–507
Structural analysis, 378–380
Structure
    family, 54–55
    teacher presentations, 170–171
    text, 457–458
Student contracting, 202
Student needs, 31
Students with special needs, 125
    ADHD, 126–131, 132
    assessment, 338–347
    at risk, 145–151
    attention, 276
    cooperative learning, 238–239
    culturally and linguistically diverse,
        138–145
    gifted, creative, and talented students,
        131, 133–138
    mathematics, 411–412
    memory, 285
    performance criteria for, 268–269
    portfolio assessment, 357
    vocational education, 493–501
Study guides, 460
Study skills, 71, 73
    listening skills, 315–319
    note taking, 319–324
    organizational skills, 306–315
    research and reference skills, 324–331
Study–test–study, 397
Stuttering, 62
Stuttering Foundation of America, 63, 66
Substance abuse, 148–149
Subtests, 358–360
Subtraction, problem solving with, 422–424
Subtraction computation, 416–417
Subtraction concepts, 415
Subtraction facts, 417–420
Suicide, warning signs for, 150
Summaries, short, 319
Summarizing, 387–388
Summative tests, 336
Support
    motivation and affect, 254–255
    research, 52–53
Supportive environment, 167
Supportive learning activities, 51
Suspension, 195

Symbolic enactments, 289
Symbolic reconstructions, 295
Symbols, 416
Syntax, 62
Synthetic touch, 92
Systematic evaluation, 181–182
Systematic teaching, 181

Tactile models, 94
Talented students, 134. See also Gifted,
    creative, and talented students
Tangible rewards, 269–270
Task analysis, 310, 311
Task-oriented classrooms, 251–252
Task-related behaviors, 209
Tasks
    interesting, 261
    meaningfulness of, 251
    writing, 327
Teacher attitudes, 23–25
Teacher behavior, on-task, 166–167
Teacher-led instruction, intensive, 281
Teacher-made tests, 343–347, 361–362
Teacher presentations, 170–176, 448–453
Teachers
    cooperative learning and, 234–238
    full inclusion and, 22–23
    See also General education teachers;
        Special education teachers
Teaching. See Co-teaching; Effective
    instruction; Inclusive teaching;
    Instruction
Teaching adaptations, emotional disabilities
    and, 85–86. See also Classroom
    adaptations
Teaching strategies
    academic engagement, 164–170
    art, music, and physical education, 488–491
    formative evaluation, 179
    learning and, 163, 164
    model lesson, 179–180
    practice activities, 176–178
    review, 178–179
    teacher presentations, 170–176
    vocational education, 501–503
Team teaching, 51
Teasing, 188
Technology
    AlphaSmart and Applet, 73
    alternative and augmentative
        communication, 102
    career information, 509
    collaborative learning, 237
    federal government updates, 15
    handwriting, 394
    hearing impairments and, 98
    IEP software, 47
    INSPECT proofreading strategy, 330
    Inspiration and Kidspiration software, 331
    mathematics, 442
    memory and, 299–300

    motivation and affect, 263
    reading, 380, 383
    recordkeeping, grading, and progress
        monitoring software, 342
    research and reference skills, 324, 326
    self-monitoring, 203
    social studies, 476
    vocational education, 500–501
    written expression, 402, 404
Technology education, 493
Teenage parents, 149–150
Teenage pregnancy, 149–150
TELLS fact or fiction, 385–386
Terminal illnesses, 109
Tests
    nondiscriminatory, 13
    types of, 336–338
    See also Assessment; Evaluation
Test-taking skills, 339, 357–362
Text formats, 391
Text organization, 457
Text structures, 457–458
Textbook-oriented teaching approaches,
    447, 448–467
Textbooks, basal, 370–371
Text enhancements, 384–385
Thinking, 71, 478–480
Three-dimensional models, 94
Three-R strategy, 323
Time, mathematics and, 434–435
Time management, 168, 358
Time sampling, 189
Time schedules, 307–309
Timelines, establishing, 37
Time-on-task, 164–170, 501
Timeouts, 198–200
Token systems, 196–197, 269
Topic selection, 327
Total communication, 96
Touch Math, 416–417
Tourette syndrome, 81
Trade education, 493
Training, for peer tutoring, 232
Training and Technical Assistance Center at
    the College of William and
    Mary, 341
Transition services, 13, 14, 48
Transitions, 168–169, 485, 503–514
Translators, pocket, 142
Traumatic brain injury (TBI), 6, 9, 103–104
TRAVEL, 461–462
Tricyclic antidepressants, 107
True–false items, 344
Tuberculosis, 100
Tutoring, peer, 75, 225–233, 383,
    465–466, 467

U.S. Department of Education, 8, 15, 61, 66,
    70, 75, 80, 92, 95, 100, 112, 117,
    131, 133, 138, 139, 141–142, 146,
    149, 150

Validity, 337
Verbal responding, 65–66
Verbalizations, inappropriate, 169
Video presentations, 286
Violence, warning signs for, 150
Virginia Department of Education, 341
Visual acuity, 92
Visual aids, 98, 286–288, 464
Visual impairments, 6, 9
    classroom adaptations, 93–95
    prevalence, definitions, and
        characteristics, 92
    social studies and science, 465
Visual representations, 436
Vocabulary checklist, 465
Vocabulary instruction, 384
Vocational education, 492–503
Vocational Rehabilitation Act, 11–12, 44,
    126, 129, 507. *See also* Section 504

Vocational Rehabilitation Act Amendments, 11
Volume concepts, 436
Volunteerism, 23

Watson v. City of Cambridge, 5
Weather-related activities, 473
Weekly planners, 309–310
Weighing, 470
Whole language approach, 371–372
Word identification, 375–382
Word meanings, 430
Working adaptation sheet, 182
Working memory, 71, 284
Worksheet activities, 452, 454
World Wide Web, 324, 326
Writing
    numbers, 416
    spelling and, 396
    thinking about, 401–402

Writing disability, 68
Writing plan, 327–328
Writing tasks, 327
Written communication, 398–405
Written expression
    handwriting, 392–394
    spelling, 395–398
    written communication, 398–405
Written tests, 361

Young parents, 149

Zaner-Bloser, 394
Zero reject, 13